MUSIC
IN THE
20TH CENTURY

VOLUME THREE

Editorial Board

SHARPE REFERENCE

An imprint of M.E. Sharpe, INC.

Sharpe Reference

Sharpe Reference is an imprint of
M.E. Sharpe, Inc.

M.E. Sharpe, Inc.
80 Business Park Drive
Armonk, NY 10504

Library of Congress Cataloging-in-Publication
Data

Music in the 20th Century/Dave DiMartino
... [et al.] editors.
p. cm.
Includes bibliographical references (p.) and
indexes.
ISBN 0-7656-8012-2
1. Music—20th century—Bio-bibliography. I.
DiMartino, Dave.
ML105.M88 1999
780'.9'0403—dc21
98-8564
CIP
MN

Printed and bound in the United States of
America

The paper used in this publication meets the
minimum requirements of American National
Standard for Information Sciences—
Permanence of Paper for Printed Library
Materials.

ANSI Z 39.48-1984

CONTENTS

COLE
PORTER

Composer and lyricist, Cole Porter crafted the most "swellegant, elegant" standards of the 1920s, 1930s, and 1940s, including "You're the Top," "Night and Day," and "I've Got You Under My Skin." According to music historian David Ewen, he "was the cynic whose love was often for sale; who could be true to you only in his fashion; to whom that seemingly crushing love affair was just one of those things." But the key to Cole's ultra-sophisticated work and extravagant lifestyle is the title of one of his most popular tunes: "Anything Goes."

Cole Porter was born in Peru, Indiana, on June 8, 1891, the only grandchild of a self-made millionaire. At six, he began studying piano and violin, and had a waltz published by his indulgent mother when he was 11. After prep school, Cole attended Yale University, where he was the big music man on campus, composing 300 songs for football games and college musicals. He dropped out of Harvard Law School for a songwriting career. Some of his songs were performed on Broadway but his first show, *See America First,* was a flop and he sailed for France in 1917. Later, Porter circulated stories that he had joined the French Foreign Legion, but he actually spent World War I partying in Paris. In 1919, he married Linda Lee Thomas, a wealthy American divorcee. Even though Porter was homosexual, he and Linda were devoted to each other and lived in grand style until her death in 1954.

While he was in Paris, Porter studied harmony and counterpoint with the French classical composer, Vincent d'Indy, and this early classical training can be heard in the chromaticism and rhythmic complexity of his songs. Porter composed the score for a 1924 revue—but he didn't have his first Broadway hit until *Paris,* in 1928, which included "Let's Do It (Let's Fall in Love)." Over the next decade, Porter wrote words and music for the wittiest shows on Broadway. In 1929, he had hits with *Wake Up and Dream* ("What Is This Thing Called Love?") and *Fifty Million Frenchmen* ("You Do Something to Me"). In 1930 he came out with *The New Yorkers* ("Love for Sale"), along with *Gay Divorce* ("Night and Day") in 1932 and *Jubilee* ("Begin the Beguine") in 1935. Two of his most successful shows *Anything Goes* ("I Get a Kick Out of You"), in 1934, and *Red, Hot, and Blue!* ("It's De-Lovely"), in 1936, starred his favorite singer, Ethel Merman. Porter's songs were also used enthusiastically by many stars of the day, including Fred Astaire and Bing CROSBY.

When Porter's legs were severely injured in a riding accident in 1937, Linda refused to let doctors amputate. After several operations (and walking with the aid of braces and a cane), he returned to the limelight with a string of successful—if formulaic—musical comedies. In 1946, *Night and Day,* a film biography of Porter, used fourteen of his songs. In 1948, he made a stunning comeback on Broadway with *Kiss Me, Kate,* a reworking of Shakespeare's *The Taming of the Shrew,* which produced classic songs such as "So in Love," "Always True to You in My Fashion," and "Too Darn Hot." He followed with more hits—in 1950, *Out of this World* ("From This Moment On"); in 1953 *Can-Can* ("I Love Paris"); in 1955 *Silk Stockings* ("All of You"). He also wrote directly for Hollywood. The movie *High Society,* starring Grace Kelly, Bing Crosby, and Frank SINATRA, was released in 1956 featuring the hit song "True Love."

Sadly, in 1958, Porter's right leg was finally amputated, and with it his desire to write—and even to live. The great sophisticate died on October 15, 1964, in Santa Monica, California, at the age of 73, and was buried back home in Indiana. In 1990, rock artists, including U2 and Annie Lennox, paid tribute to Porter on *Red, Hot, and Blue,* an album sold to benefit AIDS research.

Michael R. Ross

SEE ALSO:

FILM MUSICALS; MUSICALS; POPULAR MUSIC; U2.

FURTHER READING
Grafton, David. *Red, Hot, and Rich!: An Oral History of Cole Porter* (New York: Stein and Day, 1987); McBrien, William. *Cole Porter: A Biography* (New York: Knopf, 1998).

SUGGESTED LISTENING
American Songbook Series: Cole Porter;
From This Moment On: The Songs of Cole Porter;
Red, Hot, and Blue.

FRANCIS POULENC

Francis Jean Marcel Poulenc was a French composer and pianist whose early works exhibited qualities of wit and dissonance, so that at first he was not taken seriously by the critics. However, since World War II, he has been generally accepted as one of the most distinguished masters of the *chanson* (French song for piano and voice).

Poulenc was born on January 7, 1899, into a wealthy Parisian family. His mother was an accomplished pianist and started giving him piano lessons when he was five. When he was 16, he began studying piano with Ricardo Viñes and writing piano pieces. With five other fellow students, including Georges Auric, Arthur Honnegger, and Darius MILHAUD, he started giving concerts at which they played their own compositions, and in 1920 the group was named as LES SIX. From 1921 to 1924 Poulenc studied composition with Charles Koechlin, at the same time continuing to compose.

Poulenc's writing for piano was described as "highly idiomatic in style in a modern vein" but also as a revival of "the classical keyboard style in a new guise." His songs show clear melodic lines with intricate, restrained accompaniment. His *Rapsodie nègre* (1917) for small orchestra, brought him early recognition, while his ballet *Les biches* (1924), produced by Diaghilev, established his reputation.

Poulenc's later instrumental music included *Concert champêtre* (1927–28); the quasi-religious Organ Concerto (1938); and a piano concerto (1950), which he presented as soloist with the Boston Symphony Orchestra. His works were always melodic, and his output prolific—he wrote quantities of choral music, orchestral music, songs, and chamber music for a variety of instruments.

In 1935, Poulenc renewed his Roman Catholic faith and his Mass in G (1937) was the first of several religious pieces, including *Stabat mater* (1950) and the *Gloria* (1959). He also wrote music for films and plays, and for three operas. Of these, *Les mamelles de Tirésias* (1947) was based on a book by Guillaume Apollinaire, extolling the virtues of motherhood; *Dialogues des carmélites* (1957) was about a group of

Corbis-Bettmann

A highly talented pianist himself, Francis Poulenc wrote a wealth of memorable material for the instrument.

nuns condemned for remaining loyal to their faith during the French Revolution; and *La voix humaine* (1958) was about a distraught woman talking to her indifferent lover on the telephone.

Poulenc often performed in concerts with singer Pierre Bernac, and composed many of his songs as a result of their collaboration. Poulenc died in Paris on January 30, 1963, having made a distinguished and lasting contribution to the music of the 20th century.

Jim Whipple

SEE ALSO:

OPERA; ORCHESTRAL MUSIC; VOCAL AND CHORAL MUSIC.

FURTHER READING
Keck, George R. *Francis Poulenc: a Bio-bibliography* (New York: Greenwood Press, 1990); Mellers, Wilfrid. *Francis Poulenc* (New York: Oxford University Press, 1993).

SUGGESTED LISTENING
Les biches; Concerto for two pianos; *Dialogues des carmélites*; *Les mamelles de Tirésias*; *Rapsodie nègre*; Sextet for piano and wind.

BUD
POWELL

Earl "Bud" Powell was one of the most important pianists in the early bebop style. His highly individual approach to harmony and melody, together with his innovative ways of coupling the hands, helped transform the art of jazz piano playing in the 1940s and 1950s. At his peak Powell was a virtuoso of the highest order, but unfortunately mental illness forced him into early retirement.

Powell was born on September 27, 1924, in New York City. He began piano studies at age six, and by age 15 he was taking part in informal jam sessions at New York nightclubs such as Minton's Playhouse. Here he came into contact with Thelonious MONK and the emerging bebop jazz style. From 1942 to 1944, while playing in the band of his guardian, "Cootie" Williams, Powell refined his remarkable virtuosity. He soon created a unique piano style of long, dazzling melodic runs that were interrupted by irregularly timed chords.

RACIST ATTACK AND ITS AFTERMATH
A violent racist incident in 1945 left Powell with a head injury that brought on the first of many nervous breakdowns. Plagued after the brutal event by mental illness, he spent much of his adult life in mental hospitals. During the late 1940s and early 1950s, Powell appeared intermittently in various New York nightclubs, headlining with other leading bop soloists such as Charlie PARKER, Dizzy GILLESPIE, Sonny Stitt, and Fats Navarro. Around this time he also composed a number of memorable jazz pieces, including "Dance of the Infidels," "Tempus Fugue-It," and "Bouncing with Bud" (all 1949); and "Hallucinations" (1950), later recorded by Miles DAVIS as "Budo." His most famous piece, "The Glass Enclosure" (1953), is a remarkable musical impression of his experiences in mental institutions.

Ill-health and mental problems forced Powell to restrict his public appearances by the mid-1950s. In 1959 he moved to Paris, where he led a trio with Kenny Clarke and enjoyed country-wide celebrity status, substituting an economical primitivism reminiscent of Monk for his own lost virtuoso powers. Powell returned to the U.S. in 1964 and made an ill-advised appearance at Carnegie Hall a year later. An eagerly anticipated musical event, it turned out to be a public calamity. Powell bickered with other musicians during the performance, disappointing an audience primed by the recordings made in his heyday, and finally walked off the stage. Forced to retire ignominiously, Powell sank into obscurity and died in New York on August 1, 1966.

UNIQUE JAZZ PIANO STYLE
At the height of Powell's powers, his playing shone with technical brilliance. His style was never fastidious, however, linked as it was to an explosive intensity and a freewheeling originality. His unpredictable phrases ranged from percussive, horn-like riffs to cascading lines that displaced 4/4 bar lines. His harmonic conception, meanwhile, was based not on conventional triads, but on seconds and sevenths. This gave an exotic flavor to his interpretations of tunes such as "Night in Tunisia" and "Un Poco Loco."

The incongruity of Powell's precipitous melodic lines in the right hand, punctuated by unevenly spaced, sometimes dissonant chords in the left, represented a break from the styles of his idols, the swing pianists Art TATUM and Teddy Wilson. Because he devised new melodic ideas, harmonies, and ways of interrelating the hands, Powell remains one of jazz music's true originals. Pianists may admire his genius and imitate his style, but none can match his rich melodic invention.

Hao Huang

SEE ALSO:
BEBOP; CHRISTIAN, CHARLIE; COOL JAZZ; FREE JAZZ; SWING.

FURTHER READING
DeVeaux, Scott. *The Birth of Bebop:
A Social and Musical History*
(Berkeley, CA: University of California Press, 1995);
Owens, Thomas. *Bebop: The Music and Its Players*
(New York: Oxford University Press, 1995).

SUGGESTED LISTENING
*The Best of Bud Powell;
Bud Powell Piano Solos;
The Complete Bud Powell Blue Note Recordings;
The Genius of Bud Powell; Inner Fires.*

CHANO
POZO

Chano Pozo was a Cuban *conguero* (conga drummer) who performed with Dizzy GILLESPIE's historic Latin-influenced big band of the 1940s. Along with MACHITO and other exponents of Afro-Cuban rhythms, he was extremely influential in popularizing Latin/Afro-Cuban percussion and song forms in jazz. He was also a cowriter and arranger of some of Gillespie's greatest Latin jazz hits, including the big band anthem "Manteca."

Pozo was born Luciano Pozo y Gonzales in Havana, Cuba, on January 7, 1915. He sang, danced, and played percussion for Carnival (a Caribbean-wide celebration similar to Mardi Gras) and with local groups that included percussion greats Armando Peraza and Potato Valdes. He also became a composer of some renown, achieving success with tunes such as "El Pin Pin" and "Nague." Pozo was a follower of the Cuban Lucumi faith, which derives from West African rituals. His drumming rhythms and vocal style were firmly rooted in these African traditions, but were also influenced by indigenous Cuban musical forms such as son, *rumba*, and *comparsa*.

LATIN JAZZ IS BORN

Pozo first came to the U.S. with Cuban singer Miguelito Valdes. Miguelito had wanted to take percussionist Carlos Valdes (no relation) with him to New York, but since Carlos was a minor, he was unable to secure a passport for him. When Valdes brought Chano Pozo instead, the course of Latin jazz history was set.

Pozo was introduced to Dizzy Gillespie in 1947 by trumpeter Mario BAUZÁ, who worked with Gillespie's band as well as with the Machito Orchestra. Gillespie and Pozo had no language in common, but their musical bond was immediate. Gillespie, Bauzá, George Russell, and Gil Fuller all worked closely with Pozo to create arrangements for some of his best ideas. Many of these, such as "Manteca" and "Cubano-Be, Cubano-Bop," were destined to become jazz classics. During this period Tadd Dameron also created several original arrangements for the group.

Gillespie's big band debuted their new Afro-Cuban influenced material at New York's Carnegie Hall, in December 1947, to widespread acclaim. An international tour followed. Unfortunately, Pozo's drums were stolen sometime during the tour, and he left the band to return to New York.

TRAGIC AND MYSTERIOUS DEATH

On December 2, 1948, after a dispute over money, Pozo was shot and killed at Harlem's Rio Café. The circumstances of his death remain mysterious, and explanations for the shooting run the gamut from a drugs transaction that had gone wrong, to an altercation over royalty payments. It has even been proposed that Pozo had stolen money from members of his Lucumi sect back in Cuba, and that they were seeking revenge. According to the Rio's bartender, Pozo had just played "Manteca" on the jukebox; he died before the tune ended.

Although Gillespie and Pozo played together for only a year, their time together was extremely fruitful. Their collaboration represented the first serious attempt to fuse the jazz and Latin styles, and went on to become the starting-point for many popular and jazz musicians of the 1940s and 1950s. Recordings such as *Dizzy Goes to College* (1947), *Afro-Cuban Suite*, and *Melodic Revolution* (both 1948) showcase their unique partnership.

Chano Pozo is remembered both as a wild character and an extremely influential drummer and composer. For Gillespie, he was "the greatest drummer I ever heard." Chano Pozo's cousin, Chino Pozo, was also a noted percussionist who recorded with Gillespie, Machito, and Charlie PARKER.

Gregg Juke

SEE ALSO:

AFRICA; CUBA; LATIN AMERICA; POPULAR MUSIC; SALSA.

FURTHER READING
Suarez, Virgil. *Latin Jazz*
(New York: Simon & Schuster, 1990);
Werner, Otto. *The Latin Influence on Jazz*
(Dubuque, IA: Kendall/Hunt Publishing, 1992).

SUGGESTED LISTENING
Afro-Cuban Suite; *Dizzy Goes to College*;
Melodic Revolution.

PEREZ
PRADO

Pianist, bandleader, composer, and arranger, Perez Prado was largely responsible for establishing and popularizing the mambo in the 1950s and 1960s, and was among the first arrangers to introduce full orchestration (including strings) to Latin music.

He was born Damaso Perez Prado in Mantazas, Cuba, on December 11, 1916. By his mid-20s he had moved to Havana to pursue a musical career. While working as a pianist in clubs, cinemas, and casinos, Prado began to develop his own unique rhythmic ideas. Some of his arrangements were picked up by a famous Cuban band of the time, Orquesta Casino de la Playa, which hired Prado as pianist and arranger in 1943.

MAMBO MYTH AND MAGIC

Around this time, Prado's ideas began coalescing into mambo—an upbeat and brassy dance music in which horns and percussion provide punchy punctuation. Like the cha-cha-cha, the mambo was most likely a dance before it was a style of music; both the cha-cha-cha and mambo evolved from the traditional Cuban rumba. Perez sometimes claimed he heard the mambo emerging from the percussive cross-rhythms of five or six guitarists simultaneously jamming after hours in Cuban clubs.

Though Prado—and mambo—grew increasingly popular, he left Cuba in 1947—some biographers have suggested that Cuban music publishers considered him an upstart who dirtied their native rumba with forms like jazz, and so conspired to deny him work. Prado settled in Mexico City in 1948, and formed his own band. Through performing and recording for local labels, he gradually succeeded in becoming a multimedia sensation. He regularly performed at Mexico's most chic clubs and served as musical director for a number of Mexican films, in some of which he appeared in a musical role.

The records Prado cut for RCA in late 1949, especially "Mambo No. 5" and "Que Rico El Mambo," helped to ignite the firestorm of "mambo mania." Prado's music grew ever more popular, and began finding its way to pop stations throughout North and South America. The thousands of Cubans who had emigrated to the U.S. in the 1930s and 1940s to escape the Batista regime, and who settled in Spanish Harlem, also helped establish Prado's New York City beachhead in the 1950s.

TOP SPOT FOR "CHERRY PINK"

The mambo and Prado remained popular as he consistently recorded and toured throughout the 1950s. In 1955 he assumed the top pop spot with "Cherry Pink and Apple Blossom White," which he first recorded in 1951. But the 1955 re-recording accompanied a wriggling Jane Russell in the film *Underwater* (in which Prado himself made a brief appearance), and it spent 26 weeks in the charts, including ten consecutive weeks as No. 1.

Prado scored his second No. 1 hit in 1958 with his original "Patricia," which Nino Rota chose as the theme for Fellini's film *La Dolce Vita* in 1960. But by 1960, rock'n'roll was overshadowing the mambo on pop radio and, in 1963, RCA stopped releasing Prado's records in the U.S.

Prado returned to Mexico City in 1970 and remained popular in South America, continuing to tour and record. He recorded his final session in 1987. By that time his health was deteriorating, and he suffered a fatal stroke two years later, dying on September 13, 1989.

Perez Prado's influential relationship with the mambo was similar to Elvis PRESLEY's with rock'n'roll. He was almost certainly not the originator of the form (other candidates include Orestes Lopez, Antonio Arcano, and Arsenio Rodriguez, father of the *conjunto*), but he did more than anyone else to make mambo internationally popular.

Chris Slawecki

SEE ALSO:
CUBA; DANCE MUSIC; LATIN AMERICA.

FURTHER READING

Manuel, Peter, ed. *Essays on Cuban Music* (Lanham, MD: University Press of America, 1991).

SUGGESTED LISTENING

10 Grandes Exitos;
Voodoo Suite/Exotic Suite.

ELVIS
PRESLEY

During his lifetime, Elvis Presley was undoubtedly one of the most celebrated rock'n'roll stars of his generation. In death, however, Presley has assumed cult status, and has become one of the key cultural icons of the 20th century.

He was born Elvis Aaron Presley on January 8, 1935, in Tupelo, Mississippi, the son of a truck driver and a seamstress. His earliest musical influences were the gospel songs and psalms he heard at his Pentecostal church, but he also had a good grounding in country and blues—a combination that would create his groundbreaking musical identity. His early life was unremarkable and, like his father, he drove a truck for the Crown Electric Company of Memphis.

Presley's career started when he cut a record as a birthday present for his mother, and the studio manager contacted Sam Phillips, the owner of Sun Records. Phillips recognized that this white boy who sang in an African-American style had an astonishingly original talent. In 1954, Presley's Sun Records single "That's All Right (Mama)" electrified the Deep South thanks to the radio station WHBQ. A few other singles followed: "Good Rockin' Tonight," "Milkcow Blues Boogie," and "Baby Let's Play House," which led to Presley performing on the *Grand Ole Opry* and *Louisiana Hayride* radio programs.

In 1955, a series of live dates took Presley to clubs in Arkansas, Louisiana, and Texas, where the audience reacted enthusiastically to Presley's stage presence and suggestive semi-erotic gyrations, which earned him the nickname "Elvis the Pelvis." His last Sun single, a soaring and pulsating version of Junior Parker's "Mystery Train," confirmed his massive potential and heralded the next phase of his career.

ENTER THE COLONEL
In late 1955, Colonel Tom Parker, a former fairground huckster, took over Presley's career. He replaced DJ Bob Neal as Presley's manager and convinced Sun Records to release Elvis so he could sign with RCA. RCA paid $35,000 to gain Presley's release—an incredible figure at the time. "Heartbreak Hotel,"

released on January 27, 1956, was Presley's first RCA recording and his first nationwide No. 1 single. There followed, in remarkably short order, seven more No. 1 hit singles. One of these, the double-sided "Hound Dog"/"Don't Be Cruel," stayed at No. 1 in America for a remarkable 11 weeks, and was to be the most successful double-sided single in pop history. The diversity of Presley's musical influences and his ability as an interpreter of vocal material allowed him to cross over from rhythm and blues (R&B) into the mainstream. Along the way he changed pop music forever and lived every cliché of superstardom.

Presley's next venture was making Hollywood films. Amazingly, he completed three major motion pictures—*Love Me Tender*, *Loving You*, and *Jailhouse Rock*—in the next two-and-a-half years, and all of the

*December 3, 1968—one of the sublime moments of pop broadcasting history—*The Elvis TV Special *was networked across the States and showed Presley at his finest.*

Corbis-Bettmann/UPI

films spawned No. 1 hit songs. In 1958, Presley starred in what was arguably his greatest film, *King Creole*, but that same year, he was drafted into the U.S. Army. From 1958–1960, he served mainly in Germany. During his absence, Colonel Parker's business acumen ensured that his money-maker was not forgotten by the public. When Presley returned, he secured a series of No. 1 hits in the early 1960s, such as "It's Now or Never," and "Are You Lonesome Tonight." He also resumed his film career with *GI Blues,* which boasted the popular chart-topper "Wooden Heart."

The mid-1960s, however, were difficult years. With the advent of the BEATLES, Presley seemed to have been forgotten. His recordings were dated and his films—he made around 30 in all—seemed increasingly pointless. Even his capacity to make instant hits from mediocre material was beginning to wear thin.

Presley's fallow period was short-lived, however. In 1968, two songs—"Guitar Man" and "U.S. Male"—marked an amazing return to form. During the same year, Presley recorded a live television special, *The Elvis TV Special,* one of the most celebrated shows in pop broadcasting history, in which he appeared dressed in black leather. The success of this show personally reinvigorated Presley and the subsequent albums, including *From Elvis in Memphis,* and singles such as "Suspicious Minds," were critically acclaimed and hugely successful. Concerts followed in Las Vegas hotels and he seemed to have a new lease on life. The movie *Elvis on Tour* (1972) demonstrated his magnetism and showed his power as a performer.

THE DECLINE OF THE KING

Although Presley continued to perform, his creative inspiration again ran out and the albums started to become increasingly patchy. Presley turned into a Vegas caricature of his previous self. His personal life was fraught with difficulties: the tragedy of his still-born twin brother caused his mother to feel protective toward him, and in turn, he felt responsible for her. Meanwhile, the dissolution in 1973 of his six-year marriage to Priscilla Beaulieu further speeded his decline. He suffered an astonishing personal deterioration, gaining vast amounts of weight and becoming addicted to prescription drugs.

When not filming in Hollywood Presley performed in Las Vegas. But by this time his behavior was becoming unpredictable and he was said at some point to have stormed out of a television studio in a

fit of anger. Graceland, his relatively small but eccentric mansion on the south side of Memphis, provided him with his only refuge, and he cloistered himself there along with the same band of old Memphis buddies who had followed him since the mid-1950s.

Presley still continued to appear live, dressing in brightly colored jumpsuits and rhinestone-studded belts in a desperate attempt to disguise his obesity. He twice collapsed on stage and finally his abuse of drugs and overeating caught up with him. He died, burnt-out, on August 16, 1977. Doctors stated that he died of a heart attack, probably induced by his long flirtation with barbiturates. The world mourned and President Carter proclaimed that a part of America had died with Elvis Presley.

Despite his greatness, many feel that Presley's talent was wasted. There is also regret over his wilderness years and his untimely death. His huge talents were never fully realized, largely because neither he nor anyone else knew how to exploit them.

Colonel Tom Parker has been criticized for influencing Presley's career misdirection, but it must be recognized that without Parker's intervention at a critical time, Presley may not have achieved his enormous success.

Joseph Goldberg

SEE ALSO:

FILM MUSICALS; HALEY, BILL; LEIBER & STOLLER; LITTLE RICHARD; ROCK'N'ROLL; ROCK MUSIC.

FURTHER READING
Brown, Peter Harry, and Pat H. Broeske. *Down at the End of Lonely Street* (New York: Dutton, 1997); Escott, Peter. *Good Rockin Tonight* (New York: St. Martin's Press, 1991); Guralnick, Peter. *Last Train to Memphis: The Rise of Elvis Presley* (Boston, MA: Little, Brown & Co., 1994); Hardinge, Melissa. *Elvis Presley* (Philadelphia, PA: Chelsea House, 1997).

SUGGESTED LISTENING
Elvis' Golden Records; *Elvis! His Greatest Hits*; *Essential Elvis: The First Movies*; *I Was the One*; *King Creole*; *The Legend Begins*; *The Sun Sessions.*

ANDRÉ PREVIN

André Previn is one of the most versatile figures in music. He has made successful jazz albums, won Oscars for his film scores, conducted some of the best orchestras in the world, and even emerged as a popular personality on television.

Previn was born in Berlin, Germany, on April 6, 1929, of Russian-Jewish parents. He studied piano at the Hochschule für Musik in Berlin, and at the Paris Conservatory after his family moved to Paris in 1938. The following year they emigrated to Los Angeles, where Previn's great-uncle, Charles Previn, was music director at Universal Studios. Previn became an American citizen in 1943, at the age of 14.

JAZZ PRODIGY

While still in high school, Previn worked as a jazz pianist and wrote orchestrations for MGM. Later, he was hired as the studio's music director. His jazz trio achieved considerable success in the 1950s and his jazzed up version of *My Fair Lady* (in collaboration with Shelly Manne) started his run of jazz albums made from Broadway musical scores.

As an orchestral conductor, Previn has enjoyed a distinguished career. He has been conductor of—among others—the Houston Symphony Orchestra (1967–69), the London Symphony Orchestra (1968–79), the Pittsburgh Symphony Orchestra (1976–84), and the Los Angeles Philharmonic Orchestra (1985–90). Although Previn is immensely popular as a conductor, his repertoire is considered by many critics to be limited, generally consisting of light orchestral works ranging from Mozart to BRITTEN.

During his time with the London Symphony Orchestra, he settled in England and became well known for his television work, popularizing classical music. He also composed the music for Tom Stoppard's play for actors and orchestra, *Every Good Boy Deserves Favour* (1978).

Previn also composed film scores from 1949 until 1982, and was involved in the musical direction and supervision of many films. He received Academy Awards for his work on the scores of *Gigi* (1958),

Porgy and Bess (1959), *Irma la Douce* (1963), and *My Fair Lady* (1964). In each case, Previn was honored for his ability to adapt the musical scores of others to the demands of the screen. In addition, he has received six further nominations, mostly for adaptations of existing scores, but also for his original score for *Elmer Gantry* (1960).

One of Previn's finest scores was for Sidney Lumet's 1962 adaptation of Eugene O'Neill's stage play, *Long Day's Journey into Night*. Confining himself to piano, Previn created a highly dramatic style of writing that falls somewhere between BARTÓK and Keith JARRETT. The opening sequence is dark and tense in tone, expertly establishing the claustrophobic mood of the drama. Later, he wrote a bittersweet waltz worthy of POULENC, using it to underscore the unbalanced world of the character played by Katharine Hepburn—the drug-addicted mother of a dysfunctional family.

The score for *Two for the Seesaw* (1962) is an example of Previn's more commercial film writing. Created for solo trumpet, solo saxophone, horns, and strings, it recalls similar work by Henry MANCINI and Elmer BERNSTEIN. Even when he works in the Hollywood mainstream, however, there is a quality to Previn's melodic and harmonic language that raises his music to the level of composers such as Aaron COPLAND and Leonard BERNSTEIN.

Throughout the 1980s and 1990s, Previn has continued to work in a variety of musical styles, and one of his most recent projects was a jazz album with bass player Ray Brown and opera singer Kiri Te Kanawa.

Richard Trombley

SEE ALSO:

ARRANGERS; FILM MUSIC; FILM MUSICALS.

FURTHER READING
Bookspan, Martin, and Ross Yockey.
André Previn: A Biography
(Garden City, NY: Doubleday, 1981);
Previn, André. *No Minor Chords: My Days in Hollywood* (New York: Doubleday, 1991);
Ruttencutter, Helen Drees. *Previn*
(New York: St. Martin's/Marek, 1986).

SUGGESTED LISTENING
André Previn Plays Harold Arlen; *Long Day's Journey into Night*; *My Fair Lady*; *Two for the Seesaw*.

LEONTYNE PRICE

Leontyne Price brought to the operatic stage a generous soprano voice full of nobility and warmth. At the time she made her Metropolitan Opera debut in 1961, divas such as Maria CALLAS and Joan SUTHERLAND were at the height of their careers. But Price's dramatic presence and soaring high notes ensured that she received her own share of audience attention. Specializing in the Verdi heroines, Price was equally at home with both contemporary music and African-American spirituals.

Mary Leontyne Violet Price was born in Laurel, Mississippi, on February 10, 1927, the child of a midwife and a carpenter. She studied to become a teacher at Central State College in Wilberforce, Ohio, and sang with the college glee club. In 1949 she won a scholarship to the Juilliard School of Music in New York, and her parents mortgaged their house to enable her to attend. Further sponsorship came from the family who employed her aunt as a domestic worker.

In 1952 Price made her New York debut in a revival of Virgil THOMSON's opera *Four Saints in Three Acts.* Later that year she married the baritone William Warfield (they were separated in 1974). Following the success of *Four Saints* she was engaged as Bess in a new production of George GERSHWIN's *Porgy and Bess,* which went on to tour Europe. She stayed in the role for two years. At her New York recital debut, she presented the premiere performance of Samuel BARBER's *Hermit Songs,* a cycle based on medieval Irish texts, in which the composer accompanied her. A television appearance as the lead role in Giacomo PUCCINI's *Tosca* (1955), and as Madame Lidoine in Francis POULENC's *Dialogues des carmélites,* firmly established Price as a powerful operatic presence.

SINGING VERDI TO INTERNATIONAL ACCLAIM

It was the operas of Giuseppe Verdi, however, that brought Price true international stardom. Aida was her first professional Verdi role (she had sung Mistress Ford in a student production of *Falstaff*). Herbert von KARAJAN invited her to sing at the Vienna Staatsoper in 1958, and she was an instant success. That same year RCA signed her to an exclusive recording contract, and she went on to produce many fine recordings of operas by Puccini, Mozart, and of course Verdi.

In 1960 Price made appearances at London's Covent Garden and at La Scala in Milan. Her 1961 debut at the Metropolitan Opera, as Leonora in Verdi's *Il Trovatore,* won her 42 minutes of applause. Her other Verdi roles included Leonora in *La forza del destino,* and Amelia in *Un ballo in maschera.*

Price's repertoire also embraced Puccini's heroines Manon Lescaut and Madame Butterfly, and Ariadne in Richard STRAUSS's opera *Ariadne auf Naxos.* In 1966 she took the role of Cleopatra in Barber's *Antony and Cleopatra,* written for the opening of the Metropolitan Opera's new theater at Lincoln Center. In a performance designed to show off some elaborate new stage machinery, Price became trapped inside a pyramid and managed to wriggle out just in time for her singing cue, but was unable to complete a costume change. Despite the quality of the music, the work was a commercial failure.

PRESIDENTIAL HONORS

Leontyne Price sang at the White House for three U.S. presidents, Jimmy Carter, Ronald Reagan, and George Bush. Years earlier she had also performed for Dwight Eisenhower when he was president of Columbia University, and in 1965 she was awarded the Medal of Freedom by President Lyndon Johnson.

After she retired from the opera stage in the early 1980s, Price continued to record and to give recitals that included spirituals and the work of American composers as well as the traditional repertoire.

Jane Prendergast

SEE ALSO:
ANDERSON, MARIAN; NORMAN, JESSYE; OPERA; OPERETTA.

FURTHER READING
Sargeant, Winthrop. *Divas*
(New York: Coward, McCann & Geoghegan, 1973);
Steins, Richard. *Leontyne Price, Opera Superstar*
(Woodbridge, CT: Blackbirch Press, 1993).

SUGGESTED LISTENING
Leontyne Price in Concert at the Met;
Leontyne Price Sings Verdi;
Mozart: *Don Giovanni; Requiem.*

CHARLEY
PRIDE

The singer-songwriter and guitarist Charley Pride is one of the best-loved of all country artists, and a hero to African-Americans for his determination to break down the barriers of racial discrimination. Pride contrasted the standard country themes of loving and losing with uplifting gospel messages. His smooth baritone vocals and fondness for the "classic" country sound made him hugely popular; at the height of his career, Pride was second only to Elvis PRESLEY in his record sales for RCA.

Charley Pride was born March 18, 1938, in the northwest Mississippi town of Sledge, where his family were sharecroppers on a cotton farm. One of 11 children, he listened to country music on the radio and was drawn to the songs and style of Hank WILLIAMS. He bought his first guitar from the Sears Roebuck catalog, playing it through his teenage years. At age 16, he played baseball for the Detroit Eagles and the Memphis Red Sox in the Negro American League. By 1960 he was playing semi-pro, but his failure to reach the Major Leagues turned his attention back to music.

GOING COUNTRY

Paying his dues in small clubs and bars throughout the early 1960s, Pride refined his rich baritone and sharpened his stage performance. A backstage meeting with country star Red Sovine found Charley singing Hank Williams' "Lovesick Blues," and being encouraged by Sovine and Red Foley to try his luck in Nashville. And so it was that in 1966 the producer Chet ATKINS signed "Country Charley Pride" to RCA. Pride soon released his first single, "The Snakes that Crawl at Night."

Pride's third single, "Just Between You and Me," broke the Top 10, and his 1967 remake of Hank Williams' "Kaw-Liga" crossed over from the top of the country to the pop charts, beginning a streak of six consecutive No. 1 country hits. Keeping a low profile while releasing his first few records, Pride became a runaway success on radio before audiences ever knew he was African-American, and subsequently caused a stir in the white-dominated country music industry. The wisdom of hard labor was etched into his voice, and

his sincerity won legions of fans. In 1967 Pride debuted at the Grand Ole Opry. He was well received by the audience, and he became one of the country show's most popular performers.

In the early 1970s, Pride's career took off in earnest as he scored Top 10 hits with "I Know One" and "Does My Ring Hurt Your Finger." Meanwhile a series of gold albums—including *From Me to You* (1971), *The Best of, Volume Two* (1972), and *The Sensational* (1973)—cemented his place in country music history as he expanded his audience through regular television appearances. A 1971 gospel record, *Did You Think to Pray*, earned Pride his first two Grammy Awards.

COUNTRY'S FIRST AFRICAN-AMERICAN STAR

Pride's best-known hit, "Kiss an Angel Good Morning" (1971) led to a series of chart-topping country hits, including "It's Gonna Take a Little Time," "She's Too Good to Be True," and Merle HAGGARD's "A Shoulder to Cry On." In 1972 Pride collaborated with Henry MANCINI on "All His Children," which was featured in the movie adaptation of Ken Kesey's *Sometimes a Great Notion*. In 1977 he enlisted backing vocalists Dave and Sugar for a series of love song hits, including "I'll Be Leaving Alone" and "Someone Loves You Honey." Two Hank Williams originals, "Honky Tonk Blues" and "You Win Again," emerged from a tribute album to provide two more No.1 hits for Pride in 1980, with ten more Top 10 hits over the next three years.

Pride continues to perform in concert, and in 1994 the Academy of Country Music honored him with its prestigious Pioneer Award, in tribute to his triumph over prejudice and his many accomplishments as a recording and performing artist.

Todd Denton

SEE ALSO:

CASH, JOHNNY; COUNTRY; JENNINGS, WAYLON.

FURTHER READING

Pride, Charley, with Jim Henderson.
Pride: the Charley Pride Story
(New York: W. Morrow, 1994);
Zanderbergen, G. *Nashville Music: ... Charley Pride*
(Mankato, MN: Crestwood House, 1976).

SUGGESTED LISTENING

Essential; *Moody Woman*; *Night Games*.

PRINCE

A phenomenal talent, Prince has excelled as a singer, songwriter, instrumentalist, dancer, producer, and showman. *The New Rolling Stone Encyclopedia of Rock & Roll* hailed him as "one of the most flamboyant, controversial, influential, and popular artists of the 1980s ... and also one of the least predictable and most mysterious." And that was before 1993 when Prince changed his name first to a cryptic icon, made up of male and female gender symbols, then "Victor," and finally "The Artist Formerly Known As Prince" (TAFKAP)—informally, "The Artist."

Prince Rogers Nelson was born on June 7, 1958, in Minneapolis, Minnesota, the son of the leader of a local jazz group. A self-taught musician, he learned piano at age seven, guitar at 13, and drums at 14. After forming the band Grand Central in high school, he signed with Warner Bros. as a solo artist at age 20 and quickly released a pair of solid urban dance albums, *For You* (1978) and *Prince* (1979), the latter yielding the No. 1 rhythm-and-blues (R&B) hit "I Wanna Be Your Lover."

By 1980, when the album *Dirty Mind* was released, Prince had refined his often blatantly sexual, racially ambiguous hybrid of rock and funk. Prince's next two albums, *Controversy* (1981) and *1999* (1982), reaffirmed his mastery of contemporary R&B.

With the release of his semi-autobiographical movie *Purple Rain* (1984), Prince finally made the leap to superstar status. The soundtrack album sold 10 million copies, spent six months at No. 1 on the charts, and contained the chart-topping "When Doves Fly" and "Let's Go Crazy." The film also won an Oscar for best original score. Prince ignited a fierce controversy with his suggestive lyrics for "Darling Nikki," resulting in the formation of the "Parents' Music Resource Center" and the record industry's self-censoring sticker policy.

In the late 1980s and early 1990s, however, the extraordinary highs in the diminutive superstar's career were offset by a succession of extreme lows. He scored several No. 1 singles—"Kiss," "Raspberry Beret," and "Cream"—but the movies *Under the Cherry Moon* (1986) and *Graffiti Bridge* (1989) were both critical and commercial failures. Prince's often

Corbis/UPI

The ever-flamboyant Prince shows off his eccentric dressing style at the 1985 Grammy Awards.

eclectic albums ranged from the irresistibly funky *Sign o' the Times* (1987) to the disappointingly bland soul of the soundtrack to *Graffiti Bridge*.

In the early 1990s, Prince's behavior became increasingly eccentric. A protracted dispute with Warner Bros. became so acrimonious that the singer refused to be seen in public without the word "slave" written on his face—expressing how he felt about the terms of his contract. The dispute meant there was a lengthy hiatus in Prince's career. When the singer finally managed to free himself from Warner Bros., the resulting releases—*Emancipation* (1996) and *Crystal Ball* (1998)—were disappointing. Nevertheless, by this time, Prince's colorful career had produced enough sublime songs for such failures to be overlooked.

Michael R. Ross

SEE ALSO:
FUNK; ROCK MUSIC.

FURTHER READING
Hill, Dave. *Prince: A Pop Life*
(New York: Harmony Books, 1989);
Jones, Liz. *Purple Reign: The Artist Formerly Known as Prince* (Secaucus, NJ: Carol Publishing Group, 1998).

SUGGESTED LISTENING
1999; *Controversy*; *Dirty Mind*;
Purple Rain; *Sign o' the Times*.

PRODUCERS

The producer is an important linchpin in the music industry and is responsible for the creative, technical, and business processes of record and CD production in the studio. The producer's job is approximately equivalent to those of the producer and director in the film industry, and combines the responsibilities of both.

Of all the genres, producers are most important in popular music. Here they work with musicians, songwriters, and performers as a liaison between them and engineers in the recording studio, and working as executives for their own record labels. Producers oversee all aspects of the recording process that takes a song or album from a concept to a viable, finished musical product. As such, music producers are to popular music what directors and producers are to the theater or motion pictures: they combine the key roles of artistic adviser and business representative to create a financially successful result.

THE PRODUCTION PROCESS

The recording/studio process can be divided into three main stages—pre-production, production, and post-production. The pre-production stage involves preliminary decision making, songwriting, song selection, rehearsals, finalizing music arrangements, setting up of budgets, and settling any other details before recording begins. The production stage includes overseeing the actual recording, which involves recording all basic rhythm or bed tracks, vocals, any other additional instruments, and mixing the record. At the post-production stage all the earlier stages are tied together to complete the master recording. Mastering and duplicating mass quantities of tapes and CDs then takes place. Mastering is done by highly experienced professionals working in a specially designed environment.

The producer's role in popular music is so intertwined with the creative and business sides of the music industry that it is hard to write a definitive job description. Basically a producer is responsible for overseeing all aspects of an artist's recording. Some of these duties can overlap with those of a manager, but a producer is not a manager. By definition, a record producer is concerned with the creative, technical, and business aspects of an individual recording project, and does not extend this involvement to a life-long commitment.

A producer's involvement in a project often means not only working with the artist and engineer to get the right sound in the studio, but also being the songwriter, cowriter, and arranger, as well as managing all the business issues surrounding a recording.

THE MANY HATS OF A RECORD PRODUCER

The producer's task list includes organizing, listening, scheduling, and arranging musical, technical, and business details, so that creativity is maximized and studio time is used effectively. Producers often select material for their artists to record, studios for them to record in, and book the backing band and any additional talent needed for the recording session. The producer wears yet another hat and acts as a "director" of the session. Often having a very direct impact on the music, the producer may sometimes just act as an objective ear. Producers guide the musicians and the music during the recording process, and work with the recording engineer to achieve the best possible sound. They also handle business details such as paying the studio and hiring talent, filing union contracts, and working closely with the record company executives in charge of the act.

Sometimes pop producers are given the task of making a hit song out of a few lyrics and some chords scribbled on a piece of paper. They have a very hands-on style of working, and usually their recordings have an identifiable sound. Often producers are hired on the basis of this hit sound.

Other producers take a more removed approach, and prefer to be involved in the process only as a facilitator, offering an objective ear without being personally involved in the creative process.

Either way, the buck stops at the producer's desk; producers have the final say over all creative and business matters concerning the recording, and they have to be ready to resolve any disputes that may arise in the studio during record production.

INDEPENDENT PRODUCERS

The first independent producers were record company "A&R" (artist and repertoire) scouts—those record company executives who seek out and sign new talent. Originally, A&R executives handled all details of signing and recording new artists. However when they discovered that they could make more money from advances, royalties, and freelance production than from their fixed record company salaries, the independent producer was born.

Since that time, there has been a general division of labor between A&R representatives and producers in the record industry—with A&R people handling the scouting and signing of new talent, while the producers worked with acts during the recording process. As studio technology advanced and the recording process became more complex, the producer took on a more creative role. Some imposed a distinctive sound or approach on their artists and became famous in their own right. For example, producers of dance music are artists who create original music in the mix from sounds produced electronically or sampled elsewhere. These pioneers of electronic music boast that they can make a hit record without stirring from their own home.

Some producers started out as recording engineers and eventually worked their way up in the business. Others were successful musicians, songwriters, or arrangers who have been through the recording process many times, and therefore have invaluable experience in the creative, technical, and business aspects of music while being aware of pitfalls.

Other producers have been music critics or radio executives who have shown that they have a commercial ear for finding the next superstar.

THE NAMES BEHIND THE PRODUCERS

Many producers of popular music have had varied talents and experiences before becoming producers. Quincy JONES was a performer, a writer, and an arranger before he produced albums for artists such as Michael JACKSON, Aretha FRANKLIN, George Benson, and all-star projects like "We Are the World." George Martin, a classically trained musician, started out in A&R, then went on to sign the BEATLES, with whom he had a long and successful relationship. His main contribution was his ability to translate their ideas practically, and to add classical touches where appropriate. A millionaire by age 21, Phil SPECTOR started out writing songs. He then got backing for his recording projects and launched the careers of the Ronettes, The Crystals, and Bob B. Soxx and the Blue Jeans. He produced records of Ike and Tina TURNER and the Beatles. The ROLLING STONES were initially managed and then produced by Andrew Loog Oldham, who helped to create their rebellious pop star images.

Other notable producers were Steve Lillywhite, whose stars included GENESIS and the Pretenders; Teo Macero produced records by jazz giant Miles DAVIS; and Rick Rubin's artists were as diverse as MADONNA and Tom Petty. Berry Gordy was the founder of MOTOWN and started producing to provide an outlet for artists such as Smokey Robinson, Stevie WONDER, and Marvin GAYE. Don Was of Was (Not Was) produced Bonnie Raitt's album *Nick of Time*, which was an acclaimed best-selling release in 1989, and won Raitt a Grammy Award.

The producer is the person who has the expertise to draw the various strands of music recording together and end up with a coherent and marketable product.

Gregg Juke

SEE ALSO:

BLUES; DANCE MUSIC; ELECTRONIC MUSIC; JUNGLE; RECORD PRODUCTION; RECORDING STUDIOS; ROCK MUSIC.

FURTHER READING

Passman, Donald S. *All You Need to Know About the Music Business* (New York: Simon & Schuster, 1991); Rachlin, Harvey. *The Encyclopedia of the Music Business* (New York: Harper & Row, 1981); Ross, Courtney. *Back on the Block: A Portrait of Quincy Jones* (New York: Warner Books, 1990); Tobler, John, and Stuart Grundy. *The Record Producers* (New York: St Martin's Press, 1982); Williams, P. *Out of his Head, the Sound of Phil Spector* (New York: Outerbridge & Lazard, 1972).

SUGGESTED LISTENING

Berry Gordy: Diana Ross with Marvin Gaye, *Diana and Marvin*; Quincy Jones: Aretha Franklin, *Hey Now Hey*; Michael Jackson, *Thriller*; Steve Lillywhite: Pretenders, *Isle of View*; George Martin: The Beatles, *Abbey Road*; *Rubber Soul*; Andrew Loog Oldham: The Rolling Stones, *Out of Our Heads*; Phil Spector: Bob B. Soxx and The Blue Jeans, *Zip-A-Dee-Doo-Dah*; The Ronettes, *Presenting the Fabulous Ronettes Featuring Veronica*; Don Was: Bonnie Raitt, *Nick of Time*.

PROGRESSIVE ROCK

The term "progressive rock" is most commonly used in reference to the art-rock movement of the 1970s. The movement joined rock instrumentation with a classically influenced approach to compositional and harmonic structure. In the larger sense, the term can be applied to the journey that rock'n'roll made from being a purely commercial form of popular music to becoming a serious artistic endeavor. This journey was made more or less simultaneously in the U.K. and the U.S.

In the pre-BEATLES era of the early 1960s, rock'n'roll had been co-opted by middle-of-the-road performers such as Pat Boone and Fabian. Pop music had once again become staid and conservative. Young people with more radical tastes, then dubbed "beatniks," sought refuge in jazz and folk music.

NEW SONGWRITER POETS

Then in New York, as early as 1963, Bob DYLAN broke new ground with *The Freewheeling Bob Dylan*. The seminal singer-songwriter's second album, it departed from the Woody GUTHRIE-oriented material that had been the folk standard of the time. Dylan used a new style of songwriting that put the composer in the role of visionary poet as well as social critic, using striking imagery reminiscent of 19th-century French poets such as Baudelaire and Rimbaud. This kind of self-expressive artistic statement had previously been strictly limited to European art-song, such as was produced by Bertolt Brecht and Kurt WEILL, and Jacques BREL (both early influences on Dylan). For the first time, mainstream American pop music had been liberated from the tyranny of teenage love songs into a more cerebral, philosophical realm that offered seemingly endless possibilities.

Meanwhile, across the Atlantic, the Beatles began producing their own version of the raw, uninhibited music of rock'n'roll pioneers such as Chuck BERRY and LITTLE RICHARD. Influenced by Dylan, the Beatles (particularly John Lennon) began to inject a more intellectual form of expression into their music. Songs such as "Norwegian Wood" and "I'm a Loser" offered a more complex lyrical approach, and the group's progressive leanings resulted in *Revolver* (1966), an innovative album that incorporated avant-garde recording techniques such as running tapes backward and at different speeds, using experimental song structures, and unconventional instrumentation.

In the U.S., the progress of the BEACH BOYS from good-time surf-rockers to progressive artists paralleled that of the Beatles. Brian Wilson's masterpiece album *Pet Sounds* (1966) took Phil SPECTOR's lush wall-of-sound production techniques to new heights and featured immaculately crafted songs that stretched far beyond the capabilities of most rock'n'roll songwriters. Wilson's innovations were responsible for spurring the Beatles on to produce the revolutionary *Sgt. Pepper's Lonely Hearts Club Band* in 1967.

SGT. PEPPER'S INFLUENCE

Although many of the progressive elements used in *Sgt. Pepper's* had existed for a few of years, it was this album that truly put progressive rock on the map. Many British groups picked up on the Beatles' transmutation of American rhythm and blues (R&B) into European-style high art. One of the most progressive groups was the Zombies, with the jazzy keyboards of Rod Argent and the haunting, breathy vocals of Colin Blunstone. Badfinger signed to the Beatles' own Apple label in the late 1960s; dismissed as slavish imitators of the Beatles, they were actually a band of substance with a fine songwriter in vocalist Pete Ham. The Bee Gees, comprising Barry, Maurice, and Robin Gibb, also picked up on the Beatles' innovations. The trio's high, quavering three-part harmonies were wedded to eccentric and well-crafted pop songs about love and sometimes death with great effect.

Other innovations were being explored in Britain in the late 1960s by groups such as the Yardbirds, CREAM, THE WHO, and the Jeff Beck Group, who took American blues and R&B and added state-of-the-art technology to create a bold new electric sound. This built on the work of Muddy WATERS and Howlin' Wolf, who brought the power of the electric guitar to the blues in the 1950s. The Small Faces, led by guitarist Steve Marriot, released an early concept album, *Ogden's Nut Gone Flake*, in 1968 echoing the work on *Sgt. Pepper's*. In 1966 and 1967, psychedelic bands like PINK FLOYD, the Move, and Tomorrow

Journey, the U.S. rock group formed in 1973 by former members of Santana, started out playing European-style art-rock. A change of direction and a marketing campaign in 1978 brought huge success with the pomp rock album Infinity.

picked up on the Beatles' baroque orchestrations and free-wheeling experimentalism and combined it with their own brand of electronically enhanced pop.

THE UNDERGROUND SCENE

In the U.S., electronics and unconventional song structures found their way into the work of bands such as The Fugs (whose eponymous 1965 debut was seen as a landmark in avant-garde rock), The Holy Modal Rounders, Frank ZAPPA and the Mothers of Invention, and the VELVET UNDERGROUND. *The Velvet Underground and Nico* (1967) presented the New York band as the anti-Beatles. They were dark, decadent, and realistic, depicting street life with a grim, deadpan style.

Along with Midwestern hard rock bands such as The Stooges and The MC5, the Velvet Underground provided a blueprint for the punk rock and new wave movements of the late 1970s.

In England, Fairport Convention (featuring the singer Sandy Denny and the guitar virtuoso Richard Thompson), Pentangle, Steeleye Span, and the Incredible String Band combined traditional British folk songs with rock forms and electric instrumentation.

Their American equivalent—the Byrds, Buffalo Springfield, and later the Flying Burrito Brothers and Crosby, Stills, Nash, and Young—added American folk and country to the equation. The Byrds started out combining the jangly pop of the Beatles with the philosophical weightiness of Dylan. In fact, they had been among the first to popularize Dylan's songs by recording souped-up versions of his "Mr. Tambourine Man" and "My Back Pages." But with the arrival of singer-guitarist-composer Gram Parsons in the band in 1968, the Byrds' approach tilted toward country-rock, essentially inventing that genre with their 1968 release *Sweetheart of the Rodeo.* After leaving the Byrds, Parsons formed the Flying Burrito Brothers, releasing two classic albums, *Gilded Palace of Sin* (1969) and *Burrito Deluxe* (1970), before going solo.

From psychedelia, folk rock, and a dash of European classical music, groups like Vanilla Fudge and Deep Purple created the beginnings of art-rock. They laid the groundwork for a more fully realized version of the genre, spearheaded in Britain by Yes, the Nice, King Crimson, Jethro Tull, Genesis, and Emerson, Lake, and Palmer. The slow, heavy rhythms of Vanilla Fudge also inspired the hard rock/heavy metal sound that took bands such as Black Sabbath, Uriah Heep, Wishbone Ash, the Scorpions, and Golden Earring to the top of the 1970s album charts.

CLASSICAL INFLUENCES

The Beatles were among the first to use classical sources to spice up modern rock—from the string quartet on "Eleanor Rigby" to the sound collages of *Sgt. Pepper's*, which were derived from 20th-century "new music" techniques. The dense, angular orchestral works of Frank Zappa were doubtlessly inspired by his love of Edgard VARÈSE. Even proto-punks like the Velvet Underground brought conservatory training and modern classical theory to bear in their early, discordant pieces. Lou Reed and John Cale were both heavily influenced by the work of minimalists like John CAGE and LaMont Young.

Nowhere was the influence of classical music seen more plainly than among British art-rockers of the late 1960s and early 1970s. Some groups, such as Yes, Genesis, and King Crimson, borrowed the structure and arrangement of their lengthy, multi-part compositions from composers such as Beethoven and RAVEL. Others, such as Emerson, Lake, and Palmer and Keith Emerson's pre-ELP group the Nice, ransacked the classical repertoire, creating "rock" versions of well-known classical pieces including Mussorgsky's *Pictures at an Exhibition* and modern works like Aaron COPLAND's *Fanfare for the Common Man*.

THE ELECTRONIC PERSPECTIVE AND PSYCHEDELIA

The German take on art-rock relied less on classical sources, expanding instead on the electronic innovations of late 1960s British bands such as Hawkwind, Pink Floyd and Soft Machine and American experimentalists including the United States of America, Lothar & The Hand People, and the Monks. German bands such as Can, Faust, Amon Duul II, Sand, and Guru Guru merged these influences with various ethnic traditions to create a style that most closely resembled a rock version of the "serious music" composed by Steve REICH, Morton Subotnick, and Harry Partch. Synthesizer-oriented bands like Tangerine Dream, Cluster, and Neu took the music even further away from rock toward an exclusively electronic sound that often forsook traditional rock song structure in favor of more abstract, instrumental pieces.

Meanwhile West Coast bands such as the Grateful Dead, Quicksilver Messenger Service, Spirit, and Moby Grape combined psychedelia and folk rock in a musical amalgam whose trademark was long, improvisational passages alternated with acoustic guitar-based interludes. During this musical experimentalism exponents such as guitar virtuoso Jimi HENDRIX and West Coast "acid-rockers" Jefferson Airplane often took drugs, particularly hallucinogens like LSD, which gave birth to the San Francisco psychedelic scene, home of the hippie movement. Britain gave rise to Soft Machine, who began their

career as a spacy, organ-based psychedelic band, sharing bills with the Syd Barrett-era Pink Floyd in London. Later they transformed themselves into an instrumental jazz rock band. The fashion-conscious element of British rock produced Brian Ferry of Roxy Music, Marc Bolan of T. Rex, and David BOWIE. They were the pioneers of what became known as glam-rock. Brian Eno figured heavily in this scene, first as a pioneering rock synthesizer player with Roxy Music, then as producer-collaborator with Bowie. Eno's 1970s solo albums were critically acclaimed combinations of pop songcraft and edgy art-rock. On later recordings he created a new genre he dubbed "ambient music," which became the new age sound of the 1980s.

The progressive sounds coming from Britain found an audience in forward-looking jazz artists such as Miles DAVIS and Herbie HANCOCK. Davis began utilizing electric instrumentation as early as 1968 on *Miles in the Sky*, and in 1969 he released the hugely influential *Bitches Brew*, arguably the first jazz rock (fusion) album. Throughout the 1970s, Tony WILLIAMS, Herbie Hancock, and John McLAUGHLIN furthered the "fusion" approach, incorporating loud electric guitars, synthesizers, and rock rhythms into their jazz-based sound.

DYLAN AND POST-DYLAN INFLUENCES

On the lyrical side, the influence of Bob Dylan was still being strongly felt among American singer-songwriters in the late 1960s and early 1970s. These included the dark, satirical Randy Newman, poetic Texas troubadour Townes Van Zandt, the jazz and soul-influence Laura Nyro, and literary New Yorker Paul Simon, along with the Canadians Leonard Cohen, Joni MITCHELL, and Neil Young.

Singer-songwriters such as Britain's Nick Drake and America's Tim Buckley, Fred Neil, and Tim Hardin helped to evolve a style that combined the post-Dylan approach with a loose, jazzy feel and improvised instrumental passages. This style can be heard on the landmark albums *Happy Sad* by Tim Buckley and *Five Leaves Left* by Nick Drake, both released in 1969. However, throughout the 1970s, the specter of Dylan was inescapable as one artist after another was dubbed "the new Dylan." Those who survived the tag included Bruce SPRINGSTEEN, Loudon Wainwright III, and John Prine. Others, such as Elliot Murphy, Paul Seibel, and Sammy Walker, although equally talented, were overwhelmed by the burden of the industry's expectations and disappeared from sight.

THE LOST ROOTS OF ROCK'N'ROLL

Although the African-American roots of rock'n'roll were at the heart of most of the music's major innovations, those roots had become all but forgotten by the mid-1970s. In Britain particularly, the influence of European folk and classical music took art-rock even further away from the gospel and blues traditions that formed the core of rock'n'roll. In America, where larger-than-life blues-rock was the order of the day, high-wattage bands such as Bad Company, Ten Years After, Lynyrd Skynyrd, and the Allman Brothers offered more of a departure from than a return to their blues roots.

Most of the progressive black rock being made in the early to mid-1970s was more closely aligned with funk and R&B. These included the cosmic funk-rock of George Clinton's Parliament-Funkadelic in it's various permutations; the psychedelic soul of groups such as Mandrill, Bloodstone, and the Five Stairsteps; and the heady, eclectic mix of rock, R&B, and funk at the heart of Sly and The Family Stone's sound. But it was not until the arrival on the pop scene of PRINCE and the later work of Michael JACKSON that progressive R&B became a commercial peer to the rock of Grand Funk, Humble Pie, and Foghat.

CORPORATE ROCK, MERCHANDISING, AND MONEY

Sensing the huge amount of money to be made, the American record industry put its vast resources into promoting a genre that blended the most pretentious aspects of British art-rock and American blues-rock. Variously known as AOR, for adult-oriented-rock, corporate rock, or pomp rock, the style dominated the airwaves and charts in the mid-to-late 1970s.

Bands such as Journey, Styx, Boston, Kansas, and Foreigner—who were ex-members of the U.K.'s Spooky Tooth and King Crimson—started out aping the British art-rock currently in vogue, but watered it down for mass consumption. Merchandising became the order of the day, with albums, posters, and T-shirts making millions of dollars for these bands.

Always quick to pick up on a trend, the British produced acts such as Elton JOHN and QUEEN, who brought theatricality and a sense of humor to this otherwise earnest genre. Then there was the school of Led Zeppelin-influenced rock that included Canada's Rush, who eventually cranked up the science-fiction influence of Hawkwind and steered a course toward heavy art-rock.

INFLUENCE ON RADIO

These bands generated so much money that American radio began to build its formats around them. The resulting programming would survive as classic rock virtually unchanged throughout the 1980s and 1990s. Rock acts live and die by radio charts and airplay. Any artist not willing to fit into the strictures of mid-1970s radio was cast out. Cult artists such as Tom Waits, Captain Beefheart, and Jonathan Richman survived on the fringes, while others, such as Lou Reed and Van MORRISON, achieved the status of elder statesman due to early mainstream breakthroughs such as Morrison's 1960s hit "Brown Eyed Girl" and Reed's twin rock radio anthems "Sweet Jane" and "Rock and Roll," from the Velvet Underground's album *Loaded* (1970), even though they affected a noncommercial stance.

Ultimately, progressive rock took itself too seriously and lost its searching, adventurous spirit. The stage was set for the iconoclastic, irreverent, resolutely unprofessional sounds of punk, whose seeds had been sown nearly ten years before by the likes of the New York Dolls and Iggy Pop's Stooges.

Jim Allen

SEE ALSO:

JAZZ ROCK; PUNK ROCK; ROCK'N'ROLL; SINGER-SONGWRITERS.

FURTHER READING

Macan, Edward. *Rocking the Classics: English Progressive Rock and the Counterculture* (New York: Oxford University Press, 1997); Martin, Bill. *Listening to the Future: The Time of Progressive Rock, 1968–1978* (Chicago, IL: Open Court, 1999).

SUGGESTED LISTENING

The Beatles: *Revolver*; *Sgt. Pepper's Lonely Hearts Club Band*; Tim Buckley: *Happy Sad*; The Byrds: *Sweetheart of the Rodeo*; Nick Drake: *Five Leaves Left*; Brian Eno: *Another Green World*; Faust: *IV*; Grateful Dead: *Aoxomoxoa*; King Crimson: *In the Court of the Crimson King*; Gram Parsons: *GP/Grievous Angel*; Pink Floyd: *Piper at the Gates of Dawn*; The Small Faces: *Ogden's Nut Gone Flake*; Tangerine Dream: *Electronic Meditation*; Richard & Linda Thompson: *Pour Down Like Silver*; Tony Williams: *Lifetime*; *Spectrum*; Yes: *Fragile*.

SERGEY
PROKOFIEV

Sergey Prokofiev, born in the Ukraine on April 23, 1891, was one of Russia's greatest composers. In the hostile intellectual climate of post-revolutionary Russia, he was seen as very much a rebel. The Soviet government criticized him for being too abstract and unintelligible, and exhorted him to write for the "common man" instead of the musical élite. Ironically however, his music is now seen as technically conservative in the West, especially when compared to the innovations of composers such as STRAVINSKY, IVES, and SCHOENBERG.

Innovation, though, is not the only indication of creative genius. Prokofiev's works for the stage are exciting and genuinely theatrical, and he made major contributions in all the main musical genres. With great intellectual and emotional intensity, he made use of the musical tools available to him at the end of a musical era.

Prokofiev should be thought of as the capstone of an era rather than as an innovator, and it is the quality of his music, rather than its newness, that demands our attention and admiration.

AT ODDS WITH RUSSIA

Prokofiev was born into a middle-class family. His mother was an amateur pianist, and the young Prokofiev started composing piano pieces when he was five. His output, even as a child, was prodigious. Although his parents were worried about his being committed to a musical career so young, he was enrolled at the conservatory in St. Petersburg in 1904, when he was only 13. He stayed there until 1914, studying orchestration with Rimsky-Korsakov and counterpoint with Lyadov, although he did not form a strong bond with either teacher and got a reputation for being an impatient and rebellious youth. His first public appearance was in 1908, when he performed his piano piece, *Suggestion diabolique*, which was declared to be unintelligible and "ultramodern." During this time he came to admire the works of Richard STRAUSS and SCRIABIN, and was introduced to the early works of Schoenberg and

Stravinsky. In 1910 Prokofiev's father died, and with him, the family's income disappeared. It became clear to the young composer that he had to earn a living from his music. In his last year at the conservatory, he set himself the goal of winning the Rubinstein Prize for piano-playing, and did so with a performance of his own Piano Concerto No. 1. Besides this, his most important music of the period includes the Toccata for piano (1912), the *Scythian Suite* for orchestra (1915), the first Violin Concerto No. 1 (1917), and the *Classical Symphony* (1917).

On graduating from the conservatory, Prokofiev made a trip to London and met the ballet impresario Sergey Diaghilev, who was sufficiently impressed by Prokofiev's playing of his Piano Concerto No. 2 to commission a ballet. This contact did not bear fruit until later in the 1920s, but it fired Prokofiev's interest in ballet and the stage. His early works already showed signs of his mature musical language—one with imaginative orchestration, driving dance-like rhythms, rhythmic ostinatos (repetition of a musical phrase constantly throughout a passage), lyrical melodies, and frequent half-step modulations. The pounding rhythms and screaming sounds of the *Scythian Suite* (which were

Underwood and Underwood/Corbis-Bettmann

Sergey Prokofiev who, despite the Soviet government's censorship, was one of Russia's greatest composers.

partly inspired by Stravinsky's *Rite of Spring*), the Piano Concerto No. 2, and the ballets *Chout* (1921) and *Steel Step* help explain why his early audiences considered Prokofiev a shocking radical. But even in his most radical works, Prokofiev's music was almost always tonal, a characteristic of his style that enabled his music to win wide popular acceptance.

In the mid-1910s, Russia was in a state of political ferment. During Prokofiev's time at the conservatory, teachers were dismissed for political dissidence and the conservatory was closed for a period. Then came World War I and the Russian Revolution, which reduced the country to a state of civil war. Musical life became impossible, and Prokofiev decided to leave for the United States.

AMERICA, PARIS, AND DIAGHILEV

Prokofiev left Russia for America in 1918, and he remained there until 1920. During the voyage, he began his popular opera, *The Love for Three Oranges* (1919). However, this proved to be a mixed blessing at the time. The Chicago Opera offered to stage the work but the conductor died; the work was postponed and the composer lost much time during which he could have promoted his piano works. He did, however, complete his third piano concerto and began another opera, *The Fiery Angel*.

Prokofiev left the U.S. for France in 1920, staying there until 1936. In 1923 he married the Spanish singer Lina Llubera and settled in Paris. Here, he again met Diaghilev, who commissioned a ballet on a Soviet theme. He wanted the rawness of the newly industrialized country to be reflected in an exciting ballet. Prokofiev's response, *The Steel Step* (1925–26), was successful in Paris and London, although it was rejected by the Russian Association of Proletarian Musicians as too esoteric. Diaghilev then commissioned *The Prodigal Son* (1928–29), a ballet based on the Biblical story, which was also enthusiastically received, but Diaghilev himself became ill and died in 1929. Several other important works emerged during this period: important revisions of his operas *The Fiery Angel* (1927) and *The Gambler* (1927–28), the Symphony No. 3 (1928), the Piano Concerto No. 4 (1931), for the left hand alone, and the Violin Concerto No. 2 (1935).

Prokofiev returned to Russia (now the U.S.S.R.) in 1936, and remained there until his death in 1953—ironically he died on the same day as the Soviet dicta-

tor Joseph Stalin. Prokofiev had toured the U.S.S.R. in 1927 with considerable success, being treated as a celebrity, and returned for a visit in 1929, when an injury from a car accident prevented him performing. In 1933, the Russian film director Feinzimmer commissioned a score for his film *Lieutenant Kijé*, which remains one of Prokofiev's most popular light-hearted pieces. However, when he actually returned home as a citizen, he began to feel the effects of Soviet censorship. The Soviet government felt that any art not created for the people as a whole was meaningless, and they placed severe restrictions on all Russian artists and banned the work of European composers they considered decadent. Prokofiev responded by trying to write pieces on suitable Soviet themes of the time, but was at his happiest during these remaining years when composing works based on more traditional themes, such as the children's tale *Peter and the Wolf* (1936) and the opera *War and Peace*. In spite of continuing difficulties with government officials, he was still able to produce some of his finest work, including the ballets *Romeo and Juliet* (1935–36) and *Cinderella* (1940–44), and his Symphony No. 5 (1944).

Prokofiev died in Moscow on March 5, 1953, from a brain haemorrhage. Because of the troubled times through which he lived, a number of Prokofiev's works are lost in obscurity. Nevertheless, he is deservedly one of the most popular 20th-century composers, and many of his major works are firmly established in the standard repertoire of soloists, conductors, and ballet and opera companies.

Richard Trombley

SEE ALSO:

CHAMBER MUSIC; OPERA; ORCHESTRAL MUSIC.

FURTHER READING
Minturn, Neil. *The Music of Sergei Prokofiev*
(New Haven, CT: Yale University Press, 1997);
Samuel, Claude. *Prokofiev*
(New York: Marion Boyars Publishers, 1998).

SUGGESTED LISTENING
Alexander Nevsky; *Classical Symphony*;
The Love for Three Oranges; *Peter and the Wolf*;
Piano Concerto No. 3; *Romeo and Juliet*;
String Quartet Nos. 1 and 2; Symphony No. 5.

GIACOMO
PUCCINI

Giacomo Antonio Puccini, one of the greatest operatic composers of the Late Romantic era, was born in Lucca, Italy, on December 23, 1858, the son of a successful organist and composer. When his father died in 1864, the five-year-old Giacomo was promised his father's post when he came of age. In the meantime he studied organ with his uncle and later learned composition from Carlo Angeloni, director of the Instituto Musicale Pacini (of which Giacomo's father had been director).

By the age of 14 Puccini was the official organ player at several churches in Lucca, and soon began composing his own organ pieces. In 1876, when he saw a performance of Verdi's *Aida* in Pisa, Puccini was inspired to become an operatic composer.

In 1880 Puccini became a student at the Milan Conservatory, supported by a one-year scholarship and an allowance from his uncle. There he was taught by the composer Amilcare Ponchielli and became friends with fellow student Pietro Mascagni and with Ruggero Leoncavallo, both destined to become noted operatic composers.

STRUGGLING FOR SUCCESS

While still a student at the conservatory, Puccini decided to enter a competition for a one-act opera. Ponchielli's influence helped secure Fernando Fontana as his librettist, and Puccini's first opera *Le Villi* was entered in the competition. When the result was announced, it did not even receive a mention. However, the influential composer and music critic Arrigo Boito heard Puccini play and sing the opera at a party, and raised funds for it to be performed at the Teatro del Verne. It was an instant success, and the music publisher Ricordi bought it and then commissioned a second opera, *Edgar*.

Puccini chose the subject of his third opera. *Manon Lescaut* (1893) was based on a novel by Abbé Prévost, which had already been turned into an opera by Massenet. The libretto went through the hands of three different authors before being taken over by Giuseppe Giacosa and Luigi Illica, who were to coauthor the libretti of Puccini's most popular works. Puccini's next opera, *La bohème*, conducted by TOSCANINI, was premiered in Turin, Italy, in February 1893, and was not a success at first. The critics were initially hostile as they had expected an opera in the romantic and tragic style of *Manon Lescaut*. *La bohème*, with its lighthearted scenes of Parisian bohemian life set mainly in a garret, and its conversational style, seemed inconsequential by comparison.

MIXED REACTIONS

However, the premiere of *Tosca* in Rome in 1900 was a runaway success, and Puccini's standing was assured. Serious injury in an automobile accident slowed Puccini's rate of composition, but in 1904, *Madama Butterfly* premiered at La Scala, in Milan. This now-beloved work was so poorly received that Puccini had to return the theater's advance.

Puccini attended the New York debut of *Manon Lescaut* in 1907, and while there saw David Belasco's play, *The Girl of the Golden West,* which appealed to him as the subject for an opera. *La Fanciulla del West* had its first Metropolitan Opera performance in 1910.

By 1921, Puccini's health was declining. Although he did not know it, he was suffering from throat cancer. He raced with death to finish the score of *Turandot*, but before he could do so he died on November 29, 1924. *Turandot*, completed by the Italian composer Franco Alfano, eventually joined the repertoire of Puccini's great and enduring operas.

Jane Prendergast

SEE ALSO:

OPERA; PAVAROTTI, LUCIANO; SUTHERLAND, DAME JOAN.

FURTHER READING
Brown, Jonathan. *Puccini*
(New York: Simon & Schuster, 1995);
Jackson, Stanley. *Letters of Giacomo Puccini,*
(New York: AMS Press, 1971);
Weaver, William, and Simonetta Puccini.
The Puccini Companion
(New York: W. W. Norton, 1994).

SUGGESTED LISTENING
La bohème; *Madama Butterfly*;
Manon Lescaut; *Tosca*;
Turandot.

TITO
PUENTE

The percussionist, bandleader, composer, and arranger Tito Puente was a major catalyst in the creation of the style of music known as Latin jazz. He stood alongside other pioneers, such as Raul "MACHITO" Grillo, Dizzy GILLESPIE, and Chano POZO, as one of the genre's all-time greats. Puente's music combined Afro-Cuban rhythms and instrumentation with the harmonies and improvisations of jazz; as such he had a great influence on both modern salsa and jazz. His skills as a *timbalero* (timbale player) and composer/arranger earned him the sobriquet "El Rey" (the king).

Tito Puente was born Ernest Anthony Puente, Jr., on April 20, 1923, in New York City. His parents were immigrants from Puerto Rico, and he grew up listening to the great big bands of the day as well as the popular groups coming out of Cuba, such as Arsenio Rodriguez and La Orchestra Casino de la Playa. In his youth Puente studied piano, drums, and percussion, and later taught himself vibes and saxophone. He also studied dance and performed for a brief time with his sister Anna in a Fred Astaire–Ginger Rogers-inspired dance team.

While still in high school Puente began performing with various Latin bands, including those of Noro Morales, Jose Curbelo, Ramon Olivera, and Machito. When Machito's drummer, Uba Nieto, was drafted, Puente replaced him. Puente played drums and timbales in Machito's band until he, too, was drafted into the U.S. Navy, in 1942. Puente spent time during World War II loading artillery on a converted aircraft carrier that escorted supply and passenger ships. He also played drums and alto saxophone in his ship's big band, and began writing and arranging music.

MAMBO CRAZE HITS THE U.S.
After the war Puente enrolled at the Juilliard School of Music in New York, where he studied conducting, orchestration, theory, and composition. While studying there he continued to play with various bands, and began contracting work on his own. Eventually his band landed a steady gig at the Alma Dance

Studios. In 1949 promoter Max Hyman bought the Alma and changed the name to the Palladium; soon it was filled with dancers from all walks of life. It was the start of the "mambo craze."

In the early 1950s, the fashion for mambo (a Cuban dance form) and Afro-Cuban rhythms swept the U.S. During this time, jazz artists also began to incorporate Latin influences into their music. Dizzy Gillespie's Afro-Cuban style big band was extremely popular, as were the more commercially oriented sounds of Xavier Cugat and Perez PRADO. The Latin influence on U.S. popular culture became firmly established.

LATIN JAZZ VETERAN
Puente released over 100 albums—on various record labels, including Tico, GNP, RCA, Concord, and TropiJazz—and continued to tour and record into the late 1990s. Several of his compositions, such as "Oye Como Va" and "Para Los Rumberos," became Latin classics, and many have been recorded by best-selling artists such as Carlos SANTANA, thus extending both Puente's popularity and his influence.

A long and varied career saw Tito Puente working with big bands, small ensembles, and all-star groups such as the Latin Percussion Jazz Ensemble (a group put together by entrepreneur and instrument manufacturer Martin Cohen). He explored music in the "straight jazz" format (as on the 1956 big band album *Puente Goes Jazz*) as well as in the Latin genre. Tito Puente is still a vital and influential force not only in Latin jazz, salsa, and mainstream jazz, but also in pop and rock music.

Gregg Juke

SEE ALSO:
BIG BAND JAZZ; CUBA; LATIN JAZZ; SALSA.

FURTHER READING
Loza, Steven Joseph. *Tito Puente and the Making of Latin Music* (Urbana, IL: University of Illinois Press, 1999); Suarez, Virgil. *Latin Jazz* (New York: Simon & Schuster, 1990).

SUGGESTED LISTENING
Gozo Mi Timbal; *Mambo Mococo*; *Puente Goes Jazz*; *Salsa meets Jazz*: *Un poco loco*.

PUNK ROCK

Just when rock'n'roll looked as if it had evolved into a respectable, grown-up art form, along came punk. Punk put the rebellion back into rock, adding an injection of raw, enraged energy, laced, at least sometimes, with a smirking humor. Rejecting the overblown sounds of their contemporaries, the punk bands went back to basics, unleashing a barrage of short, sharp songs that struck a chord with a generation of angry, angst-ridden teenagers.

FOUR BOYS FROM QUEENS

The roots of punk lie in the musical adventures of the Ramones, four young hoodlums from the New York borough of Queens. The band formed in 1974, at a time when rock music was becoming increasingly intricate and self-conscious. Armed with three chords and a couple of basslines, the foursome set about bringing rock back to its roots, creating a music that was stripped down to its raw basics. The Ramones' songs were aggressive, two-minute blasts of pure energy, and their singalong choruses quickly gained the band a devoted following around New York. In 1976, the band released their self-titled debut album, a record that showcased the band's abrasive sound to the rest of the world. The Ramones' attitude struck a particular chord in London, where it inspired a generation of bands who were equally frustrated by the staid musical status quo.

By far the most important of these bands was the SEX PISTOLS, an extremely angry, loud, and outrageous quartet whose attitude toward the rest of the world could be summed up by a line from one of their songs: "… and we don't care!" The band was made up of wild-eyed, orange-haired singer Johnny Rotten, drummer Paul Cook, guitarist Steve Jones, and bassist Glen Matlock. Despite writing the majority of the band's early songs, however, Matlock was to be replaced by the man who would eventually become the most infamous punk of them all, Sid Vicious.

Dictating the general form and thrust of the band was brash young entrepreneur Malcolm McLaren, who at first envisioned the Pistols as a way of promoting the punk clothing he and fashion designer

The Ramones: four punks, three chords, two basslines, one haircut. But they changed the face of music forever.

Vivian Westwood wished to sell in their London shop, Sex. However, the impact of the group's first two singles, "Anarchy in the U.K." and "God Save the Queen," and the accompanying album *Never Mind the Bollocks* proved far greater than even the exploitative McLaren had hoped. Gleefully offending everyone within earshot, the band quickly became a cultural phenomenon. The Sex Pistols were to self-destruct in a flash at the end of their first U.S. tour, with Vicious dead soon after. However, the influence of the band would be felt for years to come.

CLASH CITY ROCKERS

The other great band to emerge from the London punk scene of the mid-1970s was the Clash. The Clash shared the Pistols' raucous, ultra-aggressive sound, but were also overtly political, playing benefit concerts for the British Anti-Nazi League at a time when fascist political organizations were highly active in the U.K. The Clash were also far more willing to incorporate other musical styles into their repertoire. Thus, while their first two albums, *The Clash* (1977) and *Give 'Em Enough Rope* (1978), were straightforward slabs of punk, their later releases such as *London Calling* (1979), *Sandinista* (1980), and *Combat Rock* (1981) incorporated reggae, funk, and rockabilly into the mix. This may have alienated some of the band's more hardcore fans, but the group's willingness to experiment resulted in some of their finest recorded material.

In the wake of these two dominant groups, dozens of British punk bands sprang up in the late 1970s. Among the chief promulgators of punk were the Buzzcocks, a Manchester band whose irrepressibly upbeat melodies earned them considerable chart success. Other notable British punk bands of the time included the Damned, who diluted their crudity and viciousness with pub-rock looniness; and the bright and breezy Generation X, whose permanently pouting singer Billy Idol went on to earn huge success as a solo singer. The late 1970s also saw two highly influential bands emerge from Northern Ireland: the improbably youthful Undertones, whose debut single "Teenage Kicks" has become a classic among punk singles, and the more overtly political Stiff Little Fingers.

BACK IN THE U.S.A.

America quickly responded to punk's call and produced its own wide variety of exponents. Perhaps the most influential, and notorious, American punk band was the Dead Kennedys. Formed in San Francisco in 1978, the band took their musical inspiration from the Sex Pistols, but eschewed the Pistols' nihilistic approach to lyrics. Instead, the Dead Kennedys used their songs to make a savage assault on the political establishment. The band's debut single, "California Über Alles," was an aggressive attack on the then governor of California, Jerry Brown, while subsequent releases such as "Holiday in Cambodia," "Kill the Poor," and "Let's Lynch the Landlord" also raised social issues, albeit in rather blunt terms. Unsurprisingly, the establishment bit back. The band's records were banned from both the airwaves and from certain stores, forcing the band's eloquent lead singer, Jello Biafra, to become a de facto spokesman for the anti-censorship lobby.

Among other punk bands to tread the same anarchic path as the Dead Kennedys were several groups based in the Los Angeles area, most notably the Germs, Black Flag, and the Minutemen, whose songs, as their name suggests, rarely lasted more than 60 seconds. The turn of the decade saw punk groups springing up in virtually every major U.S. city. On the East Coast, Washington's Minor Threat led the way, though with their staunch anti-drug, anti-alcohol stance, they were as far removed from the original punk scene as it was possible to get.

Whereas punk lost its impetus in Britain, the genre continued to flourish in the U.S. Artists such as Bad Religion and Hüsker Dü kept the punk flag flying in the 1980s, although somewhere along the line the music began to be known as "hardcore punk" and then simply as "hardcore." Toward the end of the decade, the hard-edged aggression of punk provided the inspiration for the grunge movement, with grunge standard-bearers NIRVANA owing a particularly large debt to the punk sound.

A cultural phenomenon as much as a musical genre, punk irrevocably changed the direction of rock music. Bands such as the Sex Pistols and the Clash brought with them an unprecedented sense of danger and excitement, and in so doing set the standard for countless future generations of would-be rebels.

Terry Atkinson

SEE ALSO:

FUNK; GRUNGE; ROCK MUSIC.

FURTHER READING

Boot, Adrian, and Chris Salewicz. *Punk: The Illustrated History of a Music Revolution* (New York: Penguin, 1996); McNeil, Legs, and Gillian McCain. *Please Kill Me: The Uncensored Oral History of Punk* (New York: Penguin, 1997); Savage, Jon. *England's Dreaming* (New York: St. Martin's, 1992).

SUGGESTED LISTENING

The Buzzcocks: *Singles Going Steady*; The Clash: *The Clash*; *London Calling*; The Dead Kennedys: *Fresh Fruit for Rotting Vegetables*; Hüsker Dü: *Candy Apple Gray*; The Ramones: *The Ramones*; The Sex Pistols: *Never Mind the Bollocks*.

QUEEN

British rock group Queen blended pure pop, hard rock, and quasi-classical arrangements to make some of the cleverest popular music of the 1970s and 1980s. Their flamboyant frontman, Freddie Mercury, had a keen sense of the dramatic, and his onstage theatrics were solidly backed up by the band's inventive musicianship. A combination of well-crafted albums and dynamic live presentation made them rock superstars.

The group was formed in 1970, and consisted of vocalist Mercury (b. Frederick Bulsara, September 1946; d. November 1991), guitarist Brian May (b. July 1947), and drummer Roger Taylor (b. July 1949). Bassist John Deacon (b. August 1951) joined in early 1971. Queen signed with EMI in late 1972 and, after appearing in several showcase gigs, their breakthrough finally came when their song "Seven Seas of Rhye" reached the British Top 10 in 1974.

The early to mid-1970s saw the band with a foot in both the glam rock and the heavy metal genres, but in 1975, the multilayered "Bohemian Rhapsody" set Queen apart from the less imaginative practitioners of both styles. The single made a massive impact on the British charts, staying there for nine weeks—the longest-running British No. 1 hit for 18 years. An innovative song lasting close to seven minutes, it moved swiftly from Mercury accompanying himself on piano, through a frenzied guitar cadenza, to all four members of the group singing in an operatic style. It took the band three weeks to record. The close vocal harmonies of this record became one of the strongest features of Queen's subsequent recordings. The success of "Bohemian Rhapsody" was greatly helped by a promotional video that used innovative film techniques. The single was featured on the album, *A Night at the Opera*, which was one of the most expensive albums ever made and quickly settled at No. 1 in the British charts, hitting the U.S. Top 5 soon after.

In the late 1970s, Queen subtly adjusted their style to take account of changing tastes in mainstream rock. They proved expert at creating crowd-pleasing and long lasting anthems such as "We Will Rock You" and "We Are the Champions"—popular songs for the burgeoning stadium-rock circuit. The final month of 1979 saw Queen achieve their first U.S. No. 1 hit with "Crazy Little Thing Called Love," a useful springboard into the 1980s. The next decade proved as eventful for the group as the 1970s. In 1980, *The Game* topped the album charts in the U.S., and Queen made a foray into soundtrack work, recording the music for the film *Flash Gordon*. Although a critical failure, the music blends well with the film itself. A year later, *Queen's Greatest Hits* had one of the longest chart runs in Britain.

During the 1980s, the band's output slowed as various members pursued individual projects. However, their popularity was unaffected and in 1991, Queen's last album, *Intuition*, entered the British charts at No. 1. This album was a remarkable achievement as Mercury was by this time very ill. November of that year saw Queen build on their success in the U.S., where the album *Classic Queen* reached No. 4. Sadly, having finally achieved superstardom in America, Mercury died from an AIDS-related illness later that month, after a two-year battle with the disease.

In April of 1992, a concert was held at Wembley Stadium, London, and broadcast to 70 countries to commemorate Mercury.

Queen were among the most professional of rock bands, ceaselessly seeking perfection in the production and performance of their music. They were at the forefront of an era when rock music was becoming more business-like and technologically advanced, but their innate wit ensured that the music always had a human element. As an example of how to play heavy rock with a light touch, Queen was unequaled.

Graham McColl

SEE ALSO:

HEAVY METAL; PROGRESSIVE ROCK; ROCK MUSIC.

FURTHER READING
Hodkinson, Mark. *Queen: The Early Years*
(New York: Omnibus, 1995);
Hogan, Peter. *The Complete Guide to the Music of Queen*
(New York: Omnibus, 1994).

SUGGESTED LISTENING
Classic Queen; *A Night at the Opera*;
Queen's Greatest Hits; *Sheer Heart Attack*.

SERGEY RACHMANINOV

The Russian composer Sergey Rachmaninov is best known for his piano concertos, which are among the most popular—and the most difficult—in the repertoire. He also had a successful career as a conductor, and after 1918 achieved international fame as a concert pianist and recording artist. His music was often lushly romantic, with broad and memorable melodies.

Rachmaninov was born into a landowning family on April 2, 1873, in Semyonovo, Russia. His father was a retired army officer and a spendthrift; his mother, Rachmaninov's first teacher, was an amateur pianist. The family's bankruptcy meant that they lost their last estate and had to move to an apartment in St. Petersburg. Here Sergey attended the conservatory, studying harmony and piano. At 15, he was accepted by Alexander Ziloti at the Moscow Conservatory.

For his graduation from the conservatory he wrote an opera, *Aleko*, with a libretto taken from Pushkin's *The Gypsies*. This was so successful that it was produced in Moscow in 1893, and Rachmaninov was offered a contract by the publisher Gutheil, for whom he wrote Five Short Pieces for Piano Op. 3, including the Prelude in C-sharp Minor, which was destined to become a popular encore piece.

On graduating Rachmaninov took a job teaching music to support himself while composing. But the negative reception given to his Symphony No. 1 in 1897 plunged him into depression. A hypnotist helped him overcome this, enabling him to write his famous Piano Concerto No. 2, which he performed for the first time in Moscow in late 1901, with Ziloti conducting.

CONDUCTING AT THE BOLSHOI

In 1902 Rachmaninov married his cousin, Natalia Satin, and in 1903 their first daughter, Irina, was born. The next decade was a busy and highly productive one for Rachmaninov. As well as conducting for two seasons at the Bolshoi Theater in Moscow, he composed many pieces, including his operas *Francesca* and *The Miserly Knight*, his second symphony (1907), the Piano Sonata No. 1 (1907), the Piano Concerto No. 3 (1909), and his orchestral piece, *The Bells*.

The Russian Revolution in 1917 threw the country into turmoil. An invitation to play in Stockholm gave Rachmaninov the chance to leave, and he and his family departed for Sweden, leaving Russia forever.

Since he left all his possessions behind in Russia, Rachmaninov now embarked on a punishing career as a concert pianist to earn money. He moved on to the U.S., where he gave 36 concerts in four months. At the end of the 1919–20 season, he signed a recording contract with the Victor Talking Machine Company. The constant traveling and the demands of his performing schedule meant that Rachmaninov had little time for composing after he left Russia. Nevertheless during his years of exile he composed his fourth piano concerto (1926), the *Variations on a Theme of Corelli* (1931), and the well-known *Rhapsody on a Theme of Paganini*, which was an instant success at its premiere in New York in 1934. The Symphony No. 3 was premiered` in Philadelphia in 1936. The *Symphonic Dances* (1940) was his last work. In its finale he used the *Dies Irae* ("day of wrath") chant from the Mass for the Dead, as he did in much of his music, perhaps reflecting his melancholy and pessimistic nature.

Rachmaninov continued to compose songs (79 were published during his lifetime) and to perform as a concert pianist while making classic recordings of his own and other's piano works. Early in 1943, Rachmaninov developed a cough that was ultimately diagnosed as cancer. He died on March 28, 1943.

Alan Blackwood

SEE ALSO:

CHAMBER MUSIC; OPERA; ORCHESTRAL MUSIC.

FURTHER READING
Martyn, Barrie. *Rachmaninoff: Composer, Pianist, Conductor* (Brookfield, VT: Grover Publishing Co. 1990); Norris, Geoffrey. *Rachmaninoff* (New York: Schirmer Books, 1994); Walker, Robert Matthew. *Rachmaninoff* (New York: Omnibus Press, 1984).

SUGGESTED LISTENING
Horowitz Plays Rachmaninov;
Piano Concertos;
Rhapsody on a Theme of Paganini.

RADIO

In 1906, from an experimental station in Brant Rock, Massachusetts, the first known radio broadcast in the United States was made by Reginald A. Fessenden. This broadcast, made on Christmas Eve, consisted of phonograph records, a violin solo, and a speech by Fessenden.

For the first years, radio was restricted to the sending and receiving of messages because of a wartime ban on non-military broadcasting, which lasted until 1919. After World War I, David Sarnoff, the commercial manager of the Radio Corporation of America, predicted the spread of radio so that every household would have a radio receiver. By 1952, this was true for 95 percent of American households.

A lack of government regulation promoted radio's growth and swift commercialization. The U.S. Department of Commerce was in charge of regulating stations according to the Radio Act of 1912. The act confined most domestic broadcasting to the same wavelength, thus creating a clutter of overlapping signals. In 1922, the Commerce Department allowed more powerful stations to use the 400-meters wavelength, on the condition that they play only live music. This forced large and small broadcasting systems to affiliate and share costs to bring popular live entertainment from cities to rural areas.

In 1927, Congress passed another radio act, which created a Federal Radio Commission empowered to license and regulate stations. Networks, whose influence was largely unforeseen, were free from direct FRC regulation.

RADIO AND THE GREAT DEPRESSION

It was no coincidence that interest in radio increased dramatically in the late 1920s as the Great Depression set in. The American public found radio to be a cheap source of entertainment as the effects of economic failure crippled the nation. Not surprisingly, comedy dominated the airwaves, featuring Eddie CANTOR, the star of musical comedy and vaudeville, and Fred Allen, another vaudeville star who remained in the Top 10 in the ratings until 1949, when the quiz *Stop the Music* overtook it.

Other figures who began to make a name in the new medium were Jack Benny, Burns and Allen, Fibber McGee and Molly, Ed Wynn, Rudy VALLEE, and Al JOLSON. The 1920s were a confusion of recording and experiments in the entertainment and radio business. The need for recorded music by radio stations drew artists into the studio. Fiddler Eck (A. C.) Robertson went to New York and in 1922 made the first "hillbilly" records, "Arkansas Traveler" and "Sallie Goodin."

ADVERTISING AND THE RATINGS

From the beginning, businesses were quick to see the potential of nationwide exposure on radio. Sponsors' names appeared on programs with titles such as the Firestone Orchestra, the General Motors Family Party, or the A&P Gypsies Orchestra. In 1929, Archibald M. Crossley invented the Cooperative Analysis of Broadcasting to analyze the percentage of viewers tuning in to any particular program. He gathered his figures by morning-after telephone calls and then sold the data, called the Crossley ratings, to networks and stations and, of course, to the advertisers. It was Crossley who discovered the concept of "prime time" listening, when his data revealed that most people listened to radio between 7 P.M. and 11 P.M.

In 1922, radio stations WSB in Atlanta, Georgia, and WBAP in Fort Worth, Texas, broadcast shows they called "barn dances," aptly named for the informal social dances of the frontier. WLS in Chicago, Illinois, started what was to become the *National Barn Dance* in 1924 and WSM in Nashville, Tennessee, unveiled its own barn dance—the future *Grand Ole Opry*, in November of 1925.

The need to fill up airtime meant that music of all kinds was in great demand—thus radio was the major medium for disseminating music in the early part of the century. Radio provided for every musical taste, from opera to novelty music. The Metropolitan Opera in New York began to broadcast productions every Saturday afternoon in December 1931 and continues to do so today during the opera season. The Bell Telephone Hour, The Prudential Family Hour, The NBC Symphony Orchestra, and the Longines Symphonette presented mainly classical entertainment. The *National Barn Dance* and *The Grand Ole Opry* dominated country music during the 1930s and 1940s.

In 1932, Al Jarvis introduced a new format which, in only a few years, became the standard for popular music programs. Jarvis was with KFWB in Los

Angeles when he started *Make Believe Ballroom,* a nonstop program of records and commentary. Martin Block began the same kind of show for WNEW in New York, and these two presenters are considered to be the first disc jockeys.

In the mid-1930s, the big band era brought dance music by Benny GOODMAN, Guy LOMBARDO, and others to the air-waves in programs including *Your Hit Parade,* which featured the top songs of the week performed live by singers such as Frank SINATRA, Dinah Shore, and Doris DAY. *Your Hit Parade* on the NBC Red Network was sponsored by Lucky Strike cigarettes and was the brainchild of the American Tobacco Company's president, George Washington Hill. Hill had his own ideas about the formula of the program, and forced his executives to join him in testing the "foxtrotability" of selections. For years, teenage dances were planned round this Saturday night program.

In 1935, the NBC Red Network launched another of the most popular shows of all time, *Major Bowes and the Original Amateur Hour.* This format gave amateurs a chance to be heard and the audience called in their votes. Many leading performers were launched from this program, including Frank Sinatra in its first year.

The style called Western swing began to be heard nationally in the early 1930s, with musicians like Bob WILLS. In the late 1930s, Hollywood's "singing cowboys"—Roy Rogers, Gene Autry, and Tex Ritter—brought country music to the air and made millions of fans, both nationally and internationally. New barn dances were popping up all over the place in the 1930s: the sounds of the CARTER FAMILY and Jimmy C. RODGERS were heard across the nation.

Kate Smith, remembered for her rendition of "God Bless America" on Veterans Day, had her first radio show in 1931, and continued in radio until the 1940s.

THE 1940S AND THE BEGINNINGS OF TELEVISION
Experiments with television had taken place for some time, but the medium was first seen by the public at the 1939 World's Fair in New York.

It was many years before television caught up with radio, but this was the beginning of the battle between the two broadcasting media and the gradual erosion of radio's monopoly. From the 1940s on, the chief question a radio producer had to ask was how to ensure that the audience for any particular slot was listening to the radio rather than watching television.

Popperfoto

One of America's most popular entertainers from the 1940s, Kate Smith's big career was launched on the radio.

During World War II, radio provided programs for troops overseas, probably the most popular being *Command Performance,* a variety show which featured all America's greatest stars of the time. Songs were often rather simple and patriotic, and included "Praise the Lord and Pass the Ammunition," "This is the Army, Mr. Jones," and Irving BERLIN's "God Bless America." After the war, NBC's *Kraft Music Hall* was a popular program that starred Bing CROSBY. Crosby rebelled against the live broadcasting schedule and left the show for a while, returning only after he was allowed to prerecord his songs.

THE 1950S AND MCCARTHY
The 1950s were the decade of "reds under the bed." Many artists were denounced by rivals; others by anonymous letter-writers. Once an artist had a reputation for having Communist sympathies, or even just for being liberal, he or she would not be employed by radio stations. One example was the harmonica virtuoso, Larry Adler, who was forced to leave the U.S. for Europe in search of work. Traditional radio programming lasted into the 1950s. Then the shows that had been the heart of radio programming—the variety-comedy shows, soap operas, and dramas—began moving to television.

The central radio music program of that time—*Your Hit Parade*—moved to television in 1951. However, in 1952, radio still controlled 13 percent of advertising spending, compared to television's 3 percent. Radio became an amalgam of recorded music shows, talk shows, news, and sporting events—basically the radio of today. The development of the transistor increased the availability of portable radios and the number of radios installed in automobiles multiplied rapidly. Radio promoted itself as the "intimate and mobile companion."

THE TOP 40 TAKES OVER

In the early 1950s in Omaha, Nebraska, Todd Storz and Bill Stewart introduced a format that dominated music programs for the decade and marked the marriage between record producers and radio. This was the *Top 40* program, which introduced listeners to the week's Top 40 records, which they could then go out and buy. From the point of view of the recording industry, radio was the ideal promotional vehicle.

This led to the great "payola" scandal in 1959, when the Federal Communications Commission (FCC) realized that some DJs were accepting bribes for promoting records. Many DJs were fined, including WINS's Alan FREED; others, such as Bill Randle, reported that they had been threatened with blackmail as payola takers. The result was that DJs, who for a while were known as "musicasters" in the wake of the payola scandal, had to announce both the label and the artist of each record played.

In 1955, a recording by Bill HALEY and His Comets became the No. 1 radio disc. "Rock Around the Clock" was the beginning of the rock era on radio, attracting a whole a new audience who were young and eager to buy records. Rock music became the primary popular musical form of young listeners in the United States and Western Europe, and radio stations competed fiercely for the fastest-paced, up-to-the-minute shows.

The Top 40 format reached its peak with Rick Sklar, who began to program for WABC in 1962. He researched record sales in stores and noticed that the top three songs sold more than twice as many copies as the next dozen. He cut his air-play list down to 18–24 singles a week, with the addition of some past hits from the archive. The top three songs were put on fast repeat cycles controlled by time clocks: the No. 1 was played every 60 minutes, No. 2 every 75 minutes, and No. 3 every 90 minutes. Each hit song was tagged with a jingle to introduce it to listeners. This formula invaded the air-waves like wildfire. By the late 1960s, WABC had 6 million listeners: on a typical Saturday night, one in every four radios was tuned in to the *Cousin Brucie* show.

UNDERGROUND RADIO

The Top 40 format inevitably produced a reaction, and in the 1960s, underground radio stations became the showcase for more marginal labels. "Progressive" radio was perhaps heard first on KMPX in San Francisco with Tom "Big Daddy" Donahue. Donahue played the "other" tracks from albums that had never gotten an airing, and removed the jingles from hits. He was also the man who first brought the BEATLES to San Francisco. In the liberal atmosphere of the 1960s, these stations became a counter-culture, and the prevailing use of drugs gave them the name of "voices from the purple haze" or "acid rockers."

The drug culture too brought a reaction. The FCC chairman appointed by President Richard Nixon warned broadcasters that they were responsible for the words they put on the air, and almost immediately songs like the Beatles' "With a Little Help from My Friends" were censored. At the same time, an enterprising businessman named Bill Drake undercut the DJs by supplying readymade taped programs to stations. His first package was *Hitparade,* which was followed by *Super Gold Rock'n'Roll.* Each basic library he supplied consisted of a collection of 50 one-hour tape compilations. The oldest and most successful syndicated rock program was *The King Biscuit Flower Hour,* which began in 1972 and within three years was on 175 stations.

National Public Radio (NPR) was founded in 1970, in an effort to provide radio with a more responsible public face. NPR provided more than 90 affiliated stations with news, classical, jazz, folk, and bluegrass music. NPR is a non profitmaking organization funded by grants, and smaller stations cannot afford to buy its programs, but it still struggles on.

RADIO IN THE 1980S AND 1990S

A further blow was dealt to radio in America with the birth of MTV (Music TV) in the 1980s. Pop music responded by sponsoring spectacular rock festivals and, in addition, the FCC inaugurated several deregulating efforts. First, the rules that limited stations' profits were minimized or cut out, and broadcasters were no longer obliged to apportion a part of their broadcasting day to public concerns. Second, the limit was lifted on the number of commercials a station could play per hour. Third, a radio station could keep its license for seven years before it had to apply for renewal, and was no longer required to keep a logbook to prove that it had served the public as dictated by Congress. In 1992, the FCC relaxed the conditions on the ownership of radio broadcasting stations in an effort to reinforce the industry in the face of its worst decline in many years. Many of the other restrictions disappeared following the enactment of the Congressional Telecommunications Act of 1996, which deregulated the industry even further.

Major changes of ownership followed, raising important concerns about the concentration of media power. In 1985–86 alone, Capital Cities Communication took over ABC; Fox procured Multimedia; General Electric bought RCA; Time, Inc., bought Group W. Cable; and WOR-TV (New York) was purchased by MCA, Inc. In 1995, the Disney Company purchased Capital Cities/ABC, while Westinghouse took over CBS, and the Turner cable empire was consumed by Time/Warner.

According to the Radio Advertising Bureau, in 1990 only one percent of U.S. homes had no radio, and the average household owned at least five radios. By 1995, there were over 5,000 FM stations and nearly 5,000 AM stations.

RADIO AND THE MUSICIAN

In the 1980s and 1990s, specialized minority programs took a back seat again and major stations reverted to the Top 40 format, rechristened *Contemporary Hit Radio* (CHR). This coincided with a boom in nostalgia for the music of the 1950s and 1960s, and its emphasis on DJ presenters such as Rick Dees and Scott Shannon. On their radio shows, catchy tunes epitomizing the sound of each format are used to introduce songs. Using focus artists has become more important than discovering new talent, since research showed that familiarity is vital. A clear, easily remembered identifier is used (which is why there is an overabundance of stations named Lite-, Kiss-, and Magic-.) Also, the arrival of satellite transmission has produced a new type of network. Radio producers can now broadcast shows via satellite to any station in the world with the equipment to receive them.

NEW MUSIC ON THE AIRWAVES

However, the health of the medium itself is not reflected in the welfare of the musicians. As has been the case since the early days of radio, only "hits" have a chance to be heard and the reality is that the bottom line is money, not music. With almost all of the signals owned by a few large corporations, there is little room for small, independent owners to survive, providing little or no opportunity for less mainstream musicians to be heard. Major artists get the airtime, without which albums are not heard by the audience.

Radio, via the program and music directors, is still the prime medium for hearing new music. It is also the main vehicle for creating hit artists and selling millions of records.

Renee Jinks

SEE ALSO:
COUNTRY; GOSPEL; NASHVILLE SOUND/NEW COUNTRY; POP MUSIC; POPULAR MUSIC; ROCK'N'ROLL; SOUL.

FURTHER READING
Eberly, Philip K. *Music in the Air: America's Changing Tastes in Popular Music, 1920–1980* (New York: Hastings House, 1982);
Keith, Michael C. *Voices in the Purple Haze: Underground Radio and the Sixties* (Westport, CT: Praeger, 1997);
Sklar, Rick. *Rocking America: An Insider's Story: How the All-Hit Radio Stations Took Over* (New York: St. Martin's Press, 1984).

SUGGESTED LISTENING
Big Band Themes on the Air;
Command Performance, USAF Band;
Cowboy Copas and His Friends;
Cruisin' America with Cousin Brucie;
King Biscuit Time;
Major Bowes Amateur Hour;
Make Believe Ballroom Vols. 1–20;
Old Time Radio;
Opry Time in Tennessee;
Saturday Night Barn Dance;
The Twist Goes to College;
Your Hit Parade;
Chubby Checker: *Chubby's Dance Party*;
Vincent Lopez: *Lopez Playing*.

RAGGA

A sub-genre of reggae, ragga is a modern Jamaican sound with ties to the oldest traditional music of that island-nation. The name is taken from the word "raggamuffin," a term used for disenfranchised youth. One popular ragga singer called Half Pint said, "A lot a people interpret raggamuffin as if it [is] a criminal morality."

Ragga shares many attributes with rap music, including rapid-fire lyrics chanted over a heavy bass line. It is a "hardcore" version of the Jamaican style of music called "dancehall." Dancehall is said to be more "sterile" or commercialized than ragga. In 1992, *Time* magazine described ragga as "reggae on megavitamins, bulked-up and bass-pummeled … punchy, insinuating, and prime for export."

Ragga's heritage can be traced back to the Jamaican DJ and sound-system dances from the 1950s. The latest recordings would be introduced with patter designed to pump up the excitement at dances. When migrants left to work in the Florida cane fields, they returned to Jamaica with the latest records, which they played on their homecrafted stereo systems. The local DJs became revered for their creative banter or "toasting" over the track. U-Roy was among the "toasters" whom contemporary ragga artists looked to as a pioneer.

STRONG LYRICAL CONTENT

Ragga emerged in the 1980s when it became marked by toasting of a more explicit nature. Sexual boasts, raw lyrics, and machismo, plus simulated gunfire were among its hallmarks. Chester Francis-Jackson wrote: "Figuring prominently in the music's vocabulary are the more notorious of Jamaican ghettos; references to the island's two major political parties and their strongholds; and the choicest of cusswords." The strong lyrical content was not always apparent to the uninitiated; Jamaican patois was hard for outsiders to follow. Decoding the homophobic or gangsta lyrics sometimes generated controversy, such as that which surrounded Buju Banton's notorious "Boom Boom Bye Bye." Ragga artists Steely and Clevie expressed a desire for lyrics to become "more conscious and cultured."

Several developments in the mid-1980s changed Jamaican music. Artists such as Mento, Poco, Kumina, and Revival began to cannibalize older musical forms. Much of today's ragga developed from Poco's dancehall music. In 1985, "Under Me Sleng Teng," the first song with entirely electronic tracks, launched dancehall into the computer age. Most ragga is now electronically produced. Some claim this makes it less roots-conscious, but the rhythms are derived from those used in Jamaican religious music.

INTERNATIONAL RECOGNITION

The 1990s saw artists drawing from many musical forms, including hip-hop, rap, rhythm and blues, and bhangra beat. Ragga burst onto the scene outside the Caribbean in 1991 and 1992, and performers including Shabba Ranks, Patra, Super Cat, and Tiger won contracts with major recording labels. Ini Kamoze's "Here Comes the Hot Stepper" was used in the soundtrack to the Robert Altman film *Ready to Wear,* and introduced even more people throughout the world to ragga.

These artists represent a small fraction of ragga musicians. As Peter Manuel noted in *Caribbean Currents,* Jamaica has a high record production rate, "most of which will never leave the island."

Linda Dailey Paulson

SEE ALSO:

BHANGRA BEAT; CARIBBEAN; RAP; REGGAE.

FURTHER READING

Manuel, Peter, et al. *Caribbean Currents: Caribbean Music from Rumba to Reggae* (Philadelphia, PA: Temple University Press, 1995); Potash, Chris, ed. *Reggae, Rasta, Revolution: Jamaican Music from Ska to Dub* (New York: Schirmer Books, 1997).

SUGGESTED LISTENING

Daddy Freddy: *Raggamuffin Soldier;*
Lloyd Lovindeer: *One Day Christian;*
Patra: *Queen of the Pack;*
Shabba Ranks: *As Raw as Ever; X-tra Naked;*
Super Cat: *Don Dada;*
Various Artists: *Dancehall Style: The Best of Reggae Dancehall Music;*
Just Ragga, Vols. 1–6.

MA
RAINEY

The Paramount label billed Gertrude "Ma" Rainey as "The Mother of the Blues," and rightly so. She was one of the first female singers of the blues, and one of the best of the classic blues singers of the 1920s. Her earthy vocal style made her a link between male-dominated country blues and the urban blues of contemporary female singers.

Ma Rainey was born Gertrude Pridgett on April 26, 1886, in Columbus, Georgia. Her parents had both performed in minstrel shows, and Rainey made her performing debut in 1900. She married William "Pa" Rainey of the renowned Rabbit Foot Minstrels in 1904. They formed a song-and-dance team, billing themselves as "Rainey and Rainey (or, sometimes, Ma and Pa Rainey), the Assassinators of the Blues." But it was Ma Rainey's unique singing talent that carried the team, and they eventually separated. It is believed Ma Rainey was the first singer to incorporate the blues into a minstrel show repertoire. By putting the blues on stage, she gave the music a legitimacy not previously known.

Rainey signed with Paramount in 1923, more than 20 years after she had begun performing, and cut about 100 sides for the label between 1923 and 1928. Her deep contralto voice carried great power and feeling, and even her humorous, boisterous songs conveyed an underlying sense of melancholy. Rainey's singing wore a vulnerability masked by toughness, a sense of the weary veteran who had seen it all. She sang for rural Southern African-Americans, and her songs referred to elements of folk culture, such as farming, hard times, and superstitions. She introduced a new topic into the blues, that of women's troubles with men. Other themes dealt with social outcasts, and sexuality, including homosexuality. Her hits included the raunchy "Shave 'Em Dry," "Bo Weavil Blues," "Moonshine Blues," and "See See Rider." Rainey was short and squat, but she carried herself regally, both on and off stage, and preferred to be called "Madame" to "Ma." But musicians and other admirers saw her as a mother figure, both compassionate and generous.

Michael Ochs Archives/Redferns

Ma Rainey and the Georgia Jazz Band in 1925: Thomas A. Dorsey on piano, Edward Pollack (alto sax), Dave Nelson (trumpet), and Al Wynn (trombone).

Some great musicians accompanied Rainey, including TAMPA RED, Fletcher HENDERSON, Coleman HAWKINS, and Louis ARMSTRONG. Rainey eventually formed her own performing troupe. Her recordings spread her fame from the South to cities in the North, and she joined the Theater Owners' Booking Association circuit and toured African-American theaters. As her popularity declined in the late 1920s, she returned to Southern tent shows, where she had first made her name. Rainey retired from performing in 1933, supporting herself from income from two small theaters she bought as an investment. She returned to Columbus, Georgia, where she died on December 22, 1939. Sadly, due to poor sound quality, Ma Rainey's surviving recordings do not fully convey her remarkable bluesy talent.

Stan Hieronymus

SEE ALSO:
BLUES; FOLK MUSIC.

FURTHER READING
Davis, Angela Y. *Blues Legacies and Black Feminism: Gertrude "Ma" Rainey, Bessie Smith, and Billie Holiday* (New York: Pantheon Books, 1998); Jones, Hettie. *Big Star Fallin' Mama: Five Women in Black Music* (New York: Viking, 1995).

SUGGESTED LISTENING
Ma Rainey's Black Bottom.

RAP

Few styles of music have experienced an explosion in popularity as spectacular as that of rap. As late as 1979, rap was restricted to the African-American ghettos of New York, yet by the end of the following decade, the music formed the basis of a multi-million dollar industry, and was instantly recognizable across the globe.

The roots of rap lie in the sound systems of Jamaica, mobile discos that blasted reggae out across the slums of Kingston. Thousands of Jamaicans emigrated to New York in the 1970s and they brought their sound systems with them. These became extremely popular in the summertime, when jams in parks, housing projects, and on street corners quickly became a main source of entertainment for African-Americans and Latinos. Mobile DJs grew in popularity, yet it was not until the emergence of Kool Herc, otherwise known as Clive Campbell, that the DJ became a celebrity in his own right. An immigrant from Kingston who had settled in the Bronx, Kool Herc played rhythm and blues, funk, and other records at block parties in the mid-1970s, and during this time developed a highly idiosyncratic style of DJing. Noticing that certain "breaks" or snippets of songs would drive the crowds wild, Herc would play these sections repeatedly, rewinding the records manually. In order to make the music flow, Herc would often have identical records on each turntable, cutting from one to another. This style of DJing would form the basis of rap music, otherwise known as hip-hop.

THE FIRST RAPPER

While Herc was the first hip-hop DJ, he wasn't the first rapper. Like their Jamaican predecessors, the New York DJs would use microphones to urge the crowds to dance. These exhortations gradually became more and more elaborate, and eventually DJs started to compose rhymes to deliver over the beats. Legend has it that the first to do so was a young DJ by the name of Grandmaster Flash. So that he could concentrate on DJing, Flash persuaded a group of friends to share the vocal duties. These would form the basis of the Furious Five, with whom Flash would later record some of the genre's best-loved records.

Initially, rap music circulated purely through unofficially recorded "bootleg" tapes of live sound systems, but that all changed with the phenomenal success of the Sugarhill Gang's "Rapper's Delight" (1979), which sold over 2 million copies worldwide. Soon, all of New York's rap crews—from the Treacherous Three to the Funky Four Plus One—were laying down rap tracks. The most successful were Grandmaster Flash and the Furious Five, who scored huge hits with "The Message" (1981) and "White Lines" (1982).

Gradually, as the 1980s progressed, more and more rap acts reached superstar status. Among them were LL Cool J, the Beastie Boys, and Run-DMC, who crossed over to a white rock audience when they collaborated with the heavy metal band Aerosmith on "Walk This Way" (1987). The former two were signed to Russell Simmons' Def Jam label, which was also home to Public Enemy. Led by the fiercely articulate Chuck D, Public Enemy fused radical black separatist politics with a thundering hip-hop soundtrack, and in so doing produced some of the genre's most critically acclaimed music, most notably the album, *It Takes a Nation of Millions to Hold Us Back* (1989).

Toward the end of the decade, rap plunged into controversy as "gangsta" rappers including Ice-T and NWA began to release tracks celebrating the macho exploits of ghetto criminals. The shadow of violence would continue to fall over the genre in the 1990s, when superstar rappers Tupac Shakur and the Notorious BIG were both murdered. However, in the late 1990s, artists such as Puff Daddy, the Wu-Tang Clan and the Fugees were among the most successful musicians working in the U.S. Despite the controversy, rap continues to thrive.

Nick Grish

SEE ALSO:
FUNK; RAGGA; REGGAE.

FURTHER READING
Fernando, S. H., Jr. *The New Beats*
(New York: Doubleday, 1994).

SUGGESTED LISTENING
Public Enemy: *It Takes a Nation of Millions to Hold Us Back*; Run-DMC: *Raising Hell*;
The Sugarhill Gang: *Rapper's Delight*; Wu-Tang Clan: *Enter the Wu-Tang Clan (36 Chambers)*.

MAURICE
RAVEL

Maurice Ravel was one of the eminent composers of the century, bringing a distinctive style and craftsmanship to his masterful orchestral, piano, vocal, and chamber works. Like his contemporary and fellow Frenchman DEBUSSY, Ravel has remained consistently popular with orchestras and audiences alike.

Ravel was born on March 7, 1875, in the Pyrenees region of France. Shortly after his birth, his family moved to Paris where he was based for the rest of his life, although he did travel abroad in Europe and to America in 1928. He began his piano studies at the Paris Conservatory in 1889, winning a First Medal in 1891. Between 1897 and 1899 he studied composition with Gabriel FAURÉ, and was awarded second place for composition in the Prix de Rome in 1901.

By 1905 Ravel had already written some outstanding works, including the solo piano piece *Pavane pour une infante défunte* (1899), which was transcribed for orchestra in 1910. Other notable works from this early part of his life include his String Quartet in F Major (1902-03); *Shéhérazade*, for voice and orchestra (1903), which includes the beautiful *La flute enchantée*; the solo piano work *Miroirs* (1904-05); and *Introduction et allegro*, for harp, flute, clarinet, and strings (1905). Taken together, these works, completed by the time Ravel was 30 years old, confirm a remarkable musical personality with highly individual qualities.

In 1908, Ravel completed his *Rapsodie espagnole,* following it up two years later with the comic opera *L'Heure espagnole.* Ravel's attraction to the music of Spain can be traced to the influence of Emmanuel Chabrier (1841–94), who had a profound effect on Ravel's work. This period of the composer's life also saw him compose two ballets, *Daphnis et Chloé* (1909–12) and *Ma mère l'oye* (Mother Goose, 1912), the former being the result of a commission from the Russian impresario Sergey Diaghilev.

TRAUMATIC BLOW

Ravel was declared unfit to serve in World War I, but became a driver with the transport corps. He fell ill with dysentery and was sent back to Paris. Shortly

A master orchestrator, Maurice Ravel was one of the most influential composers of the century.

afterward his mother died, which was a shattering blow to the composer. These two events had a traumatic effect on his personality. Ravel became an intensely private man who never formed close relationships with anyone else.

After the death of his mother, Ravel's emotional life seemed to become increasingly centered on childhood and its private magic. This made him a sympathetic reader of *L'enfant et les sortilèges,* a short story by Colette in which a child's toys come magically to life. Ravel turned the story into an opera, although the process took him seven years, with the composer finally completing the task in 1925.

ORCHESTRATION AND HARMONY

Ravel's numerous orchestral works include *Alborada del gracioso*, taken from the piano work *Miroirs* (1918); *Le tombeau de Couperin* (1919); *La valse* (1920); *Tzigane*, for violin and orchestra (1924); Piano Concerto in D Major, for the left hand (1929–30); and the Piano Concerto in G Major (1929–31), which makes use of American jazz rhythms. Outstanding among his chamber works is the song cycle claimed by STRAVINSKY to be Ravel's most provocative and significant composition, *Trois poèmes de Stéphane Mallarmé*, for soprano, two flutes, two clarinets, string quartet, and piano (1913).

Whatever style Ravel chose to write in, his orchestration was invariably of the highest quality, comparable with that of SCRIABIN, Debussy, Richard STRAUSS, and Stravinsky. Between them, these five composers offer some of the richest of all orchestration, taking the 19th-century orchestra to its greatest heights of opulence of sound and tone color, and demanding a high degree of instrumental virtuosity from each member of the orchestra. Ravel also created orchestral versions of several of his compositions for solo piano, including the *Pavane pour une infante défunte*. At the same time, he worked in the opposite direction: his *La valse*, for two pianos (1921), was based on an earlier orchestral work, and in 1930 he scored a version of his acclaimed ballet *Boléro* (1928), also for two pianos.

In 1922, Ravel orchestrated Mussorgsky's 1874 composition for piano, *Pictures at an Exhibition*, which is a tour de force in timbre experimentation. The ballet *Daphnis et Chloé* is another prime example of Ravel's orchestration, filled with unique timbre combinations and subtle dynamic shades.

Ravel was active as a composer during the first three decades of the 20th century, a time when most composers of his musical talent and stature were struggling to pull away from the conventions of tonality. Ravel, by contrast, seemed content with the old approach to tonality, though he did experiment with bitonality (using two keys simultaneously) once, in *L'Enfant et les sortilèges*. But that does not, of course, mean that his approach lacked imagination. His *Pavane* illustrates one of his most ingenious harmonic devices: when the beautiful though simple opening melody returns later in the piece, it now has a new harmonic accompaniment. This device can be heard, perhaps to an even greater extent, in his String Quartet.

WRONG IMPRESSIONS

Ravel and his near contemporary Debussy are often grouped together as "Impressionists," a term derived from painting, where it referred to an attempt to convey the impression of a scene rather than a precise depiction. In fact, Ravel and Debussy differed in important respects, most notably in their approach to the whole-tone scale. But impressionistic elements can be found in some of Ravel's music, such as *Jeux d'eau*, for solo piano (1901), *Miroirs* (in particular *Une barque sur l'océan*), and *Daphnis et Chloé*.

Ravel claimed that his greatest goal as a composer was to achieve technical perfection. It was in reference to this that Stravinsky once referred to him as a Swiss watch-maker, paying tribute to his intricate precision.

In Ravel's love of clarity in melody, harmony and form we can see one of the more obvious differences between his music and that of Debussy, the arch-impressionist. This tendency also led Ravel to return to earlier forms, as Stravinsky also did occasionally.

In Ravel's early works for piano, too, such as *Menuet antique* (1895) and *Pavane pour une infante défunte*, we can hear his attraction to earlier music. Another example is the later piano suite, *Le tombeau de Couperin*, which is based on 18th-century dance forms.

Ravel's use of harmony was almost invariably clear and uncomplicated He showed no interest in the more adventurous experiments of his contemporaries although his chords are often dissonant and colored with chromatic notes. He also mostly employed time-honoured musical forms, such as sonata form.

ENDURING REPUTATION

During his lifetime, Ravel received acclaim from both performers and audiences alike for most of his published works. And this reputation has endured. Although he was working at his peak when most gifted and adventurous composers were attempting to pull free of conventional tonality, Ravel happily embraced tonality and maintained his solid relationship with it.

In his last years Ravel suffered from the progressively debilitating Pick's disease, and he died on December 28, 1937.

Richard Trombley

SEE ALSO:

BALLET AND MODERN DANCE MUSIC; IMPRESSIONISM IN MUSIC; ORCHESTRAL MUSIC.

FURTHER READING

Nichols, Roger. *Ravel Remembered*
(New York: W. W. Norton, 1988);
Orenstein, Arbie. *Ravel: Man and Musician*
(New York: Dover Publications, 1991).

SUGGESTED LISTENING

Alborada del gracioso; *Bolero*;
Carmen Fantasies; *Daphnis et Chloé*;
Gaspard de la nuit; *Mother Goose Suite*;
Pavane pour une infante defunte;
Rapsodie espagnole; *Tzigane*; *La valse*;
Valses nobles et sentimentales.

RECORD COMPANIES

Record companies are commercial organizations responsible for recording musical works and releasing them to consumers. The recording industry has become highly centralized, with a few major companies controlling the distribution of the vast majority of music. But this trend appeared to be challenged somewhat toward the end of the 20th century with the reappearance of small labels and alternative forms of distribution.

While the term "record" is virtually obsolete (as it refers to recordings made on vinyl, a format largely phased out by compact discs and other digital media), the record company's role and its relationship to the music and musicians remains the same. Traditionally, if artists wanted to reach mass audiences, they had to go through a record company with mammoth recording, marketing, and distribution infrastructures. The record company acted as a middleman, a gatekeeper that only allowed what it saw as commercially viable material onto the market.

DISCOVERING NEW TALENT

Every year more than 5,000 aspiring rock stars alone send demo tapes to record companies in the hope of being awarded a recording contract. A record company's A&R person (artist and repertoire), an executive who scouts and signs new talent, might receive upward of 100 tapes weekly, but most labels will not sign an act on the basis of an unsolicited demo. Usually they take material only from a known source, or sign acts referred to them with a personal recommendation. Talent aside, getting a record company interested in a new act has a lot to do with luck and personal contacts. All but one percent of bands are discovered through a third party, such as a manager or an acquaintance. Critics say that this means the decision as to which bands get recorded and which do not is in the hands of a privileged few. On signing an act, the record company usually finances the recording costs and pays the studio

musicians. Only about 20 percent of new acts sell enough recordings to cover their costs, so the record company is taking a gamble. However, huge profits can be made when an unknown artist leaps to stardom overnight. In addition to production costs, companies can pay hundreds of thousands of dollars to promote a new artist, sponsoring free concerts and record give-aways. From the 1980s onward, this included producing the promotional music video, which costs upward of $100,000. Companies usually pay to advertise artists and recordings on large commercial radio stations, which, in the U.S., play the tracks without paying royalties to the artists.

To get their product to consumers, record companies usually go through a distributor, a firm that generally takes on a limited contract to sell the records wholesale in certain geographic areas. Distributors are often members of the same corporate family as the recording company. The record company then receives revenues from sales of the vinyl LP, cassette, or CD, and in turn pays the artist or band a royalty on sales, after deducting any advance given to the artists to cover their expenses or to induce them to sign the recording contract.

To offset their huge production and promotional expenses, record companies find various ways of maximizing profits. In the U.S. a hit is often not enough to break even; as a result, companies use a U.S. hit as a means of promoting albums in foreign markets. Often record companies boost sales by getting musicians to provide remixes, bonus tracks, and alternative "B-sides" in various different recording formats, in the hope that fans will buy more than one version. Many artists say that this generates substandard material and that artificially inflating sales in this way undermines the credibility of the charts.

In some countries, particularly the U.S. and India, cross-promotion between music and movies has become inextricably linked. U.S. companies, with their strong global presence, use films to promote their music, and vice versa. In India, many pop songs come from film soundtracks. This has led to record companies merging with movie companies, resulting in huge media conglomerates.

THE "BIG SIX"

In the late 1990s, Americans were purchasing some 670 million records per year. Roughly 80 percent of this market was controlled by the so-called "Big Six" of the music industry (and their respective labels): Time-Warner (Elektra, Warner Bros., Atlantic), Sony (Columbia, CBS, Epic), EMI Group (Capitol, Virgin), Philips Electronics NV (Polydor, PolyGram, A&M), Bertelsmann (RCA, Arista), and Seagram (Geffen, MCA, Interscope). These giants also own movie and publishing companies, distributors, and even retail outlets. Faced with an industry trend toward mergers and media consolidation, unknown artists hoping to reach large audiences via these vast corporations have faced an uphill battle.

Nonetheless, the 1980s and 1990s brought the rise of small record companies. While the Big Six were interested in rock music and spending millions of dollars promoting their artists, hundreds of small, independent companies popped up to fill the needs in smaller genres such as jazz, folk, country, new age, and alternative rock.

This development began during the PUNK ROCK era, when new bands wanted a raw, unprofessional sound that the major labels could not give them. Local record companies began to set up in small cities, picking up talent that the major labels in New York and Los Angeles were overlooking.

Although many of these independent companies were then bought out by the megacorporations, more independents kept sprouting up. Some house artists began by pressing records and distributing them to local specialty record stores themselves.

Ironically, independent companies became a major force within the musical mainstream of the 1990s, with many "independent" artists taking top awards. Many successful artists, however, used small labels merely as stepping stones to gain contracts with the Big Six.

DIGITAL TECHNOLOGY

Like the rest of the entertainment industry, record companies in the 1990s were greatly affected by revolutions in digital and communications technology. Companies had been selling music digitally on CDs since the 1980s, but the rise in information technology has made it possible to reach consumers via the Internet. Revenue from the on-line sales of recorded music was growing about $25 million per year in the late 1990s.

It began with CDs being sold by mail order from company websites, but this was gradually eclipsed by the sale of music downloaded directly from the Internet. But the digital revolution turned into a double-edged sword and the Big Six have had their fingers burned. Record companies once complained about unauthorized copies of their artists' material circulating on cassette tapes. These were usually substandard, degraded by multiple duplication. But now they have to contend with digital copies of their products that are as good as the original.

INTERNET PIRACY

The advent of Mpeg-1 Layer 3 compression (MP3) technology made it feasible for pirates to turn their CD tracks into digital files that could be distributed over the Internet. Music enthusiasts could then listen to these perfect replicas directly on a personal computer, or they could download them and store them on any number of recording media, including DAT tapes, Mini-Disks, recordable CDs, Zip disks, and Digital Video Disks.

Record companies (notably Geffen) began attacking MP3 pirate sites and servers, and the Recording Industry Association of America successfully shut down some of these sites, suing pirates for up to $1 million. But the pirates stayed one step ahead by offering files from international sites that are moving constantly.

Issues of piracy aside, the new digital technology offered high recording quality that was previously only available at the major recording studios. This allowed small or controversial artists (and even untalented ones) to sell their music for download—and bypass the record companies altogether.

Brett Allan King

SEE ALSO:

CHARTS, RECORD PRODUCTION; RECORDING STUDIOS.

FURTHER READING
Bowen, Jimmy, and Jim Jerome. *Rough Mix: An Unapologetic Look at the Music Business and How It Got that Way* (New York: Simon & Schuster, 1997);
Cimino, Al. *Great Record Labels* (New York: Apple, 1992);
Connelly, Will. *The Musician's Guide to Independent Record Production* (Chicago, IL: Contemporary Books, 1981);
Fink, Michael. *Inside the Music Industry: Creativity, Process, and Business* (New York: Schirmer Books, 1996).

RECORD PRODUCTION

Record production is the art and science of creating recorded musical works. Specifically, it refers to the work of artists, producers, and engineers, but in general record production combines the worlds of music, audio production, manufacturing, marketing, and the many other necessary tasks that have to be performed before a record can be released.

The term "record" is a generic term used to describe commercially released, recorded work. Vinyl LPs are still manufactured, but most commercial releases are now on CD or cassette tape. Modern formats currently vying for consumer acceptance, or looming on the audio horizon, include DAT tapes, mini-disks, DCC (digital compact cassette), and DVD (digital video disk—a new format that will carry more than just video information that is being touted as a revolutionary step forward).

Several distinct processes are involved in recording, and releasing a record for the commercial market, but we will concentrate here on the actual audio recording process and preparation of master recordings for eventual commercial release.

WORKING IN THE RECORDING STUDIO

There are several jobs involved in record production, and each one is vital to the creation of a successful master recording.

The A&R (artist and repertoire) person is responsible for finding and signing new talent to a record label. "Talent" is a term used to describe those individuals who are actually performing. They fall into a number of categories, such as musicians, vocalists, and voice-over artists. A&R people also act as general guides, helping new acts through the process of recording. A&R executives are assigned a stable of talent, and act as a liaison between the act and the record company. A&R people were originally in-house producers, signing talent and producing their records as well. Modern-day A&R executives do not usually produce, and theoretically are not involved in

the process, but in practice they often are. The repertoire, choice of producer, and band image are all important areas under the A&R person's control.

The producer is directly responsible for the creative, technical, and business processes of record production in the studio. A music producer's job is analogous to those of the producer and director in the film industry, combining the responsibilities of both. Producers work with the band on arrangements, song selection, and creative methodology. They also collaborate with the recording engineer on the technical process in the studio, and are responsible to the record company for keeping the project within budget. Producers directly supervise the recording process, and are responsible for the completion of the master recording. Some album recordings use different producers for each track, in which case they come under the supervision of an executive producer.

Arrangers are responsible for creating musical arrangements or orchestrations for the material being recorded. This can be the overall style and sound of the piece, or just specific aspects of the recording. For instance, a producer/arranger with limited knowledge in certain areas might call in a specialist to help with a specific recording—for example, a rhythm, vocal, horn, or string arranger. The arranger then takes the musical material and expands on it to create specific parts for individual performers. This process is known as arranging in jazz, pop, or rock music, and is called orchestration in the context of classical music.

The recording or audio engineer has the task of actually recording the material. Working with the producer, engineers mix, process, and shape the sound to create the required result. Some engineers specialize in certain areas of recording. Mix engineers, for example, are adept at mix-down (mixing and blending all the recorded tracks on a multi-track session down to one stereo mix). The assistant engineers/technicians (or A2s) help the tracking or chief engineer set up and repair the equipment, among other things.

STEPS IN THE RECORDING PROCESS

The process of producing a studio recording can be broken down into three main stages: pre-production, production/recording, and post-production. Pre-production is the preliminary work that needs to be completed before the actual recording begins—songwriting, song selection, key selection, rehearsals, finalizing musical arrangements, budgetary planning, paperwork, and any other details that need to be handled prior to recording.

Production/recording/tracking is the process of recording in the studio. This stage encompasses recording all basic (rhythm or bed) tracks, vocals, and any additional "sweetening" (strings, horns, percussion, etc.). Different styles of recording are used for different effects: live/off-the-floor recording (where all musicians and vocalists perform together and are recorded as they perform); tracking/over-dubbing (where individual instrumental and vocal parts are recorded separately to build into a completed piece); or a combination of the two approaches. The producer usually decides which approach will be used.

In post-production all the earlier phases of the process come together to create the completed master recording. The first step of post-production is mixing the recorded tracks to create a definitive version, known as the mix-down. During mixing the producer must take into account individual and overall volume of various tracks, their placement and balance in the stereo field, and the equalization or EQ, which means achieving just the right tone on each recorded track and subsequent mix.

The next step is mastering—preparing the mix-down track for manufacture (pressing or duplication). Mastering is usually handled by skilled professionals working in specially designed environments, who add just the right EQ, match the levels of all pre-recorded material, and add any corrective touches. Finally, there may be some remixing. Often a hit tune will be remixed to highlight specific aspects of the recording, and sometimes entirely new versions of a song are created (such as dance/rap remixes). This process also comes into play when reissuing catalog material.

STUDIO EQUIPMENT

The modern recording studio is a specially designed environment, generally divided into two areas—the studio (where the music is actually performed) and the control room (where the producer and engineer supervise and direct the recording). Most of the studio equipment is kept in the control room.

All modern recording studios have a recording-machine. Formerly this was a 2-track, 4-track, 8-track, 16-track, or 24-track analog tape-recorder. Now, with the popularization of various new formats and recording technologies, studios often rely on a tapeless system. New advances in technology have also led to the ability to synchronize machines and record as many as 48 discrete tracks.

THE MICROPHONE

The microphones are some of the most important pieces of studio equipment as the first items used to reproduce the source signal. Microphones come in two basic types: dynamic (which accurately record differences in volume), and condensers (which automatically adjust recording levels). Different types of microphone have different frequency response and pickup patterns, and are used in special applications.

The signals picked up by the microphones are processed through a mixing board, also known as the mixer or console. The mixer has control sections for each incoming signal and track, called channels. Each channel has a volume control and an EQ section (allowing for specific shaping of tone).

Special effects units such as reverbs (which simulate reverberation), digital delays, and filters are used to shape, enhance, and change various characteristics of incoming signals. Synthesizers and sequencers simulate sounds or create new ones, and record them for playback. Samplers are similar devices that can digitally record and manipulate short segments of sound.

As recording technology improves, new and exciting processes will continue to change record production. In the past decade, technology has facilitated the home recording boom—computers and inexpensive equipment have put the facilities of large studios in the hands of home enthusiasts. Record production, however, maintains its ties to the fundamental tenets it was built on: creating the best possible version of the song, and recording and reproducing it in the best possible way.

Gregg Juke

SEE ALSO:

PRODUCERS; RECORDING STUDIOS.

FURTHER READING

Chanan, Michael. *Repeated Takes: A Short History of Recording and Its Effects on Music* (New York: Verso, 1995);

Negus, Keith. *Producing Pop: Culture and Conflict in the Popular Music Industry* (New York: Routledge, Chapman, and Hall, 1992).

RECORDING STUDIOS

Recording studios play a vital part in the music industry. They are where state-of-the-art equipment is used to record musical performances for posterity or for release as a single or album. They may also be involved in other aspects of sound recording, such as manipulating sounds electronically to produce new or unusual effects.

The history of audio recording began with Thomas Edison's invention of the phonograph in 1877. Edison's original machine used wax cylinders as the recording medium, but these were replaced ten years later by flat discs. Initially, these early phonographs were intended to be a type of archiving device—like a dictaphone or a message machine. However, manufacturers were quick to sense the commercial potential of this new device, and introduced the first records and phonographs for the entertainment market in 1894. By 1924, thousands of phonographs and millions of records had been sold.

The growth of radio in the 1930s led to great advances in sound recording. Early recordings on Edison-type machines had used large conical "horns" as the transducer (a device that electrically or mechanically changes one form of energy into another). These horns recorded the source sounds directly onto the disk, and served as an amplifier on playback. But they were clumsy and the sound fidelity was extremely poor.

A GREAT LEAP FORWARD

Meanwhile in Germany scientists were hard at work on a technological advance in audio recording. This was not mechanical, but electric. "Wire" recording utilized a microphone as the transducer, and a spool of wire as the recording format. These wire recording machines had a much higher fidelity than the Edison machines. However, the early wire recordings were delicate and subject to accidental erasure. After World War II, inventors used wire technology as a basis to create the reel-to-reel tape recording format. In the mid-1940s, two Frenchmen, composer Pierre Henry

and acoustical engineer Pierre Schaeffer, began some of the first experiments with *musique concrète*. This used sounds from real life (automobiles, birds, etc.), or taken from other sources such as recordings, to create new musical works or "sound compositions." Often these sounds were passed through a filter (which let some frequencies through and blocked others), played backward, or manipulated in other ways. Henry and Schaeffer foreshadowed later innovations in electronic music and "sampling" technology. By 1954, avant-garde composers such as STOCKHAUSEN, VARÈSE, and MILHAUD had composed their own *musique concrète* in the recording studios of Henry and Schaeffer.

THE CONTRIBUTION OF LES PAUL

During the 1950s, along with the innovations of Henry and Schaeffer, modern analog recording equipment and multi-tracking techniques appeared. These innovations can be attributed to the tireless invention and experimentation of one man, singer-guitarist Les Paul. Paul invented one of the first functional electric guitars and a viable multi-track recording system. His first foray into recording used direct-to-disc technology; later he incorporated an analog tape machine that included a process called selective synchronization ("sel-sync"), variations of which are still used today on modern analog multi-track recorders.

Paul built a state-of-the-art studio in his home in Hollywood, where he recorded multi-tracked hits, playing all the instrumental parts, and harmonizing lead guitar and voice. He invented the eight-track recorder, which became an industry standard and the forerunner of modern analog and digital 16-, 24-, and 48-track recording machines.

MULTI-TRACK RECORDING

A multi-track recording device uses a magnetic recording head that can record more than one "track." A track is a sequence of electromagnetic pulses representing musical or audio information in the case of analog recording; or, in digital recording, the track is a series of digitally "sampled" sounds.

A stereo (short for "stereophonic") recording has two tracks, a right channel and a left channel, which when combined approximate the way sounds are heard by the human ear. Stereophonic reproduction allows different sound sources (drums, guitars, voices, natural or ambient sounds, for example) to be "panned" (placed) within the stereo field so that the listener hears sounds coming from different directions. Multi-track recorders using more than two tracks (4, 6, 8, 12, 16, 24, 32, or 48) allow each instrument, voice, or individual sound to be recorded separately before being combined into a finished stereo mix.

DESIGN OF THE RECORDING STUDIO

Several factors have to be considered in the design of a state-of-the-art recording studio. It is important to eliminate unwanted sounds from the recording environment, so studio design is an art in itself. Most studios have two discrete areas—the studio, or recording room, and the control room.

The control room is the area where all the recording equipment is kept—the analog or digital recording unit, the mixing board, the monitor speakers, the computer, and the signal processing equipment. In this room the producer and engineer work to create the best possible recordings of the source sounds.

The control room is separated from the studio by a double wall with an airtight double door. The floor is usually "floated" (an additional floor or platform is mounted on sub-flooring and is sometimes connected to shocks or springs to prevent sound transference). Most often, the control room is visually connected to the studio via a large window or windows, which must be constructed using several panes of glass set at opposing angles to prevent sound-leakage or rattling. Sometimes the visual connection is made through closed-circuit video equipment.

Because the recording equipment is often left on for long periods of time, the control room may have a specially air-conditioned room, closet, or alcove where the tape-machine is kept. To provide the best possible monitoring (listening) environment, some control rooms use acoustic foam and devices known as "bass traps." To provide a good acoustic environment, both the studio and control room must be constructed with no parallel walls, to avoid the creation of "standing waves," which are echoes or reverberations that are heard in square rooms with hard surfaces.

Studio rooms are also constructed with double walls, and often have permanently or temporarily partitioned areas or booths for recording individual instruments or vocalists. Some studios have wall areas with louvers that can be opened or closed to create different types of recording environments (smooth, hard surfaces reflect the sound; soft, angled surfaces reduce reflection or give diffused sound).

STUDIO PROFILES

Many recording studios have become identified with a particular sound or style of recording, through a combination of acoustic environment, equipment, engineering and production staff, as well as the artists who have recorded there. Some of these famous studios have been affiliated with major record labels; others have been "independents." Among the most famous recording studios of the modern pop era are Sun Studios, affiliated with Sun Records in Memphis, Tennessee and owned by Sam Phillips, the man credited with discovering Elvis PRESLEY; and Abbey Road in London, which was affiliated with Apple Records, both owned by the BEATLES. Today most of the recording studios connected with the major record labels in the U.S. are concentrated in New York, Nashville, and Los Angeles.

Technological advances in the last few years have led to a great proliferation of mid-sized and smaller commercial studios, and have created a "'home-recording" boom. Many young musicians, who would have found the cost of recording a demo or an album prohibitive, can now have sophisticated equipment at their fingertips for a reasonable price.

The art and science of studio recording is constantly changing, and the next century will provide more advances in recording technology that were unimaginable when Edison invented his first phonograph.

Gregg Juke

SEE ALSO:

AMPLIFICATION; ELECTRONIC MUSIC; PRODUCERS; RECORD COMPANIES; RECORD PRODUCTION.

FURTHER READING

Alten, Stanley R. *Audio in Media: The Recording Studio* (Belmont, CA: Wadsworth, 1996); Nisbet, Alec. *The Sound Studio* (Boston, MA: Focal Press, 1995).

SUGGESTED LISTENING

Karlheinz Stockhausen: *Studie I* and *Studie II*; *Gesang der Jünglinger*; Edgard Varèse: *Poème électronique*.

OTIS REDDING

Otis Redding was the quintessential soul man, possibly the greatest the world has ever known. A visionary artist, "The Big O" created an enduring musical legacy before his life was tragically cut short by a plane crash.

Redding was born in Dawson, Georgia, on September 9, 1941. He quit school at 16, determined to follow in the footsteps of his hometown hero, LITTLE RICHARD. While playing local talent shows, Redding met Johnny Jenkins, a flashy guitarist who hired Redding as a vocalist and roadie. After Jenkins scored a regional hit with "Soul Twist," Atlantic Records showed interest and arranged a recording session for him at the Stax studio in Memphis, in October 1962. At the session, Jenkins turned in a lacklustre performance and someone suggested that Redding sing. He sang an original ballad, "These Arms of Mine," with a lilting, nervous passion, soulfully ad-libbing the fade-out. Jim Stewart, head of Stax Records, was impressed enough to sign Redding there and then. "These Arms of Mine" sold respectably, as did the follow-up "Pain in My Heart."

Despite his lack of formal training, Redding was a prolific composer and a brilliant arranger, singing instrumental parts to teach them to the musicians. Redding's horn arrangements came to define the label's sound, and the Stax studio band (Booker T. and the MGs) played with razor-sharp intensity under Redding's leadership. By December 1964, when "Mr. Pitiful" was released, Redding had undergone a stunning maturation. On ballads, Redding would tease a vocal mercilessly with a heartbreaking "catch" in his voice. He punctuated the up-tempo numbers with stutters, shouts, and moans, all perfectly timed to increase dramatic tension. On singles like "I've Been Loving You for Too Long," "Respect," and the astounding "Try a Little Tenderness," Redding sang like a man possessed.

By 1967, Redding was headlining the Stax Revue tour of Europe, a magnetic R&B star about to cross over into mainstream fame. That fall, Otis had polyps removed from his throat and couldn't speak for two months. As he recovered, he composed new material, listening to

Otis Redding, the original "soul man," was enjoying a spectacular career before his tragically premature death.

the BEATLES and Bob DYLAN for inspiration. Once recovered, he cut dozens of tracks. Some of these, especially "(Sittin' on) the Dock of the Bay," showed Otis heading in a new direction, absorbing elements of rock and folk. Two days after the last session, Redding and his band died in a plane crash, en route to Madison, Wisconsin. He was just 26 years old.

"Dock of the Bay" was a No. 1 hit (as he had predicted), but Otis Redding died long before he had fulfilled his potential, and Stax never fully recovered from the loss of their premier artist.

Greg Bower

SEE ALSO:
COOKE, SAM; POP MUSIC; SOUL.

FURTHER READING
Bowman, Rob. *Soulsville, U.S.A.: The Story of Stax Records* (New York: Schirmer Books, 1997); Schiesel, Jane. *The Otis Redding Story* (Garden City, NY: Doubleday, 1973).

SUGGESTED LISTENING
Otis! The Definitive Otis Redding; *The Very Best of Otis Redding*.

JIMMY
REED

As a guitarist Jimmy Reed was limited, his ability on the harmonica was minimal, and he sang in a lazy rambling style. However, Reed's unique style—combining the traditional country blues of the Mississippi Delta with the urban electric guitar typical of the Chicago sound—brought him huge success during the 1950s and early 1960s, selling more records than any other blues artist of the time, except the great B. B. KING.

Reed was born on September 6, 1925, on a plantation outside Dunleith, Mississippi. A boyhood friend, Eddie Taylor, taught him to play guitar, and they would play and sing Delta standards together after a day's work in the fields. Reed moved to Chicago in 1943 and was drafted into the navy. Following his discharge, he returned to the South and worked as a sharecropper. In 1948, Reed moved north to Gary, Indiana, and found work in a steel foundry. While living in Gary, Reed met and recorded with guitarist Albert KING. In 1949, Eddie Taylor moved to Chicago, and he and Reed began performing together in South Side taverns.

SLOWLY CLIMBING THE CHARTS

Reed signed with Chicago's VeeJay label in 1953, and he and Taylor backed John Lee HOOKER on some of his singles. Reed's early recordings, although highly regarded by collectors, were not successful and VeeJay considered dropping him until his 1955 hit, "You Don't Have to Go," climbed to No. 9 on the rhythm and blues (R&B) charts. Between 1955 and 1961, Reed had 13 R&B hits, including 12 that crossed over to the pop charts. Elvis PRESLEY covered Reed's hit, "Baby, What You Want Me to Do?," while Aretha FRANKLIN and the ROLLING STONES covered "Honest I Do." Other hits from this period included "Ain't That Lovin' You Baby" in 1956, and "Big Boss Man" and "Bright Lights, Big City" in 1961. Many of these songs became R&B standards, part of the live repertoire of white R&B bands throughout the 1960s. The Byrds, for example, closed their live set with "Big Boss Man" for many years.

Unlike the gritty, urgent style of Howlin' Wolf or Muddy WATERS, Reed's guitar playing was laid-back and rhythmically relaxed. He used a neck mount so he could accompany himself on the harmonica. His warm, somewhat nasal singing voice was deliberately lazy and sexily slow, and he often stuttered. Eddie Taylor provided the rhythm to support Reed's playing, contributing a steady boogie beat that enhanced the countrified sound. Reed's wife, Mary Lee "Mama" Reed, wrote many of his songs. Often she would sit behind him in the studio, reciting the lyrics into his ear as he played. On some of Reed's recordings, you can actually hear her contribution.

Reed's style contrasted with the frenetic pace of rock'n'roll, and it proved popular with young R&B fans. His sound was tagged "swamp blues" when it was adopted by musicians on the Excello label, such as Lightnin' Slim, Lonesome Sundown, and Slim Harpo.

STRUGGLING TO FIND FAME

Reed played Carnegie Hall and the Apollo Theater in the early 1960s, and toured England, where an appreciative audience came to hear songs the Rolling Stones had made familiar. He recorded on the Exodus and ABC-Bluesway labels in the 1960s, and toured regularly in the 1970s. However, Reed's popularity was waning, and despite various gimmicks—faking live performances, dubbing 12-string guitar solos over his backing tracks, and inserting commentaries between album tracks—sales of his records fell steadily.

In his later years, Reed was often unable to perform due to illness—he was an alcoholic who also suffered from epilepsy. However, in the mid-1970s he managed to control his drinking and his career began to look up. Reed died in his sleep from respiratory failure on August 29, 1976, in Oakland, California.

Stan Hieronymus

SEE ALSO:
BLUES; COUNTRY; ROCK'N'ROLL.

FURTHER READING
Oliver, Paul. *The Story of the Blues*
(Philadelphia, PA: Chilton Book Co., 1969);
Palmer, Robert. *Deep Blues*
(New York: Penguin Books, 1981).

SUGGESTED LISTENING
Greatest Hits;
Jimmy Reed at Carnegie Hall;
Lost in the Shuffle.

JIM
REEVES

When Jim Reeves started out, he was a traditional country singer, following the lead of other popular artists. But by combining the relaxed singing style of pop balladry with country music, he reached the top of the pop charts. He was the first crossover star of country music and his success led to the birth of the new Nashville Sound. Other artists followed him, including Patsy CLINE and Eddy Arnold. Together their new sound took the nation by storm. Since his death, many have tried to follow in Reeves' footsteps, but his deceptively simple style has proved a very hard act to follow.

Born in 1923 (the Country Music Hall of Fame mistakenly gives the date as 1924) in Panola County, Texas, Reeves had an early passion for baseball. After high school, Reeves entered the University of Texas on a scholarship and his superior ability on the mound attracted attention from the majors. Reeves was soon signed up by the St. Louis Cardinals, but his ballplaying career was cut short by an unlucky fall. The resulting ankle injury was severe enough to put him out of the game for good.

SINGING DJ

After his marriage in 1947, Reeves and his wife, Mary, moved to Shreveport, Louisiana. There, he landed an announcer's job with radio station KWKH. Reeves had overcome an early stammer while at the university and thereafter was known for his perfect diction. One of his new responsibilities was to announce the Saturday night shows, and occasionally he was allowed to sing on air.

The turning point in Reeves' musical career came in 1952. Hank WILLIAMS, booked for a live radio performance, failed to show, and Reeves was asked to fill in. In the audience that night was Fabor Robinson, owner of Abbott Records. Robinson was impressed enough to sign Reeves to his label. In 1953, Jim scored his first No. 1 record with "Mexican Joe." Two years later, Jim signed with RCA and joined the *Grand Ole Opry* at the urging of friends Ernest TUBB and Hank Snow. In 1957 "Four Walls" was released, and it proved to be one of Reeves' most memorable songs. Chet ATKINS thought "Four Walls" was a "girl's song" and was unhappy at the idea of Reeves recording it. However, Reeves persisted, and he used this song to establish a new singing style. Lowering his voice and moving close to the microphone, he created an intimate ballad style unlike his earlier hillbilly tracks. "Four Walls" became a huge crossover hit. After this Atkins recorded Reeves as a balladeer, replacing steel guitars and fiddles with piano and strings. The 1959 release of "He'll Have to Go" was perhaps the musical highpoint for Reeves, and is generally considered to be his greatest hit—topping the country charts for 14 weeks and making No. 2 in the pop charts. Over the next few years, Reeves continued to dominate the charts with recordings such as "Guilty" and the unforgettable "Welcome to My World."

On July 31, 1964, Reeves and his manager were returning to Nashville from Arkansas. They flew into bad weather attempting to reach Nashville's Beery Field, a few miles away. The plane crashed in dense woodland outside Nashville. Despite 500 volunteers helping to search—including some of Reeves' fellow country stars—the bodies weren't found for three days.

Before his death, Jim Reeves had built up a large catalog of unreleased recordings, and over the next decade his widow continued to release new Jim Reeves records. In 1966, recordings including "Distant Drums," "Is It Really Over?" and "Blue Side of Lonesome" were released.

Other recordings were remastered, and posthumous duets were created with country legends such as Patsy Cline. In 1975, more than ten years after Reeves' death, his *40 Golden Greats* reached No. 1.

Renee Jinks

SEE ALSO:
CASH, JOHNNY; HILLBILLY MUSIC; NASHVILLE SOUND/NEW COUNTRY; POP MUSIC.

FURTHER READING
Streissguth, Michael. *Like a Moth to a Flame: The Jim Reeves Story* (Nashville, TN: Rutledge Hill Press, 1998).

SUGGESTED LISTENING
Gentleman Jim 1955-59; *Welcome to My World: The Essential Jim Reeves Collection*.

REGGAE

Reggae is the most influential popular music of Jamaica. Although it is a uniquely original form, it has its roots in both American rhythm and blues (R&B) and Caribbean calypso and mento. Some of its most famous Jamaican performers include Bob MARLEY and the Wailers, Peter Tosh, and Jimmy Cliff; although reggae is a style that is now performed by artists throughout the world and has influenced many other genres of popular music since its inception in Jamaica in the late 1960s and early 1970s.

JAMAICAN ROOTS OF REGGAE

In the 1950s the sound of calypso was at the height of its popularity in the U.S. and abroad, popularized by singers such as Harry Belafonte. At the same time young Jamaican musicians were becoming interested in American jazz, soul, rock'n'roll, and, in the early 1960s, the pop and R&B sounds coming out of MOTOWN and New Orleans. But the Jamaican bands and recording studios lacked the sophisticated technology that allowed the American producers to create their signature sounds (using reverbs, echos, and other equipment that was then state-of-the-art). Instead, the Jamaican musicians created two essential elements of the reggae rhythm, the "one-drop" and the "skank" (also known as the "changa," or "shank" in England). While the one-drop rhythm is played in 4/4 time, it differs from a standard pop-rhythm in that the accent is felt on the third beat of the 4/4 measure. This creates what is known as a "half-time" feel. The skank is a rhythmic figure (usually performed on electric guitar) that plays on the upbeat eighth notes of the 4/4 measure, and competes with, but also complements, the one-drop. The rhythmic tension created when the one-drop and the skank are played together is responsible for the floating, dancing quality of most reggae music, and the skank guitar part is regarded as pivotal to the music.

Other characteristics of reggae include the "bubble," the two-handed rhythmic figure played by keyboardists; and the tendency of the bass to play "off the one" (meaning in a syncopated fashion, leaving out the first beat of the bar), but the harmonies are simple.

In addition to the one-drop, some of the drum rhythms heard in reggae music include "steppers" or "military-style" (a heavy four-to-the-bar feel), the 16th-note straight "back-beat" rhythm, and what has become known as "dancehall," a three-note repetitive figure played over a straight four quarter-note beat that has established itself as an independent Reggae style.

SIGNATURE SOUND OF SKA

Jamaican guitarist Ernest Ranglin is usually credited as the first player to use the skank rhythm. This rhythm became a signature sound in the pop and R&B imitations of Jamaican groups, which eventually became the proto-reggae style known as "ska." An early hit in this ska/Jamaico-R&B style was Millie Small's "My Boy Lollipop," a novelty number that appealed to the teen market and charted in 1964.

Ska is a fast dance music with horn-section arrangements, a driving beat, and an uptempo version of the skank rhythm. Toots and the Maytals were one of the earliest Jamaican groups to popularize the ska style, which has made comebacks in recent years—first in

Jamaican reggae legend Desmond Dekker, who scored his biggest hit in 1969, with the single "Israelites," was one of the first internationally known reggae artists.

Gems/Redferns

the 1980s with British 2-Tone label bands such as Selector and the English Beat, and again in the 1990s with groups like the Mighty Mighty Boss-Tones.

BIRTH OF REGGAE WITH DESMOND DEKKER

As Jamaican pop evolved, the earliest reggae music began to surface. Groups or recording artists that contributed to the beginnings of reggae sound include the Skatelites, Johnny Nash, and Desmond Dekker. The first Jamaican tune to mention the new musical style by name was the Maytals' "Do the Reggay," (1968) although many students of the music agree that Dekker's song "Israelites" (1969) qualifies as the first true reggae song. It contains many of the elements that make up the reggae rhythm (a much slower tempo than ska, a one-drop-like beat, and the skank rhythm), and the lyrics deal with the ideology of Rastafarianism, a religious cult based on a messianic belief in Africa as the Promised Land, and on the worship of Haile Selassie as a deity. Rastafarianism and reggae have become closely linked, and it is hard to find a Jamaican reggae song that is not based on Rastafarian ideas.

SOUND-SYSTEM MAN

Due to the increased demand in Jamaica for American sounds in the mid-1960s, a curious phenomenon arose that has profoundly affected not only reggae, but also its American cousins, dance and rap/hip-hop. The Jamaican "Sound System Man," a mobile DJ and sound-system operator, became the precursor to U.S. disco, party, and rap DJs. Often using an old vehicle, crude equipment, and home-made speaker cabinets, Jamaican DJs would travel to events, parties, and street corners throughout the capital city of Kingston to play recorded music for the masses. These DJs or MCs initiated the practice of rhyming over instrumental B-sides of Jamaican and American hits; they often "rapped" about their own prowess as DJs or the superiority of their sound-system. This early form of rap was known as "toasting," which usually had the connotation of good-natured ribbing or insulting the competition. The DJs were also responsible for the creation of another of reggae's hallmark musical offerings, "dub."

Dub music is the musical antecedent to the modern "dance re-mix." DJs and Jamaican recording engineers used equal parts primitive equipment and ultra-ingenious flash to create a new style, a remix of prerecorded tracks that usually left some portion of the rhythm intact, while dropping in bits and pieces of various vocal tracks or musical accompaniment in seemingly random places. Distorted or over-generated echo or reverb adds a rhythmically disorienting effect. Dub became the basis for the newer Jamaican sounds of dancehall, a modern dance/rap-oriented version of reggae practiced by artists such as Mad Cobra, Shabba Ranks, Buju Banton, and Patra.

Despite the popularity of other versions of reggae, the most famous reggae performer of all time remains the late Bob Marley. His recordings with the Wailers have sold millions in North America, England and Africa. His music dealt with tough socio-political issues, but also dealt with topics everyone understands—spirituality, life, love, and loss. His best-known song is probably "I Shot the Sheriff" (1973). Marley died in 1981, but his musical legacy lives on with the Marley-family band (the Melody Makers) led by his son, Ziggy.

Other famous "roots" (mid-1970s) style reggae performers included Jimmy Cliff, Burning Spear, Culture, the Gladiators, the Mighty Diamonds, and Black Uhuru. Probably the most recorded reggae rhythm section is the combination of drummer Sly Dunbar and electric bassist Robbie Shakespeare. The pair appeared on countless recordings, crossed over to the rock/pop field and worked with performers such as Mick Jagger and Keith Richards, and also became involved in producing.

Reggae music continues to be a vital, evolving musical force, as well as an influence on modern rock, pop, jazz, rap, and R&B.

Gregg Juke

SEE ALSO:
CARIBBEAN; RAGGA.

FURTHER READING

Potash, C., ed. *Reggae, Rasta, Revolution: Jamaican Music from Ska to Dub* (New York: Schirmer Books, 1997).

SUGGESTED LISTENING

Rhythm Come Forward: A Reggae Anthology;
Black Uhuru: *Red*; Culture: *Two Sevens Clash*;
Desmond Dekker: *007 (Shanty Town)*;
Bob Marley: *Birth of a Legend*; *Exodus*;
Augustus Pablo: *King Tubby Meets Rockers Uptown*;
Lee Scratch Perry: *Island Masters*.

STEVE
REICH

The composer Steve Reich is one of the leading figures in minimal music. His important contributions to minimalism were his unique use of sustained repetition and electronic resources.

Reich was born in New York City on October 3, 1936. He studied philosophy at Cornell University, graduating in 1957, and then enrolled at the Juilliard School of Music in New York, where he trained to be a composer. In 1962 he moved on to Mills College in Oakland, California, where he was taught by the composers Luciano Berio and Darius MILHAUD. While at Mills college he supported himself by working as a drummer and playing keyboards.

In 1966, he began composing when he formed his group, Steve Reich and Musicians, to play his own pieces. (Before 1980, he did not permit perfomances of his work by other groups.) Reich became increasingly interested in reducing music to pulse-generated sounds, rejecting traditional concepts of harmony and melody.

PHASE SHIFTING AND REPETITION

Early in his career Reich became fascinated by the technique of repetition, and by the potential of electronic music. He began to experiment with tape loops, and devised the technique of playing two tape loops at slightly different speeds, which he called "phase shifting." His first compositions to use this were *It's Gonna Rain* (1965) and *Come Out* (1966). *Come Out* was inspired by an incident during the Harlem riots in 1964, when six boys were arrested. They were beaten by police, and those who were bleeding were taken to the hospital. One of the boys who was not bleeding decided that, in his words, "I had to, like, open the bruise up and let some of the bruise blood come out to show them," in order to be hospitalized.

Reich recorded the phrase "come out to show them" on two channels, then manipulated them so that one channel began to move slightly faster than the other— phase shifting. In the composition there is a building of volume, and what begins as two voices becomes four, and then eight. *Come Out* is an early example of minimalism and a forerunner of repetitive "rap" styles.

After his first experiments involving tape loops, Reich then turned to instruments, producing *Piano Phase* (1967), *Violin Phase* (1967), and *Four Organs* (1970). *Pendulum Music* (1968) represents the ultimate in electronic music: microphones swinging over amplifiers set up feedback pulses that eventually merge into one continuous drone.

After a summer spent in Ghana studying African drumming, Reich produced the album *Drumming* in 1971. The next year he composed the piece *Clapping Music* (1972), which, as an example of pure minimalism, is simply the sound of two sets of hands clapping to prescribed rhythmic patterns.

From 1973, Reich demonstrated a new-found interest in harmony, instrumentation, and melody rather than in pure pattern-making. His *Music for Mallet Instruments, Voices, and Organ* (1973) used harmonic modulation for the first time. In his *Music for 18 Musicians* (1976), Reich featured woodwinds, strings, and female voices to create instrumental and vocal color, while in *Tehillim* (1981), he went even further in his use of melody, now allowing the voices—with text—to sing substantial melodies. *The Desert Music* (1986) is fully orchestrated, and *The Four Sections* (1990), a concerto for orchestra, takes Reich furthest from his early minimalism. *Different Trains* (1988), meanwhile, also demonstrates a further development in terms of subject matter with its exploration of Reich's own personal memories of childhood.

Although minimalism has remained on the fringe of modern classical music, Reich nevertheless continues with his individual approach to music.

Richard Trombley

SEE ALSO:

ELECTRONIC MUSIC; MINIMALISM.

FURTHER READING

Duckworth, William. *Talking Music: Conversations with John Cage, Philip Glass, Laurie Anderson, and Five Generations of American Experimental Composers* (New York: Schirmer Books, 1995); Mertens, Wim. *American Minimal Music* (New York: Broude, 1983).

SUGGESTED LISTENING

Come Out; *Drumming*; *Music for 18 Musicians*; *Tehillim*.

DJANGO REINHARDT

Django Reinhardt was an innovative virtuoso on the guitar and, to this day, the group he led with Stéphane Grappelli remains a legend in European jazz.

Born in Liverchies, near Charleroi, Belgium, on January 3, 1910, Jean Baptiste Reinhardt was the son of a traveling Gypsy entertainer. By age 12, he began playing with local bands at dances and bars, and then moved on to solo engagements in the cafés of Montmartre in Paris. At 18, a fire in his caravan left him without the use of the last two fingers on his left hand. He had to retrain himself on the guitar, but was soon able to play the most intricate progressions with unprecedented sophistication. He bent and stretched notes to make the guitar sound like a singing voice, and played incredibly fast solos in a style partly derived from his Gypsy ancestry.

Inspired by the music of Louis ARMSTRONG and guitarist Eddie Lang, Reinhardt made his first recordings in 1934 with the Michael Warlop Orchestra, and played with French violinist Stéphane Grappelli in Louis Vola's band. Reinhardt and Grappelli soon split from the group to form their famous all-string ensemble, the Quintette du Hot Club de France. Their premiere at Paris's Hot Club was followed by a performance with Coleman HAWKINS, and performances with other visiting Americans (Benny CARTER, Eddie South, and others), each of which brought them greater international acclaim. By the time the quintet disbanded in 1939, the group had recorded over 200 tunes and had become the first non-Americans to make a significant impact on the development of jazz.

During World War II, Reinhardt recorded with the Air Transport Command for broadcast on the American Forces Network. He then formed another quintet, with clarinetist Hubert Rostaing, and began composing original music, including the famous "Nuages," his own "Bolero," and even a symphony, parts of which were used in the 1946 film *Le Village de la Colère*. Reinhardt's trip to the United States in 1946, to perform with the Duke ELLINGTON Orchestra, met with mixed results. He was struggling for the first time with the electrified guitar, and was eager to conform to the new concepts of jazz created by the bebop style. He was exposed to bebop as it was being developed by Dizzy GILLESPIE, Charlie PARKER, and others, and to the electric guitar playing of Charlie CHRISTIAN, which had a profound influence on his music.

Back in Paris, Reinhardt temporarily reformed the Hot Club with Grappelli in a more informal setting. He toured Europe with his small ensemble, recorded with trumpeter Rex Stewart's band in 1947, and in 1949 reunited with Grappelli to make their final recordings together. Reinhardt died at age 43 in May 1953, after suffering a stroke. More than 40 years after his death, he remains a seminal figure and his recordings are greatly sought after.

Todd Denton

SEE ALSO:
EUROPEAN JAZZ; GYPSY MUSIC; JAZZ.

Stéphane Grappelli (violin) and Django Reinhardt leading the Quintette du Hot Club de France in Paris.

Corbis

FURTHER READING

Delaunay, Charles, trans. Michael James, *Django Reinhardt* (New York: Da Capo Press, 1982).

SUGGESTED LISTENING

Best of Django Reinhardt;
Compact Jazz in Brussels; *Indispensable: 1949–50*;
Verve Jazz Masters, Vol. 38.

R.E.M.

R.E.M.'s sound is impossible to mistake: layers of jangling guitars, haunting melodies, oblique lyrics, and Michael Stipe's reedy vocals. Declared "America's best rock'n'roll band" by *Rolling Stone* magazine in 1989, R.E.M. grew from a garage band to a cult favorite to superstars as the most popular alternative (rather than mainstream) group of the 1980s. With a name taken from the phrase "rapid eye movement," the term for the sleep cycle in which dreaming takes place, R.E.M. remains one of rock's most durable—and visionary—bands.

In 1978, Stipe (b. Decatur, Georgia, January 4, 1960), an art student at the University of Georgia, met Peter Buck (b. Berkeley, California, December 6, 1956) in an Athens, Georgia, record store where Buck worked and practiced guitar between customers. Both were fans of British new wave music, and Stipe had performed with a band that had covered punk songs. Stipe and Buck formed R.E.M. in 1980 with two struggling musicians—drummer Bill Berry (b. Duluth, Minnesota, July 31, 1958) and bassist Mike Mills (b. Orange County, California, December 17, 1956). The next year, the band recorded a demo tape that included "Radio Free Europe," chosen as the *Village Voice*'s "best independent single of the year." In 1982, R.E.M. released a self-produced mini-LP *Chronic Town* on Miles Copeland's I.R.S. label.

FIRST ALBUMS AND TOURS

R.E.M.'s first two full albums, *Murmur* (1983) and *Reckoning* (1984), became immediate college radio favorites. In 1985, the group traveled to England to record the darkly atmospheric *Fables of the Reconstruction*. The harder-edged, but more accessible, *Life's Rich Pageant* (1985) was R.E.M.'s first gold album. *Document*, their first Top 10 album, in 1987, yielded the hit single "The One I Love," a typically misinterpreted song about betrayal.

In 1988, *Green,* the band's first album for Warner Bros., produced another hit song, "Stand," and other radio-friendly tunes such as "Pop Song 89" and "Orange Crush." Many of the songs from the albums *Document* and *Green* demonstrated clearly the band's

increasing political orientation, with pertinent lyrics commenting, however obscurely, on some of the current issues of the environment and society.

In 1991, after a three-year stretch during which they toured and pursued side-projects, R.E.M. resurfaced with their first No. 1 album. The eclectic *Out of Time* featured the hit singles "Losing My Religion" and "Shiny Happy People." The album won three Grammys, including best alternative album, and the haunting *Losing My Religion* video won six awards at the MTV Video Music Awards. *Automatic for the People* in 1992 (with the title based on a sign in an Athens soul food diner) also went to No. 1, and boasted such ethereal, heavily atmospheric hits as "Everybody Hurts," "Drive," and "Man on the Moon."

Monster, in 1994, described by Stipe as sounding "like punk rock, but loud," was dedicated to the late actor, River Phoenix. It featured the hit "What's the Frequency, Kenneth?" as well as "Let Me In," an ode to NIRVANA's Kurt Cobain. The *Monster* tour itself was plagued with misfortune—Berry suffered an aneurysm, Stipe had a hernia operation, and Mills underwent abdominal surgery.

The band's latest album, *New Adventures in Hi-Fi* (1996), was a commercial disappointment. "The secret to R.E.M.'s success over the years has always been its ability to remain focused on the music, regardless of outside pressures," observed *Time* magazine critic, Christopher John Farley. "Good bands hit and fade. Great bands, like R.E.M., endure." In the late 1990s R.E.M. played less frequently but continued to endure.

Michael R. Ross

SEE ALSO:
INDIE BANDS; ROCK MUSIC; ROCK'N'ROLL.

FURTHER READING
Bowler, Dave, and Bryan Dray.
R.E.M.: From "Chronic Town" to "Monster"
(Secausus, NJ: Carol Publishing Group, 1995);
Gray, Marcus. *It Crawled from the South:
An R.E.M. Companion*
(New York: Da Capo Press, 1997).

SUGGESTED LISTENING
Automatic for the People; *Document*;
Green; *Murmur*; *Out of Time*.

OTTORINO
RESPIGHI

Ottorino Respighi was an Italian composer best known for his rich and colorful orchestral pieces. Respighi was born in Bologna, Italy, on July 9, 1879. While studying at the Liceo Musicale, Bologna (1891–1901), he visited Russia, and returned in 1902–03 to take lessons from Rimsky-Korsakov, a master of orchestration who also taught STRAVINSKY.

Back in Italy, Respighi worked as a pianist and string player, and rather early made a contribution to authentic performance with his interest in early Italian lute music. In 1913, he was made a professor of composition at the Conservatory of St. Cecilia in Rome. Though he was promoted to director in 1923, he resigned in 1925 to devote himself to composition. However, he still conducted in Europe and the U.S., and provided piano accompaniment to singers, including his wife, Elsa Olivieri-Sangiacomo, who was herself a composer.

Respighi's works, although never adventurous, were promoted by the major conductors of the century, including his fellow countryman, Arturo TOSCANINI. Respighi's lessons with Rimsky-Korsakov and his study of the music of Giacomo PUCCINI, Claude DEBUSSY, and Richard STRAUSS resulted in a deep love and understanding of melody and orchestration. He never abandoned the traditional use of harmony and melody, and he excelled in creating rich and colorful orchestrations. This approach to composition appealed to the Hollywood composers of the 1930s and 1940s. It is rare to hear a score by Max STEINER, Dimitri Tiomkin, or Miklos Rozsa without sensing at least some influence of Respighi.

Although classification of Respighi's music is difficult, it can be said to belong to the school of "Neo-Impressionism." Generally, such music attaches great importance to atmosphere and often tends to be descriptive of a scene or event. Thus, the sounds of the scene—the sighing of wind in trees, the splash and tinkle of water—become molded into the piece. Others of this school include the American Charles Griffes, the Englishman Arnold Bax, and the Swiss-born Ernest Bloch. In addition to original compositions, Respighi reworked the music of earlier composers and periods (as did Stravinsky, although Respighi's musical language was less innovative). His works of this kind include the *Rossiniana* (1915), based on piano works by Rossini; *Antiche arie e danze per liuto*, based on airs and dances for lute (1916, 1923, and 1931); and *Gli Uccelli* (1927), based on themes by Rameau and others. Later, he became interested in Gregorian plainchant (again, well before the revival of chant in the later years of the 20th century) and incorporated the serene and timeless melodic lines in the orchestral tone poem, *Vetrate di chiesa* (1925).

Among Respighi's most successful and popular compositions are three highly programmatic tone or symphonic poems that dramatically depict the Roman landscape. The orchestration in *Fountains of Rome* (1917), *Pines of Rome* (1924), and *Roman Festival* (1928) is the work of a master craftsman.

Respighi also wrote chamber music and operas. Indeed, the latter represent over half of his complete catalog, and include *Re Enzo* (1905); *Semirama* (1910); the charming *La bella addormentata nel bosco* (1922), originally a puppet play for children; *Orfeo* (1935); and *Lucrezia* (published in 1937).

Finally, Respighi's *Lauda per la Natività del Signore* (1928–30), a medley of carols and other early material for soprano, mezzo-soprano, tenor, chorus, and a chamber ensemble, is an especially attractive work that is seldom heard, but which deserves to be reinstated in the repertoire.

Respighi's last work was an opera, *Lucrezia*, which he started in 1935. It was completed by his wife, Elsa, after he died in Rome on April 18, 1936.

Richard Trombley

SEE ALSO:

AUTHENTIC PERFORMANCE; OPERA; ORCHESTRAL MUSIC; VOCAL AND CHORAL MUSIC.

FURTHER READING

Alvera, Pierluigi, trans. Raymond Rosenthal. *Respighi* (New York: Treves Publishing Company, 1986); Respighi, Elsa, trans. Giovanni Fontecchio and Roger Johnson. *Fifty Years of a Life in Music, 1905–55* (Lewiston, NY: E. Mellen Press, 1993).

SUGGESTED LISTENING

Ancient Airs and Dances; *Fountains of Rome*; *Roman Festival*; Toccata for piano and orchestra.

MAX
ROACH

Drummer-percussionist Max Roach is credited, together with Kenny Clarke, with creating the bebop and modern jazz style of drumming. During his illustrious 50-year career as a jazz musician, he played with Charlie PARKER, Dizzy GILLESPIE, and other key artists involved in the evolutionary process that metamorphosed swing into bebop.

Max Roach was born in New York City on January 10, 1924, and grew up listening to the big-band sounds of Chick Webb, Count BASIE, Duke ELLINGTON, and the Savoy Sultans. He was influenced by drummers Webb, "Papa" Jo Jones, "Big Sid" Catlett, O'Neil Spencer, and Razz Mitchell. Always interested in jazz, he also studied percussion and classical composition.

Roach's big break came at 19, when he was asked to substitute for Sonny Greer with the Duke Ellington Orchestra at New York's Paramount Theater. After that high-profile start, Roach performed a variety of gigs and eventually found himself working with Dizzy Gillespie on 52nd Street. Gillespie then introduced him to Charlie Parker.

BIRTH OF BOP

A variety of sounds from Dixieland to Swing could be heard at the 52nd Street clubs during the 1940s, and it was here that the serious music frivolously dubbed "bebop" was born. Parker, Gillespie, Thelonious MONK, and others began experimenting with a new formula for jazz improvisation—extremely fast tempos, chord substitutions and alterations, the use of new intervals, and extended melodic lines. Solos were much longer, and bebop was meant to be listened to and was not dancing music. The bebop innovators wanted to take the focus off jazz as entertainment, and instead focus on its musical virtuosity. Minton's Playhouse in Harlem and the 52nd Street clubs held all-night jam sessions where the musicians worked to hone their craft.

In Parker's group, Max Roach's improvisational talents flourished. He was one of the first (along with Clarke) to move the swing rhythm from the hi-hat—a cymbal that is played with the foot—to the ride cymbal, a large cymbal played with a drumstick, keeping steady time on the hi-hat on beats 2 and 4. This allowed for much more interaction and punctuation between the drummer's bass drum and snare, and the rest of the ensemble. Roach also used his tom toms and snare to play melodic patterns that introduced new solo possibilities for drummers, well demonstrated by his solo features on Miles DAVIS's influential album *Birth of the Cool*.

THE TOP OF HARD BOP

In the 1950s Roach jointly led a quintet with trumpeter Clifford BROWN, releasing a series of classic recordings that featured innovative originals and unique arrangements, including "Brown/Roach Incorporated," and "Live at the Bee-Hive." This collaboration was the zenith of that era's hard bop scene, but sadly came to an end following the deaths of Brown and the group's pianist Richie Powell in a car crash in 1956.

Roach later worked with an endless list of jazz luminaries and led his own groups. Among those he performed or recorded with were Bud Powell, Kenny Dorham, Booker Little, George Coleman, Miles Davis, Clifford Jordan, Sonny ROLLINS, Cecil Taylor, Eric DOLPHY, Anthony Braxton, Oscar Brown, Jr., and Abbey Lincoln (to whom he was married for a time).

Max Roach was also a pioneer of solo percussion composition, and wrote several drumset pieces that have been performed in jazz club venues as well as on the concert stage. These include "Tribute to Big Sid," "Dr. Free-Zee," and "The Drum also Waltzes."

Roach also held a teaching position in the music department at the University of Massachusetts, Amherst, until his retirement in the mid-1990s.

Gregg Juke

SEE ALSO:
BEBOP; HARD BOP; JAZZ; SWING.

FURTHER READING
Rosenthal, David H. *Hard Bop: Jazz and Black Music, 1955–1965* (New York: Oxford University Press, 1992); Taylor, Arthur, ed. *Notes and Tones: Musician-to-Musician Interviews* (New York: Da Capo Press, 1993).

SUGGESTED LISTENING
In the Light; *It's Time*; *The Max Roach 4 Plays Charlie Parker*; *Percussion Bitter Sweet*; Miles Davis: *Birth of the Cool*.

PAUL ROBESON

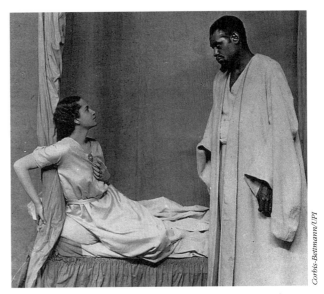

Paul Robeson in a scene from the 1943 production of Shakespeare's Othello, *in which he played the leading role.*

Paul Robeson had a career that spanned opera, theater, and film. The warmth of his bass-baritone voice and of his personality made him widely loved in America and Europe. He performed in 11 motion pictures, the most famous of which was the 1936 film of Jerome KERN's musical *Show Boat*. Although the conventions of the time limited the roles available to an African-American artist, Robeson was active in the cause of civil rights, and his advocacy helped to ease the way for African-American artists to be accepted into the mainstream of classical music.

Robeson's father was born a slave, but escaped and later had a university education. Upon graduation, he moved to Princeton, New Jersey, where Paul was born on April 9, 1898. Paul's mother, a Quaker school-teacher, died in an accident early in his childhood. Throughout his youth Robeson placed great emphasis on education, and in his spare time he sang spirituals in church and played football. He attended Rutgers University, where he became the first black All-American football player and was elected to Phi Beta Kappa. Afterward, he enrolled at Columbia University Law School. Robeson supported himself by playing professional football and working as a postal clerk. He married Eslanda Cardozo Goode, a fellow student, and acted in student performances.

He graduated from Columbia in 1923, but never practiced law. In 1924, he appeared with the Provincetown Players in Eugene O'Neill's *The Emperor Jones*. Although Jerome Kern wanted him for the 1927 Broadway production of *Show Boat*, Robeson only appeared in the English production in Drury Lane, London, in 1928.

By the early 1930s Robeson had earned an international reputation as an actor and as a concert singer. He also became increasingly involved in human rights and was horrified by the rise of fascism in Europe. In 1934 he visited the Soviet Union, and in 1938 he entertained the anti-fascist International Brigade in Spain. Robeson returned to America during the war to act in *Othello*, but his pro-Soviet statements attracted the interest of the House Un-American Activities Committee, and he was blacklisted and unable to work. In 1949, Robeson made a speech in which he said he did not have unquestioning loyalty for his native land because of its treatment of African-Americans. This cost him the support of influential members of the black community. His passport was taken away in 1950, the Ku Klux Klan stoned the audience at an outdoor concert in Peekskill, New York, and his records were withdrawn from sale.

In 1958 Robeson regained his passport and undertook several world tours. He retired in 1961 due to depression. A comeback in the late 1960s was not a critical success because his voice had lost its powerful clarity. He died in Philadelphia on January 23, 1976.

Jane Prendergast

SEE ALSO:

MUSICALS; OPERA; VOCAL AND CHORAL MUSIC.

FURTHER READING

McKissack, Pat. *Paul Robeson: A Voice to Remember* (Hillside, NJ: Enslow Publishers, 1992); Wright, David K. *Paul Robeson: Actor, Singer, Political Activist* (Springfield, NJ: Enslow Publishers, 1998).

SUGGESTED LISTENING

Carnegie Hall Concerts Vol. 1; *The Odyssey of Paul Robeson*; *The Power and the Glory*.

ROCK FESTIVALS

A creation of the 1960s, rock festivals began as the ultimate expression of the counter culture. They set out to show that rebellious youth could organize huge events without the help of the older generation or its institutions. With the huge amounts of money these festivals generated, however, it did not stay that way for long. But rock festivals have never entirely lost their idealism.

The first major rock festival was the Monterey International Pop Festival. It took place in 1967 from June 16 to 18, in Monterey, California. Monterey was the site of a well-known jazz festival, and promoter Alan Pariser decided that rock deserved a similar showcase. The festival drew around 90,000 people, many of whom did not have tickets. Performers included the Grateful Dead, the Paul Butterfield Blues Band, Booker T and the MGs, Big Brother and the Holding Company (featuring Janis Joplin), the Steve Miller Band, Jefferson Airplane, Jimi HENDRIX, the Byrds, Simon and Garfunkel, Lou Rawls, and THE WHO. But it was soul singer Otis REDDING who stole the show, and the festival launched Redding's career nationally, as it did for Joplin, Hendrix, and The Who.

THE FIRST WOODSTOCK

The most famous of all music festivals was Woodstock, held between August 15 and 17 in 1969, on a farm in Bethel, New York. It is estimated that as many as 500,000 people attended. Woodstock is remembered as much for the rain and mud, lack of food, drug overdoses, births, deaths, miscarriages, sex, and nudity as it is for the music. It was understaffed and poorly planned. Every road within a 20-mile radius, including the New York State Thruway, was blocked, and opening act Richie Havens had to play for three hours because the other performers were stuck in traffic. Still, Woodstock is remembered as the high point of the "flower power" movement of the late 1960s. Among those who performed there were Joan BAEZ, The Who, Country Joe and the Fish, Sly and the Family Stone,

SANTANA, Janis Joplin, Joe Cocker, The Band, the Grateful Dead, the Incredible String Band, Creedence Clearwater Revival, Bob DYLAN, Ten Years After, and Crosby, Stills, Nash and Young, who were formed especially for the festival, and the oldies band Sha Na Na. But it was not as idealistic a venture as it appears in memory. The organizers had sold the movie rights to Warner Bros. even before they staged the event.

The "good vibrations" spread by Woodstock died four months later at Altamont, a music festival held on December 6, 1969, at Altamont Speedway, in California. The free event featured the ROLLING STONES, Santana and Jefferson Airplane, but is best remembered for bloody fights spawned by the Hells Angels. The Rolling Stones had hired the Hells Angels as marshals, but the motorcycle gang stabbed a young man to death, and the incident was caught on camera.

Despite these problems rock festivals did not die out, partly because money could be made if they were staged properly. Summer Jam, held on July 28, 1973, at Watkins Glen Raceway in upstate New York, was the largest one-day outdoor rock event ever held. It is estimated that more than 600,000 people came to see just three bands: the Band, the Grateful Dead, and the Allman Brothers.

Steve Wozniak, cofounder of Apple Computers, put together the three-day Unite Us In Song (or Us) Festival that took place in Devore, California, in September 1982. It featured more than a dozen musicians and groups, including Fleetwood Mac, Tom Petty, and the Talking Heads.

A second Us Festival took place in San Bernardino, California, in 1983. But that festival was marred by an onstage fistfight involving the Clash, as well as by crowd violence and by numerous drug overdoses. Neither event was a financial success, with estimated losses of $20 million.

ROCK IN RIO

The largest multi-day rock event in the world took place over ten days in January 1985 in Rio de Janeiro. QUEEN, the Scorpions, AC/DC, Ozzy Osborne, James Taylor, George Benson, and Rod Stewart were some of the headliners at Rock in Rio, referred to as "the peak moment in 1980s-style pop music consumerism." More than 1.5 million people attended, but an attempt to repeat the event in 1991, known as Rock in Rio II, was not as successful. Rock festivals that were also fundraising events—such as George Harrison's

"Concert for Bangladesh" in 1971, Musicians United for Safe Energy's No Nukes concerts of 1979, and Willie NELSON's Farm Aid concerts, which started in 1985—were more successful. The largest fundraising concert ever held was Live Aid, which took place simultaneously at J.F.K. Stadium in Philadelphia, Pennsylvania, and Wembley Stadium in London, England, on July 13, 1985. Live Aid was organized in just ten weeks by Bob Geldof of the Irish group the Boomtown Rats. It ran for 16 hours and was televised live, reaching an audience of an estimated 1.5 billion people in 160 countries.

Joan Baez opened the Philadelphia show, which drew a crowd of 100,000 and featured Tina TURNER; Mick Jagger; Eric Clapton; MADONNA; Neil Young; the BEACH BOYS; the Four Tops; Crosby, Stills and Nash; LED ZEPPELIN; and Bob Dylan. The London show, which drew 72,000, included performances by STING, The Who, Paul McCartney, Peter Gabriel, and U2. Phil Collins played at both events, performing in London and then flying to the U.S. to drum with Led Zeppelin. These concerts raised about $120 million for famine relief in Africa. Live Aid was followed in 1986 by the Conspiracy of Hope Tour, which marked the 25th anniversary of the human rights organization Amnesty International. The "supertour" presented a series of five-hour concerts featuring Sting, Lou Reed, Peter Gabriel, Jackson Browne, Bono, and others.

BANDING TOGETHER

Some festivals feature a group of musicians who travel together and play at outdoor venues. These tours are produced in part for financial reasons, as it has become difficult for individual bands to fill large arenas and stadiums. One such event is Lollapalooza, which was started by Perry Farrell of the band Jane's Addiction, in 1991. Farrell wanted to create an event similar to England's Reading Festival, which features alternative bands. Lollapalooza has boasted big-name performers such as the Red Hot Chilli Peppers on its main stage, with lesser-known and local bands on a second stage.

In 1992 the first Horizons of Rock Developing Everywhere, or H.O.R.D.E., festival took place. This is a traveling tour, like Lollapalooza, which features rock performers who are influenced by roots music and world music. Peter Gabriel began headlining the World of Music, Arts, and Dance, or W.O.M.A.D., festivals in the early 1980s. He brought the tour to the U.S. in 1993, adding an international flavor to rock festivals.

Henry Diltz/Corbis

Shannon Hoon of the band Blind Melon at Woodstock '94, which was an attempt to re-create the highs of 1969.

Woodstock '94, a festival to mark the 25th anniversary of the original Woodstock, was held in August 1994 in Saugerties, New York. Stars from the first Woodstock were joined by several 1990s performers. The event was criticized for its high prices and commercialism, and protesting musicians held a small counter-festival at the site of the first Woodstock.

Despite uncomfortable and sometimes unhealthy conditions at many rock festivals, their popularity remains undiminished in Europe, the U.S., and the U.K.

Daria Labinsky

SEE ALSO:

FOLK MUSIC; POP MUSIC; ROCK MUSIC; ROCK'N'ROLL.

FURTHER READING

Hillmore, Peter. *Live Aid: World-Wide Concert Book* (Parsipanny, NJ: Unicorn Publishing House, 1985); Makower, Joel. *Woodstock: The Oral History* (New York: Doubleday, 1989); Selvin, Joel. *Monterey Pop* (San Francisco, CA: Chronicle Books, 1992).

SUGGESTED LISTENING

The Concert for Bangladesh; *No Nukes*; *Woodstock: Three Days of Peace and Music.*

ROCK MUSIC

The term "rock music" is a generic one for the rhythm-and-blues based music that dominated the world music scene for the second half of the 20th century. Rock music may be divided into rock'n'roll, which developed in the U.S. from 1954 to about 1964, and rock, which developed in the U.S. and the U.K. from early 1963. The evolution of rock worldwide occurred during the last quarter of the 20th century.

Rock as a genre can be subdivided into subgenres such as classic, progressive, acid, art, country rock, folk rock, jazz rock, and hard rock. Each of these subgenres has specific musical traits, and is related to the others through the general characteristics of rock.

BIRTH OF ROCK

Rock evolved in the early 1960s, when rock musicians began combining the musical characteristics of different rock'n'roll styles. Of particular influence were the Chicago style of rock'n'roll, represented by Chuck BERRY and Bo DIDDLEY, and country rock, exemplified by Scotty Moore. Singing styles of rock performers were influenced by Elvis PRESLEY, LITTLE RICHARD, and Buddy HOLLY; vocal harmonies were inspired by vocal group rock'n'roll and by the EVERLY BROTHERS. Many early rock bands were influenced by the urban blues style of Muddy WATERS and Howlin' Wolf. The ROLLING STONES based their early career on new interpretations of Chicago blues. Bands such as the Hollies, the Stones, the BEATLES, THE WHO, and the BEACH BOYS were greatly indebted to rhythm-and-blues (R&B) and soul artists such as Ray CHARLES and Marvin GAYE.

The rock bands of the 1960s were guitar-oriented, featuring lead and rhythm guitars. The standard format was a lead guitar, rhythm guitar, bass, and drums, with all band members singing. Although some bands, such as the Rolling Stones, had an extra person singing, the basic format was two guitars, bass, and drums.

In the early 1960s, rock bands mostly played songs previously recorded by other groups. By 1965, rock bands were including traditional orchestral instruments, such as in the Beatles' "Yesterday" (1965) and the Rolling Stones' "As Tears Go By" (1965). Folk rock and psychedelic bands incorporated musical elements from India and others used Western folk instruments. Several rock composers began to conceive their music as multiple-movement works, and the concept album was developed. Early examples include *Freak Out* (1966) by Frank ZAPPA and the Mothers of Invention, and *Sgt. Pepper's Lonely Hearts Club Band* (1967) by the Beatles. Later rock groups experimented with the form, yielding classic albums such as *The Village Green Preservation Society* by the KINKS (1968).

In the 1960s, rock styles were represented by mainstream or commercial rock; the music that was prominently performed on radio and television and that sold well. There were many rock subcategories, including ragga rock and baroque rock, but only a few have stood the test of time. The most prominent and influential of these subcategories were surf rock, folk rock, and psychedelic (acid) rock.

Surf rock developed in southern California in the subculture of surfing enthusiasts. Much of the surf style was instrumental, performed by guitar-oriented groups like the Ventures, the Surfaris, and the "King of the Surf Guitar," Dick Dale. Dale's sound is augmented by an affinity for Middle Eastern modes ("Miserlou," 1962). Vocal surf rock, celebrating the southern California lifestyle of fun in the sun, is represented primarily by the Beach Boys. The sound of the Beach Boys is characterized by strong four- and five-part vocal harmonies and clear, high-pitched lead vocals. Their vocal style was influenced by vocal group rock'n'roll, primarily the Four Freshmen, while their instrumental style was inspired by Chuck Berry. Although leader Brian Wilson attempted a more experimental rock style in the song "Good Vibrations" (1966) and the album *Pet Sounds* (1966), the Beach Boys largely remained within their surf sound.

EVOLUTION OF FOLK ROCK

Folk rock was developed in the mid-1960s by Bob DYLAN and the Byrds. The style combines elements of rock and folk music, with folk instrumental playing styles. Prominent folk rock acts include Buffalo Springfield, Crosby, Stills, and Nash, and Simon and Garfunkel. Folk rock evolved in the 1970s to include country rock represented by groups such as the EAGLES, Poco, and the Flying Burrito Brothers. Other offshoots in the 1970s were the singer-songwriters such as James

Taylor and Carole KING. Southern rock, related to folk rock, developed in the late 1960s and was very popular through the 1970s. It combines musical elements from rock, blues, and country music, each band varying the mixture to create their own sound. Southern rock defines a rock spectrum from blues-based (the Allman Brothers), through rock-oriented (Lynyrd Skynyrd), to country-based (Charlie Daniels Band).

Psychedelic rock developed in the mid-1960s, in an attempt to duplicate the acid trip through sound. Important acid rock groups include Jefferson Airplane, the Doors, and the Grateful Dead. Several psychedelic bands chose names that were ambiguous or presented cross-images: Iron Butterfly, Electric Flag, and the Grateful Dead. In the 1970s, elements of psychedelic rock evolved into hard rock or heavy metal, represented by bands such as Deep Purple, LED ZEPPELIN, and Black Sabbath, and into progressive rock represented by groups such as PINK FLOYD and YES.

DEVELOPMENT OF JAZZ ROCK

In the late 1960s, several bands began combining elements of jazz—horn improvisation, extended chords, and complex chord progressions—with rock sounds. The most successful of the jazz rock bands included Blood, Sweat and Tears. Other bands combined jazz and funk elements with soul characteristics to create funk rock. Funk rock, represented by bands such as Sly and the Family Stone, was popular through the 1970s and the 1980s. The thudding drumbeat, the rhythmically intricate bass lines, and the punching horn arrangements became crucial to the funk-pop sound of the 1980s, as well as in rap.

Rock after about 1973 turned to more pop-oriented sounds. Groups that were popular at this time included America, with a folk-rock sound, and Bread. Pop artists such as Barry MANILOW and Neil Diamond enjoyed great success in the 1970s, along with singer-songwriters such as Billy Joel and Bruce SPRINGSTEEN. Fleetwood Mac created a successful pop/rock band with their album *Rumours* (1977). Also extremely popular in the mid-1970s was disco, which influenced songs such as the Rolling Stones' "Miss You" (1977) and Paul McCartney's "Good Night Tonight" (1979).

As a reaction against pop/rock and disco, punk rock arose in the mid-1970s in London, Los Angeles, and New York. Punk was derived from the styles of New York's the VELVET UNDERGROUND and the Ramones. Punk rock fought against all kinds of established

authority and social norms. The lyrics were antisocial simply for the sake of being antisocial, as in the SEX PISTOLS' "Anarchy in the U.K." (1977), or else they explored social injustice, as in the Clash's "White Man in Hammersmith Palais" (1977). With the addition of synthesizers and pop-oriented lyrics, bands like the Cars and Elvis Costello established what became known as "new wave." The computer technology used in new wave led to the techno rock of the 1980s, represented by bands such as the Talking Heads.

BACK TO ROCK'N'ROLL

In the mid-1980s, the most popular rock styles were heavy metal, techno rock, and rap. Heavy metal was characterized by extreme instrumental technique and loud volume. Techno rock, on the other hand, was highly dependent on computers and synthesizers. In the late 1980s and early 1990s, groups such as NIRVANA and Pearl Jam returned to the hard-edged sound of the 1960s, with lyrics about the problems of the 1980s and 1990s. Their desire was to create an alternative to the flashy styles of heavy metal and techno rock, returning to the root sound of rock'n'roll.

Steve Valdez

SEE ALSO:
FOLK ROCK; HEAVY METAL; NEW WAVE; PROGRESSIVE ROCK; PUNK ROCK; ROCK'N'ROLL; SINGER-SONGWRITERS.

FURTHER READING

Cooper, B. Lee, and Wayne S. Haney. *Rock Music in American Popular Culture II: More Rock'n'Roll Resources* (New York: Harrington Park Press, 1997); Covach, John, and Graham M. Boone, eds. *Understanding Rock: Essays in Musical Analysis* (New York: Oxford University Press, 1997); De Barres, Pamela. *Rock Bottom: Dark Moments in Music Babylon* (New York: St. Martin's Press, 1996).

SUGGESTED LISTENING

AC/DC: *Back in Black*; Elvis Costello and The Attractions: *Imperial Bedroom*; Grateful Dead: *From the Mars Hotel*; Led Zeppelin: Boxed Set 2; Nirvana: *Bleach*; Oasis: *Be Here Now*; Pink Floyd: *Delicate Sound of Thunder*; Lou Reed: *Walk on the Wild Side: The Best of Lou Reed*; Rolling Stones: *Rewind*; Soundgarden: *Ultramega OK*; Frank Zappa: *The Best Band You Never Heard in Your Life*.

ROCK'N'ROLL

The musical style of rock'n'roll is generally considered to have derived from rhythm and blues (R&B), and became popular principally with teenagers in the 1950s. It developed in various regions of the United States, roughly from 1954 to 1964, as an extension of the R&B that had become popular in the 1940s, during and especially after World War II.

THE RISE OF R&B

R&B developed in Southwestern and Midwestern urban centers such as Kansas City, Chicago, and St. Louis, and was influenced by jazz, the blues, and black gospel music. R&B bands were similar to small jazz combos: they had a lead singer backed by bass, drums, piano, and electric guitar as the rhythm section, and a horn section consisting of one to three saxophones and perhaps a trumpet. From the blues, R&B borrowed its textual structure, chord progression, performance style, and song subject matter; it also borrowed the enthusiastic, exciting performance style of African-American gospel music.

The rhythm section played a continuous rhythmic ostinato derived from boogie-woogie that placed a strong accent on the second and fourth beats of the quadruple measure. This accented beat (the "rhythm" in "rhythm and blues") became known as the backbeat, and was to figure prominently in the development of rock'n'roll. The popularity of R&B gradually spread throughout the country during the postwar years, in some markets completely supplanting jazz or blues styles.

THE FIRST ROCK'N'ROLL PARTY

In the early 1950s, disc jockey Alan FREED noticed that African-American R&B was attracting a new audience: middle-class, suburban, white teenagers. Freed began broadcasting a late-night R&B radio program, sponsored by a local record store, from Cleveland station WJW in June 1951, calling his program *Moondog's Rock'n'Roll Party*. The term "rock'n' roll"—a phrase frequently used in the lyrics and titles of the R&B songs Freed played on his program—was originally a euphemism both for dancing and for sex. However, in Freed's thinking "rock'n'roll" was the R&B he played for his white teenage audience.

"Rhythm and blues" for Freed became a heavily backbeat-accented music performed by black musicians for a black audience, while "rock'n'roll" was the same music by the same performers, but for a white audience. Freed's radio program became so popular that he was eventually hired by New York City station WINS to broadcast nationally.

Around 1953, it became an accepted practice for white performers to copy R&B songs, often changing the more risqué lyrics to more acceptable versions, and to release these new "cover" versions to compete with the original R&B recordings. With more radio stations playing music by and for white Americans than by African-Americans, the cover versions became better known than the originals,

The driving guitar style of Carl Perkins produced some of the most exciting rockabilly music. His recording of his own song "Blue Suede Shoes" was a smash hit in 1956.

Michael Ochs ARchives/Redferns

with the result that more performance royalties were paid to the cover artists than to the original performers. Some of the best-known examples of this include Pat Boone's recordings of LITTLE RICHARD's "Tutti Frutti" and Fats DOMINO's "Ain't That a Shame," Elvis PRESLEY's version of Willie Mae Thornton's "Hound Dog," and Bill HALEY's cover of Big Joe Turner's "Shake, Rattle and Roll." By 1954, "rock'n'roll" had come to denote R&B songs covered by white performers, as well as original material by these performers written to imitate the R&B style.

However, there is more to the musical style of rock'n'roll than white performers copying black R&B. Both black and white artists contributed to the development of rock'n'roll in the 1950s by combining elements of the blues and other musical styles in which they had been raised. Rock'n'roll developed slightly differently in different areas of the country—in the Northeastern U.S. and in New Orleans, in Memphis, and in Chicago—through the fusion of African-American blues, R&B, and the popular music styles in those areas. The music that came out of these areas exerted a strong influence on music produced in other parts of the country throughout the 1950s.

BILL HALEY AND HIS COMETS

The rock'n'roll that came out of the Northeastern U.S. was represented by Bill Haley and His Comets, and by vocal groups usually referred to as "doo-wop." Bill Haley was originally a country singer known for his yodeling skill, and was popular in Pennsylvania, New Jersey, Delaware, and Ohio. In 1949, backed by his group the Four Aces of Western Swing, Haley began to perform R&B songs at his live shows. After reorganizing his band into the Western swing group the Saddlemen, Haley made his first record, a cover of Jackie Brenston's "Rocket 88." Eventually the Saddlemen became the Comets, and in 1954 the group recorded their classic "Rock Around the Clock."

Originally issued as a B-side, when "Rock Around the Clock" was used for the opening credits of the film *The Blackboard Jungle* in 1955, the film's popularity with teenagers raised the song to the top of *Billboard* magazine's sales charts, making it the first No. 1 rock'n'roll song. The song has since become synonymous with 1950s nostalgia, having appeared on the soundtrack of the film *American Graffiti* (1973), and as the title song for the first season of the hugely successful television show *Happy Days* (1974).

The Comets' music is a combination of elements from R&B and country music, with jazz guitar performance techniques added. Their style is characterized by a steady, mechanical approach to meter, fast tempos, even melodic rhythms, slapped bass technique, and steel guitar. One can also hear vocal techniques borrowed from country music, combined with the emphasized backbeat, boogie-woogie accompaniment, and the harsh tenor saxophone sound of R&B. The lead guitarists were influenced by the playing style of jazz guitarist Charlie CHRISTIAN. Bill Haley and His Comets were immensely popular from roughly 1954 to 1957.

DOO-WOP VOCAL GROUPS

The other type of rock'n'roll from the Northeast—vocal group rock'n'roll—is a diverse category of music. The vocal groups were primarily made up of African-American singers from the large urban centers like Philadelphia, New York, Detroit, and Los Angeles. The type of song ranges from fast-tempo novelty songs by the Coasters to slow-tempo love ballads by the Platters. While vocal groups were as individual as their members, there are some general style characteristics that set it apart from other rock'n'roll styles. The main focus is on the vocals—usually a high tenor lead vocal supported by three to four singers in close harmony. The entire group is supported by an R&B band kept deep in the background so as not to intrude over the vocals. The supporting vocals often vocalize syllables (ahs, oohs) or sing syllables like "d-doo wah" (giving the style its name "doo-wop").

While the other rock'n'roll styles depend heavily on the 12-bar blues progression, many doo-wop songs are built on the progression using tonic–submediant –subdominant–dominant (I-VI-IV-V). These doo-wop vocal groups, which were heavily influenced by popular male singing groups such as the INK SPOTS and the Mills Brothers of the 1930s and 1940s, include the Orioles, Penguins, Platters, Coasters, Drifters, Dion and the Belmonts, and the FOUR SEASONS.

NEW ORLEANS STYLE

The New Orleans style of rock'n'roll is based on the rhythm and blues associated with that city, in combination with musical elements from boogie-woogie

Michael Ochs Archives/Redferns

Gene Vincent's career was launched in the late 1950s when he recorded the Elvis Presley-sounding "Be-Bop-A-Lula."

piano. The principal rock'n'roll artists to rise to popularity in New Orleans from around 1953 to 1963 included Clarence "Frogman" Henry, Professor Longhair, Lloyd Price, Smiley Lewis, Antoine "Fats" Domino, and "Little" Richard Penniman.

The J&M recording studio owned by Cosimo Matassa was instrumental in developing the New Orleans sound. The sound is characterized by a deep bass foundation, concentration on the lower range of instruments, loose rhythms based on boogie-woogie rhythms, melodic surface rhythms that varied from a lively, bounced beat to a slow, intense shuffle, and an emphasis on vocal expression making songs either exuberantly joyful or incredibly depressed. The saxophone- and piano-oriented New Orleans style of rock'n'roll gradually declined in popularity during the early 1960s in favor of the electric guitar bands of rock.

MEMPHIS ROCKABILLY

The rock'n'roll style that developed in Memphis came into prominence in 1954; it combined musical elements of rhythm and blues with those of country. The style was referred to as "country rock" by the

musicians who played it, though it is now most often referred to as "rockabilly," a combination of rock'n'roll and hillbilly (country) music.

Bands were essentially country string bands with electric and acoustic guitars, and acoustic bass; after 1955 piano and drums were often included. The sound is dominated by a tinny, treble foundation in the guitars and nasal vocals influenced by country music. Vocals are characterized by yelps, stuttering, and yodels from country music, and growls, wails, and slurred words from the blues.

The Memphis country rock style was largely the product of Sam Philips's Sun Recording Studio, where leading artists such as Elvis Presley, Carl Perkins, and Roy Orbison recorded. Jerry Lee LEWIS, the self-styled "king of rock'n'roll," also recorded with Sun.

ELVIS THE PELVIS

Elvis Presley came to the notice of Sam Philips when as a teenager he paid to record a track at the studio for his mother's birthday. He cut some singles for Sun, appeared on the *Grand Ole Opry*, and toured clubs. He was 21 when he recorded "Heartbreak Hotel" for the RCA label in January 1956—an event now considered to be the beginning of rock. It shot to the No. 1 spot where it remained for two months. Other hits swiftly followed—"Hound Dog," "Blue Suede Shoes," and "Love Me Tender." His appearances on stage caused hysteria among his teenage fans, encouraged by his suggestive hip gyrations. But at the end of the decade he was drafted into the U.S. Army, and by the time he was discharged his importance on the rock'n'roll scene had begun to fade.

Carl Perkins's abrasive, driving guitar style was the epitome of rockabilly and influenced many later groups, in particular the BEATLES. Soon after his own recording of "Blue Suede Shoes" was a huge hit, he was seriously injured in a car accident and his career lost momentum. Nevertheless, many of his later singles are regarded as rockabilly standards.

Other performers associated with the rockabilly style, though not through Sun Studios, include the EVERLY BROTHERS, Eddie Cochran, Gene Vincent, Dale Hawkins, and Rick Nelson.

Gene Vincent's career was launched hot on the heels of Presley's debut, as the record labels competed to find the next rock sex symbol. Vincent's first (and biggest) hit was the exciting "Be-Bop-A-Lula," which almost convinced Presley's mother that it was cut by her son. The record was a huge hit in both the U.S. and Britain. But Vincent's sultry, menacing image made him difficult to promote in the U.S., and he eventually found a manager in Britain to handle his declining career. Eddie Cochran was a great rockabilly guitarist who shot to fame in 1958 with his smash hit "Summertime Blues." Although his career was short (he died in a road accident in 1960, at age 22), his influence on rock'n'roll was considerable.

Memphis country rock'n'roll remained a popular style into the 1960s and was extremely influential on the growth of rock in the 1960s and beyond. The 1980s saw a renewed interest in the rockabilly style with groups like the Stray Cats and the Cramps becoming popular.

CHICAGO ROCK'N'ROLL

Chicago rock'n'roll developed in the mid-1950s from the urban blues and R&B that had been popular there in the 1940s and 1950s. Chicago rock'n'roll is a guitar-based style, as opposed to the hard-edged saxophone sounds of Chicago R&B. The Chicago rock'n'roll guitar, derived from urban blues techniques, features frequent sliding on the strings, bent notes, and multiple-stopped strings. There are generally faster tempos and harder-driving backbeat emphases than in either urban blues or rhythm and blues. The rock style also features more even beat subdivisions, rather than the boogie-woogie swung beat heard in R&B, and performers generally stay closer to the beat than do blues performers.

The two main exponents of Chicago rock'n'roll are Chuck BERRY and Bo DIDDLEY. Berry's guitar style is melodic, featuring repeated riffs, bent notes, and bent multiple stops, a straight eighth-note accompaniment that has become the trademark of the rock'n'roll sound, and a frequent use of syncopated rhythms. Many of Berry's songs ("Roll Over Beethoven," "Johnny B. Goode," "Carol") begin with a guitar introduction that has become a cliché in rock music.

Berry was to become a role model for many young rock'n'roll bands, and was to have a seminal influence on the rock bands of the 1960s, including the BEACH BOYS, the Beatles, and the ROLLING STONES.

Bo Diddley grew up in Chicago, playing street music as a boy, and was launched in 1955 by the new Chess label, along with Chuck Berry. Diddley's guitar style is harder and more rhythm-oriented than Berry's, defined by a heavy-handed picking style,

full-chorded rhythmic patterns, and solos based on rhythms rather than melodies. The classic Bo Diddley rhythm—which he refers to as the "Bo Diddley beat"—is derived from the African juba rhythm heard frequently in children's games—the same rhythm as the shoeshine chant "shave and a haircut, two bits."

BUDDY HOLLY—ROCK'N'ROLL LEGEND

The music of Buddy HOLLY is also a part of the 1950s rock'n'roll scene, being a fusion of elements from Chicago and Memphis rock'n'roll styles combined with his own personal style. "That'll Be the Day," released in 1957 when he was 21, was an instant hit, and was quickly followed by what are now regarded as rock'n'roll standards—"Peggy Sue," "Oh Boy," and "Maybe Baby."

Holly's group, the Crickets, featured a self-contained line-up of two electric guitars, bass, and drums that would set the pattern for rock groups of the 1960s and beyond. He also experimented with and pioneered innovative techniques in the recording studio that were to become widely used.

The different styles of rock'n'roll that developed simultaneously in the mid-1950s blended musical elements of the blues, country, R&B, jazz, and a variety of American folk music into a unique style that has dominated the pop music landscape for the second half of the 20th century.

Steve Valdez

SEE ALSO:
BLUES; BOOGIE-WOOGIE; DOO-WOP; GOSPEL; ROCK MUSIC.

FURTHER READING

Clifford, Mike, ed. *The Harmony Encyclopedia of Rock* (New York: Harmony Books, 1992);
Gillett, Charlie. *The Sound of the City: The Rise of Rock and Roll* (New York: Pantheon Books, 1983);
Logan, Nick, and Bob Woffinden. *The Illustrated Encyclopedia of Rock* (New York: Harmony Books, 1977).

SUGGESTED LISTENING

The Buddy Holly Collection; *Chuck Berry on Stage*; *Legendary Masters: Eddie Cochran*; Bo Diddley: *I'm a Man*; Bill Haley: *Rock Around the Clock*; Elvis Presley: *The Sun Sessions*.

JIMMIE
RODGERS

Jimmie Rodgers has been described as the "father of country music." Combining blues from his native Mississippi with a hillbilly style (including a distinctive highland yodel), Rodgers crafted a form that became the template for virtually all subsequent country music. During his brief career, Rodgers left a musical legacy from which generations of musicians have drawn inspiration.

James Charles Rodgers was born on September 8, 1897, in Meridian, Mississippi. Meridian was home to an active vaudeville and dance hall scene which quickly entranced young Jimmie. Before pursuing a show-business career, however, in the late 1910s Rodgers followed in his father's footsteps and took a job as a brakeman, inspecting passenger trains and assisting the conductor. After being diagnosed with tuberculosis in 1924, Rodgers left railroading, worked for a while as a private detective, and then formed a band, aiming for an easier life as a musician.

In the mid-1920s, Rodgers moved to Asheville, North Carolina, hoping the crisp mountain air would be easier on his failing lungs. His band, the Jimmie Rodgers Entertainers, began working at the city's WWNC radio station. In August 1927, Ralph Peer, the talent scout for the Victor Talking Machine Company, was holding a recording session across the mountains in Bristol, Virginia. Rodgers' group had planned to audition, but the night before they were scheduled to leave, Rodgers and his bandmates parted company over the issue of the band's name. Rodgers ended up recording "The Soldier's Sweetheart" and "Sleep Baby Sleep" as a solo act.

BLUE YODELING DAYS

Rodgers' first record met with little public reaction. But "Blue Yodel (T for Texas)," recorded a few months later, became the first country record to sell over a million copies, and made Jimmie Rodgers a household name among hillbilly music fans.

Rodgers eventually recorded 110 singles for Victor between 1927 and 1933, including ten more "Blue Yodels." He sang against a wide variety of backdrops,

including Hawaiian music, jazz (most famously, a session with Louis ARMSTRONG), small orchestras, cowboy music, and gospel (recorded with the CARTER FAMILY, the era's other country superstars). Rodgers himself was never a proficient guitarist: he introduced the characteristic slides of the Hawaiian guitar into his band, complementing his yodeling technique. His record sales were consistently strong until the onset of the Great Depression, when record sales dropped dramatically for almost everyone.

Unfortunately, Rodgers' health continued to decline, despite the wishful thinking of songs like "Whipping that Old TB." He refused to slow down his pace, telling his wife, "I want to die with my boots on." On May 24, 1933, he recorded a dozen sides in one session, including some of his finest work. Two days later, the father of country music was dead of a lung hemorrhage.

Country music (and in turn, rock'n'roll) owes a great debt to Jimmie Rodgers. Countless country singers integrated Rodgers' work into their repertoires and, until Hank WILLIAMS, every country singer began their career imitating Rodgers. In 1997, some 64 years after his death, he was the subject of a tribute album featuring Bob DYLAN, Steve Earle, Aaron Neville, Dwight Yoakam, and Jerry Garcia, among others.

Rodgers was the first member inducted into the Country Music Hall of Fame, and he was also celebrated by the Rock and Roll Hall of Fame as an early influence.

Greg Bower

SEE ALSO:

BLUES; COUNTRY; HILLBILLY MUSIC.

FURTHER READING
Porterfield, Nolan. *Jimmie Rodgers: The Life and Times of America's Blue Yodeler* (Champaign, IL: University of Illinois Press, 1992); Rodgers, Carrie C. W. *My Husband, Jimmie Rodgers* (Nashville, TN: Country Music Foundation, 1975).

SUGGESTED LISTENING
The Best of Jimmie Rodgers; *Jimmie Rodgers: The Early Years*; *Jimmie Rodgers on Record: America's Blue Yodeler*; *My Old Pal*; *Train Whistle Blues*; *Way Out on the Mountain*.

RICHARD
RODGERS

Broadway's two most successful teams of songwriters shared one essential ingredient—the same composer, Richard Rodgers. Paired first with lyricist Lorenz Hart (from 1920 to 1943) and then Oscar HAMMERSTEIN II (1943 to 1960), Rodgers' enormous success as a songwriter was based on craftsmanship, talent, and longevity. As fellow composer Leonard BERNSTEIN said, he "established new levels of taste, distinction, simplicity in the best sense, and inventiveness."

Richard Charles Rodgers was born in Hammels Station, Long Island, New York, on June 28, 1902, the younger son of a successful doctor. When he was just four, he began composing songs on the piano and was soon emulating the operatic melodies of Franz Lehár and Victor HERBERT. In 1918, a mutual friend introduced the 16-year-old Rodgers to Hart, the brilliant if mercurial lyricist who would be his partner for the next quarter-century. The team contributed several tunes to the 1920 musical *Poor Little Ritz Girl,* but after two years of failure, Rodgers entered the Institute of Musical Art in New York for formal musical training. However, just as Rodgers was about to abandon songwriting for a career as a children's underwear salesman, he and Hart were asked to write songs for a 1925 revue, *The Garrick Gaieties.* One of their tunes, "Manhattan," became a big hit, and was the team's ticket to Broadway.

FROM HART TO HAMMERSTEIN
Between 1925 and 1942, Rodgers and Hart produced the scores for 28 successful shows, including *A Connecticut Yankee, Babes in Arms,* and *Pal Joey,* plus several other musicals. For *On Your Toes* (1936), which explored the world of dance, Rodgers composed the memorable symphonic-jazz ballet *Slaughter on Tenth Avenue.*

By 1943 Hart's self-destructive lifestyle had made it impossible for him to work, and Rodgers was forced to find a more stable partner—48-year-old librettist-lyricist Oscar Hammerstein II, best known for collaborating with Jerome KERN on the 1927

masterpiece *Show Boat.* (Actually Rodgers and Hammerstein had previously written songs for an amateur production in 1919.) Their first project was *Oklahoma!,* the landmark 1943 musical, which featured instant classics such as "Oh, What a Beautiful Morning" and "People Will Say We're in Love." In the new partnership, the sophisticated musical comedies of Rodgers and Hart gave way to fully realized musical plays: often homespun, usually optimistic, always universal in theme and melody.

SUCCESS ON STAGE AND SCREEN
For the next 17 years, Rodgers and Hammerstein wrote the scores for an almost unbroken string of Broadway classics—*Carousel* (1945), *South Pacific* (1949), *The King and I* (1951), *Flower-Drum Song* (1958), and *The Sound of Music* (1959)—all of which became successful movies. The team also received a 1945 Academy Award for "It Might As Well Be Spring" from the film *State Fair.*

Following Hammerstein's death in 1960, Rodgers continued to write for the Broadway stage—sometimes acting as his own lyricist (*No Strings,* 1962), and often collaborating with others (including Hammerstein's disciple, Stephen SONDHEIM on 1965's *Do I Hear a Waltz?*).

Rodgers published his autobiography, *Musical Stages,* in 1975, and the following year composed his final musical, *Rex,* which closed after only 42 performances. The grand old man of the American musical stage died of cancer in New York City on December 30, 1979, at the age of 77.

Michael R. Ross

SEE ALSO:
FILM MUSICALS; MUSICALS.

FURTHER READING
Hyland, William G. *Richard Rodgers* (New Haven, CT: Yale University Press, 1998); Rodgers, Richard. *Musical Stages: An Autobiography* (New York: Da Capo Press, 1995).

SUGGESTED LISTENING
Babes in Arms; Carousel; Musicals: Selections; Rodgers and Hart: On Your Toes; The Sound of Music.

JOAQUIN RODRIGO

The place in history of the Spanish composer Joaquin Rodrigo is secured by a single work, the *Concierto de Aranjuez*, composed more than 50 years ago, but so popular in the 1990s that over 40 recordings are currently available. The work has been transcribed from the original guitar to other instruments, including voice and trumpet.

Rodrigo was born in Sagunto, Spain, on November 22, 1901, one of ten children. At the age of three, his vision was affected by diphtheria, and he was nearly blind throughout his life. Nonetheless, he learned to play the violin, and at 14 was studying harmony and counterpoint. He was encouraged in his studies by the great Spanish composer and pianist Manuel de FALLA. Rodrigo also studied under the composer Paul DUKAS at the Paris Conservatory beginning in 1927, aided by his secretary/copyist, Rafael Ibanez.

MAN OF MANY PARTS

Although he was in touch with all compositional styles current in Europe during his studies in Paris, Rodrigo never abandoned his Spanish roots and his love for the guitar and Spanish folk song.

Rodrigo's first major work, *Juglares* (1924), was given a premiere by the Valencia Symphony Orchestra, and it was this success that persuaded the Turkish pianist Victoria Kamhi to perform his orchestral work *Cinco Piezas Infantiles* in 1929. The pieces won second prize in the Spanish National Competition and remain popular teaching pieces to this day. Rodrigo married Kamhi in 1933.

For the duration of the Spanish Civil War Rodrigo lived abroad, but he returned to Spain in 1939 to become the musical advisor of the National Spanish Radio, and the chairman of art and publicity of the Spanish National Organization for the Blind. In 1948, he became the head of the latter organization, and taught and worked as a music critic for the newspaper *Pueblo*. It may have been Rodrigo's experiences with the Spanish bureaucracy that led to the *Gran Marcha de los Subsecretarios* (Grand March of the Bureaucrats) duet for piano.

The *Concierto de Aranjuez* for guitar and chamber orchestra was composed in 1940, and has been recorded by every major classical guitarist including Angel and Pepe Romero, Narciso Yepes, Julian Bream and John WILLIAMS, and also by the cellist Julian Lloyd Webber. The jazz trumpeter Miles DAVIS recorded a version of the slow movement, arranged by Gil Evans, on the album *Sketches of Spain*.

WORLDWIDE FAME

For 30 years beginning in 1948, Rodrigo occupied the Manuel de Falla chair at the University of Madrid. His interest in folk music, which he taught, led to the *Doce Canciones Espanolas* (1951) and the *Cuatro Canciones Sefardies* (1967).

Rodrigo's reputation continued to grow during this period. The English composer Robert Shaw brought his work to New York, and the harpist Nicholas Zabaletta commissioned a harp concerto from him in 1956. In 1958, the legendary guitarist Andrés SEGOVIA played Rodrigo's *Fantasia para un gentilhombre* with the San Francisco Symphony. Rodrigo festivals were held in Japan in 1972 and in Mexico City in 1981. A week-long festival in Jerusalem, underwritten by the publisher Schott, took place in 1983, and Rodrigo's music was the focus of concerts spread over two weeks in London in 1986. In 1994, a short film, *Shadows and Light*, was made by Bullfrog Films, recording the composer in his 90s.

Although Rodrigo has not had a significant impact on music history, he was one of the most popular composers of his day.

Jane Prendergast

SEE ALSO:

FOLK MUSIC; ORCHESTRAL MUSIC.

FURTHER READING

Kamhi de Rodrigo, Victoria, trans. Ellen Wilkerson. *Hand in Hand with Joaquin Rodrigo: My Life at the Maestro's Side* (Pittsburgh, PA: Latin American Literary Review Press, 1992).

SUGGESTED LISTENING

Concierto andaluz; *Concierto de Aranjuez*; *Concierto Galante*; *Fantasia para un gentilhombre*; *Tonadilla*.

KENNY
ROGERS

A pop and country music superstar, Kenny Rogers can be credited with helping to redirect American country music toward the mainstream. As a singer, songwriter, and actor, he continues to please crowds with his mellow sound and friendly smile.

Kenneth Ray Rogers was born on August 21, 1938, in Houston, Texas. As a young child he would listen to his uncles playing guitar and fiddle, and by age 14 he had decided to be a professional musician, saving the money he earned as a busboy to buy his first guitar. He joined with friends to form the Scholars, and the rockabilly combo's early recordings led to a few regional hits and a succession of live bookings.

One of Rogers' 1957 solo recordings, "That Crazy Feeling," became a million-copy hit and landed him an appearance on *American Bandstand*. He studied briefly at the University of Houston, where he joined a jazz group, the Bobby Doyle Trio, and later the Kirby Stone Four.

In 1966 Rogers was playing with the Lively Ones jazz combo when he was offered a position in the New Christy Minstrels, a folk pop ensemble. This provided him with the national exposure he needed.

Rogers and fellow Minstrels Mike Settle, Terry Williams, and Thelma Lou Camacho founded the First Edition in 1967, with their eyes on the more adventurous folk rock being played by Bob DYLAN and others. The group changed their name to Kenny Rogers and the First Edition in 1969, and eventually disbanded in 1976 with two gold records to their credit: 1969's "Reuben James" and a cover of Mel Tillis's "Ruby, Don't Take Your Love to Town."

After an initially fallow period as a soloist, Rogers broke onto the charts with "Love Lifted Me" in 1976, and followed with Don Schlitz's martyr ballad, "Lucille." Platinum albums and major hits continued with "The Gambler," and "We've Got Tonight," which he sang with Sheena Easton. "Islands in the Stream," and "What Are We Doin' in Love," his pop hit duets with Dolly PARTON and Dottie West, continued to win major awards as Rogers became one of the most sought-after performers in the music business.

Throughout the 1970s and 1980s, Rogers received a string of awards while continuing to score many solo hits. In 1980, Rogers moved from EMI to RCA Records, married his fourth wife, actress Marianne Gordon, and scored smash hits with two songs "Don't Fall in Love with a Dreamer" (with Kim Carnes 1980), and "Lady," written by Lionel Richie. The same year the television movie *The Gambler*, based on his story-song "The Gambler," starred Rogers, who began to explore a career in television.

In the 1980s he recorded duets with Dottie West, Sheena Easton, Ronnie Milsap, Anne Murray, Dolly Parton, and Holly Dunn. He also made two more television mini-series.

CHARITY WORK

Rogers' extensive charity work to combat hunger and diabetes included his participation in the "We Are the World" project, the Hands Across America organization, and several benefit concerts. In 1985, he received the prestigious Roy ACUFF Award. Since then, he has recorded several more albums and television specials. "If You Want to Find Love," with Linda Davis, was perhaps the only standout hit for Rogers in the 1990s, though television paired him with Reba McEntire, Naomi Judd, and Travis Tritt.

With 40 years in the music business, 11 platinum records, 18 gold records, and 50 major music awards to his credit, Rogers remains one of America's best known entertainers. He is a rare case of a pop artist who crossed over into country, rather than vice versa, and he has proven that changing with the times can ensure long-term success for a recording and performing artist.

Todd Denton

SEE ALSO:
COUNTRY; FOLK ROCK; POP MUSIC.

FURTHER READING
Martha Hume. *Kenny Rogers:
Gambler, Dreamer, Lover*
(New York: New American Library, 1980).

SUGGESTED LISTENING
A Decade of Hits; *Lucille & Other Classics*;
Ten Years of Gold; *Timepiece*;
We've Got Tonight.

THE ROLLING STONES

The British rock group the Rolling Stones have often been described as the greatest rock'n'roll band in the world. Despite its complimentary nature, however, this label is inaccurate. The Stones did not just play rock'n'roll: they also put black rhythm and blues (R&B) firmly into the mainstream of international popular music, and thus laid the foundations for all rock music since the 1960s.

The group was formed in 1962, and, after various early changes of personnel, the line-up featured vocalist Mick Jagger (b. July 1943), guitarist Keith Richard (b. December 1943), guitarist Brian Jones (1942-69), drummer Charlie Watts (b. June 1941), and bassist Bill Wyman (b. October 1936). Jones was

The Rolling Stones in 1964. From left: Bill Wyman, Brian Jones, Charlie Watts, Mick Jagger, and Keith Richard.

David Redfern/Redferns

asked to leave the group in June 1969, when his drug habit began to have a detrimental effect on the band's music, and was found drowned in the swimming pool of his home the following month. He was replaced by Mick Taylor (b. January 1948), an accomplished blues guitarist. When Taylor left in 1974, he was in turn replaced by Ronnie Wood (b. June 1947), who had previously backed Rod Stewart in the Faces. In 1993 Wyman quit the band, but the Stones did not replace him.

The Stones were originally inspired by a shared love of rock'n'roll artists such as Chuck BERRY, and bluesmen such as Muddy WATERS, from whose song they took their name. After earning a reputation as a stunning live act, their third single, a version of Buddy HOLLY's "Not Fade Away," made No. 3 in Britain in March 1964. The following month, they released their eponymous first album, and knocked the BEATLES off the No. 1 spot in the album charts for the first time in 51 weeks.

The Rolling Stones album (released with additional tracks in the U.S. as *England's Newest Hit Makers: The Rolling Stones*) was crammed with songs written by the artists who had inspired them, and introduced black R&B to a mass white audience for the first time. In the summer of 1964, "It's All Over Now," a cover of a song by soul artist Bobby Womack, became the first of the Stones' eight No. 1 singles in their homeland during the 1960s.

The biggest rivals to the Beatles in the mid-1960s, the Stones were scruffier, angrier, and appeared to advocate drugs and casual sex—in 1967, Jagger and Richards were briefly imprisoned for drugs offenses. With their roots in black music, the Stones were seen as a bigger threat to established social mores than were the Beatles. This mix ensured that the Stones initially appealed mainly to young outsiders, an identity that remained with the band until the members were well into their 30s, and had themselves become part of a new musical establishment.

REVOLUTIONARY WRITING

In 1965, the group's manager, Andrew Loog Oldham, locked Jagger and Richard in a room until they wrote a song. "The Last Time," with its lively looping riff, was the first of a series of action-packed singles that made Jagger and Richard a key writing partnership of the 1960s. Their run of hits included "(I Can't Get No) Satisfaction," which shot to No. 1 in both Britain and the U.S., and was to be the first of nine U.S. No. 1 singles. Other hits from the Jagger-Richard partnership included "Get Off My Cloud," "Paint It Black," "19th Nervous Breakdown," "Let's Spend the Night Together," "Ruby Tuesday," "Jumpin' Jack Flash," and "Honky Tonk Woman."

RELENTLESS POWER

These singles were perfectly crafted: few groups understood the importance of a strong song-intro in the way the Stones did, while their tight playing drove their three-minute rushes of rhythm with relentless power from beginning to end. Jagger's strident vocals commanded attention, while Richard sometimes used unusual guitar tunings to achieve a distinctive sound. A solid beat from bass player Wyman and drummer Watts then provided the perfect backing for Jagger's sensuality and athleticism, making the Stones a riveting stage act.

With their sell-out concerts, and their singles topping the charts on both sides of the Atlantic, the Stones had to put their energies into albums in the late 1960s. This coincided with the fact that the rock audience had suddenly moved its affections from singles to albums. The Stones—with the invaluable help of their new producer, Jimmy Miller—seamlessly switched their focus onto the long-playing medium.

FOUR HIGH-OCTANE ALBUMS

The album *Beggar's Banquet* (1968) featured country rock and a rock samba in the song "Sympathy for the Devil." The brutal *Let It Bleed* (1969) saw them attain new heights (or depths) of decadence, with tracks such as "Gimme Shelter" and "Monkey Man." It also featured one of the great rock ballads, "You Can't Always Get What You Want," which used the London Bach Choir to sing the opening lines and the climactic ending. The live album *Get Yer Ya-Ya's Out!* (1970) captured the unrestrained excitement of which the group was capable, and is still regarded by many as one of the best live rock albums ever made. The album *Sticky Fingers* (1971) found the band at its zenith, kick-starting with the high-octane hit single "Brown Sugar," before moving on to jazz rock, blues, country, and entrancing ballads. The lyrical content was provocative as was usual for the Stones. In this instance, they peppered the songs with drug references and lascivious sex, notably in Marianne Faithfull's "Sister Morphine" and "Wild Horses."

LATER WORKS

After those four albums, it was hard for the Stones to reach such heady heights again, although they did have their moments. The double album *Exile on Main Street* (1972) found them still close to their best, if somewhat weary. *Goat's Head Soup* (1973) and *It's Only Rock'n'Roll* (1974) featured some passable songs, but the band seemed to be treading water. *Black and Blue* (1976) experimented with reggae with some success, while *Some Girls* (1978) was an energetic response to the jibes of Britain's punks. *Tattoo You* (1981) was their last fully satisfying album, although they still produced excellent singles, such as "Tumbling Dice," "Angie," "It's Only Rock'n'Roll," the disco-influenced "Miss You," and "Start Me Up." In 1997, they brought out a new album, *Bridges to Babylon*. They also remained a potent live act into the 1990s.

The Rolling Stones molded the blues, R&B, and rock'n'roll in their own inimitable image to make music that was always restless, intriguing, exciting, and usually good for dancing. They created a unique style of rock music, and although they spawned many imitators, they have yet to be matched for originality and panache.

Graham McColl

SEE ALSO:

BLUES; COUNTRY; JAZZ ROCK; REED, JIMMY; ROCK FESTIVALS; ROCK MUSIC; ROCK'N'ROLL.

FURTHER READING
Flippo, Chet. *On the Road with the Rolling Stones* (New York: Doubleday, 1985);
Hotchner, A.E. *Blown Away: The Rolling Stones and the Death of the Sixties* (New York: Simon & Schuster, 1990);
Miller, Jim. *The Rolling Stone Illustrated History of Rock & Roll* (New York: Random House/Rolling Stones Press, 1980).

SUGGESTED LISTENING
Beggar's Banquet; *Black and Blue*;
Exile on Main Street;
Get Yer Ya-Ya's Out; *Let It Bleed*;
Singles Collection: The London Years;
Some Girls; *Sticky Fingers*;
Tattoo You.

SONNY ROLLINS

A master of the tenor saxophone, a jazz icon in the same league as Charlie PARKER or John COLTRANE, and a fiercely unique and creative improviser—all this and more can be said of saxophonist and composer Sonny Rollins. He would regardless deserve a place in jazz history purely on the strength of his unparalleled sound on his instrument, and on the extent to which he influenced several generations of jazz artists.

Theodore Walter Rollins ("Sonny" or "Newk") was born in New York City on September 9, 1930. His parents were immigrants from the Virgin Islands, and Rollins' brothers and sisters all studied classical music, while his uncle played saxophone and listened to the blues. When Rollins began studying the sax he was influenced by Louis Jordan and jazz masters Parker, Coleman HAWKINS, and Lester YOUNG.

Early on Rollins worked with Babs Gonzales, the Bud POWELL–Fats Navarro combo, and Miles DAVIS, as well as with Parker; but he gained serious exposure and arrived musically during his tenure with the Clifford BROWN–Max ROACH group, from 1956 to 1957.

Rollins worked with Roach on several of his albums, and the collaboration yielded a jazz masterpiece, *Saxophone Colossus*, from which the original composition "St. Thomas" became a classic. "St. Thomas" is a Calypso, exploring melodic and rhythmic material from Rollins's Caribbean roots. *Saxophone Colossus* also included Rollins's extended improvisation on "Blue 7." Here, he improvised by exploiting short melodic motives in a way that was influential for other hard bop musicians.

Rollins continued to release groundbreaking material, such as 1957's *Way Out West*, which showed his interest in odd improvisational vehicles like "Wagon Wheels" and "I'm an Old Cowhand." Rollins composed the noteworthy *Freedom Suite* in 1958, after which he took the first of several sabbaticals from recording and public performance.

Sonny Rollins' unique style came from blending swing era and bebop influences, and his interest in both the blues and Caribbean music. He tended to approach solos melodically or thematically (quoting tunes that are related lyrically in some way to the composition he was performing), rather than by simply playing strings of scales that fit over the chord changes. His sound on the tenor was thick and rough, with vibrato that is very evident but not overwhelming. His sound, like that of Joe HENDERSON, is very distinct from that of his contemporaries.

AN ECCENTRIC CHARACTER

Rollins' output was prolific, but his unique musicianship and contribution to the jazz vocabulary were often overshadowed by his eccentric tendencies and the mystique that surrounded him. Long before the styles were popular, Rollins sported a "Mohawk" haircut and then a shaved head, and a legend grew up around his penchant for practicing his instrument late at night on the catwalk of the Williamsburg Bridge over New York's East River.

In later years, Rollins worked with younger musicians, especially those performing on electric rather than acoustic instruments. He even recorded with the ROLLING STONES ("Waiting on a Friend," from the 1981 release *Tattoo You*); but Rollins' music never strayed too far into the "fusion" genre; he remained a unique voice in post-bop jazz. His 1984 recording, *Sunny Days and Starry Nights,* featured a future classic in the form of his original ballad, "Wynton."

In addition to Roach, Brown, Davis, and MONK, Rollins worked with Billy Higgins, Don Cherry, Bob Cranshaw, Jack DeJohnette, Philly Jo Jones, Shelley Manne, Ray Brown, Victor Bailey, Mark Soskin, and Tommy Campbell, among others.

Sonny Rollins continued to have a unique voice on the tenor sax, and to exert a solid influence on modern jazz through his style and compositions.

Gregg Juke

SEE ALSO:
CARIBBEAN; HARD BOP; JAZZ.

FURTHER READING
Blancq, Charles. *Sonny Rollins, The Journey of a Jazzman* (Boston, MA: Twayne, 1983).

SUGGESTED LISTENING
The Complete Blue Note;
The Essential Sonny Rollins on Riverside;
Saxophone Colossus: Sunny Days, Starry Nights.

DIANA
ROSS

After several years as the lead singer of the MOTOWN group, the Supremes, Diana Ross achieved superstardom in the 1970s and 1980s, appearing in cabarets and films, as well as making a series of albums and singing on several records that reached No. 1 in the charts.

Born in Detroit, Michigan, on March 26, 1944, Diane Ernestine Ross joined the female group, the Primettes, while still in high school. The group was signed by Berry Gordy's Motown label in 1961 and renamed the Supremes. Diana was soon promoted to lead singer as Gordy valued her looks and style over Florence Ballard's superior vocal abilities.

As the Supremes vaulted to the upper echelons of pop music in the early 1960s, Gordy groomed Ross for a solo career, changing the name of the group to "Diana Ross and the Supremes" in 1967. These machinations (along with persistent rumors of romantic involvement between Ross and Gordy) led to considerable tension within the group.

DIANA ON HER OWN

After the Supremes disbanded in 1970, Ross's solo career began with the hits "Reach Out and Touch (Somebody's Hand)," and "Ain't No Mountain High Enough." She married a businessman, Robert Silberstein, in April 1971, but the marriage ended in divorce five years later.

Ross's career branched out in 1971 when she hosted a television show *Diana!* The following year, Motown used Ross's star power to launch its foray into the movie business. Her surprisingly strong performance in *Lady Sings the Blues*, a film biography of Billie HOLIDAY, earned Ross an Oscar nomination. Ross's subsequent starring roles, unfortunately, ranged from mediocre (*Mahogany,* 1975) to forgettable (*Wiz,* 1978, in which she played Dorothy in a modern version of *The Wizard of Oz*).

Ross continued to score hits, including "Touch Me in the Morning" (1973) and "Theme from *Mahogany*" (1975), although she seemed headed for the cabaret spot of the supperclubs with this material.

Ross signaled a change of direction in 1976, however, with the seven-minute disco epic "Love Hangover." She followed this path through 1980, when she released her funkiest single, the No. 1 hit "Upside Down," produced by Chic's Nile Rodgers and Bernard Edwards. Refreshing as this material was, her treacly 1981 duet with Lionel Richie, "Endless Love," nevertheless proved to be her biggest hit of this period.

BREAKING WITH THE PAST

At this point in her career, Ross severed her links with Motown and signed with RCA. She appeared more interested in being a media star than a musical artist, and her prima donna-like behavior prompted severe criticism in the press. During the taping of Motown's 25th anniversary television special in the spring of 1983, Ross was seen giving ex-Supreme Mary Wilson a hefty shove. That summer, her concert in New York's Central Park was a fiasco, costing the city $650,000 in damages and police overtime.

Ross's record sales were declining as well. Other than "Missing You," her tender 1984 tribute to Marvin GAYE, Ross's showings on the American charts dropped precipitously. She remained popular overseas, however, scoring a No. 1 hit in Britain in 1986 with "Chain Reaction."

The 1990s found Ross focusing on non-musical pursuits. Her 1993 memoir, *Secrets of a Sparrow,* allowed Ross to reflect on her legacy as a superstar: "Through the burden of my celebrity, I have learned certain ways to carry myself and my loads. I always try to see the bigger scheme of things and in so doing find a form of grace with which to live my life."

Greg Bower

SEE ALSO:
MOTOWN; PHILADELPHIA SOUND; SOUL.

FURTHER READING
Ross, Diana. *Secrets of a Sparrow: Memoirs* (New York: Villard Books, 1993); Taraborrelli, J. Randy. *Call Her Miss Ross: The Unauthorized Biography of Diana Ross* (New York: Ballantine Books, 1989).

SUGGESTED LISTENING
Diana Ross & the Supremes; *The Force Behind the Power*; *Ross*; *Why Do Fools Fall in Love.*

MSTISLAV ROSTROPOVICH

One of the preeminent cellists of the 20th century, Mstislav Rostropovich is also an important conductor and sponsor. He has recorded practically all works written for cello, and continues to inspire additions to the repertoire.

Rostropovich was born in the city of Baku, in present-day Azerbaijan, on March 27, 1927. Both his parents were musicians, and he began musical studies in early childhood. He played his first cello concerto with an orchestra at age 13. At 16, he was accepted at the prestigious Moscow Conservatory, and two years later won a Soviet competition that launched his career. He joined the faculty of the conservatory shortly after graduation.

Rostropovich was recognized early as an outstanding talent, capable of combining great accuracy of intonation with a tremendous feel for the material he performed. A number of prominent Russian composers wrote pieces specifically for him, including Dmitry SHOSTAKOVICH and Sergey PROKOFIEV.

The cellist Mstislav Rostropovich earned respect as both a musician and as a staunch defender of human rights.

Lebrecht Collection

In 1956, Rostropovich made debut appearances at the Festival Hall in London, and at Carnegie Hall in New York, becoming one of the first Soviet artists to perform in the United States. He returned to the U.K. in 1960, where he met the composer Benjamin BRITTEN. The pair formed a lasting friendship, and Britten went on to write a series of pieces for him, including his Sonata for cello and piano (1961), and his Symphony for cello and orchestra (1968).

In 1969, Rostropovich publicly supported the novelist Alexandr Solzhenitsyn, who was being persecuted because of his criticisms of the Soviet regime. Despite their popularity, Rostropovich and his wife, the soprano Galina Vishnevskaya, had their foreign tours canceled and their recording projects suspended by the Soviets. Rostropovich turned down a chance at official rehabilitation when he refused to denounce another dissident, the scientist Andrei Sakharov. He and Vishnevskaya were not granted exit visas until 1974, when pressure from the West was put on the Soviet government to do so. They were welcomed in the U.S., where Rostropovich made his conducting debut in 1975. Rostropovich went on to become music director of the National Symphony Orchestra in Washington in 1977, a post which he held for 17 years.

An international celebrity and, for the West, a symbol of post-communist Russia, Rostropovich flew to Berlin to play atop the Berlin Wall when it was demolished in 1989. He subsequently went to Moscow to lend his support to President Mikhail Gorbachev when the Soviet leader was threatened by a reactionary coup in 1991, and he still performs in the former Soviet Union to raise funds for humanitarian projects.

Jane Prendergast

SEE ALSO:
CHAMBER MUSIC; ORCHESTRAL MUSIC.

FURTHER READING
Rostropovich, M., with C. Samuel. *Mstislav Rostropovich and Galina Vishnevskaya: Russia, Music and Liberty* (Portland, OR: Amadeus Press, 1988).

SUGGESTED LISTENING
J. S. Bach: Suites for Solo Cello;
Dvořák: Cello Concerto; Elgar: Cello Concerto;
Messiaen: *Concert à quatre.*

ALBERT ROUSSEL

Born four years after the American Civil War and dying shortly before World War II, Albert Roussel bridged the music of the 19th and 20th centuries. His harmonies were evocative of the post-Wagnerians, but he employed innovations such as the melodies and repetitions of Indian music, which gave his compositions a unique voice.

Albert Charles Paul Marie Roussel was born on April 5, 1869, in Tourcoing, France. His father died in 1870, and until her own death in 1877, his mother taught him music theory and piano. Afterward he lived with his grandfather, who passed away in 1880, when Roussel's care fell to his aunt. In 1887, Roussel was accepted as a cadet in the French naval college. After graduating, he served as a midshipman on the battleship *Devastation*, which was equipped with a piano on which he was able to compose. His first piece, an Andante for string trio and organ, was played in a church in Cherbourg in 1892.

In 1894, Roussel resigned his commission and went to Paris to take lessons from Eugène Gigout. Four years later, he was accepted at the new Schola Cantorum into the class of Vincent d'Indy, a Wagnerite opposed to the Impressionist music being written by Claude DEBUSSY and others. Roussel continued there for nine years, and became professor of counterpoint in 1902. Among his students were Bohuslav MARTINU and Erik SATIE.

ORIENTAL INFLUENCES

In 1908, Roussel married Blanche Preisach, and the couple honeymooned in India and Asia. *Evocations* for chorus, soloists, and orchestra was a tonal picture of that honeymoon. Among the melodies is the song of the fakirs (itinerant religious men who have renounced worldly goods) at Benares. The opera-ballet *Padmâvatî* is also based on a Hindu legend. Roussel's first success was the ballet *Le festin de l'araignée* (1913). Its popularity led to his appointment as director of the Théâtre National de l'Opéra in 1914, and was thus able to resign from the Schola Cantorum, where his drift away from the precepts of the post-Wagnerians had led to friction.

Military service in World War I interrupted Roussel's musical career, but he finished his opera, *Padmâvatî*, and his second symphony in 1922. The latter was heard by Sergey KOUSSEVITZKY, who promoted Roussel's music in America. In 1929, France acknowledged his position as one of the country's leading composers by holding a Roussel Festival in Paris for his 60th birthday. The Suite in F (1927) was dedicated to Koussevitzky, and the composer visited America for Koussevitzky's premiere of Roussel's Third Symphony, written for the Boston Symphony Orchestra's 50th anniversary in 1930. In 1931, he also visited the U.K. for the London performance of his choral work, *Psalm lxxx*.

During the 1930s, while living in Normandy, France, Roussel continued to compose at a rapid rate, despite illness. The ballet *Bacchus et Ariane* was performed at the Paris Opera in 1931, as well as the *Psalm lxxx*. Although Roussel's ballets are seldom performed now, the *Bacchus et Ariane* music is frequently programmed. His last orchestral work was the *Rapsodie Flamande*, which echoed the Belgian folk music he had heard as a child.

Toward the end of his life, Roussel continued to compose and travel, despite warnings from his doctor. He died on August 23, 1937. Although Roussel saw his own music as being outside the mainstream of French classical music at the time, he took an active part in the nation's musical life by teaching and promoting the work of younger composers. A Roussel Festival, promoted by the Centre International Albert Roussel, was held in France in 1997.

Jane Prendergast

SEE ALSO:
BALLET AND MODERN DANCE MUSIC; CHAMBER MUSIC; OPERA; ORCHESTRAL MUSIC; VOCAL AND CHORAL MUSIC.

FURTHER READING
Deane, Basil. *Albert Roussel*
(New York: Greenwood Press, 1980);
Follet, Robert. *Albert Roussel: A Bio-bibliography*
(New York: Greenwood Press, 1988).

SUGGESTED LISTENING
Bacchus et Ariane; Concerto for Piano and Orchestra; *Evocations*;
Padmâvatî; Symphonies Nos. 3 and 4.

ARTUR RUBINSTEIN

Artur Rubinstein was a Polish pianist best remembered for his style and vivacity. He was born in Lodz, Poland, on January 28, 1887, the youngest child of Ignacy Rubinstein, a textile producer, and Felicia Heyman Rubinstein. He began piano lessons at the age of three, and exhausted the resources of the Warsaw Conservatory of Music by age eight, when he was sent to Berlin to perform for the eminent violinist, Joseph Joachim. Joachim not only undertook supervision of the prodigy's musical education, but also conducted at Rubinstein's Berlin debut in December 1900. Public success in Berlin led to recitals in Dresden, Hamburg, and Warsaw, as well as a visit to Ignacy Paderewski in Switzerland. He was later taught privately by Paderewski. Launched on the concert stage in 1910, Rubinstein's natural facility and exuberant temperament propelled him into the first rank of European concert pianists. His gift for sight-reading and sensitive musicianship made him a favorite of singers and chamber musicians. The great violinist Eugène Ysaÿe chose him to be his main accompanist.

During the early part of World War I, Rubinstein gave recitals for the Allied cause and became so enraged by German treatment of Poles and Belgians that he vowed never to appear in Germany again. From 1916, tours of Spain and South America earned critical acclaim. Rubinstein reappeared at Carnegie Hall in 1919, but was rebuffed by American critics who found his playing marked by high spirits and little preparation, as they had with his first appearance as a boy in 1906.

DEDICATION AND DISCIPLINE EARN ACCLAIM

This casual approach changed after his marriage to Aniela Mlynarski in 1932. Rubinstein began to dedicate himself more fully to becoming a serious pianist—he practiced six to nine hours a day, restudied his repertoire, and began to record. This process brought discipline to his robust temperament and intelligence to his charismatic manner. Rubinstein's third tour of America in 1937 wrung the highest critical acclaim from previously skeptical critics. A love affair between the charismatic Pole and the American musical public

began and never flagged. World War II forced Rubinstein to relocate his family from Paris to Beverly Hills, where he played the piano in films about Schumann, Liszt, Brahms, and others, including *Of Men and Music* (1950), in which he played himself. In 1946, Rubinstein took American citizenship, and he moved to New York in the 1950s. His prodigious concert career continued unabated, and he also collaborated with the likes of Piatigorsky, Szeryng, and the Guarneri Quartet.

MATURE PERFORMANCES

Through his 70s and 80s, Rubinstein held pride of place as the complete pianist—his playing was always forthright and natural. He gave his last recital in London in 1976, when failing eyesight put an end to his public appearances. His recorded legacy includes the complete piano works of Chopin, three versions of the complete Beethoven piano concertos, and an enormous repertoire of works by Mozart, de FALLA, DEBUSSY, RAVEL, POULENC, Brahms, and others. However, he was known in his maturity above all as a Chopin interpreter. In his early years, Rubinstein's interpretations of Chopin were criticized as cold and colorless; but his rich, glowing sonority and lyric legato phrasing eventually converted critics to his approach.

Rubinstein died in Geneva on December 20, 1982.

Hao Huang

SEE ALSO:

CHAMBER MUSIC; ORCHESTRAL MUSIC.

FURTHER READING

Rubinstein, A. *My Many Years*
(New York: Knopf, 1980);
Sachs, H. *Rubinstein: A Life*
(New York: Grove Press, 1995);
Schonberg, H.C. *The Great Pianists*
(New York: Simon and Shuster, 1963).

SUGGESTED LISTENING

Beethoven: Concerto No. 5 in E flat (*Emperor*);
Brahms: Four Ballades; Concerto No. 1 in D;
Chopin: Ballades; Mazurkas; Scherzi;
Rachmaninoff: Concerto No. 2, in C; Rhapsody;
Ravel: *Valses nobles et sentimentales*;
Saint-Saens: Concerto No. 2 in G minor;
Schubert: Fantasy in C;
Schumann: Three Fantasies; Quintet in E flat Major.

SALSA

The salsa style emerged in New York in the 1970s when Latin musicians, searching for a tougher, more strident sound, started updating big band arrangements that had been used by Cuban bands for the previous 20 or 30 years. Salsa is a mixture of Afro-Cuban, Puerto Rican, and other indigenous Caribbean styles combined with pop and jazz styles of the U.S.

The origin of salsa can be traced to the explosion of the Afro-Cuban "mambo craze" in the U.S. in the late 1940s and early 1950s, and to the increased numbers of Latin immigrants in the U.S. (The name "salsa" derives from the Spanish word for "hot sauce," which was often shouted by Latin American musicians as praise for outstanding playing.) The popularity of salsa was boosted by record labels dedicated to it and Latin American music (such as the New York–based Fania label), and by the popularization of Latin musical instruments in general.

THE CLAVE RHYTHM

Salsa, like its musical cousin Latin Jazz, and its predecessor the Cuban son, is based around the clave rhythm. Clave is a two measure beat-cycle that comes in two basic varieties: son clave and rumba clave. The rhythm is divided into a "three-beat" side and a "two-beat" side (depending on which measure is the starting point); and all rhythmic and melodic phrasing must conform to the clave. Confusingly, the word also refers to a percussion instrument made up of two small cylindrical sticks. Whether this instrument is actually played or not, salsa musicians need to understand clave and base their music on it.

Salsa borrows heavily from the Afro-Cuban rhythmic tradition, and therefore includes elements of traditional rhythms such as the mambo, bolero, and the Dominican merengue. The tumbao, a basic Afro-Cuban beat, is played on the congas (*tumbas* or *tumbadora* in Spanish), while the acoustic or electric bass plays a specific pattern that includes the "bombo

Veteran percussionist and conga player Ray Barretto was an early enthusiast of salsa, helping to establish the Fania record label dedicated to salsa and Latin American music.

David Redfern/Redferns

note" (a note that helps define the placement of the rhythm within the clave). The bass and congas, together with the clave rhythm and *guajeos* ("gwa-hey-yos") or *montunos* played on the piano form the foundation on which salsa is built.

MAKING THE SALSA SOUND

Other instruments in salsa include bongos, timbales, various bells and shakers, and in some cases, a drumset or guitar. Horn sections may be made up of various combinations of saxes, trumpets, and trombones (a section sound popularized by pioneer salsa trombonist Willie COLÓN features only trombones).

Other musical elements of salsa include *coro* sections (background voices singing in harmony or unison), the use of the nasal, high-pitched *jíbaro* lead vocal style (deriving from a singing style that comes from the rural parts of Puerto Rico), and the use of *descarga/montuno* vamps (rhythm section "jams" over which the lead vocalist acts as a soloist or improvising instrument, trading musical phrases with other instrumentalists or *coro* in a jazz-like dialogue).

Salsa styles include "salsa tradicional" (as exemplified by artists such as Eddie Palmieri) and "salsa dura" or *nueva canción* (typified by performers such as Willie Colón and Rubén BLADES), and the more modern sounds of "salsa romantica." This usually features lush string and synthesizer arrangements, and puts less emphasis on improvisation and more on romantic or ballad lyrics, often sung in English in an attempt to broaden the salsa market. Famous salsa bandleaders include Tito PUENTE and Ray Baretto, both of whom played Latin jazz as well as salsa, and Eddie Palmieri, Rubén BLADES, and Willie Colón.

SONGS AND SINGERS

Salsa singers have a technique all their own, encompassing ad-libbing, improvising, and scatting (jazz singing with nonsense syllables) to rhythm. The Cuban singer Celia CRUZ sang with the Tito Puente Orchestra in the 1960s, and then shot to fame in 1974 when she collaborated with percussionist Johnny Pacheco on an album that went gold. Her energy, formidable technique, and rich, vibrant voice earned her the name "queen of salsa."

Although most salsa lyrics are purely escapist, some singers and groups, such as Rubén Blades and the Cuban group LOS VAN VAN, dealt with issues that carried a political message.

UNIVERSAL APPEAL

Salsa is accessible to and generates excitement in audiences everywhere, and has created a bridge between the traditional Afro-Cuban sounds, their American jazz interpretations, and popular music. It has also had tremendous influence on the development of Latin music, and has influenced generations of performers and music fans worldwide. Although salsa began in New York, it enjoys an international following, with bands coming from throughout the Spanish-speaking world, and even from places such as Germany and Japan.

While salsa has had an effect on the traditional music of countries such as Spain (modern flamenco music includes elements and instrumentation borrowed from salsa), it is also a vital musical force that is constantly evolving, as evidenced by the rise of newer styles that combine traditional sounds with Latin hip-hop and pop dance music. Salsa styles, instrumentation, and sounds have also had a great influence on the emerging musical style known as Afro-pop.

Salsa is so vital and so much a part of Latin American life that most large Latin American cities have their own separately evolving salsa scene. This fact alone ensures that salsa will remain a dynamic and growing force in music.

Gregg Juke

SEE ALSO:

CARIBBEAN; CUBA; LATIN AMERICA; LATIN JAZZ.

FURTHER READING
Ayala, Cristobal Diaz. *The Roots of Salsa: The History of Cuban Music* (New York: Excelsior Music Publishing, 1995); Figueroa, Rafael. *Salsa and Related Genres: A Bibliographical Guide* (Westport, CT: Greenwood Press, 1992).

SUGGESTED LISTENING
Adalberto Alvarez: *La Salsa Caliente*; Rubén Blades: *Siembra*; Willie Colón: *Grandes Exitos*; Fania All Stars: *Live at Yankee Stadium*, Vols. 1 and 2; Fruko y sus Tesos: *The Godfather of Salsa*; Various artists: *Super Salsa Hits*; *Viva Salsa!*

ARTURO SANDOVAL

An award-winning trumpet player and sometimes flugelhorn player, Arturo Sandoval is among many Cuban-born musicians who found greater international fame after leaving their island-nation. He also was perhaps the most notable Latin jazz trumpet player performing in the 1990s.

Arturo Sandoval was born in Artemisia, Havana, on November 6, 1949, and grew up listening to and playing traditional Cuban music. He started learning classical trumpet at the age of 12 (he also played keyboards and percussion), and attended the Cuban National School of Arts to study classical music. While a student, he performed with the BBC Symphony Orchestra and Leningrad Symphony Orchestra as a guest artist.

AN INTRODUCTION TO JAZZ

A fellow trumpet player introduced Sandoval to a recording by Charlie PARKER that featured Dizzy GILLESPIE on trumpet. Sandoval told *Down Beat* that he didn't understand the music, but it pushed him to explore jazz. "And I'm still trying to find out what they were doing."

With Chucho Valdes, and other former members of the Orquesta Cubana de Música Moderna, he was a founder member of the group IRAKERE in 1973. The Irakere line-up included top Cuban musicians, many of them—like Sandoval—classically trained.

After the 1959 revolution in Cuba, relations with the U.S. were severed. Nevertheless, the Castro government was highly supportive of musicians, and some cultural exchange continued. Irakere and its individual members were strongly influenced by Dizzy Gillespie, who had visited Havana while on a cruise with Stan GETZ in the late 1970s. None was influenced more than Sandoval.

The young trumpeter introduced himself to Gillespie, then offered to escort him to neighborhoods where street musicians convened and played. Sandoval had not told the elder statesman of jazz that he was also a musician—that is until they played together on stage later that same night. The two became fast friends. Gillespie and Sandoval eventually toured and recorded together. Sandoval also played for three years with Gillespie's United Nations Orchestra and was featured on their album *Live at the Royal Festival Hall.*

LEAVING CUBA

Sandoval parted company with Irakere in 1982 to form his own group, which toured extensively in Europe and South America. He was voted Cuba's best instrumentalist from 1982 through 1984. It was while on tour with Gillespie in Rome in 1990 that Sandoval decided to defect and seek political asylum in the U.S. That same year he settled in Miami, Florida, where he has remained ever since.

After leaving Cuba, Sandoval expanded his musical horizons. Among the projects he undertook were teaching music, performing on the soundtrack of the film *Havana* as well as with the GRP All Star Big Band, contributing to Gloria ESTEFAN's pop recording *Into the Light*, and recording an album of trumpet concertos.

"[It] has been my goal all my life to play as many things as I can," he said in a *Down Beat* interview. "I don't want any sign on me that says "jazz" or "salsa" or "blues." I'm a musician, man."

Linda Dailey Paulson

SEE ALSO:
CUBA; D'RIVERA, PAQUITO; JAZZ; LATIN JAZZ.

FURTHER READING

Alkyer, Frank, and John McDonough, eds.
Down Beat: 60 Years of Jazz
(Milwaukee, WI: Hal Leonard Publishing Corp., 1995);
Manuel, Peter, et al. *Caribbean Currents:*
Caribbean Music from Rumba to Reggae
(Philadelphia, PA: Temple University Press, 1995);
Sandoval, Arturo. *Playing Techniques and*
Performance Studies for Trumpet
(Milwaukee, WI: Hal Leonard Publishing Corp., 1995).

SUGGESTED LISTENING

Arturo Sandoval and the Latin Train;
Arturo Sandoval Plays Trumpet Concertos;
Breaking the Sound Barrier;
Danzón; Straight Ahead;
Tumbaito.

SANTANA

Carlos Santana was one of the major rock musicians of the late 1960s "flower power" era, exerting a major influence on the fusion of jazz, Latin, and rock.

Born in 1947 in Autlán, Mexico, Carlos Santana was brought up in a family of professional musicians. First his father taught five-year-old Carlos the violin; a few years later he switched to guitar. Santana learned blues and rock styles by listening to recordings of Chuck BERRY, B. B. KING, and T-Bone WALKER. In the early 1960s, Santana added the music of jazz performers such as John COLTRANE and Miles DAVIS to his long list of musical influences.

JOINING LATIN MAGIC TO ROCK

Santana assembled his first band, the Santana Blues Band, in 1966 in San Francisco; the name of the band was soon shortened to Santana. The band created its unique sound by adding conga drums, timbales, agogo bells, and other Latin American percussion instruments to the standard rock instrumentation of electric guitars, electric bass, drums, and organ. Original band members included Santana (guitar, vocals), Mike Carabello (conga, percussion), Dave Brown (bass), José Chepito Areas (timbales, percussion), Mike Shrieve (drums), and Gregg Rolie (keyboards, vocals). The intricate African and Latin American polyrhythms of the percussion, in conjunction with the rock rhythms of the rhythm section, created a new tone color in the otherwise blues-based outfit. The group appeared at the Woodstock Festival in the summer of 1969, virtually unknown, and played the song "Soul Sacrifice." The song electrified the crowd, and firmly established the band on the rock scene. The group's popularity increased dramatically after Woodstock, as did sales of the band's first album, *Santana* (1969).

The Latin American background of the tune "Black Magic Woman," which was originally a blues-based song written by Fleetwood Mac's guitarist Peter Green, as well as the group's own recording of Tito PUENTE's "Oye Como Va" and the instrumental "Samba Pa Ti" helped Santana's second album, *Abraxas* (1970), achieve great commercial success. On the strength of *Santana* and *Abraxas*, Santana became one of the most popular bands of the early 1970s, both in America and throughout the world. Santana's popularity was greatly enhanced by extensive international tours.

In the early 1970s Carlos Santana became attracted to Indian religion and philosophy, an influence that resulted in the albums *Love, Devotion, Surrender* (1973; with John McLAUGHLIN), *Illuminations* (1974; with Alice Coltrane), and *Oneness* (1979).

CHANGING WITH THE TIMES

Santana adopted a more Latin, jazz, and rock fusion sound on the albums *Caravanserai* (1972) and *Welcome* (1973), but not all of the group's members shared Carlos's artistic views. Organist Gregg Rolie and guitarist Neal Schon left the group to form the band Journey. In all, Santana went through some 35 different musical versions, reflecting the stylistic changes it witnessed since its inception. Former members of Santana include Buddy Miles, Alphonso Johnson, Mingo Lewis, Coke Escovedo, and Ndugu Chandler. In the early 1980s, Santana had occasional single hits, such as "Winning," and a best selling album *Zebop* (1981). Through the 1980s, Santana continued performing live and recording, earning a Grammy for the album *Blues for Salvador* (1989).

Although it is unlikely that Santana will ever command the popularity he enjoyed in the 1970s, he remains a strong voice in rock, recording and touring extensively with his band and as a guest artist with artists such as Buddy Miles and Willie NELSON.

Steve Valdez

SEE ALSO:

JAZZ ROCK; LATIN JAZZ; ROCK MUSIC.

FURTHER READING

Charlton, Katherine. *Rock Music Styles: A History* (Madison, WI: Brown & Benchmark, 1994); DeCurtis, Anthony, and James Henke with Holly George-Warren, eds. *Illustrated History of Rock & Roll* (New York: Random House, 1992); Stuessy, Joe. *Rock and Roll: Its History and Stylistic Development* (Englewood Cliffs, NJ: Prentice-Hall Inc., 1994).

SUGGESTED LISTENING

Abraxas; *Blues for Salvador*; *Caravanserai*; *Moonflower*; *Santana*; *Santana (III)*; *Viva Santana!*

ERIK
SATIE

The composer Erik Alfred-Leslie Satie is remembered as a writer of fairly modest music, and also for the considerable influence he had on composers such as RAVEL, DEBUSSY, and CAGE.

Satie was born in Honfleur, France, on May 17, 1866, to a French father and a Scottish mother. The family moved to Paris in 1870, and when Satie's mother died, he went to live with his grandmother until she too died. He returned to Paris and in 1879 attended the Paris Conservatory to study harmony and piano. The records show that he was talented, but given to truancy, and he was dismissed in 1882. However, he managed to write a few songs and other pieces, and in 1884 published a piano piece that he called Opus 62. He gave other piano pieces extraordinary titles that poked fun at both classical and modern compositions.

In 1887 Satie produced his first major work, the triptychs of *Sarabandes* for piano. The following year, at the age of 22, he wrote the piano suite *Gymnopédies*. The economical style of these pieces reflects his earlier interest in Gregorian chant, mystical religion, and Gothic art, and were a reaction to the often complex music of Wagner and the post-Romantic composers.

In the early 1890s Satie took lodgings in Montmartre, where he joined, and wrote music for, the Rosicrucians, an organization founded in the 17th century and devoted to spiritual enlightenment. He met Claude Debussy, who was to be his friend and supporter for the next 25 years. At this time, Satie was a rather eccentric, bohemian character. He wore his hair long, and bought 12 identical gray velvet suits. In 1898, he dropped his bohemian lifestyle and moved to a suburb of Paris. There followed many unhappy years, in which the only high point was the composition of cabaret melodies to which he gave the bizarre name, "Trois morceaux en forme de poire," or "Three Pieces in the Shape of a Pear."

BACK TO SCHOOL

In 1905 he entered the Schola Cantorum as a student and studied orchestration and counterpoint. He wrote various pieces of piano, ballet, symphonic, and chamber music, but his fortunes did not change until 1911, when Maurice Ravel performed the *Sarabandes* at a concert, and Debussy conducted a performance of two numbers from *Gymnopédies* that Debussy had orchestrated. Both performances were well received, and from this time Satie's music gradually began to be performed and published.

The poet Jean Cocteau heard some of Satie's music in 1915, and this led to a commission to write the music for a new ballet *Parade* for the impresario Diaghilev. The opening night of *Parade* in 1917 caused a sensation, and at last Satie was established. The scenario was by Cocteau, the sets and costumes by Picasso, and Satie's eccentric score called for sirens and typewriters.

Satie's masterpiece was perhaps the cantata *Socrates* (1920), for four sopranos with orchestra; the soprano parts were mostly recitative as opposed to arias, and the orchestral parts often seemed unrelated to the voices. This was music stripped of all embellishments, reminiscent of plainsong (the unaccompanied chants of the medieval church).

Many younger French composers claimed to be following Satie's lead. A 1920 newspaper article by Henri Collet in *Comoedia* described a group of modern composers whose spiritual leader was Satie, as "Les Six." They were Georges Auric, Louis Durey, Arthur Honegger, Darius MILHAUD, Francis POULENC, and Germaine Tailleferre. Satie's musical innovations also helped pave the way for composers of ALEATORY MUSIC such as John CAGE, making Satie ahead of his time.

Satie died in Paris on July 1, 1925, in a small bare room that contained a few pieces of furniture, his music, and his velvet suits piled on top of a cupboard.

Jim Whipple

SEE ALSO:

IMPRESSIONISM IN MUSIC; MINIMALISM; SIX, LES.

FURTHER READING
Orledge, Robert. *Satie the Composer*
(New York: Cambridge University Press, 1990);
Whiting, Steven Moore. *Satie the Bohemian:
From Cabaret to Concert Hall*
(New York: Oxford University Press, 1998).

SUGGESTED LISTENING
Gnossiennes; *Gymnopédies*; *Parade*; *Socrate*;
Trois morceaux en forme de poire.

ARTUR
SCHNABEL

Pianist and composer Artur Schnabel was born on April 17, 1882, in Lipnik in Austrian Silesia. The Schnabel family moved to Vienna when Artur was two, and at the age of six Schnabel was accepted as a pupil by Hans Schmitt of the Vienna Conservatory. As a nine-year-old, he was precocious enough to be accepted as the youngest pupil of the Polish pianist and composer Theodore Leschetizky, who later told the young Schnabel, "You will never be a pianist; you are a musician."

Theory lessons with Eusebius Mandyczewski, who was archivist to the historic archives of the Musikverein in Vienna, gave Schnabel access to the authentic scores of Mozart, Beethoven, and Schubert, the composers who were to remain Schnabel's lifelong passions. In 1896, Schnabel made his official Vienna debut as a Leschetizky protégé to popular and critical acclaim.

At 18 Schnabel moved to Berlin, and became recognized as a superb interpreter of Brahms, Schubert, and Beethoven. The extraordinary musical perceptiveness that characterized his playing led to collaboration with other musicians, among them the admired contralto Therese Behr, whom he married in 1905. They gave many recitals together, and later Schnabel also recorded piano duets with their son, Karl Ulrich. As a soloist, Schnabel established an international reputation in Europe that extended to Russia. A friendship with Arnold SCHOENBERG not only resulted in material support from the successful pianist to the poor composer, but also inspired Schnabel to explore advanced atonality in his own compositions.

SCHNABEL AS COMPOSER

Schnabel's compositions include three symphonies, a piano concerto, five string quartets, and miscellaneous songs and pieces for the piano. *Duodecimet*, for wind, strings, and percussion, was his last work.

From 1925 to 1930 he taught at the Hochschule für Musik at Berlin; also at that time he began a series of recitals with the eminent violinist Carl Flesh, with whom he edited the violin sonatas of Brahms and

Mozart. In 1934, Schnabel visited the U.S. to perform all of Beethoven's piano works in a series of seven concerts at Carnegie Hall; he also recorded all of the sonatas for the Beethoven Sonata Society. This earned him public lionization as the foremost Beethoven interpreter of his time. His acclaimed edition of Beethoven's sonata scores continues to offer to musicians today a unique blend of interpretative insights and scholarly integrity.

AN AMERICAN CITIZEN

World War II spurred Schnabel to emigrate to the U.S. in 1939, where he lectured at the University of Chicago in 1940 and taught at the University of Michigan in Ann Arbor from 1940 to 1945; he became an American citizen in 1944. Once the war ended, Schnabel eagerly returned to Europe, concentrating his performances in England and Switzerland. His eyesight and his health began to decline, and he died on August 15, 1951, in Axenstein, Switzerland.

Schnabel believed in the importance of spontaneity in artistic performance, even at the risk of technical imperfection. His own performing repertoire was drawn from music that was, in his own words "better than it can be played." "I hope," he said, "never to see the day when I sit at a piano uninspired." His performances of Beethoven's late piano sonatas remain unequalled as luminous and almost mystical expressions of a visionary world.

Hao Huang

SEE ALSO:
CHAMBER MUSIC; LATE ROMANTICISM.

FURTHER READING

Saerchinger, César. *Artur Schnabel: A Biography* (Westport, CT: Greenwood Press, 1973); Wolff, Konrad. *Schnabel's Interpretation of Piano Music* (New York: W. W. Norton, 1979).

SUGGESTED LISTENING

Duodecimet for wind, strings, and percussion; Rhapsody for Orchestra; Beethoven: Complete Piano Sonatas; *Diabelli Variations*; Mozart: Piano Concertos; Schubert: Impromptus; Piano music for four hands; "Trout" Quintet (with Karl Ulrich Schnabel).

ALFRED SCHNITTKE

The Russian Alfred Schnittke is one of the most famous composers to emerge from the U.S.S.R. since World War II. Avant-garde music was suppressed in the Soviet Union until the early 1980s, and Soviet musicians had little access to the music of the West. Because of this isolation, Russian modern music did not follow European lines. When it was finally heard in the West, Schnittke's brand of modern music grew increasingly popular partly because of its accessibility.

Alfred Schnittke was born in Engels, Russia, in 1934, to a German Jewish father and a Catholic Volga German mother. His father was posted to Vienna during the Soviet occupation, and from 1946 to 1948 Schnittke studied music there. The family returned to Russia after the occupation, and Schnittke attended the Moscow Conservatory between 1953 and 1961, where he studied instrumentation under Nikolay Rakov. He taught at the school from 1962 until 1972, when his membership of the Composer's Union allowed him to resign and devote himself to composition without being labeled as a parasite on the state.

During this period, Schnittke supported himself in part by composing music for films; his other work included three symphonies, several string quartets and sonatas, and concertos for violin, viola, oboe and harp, and cello. In these compositions, Schnittke employed a mix of styles, including elements of serialism and conventional tonality. The *Requiem*, which used traditional harmonies, ensured his success in the USSR, although critics were reproached for heaping "excessive praise" on the composer.

THE SHIFT FROM REALISM

Schnittke began to move away from Soviet Realism, experimenting with the new techniques that were beginning to penetrate from the West, such as graphic notation (where symbols, spatial distance, or linear diagrams are used instead of traditional notes and staves), and incorporating periods of silence (up to ten seconds or longer). In his Sonata No. 2, he incorporated the B-A-C-H motif (German B flat, A, C, and B natural—given as "H" to denote the composer's name), which J. S. Bach first used in the *Art of Fugue* and which has been used in homage by several other composers, including serialists such as SCHOENBERG and WEBERN. The *Concerto Grosso* followed, a work in six movements for prepared piano (where the individual notes have been altered by placing objects between the strings), harpsichord, and 21 string soloists, which mixed baroque, popular, and even serial elements, and contained a quote from Tchaikovsky.

RECOGNITION IN THE WEST

Schnittke's music arrived in the U.S. in the 1980s, together with the recordings and scores of other composers whose work was not officially sanctioned in the Soviet Union. Although American musicians were impressed by what they heard, it was at first difficult to program these works because of the difficulty in obtaining scores. However, once the scores were made available in the U.S. by the publisher G. Schirmer, this obstacle was overcome, and Schnittke's work was presented to a broader audience. In addition, the violinist Gidon Kremer commissioned several new works by the composer.

Despite suffering a stroke in 1985, Schnittke continued to work, and completed his Symphony No. 5 in 1988. His ever-growing popularity in the West encouraged him to move to Hamburg in 1990, where he continued to live for the rest of his life. During this period, Schnittke taught and traveled extensively. He also produced several operas, the best known of which are *Gesualdo* (1993), a study of the madrigalist and murderer, and *The History of Dr. Johann Fausten* (1994). Schnittke died on August 3, 1998.

Jane Prendergast

SEE ALSO:
ORCHESTRAL MUSIC; VOCAL AND CHORAL MUSIC.

FURTHER READING
Brown, Malcolm Hamrick. *Russian and Soviet Music* (Ann Arbor, MI: University of Michigan Research Press, 1984); Ivashkin, Alexander. *Alfred Schnittke* (New York: Phaidon Press Inc., 1996).

SUGGESTED LISTENING
Concerto Grosso; *Quasi una sonata*; Requiem; *Sacred Hymns*; Symphony No. 4; Violin Concertos Nos. 3 and 4.

ARNOLD
SCHOENBERG

P ossibly this century's most controversial composer, Arnold Schoenberg was born in Vienna on September 13, 1874. He began learning the violin at the age of eight and composing little pieces when he was about 12, but he did not decide on music as a career until he was well into his teens. Even then, Schoenberg did not attend a major school or conservatory of music, but studied privately with the composer Alexander Zemlinsky (1871–1942), who was only three years older. Schoenberg is said to have acquired Zemlinsky's passion for the music of Richard Wagner while studying with him.

Schoenberg married Zemlinsky's sister, Mathilde, in 1901. They spent two years in Berlin, where he made his living by orchestrating operettas and directing a cabaret orchestra. Mathilde died in 1923, and the following year Schoenberg married Gertrud Kolisch, the sister of the violinist Rudolf Kolisch who championed his music.

Corbis-Bettmann

Arnold Schoenberg was one of the most innovative composers of the early 20th century, leaving a profound legacy and transforming the notion of music.

LATE ROMANTIC INFLUENCES

Schoenberg's own early music belongs to the Late Romantic period. Music during this era was dominated by Wagner's psychological music-dramas, with their rich harmonies and orchestration. Schoenberg's early works were very much a part of all this: the orchestral piece *Verklärte Nacht* of 1899; the "monodrama" for singer-actor and orchestra *Erwartung* of 1909; the orchestral tone poem *Pelleas und Melisande*; and the massive choral and orchestral cantata, *Gurrelieder*, finished in 1911. These works are full of feelings of guilt and anxiety, use symbolic images such as moonlight and dark forests, and are deeply influenced by Wagner's lush and dramatic chromatic and sometimes atonal harmonies.

It was Schoenberg's growing belief that this kind of post-Wagnerian music had gone as far as it could that made him look for new musical paths. A key work in this process was Schoenberg's song-cycle *Pierrot lunaire* of 1912. To capture the dream-like, sometimes nightmarish imagery of the songs, Schoenberg turned to a not uncommon style of vocal delivery known in German as *Sprechstimme* (speech song), which hovers between speech and pitched notes. For each of the 21 songs of the cycle, the accompanying chamber ensemble played a different combination of instruments.

Such a style was not entirely new in itself, but Schoenberg's daring and imaginative use of it in *Pierrot Lunaire* certainly shook the whole artistic world at the time. "If this is music," wrote one critic who attended the first performance of the song-cyle in Berlin, "Then I pray to my Creator not to let me hear it again." Schoenberg's *Five Pieces for Orchestra,* composed in the same style as *Pierrot lunaire*, also had its first performance in 1912.

THE 12-TONE SYSTEM

Schoenberg bitterly resented the many attacks on his work, but he would not allow himself to be distracted by them. He soon came to the conclusion that music needed an entirely new kind of "alphabet" or "grammar." This led him to the momentous decision to abandon entirely the system of 24 major and minor keys and scales that had formed the basis of Western music for hundreds of years. In its place, he based his compositions on "tone-rows" or "note-rows." This used all 12 notes of the chromatic scale in a particular order that was chosen by the composer. This was Schoenberg's new system of "dodecaphonic" or "12-tone" composition, also known more generally as "serial" composition, since the "tone-rows" or "note-rows" were played in series.

Serialism was not an entirely new concept: it had appeared in works by Reger and Liszt, but not as the actual basis of composition.

Schoenberg first used this new method of composition in his *Five Piano Pieces* of 1923. With it, he also divided the musical world between those who were totally baffled by what he was doing and derided it, and those disciples and pupils, notably Anton WEBERN and Alban BERG, who admired and developed his technique. He also ensured that he would become one of the most influential, and perhaps the most controversial, composers of the century.

EXILE FROM BERLIN

While Schoenberg was shaking music to its foundations, events in the outside world were catching up with him. In 1925, he had taken up a major teaching post at the Prussian Academy of Arts in Berlin. But the arrival of the new Nazi regime quickly made life in Germany impossible for him, not only because he was a Jew, but because his radical ideas were unacceptable to the Nazis.

Schoenberg had converted to Christianity in 1898, but as an act of defiance in the face of Nazi anti-Semitism, he reaffirmed his Jewish faith. This can be heard in the opera *Moses und Aron,* composed between 1930 and 1932. He left Germany in 1933 and stayed briefly in Paris before emigrating to the U.S. He lived in Boston for a short time before settling in Los Angeles, where he taught at UCLA between 1936 and 1944.

Schoenberg became an American citizen in 1941. He continued to compose until the end of his life, sometimes using 12-tone or serial methods, sometimes returning to more conventional styles. Among his works from this period are the Violin Concerto (1936), the Piano Concerto (1942), and the String Trio (1946). At his death, he was still working on the last part of his Opus 50, consisting of three religious choruses which explore the relationship between man and God. These pieces are the culmination of a strain in his

music that began with the unfinished oratorio *Die Jakobsleiter* (begun in 1917) and found its most intense expression in *Moses und Aron.* Schoenberg died at his Los Angeles home on July 13, 1951.

Schoenberg was the most conspicuously revolutionary figure in 20th-century music. Many of his compositions sound perplexingly difficult, even 60 or 70 years later. Some critics have argued that his system, while revolutionary in principle, simply replaced one set of rules with another even more rigid and complicated one. But his musical influence has been enormous. Many other major 20th-century composers, from Webern and Berg to Igor STRAVINSKY, Aaron COPLAND, Karlheinz STOCKHAUSEN, and Pierre BOULEZ, have used or developed his ideas.

For all the emphasis on theory in Schoenberg's music, it is far from sterile. Schoenberg was deeply affected by the turbulent and terrible events of his age, as is heard in works such as his opera *Moses und Aron* (1932), and his cantata *A Survivor from Warsaw* (1947), which deals with the grim subject of Nazi persecution and war crimes. He also made several arrangements of other composers' music, including an enchanting one of Johann Strauss II's "Emperor Waltz," recalling his own childhood in Vienna.

Richard Trombley

SEE ALSO:

CHAMBER MUSIC; ORCHESTRAL MUSIC; SERIALISM; VOCAL AND CHORAL MUSIC.

FURTHER READING

Bailey, Walter B., ed. *The Arnold Schoenberg Companion* (Westport, CT: Greenwood Press, 1998); Rosen, Charles. *Arnold Schoenberg* (Chicago, IL: University of Chicago Press, 1996).

SUGGESTED LISTENING

Das Buch der hängenden Gärten;
Erwartung; Five Orchestral Pieces
Five Piano Pieces; Gurrelieder;
Moses und Aron; Ode to Napoleon Bonaparte;
Pelleas und Melisande; Piano Concerto;
Pierrot lunaire; Serenades;
A Survivor from Warsaw;
Verklärte Nacht ;
Violin Concerto.

ARTHUR
SCHWARTZ

Arthur Schwartz may not be the best known, or have written as many hits, or been as prolific, as some other composers in the field of popular music. But in his particular area of specialization—literate, sophisticated songs for intimate Broadway revues— he was a master craftsman. The composer and music historian Alec Wilder, in his classic book *American Popular Song*, noted that "Schwartz wrote with total self-assurance and high professional skill and never lingered by the wayside to gaze with longing at the musically greener grass of Culture. He rolled up his sleeves and went to work."

Schwartz was born in Brooklyn, New York, on November 15, 1900. Although his father, a prominent Manhattan attorney, insisted that his son follow in his footsteps, Arthur secretly taught himself piano. By age 14, he was accompanying silent films at a local movie house. Eventually, though, Schwartz submitted (at least temporarily) to his father's wishes, earning two law degrees from New York University and setting up practice on lower Broadway. During this time he published his first tune, "Baltimore, MD, You're the Only Doctor for Me," which was later featured in *The Grand Street Follies*. In 1924, while working as a counselor at a boys' summer camp in the Adirondacks, Schwartz formed a short songwriting partnership with lyricist Lorenz Hart.

PARTNERSHIP WITH DIETZ

In 1928, Schwartz persuaded Howard Dietz, an MGM film publicist who had written lyrics for composer Jerome KERN, to collaborate with him. During their on-again, off-again 35-year relationship, Schwartz and Dietz crafted numerous scores for smart revues. Among their first collaborations was *The Little Show* (1929), which featured "I Guess I'll Have to Change My Plan," a radical reworking of a song that Schwarz had earlier written with Hart. This was followed by *Three's a Crowd* (1930) and *Flying Colors* (1932). The team also composed four Broadway musicals—*Revenge with Music* (1934), *Between the Devil* (1937), *The Gay Life* (1961), and *Jennie* (1963).

The Band Wagon, the 1930 revue that featured Fred Astaire and his sister Adele in their final appearance together, is the musical most critics consider Schwartz and Dietz's masterpiece. Schwartz's most famous melody, "Dancing in the Dark," was literally composed overnight, he recalled, when the show needed "a dark song, somewhat mystical, yet in slow, even rhythm." In 1953, Schwartz and Dietz's greatest hits were to be compiled in another version of *The Band Wagon*, which bore little resemblance to the 1930s Astaire hit. "That's Entertainment," a new tune written for the movie, became an instant showbiz anthem, as well as the title of two film anthologies of MGM musicals.

TRYING IT OUT IN HOLLYWOOD

In the late 1930s, Schwartz moved to Hollywood where he teamed, often unsuccessfully, with other lyricists such as Frank LOESSER and Leo Robin. In 1944 he produced the Gene Kelly musical *Cover Girl*, and two years later the Cole PORTER film biography, *Night and Day*. He returned to Broadway in the late 1940s, joining up with Ira Gershwin to create the badly received *Park Avenue* (1946). More successful was his partnership with Dorothy Fields, which produced both *A Tree Grows in Brooklyn* (1951) and *By the Beautiful Sea* (1954). In the late 1960s Schwartz briefly relocated to London, where he worked on a stage version of *Nicholas Nickleby* by Dickens.

Arthur Schwartz died in Kintnersville, Pennsylvania, on September 3, 1984. In summing up his splendid legacy, Alec Wilder wrote: "… quality was his style. And that's plenty."

Michael R. Ross

SEE ALSO:
FILM MUSICALS; MUSICALS; POPULAR MUSIC.

FURTHER READING

Hemming, Roy. *The Melody Lingers On: The Great Songwriters and Their Movie Musicals* (New York: Newmarket Press, 1986); Wilder, Alec. *American Popular Song: The Great Innovators, 1900-1950* (New York: Oxford University Press, 1990).

SUGGESTED LISTENING

American Songbook Series: Arthur Schwartz; *At Home Abroad*; *The Band Wagon*; *Musicals—Selections*.

ELISABETH SCHWARZKOPF

The elegance of Elisabeth Schwarzkopf's soprano, particularly in the operas of Mozart and Richard STRAUSS, will be long remembered, as will her attractive and believable presentation of the dramatic aspects of these roles. Her extensive recordings contain gems of the Viennese operetta, as well as recitals of German lieder, distinguished by exquisite control and apparent effortlessness.

Schwarzkopf was born on December 9, 1915, in the small town of Jarotschin near Poznan, Poland. Her parents moved to Germany when she was still a small child, and she attended school in Magdeburg, where she studied viola and organ, and played the glockenspiel in the school marching band. From early youth her voice was in demand, and she played Eurydice in Gluck's *Orfeo* in a school production when she was only 13. In 1934, she entered the Hochschule für Musik, where she studied for a year with the famous singer Lula Mysz-Gmeiner, who tried to make a contralto (the lowest female voice) of her.

UNEXPECTED DEBUT

Schwarzkopf was accepted into graduate studies at the Opera School, Berlin, and joined the semi-professional Favre Solistenvereinigung ensemble. Her debut at the Berlin Städtische Oper came in 1938, where within only 36 hours, she prepared for the role of the Second Flower Maiden in *Parsifal*. She studied later with Maria Ivogün to develop her true soprano range, and Michael Rauchiesen, Ivogün's husband, became Schwarzkopf's accompanist in lieder recitals.

From 1938 to 1940, she appeared in small solo parts including the First Boy in Mozart's *Die Zauberflöte* and the Woodbird in Wagner's *Siegfried.* By 1941, she was assuming secondary principal roles such as Oscar in Verdi's *Un ballo in maschera* and Musetta in PUCCINI's *La bohème.*

From 1942 to 1944, Schwarzkopf made guest appearances at the Vienna State Opera. After an assassination attempt on Hitler was made in 1944, the artists at the opera were instructed to become part of the labor force at an armaments factory, but in defiance of this order, she continued to sing at the opera until it was destroyed in the Allied bombing. She was able to escape from Vienna only a few hours before the Soviet occupation began.

The end of the war meant wider opportunities for German artists, and Schwarzkopf toured England in 1947, appearing at the Royal Opera House in Covent Garden as Donna Elvira in Mozart's *Don Giovanni,* and as Marzelline in Beethoven's *Fidelio.* She was invited to join the Covent Garden opera company and stayed until 1951, singing the roles of Verdi's heroines Violetta and Gilda, and Puccini's Mimi, Manon, and Butterfly, in English, as well as German roles.

Schwarzkopf's association with the conductor Herbert von KARAJAN began when he became producer and conductor at La Scala, Milan, in 1948, where Scharzkopf made her debut as the Countess in Mozart's *Le nozze di Figaro.* She sang at the Salzburg Festival in 1949, and in 1953 made her American debut with a recital in New York. Her first opera appearance in the U.S. was in San Francisco in 1955, where she sang Donna Elvira, and the Marschallin in Richard Strauss' *Der Rosenkavalier*, a role with which she was identified for many years.

In the concert hall, she was best known for her lieder recitals, but also sang in oratorio from Bach's Passions to TIPPETT's *A Child of Our Time.* Her interpretations of the songs of Hugo Wolf were outstanding, and she made many superb recordings with the famous accompanist Gerald Moore. Schwarzkopf married EMI record executive Walter Legge in 1953, and her performances are well represented in the EMI record catalog.

Jane Prendergast

SEE ALSO:

OPERA; OPERETTA; VOCAL AND CHORAL MUSIC.

FURTHER READING
Jefferson, Alan. *Elisabeth Schwarzkopf*
(Boston, MA: Northeastern University Press, 1995);
Rasponi, Lanfranco. *The Last Prima Donnas*
(New York: Alfred A. Knopf, 1982).

SUGGESTED LISTENING
Mozart: *Lieder*; *Die Zauberflöte*;
Richard Strauss: *Der Rosenkavalier* (highlights);
Verdi: *Four Sacred Pieces*; *Requiem.*

ALEXANDER
SCRIABIN

Alexander Scriabin is most well known for his idiosyncratic but exciting piano music, although he also composed a handful of orchestral works. His work was colored by his interest in mysticism and theosophy, but is powerful and direct in its appeal.

Alexander Nikolayevich Scriabin was born in Moscow, Russia, on January 6, 1872. His mother died when he was only one year old, and his father spent the rest of his life abroad, so Scriabin was brought up by a great-aunt. The wilfulness apparent in his music is sometimes ascribed to his being a pampered boy. He entered the Conservatory of Music in Moscow at the age of 16, studying piano and composition. Here he met Sergey RACHMANINOV, with whom he remained lifelong friends. When they graduated from the conservatory, Rachmaninov won the first gold medal and Scriabin the second.

Scriabin's early piano pieces show the influence of Chopin, both in the intelligent use of the piano's resources and texture, and in the sensuous evocation of mood. Thanks to the financial support of a well-to-do Russian patron and music publisher named Belyayev, Scriabin was able to move to Switzerland in 1904 to concentrate on composition.

Scriabin was in America for a few months during 1906 and 1907, and then settled in Paris. In 1908 he was befriended by Sergey KOUSSEVITZKY, who did much to encourage acceptance of Scriabin's music. Scriabin came under the influence of the ideas of the German philosopher Nietszche, and later those of the theosophist Madame Blavatsky.

These concepts of the spiritual nature of the universe, coupled with an interest in Eastern mysticism, were sweeping Europe at the time and were eagerly embraced in Russia.

MUSIC AND COLOR

Scriabin had many discussions with Rimsky-Korsakov, the Russian composer, about the association of music and color. They discovered that they both felt that musical notes could be related directly to colors—therefore mixing art with the senses.

Scriabin attempted to convey this discovery in his work. He even attempted to design a keyboard that would create colors during performance, but it proved unworkable.

As his music matured, Scriabin's work became very adventurous harmonically, and even approached atonality. He developed what has been called the "mystic chord," which is based on intervals of fourths rather than the traditional thirds. Scriabin also used tritones—intervals of three whole tones—and scales built entirely from whole tones. Increasingly, a sense of a tonal center was weakened in his compositions.

This approach to harmony already interested Claude DEBUSSY, and was to be further developed by Arnold SCHOENBERG. Scriabin's orchestral tone poem *Prometheus* (1911) is a good example of his use of his "mystic chord." Thus, already aware of Debussy's work, Scriabin was working in the same direction as Schoenberg, moving ever further from conventional tonality, pushing it to an extreme that might have been revealed had he lived longer.

Scriabin's works for the orchestra include a piano concerto (1897), *Reverie* (1899), three symphonies, and *Le poème de l'extase* (1908). For piano, he wrote preludes, études, and mazurkas, for which only the titles of some of the movements—"Ironies," "Danse languide," and "Désir"—betrayed their character.

After a tour of Russia in 1914, Scriabin became ill, and died of blood poisoning after developing a sore on his lip. He died in Moscow, and his friend Koussevitzky organized a memorial concert devoted to Scriabin's music.

Richard Trombley

SEE ALSO:

CHAMBER MUSIC; ORCHESTRAL MUSIC.

FURTHER READING

Baker, James M. *The Music of Alexander Scriabin* (New Haven, CT: Yale University Press, 1986); Bowers, Faubion. *Scriabin, A Biography* (New York: Dover, 1996).

SUGGESTED LISTENING

Fantasy for pianoforte; Piano sonatas Nos. 5, 9, and 10; *Poème nocturne*; *Prometheus*; Symphony No. 3; Two dances for pianoforte; *Vers la Flamme*.

EARL
SCRUGGS

During his illustrious musical career, which has spanned more than five decades, legendary bluegrass banjoist Earl Scruggs has not only motivated others to take up the banjo, but has brought recognition and respect to country music all over the world.

Scruggs was born in North Carolina on January 6, 1924. He taught himself the five-string banjo at the age of four and developed his trademark three-finger picking style before he reached his teens. At age 15 he was playing with a band that performed on a local radio station in Knoxville, Tennessee.

FOGGY MOUNTAIN BOYS

In 1944 Scruggs joined Bill MONROE's Bluegrass Boys, where he met his future partner, the guitarist Lester Flatt. Scruggs stayed with Monroe until January 1948. Soon after, Earl and Lester teamed up to form Flatt and Scruggs, the beginning of the Foggy Mountain Boys group.

Mercury Records was immediately attracted to the pair and signed them to a recording contract in 1948 that lasted until October 1950. While at Mercury they recorded "Foggy Mountain Breakdown," which was used later as the background music for the 1967 movie *Bonnie and Clyde*.

In 1950 they switched to Columbia Records, where they recorded for the rest of their career together. In 1953 Flatt and Scruggs began presenting their own show on radio station WSM in Nashville, Tennessee. They were also performing regularly at the Grand Ole Opry in Nashville, which they officially joined in 1955.

Other songs that Flatt and Scruggs are credited with from this period include the themes from the television shows *Petticoat Junction* and *The Beverly Hillbillies*. With "The Ballad of Jed Clampett," from the latter, bluegrass had its first No. 1 single on the country chart and, in addition, crossed over into the pop charts. Scruggs himself appeared in seven episodes of *The Beverly Hillbillies*, which was screened in 78 countries and brought worldwide recognition of country and bluegrass music. Another

success for Scruggs was the syndication of his television program entitled *Earl Scruggs: His Family and Friends*, which was broadcast on local stations throughout the Southeast.

During their 20 or so years together, Flatt and Scruggs remained one of the most popular duos on the American country music circuit. Their last performance together was on February 22, 1969. Their breakup was due mostly to their divergent tastes in music. Scruggs was more likely to introduce slide electric guitar and banjo riffs into a piece, while Flatt was more traditional.

BACK IN THE MOVIES

When Flatt and Scruggs split, Scruggs formed the Earl Scruggs Revue band with his three sons, Randy, Gary, and Steve, plus Josh Graves and Jody Maphis. The revue was recorded by Scruggs' long-time label Columbia, and his music made it to the movies once more: in 1973, he recorded the theme for *Where the Lilies Bloom*. Since Graves left the band in the mid-1970s, the revue has continued to perform regularly.

During his long career, Scruggs has been nominated for eight Grammy Awards, winning one for "Foggy Mountain Breakdown" in 1975. He was inducted into the Country Music Hall of Fame in 1985 and in 1993 was presented with the National Medal of Arts. Scruggs has also won numerous country and bluegrass awards.

Renee Jinks

SEE ALSO:
COUNTRY; HILLBILLY MUSIC.

FURTHER READING
Artis, Bob. *Bluegrass: The Story of an American Musical Tradition* (New York: Hawthorn Books, 1975); Scruggs, Earl. *Earl Scruggs and the Five String Banjo* (Philadelphia, PA: Theodore Presser, 1980).

SUGGESTED LISTENING
Anniversary Special, Vol. 1; *The Complete Mercury Sessions*; *The Earl Scruggs Revue*; *Foggy Mountain Jamboree*; Flatt and Scruggs: *The Essential Flatt and Scruggs*.

ANDRÉS
SEGOVIA

Andrés Segovia is considered one of the most important and influential classical guitarists of the 20th century. He established the classical guitar as a serious concert instrument, transforming it from a parlor instrument to one respected in recital.

Segovia was born in the Andalusian town of Linares, Spain, on February 21, 1893. He took up the guitar despite the objections of his family, who wanted him to study the violin, and was largely self-taught. In 1912, he made his official debut at the Ateneo in Madrid. His debut in Paris in 1924 was attended by the composers Paul DUKAS and Manuel de FALLA. In 1928, Segovia made his United States debut at New York's Town Hall, followed by a tour of Asia. Because of the Spanish Civil War, Segovia left Spain in 1936 and lived in Montevideo, Uruguay, and New York until returning home in the early 1950s.

While in the Americas, Segovia performed and taught extensively, inspiring many young guitarists to study the classical instrument and repertoire. His dedication to the guitar was all-consuming, and he performed regularly for 78 years until his death in Madrid, on June 2, 1987 at age 94.

Segovia recognized that the limited repertoire for the classical guitar was an obstacle to its being accepted as a serious concert instrument, so he expanded the repertoire by transcribing existing works and by commissioning new pieces. His transcriptions included Spanish *vihuela* (a plucked string instrument of the viol family), Renaissance and Baroque lute music, and the Spanish piano music of Isaac Albéniz and Enrique GRANADOS. He also expanded the repertoire by commissioning works from noted composers such as Heitor VILLA-LOBOS, Joaquín RODRIGO, Mario Castelnuovo-Tedesco, and Manuel Ponce.

Segovia advanced classical guitar by absorbing practices from 19th-century guitarists such as Fernando Sor and Francisco Tárrega, and combining them with his own idiosyncratic technique. His rich tonal palette, flexible pulse, and clear articulation were characteristic of what came to be known as the

The preeminent Spanish classical guitarist Andrés Segovia transformed the repertoire and status of the instrument.

Hulton-Deutsch Collection/Corbis

"Segovia sound." He also worked with Albert Augustine and the Du Pont corporation to create the nylon guitar string, a major technical innovation which also contributed to the new guitar sound.

Through his legendary master classes, Segovia inspired many of the succeeding generation of classical guitarists, including John WILLIAMS. He was also a pioneer in recording. His first recording was made in 1927 and ultimately he made over 30 records which continue to form a springboard for later performers.

Jim Tosone

SEE ALSO:
CHAMBER MUSIC.

FURTHER READING

Segovia, Andrés. *Andrés Segovia: An Autobiography of the Years 1893–1920*
(New York: Macmillan, 1976);
Wade, Graham. *Segovia: A Celebration of the Man and His Music*
(New York: Allison & Busby, 1983).

SUGGESTED LISTENING

Bach, J. S.: *Solo cello suites*, arr. for guitar;
Castelnuovo-Tedesco: Guitar Works;
Ponce: *Concierto del sur*; Sonatas;
Rodrigo: *Fantasía para un gentilhombre*;
Turina: Guitar works.

SERIALISM

Serialism developed as a way forward from what was felt by adventurous composers to be the dead end of tonality reached by 19th-century composers, notably Richard Wagner. Wagner had stretched tonality to its limits with his music, culminating with his opera *Tristan und Isolde* in 1859. Later composers, such as Gustav MAHLER and Richard STRAUSS, continued in the same tradition, but others, beginning with Arnold SCHOENBERG, wanted to take music to another level of modernity.

THE ROOTS OF SERIALISM

Western classical music was traditionally based on the diatonic scale—the series of seven ascending notes spaced at prescribed intervals, with the first of these notes, called the keynote or tonic, giving its name to the "key" of the scale. The sense of development and progress in a piece of music was built-in by modulating from the "home" key to a related key, and on to other keys before ending in the original key. Notes that did not "belong" to the tonality of the piece were called chromatic—a word meaning "colored"—in the sense that these notes gave piquancy to the sound.

Gradually, composers modulated to more and more distant keys, or composed in two or more keys simultaneously (polytonality), and chromaticism undermined the sense of key. In the modernistic atmosphere of the post–World War I era, the time was ripe for a new basis for music.

THE TONE-ROW

Arnold Schoenberg, a Viennese composer teaching in Berlin, began to experiment with freeing music from the scale altogether. He evolved a system based on the tone-row. This was a series of 12 tones related only to one another. The tone-row was an arrangement of all 12 notes of the chromatic scale, in which no note might appear twice.

Once fixed, the 12-note arrangement became the "series" on which a composition would be based. The series might be quoted backward, or "retrograde," or the intervals might be inverted from down

to up and vice versa, in the "inversion." Both retrograde and inversion modifications might be applied together. Any note of the series might be transposed to a different octave, and the whole tone-row might be transposed, or parts of it played together in a tone cluster. However, the composer had to bear in mind that single tones could not be quoted out of order. As formulaic as it appeared, Schoenberg's rules meant that the underlying tone-row, in its varying treatments, gave cohesion to the composition.

EXTENSIONS OF SERIALISM

Strict serialism was in fact practiced in very few works, although once Schoenberg's pupil Anton WEBERN had adopted the 12-tone system in 1924, he used it for the rest of his life. But other composers used the principle as a launchpad for other ideas. Schoenberg himself composed in a series of nine notes (*Five Piano Pieces*, 1920) and 14 notes (*Serenade*, 1920–23) and Igor STRAVINSKY's *In Memoriam Dylan Thomas* uses a tone-row of only five notes. The 12-tone row offers all the semitone intervals of the octave, but French composer Pierre BOULEZ extended this to 24 microtonal intervals in his cantata *Le visage nuptial* for female voices and chamber orchestra (1946).

Serialism can also be extended to other elements of music, notably the rhythmic organization of a piece. Here, time values can be arranged in a series and repeated, mirrored (retrograde), or multiplied by the same value throughout (transposed). Boulez again experimented with series of durations in *Structures Ia* for two pianos. The French composer Olivier MESSIAEN also used something similar that he had devised from a study of Hindu classical *talas*, or rhythmic patterns.

MAKING AND BREAKING THE RULES

Schoenberg's earliest works were in post-Wagnerian style, and it was not until the beginning of the 1920s that he formulated the rules of serialism and wrote his first serial music. He first used 12-tone composition in his *Five Piano Pieces* Op. 23, which he wrote between 1920 and 1923.

Schoenberg was to write many other works that adhered strictly to the principles of 12-tone composition. However, having established the rules of serialism, Schoenberg soon began breaking them, placing notes out of sequence or doubling parts of the lines.

Many examples of this rule-breaking can be found in his later works, such as the piano concerto of 1942 and the cantata *A Survivor of Warsaw* (1948).

Schoenberg's system of composition was naturally emulated by his students, the most illustrious of whom were Webern and Alban BERG. Berg is best remembered for his opera *Wozzeck* (1922). His second opera, *Lulu* (1935), which was unfinished at the time of his death, was based on a single tone-row and four variations derived mathematically from it. The intense drama of *Lulu*, which ends when the streetwalker heroine is murdered by Jack the Ripper, brands itself on the listener through the inventiveness of the orchestration, above all, with the blaring of the predominant brass section. But the opera is held together by Berg's extensive and systematic manipulation of the tone-row.

Followers of Berg reintroduced tonal elements to lessen the tension generated by the extended "dissonances" resulting from strict adherence to the rules of serialism. These included the Italian Luigi Dallapiccola (1904–75). He chose his tone-rows so as to exploit their tonal implications, and looked backward to the 17th century, using musical forms of that period.

Tonal elements are even more prevalent in the music of the German composer Hans Werner HENZE, the American Wallingford Riegger (1885–1961), and the Swiss composer Frank Martin (1890–1974), who actually reintroduced major and minor triads.

MUSIC STRIPPED TO THE BONE

Webern's music was ascetic and stripped to the barest essentials. Many of his compositions last only a minute or two. His strict adherence to the rules of serialism means that the tone-row itself dictates the musical form of the piece. Webern also applied Schoenberg's rules regarding repetition to the registers and instrumental timbre in which each tone was played. This repetition forced the listener to concentrate on the tone itself as well as its role in the statement of the row.

Many modern composers took Webern as a starting point for their own work, applying strict serialization to elements such as rhythm, tempo, and instrumentation as well as to the tone-row. For example, Boulez wrote serial music for exotic and conventional instruments, introducing aleatoric (random or performer's choice) elements in his second sonata for piano.

Also, the German composer Karlheinz STOCKHAUSEN found in the mathematical complexities of electronically produced wave-forms a complement to the rules of serial music, and his works include music for synthesized sound, alone and in combination with conventional instruments.

Although serial music was controversial when first introduced, today's audiences appear to accept it with less difficulty. The post-serial generation of composers has taken on aspects of the organizational philosophy of serialism rather than the system itself, and this aspect of serialism has had a greater influence on 20th-century music than the serial compositions themselves.

POST-SERIAL INFLUENCE

The 20th-century composers who are performed more often than many of the hard-line serialists include major figures such as Witold LUTOSLAWSKI, Harrison Birtwistle (b. 1934), and Peter Maxwell Davies (b. 1934). These were never true serial composers, but their music would have been vastly different had serial music never happened.

Jane Prendergast

SEE ALSO:

ALEATORY MUSIC; ELECTRONIC MUSIC.

FURTHER READING

Griffiths, Paul. *Modern Music: A Concise History*
(New York: Thames and Hudson, 1994);
Schoffman, Nachum. *From Chords to Simultaneities:*
Chordal Indeterminacy and the Failure of Serialism
(New York: Greenwood Press, 1990).

SUGGESTED LISTENING

Babbitt: *All Set*; *My End Is My Beginning*;
Relata I and II;
Berg: *Altenberg Lieder*; *Lulu*;
Three Pieces for Orchestra;
Berio: *Nones*;
Boulez: *Le marteau sans Maître*;
Polyphonie X; *Structures*;
Nono: *Allelujah II*;
Schoenberg: Piano concerto; String Quartet No. 4;
Variations for Orchestra; Violin Concerto;
Webern: Cantatas Nos. 1 and 2;
Concerto for Nine Instruments.

THE SEX PISTOLS

The Sex Pistols were the British band that epitomized the punk rock movement's antisocial music and lifestyle. The group's aggressive songs, strewn with obscenities, and their anti-glamor image—cropped hair, torn clothes, pierced features, and "bondage" gear, spawned a new era of street fashion.

Formed in 1975 by fashion boutique owner Malcolm McLaren, the first Sex Pistols line-up featured vocalist Johnny Rotten (b. John Lydon, January 1956), guitarist Steve Jones (b. May 1955), drummer Paul Cook (b. July 1956), and bassist Glen Matlock (b. August 1956)—replaced in March 1977 by the more threatening presence of Sid Vicious (b. John Simon Beverley, 1957; d. 1979).

During the mid-1970s, Britain was in economic decline, and the Sex Pistols, in reaction to the escapism of much early 1970s mainstream rock,

Sid Vicious (left) and Johnny Rotten of the Sex Pistols helped make rock'n'roll dangerous again.

Corbis-Bettmann

seized upon a powerful, angry current of political and social disaffection. After using obscenities on TV, the group was dropped by its record label, EMI, in 1977, signed to A&M, was dropped again six days later, and finally signed to Virgin Records.

After seven hit singles in Britain, the Sex Pistols released their one studio album, *Never Mind the Bollocks—Here's the Sex Pistols*, in January 1977. The sound of marching soldiers introduced the listener to some of the most raw, aggressive music ever recorded. Jones's highly charged, garage-rock guitar complemented Rotten's twisted, cockney vocals—unlike other British rock stars, Rotten shunned the then almost obligatory American-like accent.

The group visited the U.S. in January 1978 but, after just seven appearances, personality clashes tore the band apart. After a gig in San Francisco, Rotten left the group. Later that year Vicious, by now a heroin addict, was charged in New York with the murder of his American girlfriend, Nancy Spungen. While awaiting trial, Vicious died from a drug overdose. Within months of the breakup of the Sex Pistols, Rotten—reverting to the name Lydon—had formed Public Image Ltd., which achieved moderate success. In 1996, the Sex Pistols reformed, with Matlock, for "The Filthy Lucre Tour" of the U.S. and Britain.

The influence of the Sex Pistols was most deeply felt in Britain, where they helped to inject new energy into British rock music. It took longer to reach the U.S. Among the first to pick up on the more streetwise music was Neil Young, who paid homage to Rotten on his album *Rust Never Sleeps*, which saw Young adopt punk-style guitar. The influence of the Sex Pistols continued into the late 1990s in the music of bands as diverse as Bush, OASIS, and the British techno-punks, the Prodigy.

Graham McColl

SEE ALSO:

GRUNGE; INDIE BANDS; NEW WAVE; PUNK ROCK.

FURTHER READING
Savage, Jon. *England's Dreaming*
(New York: St. Martin's Press, 1977).

SUGGESTED LISTENING
Flogging a Dead Horse;
Never Mind the Bollocks—Here's the Sex Pistols.

RAVI SHANKAR

Sitar virtuoso and composer Ravi Shankar has done a great deal to popularize Indian music in the West. Known for his charisma and enthusiasm as a performer, and for his association with Western classical musicians and pop stars, Shankar is the quintessential Indian musician for the West.

Born in Uttar Pradesh, India, on April 7, 1920, the young Shankar showed extraordinary early promise as a musician and dancer. His cosmopolitan life began when, as a boy, he went to live with his older brother Uday and his dance troupe in Paris, but in his late teens he decided to return to India to study classical Indian music. This involved many years of disciplined study with Ustad Allauddin Khan, who became both his musical and spiritual teacher, and later his father-in-law. Shankar chose to study one of the classical Indian instruments, the 17-plus-stringed, plucked sitar, and had to learn the complex system of *ragas* (melodic patterns) and *talas* (rhythmic patterns) that provide the basis for classical Indian music.

FAME AT HOME AND ABROAD

Shankar's debut concerts in the mid-1940s were widely acclaimed in India and he became a central figure in the musical life of the country. In 1949 Shankar became director of music for All-India Radio and remained in the post until 1956. He composed for films, including Satayajit Ray's Apu trilogy in the mid-1950s. He also composed the music for ballets, including *Immortal India, Discovery of India* (1944), based on a book by the first prime minister of India, Pandit Nehru, as well as *Samanya Kshati* (1961) and *Chanadalika* (1962), both based on texts by the famous Bengali poet, Rabindranath Tagore.

In the mid-1950s, Shankar left for a tour of Europe and the U.S. He played for a UNESCO concert in Paris (1958), and later performed at the United Nations Human Rights Day concert in New York (1967), where he played a duet with classical violinist Yehudi MENUHIN. In 1966, George Harrison briefly became his pupil and began incorporating the sitar on the BEATLES' experimental albums (for example, in the song

"Norwegian Wood" from the album *Rubber Soul*, 1965). This pop connection made Shankar a hippy superstar, and he appeared with Harrison at the Woodstock Festival in 1969, and in two fund-raising concerts to benefit Bangladesh. "I was happy that I could reach the young people so quickly," he said "but the unfortunate side was that it was very superficial." Shankar himself came under some criticism from classical Indian purists, who accused him of sacrilege and having harmed Indian music by this exposure to the West. From then he gradually withdrew from the pop scene.

ECLECTIC ASSOCIATIONS

Shankar continued to be associated with an eclectic group of musicians, from jazz to classical: among his many students and collaborators were John COLTRANE, just prior to the jazz saxophonist's premature death; minimalist composer Philip GLASS; and fellow countryman and conductor Zubin MEHTA.

Shankar continued these activities, including classical concerts with Ali Akbar Khan and others, through the 1970s to the 1990s, despite heart problems that led to bypass surgery in 1986. In 1981, his daughter, Anoushka, was born to his second wife, Sukanya, and the family divided their time between their homes in California and New Delhi.

Shankar founded a school of Indian music in Los Angeles, and has taught privately and at institutions. He taught his daughter, Anoushka, who participated on sitar in some of the concerts honoring her father's 75th birthday, in 1995. He remains a spiritually attuned, humble, and influential musician.

Jeff Kaliss

SEE ALSO:

MEHTA, ZUBIN; RAGGA; SOUTH ASIA.

FURTHER READING

Shankar, Ravi. *Drops of Light: Discourses in Santa Barbara* (Santa Barbara, CA: Art of Living Foundation, 1990); Shankar, Ravi. *Learning Indian Music: a Systematic Approach* (Ft. Lauderdale, FL: Onomatopoeia, 1979).

SUGGESTED LISTENING

Raga Charukauns; Raga Jogeshwari; Philip Glass: *Passages.*

WAYNE SHORTER

Wayne Shorter has been one of the cornerstone saxophone players in some of the most important ensembles in jazz history. He was also a composer and soloist of great originality. Influenced by Coleman HAWKINS, John COLTRANE, and Sonny ROLLINS, Shorter developed a spare, fragmented style of improvisation, and his compositions show a marked originality in their melodic and rhythmic elements.

Born on August 25, 1933, in Newark, New Jersey, Shorter began learning the clarinet at age 16. He studied music at New York University, after which he served in the United States Army from 1956 to 1958.

Hearing bebop music on the radio, Shorter became interested in the roots of jazz and was eager to be a part of the burgeoning jazz scene. He studied the saxophone and was soon invited on stage at New York's Café Bohemia with Art BLAKEY, Jackie McLean, Oscar Pettiford, and Max ROACH, where he astonished the audience and the band with his adventurous solos.

Shorter joined Art Blakey's Jazz Messengers in 1959, and became music director, where he was inspired by the drumming of the band's leader, and by virtuoso trumpeter Lee MORGAN. While he was with Blakey, Shorter cut his first two albums as a leader for Veejay records, *Blues à la Carte* and *Second Genesis*, both of which showcased his fine compositions.

SHORTER JOINS ENSEMBLE

Shorter left Blakey in the summer of 1964 to join Miles DAVIS in his second great quintet, with Herbie HANCOCK, Ron Carter, and Tony WILLIAMS. As in Blakey's band, Shorter's originals ("ESP," "Footprints," "Dolores," "Nefertiti," and others) provided much of the material for this groundbreaking ensemble. Shorter stayed with Davis until 1970, and during this time also took up the soprano saxophone to extend the ensemble. A tender, melancholy mood pervaded much of this work for Shorter, who was learning from Davis the fine art of understatement.

A new, more experimental style pervaded Shorter's own Blue Note recordings of the 1960s (his most prolific period), including "Night Dreamer" (1964),

"Speak No Evil" (1965), "Juju" (1965), and "Super Nova" (1969). After leaving Davis's band in the spring of 1970, Shorter cofounded Weather Report, the avant-garde quintet that combined jazz, rock, and funk ideas, with the keyboard player Joe Zawinul. This ensemble charted new territory and set the standard for the jazz rock (fusion) subgenre. Exploration with electronics and free-form arrangements were the early hallmarks of the quintet, but they gave way to more structured forms, and Shorter, who found less room for his originals, left in 1985.

NEW IDEAS, MUSICAL HARMONIES

Shorter continued to record as a leader during his 15 years with Weather Report, later finding an outlet for his compositions of Afro/Latin-flavored music. His quest for new ideas and musical harmonies led him to collaborate with Airto Moreira, Milton Nascimento, Chick COREA, Bobby McFerrin, and (most recently) Joni MITCHELL and Herbie Hancock. He also featured in the film *Round Midnight* in 1986, which portrayed the 1950s jazz scene in Paris.

With more than 75 albums and several jazz standards to his credit, Shorter's music continues to inspire a younger generation of composers and players, including George Howard and Branford Marsalis. His Verve debut, "High Life"—his first as a leader after a seven-year hiatus—won a Grammy award for best contemporary jazz performance, which was his first Grammy for one of his own albums.

Todd Denton

SEE ALSO:
HARD BOP; JAZZ ROCK.

FURTHER READING
Gridley, Mark C. *Jazz Styles* (Englewood Cliffs, NJ: Prentice Hall, 1985); Santoro, Gene. *Dancing in Your Head: Jazz, Blues, Rock, and Beyond* (New York: Oxford University Press, 1994).

SUGGESTED LISTENING
"Night Dreamer"; *Speak No Evil*; *Super Nova*; Art Blakey: *The Complete 1960 Jazz Messengers*; *Free for All*; Miles Davis: *Bitches Brew*; *The Complete Live at the Plugged Nickel*; *E.S.P*; *In a Silent Way*; Weather Report: *Heavy Weather*; *I Sing the Body Electric*; *Sweetnighter*.

DMITRY SHOSTAKOVICH

Dmitry Shostakovich was a leading composer of the Soviet Union, and also one of the towering figures of 20th-century music. He was born in the Tsarist capital of St. Petersburg on September 25, 1906. In 1919, two years after the Bolshevik Revolution, he entered the Petrograd (now St. Petersburg) Conservatory. Times were very hard in the aftermath of the 1917 Revolution, with strict food rationing, but the young Shostakovich was given extra food as a reward for his exceptional talents. He repaid this faith in him in 1925, when at age 19 he graduated from the conservatory with a symphony that was soon hailed all over the world as a masterpiece.

Throughout the remainder of the 1920s and into the 1930s, official Soviet attitudes toward the arts remained relatively liberal, allowing composers, writers, and artists some degree of creative freedom. The young Shostakovich took full advantage of this in such wildly "modern" and experimental works as his Symphony No. 2 ("To October," 1927), which celebrates the tenth anniversary of the revolution. But, as Joseph Stalin tightened the grip of the state on all aspects of Soviet life and became a hard-line dictator, the whole social and artistic climate changed.

CHAOS INSTEAD OF MUSIC

The turning point for Shostakovich's career came in 1936, when Stalin himself attended a performance of Shostakovich's opera, *Lady Macbeth of the Mtsensk District*. Stalin disliked the opera, and the government newspaper *Pravda* predictably attacked the piece under the headline "Chaos Instead of Music." Shostakovich was in political disgrace. He reacted by writing his Symphony No. 5 (1937), which was described as "a Soviet artist's practical creative reply to just criticism," although this epithet did not originate from the composer himself. This critical success restored Shostakovich to favor, and indeed the symphony, dramatic and suitably triumphant by turns, has since become the most popular of all his works, though many commentators now claim that behind his show of contrition and obedience, Shostakovich was secretly mocking Stalin himself. Whatever the case with Symphony No. 5, as long as Stalin lived, Shostakovich continued to be in and out of trouble, although his Piano Quintet (1940) won him a Stalin Prize.

WORLD WAR II

Shostakovich became a hero during World War II, when he was a firefighter in the defense of Leningrad (formerly Petrograd and now St. Petersburg) against the German invasion. He then wrote his patriotic Symphony No. 7 ("Leningrad," 1941) which was flown in microfilm form to the U.S. where it had its first performance there under the baton of Arturo TOSCANINI. During the war years, this symphony was performed many times in America and in other Western countries, becoming symbolic of the heroic resistance to fascism.

Later in the war, Shostakovich was appointed professor of composition at the prestigious Moscow Conservatory. But he fell into official disfavor again in 1948, together with eminent colleagues such as Sergey PROKOFIEV, when the authorities accused him of "formalism." This was an odd political term that referred to writing music that did not have mass appeal, and therefore sinned against Soviet artistic policy. As a result, Shostakovich was dismissed from his post at the Moscow Conservatory. He reacted to this censorship by splitting his musical personality to produce some acceptable, simpler works, while continuing to write more adventurous pieces to satisfy

The Russian Dmitry Shostakovich is widely regarded as the greatest symphonist of the mid-20th century.

himself, including the Violin Concerto No. 1, the String Quartet No. 4, and the song-cycle *From Jewish Folk Poetry* (1948), which would have been unacceptable in the anti-Semitic attitude prevailing under Stalin.

LIBERATION FROM CENSORSHIP

Stalin died in 1953, and Nikita Khrushchev eventually became premier. Life for the composer, as for others in the Soviet Union, gradually became easier. Several earlier works which he had withdrawn from publication and performance for fear of political attack, were now given a hearing. Shostakovich quickly finished his immensely powerful Symphony No. 10, and in 1959 composed another of his most inspired concert works, the Cello Concerto No. 1.

In some ways, Shostakovich reacted to this liberalism with suspicion. His Symphonies No. 11 ("The Year 1905") and No. 12 ("To the Memory of Lenin") are an almost nostalgic look back at the early days of Bolshevism: the composer who had been a boy in the revolution could not betray those principles. But it was always in his chamber works that he allowed himself to write in a more personal style and with exciting new textures.

Shostakovich received further high honors. He was awarded the Order of Lenin in 1956, and was the first musician to receive the title of Hero of Socialist Labor. He was also free to travel abroad, back to the United States (which he had first visited as part of a delegation in 1949, at the beginning of the Cold War), and to Britain, where he struck up a warm friendship with the English composer Benjamin BRITTEN. And he continued to compose prolifically, even after a serious heart attack. His Symphony No. 15 (1971) is one of his most original and enigmatic works. His last piece, in 1975, was a viola sonata in three movements. The first two movements are serene and lyrical, while the final adagio, which is the longest, is more melancholy in tone. Shostakovich died at age 69 in a Moscow hospital on August 9, 1975.

STYLE AND TECHNIQUE

Shostakovich's musical output was shaped by a number of contrasting and sometimes conflicting influences. To begin with, he was a Soviet artist, and a servant of the state. In that capacity, he was expected to write music that praised government achievements and lifted the morale of the people with the same intent as all those paintings of heroic but joyful workers toiling in factories or fields. In contrast to this official optimism, he lived through some of the most grim and traumatic events in modern history. Shostakovich's personality was also a shaping factor: he had something of the same temperament as his great Russian predecessor Tchaikovsky, swinging between emotional extremes. He also shared Gustav MAHLER's taste for composition on an epic scale, and struggled to reconcile all these pressures, impressions and impulses in his music.

After his early experimental period, Shostakovich settled for a generally conservative mode of expression. He chose to write much of his music in the long-established forms of the symphony and the string quartet (15 examples of each), using fairly familiar patterns of harmony and rhythm. But, at its best, his music carries tremendous power and conviction, ranging from tenderness and pity, through irony and satire, to blackest doom and tragedy. It adds up to a mighty testimony to a tumultuous age.

One unique feature of the music is Shostakovich's use of the four notes D, E flat, C, and B natural. In German notation, the notes are DSCH, and he made them stand for the initials of his own name. They run throughout his compositions, like a defiant gesture in the face of hardship and catastrophe.

Richard Trombley

SEE ALSO:

CHAMBER MUSIC; OPERA; ORCHESTRAL MUSIC.

FURTHER READING

Volkov, Solomon, ed. and Antonia W. Bouis, trans. *Testimony: the Memoirs of Dmitry Shostakovich* (New York: Limelight Editions, 1984); Wilson, Elizabeth. *Shostakovich: a Life Remembered* (Princeton, NJ: Princeton University Press, 1994).

SUGGESTED LISTENING

Cello Concerto No. 1; Piano Concerto No. 1; Piano Quintet; String Quartets Nos. 8 and 11; Symphony No. 1; Symphony No. 2 ("To October"); Symphony No. 5; Symphony No. 7 ("Leningrad"); Symphony No. 9; Symphony No. 10; Symphony No. 11 ("The Year 1905"); Symphony No. 13 ("Babi-Yar"); Symphony No. 15.

JEAN
SIBELIUS

Finland's great composer Jean Sibelius was born on December 8, 1865, in Tavastehus, a small town north of Helsinki. The son of an army doctor, he was baptized Johann, but adopted the name of Jean. His father died of cholera when Jean was two, and he was brought up, along with his elder sister and younger brother, by his mother and grandmother.

As a small child, Jean learned to play the piano and then the violin, the latter becoming his favorite instrument. The whole family was musical, and Jean showed an early talent for composition. His first piece, *Waterdrops*, was written at the age of nine. From the age of 14, he studied the violin seriously with a local bandmaster, and played chamber music at home with the other members of his family. By the time he was 17, he had also written a piano trio in A minor and a piano quartet in E minor.

It was while he was at school that Sibelius first became deeply interested in the Finnish national epic poem *Kalevala* that was to be a major inspiration for much of his music.

In 1885, Sibelius went to Helsinki to study law, but soon abandoned this in favor of the music school of Martin Wegelius, where he took lessons in composition and played the violin in the school's string quartet. He continued to study the violin, and had ambitions to be an orchestral violinist, even auditioning for the Vienna Philharmonic in 1891. He also made friends with the composer and pianist Busoni, who was teaching at Wegelius's music school.

Sibelius went next to Berlin to study counterpoint with Becker, and here for the first time he was able to hear much of the musical repertoire of the time—including Richard STRAUSS's *Don Juan*. He completed his musical studies in Vienna, and in 1891 returned home to take up a teaching post in Helsinki.

MUSIC OF NATIONALISM

Finland at the time was ruled by Tsarist Russia, and there was a growing movement for political independence. Sibelius identified himself with this, writing works that openly expressed his nationalist feelings.

The first of these was the five-movement choral symphony *Kullervo*, which was inspired by the *Kalevala*. This was premiered in April 1892 and was an immediate success, placing Sibelius (at the age of 26) firmly in the position of Finland's foremost composer. That June he married Aino Järnefelt, sister of fellow composer Armas Järnefelt.

During the 1890s Sibelius wrote several symphonic pieces, all expressing his patriotism through Finnish mythology. These included the tone-poem *En Saga* (1892) and the *Lemminkäinen* legends (four tone poems based on tales of a legendary hero). *Finlandia* (1899), written as part of the music for a patriotic pageant, caught the public imagination and turned Sibelius into a national hero. Only the highly romantic *Valse Triste*, written a few years later, has rivaled *Finlandia* in popularity. These and other early compositions may still belong to the 19th century in time, style, and mood, but they are already marked by their highly individual, rugged strength.

Sibelius continued writing descriptive "program" music, incidental music for the theater, piano pieces, and songs in the years to come. But it is his seven symphonies that stand at the heart of his output, and distinguish him as one of the great composers of the 20th century. Sibelius finished his Symphony No. 1 in 1899, on the threshold of the new century. The brooding clarinet solo at the very start must certainly have made the first-night audience sit up and take notice. Otherwise, the symphony is generally written in a fine, Late Romantic style, with perhaps some echoes of Tchaikovsky.

INTERNATIONAL RECOGNITION

At the turn of the century, Sibelius's standing in his own country was unchallenged, yet his music had not been heard outside Finland. All that was to change in 1900, when the Helsinki Philharmonic Orchestra, led by Robert Kajanus, went on its first European tour, including an appearance at the Paris World Exhibition. They played Sibelius's Symphony No. 1, *Finlandia*, and two of the *Lemminkäinen* legends. These were so well received that Sibelius was invited to Heidelberg the following year to conduct his own music, and to Berlin the year afterward.

The Symphony No. 2 (1902) has a rousing finale, in the spirit of *Finlandia*. But its opening and its slow movements are much more striking in terms of form and instrumental sound. Sibelius introduced a revolution in symphonic form, bringing in a sequence of apparently isolated and random ideas, then forging them together into a powerful and convincing whole.

A HOUSE IN THE COUNTRY

In 1904 Sibelius decided to live outside Helsinki, where he was inclined to indulge in heavy drinking, running up increasing debts. He bought a plot of land in a pleasant spot not far from the capital and built a house, which he called Ainola, after his wife. It was there at Järvenpää that he was to spend the rest of his life.

Sibelius completed his Symphony No. 3 at Ainola in 1907. In 1908 he became ill and underwent several operations for suspected cancer. The concern that he felt about his illness may well have influenced his subsequent works, and Symphony No. 4 (1911) astonished its audience with its originality. It opens with a strange passage on the lower strings, like a plunge into one of Finland's deep, cold lakes. The rest of the symphony is nearly as bleak, as the composer strips his ideas down to the bone.

Sibelius worked on his fifth symphony during the grim period of World War I, when Finland itself was on the brink of civil war leading to independence. The symphony, however, is mostly bright and optimistic in spirit, ending famously with a series of chords spaced like mighty hammer blows. It also marks advances in Sibelius's symphonic thinking. The two middle movements are linked in a highly original way, so that one merges seamlessly into the other. In other parts of the score Sibelius repeats a phrase while changing it slightly, a technique developed by the later minimalist composers. The Symphony No. 6 is a luminous, pastoral work played less often than some of the others, but is nevertheless highly regarded by many admirers of Sibelius.

A SUMMING UP

The Symphony No. 7 of 1924 is a superb summing up of all that came before. In it, the traditional four movements of a symphony are compressed into one monolithic, single movement, ending with a great upward sweep of the violins back into the original key of C major, as if a line were drawn beneath a lifetime's achievement.

Sibelius was then 59 years old, honored in his own country and famous all over the world. Only two more major works followed, incidental music for

Shakespeare's *Tempest,* and the tone poem *Tapiola* (1926), inspired by Finland's great dark forests and including one remarkable passage evoking a blizzard. Sibelius then settled into a long retirement. He worked on an eighth symphony, which was eagerly awaited by the musical world, but he never completed it and burned what he had written. Sibelius died at Ainola on September 20, 1957.

WANING AND WAXING

After his death, Sibelius's popularity and reputation tumbled. From being regarded by many music-lovers as the greatest living composer, he was suddenly dismissed as old-fashioned. But his status has long since been revived. His music is Romantic in the way it recalls Finnish myth and legend, or holds up a mirror to Finland's beautiful, if sometimes austere, landscape. At the same time, his music—particularly the symphonies—belongs firmly to the 20th century. In contrast with those of his contemporary, Gustav MAHLER, Sibelius's symphonies move toward increasing brevity, economy, and clarity of sound. His music was very modern at the time, and has lost none of its strength and originality over the years.

Richard Trombley

SEE ALSO:

CHAMBER MUSIC; LATE ROMANTICISM; ORCHESTRAL MUSIC; VOCAL AND CHORAL MUSIC.

FURTHER READING
Goss, Glenda Dawn, ed.
The Sibelius Companion
(Westport, CT: Greenwood Press, 1996);
Howell, Tim. *Jean Sibelius: progressive techniques in the symphonies and tone poems*
(New York: Garland Publications, 1989);
Layton, Robert. *Sibelius*
(New York: Schirmer Books, 1993).

SUGGESTED LISTENING
Aollottaret; *En Saga*; *Finlandia*;
In Memoriam (Funeral March);
Kullervo; *Lemminkäinen Suite*;
Luonnotar; *Pelléas et Mélisande*;
Symphony No.1; Symphony No. 2;
Tapiola; *Valse Triste*;
Violin concerto.

HORACE SILVER

Among the funky piano players in modern jazz, Horace Silver reigns supreme. A master at composing simple, memorable tunes for the hard bop quintet, his resoundingly soulful compositions such as "Filthy McNasty," "Señor Blues," "Song for My Father," "Nica's Dream," and "Opus de Funk" have become staples in the jazz canon. Silver and drummer Art BLAKEY are the two jazz artists most responsible for emphasizing the "hard" part of hard bop.

Silver was born in Norwalk, Connecticut, on September 2, 1928, and raised there mainly by his father, a Portuguese folk musician (his mother died when he was ten). He studied piano and saxophone in high school, and moved on to heading a piano trio that backed musicians visiting local clubs. One such visitor, Stan GETZ, sat in with Silver's trio in 1950 and was impressed enough to ask the pianist to join him on tour. Silver took to the road with Getz, making his first recorded appearance with the star in 1951. Then Silver relocated to New York City. From 1951 to 1954 Silver worked as a pianist and composed for small groups led by Blakey, Coleman HAWKINS, Oscar Pettiford, and Lester YOUNG, recording with Lou Donaldson and Miles DAVIS. He also began to record as a bandleader, most notably with Blakey.

HARD BOP QUINTETS

The Horace Silver Quintets of 1954 and 1955—with Donald Byrd or Kenny Dorham on trumpet, Silver, Blakey, tenor Hank Mobley, and bassist Doug Watkins—were the seminal hard bop quintets of the mid-1950s. Silver's compositions, most notably "Quicksilver" and "The Preacher," could be described by the loose term "funky." At their core lay a mixture of gospel and blues (frequently in the "call-and-response" format of the African-American church) riding roughshod over frenetic, hard-rocking beats. These quintets became the foundation for Art Blakey's Jazz Messengers when Blakey and Silver split up in 1956. Along with gospel, blues, and jazz, Silver was one of the first composers to incorporate the influence of Caribbean music into jazz.

Recording for Blue Note from 1953 to 1981, Silver became an acknowledged master at composing and arranging for what became the prototypical bop quintet (tenor saxophone, trumpet, bass, piano, and drums). He was a soloist fond of sly references, emotional forthrightness, and strong emphasis on the "blueness" of the notes. As an accompanist, Silver tried, he said, to "goose" soloists into more explosive playing. Among the memorable works produced by Silver in this period were *Doing the Thing: Live at the Village Gate* (1961), *Silver's Serenade* (1963), and *Song for My Father* (1964).

Silver's albums began to include more songs with vocals and lyrics toward the end of the 1960s. His 1970s albums often featured expanded groups including guitars and singers (*The United States of Mind*) and larger instrumental ensembles (*Silver & Strings*, *Silver & Voices*, *Silver & Percussion*). In 1981 he founded his own label, Silveto Records, then signed with Columbia in 1993.

The Horace Silver Quintet has served as a traveling "finishing school" for jazzmen. Its alumni include Blue Mitchell, Joe HENDERSON, Hank Mobley, Kenny Dorham, Clifford BROWN, Donald Byrd, Benny Golson, Randy and Michael Brecker, Woody Shaw, Louis Hayes, and Art Farmer.

Silver became one of the first hard bop pianists, playing a funky mixture of gospel and blues, which greatly influenced contemporaries such as Ray CHARLES, Herbie HANCOCK, Bobby Timmons, Ramsey Lewis, Bill EVANS, and Les McCann. He is one of the premier composers for the modern jazz quintet, and stripped away much of the multi-note complexity of bebop to employ a more direct, percussive, and on-the-beat approach with charming humor and humanity.

Chris Slawecki

SEE ALSO:
BEBOP; FUNK; HARD BOP; JAZZ.

FURTHER READING
Lyons, Len. *The Great Jazz Pianists* (New York: Da Capo Press, 1989).

SUGGESTED LISTENING
Blowin' the Blues Away;
Hard-Bop Grandpop;
Horace Silver and the Jazz Messengers.

NINA
SIMONE

The fiercely independent spirit of Nina Simone is summarized by her claim, "I've never changed my hair. I've never changed my color. I have always been proud of myself." A performer for the past four decades, and crowned the "high priestess of soul" for the soul-wrenching intensity of her singing, she is equally at home performing jazz, rhythm and blues (R&B), folk, gospel, protest songs, or material from Broadway musicals. Simone's smoky, often hard-edged voice and genre-bending style have made her one of 20th-century popular music's most provocative artists. "Her extraordinary faculty for communicating," wrote jazz critic Leonard Feather, "is based in part on the urgent topicality of her songs, and in equal measure, on the power, sometimes tantamount to fury, with which she drives home her point."

Born Eunice Kathleen Waymon on February 21, 1933, in Tryon, North Carolina, she was the sixth of eight children of a handyman (and ordained minister) and a housekeeper. Early on she displayed such a prodigious musical talent that, when she was six years old, a local benefactor paid for her first piano lessons. In 1943, ten-year-old Eunice gave her debut recital at the local library—and experienced racism firsthand when her parents were removed from the front row to make room for whites. This traumatic episode may have reinforced her lifelong commitment to the fight for racial equality.

CLASSICAL TRAINING

In 1950, Eunice Waymon moved to New York to study classical music at Juilliard, but by 1954 the poor state of her finances forced her to take a summer job as pianist-singer at the Midtown Bar in Atlantic City, New Jersey. She took the stage name "Nina Simone," afraid that her parents would find out she was performing in a bar. "Nina" was a nickname a boyfriend had given her, and the "Simone" came from the glamorous French actress Simone Signoret. When Simone was signed to Bethlehem Records in 1957, her first album yielded a million-selling single, George GERSHWIN's "I Loves You Porgy." When

Simone switched labels to Colpix in 1959, the five-year association produced ten eclectic albums (ranging from ELLINGTON standards to folk songs and movie themes) and hits such as "Wild Is the Wind" and "The House of the Rising Sun."

Simone moved to Philips in 1964, where she recorded signature songs such as "Don't Let Me Be Misunderstood" and "I Put a Spell on You," and composed her first protest tune, the fiery "Mississippi Goddam!" in response to the 1963 murder of civil rights activist Medgar Evers.

In 1966 Simone joined RCA for an eight-year stay that produced some of her most commercial records—including "Ain't Got No/I Got Life" (from the musical *Hair*), "To Love Somebody," and her uplifting African-American pride anthem "To Be Young, Gifted, and Black."

DEPARTURE FROM THE U.S.

Embittered by racism, the self-proclaimed "rebel with a cause" left the U.S. in 1969. Since then she has lived in numerous places including Liberia, Barbados, Switzerland, Trinidad, Belgium, and the south of France. Returning to the U.S. in 1978, she was briefly arrested for having withheld income tax payments in protest against the Vietnam War.

Simone's recording of "My Baby Just Cares for Me" made it to No. 5 in the U.K. charts in 1987, and was used to advertise Chanel No. 5 perfume on television in America and Europe. Her music also featured prominently in the 1992 movie *Point of No Return*, a remake of the French thriller *La femme Nikita*, in which the heroine takes both Nina's name and songs as inspiration. Simone's passionate autobiography, *I Put a Spell on You*, was published in 1991.

Michael R. Ross

SEE ALSO:
BLUES; FOLK MUSIC; GOSPEL; JAZZ; SOUL.

FURTHER READING

Simone, Nina, and Stephen Cleary.
I Put a Spell on You
(New York: Pantheon, 1991).

SUGGESTED LISTENING

The Colpix Years; *The Essential Nina Simone*;
Wild Is the Wind/High Priestess of Soul.

FRANK SINATRA

Frank Sinatra is considered one of the greatest popular singers of his generation. Thanks to his outstanding technical ability, instantly recognizable, mellow baritone, and overwhelming charisma, Sinatra remained at the top of his profession for five decades, earning himself legendary status in the process.

Francis Albert Sinatra was born on December 12, 1915, in Hoboken, New Jersey. He began to sing in local clubs at age 18, and in 1939 became the vocalist for trumpeter Harry JAMES's big band. By 1940 he had moved on to the Tommy DORSEY band, recording songs that are still among his best loved, such as "I'll Never Smile Again," and "I'll Be Seeing You."

While he was with Dorsey, Sinatra began to perfect a rhythmic, jazzy style that worked well with the band's swing arrangements. Sinatra's elastic phrasing and relaxed, yet strong approach made him stand out from other big band singers. With his gangly frame, Sinatra cut an awkward, vulnerable figure on stage, and this image helped to earn him a following of young female admirers, known as "bobby-soxers."

In 1943 the ambitious Sinatra parted ways with the Dorsey band to go solo. He signed with Columbia Records, teaming up with arranger Axel Stordahl to produce a string of hits including "Nancy (With the Laughing Face)," and "Dream." Sinatra also began a highly successful film career, appearing in lightweight musicals such as *Higher and Higher* (1944) and *Anchors Aweigh* (1945).

Sinatra's fortunes started to wane towards the end of the decade, but his career was kickstarted by his highly acclaimed performance in the film *From Here to Eternity* (1953), for which he won an Oscar for best supporting actor. He also starred in *Ocean's Eleven* (1960), and *The Manchurian Candidate* (1962). Sinatra moved to Capitol in 1953, where he began his long collaboration with arranger Nelson Riddle, whose unconventional, atmospheric orchestrations perfectly matched Sinatra's style. During this time, Sinatra began to record theme albums such as *In the Wee Small Hours* (1955), *Songs for Swingin' Lovers* (1956), and *Sinatra Sings for Only the Lonely* (1956). This period saw

Frank Sinatra, known affectionately as "ol' blue eyes," giving one of his professional, polished performances.

Corbis-Bettmann/UPI

Sinatra produce his best material, though it wasn't until 1969 that he recorded "My Way," the song that would become his signature tune.

Sinatra continued to record during the 1970s and 1980s, but increasingly concentrated on live performances, particularly at his "second home" of Las Vegas. By this time, Sinatra's voice was beginning to show signs of wear and tear, yet audiences were still won over by the singer's showmanship and charisma. Even with much of his vaunted range gone, Sinatra never lost his ability to throw himself completely into a song.

The 1990s saw several "farewell" performances, as well as a series of collaborations with contemporary artists such as Bono of U2. Frank Sinatra died on May 15, 1998, mourned by millions throughout the world.

Jim Allen

SEE ALSO:

ARRANGERS; FILM MUSICALS; POPULAR MUSIC.

FURTHER READING

Freedland, Michael. *All the Way: A Biography of Frank Sinatra* (New York: St Martin's Press, 1998); Hawes, Esme. *The Life and Times of Frank Sinatra* (Philadelphia, PA: Chelsea House, 1997).

SUGGESTED LISTENING

In the Wee Small Hours; *Sinatra Sings for Only the Lonely*; *Songs for Swingin' Lovers*.

SINGER-SONGWRITERS

There have always been singers who wrote their own songs, or songwriters who performed. Indeed, it was only after music was written down or recorded that people began to perform songs written by others. In the 20th century, the works of singer-songwriters have usually provided some specific message, social or political, with articulate, poetic lyrics that tend to be at least as, if not more, important than the musical setting.

Variants of the singer-songwriter can be found in all the different strands of American popular music including blues, country, and jazz. However, the major legacy of being a singer-songwriter as we know it today comes from the folk revival of the early 1960s, when young folksingers popularized the socially aware protest song.

In the 1920s and 1930s, early blues singers such as Charley PATTON and Robert JOHNSON, whose work was the first to be recorded, helped to spread music previously heard only in the singers' immediate community. Blues songs were mostly derived from the urban squalor and poverty of their surroundings, and found a ready audience in people for whom these problems were being voiced for the first time.

Patton and Johnson were followed in the 1930s and 1940s by rural blues singer LEADBELLY and folk songwriter Woody GUTHRIE, who laid the groundwork for much of what was to follow in the second half of the 20th century. Guthrie was one of the first performers in folk music to sing his own songs almost exclusively, thus widening the terms of reference of folk music.

By the early 1940s, American popular music had begun to dominate the listening habits of not just the U.S. but much of Europe, effectively ghettoizing the American folk tradition in all its forms. The pop vocalists of that time, like Bing CROSBY and Frank SINATRA, were strictly performers dependent on the song mills of their record labels and publishing houses for material, while songwriters like Sammy Cahn, Harold ARLEN, and Irving BERLIN never enjoyed the spotlight themselves. The work of these songwriters could conceivably be recorded convincingly by any number of popular singers.

This meant that the folk, country, and blues traditions were largely being ignored by the mainstream, but were still fermenting in the background. The more individualistic style these genres demanded, and an impatience (on the folk scene) with the superficiality of the work of the pop vocalists, helped fuel the rebirth of the singer-songwriter.

Rhythm-and-blues (R&B) singers like Louis Jordan and Charles Brown began writing their own compositions, influencing rock'n'roll songwriters such as Chuck BERRY, Bo DIDDLEY, and LITTLE RICHARD. The same thing was happening in country music, where Lefty Frizell, Roy ACUFF, and Ernest TUBB paved the way for performers such as Johnny CASH and Hank WILLIAMS, who brought a new level of sophistication to country songwriting. Throughout the 1950s, artists like Muddy WATERS, Willie DIXON, Buddy HOLLY, and Roy Orbison emerged, bringing their own styles to the blues, rock, and country that vied with popular music in the charts.

THE INFLUENCE OF DYLAN

In 1961, a young Minnesotan folksinger named Bob DYLAN arrived in New York City. He was as contemptuous of the output of commercially oriented popular singers as he was obsessed with the songs of Woody Guthrie and Ramblin' Jack Elliott. Dylan attempted to cast himself in their mold, writing songs in a style that was associated with the folk music of 30 years earlier. However, he also recognized the need for a contemporary voice on the folk scene, and gradually developed his compositional style, moving away from the Dust Bowl balladry of Guthrie to revolutionary song-poetry.

Several factors contributed to Dylan's subsequent success, not least of these was his sensitivity to the politics of the time. Politically committed performers were not new; along with Dylan's mentor Guthrie were the WEAVERS—who included one-time Guthrie band member Pete Seeger—a group that set a precedent among folk musicians during the late 1940s and early 1950s of achieving commercial success without compromising their commitment to voicing concern over social injustice. (The Weavers were also the major historical influence for the folk revival of the 1960s.) Unique to Dylan, however, was the

Neal Preston/Corbis

Beck, the 1990s singer-songwriter, combines 1960s-style songwriting talent with post-punk spirit.

concurrence of his poetic vision and political views with the events of the 1960s, including the Civil Rights movement and the anti-Vietnam War protests. He created a radical commentary on the time, and confirmed himself as the spokesman for a large part of the counterculture of the 1960s. By the mid-1960s, his music had become a clarion call, inspiring others to create music criticizing the establishment. Dylan and allied singer-songwriters such as Joan BAEZ also established the yardstick of artistic authenticity. It was never again easy for pop entertainers to produce crass material without fear of critical appraisal from less commercially successful, but better respected musicians.

At first, Dylan's influence was felt mostly among other folksingers, like Eric Anderson, Tom Paxton, Joni MITCHELL, and Phil Ochs. Eventually, his style and concerns filtered through to rock'n'roll, influencing groups like the Byrds, the Lovin' Spoonful, and the BEATLES, who, after initially reworking rock'n'roll material from the 1950s, had by 1965 begun to write more original material that reflected contemporary life and politics.

At the same time, a young Dylan disciple from Buffalo, New York, named Jackson C. Frank had begun to cause a stir among British folk music fans.

Frank brought a personal, artistic approach to the "solo singer-songwriter with an acoustic guitar." Though he soon disappeared from the spotlight, Frank was a direct influence on many of the finest singer-songwriters in England at the time—from Nick Drake, Sandy Denny, and Bert Jansch, to American expatriate, Paul Simon—proving to be almost as influential there as Dylan was in America.

ROCK SINGERS

By 1967, the work of artists such as Dylan and the Beatles had liberated musical expression, encouraging a personal freedom that was previously unthinkable. Political issues like world peace began to give way to a sympathy for minorities and social misfits, captured best perhaps in Lou Reed's 1972 song "Walk on the Wild Side". Reed and others explored rock music's darker side with a literary sensibility leavened by a sense of humor. However, it was folk-rock artists who popularized the notion of the singer-songwriter. On the one hand, there were the arty, impressionistic, jazz-inflected works of Tim Buckley, Fred Neil, Tim Hardin, Van MORRISON, Joni Mitchell, and Nick Drake. On the other, were the more traditional, earthy sounds of Carole KING, James Taylor, Jackson Browne, and Arlo Guthrie that led the way to the soft, country-rock that dominated the early 1970s, as practiced by Jonathan Edwards, and Crosby, Stills, and Nash. And Loudon Wainwright, John Prine, Paul Siebel, Townes Van Zandt, Leonard Cohen, and Richard Thompson upheld the tradition of the thoughtful, incisive singer-songwriter throughout the 1970s.

Many rock musicians of the early 1970s were classically trained, producing elaborate performances and progressive rock "concept" albums. But audiences grew impatient: there was a demand for a return to short, simple, energetic songs that had characterized early rock'n'roll. Punk was born with bands like the SEX PISTOLS and the Ramones. In the U.K., Elvis Costello produced hard-hitting albums including *My Aim Is True* (1977), and the single "Shipbuilding," a blistering indictment of the Falklands War in 1982. Meanwhile, Billy Bragg carried the baton for the more traditional-sounding singer-songwriters, with his socialist songs highlighting the plight of the coal miners and the urban poor.

In Brazil, the *Música popular brasileira* movement had yielded sophisticated, poetic singer/composers like Milton Nascimento, Gilberto Gil, Caetano VELOSO, and Jorge Ben Jor, who had a major impact when "world music" gained popularity in the late 1980s.

SISTERS UNITED

Several outstanding women singer-songwriters, influenced by artists such as Joan Baez and Carole King, emerged in the 1980s and 1990s. Joan Armatrading was born on the Caribbean island of St. Kitts, but moved to the U.K. as a child. Her songs took up the cause of the urban poor and the position of blacks in white society. At the same time, in the U.S., Suzanne Vega was writing songs about issues such as child abuse and urban loneliness, Michelle Shocked was drawing on her poor upbringing to describe rural poverty, and Tracy Chapman also joined this feminist vanguard. In the late 1980s, the Canadian k. d. lang—who started out as a "new country" writer—allied cultural politics with a smooth style and velvet voice.

A platform for new women singers was created in 1997 with the Lilith Fair in the U.S. The brainchild of Canadian artist Sarah McLachlan, this is a touring summer music festival that has featured rising stars such as N'Dea Davenport, from the Brand New Heavies, and the Alaskan singer Jewel, producing eccentric, intellectual art-punk.

While R&B artists of the 1970s like Stevie WONDER, Marvin GAYE, Curtis Mayfield, and Al Green were defining soul, a crop of innovators were doing the same for country music, cutting through the ubiquitous Nashville sound. Singer-songwriters including Waylon JENNINGS, Willie NELSON, and Kris KRISTOFFERSON injected both the rebel attitude of rock'n'roll and the high-minded philosophizing of the Dylan school of folk into the traditional country sound, thus revitalizing the idiom.

In the 1980s, singer-songwriters were back in the mainstream with the success of Bruce SPRINGSTEEN, Tom Waits, and Elvis Costello, artists who used advances in recording technology to frame their songs in an innovative way—something that had generally been shunned by earlier folk-based singer-songwriters.

By the 1990s singer-songwriters such as Beck, Mark Eitzel, Palace's Will Oldham, Simon Joyner, and Pavement's Steve Malkmus combined the literary, introspective songcraft of the 1960s with a post-punk spirit to produce some new, emotionally complex music.

It remains clear that, whatever musical style is in vogue, there will always be room for singer-songwriters to put a human face to it.

Jim Allen

SEE ALSO:

BRAZIL; COUNTRY; FOLK MUSIC; FOLK ROCK; POP MUSIC; POPULAR MUSIC; PROGRESSIVE ROCK; ROCK MUSIC; ROCK'N'ROLL; SOUL.

FURTHER READING

Cantwell, Robert S. *When We Were Good* (Boston, MA: Harvard University Press, 1996); Wolliver, Robbie. *Hoot!* (New York: St. Martin's, 1994).

SUGGESTED LISTENING

Beck: *Odelay*;
Leonard Cohen: *Songs of Love and Hate*;
Bob Dylan: *Blonde on Blonde*;
Bringing It All Back Home;
Jackson C. Frank: *Blues Run the Game*;
Woody Guthrie: *Dust Bowl Ballads*;
Kris Kristofferson: *Me & Bobby McGee*;
Joni Mitchell: *The Hissing of Summer Lawns*;
Randy Newman: *Sail Away*;
Palace: *Lost Blues and Other Songs*;
Tom Waits: *Bone Machine*;
Hank Williams: *The Original Singles Collection*.

LES SIX

The "French Six," as they were named by music critic Henri Collet in 1920, were a loosely linked group of six young composers who had all been students at the Paris Conservatory. They were Arthur Honegger, Darius MILHAUD, and Georges Auric, who had met as students and were later joined by Louis Durey, Germaine Tailleferre, and Francis POULENC. Their spiritual leader was Erik SATIE, and they were dedicated to producing a new style of music in reaction to the epic works of Wagner and other late Romantic composers. Collectively they were enthusiastic about modernism, simplicity, and elegance, although each had an individual style.

Under the influence of the poet Jean Cocteau, who was a fierce nationalist, and wanted French music free from the taints of foreign influences, the young composers sought to be the *enfants terribles* of the musical world. Their works were to be short and straightforward to reflect the machine era and the jazz age. Inspiration, for some of the composers, came from jazz bands, music halls and the circus.

Les Six held concerts to promote their own works and also collaborated on other projects. The *Album des Six* was a collection of piano pieces written by members of the group. In 1921, all but Durey wrote dance music for a ballet-cum-play written by Jean Cocteau, called *Les mariés de la tour Eiffel*. This consisted of a near-Surrealist mime about a wedding interrupted by an ostrich-pursuing hunter, a bather, a cyclist, and a lion. In the years following this concert, however, the six composers began to follow increasingly divergent musical paths and, by the mid-1920s, there was little cohesion remaining in the group.

THE WORKS OF THE SIX

Francis Poulenc is perhaps the best-remembered of the group. His early pieces displayed a sardonic musical wit, and the influence of jazz is heard in his 1922 Sonata for clarinet and bassoon. He wrote many pieces of chamber music, piano music, orchestral music, and music for the stage and for films. His best-known work is the ballet music for *Les biches* (1924). Other well-known works include the Concerto in G for organ, strings, and tympani (1941); the opera *Dialogues des carmélites* (1953–56); and his sextet for piano and wind (1932). Darius Milhaud wrote operas, ballets, symphonies, concertos, chamber music (including 15 string quartets), songs, and piano works. His best-known pieces are the jazzy ballet *Creation of the World* (1923) and the suite *Scaramouche* (1937), for two pianos. Arthur Honegger (1892–1955) was a Swiss who studied at the Paris Conservatory and was grouped with the others as the French Six. In fact he had little sympathy with the music of Satie, who was so admired by the rest of the group. When discussing his opera *Antigone* (1927)—which had a text by Jean Cocteau—Honegger said his aim was "as an honest workman to produce an honest piece of work." He wrote operas, cantatas, choral works, symphonies, concertos, numerous chamber works, and scores for radio and films. His best-known composition is the dramatic oratorio *King David* (1921).

Georges Auric (1899–1983) is best remembered as a composer of scores for films, such as Cocteau's *Beauty and the Beast* (1946) and *Orpheus* (1949). Louis Durey (1888–1979) and Germaine Tailleferre (1892–1983) are the least-known of Les Six. In addition to writing piano pieces, songs, chamber music, and works for chorus and orchestra, Durey became music critic of *L'Humanité* in 1950. Germaine Tailleferre was the only woman in the group. Her work includes several chamber pieces for mixed ensembles, songs, and piano pieces.

Richard Trombley

SEE ALSO:

BALLET AND MODERN DANCE MUSIC; CHAMBER MUSIC; OPERA; ORCHESTRAL MUSIC.

FURTHER READING

Halbreich, Harry, trans. Roger Nichols. *Arthur Honegger* (Portland, OR: Amadeus Press, 1998); Hill, Edward Burlingame. *Modern French Music* (Westport, CT: Greenwood Press, 1970); Shapiro, Robert. *Germaine Tailleferre: A Biobibliography* (Westport, CT: Greenwood Press, 1994).

SUGGESTED LISTENING

Auric: *Orpheus*; Honegger: Symphony No. 2; Milhaud: *Creation of the World*; Poulenc: Sextet for piano; Woodwind Quintet.

BESSIE
SMITH

Most critics consider Bessie Smith to be the greatest of women blues singers. She set the standard for the classic blues singers of the 1920s and influenced later ones such as Billie HOLIDAY and Janis Joplin. Her flamboyance on and off stage befit a woman known as the "empress of the blues."

Smith was born on April 15, 1894, in Chattanooga, Tennessee. She was orphaned at around the age of seven and had to sing in the streets for pennies. Smith first performed on stage in 1912, starting out as a dancer and later becoming a chorus girl. Her big, lush singing voice soon commanded attention, and she quickly became a featured singer with traveling tent shows such as the Moses Stokes Company. The latter featured Ma RAINEY, the first of the great female blues singers, who may well have influenced Smith's singing style.

By the end of the 1910s, Smith was leading the *Liberty Belles Revue*, based in Atlanta. In the early 1920s, she worked in vaudeville and with various bands in Philadelphia and Atlantic City.

Smith is said to have auditioned for several recording companies before Columbia Records took her on in February 1923. That same month she cut her first and what would become her most successful record, "Down Hearted Blues," which was backed on the other side with "Gulf Coast Blues." The single sold 780,000 copies in six months. "Down Hearted Blues" was similar to many of Smith's hit recordings in that it was a new version of another woman's song, in this case Alberta Hunter's 1922 hit.

JAZZ INFLUENCES

Smith was a master of the "classic blues," a jazz-influenced style of singing that brought the inflections and expressions of blues to popular vaudeville tunes such as "There'll Be a Hot Time in the Old Town Tonight." Smith worked with many jazz musicians, including Clarence Williams, Louis ARMSTRONG, Fletcher HENDERSON, Sidney Bechet, and Coleman HAWKINS. From each of these master artists Smith learned a keen sense of timing and phrasing,

and sophisticated vocal techniques. She was also a deeply emotional, earthy singer, which stemmed in part from her tortured, volatile personality. She drank heavily, often got into fights, and had wild affairs with both men and women. However, she was also capable of being kind and generous. Both her music and her lifestyle reflected the fact that she was an emancipated, urban black woman, something rare for the time. Smith's career flourished in the mid- to late 1920s, when she recorded memorable songs such as "Young Woman's Blues" (1926) and "Back-Water Blues" (1927). Besides recording, Smith toured the country with her own highly successful shows, including *Harlem Frolics*, *Yellow Girl Revue*, and *Steamboat Days*.

Smith's last big blues hit, "Nobody Knows You When You're Down and Out," was recorded in 1929, the same year she made the short film *St. Louis Blues*, featuring the eponymous W. C. Handy song that was one of her signatures.

TRAGIC END

The Great Depression and the fading popularity of the classic blues singers led Columbia to release Smith from her contract in 1931. When producer John Hammond brought her back into the studio in late 1933, she refused to record blues, wanting to do something more modern. Hammond produced a reissue of her work for Columbia in 1936, and her career was picking up when she died on September 26, 1937, in Clarksdale, Mississippi, from injuries suffered in an auto accident while on tour.

Stan Hieronymus

SEE ALSO:
BLUES; NEW ORLEANS JAZZ/DIXIELAND.

FURTHER READING
Friedwald, W. *Jazz Singing*
(New York: Da Capo Press, 1996);
Harris, D. *Black Pearls: Blues Queens of the 1920s*
(New Brunswick, NJ: Rutgers University Press, 1988);
Jones, Hettie. *Big Star Fallin' Mama: Five Women in Black Music* (New York: Viking, 1995).

SUGGESTED LISTENING
The Bessie Smith Collection;
The Complete Recordings, Vols. 1 and 2.

SIR GEORG
SOLTI

S ir Georg Solti was the last of the great generation of European autocrats who wielded the conductor's baton, including Wilhelm FURTWÄNGLER, Otto KLEMPERER, and Bruno WALTER. He was personally responsible for the development of the acclaimed and exciting "Chicago sound" that characterized his 22 years as music director of that city's symphony orchestra.

Georg Solti was born in Budapest, Hungary, on October 21, 1912. He started playing the piano at the age of six and gave his first concert at 12. The following year, he was enrolled at the Franz Liszt Academy of Music, where he studied under the composers Ernö Dohnányi, Béla BARTÓK, and Zoltán KODÁLY. He graduated in 1920, and subsequently found work as a rehearsal pianist at the Budapest Opera. In 1935, he became assistant to Walter, and was Arturo TOSCANINI's assistant in the 1936 and 1937 Salzburg Festivals. Solti made his own conducting debut in Mozart's *Le nozze di Figaro* with the Budapest Opera in 1938.

In 1939, the Horthy government of Hungary restricted his musical activities because he was Jewish, and he was forced from his position with the opera. He took refuge in Switzerland, where he supported himself as a pianist. Ordered to leave by the Swiss in 1942, the desperate Solti gained permission to stay by winning the important Geneva International Competition, but he was allowed to teach only five students and passed the war years in poverty. In 1944, however, he was allowed to conduct on Swiss radio.

The war over, Solti applied to the U.S. occupation forces in Germany for the position of conductor at the Bavarian State Opera in Munich. He spent the next six years in Munich, moving to the Frankfurt Opera in 1952. In both houses, Solti established a reputation for hard-driving rehearsals and consummate professionalism. In 1961 he was made the music director of the Los Angeles Philharmonic, but resigned soon after the arrival of Zubin MEHTA who had been appointed associate conductor without consulting Solti.

Solti's guest appearances during 1959 at Covent Garden in London had been extremely well received, and in 1961 he was hired as music director, replacing Rafael Kubelik. Kubelik's resignation had been prompted by attacks in the press because he was not British, and Solti encountered opposition for the same reason. However, his manifest ability and promotion of British singers turned the tide in his favor. During this period he completed the first recording of the entire cycle of Richard Wagner's *The Ring* with the Vienna Philharmonic.

Through guest appearances that began at the Ravinia Festival in Chicago in 1954, Solti established a relationship with the Chicago Symphony, of which he became music director in 1969. He remained there for more than two decades, although he continued to live in England, and made guest appearances and recordings with orchestras throughout the world. Solti retained his position at Covent Garden until 1971, and was music director of the Orchestra of Paris from 1972 to 1975, touring China with that orchestra in 1974.

Solti never actually retired as such. In 1983, he conducted a full performance of *The Ring* at the Bayreuth Festival in Germany. At the age of 80, he appeared as a duet partner of pianist Murray Perahia. At the time of his death on vacation in France on September 5, 1997, he still had several musical projects in the pipeline.

Jane Prendergast

SEE ALSO:
OPERA; ORCHESTRAL MUSIC.

FURTHER READING
Chesterman, Robert. *Conductors in Conversation*
(New York: Limelight Editions, 1992);
Furlong, William B. *A Season with Solti:*
A Year in the Life of the
Chicago Symphony
(New York: Macmillan, 1974);
Robinson, Paul. *Solti*
(Toronto, Canada: Lester and Orpen, 1979).

SUGGESTED LISTENING
Bartók: Music for strings, percussion, and celesta;
Beethoven: The Nine Symphonies;
Mozart: *Die Zauberflöte*;
Wagner: *The Ring*.

STEPHEN SONDHEIM

As a youth in rural Pennsylvania in the 1940s, Stephen Sondheim had the good fortune to count among his neighbors the already eminent lyricist Oscar HAMMERSTEIN II, whose songwriting team with composer Richard RODGERS would help raise Broadway shows and Hollywood musicals to a peak of sophistication and entertainment rarely scaled before or since. Sondheim himself would later take the musical theater into areas of psychological examination never attempted before. But his first schoolboy efforts met with harsh yet invaluable criticism from his distinguished neighbor.

A STROKE OF GOOD LOOK

Sondheim studied music at Williams College and trained in New York under the tutelage of Milton Babbitt. After writing scripts for the popular early 1950s sitcom *Topper*, Sondheim stumbled across another piece of good fortune. He met the playwright Arthur Laurents at a party, who told him that Shakespeare's *Romeo and Juliet* was being updated and turned into a musical with a score by Leonard BERNSTEIN. The musical became *West Side Story* (1957), and as a result of this chance encounter, the young Sondheim got to write the lyrics for the Broadway hit. Sondheim also worked with Laurents and composer Jule STYNE on the musical *Gypsy* in 1959. Both shows were also made into hit movies.

Sondheim became responsible for both the music and the lyrics in *A Funny Thing Happened on the Way to the Forum* in 1962, which has enjoyed many successful revivals. He continued writing for Broadway and television throughout the 1960s, but had to wait until the 1970s for new hits, *Company* in 1970 and *Follies* in 1971.

Company was directed by Harold Prince, a collaborator from *West Side Story*, and it began Sondheim's fascination with the minutiae of domestic relationships. *A Little Night Music* (1973) is perhaps best remembered for one song, "Send in the Clowns," a touching and truthful number which became a popular hit for singer Judy Collins.

Sondheim continued to crave experimentation and innovation to sustain his interest and output. *Pacific Overtures* made use of Japanese musical conventions and kabuki. *Sweeney Todd: The Demon Barber of Fleet Street* (1979) turned the unlikely fare of murder and cannibalism into a musical comedy with operatic overtones. *Merrily We Roll Along* (1981) moved its action backward in time. *Sunday in the Park with George* (1984) was a fictionalized biography of French pointillist artist Georges Seurat that brought the painter's work to life on stage. *Into the Woods* (1987) reexamined children's fairytales from the perspective of adult aspirations. In 1990, the same year he won an Oscar for the song "Sooner or Later" sung by MADONNA in the film *Dick Tracy*, Sondheim opened the short musical *Assassins*, about America's historical gallery of successful and would-be murderers of its presidents.

It is an interesting paradox that out of such a long list of critically acclaimed works, Sondheim produced only one popular hit song. However, two hugely successful revues—*Side by Side by Sondheim* (1976) and *Putting It Together* (1993)—have celebrated the composer/lyricist's outstanding output.

Unlike the musicals of overtly populist composers such as Andrew LLOYD WEBBER, Sondheim's pieces tend toward finding a balance between the emotional, the intellectual, and the entertaining. Although some have criticized him for being too high-brow, Sondheim, who has won numerous Tony awards, is far too savvy not to understand the financial realities of musical theater. Making money is easy; making art is the hard part.

Jeff Kaliss

SEE ALSO:
FILM MUSICALS; MUSICALS; POPULAR MUSIC.

FURTHER READING
Secrest, Meryle. *Stephen Sondheim: A Life* (New York: Alfred A. Knopf, 1998); Zadan, Craig. *Sondheim and Company* (New York: Da Capo Press, 1994).

SUGGESTED LISTENING
Anyone Can Whistle; *Company*; *Follies*; *Into the Woods*; *Side by Side by Sondheim*; *Sunday in the Park with George*; *Sweeney Todd: The Demon Barber of Fleet Street*; *West Side Story*.

MERCEDES SOSA

K nown as the voice of inspiration to many people struggling for justice, Mercedes Sosa is a singer whose political activism has brought her international recognition. During her life, Sosa has experienced the pain of poverty, the oppression of Argentina's dictatorship, and the banishment of herself and her music from her native country. She became one of the figureheads of the Latin American *nueva canción* (new song) movement.

Sosa was born on July 9, 1935, in Tucuman, Argentina. She enjoyed singing as a child and, at the age of 20, won a singing competition, the award for which was a two-month contract with a local radio station. She made her professional singing debut at a regional folk music festival in Cosquin.

SONGS OF STRUGGLE

In 1962 Sosa joined with Armando Tejado Gomez and others in launching a musical manifesto, known as *nueva canción*, that aimed to rehabilitate the music of the people and give it a new impetus. Up until then, native folk songs had only rarely acknowledged the limiting social conditions faced by *campesinos* (field workers). The "new" songs, while retaining the stylistic elements of the folk tradition, began to address social issues such as human rights, and the need for a realistic living wage and proper working conditions. When she was asked whether these were "protest" songs, Sosa said in an interview: "I've never liked that label. They were honest songs about the way things really are."

During the 1970s, Sosa attracted a significant following with her warm voice, perfectly suited to the indigenous song styles. She occasionally wrote her own songs, but was known primarily for performing the body of "new" songs by Argentine artists such as Atahualpa Yupanqui and Leon Gieco. Toward the end of the 1970s, the songs she performed began to deal more pointedly with agrarian reform and democracy. This resulted in her being targeted for harassment by the military government. She was repeatedly arrested and, eventually, the government banned her music from Argentine radio and television. After her performances were banned in 1979, Sosa was unable to earn a living and was forced to leave the country in order to support herself.

LIFE IN EXILE

Sosa lived in exile in France and Spain for the next three years, experimenting with other musical styles and performing throughout Europe, England, Canada, Colombia, and Brazil. The pain of exile exacted an emotional toll on Sosa. She said in a *New York Times* interview: "When you are in exile, you take your suitcase, but there are things that don't fit. There are things in your mind like colors and smells and childhood attitudes, and there is also the pain and the death you saw. You can't deny those things because to do so can make you ill."

Sosa returned to Argentina in 1982, shortly before the collapse of the military government, which was replaced with a new civilian government. Sosa performed for sell-out audiences in Buenos Aires for her old fans and new followers who shared her restored optimism and faith. She also appeared in Europe, in other parts of Latin America, and at Carnegie Hall in New York.

In 1995, during a tour of the U.S. and Canada, Sosa was honored in a special ceremony in New York by UNIFEM, the United Nations Development Fund for Women, with their Anniversary Award. She continues her mission of building bridges between people through her music, offering herself as a voice and model for the under-represented.

David Brock

SEE ALSO:

CUBA; FOLK MUSIC; LATIN AMERICA.

FURTHER READING
Lacoren, Nelson. *Mercedes Sosa Poems: The New Woman*
(New York: Latin Culture Productions, 1990).

SUGGESTED LISTENING
Canciones con fundamento;
Chants de ma terre et de mon peuple;
El gran concierto;
Lo mejor de Mercedes Sosa;
Mercedes Sosa Live in Argentine.

SOUL

For many listeners, the soul music of the 1960s represents the essence of African-American musical expression. Soul singers are characterized by their dramatic delivery of strongly emotional lyrics so that the listener is swept irresistibly into the same tide of feeling. Many soul singers, like Aretha FRANKLIN, move on from the religious fervor of gospel to the exposition of personal emotions.

Historically, soul music was the logical progression of African-American music, a hybrid genre created from fervent Southern gospel and gritty Southern rhythm and blues (R&B). Yet, much of soul music's powerful emotional resonance was never the conscious intention of its creators. Inexorably linked by history to the civil rights movement of the 1960s, soul music provided an impassioned voice for the aspirations of the black American community. And as one of the first truly integrated genres of music, where blacks and whites collaborated as musical equals even in the Deep South, soul music provided a glimmer of hope in the face of racism.

RISING OUT OF GOSPEL

Before soul, gospel music was sacred, the blues were profane, and that was that. However, most Southern blacks at that time went to church, so it was inevitable that the styles influenced one another. Vocal ensembles such as the Orioles and singers like Jackie Wilson and Little Willie John added an obvious gospel-based element of emotional intensity to their performances. One gospel group, Royal Sons, from Winston-Salem, North Carolina, abandoned spirituals and took up raunchy double entendres. They changed their name to the Five Royales, becoming a major draw throughout the rural South. The Royales' fiery guitar player Lowman Pauling emerged as an enormous influence on every guitarist in soul music.

Soul's "big bang" came from Ray CHARLES. Charles had begun recording in 1949, but his style did not change from "cool" to emotional until 1954, when he

Wilson Pickett, whose soul hit "In the Midnight Hour" was one of the major crossover songs of the 1960s.

transformed a gospel number into an R&B stomp with "I Got a Woman." The song created considerable repercussions in churches and on the gospel circuit. Charles' style embraced both the fervent call and response of "What'd I Say" and slow ballads. The fire of his vocals delivered the sound of gospel, both to blacks and to young whites, who were entranced by the music's exotic qualities.

Soon afterward, the Soul Stirrers' Sam COOKE, gospel's most magnetic young star, began recording secular material. Although Cooke's style was more pop than the soul singers who followed, he was the one they would all emulate—cool, suave, with an underlying passion and a heart-rending melisma (a group of more than five or six notes sung to a single syllable). Charles and Cooke also set an example by being canny businessmen who showed that music could be a paying profession for ambitious African-Americans at the time.

THE RECORD COMPANIES DISCOVER SOUL

Crucial to the development of soul was Jerry Wexler of Atlantic Records. Atlantic had assembled an impressive roster of R&B talent and had wisely given Ray Charles enough artistic latitude to make his breakthrough. In 1960, Wexler signed the dynamic Solomon Burke, one of soul's greatest showmen and a classic gospel-inspired singer. Burke scored a string of hits in the early 1960s, including the country-flavored

"Empty Arms," and the hugely popular "Everybody Needs Somebody to Love," later recorded by many other artists including the ROLLING STONES.

Burke's rival as a soul showman was a young Georgian named James BROWN. Brown also began as a gospel singer (in prison), and had scored R&B hits with the histrionic "Please, Please, Please" and the tender "Try Me." Large-scale success eluded him, however, until he recorded a live show from New York's Apollo Theater. *Live at the Apollo 1962* reached No. 2 on the album charts (unheard of for an R&B LP) and solidified Brown's reputation as an explosive live act. Of the soul era's early stars, Brown was also its most restless; by 1965 the "Godfather of Soul" was devoting his energies toward his new musical creation, funk.

Because the gospel influences that fueled soul music's development were more ingrained in the Deep South than elsewhere, this is where the genre would thrive. In 1960, a white recording hobbyist named Jim Stewart set up a studio in a vacant movie theater on McLemore Avenue in Memphis, Tennessee. The studio and its record label, Stax, had an undistinguished beginning. Their first regional hit was a duet by local DJ Rufus Thomas and his daughter Carla. Atlantic's Jerry Wexler heard about the fledgling label and offered to distribute their records, a decision that helped Carla's teenage ballad "Gee Whiz" become a national hit. A few months later, an unlikely mélange of local black music veterans and young white musicians, dubbed the Mar-Keys, scored a huge hit with the instrumental "Last Night."

In 1961, William Bell's gorgeous, gospel-flavored "You Don't Miss Your Water" crystallized the style that would become the dominant sound at Stax. In 1962, Booker T. and the MGs scored another huge instrumental hit with "Green Onions." These musicians—Booker T. Jones on organ, Steve Cropper on guitar, Lewis Steinberg on bass (replaced in 1964 by Donald "Duck" Dunn), and Al Jackson, Jr., on drums—played on virtually every Stax recording over the next eight years. When the great Otis REDDING arrived a few months later, Stax had all the elements it needed to perfect the Southern soul sound.

Jim Stewart followed the principles of fellow Memphian Sam Phillips, who a few years earlier had discovered Elvis PRESLEY, Carl Perkins, Jerry Lee LEWIS, and Johnny CASH. Stax's emphasis on the unique qualities of the individual performer set the company apart from the more urbane pop/soul of Detroit's MOTOWN, where the tightly controlled studio environment produced a more formulaic sound. An artist as unrefined as Redding could never have been a key player at Motown. (As Carla Thomas observed during their 1966 duet, "Tramp": "Otis, you're country. You're straight from the Georgia woods," to which Otis replied, "That's good.") But at Stax, Redding became the heart and soul of the label.

Impressed by Redding's recordings at Stax (released on Stax's subsidiary label Volt), Jerry Wexler began sending the talent he discovered down to Memphis. In 1965, a Florida duo named Sam and Dave arrived at Stax and were assigned to the songwriting team of David Porter and Isaac Hayes. (Hayes was also the Stax studio's primary piano player.) Hayes and Porter's songs for Sam and Dave, including "Hold On! I'm Comin'," "Soul Man," "I Thank You," brought out the potential of the duo and established them as one of the hottest soul acts of the 1960s. Another new arrival was Eddie Floyd, who scored one of Stax's biggest hits ("Knock on Wood") and became one of the label's key songwriters. The relationship between Stax and Wexler became strained however, when the fast-talking, New York-bred Wexler attempted to exercise too much control over a session for another of his discoveries, singer Wilson PICKETT.

THE FAME LABEL

Although the sessions at Stax produced two hits ("In the Midnight Hour" and "634–5789"), Wexler and Pickett (no stranger to abrasive behavior himself) left Stax for Rick Hall's Fame studio in Muscle Shoals, Alabama, in 1967.

At Fame, Pickett recorded much of his definitive work, including "Land of 1,000 Dances," "Mustang Sally," "Soul Dance Number Three," and "Funky Broadway." The studio, located in northwestern Alabama, was staffed by a motley assortment of what Wexler called "white Alabama country boys who took a left turn to the blues"—Dan Penn, Spooner Oldham, Donnie Fritts, Jimmy Johnson, Roger Hawkins, and Roger Cogbill—under the autocratic rule of producer/studio owner Rick Hall. Through Fame's recordings of Arthur Alexander, Jimmy Hughes, Joe Tex, Clarence Carter, and Pickett, Muscle Shoals established itself as another hotbed of Southern soul recording in the 1960s. Fame also spawned more musical activity in the area; the tiny

Quinvy studio (using many of Hall's musicians) recorded one of the soul era's biggest hits, Percy Sledge's "When a Man Loves a Woman."

QUEEN OF SOUL

In one of Wexler's most inspired moves, he brought Aretha Franklin to Muscle Shoals. Franklin, a gospel singing prodigy, had signed with Columbia Records as a teenager in 1961. Unfortunately, at Columbia, she was given material and musical settings ill-suited to her dramatic vocal abilities. When her contract expired in 1966, Wexler quickly signed her. At Fame, she managed to record a single track, the magnificent "I Never Loved a Man (the Way I Love You)" before the session disintegrated due to a volatile mix of racial tension and alcohol, culminating in a fistfight between Hall and Franklin's husband, Ted White.

Wexler severed his relationship with Hall, and surreptitiously hired Hall's musicians to finish the sessions at Atlantic's studios in New York. Backed by this inspired group of musicians (including Franklin on the piano), Franklin translated the bruised emotionalism of her troubled life into some of the most thrilling soul music of the era. She transformed Otis Redding's "Respect" into a powerful declaration of ethnic and female pride, and her other hits over the next year—"(You Make Me Feel Like) A Natural Woman," "Chain of Fools," "Baby, I Love You," "Since You've Been Gone,"—led to her being dubbed "the Queen of Soul."

THE END OF AN ERA

Led by Franklin's remarkable breakthrough, 1967 was the last great year of Southern soul. But, with a series of disasters, the world that had created soul crumbled. In October 1967, Atlantic was sold to Warner Brothers, throwing into confusion the distribution deal Wexler had developed with Stax. In December, Otis Redding and his road band the Bar-Kays (the second unit at the Stax studio) perished in a plane crash. Still reeling from this shock, Stax discovered that their contract gave Atlantic (and now Warner Bros.) ownership of Stax's recordings up to that point. Warner/Atlantic, concluding that Stax was a far less valuable entity without its flagship artist, severed their business relationship. And to add insult to injury, Sam and Dave, who had initially been under contract with Atlantic, were taken from Stax. In one brief period, Stax had lost their two biggest acts, their distributor, and their entire back catalog.

A few months later, Martin Luther King, Jr. was assassinated in Memphis. Without warning, the delicate racial balance that had allowed whites like Steve Cropper and "Duck" Dunn, and blacks like Booker T. Jones and Al Jackson, Jr., to create music as equals was shattered. The civil rights movement that had empowered Southern blacks festered into an angry militancy in King's absence; urban America became a war zone, and the crumbling Memphis neighborhood where the Stax studio stood was much closer to ground zero than anyone who worked there had ever realized.

The Stax label managed a few more successful years before disintegrating in a flurry of financial mismanagement suits and tax audits. At Muscle Shoals, musicians who had once backed soul singers such as Aretha Franklin and Wilson Pickett instead did sessions for pop stars including Simon and Garfunkel. Aside from Franklin, only Al Green, on the strength of a remarkable series of records in the early 1970s, kept Southern soul's flame alight. But, as disco came to dominate commercial music, soul became the sound of a bygone era, a powerful force in American popular music relegated to nostalgic radio. The 1980 film *The Blues Brothers* briefly brought the faces and voices of some of soul's stars back to middle-America, but the life force was lost.

Soul singing styles have influenced all popular music since, while the rhythmic vitality of the great soul records has never been surpassed.

Greg Bower

SEE ALSO:
BLUES; GOSPEL; MOTOWN; RECORD COMPANIES.

FURTHER READING
Haa, Erikka. *Soul*
(New York: Friedman/Fairfax Publishers, 1995);
Hirshey, Gerri. *Nowhere to Run:
The Story of Soul Music*
(New York: Da Capo Press, 1994).

SELECTED LISTENING
Aretha Franklin: *Lady Soul*;
Eddie Floyd: *Knock on Wood*;
Al Green: *Greatest Hits*;
Otis Redding: *Otis Blue*;
Sam and Dave: *Soul Men*.

JOHN PHILIP SOUSA

John Philip Sousa crafted most of the timeless patriotic marches that gave Americans pride and embodied their national spirit. For over half a century, he was an imposing, almost mythic, figure on the musical scene, resplendent in an embroidered uniform while energetically conducting with a gold-tipped baton. His efforts in the late 19th and early 20th centuries produced an astounding body of work, including many of America's best-loved and most-performed melodies. *The Stars and Stripes Forever*, his most famous composition, symbolizes the Fourth of July as much as fireworks and barbecues, and has been designated the official national march of the U.S.

John Philip Sousa was born in Washington, D.C., on November 6, 1854, the third of ten children of a Bavarian mother and a Portuguese father who played trombone in the U.S. Marine Band. During the Civil War, the young boy became infused with the spirit of marching men and martial music. He began studying the violin and trumpet in a musical conservatory when he was ten.

At 13, after Sousa ran away to join a circus band, his father enlisted him in the Marines as an apprentice violinist. After his discharge in 1875, he composed comic operettas, toured in vaudeville bands, and conducted theater orchestras. In 1880, 25-year-old Sousa was named the Marine Band's first American-born conductor. Under his leadership, the ensemble became world famous, and Sousa's own rousing compositions, including *El Capitan, The Washington Post*, and *Semper Fideles* (the Marine anthem) earned him the nickname of "the march king." Resigning in 1892, he formed the celebrated Sousa's Band (originally called "the New Marine Band"), which toured the world bedecked in blue-and-black military uniforms.

THE STARS AND STRIPES FOREVER

In 1896, while on the deck of an ocean liner sailing back to America, Sousa was inspired to compose his most famous march. In his mind's eye, "I could see the Stars and Stripes flying from the flagstaff of the White House," he recalled, "... and to my imagination it seemed to be the biggest, grandest flag in the world, and I could not get back under it quick enough." Sousa made an estimated $1 million from the sale of sheet music and recordings of the march. In 1952, it was used as a title for a heavily fictionalized movie biography of the composer.

When the U.S. entered World War I in 1917, 62-year-old Sousa enlisted in the Naval Reserve Force and marched across the country with his 300-piece musical battalion, raising millions of dollars for the war effort. In the 1910s and 1920s, Sousa's Band recorded his most famous compositions for the Victor label.

THE END OF THE MARCH

Always an energetic worker, Sousa found time to write well over 100 marches, plus novels and a best-selling autobiography, *Marching Along*. He also invented the tuba-like instrument called the sousaphone. Sousa died of a heart attack on March 6, 1932, shortly after conducting *Stars and Stripes Forever* for the last time. While still alive "the march king" was already a national treasure, and in 1973, in honor of his legacy, he became one of only three composers to be honored with election to the Hall of Fame for Great Americans.

Michael R. Ross

SEE ALSO:

OPERETTA; ORCHESTRAL MUSIC.

FURTHER READING
Bierley, Paul E. *John Philip Sousa, American Phenomenon* (Columbus, OH: Integrity Press, 1986);
Newsom, Jon, ed. *Perspectives on John Philip Sousa* (Washington, D.C.: Library of Congress, Music Division, 1983);
Sousa, John Philip. *Marching Along: Recollections of Men, Women, and Music* (Westerville, OH: Integrity Press, 1994).

SUGGESTED LISTENING
El Capitan; Showing off Before Company; Stars and Stripes Forever; The Trooping of the Colors; Under the Double Eagle; U.S. Field Artillery; The Washington Post.

SOUTH AFRICAN JAZZ

The story of South African jazz is inextricably linked with the growth of the townships in the 1950s and with the story of apartheid. After World War II, the South African economy expanded rapidly, and people from rural areas flooded into the townships. Rejecting tribalism and traditionalism, the new urban population aspired to an African-American lifestyle. Homegrown jazz flourished in the black urban ghettos, and artists such as Abdullah Ibrahim, Kippie Moeketsi, Hugh Masekela, and Jonas Gwangwa fused local music with American jazz and other global sounds to create a potent indigenous sound.

Jazz found a natural home in South Africa. As an American music born of racial injustice, the struggle for freedom, and ethnic musical fusion, it was embraced by black South Africans as both a cultural and political expression. Black townships of the 1950s were a lively cauldron of musicians, gangsters, prize-fighters, and prostitutes.

This vibrant subculture was portrayed in Todd Matshikiza's 1959 Broadway-type hit musical *King Kong,* which horrifyingly related the story of a boxer who kills his girlfriend and then dies in prison. The production, with its *kwela* dance rhythms, included now-famous cast members such as Miriam Makeba. Nelson Mandela, destined to be the country's first black president, attended the show's debut hours before facing trial for treason.

MUSICAL INHERITANCE
Back in the 1920s, revelers in Johannesburg's black ghettos had gathered in the evenings to listen to the trance-inducing monotonous rhythms of *marabi.* This would be played on a rickety piano with a primitive percussion accompaniment—the style employed a basic, endlessly repeated, three-chord, two- or four-bar sequence, over which the melodic line could be improvised. Over the next decade,

other instruments began to be used—organ, accordion or guitar—and solo vocals. It was from this *marabi* base that South African jazz was to emerge.

FINDING AN INSTRUMENT
The instruments used by the township bands were those that were cheap and readily available—fiddles, banjos, accordions, and harmonicas. The brass instruments that the players heard on imported jazz records—trumpets and saxophones—were far too expensive for most musicians to buy. Sometimes they could be borrowed from the Salvation Army, but they were only incorporated gradually into the South African bands.

In Johannesburg in the late 1930s, "Zuluboy" Cele was playing with his Jazz Maniacs, with modern instrumentation. This band was followed after World War II by the Harlem Swingsters. Players from both bands, such as the Jazz Maniac alto sax player Zacks Nkosi, later led their own groups, which started to sound increasingly like American swing bands.

These township bands were composed of musically literate players who sometimes played from American band parts. Although influenced by Louis ARMSTRONG and Duke ELLINGTON, swing, big band, and bebop sounds from the U.S., these South African jazz bands had their own exciting style that still incorporated the characteristic improvisation and chord progression of *marabi.* In fact by the 1950s, people were beginning to refer to *marabi* as jive.

PENNY WHISTLES
A key instrument in the 1950s was the penny whistle. It was easy to obtain, and became an enormously popular instrument with young street musicians. What came to be called "penny whistle jive" would be played in the townships by groups of three or four players, perhaps with banjo and guitar, imitating swing, jive, and jazz as best they could. This basic street music was given the name *kwela.*

From Cape Town came "Cape jazz," which drew on the musical influence of the Western Cape. Alongside Latin and African rhythms were the South Asian sounds of the area's Malay community. This eclectic sound was characteristic of bands like Pacific Express and Oswietie, and artists such as Basil Coetzee, Ngozi, the Ngcukana brothers, and Robbie Jansen. A new wave of South African jazz became apparent in the early 1960s. While *marabi*-type jazz continued on its way, another strand was emerging, led by Kippie "Morolong" Moeketsi, an alto saxophone player revered for his bebop-inspired improvisation. This progressive jazz was more politically motivated—it constituted a protest against apartheid and the accompanying oppression.

THE JAZZ EPISTLES

In the late 1950s, Moeketsi guided musicians like pianist and composer Abdullah Ibrahim (also known as Dollar Brand), trombonist Jonas Gwangwa, and trumpeter Hugh Masekela. All four men formed the core of the first real jazz band—Ibrahim's township band the Jazz Epistles, which released the first black album (with less than 500 copies) in 1960.

Ibrahim was a disciple of Ellington and admirer of Thelonious MONK, whose strong, spiritual melodies and talents as soloist and bandleader made him a premier figure in the world of jazz. Ibrahim was an apt disciple, and was soon to leave South Africa for the greater artistic freedom of Europe.

Masekela had started playing trumpet as a teenager in the Father Huddleston Band (the "hoodlum priest" Trevor Huddleston had provided a venue and training ground for several aspiring jazzmen, and had even given Masekela his first trumpet). Masekela then played with a small band called the Jazz Dazzlers, along with Jonas Gwangwa and Kippie Moeketsi.

Masekela also left South Africa in the early 1960s, to remain an exile for nearly 30 years. He became a world fusion pioneer, his trumpet and flugelhorn style making hits in the worlds of jazz, rhythm and blues (R&B), Afropop, disco, and pop. He was joined in exile in the early 1970s by Jonas Gwanga, who then played in Masekela's Union of South Africa group.

THE BLUE NOTES

Despite its black township roots, South African jazz was not entirely a blacks-only phenomenon. Chris McGregor, a white pianist from the Transkei, joined four black musicians to form the Blue Notes in 1962. Along with trumpeter Mongezi Feza, saxophonist Dudu Pukwana, bassist Johnny Dyani, and drummer Louis Moholo, the band developed a strong, distinctive style that has been compared to the music of John COLTRANE and Ornette COLEMAN. But apartheid made life increasingly difficult for multiracial bands. In 1964, the Blue Notes moved to Europe and settled in London, where they revolutionized the British jazz

scene with their aggressive, emotional style. Despite the success of his exiled protégés, Moeketsi stayed in South Africa, playing the country's black townships. He was an almost mythical figure in South African music when he died in 1983. With some of its top players living in Europe or the United States, township jazz was largely a music in exile.

Apartheid laws continued to hinder multiracial bands. Record companies paid meager sums for all rights to a performer's music, and the South African Broadcasting Corporation pressured artists to record short pop songs with lyrics conforming to its standards of "tribal purity." Musicians often responded with protest songs about the tribal pass system, bus boycotts, and even revolution. The 1980s brought the foreign influence of jazz rock (fusion), and a generation of fusion bands like Sakhile.

THE BEGINNING OF A NEW ERA

The 1990s saw the end of apartheid and a new multiracial democracy. Jazz greats like Ibrahim and Masekela were able to return to South Africa, while younger groups continually gained ground on World Music charts. South African jazz today has a vitality that is a result of the musicians mixing African styles with acid jazz, *marabi* piano, Shangaan guitar, Asian flute, *marrabenta* rhythms, and anything else they can think up. This heady mix is what makes South African jazz so intensely alive.

Brett Allan King

SEE ALSO:

BEBOP; BIG BAND JAZZ; JAZZ; SWING.

FURTHER READING

Card, Caroline, ed. *A Tribute to Alan P. Merriam* (Bloomington, IN: Indiana University Press, 1981); Kaufman, Frederick, and John P. Guckin. *The African Roots of Jazz* (Sherman Oaks, CA: Alfred Publishing, 1979).

SUGGESTED LISTENING

African Jazz Pioneers; Township Swing Jazz; The Blue Notes: *Blue Notes for Mongezi;* Johnny Dyani: *Song for Biko;* Abdullah Ibrahim and Ekaya: *Water from an Ancient Well;* Hugh Masekela: *Hope;* Bheki Mseleku: *Timelessness.*

SOUTH ASIA

The sounds of South Asia have become increasingly familiar to Western ears, through the involvement of Western popular musicians in Indian traditional music in the latter half of the 20th century, and through the wider distribution of Indian films. Nonetheless, the extremely complex and subtle classical music of the region—defined here as the Indian subcontinent, including neighboring nations such as Afghanistan, Nepal, and Tibet—is probably more alien to the Westerner than that of other Eastern countries such as China and Japan.

INDIA AND PAKISTAN

The chief influence on the life of the region was the Islamic invasion from the tenth to the 13th centuries A.D. The Islamic armies came from the west via Afghanistan and only slackened in force when they reached South India. This has resulted in the southern Indian, or Carnatic, tradition being markedly different from the rest of the region. The Hindu religion remains the chief faith, and the music is still religious in nature. Buddhism has largely been pushed out to the fringes of the region, being the main religion in Sri Lanka and surviving, although under pressure, in Tibet.

The religious affiliations affect the music because, in most areas, vocal music is considered the peak of the performer's art and, in Hindustani music, the texts and stories used still derive chiefly from the ancient myths and epics. Islamic music is based on religious songs celebrating the glory of Allah. Moreover, in the Hindustani tradition, music is closely linked to other performing arts, including plays, puppet-shows, shadow theater, dance-drama, and opera, but the Islamic religion prohibits representation of one person by another, as in acting.

The instrumentation of the region also varies from north to south, although the instruments can be discerned as belonging to the same families. Probably the most important type is the large plucked lute-type—the *sitar* and the *sarod* in the north, which are distinguished by their sympathetic strings under the played strings, and the *veena* in the south, which does not have the sympathetic strings. The bowed, gut-stringed *sarangi* from the north can also have up to 40 metal sympathetic strings under the three or four bowed ones, and is reputed to be one of the most difficult instruments to play, while in Carnatic music, the Western violin was adopted in the 18th century and is admirably suitable for the slides and ornamentation of the music.

Reed instruments and flute-types are also used, although more in folk music than in the classical ensembles, but the greatest variety of instruments is in the drum family. The most common type is the barrel drum, with two heads tuned to different pitches, the *pakhavaj* in the north and the *mrdangam* in the south. Northern ensembles also use the *tabla*, a pair of smaller drums that can produce a variety of pitches. With the violin, Carnatic musicians also adopted the harmonium, which they took over from Christian missionaries, but the use of the instrument is confined to producing drones (sustained pitches) that provide the foundation over which the string players and singers improvise.

The basis of Indian classical music is an improvisation above set patterns called *ragas* and *talas*. *Ragas* are patterns of notes incorporating both the idea of the scale, in that some notes are pivotal to the structure of the music, and the idea of melody, in that the shape of the sequence is also to some extent determined. There are about 200 *ragas* in use, although they fall into groups with recognizably similar patterns. As well as determining the pattern of the music, the *raga* has another function, however, because it fits the music into the complex structure of Indian life. There are specific *ragas* for the different seasons, for different weathers, for different times of day, and for different voices, so that the performance always has an affinity with ceremony.

Talas are rhythmic patterns—the word is derived from the clapping of hands—and again there are hundreds of different cycles of these patterns. The cycles are repeated but overlap and can be very long. However, a large part of the performance of a *raga* is improvised independently of the time cycle, and without a beat at all. The performance of a *raga* can sometimes take several hours and follows a set pattern, with a basic exposition of the *raga* followed

Ravi Shankar performs traditional Indian music on sitar at the Monterey Pop Festival, California, in June, 1967.

by variations, and only in the last section is the drum introduced. The instrumentalist or singer improvises a continuous stream of subtle variations on the phrases of the *raga*, with the underlying drone providing a groundwork.

The ambience of the performance also plays a considerable part in the music. Western listeners who have heard *ragas* in large concert halls cannot appreciate the intimate and meditative nature of the traditional Indian performance. These used to be in the palaces of princes or sheikhs, and are now often performed in the private houses of rich people who can provide the space for a *mahfil*, or private concert. Another factor, which contributes to the deep concentration with which the music is played and heard, is that the transmission of music from teacher to pupil is oral, and the relationship built up is both long and intense. Often, a son will become the pupil of his father, and a school or *gharana* is made up of generations of the same family. Ravi SHANKAR is the most famous Indian musician to have toured widely throughout the West; he learned the sitar in the traditional way and now plays with his daughter.

In Pakistan, the pressures of orthodox Muslim religion have relegated music to a lower social level. Performers are regarded as entertainers and art music plays a much smaller part in life. Folk music, however, is used to cement all the various ceremonies of rural life, at the elaborate and prolonged weddings, at festivals, and as an accompaniment to manual work.

One religious type of music is *qawwali*, or devotional songs of the ecstatic form of Islam known as Sufism. Nusrat Fateh Ali Khan was a native of Pakistan best known for performing *qawwali*. He made more than 100 recordings, which included film soundtracks for *The Last Temptation of Christ* and *Dead Man Walking*. *Qawwali* is a complex vocal music that has been compared by Western listeners to yodeling. It is more than seven centuries old, and is passed orally from father to son (and, very occasionally, to daughters) by Sufi masters. The songs are accompanied by drums, and often use the harmonium for the supporting drone. These ritual performances must include songs of praise to Allah, Muhammad, and the saints. The audience often dances in accompaniment.

Henry Diltz/Corbis

In popular music, Indian film music is a genre in itself. It combines folk music with other styles, notably the *qawwali* and *ghazal* (soulful love songs). Western influences have changed music throughout India and Pakistan as musicians have come into contact with rock and pop music.

AFGHANISTAN

Afghanistan has a heritage unlike that of its other Asian neighbors. The traditional music is a result of the mingling of sounds from India, Persia, and China, and from different ethnic groups such as the Pashtuns, Uzbeks, Tadzhiks, Kazakhs, and Turkmens.

One unique instrument that makes Afghani music distinct is the *rabab*, a lute with a metal soundboard, which gives it a plangent, carrying quality. Other instruments include reed instruments and flutes: the frequently nomadic lifestyle demands instruments that are loud rather than intimate in tone, and therefore suitable for outdoor use.

The folk songs are often long, complicated tales, developed to amuse groups around campfires or in tea houses along the nomads' routes. Folk poetry has been augmented by imported music heard on the radio—a relatively recent introduction in this nation. Radio has also raised the status of musicians. Indian and Pakistani *ghazals* have been popular in recent decades as has Indian film music.

Kiliwali, which has developed as a mix of folk music and imported styles, is said to be the closest genre to a national music, but, during the civil war of the 1990s, most prominent *kiliwali* performers fled from Afghanistan.

BANGLADESH

Music in Bangladesh does not use the classical *ragas.* Its forms are much simpler; because of the national love of poetry, many musical forms provide a setting for narrative or dramatic verse. These include *kabigan,* which is a poetic contest having a simple accompaniment in which wit and topical references are keenly judged by the audience.

Jatra is a form of music theater for the predominantly rural population. It uses local religious and historical legends, and the miscellaneous musical ensemble consists of a mix of Western instruments, from saxophones to harmoniums, and brass cymbals, gongs, and drums. The entertainment can go on all night and includes musical interludes and dancing.

Ali Akbar Khan, who grew up in what is now known as Bangladesh, is a preeminent player of the *sarod,* a 25-string instrument similar to a lute. He is credited with having made the first Western recording of Indian classical music and the first televised performance of Indian music in the 1950s.

KASHMIR

The high valley of Kashmir is a distinct area of the Himalayas with its own culture. It includes parts of India, Pakistan, and China, and its musical culture has its roots partly in Iran and partly in India to the south. The two primary genres are the *Sufiana kalam,* which is a form of devotional music related to the Pakistani *qawwali,* and Kashmiri folk song. The devotional songs are accompanied by instruments bearing a distinct resemblance to those of Iran to the west, the *sehtar,* or long-necked lute, and the *santur,* a zither played with hammers.

Kashmiri folk song, on the other hand, uses instruments more akin to those of India, the bowed *sarang* (a smaller version of the *sarangi*) and a plucked *rabab* similar to the *sarod.*

MYANMAR (BURMA)

Burmese instruments are more akin to those of Southeast Asian ethnic groups than to those of India, although the subject matter of its dramatic music is tied to Indian folklore. The content typically originates in the *Ramayana* or *Mahabharata* epics. *Hsaing-waing* music has taken its name from the chief instrument of the ensemble, a set of gong-chimes that is more like a gamelan than any Indian instrument. The player sits inside a circle of tuned drums and chimes. Typical ensembles might also include oboes, additional percussive instruments, flutes, and mouth organs. Traditional Burmese orchestras use a common melody, but instrumentalists can freely improvise within this framework.

These ensembles are used for theatrical performances, at festivals, and for religious ceremonies. Contemporary recordings are commonly made by professional government-sponsored groups, playing both solo and in ensembles.

NEPAL, TIBET, AND BHUTAN

There is a common thread of culture and history linking Bhutan, Nepal, and Tibet. The religion in the high mountains is Buddhism and ceremonies typically use loud wind instruments, long shawms (double-reed instruments), trumpets, and drums. In Tibet, before the Chinese invasion in 1950, the Buddhist monks spent a large part of their lives chanting hymns and scriptures. Since the refugee monks moved to the West, this type of music has been heard and studied outside Tibet. Typically, the monks sing in unison on very deep notes but create chords by altering the resonating cavities in the mouth, which adds harmonics to the fundamental note (overtone singing).

Ritual drumming and dance are also popular. The mask dances of Bhutan, for example, typically associated with religious festivals, are performed by monks and laity. These dance and music pageants represent the Buddha in various manifestations.

In Nepal, musicians belong to two untouchable castes (groups of the lowest class in India, whom members of the four main castes were once forbidden to touch), the Damai and the Gaine. The ensembles are known as *panche baja* or *damai baja*, and use instruments such as shawms, drones, drums, and cymbals, and play for ceremonies and festivals.

SRI LANKA

Music in Sri Lanka is almost invariably associated with dance, and uses many different types of drums and conch trumpets. The dances are elaborate enactments of traditional stories with costumed mime actors. *Kandyan* ceremonies can include processions of Buddhist monks, elephants, singers, and dancers. Another popular genre is the masked devil dance, used to exorcise evil spirits. With Sri Lanka's strong orientation toward entertaining tourists, there has been an active move to preserve these traditional and colorful performances.

SOUTH ASIAN POPULAR MUSIC AND THE WEST

In South Asia, it is popular music that has been most influenced by the West, while musicians such as Ravi Shankar, Nusrat Fateh Ali Khan, and Ali Akbar Khan, introduced by pop figures such as the BEATLES and Peter Gabriel, have done much to popularize Indian music in the West.

Western influences have also been felt in South Asia. Although the musicians might be singing in Urdu or Tamil, their popular music has absorbed a range of Western musical forms, such as rock, country, blues, and disco. Nepalese and Pakistani rock music became so popular that Western-style

radio stations, like Nepal's Hits FM 100, were instituted in part to promote indigenous artists. These include Junoon and Saroor, Pakistani pop groups, and Nepal's Kandara and Om Mane Padme. Some younger Burmese musicians typically graft Burmese lyrics to Western music or choose to perform French and English songs to a Burmese beat. At the same time, an increased consciousness of their invaluable heritage has encouraged the preservation of traditional music.

Linda Dailey Paulson

SEE ALSO:

BHANGRA BEAT; GAMELAN; INDIAN FILM MUSIC; MIDDLE EAST; SOUTH EAST ASIA.

FURTHER READING

Kaufmann, Walter. *The Ragas of South India* (Bloomington, IN: Indiana University Press, 1976); Titon, Jeff Todd, ed. *Worlds of Music* (New York: Schirmer Books, 1984).

SUGGESTED LISTENING
Afghanistan, Bangladesh, Bhutan, Burma
Folk Music of Afghanistan Vols. 1 and 2; *The Garos of the Madhuphur, Hsain Waing of Myanmar, Rituals of the Drukpa Order, Songs of the Pashai.*

India
Balachander: *Veena Virtuoso*; Sheila Chandra: *Weaving My Ancestors' Voices*; Ali Akbar Khan with Asha Bhosle: *Legacy*; Ustad Nizamuddin Khan: *Tabla*; Ravi Shankar and Ali Akbar Khan: *Ragas*; Ravi Shankar: *Pandit Ravi Shankar*; Ramnad Krishnan: *Vidwan—Songs of the Carnatic Tradition*; Vadya Lahari: *South Indian Instrumental Ensemble.*

Kashmir, Nepal, Pakistan
Kashmir Traditional Songs & Dances; Singh Tara Bir: *Nepal Sitar*, *Folksongs of Nepal*; Khamisu Khan: *L'Algoza du Sind*; Nusrat Fateh Ali Khan: *The Day, the Night, the Dawn, the Dusk.*

Sri Lanka, Tibet
Singhalese Music-Singing and Drumming; *Sri Lanka: Comic Theatre and Folk Operas*; Ache Lhamo: *Tibetan Musical Theatre*; Gyuto Monks: *Tibetan Tantric Choir.*

SOUTH EAST ASIA

Since the days of Marco Polo, the West has been fascinated by the East. More recently, Western composers from Claude DEBUSSY to John CAGE have cited Asian music as having influenced their work. Although today many types of traditional music can still be heard in Asia, the last hundred years of Western influence has had a tremendous effect on music there and much of it has become Westernized. Nonetheless, the music discussed here is primarily concerned with genres that are indigenous to Asia, despite the prevalence of many diverse, multicultural genres in recent Asian music.

CHINA

Chinese instrumental and vocal music has existed for thousands of years, but the one predominant theme that runs throughout its history is its connection to culture and politics. From the very beginning, music in China, which geographically dominates central and east Asia, has been considered an instrument of government, and an important part of an ancient Chinese nobleman's education was instruction in music. In fact the Chinese government established a ministry of music (*Yuefu*) as far back as the Han Dynasty (206 B.C.–220 A.D.).

The two main elements of traditional Chinese music are melody and timbre (instrumental tone color). Harmony, as known in the West, is largely absent; instead, melodies are played in unison, and the resultant sound is colored by the rich cloud of upper harmonics that are generated by the different timbres playing simultaneously. There is an incredibly wide range of musical genres found in China, but one of the most prominent in the vast realm of Chinese art music is that of regional opera. There are several hundred types of regional Chinese opera, the most famous being Beijing opera. Beijing opera combines singing, heightened speech, mime, dance, and acrobatics. One of its most distinctive qualities is the actors' highly stylized voices, with each actor

employing a specific type of vocal style based on the role that is portrayed. Music in Beijing opera is adapted and arranged from a traditional repertoire of stock arias, and is accompanied by an orchestra primarily made up of stringed instruments, gongs, and drums. Another respected form of art music in China is that of the *qin* or *ch'in* (a seven-stringed zither) usually played by a virtuoso soloist for both ritual music and refined art music. It was associated with the teachings of Confucius.

Traditional Chinese music has changed in the last century due to the influence of Western music. After the overthrow of the last imperial dynasty in 1911, music in China enjoyed a time of interesting combinations as composers struggled to write new works using both Eastern and Western musical techniques.

However, after the Communist victory of 1949, the new government began clamping down on anything they deemed either feudal, religious, or bourgeois, including most traditional folk customs and music. Any new music was "revolutionized," and focus was taken off individuals as the composers—instead, committees of composers were credited for pieces. By the time of the Cultural Revolution (1966–76), music was so restricted that only eight state-approved operas were allowed to be performed. Since the end of the Cultural Revolution, however, the government has relaxed these sanctions somewhat and many kinds of music in China are enjoying a moderate amount of freedom, although still closely monitored by the government.

In most Chinese villages, the folk tradition has survived despite the Communist government's disapprobation. There one can hear many modern forms of traditional Chinese music from the Silk and Bamboo folk ensembles, mostly amateurs who gather in teahouses to "jam" on an eclectic mix of Eastern and Western instruments, most often Chinese fiddles, flutes, and banjos. However, the only music resembling ancient court ritual music is performed for Confucius's birthday (September 28) in non-Communist Taiwan, where there are no government restrictions on music.

Buddhist and Taoist priests also perform music for temple rituals, and in recent years some traditional genres have even been performed in concert halls and music conservatories. However, such performances are subject to government approval which continues to severely limit what it will allow to be performed in public. A concert of "classical" Chinese music today may include pieces performed on the *qin*, the *zheng* (a 16-stringed zither with movable bridges), the *sheng* (mouth organ), the *hsiao* (vertical flute) and folk and theater instruments such as the *p'ip'a* (a pear-shaped lute), the *ti* (transverse flute), and the long or conch trumpet, in combination with Western instruments such as the violin, cello, or piano.

KOREA

Korean music has formed a musical identity distinctly different from its neighbors, and it retains a characteristic triple meter not found in the traditional music of either China or Japan. Korean classical music is undeniably old, and its repertoire has evolved and developed over centuries—this may be why the music has an almost timeless and organic flavor to it. Korean traditional music can be roughly divided into two major categories, *chong-ak* (music for the ruling class) and *sog-ak* (music for the common people). *Chong-ak* consists primarily of *p'ungnyu* (a type of ensemble music), *kagok* (the most sophisticated form of Korean vocal music), and *sijo* (popular songs indigenous to North and South Korea).

Instruments used for accompaniment may include the *komungo* (a zither with six strings of twisted silk), the *kayagum* (another type of Korean zither, related to the Chinese *zheng* and the Japanese *koto*, having 12 silk strings supported by 12 movable bridges), the *taegum* (a large transverse wooden flute), the *haegum* (a two-stringed fiddle without a fingerboard), the *p'iri* (a cylindrical oboe) and the *changgo* (an hourglass drum).

Sog-ak includes shamanistic music, Buddhist music, folk songs, *nong-ak* (farmers' music), *p'ansori* (opera-like dramatic songs performed by one singer storyteller, accompanied by a drum) and *sanjo*, an instrumental solo music.

As Korea (now the countries of North and South Korea) has traditionally been an agricultural region, the farmer's life has figured greatly in its rich musical history. The most interesting characteristic of farmers' music is its 12 different rhythmic patterns called *shipich'ae*, which are led by playing a small gong. However, the most widely known Korean music is the *samulnori*, performed on drums and gongs by a quartet of musicians. The *samulnori* repertoire is based on ancient dances by farmers and the shamanistic music of rural Korea.

Tiziana and Gianni Baldizzone/Corbis

"Yellow Hat" Tibetan Buddhist monks playing conch trumpets at the Xinglong Festival in Sichuan Sheng, China.

JAPAN

Japan owes much of its musical heritage to China, whose culture came to Japan through Korea. Japan embraced Chinese court music (which became *gagaku* in Japan and is the oldest orchestral music in existence, dating back to 600 A.D.) and Buddhism, and even adopted Chinese musical theory and some of its instruments. For instance, in Japanese music the primary instruments are the *koto*, a type of zither, an example of which is indigenous to Japan while the other is derived from the Chinese *qin*; the *biwa*, a short-necked lute derived from the Chinese *p'ip'a*; the *sho*, a mouth organ developed from the Chinese *sheng*; the *hichiriki*, a small high-pitched double-reed instrument; and the *shamisen*, a fretless stringed instrument that also came from China. In addition, the chants and hymns (*shomyo*) that accompany Buddhist ritual are also derived from China. Although Japan was greatly influenced by China (and also by Korea, Manchuria, and India), its self-imposed isolation during the Edo era (1615–1868) gave Japanese culture an incubation period in which to develop its own distinctive quality. In fact, much of the music we think of as Japanese developed during this time. Solo music for the *koto* (a 13-stringed zither whose most striking feature is its wide ranging tonal leaps) and the *shakuhachi* (an end-blown bamboo flute capable of an extraordinary variety of tone colors) flourished, and the *shamisen* rose in popularity, eventually becoming the chief instrument used in both the *bunraku* (puppet drama) and the *kabuki* (popular theater) performances. The *shamisen* was also important in both instrumental and vocal music.

Gagaku court music is the oldest surviving music in Japan. *Gagaku* includes orchestral music, either with dance (*bugaku*) or without (*kangen*); court songs; and ritual music used in Shinto (religious) ceremonies. With the exception of *kangen*, *gagaku* is mostly monophonic, which means that it consists of a single melodic line without additional parts or accompaniment. It is now mainly heard only at the Imperial Court and in a few temples.

In addition to *gagaku*, theater music plays a large role in the musical heritage of Japan. The highly formalized Noh theater, with its codified gestures whose meaning is known instantly by its audience, is performed by either the main actors or a unison chorus and is accompanied by four musicians known as the *hayashi*. The *hayashi* accompany the drama with three *shamisen*, a transverse flute, and three types of drum. The drums keep a regular pulse throughout the action, and the vocal music is broken up into song and chant-like sections. Both *bunraku* puppet theater and *kabuki* (similar to Noh, but less bound by artistic conventions) developed out of the Noh tradition.

THAILAND

The Thai people have only inhabited present-day Thailand since the latter part of the 13th century. Originally, they came from southern China, and the emergence of the Thai as a culture can probably be traced to sometime during the Han Dynasty (206 B.C.–220 A.D.). The Mongol invasions of China in the tenth century forced many wealthy and cultivated Chinese to flee south into Thailand, and also resulted in the Thai migrating even further south, into Laos, northern Vietnam, northern Burma, and into what is now present day Thailand. In 1450, the Thai conquered the last of the Khmer kingdoms (the Khmer were then rulers of Cambodia and much of South East Asia) and a great deal of the highly civilized Khmer culture was also absorbed by the Thai. Traditional Thai music, therefore, is an amalgamation of the music of the cultures the Thai were in

contact with. They combined the music of China, Burma, Khmer (and through the Khmer, Indian and Javanese music) with those elements indigenous to the Thai themselves to create their unique sound.

Thai music primarily employs "polyphonic stratification," meaning that one main melody is played simultaneously with a number of versions and variants of itself. Vocalists use little or no vibrato, and often pitches other than those in the fixed tuning system are used, particularly in vocal ornaments. As Thai is a tonal language (that is, words pronounced with different pitches carry different meanings), at some time in the past vocal and instrumental sections began to be alternated because the tonal aspects of the language restricted the free melodic style more suitable to instruments.

The main ensemble in Thailand is the *pi-phat*, which includes a large array of percussion instruments made up of gongs, xylophones, metallophones, and drums, as well as the *pinai* (a type of oboe). The *pi-phat*'s repertoire is generally characterized by fairly regular repeating rhythms, and has few dynamic changes insofar as its instruments have a limited dynamic range. Consequently it can seem somewhat monotonous to the Western ear, but the beauty in this music is present in the subtle and hypnotic interaction of its simultaneous melodies constantly intermingling and interweaving.

Thai folk music is usually either text dominated (sounding more like chants than true songs and incorporating heightened speech) or melodic, generally pentatonic, and independent of stresses employed in speaking. Instrumental folk music follows the same rules as Thai art music, but is characteristic of most folk music in that it is more relaxed in its conventions.

In the late 19th to early 20th centuries, a new Thai style developed known as *thao*—meaning "a set of something in graduated sizes." Pieces in this genre are constructed in the following way. First a composer chooses an existing piece of music of about 16 measures, which he enlarges to twice its original length. He then also reduces it to half its original length. In both cases, the composer must retain the same pitches at the essential structural points, and the enlarging and condensing must be done in order to retain the style of the original. The three divisions are then played in order: extended, middle (original), and short.

INDONESIA (JAVA/BALI)

Despite successive periods of foreign influence the music of Indonesia is unique and instantly identifiable. Central to Indonesian music is the gamelan. A full gamelan can create an acoustic range as great as six or seven octaves, and the effect can be described as a shimmering cloud of sound. When French composer Claude DEBUSSY first heard a Javanese gamelan at the Paris international exhibition in 1889, it had a profound effect on him and his music, and many 20th-century composers have studied and emulated its effects in their own works.

The gamelan is an ensemble of tuned percussion consisting mainly of gongs, metallophones (instruments similar to xylophones but with bars made of bronze or iron instead of wood), and drums. A gamelan may range in size from a few instruments to over 75, but no matter what size a gamelan is, each instrument will perform one of three functions: it will either play the central melody (the *balungan*); or it will add layers of elaboration around the *balungan*; or it will punctuate or divide the melody into various independent sections. Instruments in the present-day gamelan are generally tuned to one of two scale systems: either the five-tone *slendro*, or the seven-tone *pelog*. Some gamelans are tuned entirely to *slendro*, others entirely to *pelog*, but some are actually tuned to both, combining a full set of instruments for each tuning.

In Java, music for the gamelan is much more stately and contemplative than the more fiery music that is favored in neighboring Bali. Balinese gamelan music is called *Kebyar*, meaning "like the bursting open of a flower." In both cultures, gamelan music holds great importance, and may be heard at temple ceremonies in conjunction with dance and theater, at *wayang kulit* (shadow puppet theater, whose performances often last all night) or at weddings and funerals—almost any social occasion is marked by the presence of a gamelan.

In Java, the major instruments are the *saron* (a metallophone without resonators, played with hard mallets), the *bonang* (small kettle gongs mounted in a frame), a row of different sized gongs, the two-headed drum, the metal drum, and many other types of xylophones and metallophones. Often the *rebab* (two-stringed fiddle), the *suling* (bamboo flute), and singers are also included in an ensemble. The largest Javanese gong is called the *gong ageng*, and it is the most important instrument in the gamelan. No piece of music can begin or end without it, and it is believed that the soul or spirit of the mystical gamelan resides within it.

Bali has similar instruments but they are known by different names, and they are usually played in pairs. Each instrument is tuned slightly differently from its twin, and when the pair are played together it creates a kind of "harmonic beating" that gives the Balinese gamelan its characteristic shimmering sound.

The traditional music of all these different Asian cultures is changing very fast with the spread of Western influence. However, perhaps the Western appreciation of other cultural heritages will also save the music of South East Asia in time.

Llyswen Vaughan

SEE ALSO:

GAMELAN; SOUTH ASIA.

FURTHER READING

Malm, William P. *Music Cultures of the Pacific, the Near East, and Asia* (Englewood Cliff, NJ: Prentice Hall, 1995); Titon, Jeff Todd, et al. *Worlds of Music: An Introduction to the Music of the World's Peoples* (New York: Schirmer Books, 1996).

SUGGESTED LISTENING

China

China's Instrumental Heritage; *Eleven Centuries of Traditional Music of China.*

Indonesia

Gamelan Music of Bali; *Javanese Court Gamelan*; *Traditional Music of Indonesia.*

Japan

Gagaku: Court Music of Japan; *Japanese Shinto Ritual Music*; *Japanese Traditional Music*, Vols. 1–9.

Korea

The Seoul Ensemble Traditional Music.

Thailand

Thailand: Classical Instrumental Traditions.

OTIS
SPANN

Otis Spann rose to fame as the piano player for Muddy WATERS, whose band, more than any other, defined the postwar Chicago blues sound. He went on to become as highly regarded as a solo performer as he was as an accompanist.

Spann was born on March 21, 1930, in Belzoni, Mississippi. He worked in the cotton fields at an early age, but began playing piano at age seven, later playing organ and harmonica as well. An early inspiration was a barrelhouse piano player named Friday Ford. By the time Spann had reached his mid-teens, he was performing regularly in juke joints in and around Jackson, Mississippi.

Spann served in the army from 1946 to 1951, then settled in Chicago, where he worked as a house plasterer by day and musician at night. Among the artists he played with during this period were MEMPHIS SLIM and Roosevelt Sykes.

PLAYING WITH MUDDY WATERS

Spann first recorded with legendary singer/guitarist Muddy Waters in 1952, but only joined the Muddy Waters Band as a full-time member in 1953, when he replaced singer pianist Big Maceo, whose husky singing style influenced the young newcomer. Spann remained a loyal member of the band while others, such as harmonica player LITTLE WALTER, were embarking on solo careers. Spann played on many of Waters' hits, including "I Just Want to Make Love to You" and "Hoochie Coochie Man."

As a member of Waters' band, Spann played hard-rocking, loud piano blues. Waters liked the full sound Spann's piano provided, the piano serving as a subtext to the guitar and harmonica, moving the rhythm along and embellishing the lyrics. Spann also became something of a house pianist for Chess Records, playing on hits by Howlin' Wolf, Bo DIDDLEY, and Chuck BERRY, among others.

Spann was a master accompanist. Willie DIXON once explained why as a producer he called on Spann to play so often: "He was a *good* musician. You see, a good musician knows how to make the

other fellows sound good. Otis was the type of guy who could play with anybody and play behind you enough to make you sound good. When it came his time, he would do his thing, but he would get out in time to let *you* do yours."

Spann's solo career evolved concurrently with his other work. Blues scholar Paul Oliver traced its beginning to a 1958 festival in Leeds, U.K., where Spann performed with Waters and "all but stole the show." His first solo recording was *Otis Spann Is the Blues* in 1960. That album, and others that he recorded for the Candid label, show to great effect the breadth and depth of Spann's talent.

Spann toured Europe with Muddy Waters from 1963 to 1964 with the American Folk Blues Festival. During this tour he recorded *The Blues of Otis Spann* in Great Britain. He also recorded two tracks with Yardbirds guitarist Eric Clapton: "Pretty Girls Everywhere" and "Stirs Me Up."

Spann's solo career took off when he returned to the U.S., and produced a series of albums. In his solo work he showed a preference for the slower blues, which he played in the barrelhouse style, laying down bass chords with his left hand and rolling complex, rippling phrases with his right. His singing voice was deep and soft, with hints of a shout and a slight lisp. "When he sings, his eyes are shut and his words are spun out as if he is reluctant to let them go," Oliver said.

Spann performed regularly and recorded for many labels throughout the 1960s while continuing to play with Waters. The two men remained close friends and colleagues until Spann's death from cancer on April 24, 1970, in Chicago.

Daria Labinsky

SEE ALSO:
BLUES.

FURTHER READING
Cohn, Lawrence, ed. *Nothing But the Blues: The Music and the Musicians* (New York: Abbeville Press, 1993); Rooney, James. *Bossmen: Bill Monroe and Muddy Waters* (New York: Da Capo, 1991).

SUGGESTED LISTENING
Complete Candid Recordings; *Down to Earth*; *Otis Spann Is the Blues.*

PHIL SPECTOR

Creator of the "Wall of Sound," a millionaire at the age of 21, and one of the first independent producers to generate musically and financially successful records based on a producer-driven, rather than artist-centered approach, Phil Spector firmly established the record producer as a creative artist in the 1960s.

Philip Harvey Spector was born on December 26, 1940, in New York City. His father died when he was nine and the family moved to Los Angeles. Spector was withdrawn and nondescript as a youth—nothing pointed to his future as a rock'n'roll mogul—but he did play guitar and seemed driven to find success in the music business. In 1958 he recorded a tune he had written with a high school group he called the Teddy Bears. The track was called "To Know Him Is to Love Him"—from the epitaph on his father's grave. He convinced the Los Angeles-based Dore label to release the recording and it became an instant hit.

Back in New York, Spector began networking, eventually making connections at Atlantic Records and the Brill Building (the Tin Pan Alley of rock and pop publishing), and he got backing for some of his recording projects. Working with songwriter-producers LEIBER AND STOLLER, Spector created hits for Curtis Lee and Ray Peterson, and wrote "Spanish Harlem" for Ben E. King.

With the capital from these hits, Spector financed his record label, Philles Records, and launched the careers of genre-defining artists such as the Crystals, Darlene Love, the Ronettes, and the Righteous Brothers.

Spector used orchestration and over-dubbing on a grand scale, in a process and product widely called the "Wall of Sound"—pounding rhythms, smooth strings, choral vocals, and emphatic percussion. He often mixed his recordings using transistor radio speakers rather than studio monitors, to ensure that every nuance was audible on the cheapest equipment. Spector called his records "little symphonies for the kids."

By the time the BEATLES arrived in America, Spector's popularity had already begun to wane. In 1966, he produced his best work, Ike and Tina TURNER's "River

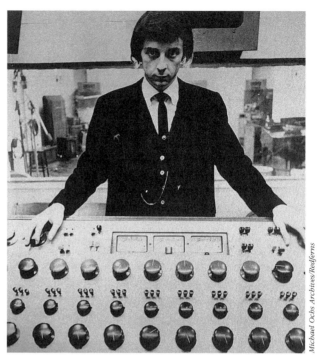

Michael Ochs Archives/Redferns

A genius at producing well-crafted and memorable pop songs, Phil Spector has left an indelible mark on music.

Deep, Mountain High." The single was an artistic success but a commercial flop, and Spector announced his retirement soon afterward. He returned briefly to work on the Beatles' *Let It Be*; and also produced John Lennon's *Imagine*. He continued to make hits, but the creative luster was all but gone.

In 1989, Spector was inducted into the Rock and Roll Hall of Fame, and that same year produced the Ramones' album *End of the Century*. Since then his involvement in the music industry has faded, but his innovative contributions to pop music and the recording process have afforded Spector a lasting place in musical history.

Gregg Juke

SEE ALSO:
POP MUSIC; PRODUCERS; ROCK MUSIC.

FURTHER READING
Ribowsky, Mark. *He's a Rebel*
(New York: Dutton, 1989).

SUGGESTED LISTENING
Phil Spector: Wall of Sound, Vols. 1–6.

BRUCE SPRINGSTEEN

Gruff-voiced singer-songwriter Bruce Springsteen, also known as "the Boss," is regarded by many as the very embodiment of blue-collar American rock. He gave the disaffected white underclass its voice, both with his 1975 single "Born to Run" and with his 1984 album *Born in the U.S.A.* Springsteen has appeared in a great many guises during a 25-year recording career. He has been a wild-eyed, leather-jacketed street punk, a socially conscious folk troubadour, a musclebound stadium rocker, and a sensitive commentator on the American experience.

Springsteen was born on September 23, 1949, in Freehold, New Jersey, about an hour's drive from New York City. Inspired by Elvis PRESLEY, he picked up the guitar as a teenager and played in bands in and around nearby Asbury Park. There he met many of the musicians who would later back him in his E. Street Band. Legendary talent scout John Hammond, whose previous finds included Bob DYLAN and Aretha FRANKLIN, signed him to Columbia Records.

Springsteen's early songs were rambling street poetry, and he was touted as a "new Dylan." His concerts were revival-like affairs, in which he told long autobiographical tales while rocking deep into the night. In 1974 critic Jon Landau saw one of these shows in Cambridge, Massachusetts, and wrote the famous line: "I have seen rock'n'roll's future—it's called Bruce Springsteen."

"BORN TO RUN"

Landau coproduced Springsteen's third album, *Born to Run* (1975), an epic collection that quickly sold a million copies. However, a lawsuit over the right to choose his producer kept Springsteen out of the studio until 1978, when he emerged (with Landau in tow) with the hard-rocking but bleak *Darkness on the Edge of Town*. That marked the beginning of a new phase, in which songs about cars and girls were replaced by songs about work, struggle, marriage, and death. *The River* (1980) mixed sad, poignant songs with sing-along rockers, and earned Springsteen his first pop hit single, "Hungry Heart."

On the brink of superstardom, he released the surprising *Nebraska* (1982), an acoustic folk album made on a portable four-track recorder and featuring sympathetic portraits of murderers and other outcasts. *Born in the U.S.A.* (1984) maintained that downcast feel while returning to a full-band rock sound. The result was a quintessential pop album that was also a perfect distillation of the anger and bitterness seething beneath the surface of Reagan-era America. The title song, about a bitter Vietnam War veteran, was one of seven singles from the album to reach the Top 10. Springsteen spent the next 18 months touring the world, spreading a gospel of populism, political engagement, and hard-rocking defiance.

Springsteen's next studio album, *Tunnel of Love* (1987), was ballad-heavy and quite different from the big rock sound of *Born in the U.S.A.* Springsteen married actress Julianne Phillips in 1985, but they were divorced soon afterward. He later married E. Street Band backup singer Patti Scialfa.

In 1993 Springsteen recorded a synthesizer-and-drum-machine ballad, "The Streets of Philadelphia," for the movie *Philadelphia*, and won an Academy Award. Then came *The Ghost of Tom Joad* (1996), his starkest album since *Nebraska*, full of modern-day sagas about economic hardship.

Matty Karas

SEE ALSO:
ROCK MUSIC; ROCK'N'ROLL.

FURTHER READING
Cavicchi, Daniel. *Tramps Like Us:*
Music and Meaning among Springsteen Fans
(New York: Oxford University Press, 1998);
Cross, Charles R. *Backstreets: Springsteen:*
The Man and His Music
(New York: Crown, 1992);
Goodman, Fred. *The Mansion on the Hill*
(New York: Times Books, 1997);
Marsh, Dave. *Born to Run*
(New York: Thunder's Mouth Press, 1996).

SUGGESTED LISTENING
Born in the U.S.A.; Born to Run;
Darkness on the Edge of Town; Nebraska;
The River; The Streets of Philadelphia; Tunnel of Love;
The Wild, the Innocent and the E. Street Shuffle.

MAX STEINER

Maximilian Raoul Steiner, "the father of Hollywood film music," was born in Vienna on May 10, 1888, and proved to be a musical prodigy. He graduated from the Academy of Music in Vienna with high honors at the age of 13, and wrote his first operetta, *The Beautiful Greek Girl,* in 1902. He studied with Gustav MAHLER and Robert Fuchs, and launched a career as a conductor before leaving for America in 1914, at the invitation of Florenz Ziegfeld. While working for Ziegfeld, Steiner also conducted Broadway operettas for George White and Victor HERBERT.

A HOLLYWOOD PIONEER

Steiner left New York for Hollywood in 1929 when sound films were beginning to be introduced. There at the start, he stands out among the film composers whose style dominated Hollywood cinema in the 1930s and 1940s, a group which includes Dimitri Tiomkin, Alfred NEWMAN, and Miklos Rozsa.

Steiner's compositional style was post-Romantic, with strong leanings toward a light, sentimental treatment. From his earliest scores he used music in the service of the film, helping to establish time, place, and mood. He treated film as if it were operetta. Music was used throughout the drama, not just at salient points, and related very closely to what was being shown on the screen. In doing so, he was following the style of music written to accompany silent films in the 1920s, and established this approach as the norm for Hollywood's sound era. Steiner was also one of the first composers to use the click-track to ensure that the film's action and music were precisely coordinated.

For more than two decades Steiner's style, and that of people who followed immediately in his wake, was imitated in Hollywood. In this style, music had considerable prominence in helping the action of a film to unfold, and it was fully incorporated into the medium. It became so natural to expect music to take great prominence in a film that when, as late as 1963, Ingmar Bergman's *The Silence* was made without any music, the result seemed startling and unsettling.

During the course of his illustrious career, Steiner's film scores won him three Academy Awards, for *The Informer* (1935), *Now, Voyager* (1942), and *Since You Went Away* (1944). The second of these scores produced a hit record for singer Dick HAYMES with the theme song "It Can't Be Wrong." Steiner was also nominated for a further 23 Oscars, among others for the scores of two of the most celebrated motion pictures in cinema history, *Gone with the Wind* (1939) and *Casablanca* (1943). Steiner's score for *Casablanca* is an effective demonstration of his characteristically emotive sound. Its rich, 19th-century orchestration adds a shimmering, dream-like quality to the film, beautifully complementing the tense and romantic action.

MEMORABLE SCORES TURNED INTO HIT TUNES

The lushly memorable central tune from *Gone with the Wind*, known as "Tara's Theme," was a hit twice over, firstly as an instrumental by Leroy Holmes and his orchestra, and then with lyrics by Mack David for singer Johnny Desmond, called "My Own True Love." His 1959 score for *A Summer Place* produced another massive hit, when Percy Faith and his orchestra recorded the theme song.

Steiner also worked in television, where one of his most familiar themes was for the long-running courtroom drama *Perry Mason.* He died in Hollywood on December 28, 1971.

Richard Trombley

SEE ALSO:

FILM MUSIC; OPERETTA.

FURTHER READING

Darby, W., and J. Dubois. *American Film Music: Major Composers, Techniques, and Trends 1915–90* (New York: Schirmer Books, 1997); Marmorstein, Gary. *A Hollywood Rhapsody: Movie Music and Its Makers 1900–75* (New York: Schirmer Books, 1997); Prendergast, Roy. *Film Music: A Neglected Art* (New York: W. W. Norton, 1977).

SUGGESTED LISTENING

Casablanca; *Gone with the Wind*; *Now Voyager: The Film Scores of Max Steiner.*

ISAAC STERN

The violinist Isaac Stern has been the primary exponent of the Russian school of violin playing in America. In recent years, he has become, as well as a devoted teacher, a tireless advocate of musical causes throughout the world.

Isaac Stern was born in Kremenets, in the Ukraine, on July 21, 1920. His family emigrated to America in 1921, a year after his birth. They settled in San Francisco, and at eight years of age, Stern was brought to Louis Persinger for violin lessons. Persinger was the concertmaster of the San Francisco Symphony and taught Yehudi MENUHIN. He stayed only a short while with Persinger, however, and continued lessons from 1932 to 1937 with Persinger's successor as concertmaster, Naoum Blinder, a violinist who had been trained in the Russian school of violin.

Stern made his orchestral debut at the age of 15, with the San Francisco Symphony under the baton of Pierre MONTEUX, playing Bach's Double Violin Concerto with his teacher. A year later, he was the soloist in the same orchestra's performance of Brahms's Violin Concerto, broadcast nationally on the radio. His first New York recital came in 1939, and he was immediately signed by Columbia Artists. During World War II, he gave recitals for the Allied troops from the South Pacific to Iceland.

DEBUT IN EUROPE

Stern played in Europe in 1948 at the Lucerne Festival, and at the CASALS Festival in Puerto Rico in 1950 and in 1953, where he formed a trio with pianist Eugene Istomin and cellist Leonard Rose. During the early days of the Soviet/American artists' exchange, he toured the Soviet Union, where he played duets with David Oistrakh. Those who heard this concert were amazed at how well these violinists blended with each other. Trained on opposite sides of the globe, they were nevertheless from the same tradition.

In Israel, Stern not only gave concerts, but was also active in founding the Jerusalem Music Center, which fostered the careers of violinists Itzhak Perlman, Pinchas Zukerman, and Schlomo Mintz, among others. In 1960, when New York's Carnegie Hall was threatened with demolition, Stern led the crusade that ultimately saved and renovated the venerable concert hall. In 1964, President Lyndon Johnson appointed him as advisory member of the new National Endowment for the Arts, and Stern performed at the White House on several occasions.

FILM FAME

Among the composers whose works were premiered by Isaac Stern were George Rochberg, Krzysztof PENDERECKI, and Leonard BERNSTEIN. In 1981, the film *From Mao to Mozart*, which chronicled Stern's tour of China, won the Academy Award for best full-length documentary. Stern's playing can also be heard in the sound track of the film *Tonight We Sing* (1953), in which he played the legendary virtuoso violinist Eugène Ysaÿe. The film *A Journey to Jerusalem* (1967) records his performance of the Mendelssohn Violin Concerto with the Israel Philharmonic Orchestra under Bernstein after the Six Days War, and he can also be heard in the motion picture version of the musical *Fiddler on the Roof* (1971).

Stern played violins made by the 18th-century Italian violin-maker, Guarneri "del Gesù," one of which was Ysaÿe's own instrument.

In the early 1990s, Stern sponsored music workshops for talented young players in New York that culminated in Carnegie Hall concerts.

More than 50 years of Isaac Stern's performances have been documented on recordings. The most recent, in 1994, was of classical chamber music with the trio of Emanuel Ax, Jaime Laredo, and Yo-Yo Ma.

Jane Prendergast

SEE ALSO:
CHAMBER MUSIC; ORCHESTRAL MUSIC.

FURTHER READING

Roth, Henry. *Great Violinists in Performance* (Los Angeles, CA: Panjandrum Books, 1986); Schwartz, Boris. *Great Masters of the Violin* (New York: Simon and Schuster, 1983).

SUGGESTED LISTENING

Bartók: Sonatas for violin and pianoforte; Beethoven: Piano trios; Berg: Violin Concerto; Brahms: Violin Concerto.

STING

Sting, rock singer and bass guitarist, was the founder and focus of the Police, a British band that blended rock and reggae to create a classic style of pop music. On going solo, Sting changed direction to produce a series of jazzy albums that created a genre of intelligent adult rock music.

Sting, who was born Gordon Sumner on October 2, 1951, in Wallsend, England, was formerly a school teacher and began his musical life as a jazz-rock musician in the early 1970s. (He became known as "Sting" because of the bee-like black-and-gold hooped jersey that he wore.)

In 1977, he formed the Police—a trio in which he was vocalist and songwriter—with guitarist Andy Summers (b. December 1942), and innovative U.S. drummer Stewart Copeland (b. July 1952). The group had a number of hit singles, and their albums *Outlandos D'Amour* (1978), and *Regatta de Blanc* (1979) are two of the most enjoyably original of the era. The album *Zenyatta Mondatta* (1980) was their breakthrough in the U.S. and in the rest of the world.

Sting starred in a television film in 1982, *Brimstone and Treacle*, and one of its songs, "Spread a Little Happiness," was released and became a Top 20 hit.

In 1983, their album *Synchronicity* became No. 1 in the U.S., and, as always, it was dominated by Sting's distinctly high yet rough voice and lyrical imagery. That year, however, disillusioned with life in a rock band, Sting decided to go solo.

ON HIS OWN AND SEEKING SOMETHING NEW

Sting had always appeared coolly detached in contrast to his often soul-searching lyrics, and his solo albums, starting with *The Dream of the Blue Turtles* in 1985, further developed that image.

Sting moved into a swinging, jazzy mode, introducing an up-tempo rock beat to his music. The album's opening track, "If You Love Somebody, Set Them Free," was a declaration of independence from his rock-star image. It was an impressive debut album, and made the Top 3 in both the U.S. and Britain. He then made a documentary and album, *Bring on the Night*. The documentary showed his

girlfriend giving birth to their child. His next album, *Nothing Like the Sun* (1987), featured the sublime "Englishman in New York," and Latin-tinged numbers such as "They Dance Alone," and "Fragile," which emphasized Sting's concern for the victims of repression in Argentina. Sting assembled an impressive line-up of stars for the album, including Mark Knopfler of DIRE STRAITS, Eric Clapton, and Miles DAVIS's arranger Gil Evans.

The Soul Cages (1991) and *Ten Summoner's Tales* (1993), with hit singles "If I Ever Lose My Faith in You," and "Fields of Gold," demonstrated Sting's continuing appeal. *Mercury Falling* (1996), featuring the haunting "The Hounds of Winter," and "La Belle Dame Sans Regrets," consolidated his reputation.

ENVIRONMENTAL ACTIVIST

Sting's interest in Amnesty International influenced many of his lyrics, and he has toured with Bruce SPRINGSTEEN, Peter Gabriel, and Tracy Chapman to support the cause of human rights.

From 1988 to 1990, through his Rainforest Foundation, he accompanied a tribal chief on a publicity tour and successfully highlighted the plight of the Brazilian Indians.

A serious thinker and campaigner on conservationist issues, Sting's literate music and consistent preference for subtlety over screeching guitars made him one of the few solo artists to have successfully found new directions in rock music.

Graham McColl

SEE ALSO:
NEW WAVE; REGGAE; ROCK MUSIC.

FURTHER READING
Nikart, Ray. *Sting and The Police* (New York: Ballantine Books, 1985); Sellers, Robert. *Sting: A Biography* (New York: Omnibus Press, 1989).

SUGGESTED LISTENING
The Dream of the Blue Turtles;
Fields of Gold: The Best of Sting;
Ten Summoner's Tales;
The Police: *Every Breath You Take—The Singles*;
Regatta de Blanc.

KARLHEINZ
STOCKHAUSEN

The work of Karlheinz Stockhausen has been a seminal influence on music and composition in the latter half of the 20th century. Starting from the strict application of the rules of SERIALISM, he pioneered and developed electronic music, continuing into aleatory music, intuitive music (folk music or other indigenous music that is not taught formally), and collective composition (compositions written by two or more composers in collaboration). His work has always been at the forefront of the avant-garde.

Stockhausen was born in Mödrath, Germany, on August 22, 1928. His father was a schoolteacher and his mother a housewife and amateur musician. Recurring mental health problems forced her to seek treatment in a sanatorium in 1932, where she remained until she was murdered in 1942 as part of the Nazi government's policy of killing the mentally ill. His father also died during World War II.

Stockhausen first went to school in Altenberg, where he learned piano, violin, and oboe. In his later school years in Cologne, from 1944 to 1947, he took various jobs to earn money, working as a farmhand and a stretcher bearer during the difficult postwar years in Germany. In the evenings he pursued his musical career—as a rehearsal pianist for an operetta society, of which he became the director in 1947.

That year he started a four-year course at the Hochschule für Musik at Cologne, where he majored in piano under Hans-Otto Schmidt-Neuhaus. He also studied musical form and composition. At the same time, he attended Cologne University, studying musicology and philosophy.

EARLY BROADCAST

At music school, Stockhausen studied the works of major contemporary composers, principally BARTÓK, SCHOENBERG, and STRAVINSKY. His graduation thesis was on Bartók's Sonata for two pianos and percussion. This came to the attention of Herbert Eimert at Cologne Radio, who arranged for a radio script to be made of the thesis, and for Stockhausen's work to be broadcast to the radio audience. Eimert also arranged for the

23-year-old Stockhausen to give several talks on radio on the subject of mid 20th-century music. In 1951, Stockhausen attended the Darmstadt summer school, which was a center for avant-garde composition. There he became familiar with Anton WEBERN's serial compositional techniques, and encountered the work of Olivier MESSIAEN. In this period in the history of serialism, composers had begun to experiment with serial treatment of musical elements other than pitches.

Kreuzspiel (1951) for wind, piano, and percussion, was written as a direct result of this first encounter with serialism, and was regarded by Stockhausen as his first serious work. In *Kreuzspiel,* durations of one to 12 multiples of a fundamental unit are assigned to various pitch classes and permuted throughout the piece. The influence of Stockhausen's part-time job as a jazz pianist can also be heard in this work, where the various instruments have solo "breaks" in the style of a jazz band.

After marrying his college girlfriend, Doris Andreae, Stockhausen took off for Paris to study with Messiaen for 14 months. It was in Paris that he had his first contact with electronic music, in the French radio studio for *musique concrète.*

In the compositions that he wrote in Paris, Stockhausen was already expanding the boundaries of serialism, and gradually working toward the idea of replacing the single notes of serial composition with a larger unit of a number of interrelated notes (the group). In his chamber piece for ten instruments, *Kontrapunkte* (1952, his first published work), Stockhausen used groups and also extended the idea of serialism to include the tempos of the piece, making a series out of the metronome markings 120, 126, 132, 152, 168, 184, and 200.

FIRST ELECTRONIC PIECES

On his return to Cologne, Stockhausen was invited by Eimert to work in the newly established West German Radio recording studio for electronic music, of which Eimert was director. He started work on his revolutionary piece *Studie I,* which used only sounds produced by the sine-wave generator. This was followed by the equally innovative *Studie II.*

From 1953 to 1956, Stockhausen studied phonetics and communications theory at the University of Bonn, and became increasingly interested in the part played by the performers and the audience in music. This interest led to the second set of *Klavierstücke* (piano pieces), which gave the performer considerable freedom of interpretation. His woodwind quintet, *Zeitmasze* (1956), bases its tempos on the longest and shortest time the performers can sustain a note.

In *Gesang der Jünglinge* Stockhausen introduced to his work two new elements: the human voice and the idea of physical space as a musical component. The piece is composed of electronic sounds mixed with the voice of a choirboy singing the *Benedicite*, and is played through five groups of loudspeakers so that the sound issues from different directions at different moments. He experimented during this period with the relation between audience and performers, surrounding the former with three orchestras in *Gruppen* (1957).

Another musical element that Stockhausen subjected to permutation was that of the order of sections within a suite. *Klavierstück XI* (1956) is a suite of pieces that the pianist can play in any order. Three repetitions of any single section ends a performance of *Klavierstück IX*, in which the player may choose any of six designated tempi, dynamic intensity, and stroke articulation.

TEACHING COMPOSITION AT DARMSTADT

In the summer of 1957, Stockhausen returned to Darmstadt to teach composition for the first time. Over the years that he taught at Darmstadt, he gradually evolved a technique of collective composition with his students that was to be reflected in the direction of his own music. An early test piece that he wrote at Darmstadt for percussion players is *Zyklus*, in which the player is surrounded by his instruments. He begins on one instrument at any page of the score, which is bound in a spiral notebook, and completes the work in sequence while completing the physical circle of instruments.

THE CONCEPT OF MOMENTS

Stockhausen also conceived the idea that a piece of music is composed of experiential "moments," each of which has an equal claim to the listener's attention. This was the basis of *Kontakte* (1960), which had two versions, one purely electronic, and one in which electronic sounds were combined with piano and percussion. This was followed by *Momente* (1961), in which a soprano voice, four choral groups, and 13 instruments are used to produce a succession of "moments." The structure is so free that additional moments can be added or the original ones dropped, without noticeable effect on the piece.

An essential element in Stockhausen's development has been working with live performers while composition is in progress. This started at Darmstadt, and continued when he established his own group in 1964. This group performed the live-electronic piece *Mikrophonie I* in December 1964, in Brussels. Other pieces followed, including the two-hour *Hymnen* (1966), in which melodies are enhanced by "found sounds" produced by both concrete and electronic means.

MAGIC AND MANTRA

In the 1960s, Stockhausen became increasingly interested in magic, ritual, and the religion of the East. In the vocal piece *Stimmung* (1968), the six performers sit cross-legged in a ritualistic circle. In *Mantra* (1970), he mixed two pianos, two woodblocks, and crotales (finger cymbals) with two sine-wave oscillators—here each note of the chromatic scale produced on one oscillator is mixed with the held pitch on the other oscillator. The effect is hypnotic—similar to that of a mantra chanted in meditation.

In the 1970s, Stockhausen's music became more explicitly theatrical, including works such as *Inori* (1974), and *Sirius* (1977). The same year, he started on a seven opera series, *Licht*, which was designed to fill seven consecutive evenings. The work began with *Donnerstag* (1980), and continued through the days of the week with *Samstag* (1984), and *Montag* (1988), and used combinations of dancers, an actor, chorus, and conventional instruments with or without electronic tape. He continues to be a pioneer, generating excitement through his own charisma and the conviction and drama of his works.

Jane Prendergast

SEE ALSO:
ALEATORY MUSIC; DARMSTADT SCHOOL; ELECTRONIC MUSIC.

FURTHER READING
Kurtz, Michael, trans. Richard Toop. *Stockhausen: A Biography* (Boston, MA: Faber and Faber, 1992); Maconie, Robin. *The Works of Karlheinz Stockhausen* (New York: Oxford University Press, 1990).

SUGGESTED LISTENING
Atmen gibt das Leben;
Aus den Sieben Tagen; *Kontakte*;
Licht: Donnerstag; *Mantra*; *Zyklus*.

LEOPOLD STOKOWSKI

For many, Leopold Stokowski was the quintessential conductor, thanks mostly to his appearance in Disney's film *Fantasia*. He was a master of orchestral sound, and under his leadership the Philadelphia Orchestra became one of the finest in the world. Stokowski was also a champion of many contemporary composers and took a keen interest in the emerging technologies of music recording and filmmaking.

Stokowski was born in London, England, on April 18, 1882, to an Irish mother and a Polish father. He studied piano and organ at the Royal College of Music from the age of 13, becoming the youngest student ever to have been accepted. At 20, he was appointed organist and choirmaster at St. James's Church in London's Piccadilly, and the following year took a degree in music from Oxford University. In 1905, the Rev. Leighton Parks of the prestigious St. Bartholomew's Church in New York heard him play and hired him as organist on the spot.

Stokowski made influential friends at the church, among them prominent musicians including pianist Olga Samaroff, whom he married in 1911. He became conductor of the Cincinnati Symphony Orchestra in 1909, despite his lack of symphonic experience.

After three successful years in Cincinnati, Stokowski left in 1912 to go to the Philadelphia Orchestra, where he remained for the next 25 years. Under Stokowski, the orchestra developed a lush sound. Among his innovations were free bowing, doubling the brass to avoid breathing breaks, and experiments with different seating for members of the orchestra. He gave American premieres of many pieces, including MAHLER's Symphony No. 8 and the equally massive *Gurrelieder* by Arnold SCHOENBERG. During his Phildelphia years, Stokowski made many controversial transcriptions of music by Bach and other composers for modern orchestra. He also premiered works by composers such as VARÈSE.

Stokowski began recording with the orchestra in 1917, studying electronics in order to improve the sound. In 1937, he starred as a conductor in the film *100 Men and a Girl*, and in 1939 Walt Disney proposed collaborating on *Fantasia*, in which Disney animations were set to works conducted by Stokowski, including STRAVINSKY's *Rite of Spring* and Mussorgsky's *Night on the Bald Mountain*.

Stokowski went on to found several orchestras, including the All-American Youth Orchestra, the New York Symphony Orchestra, and the American Symphony Orchestra, among others. He continued working and conducting until his death in a recording studio on September 13, 1977, at the age of 95.

Jane Prendergast

SEE ALSO:
FILM MUSIC; ORCHESTRAL MUSIC.

Corbis-Bettmann

Quintessential conductor, Leopold Stokowski, cuts an imposing figure while conducting his orchestra.

FURTHER READING
Chasins, Abram. *Leopold Stokowski: A Profile* (New York: Da Capo Press, 1979);
Daniel, Oliver. *Stokowski: A Counterpoint of View* (New York: Dodd, Mead, 1982).

SUGGESTED LISTENING
Bach: Toccata and Fugue in D minor;
Beethoven: Symphonies Nos. 5 and 7;
Debussy: *La mer*;
Mendelssohn: *A Midsummer Night's Dream*;
Schoenberg: *Gurrelieder*.

RICHARD STRAUSS

Richard Strauss, creator of some of the greatest tone poems and operas ever written, combined in his long life a career as a prolific composer with the punishing schedule of the conductor and musical director of some of Europe's major orchestras and opera houses.

Strauss was born in Munich on June 11, 1864. His father played the horn in the Munich Court Orchestra, and Richard started piano and violin lessons at an early age. He also studied composition, and from the age of 13 was allowed to sit at the back of his father's own semi-professional orchestra and play along with the violins. He started composing at an early age, and many of his youthful compositions were performed in Munich as they were written.

In 1883 he became assistant conductor to the Meiningen Orchestra, directed by Hans von Bülow. Strauss became its chief conductor in 1885, by which time his Symphony in F Minor had been performed for the first time in the U.S.

THE TONE POEMS

In 1886, Strauss became one of the conductors of the Munich Opera, and three years later he went to the Weimar Opera as assistant conductor. It was in Weimar that he conducted the first performance of his tone poem, *Don Juan* (1889).

The symphonic poem—or tone poem as Strauss preferred to call it—was a genre made popular by Liszt. It is a symphonic piece of music based on a poetic idea. Strauss's tone poems became the culmination of the genre, and in their time were regarded as the forefront of modernist music. *Macbeth* and *Don Juan* were quickly followed by *Tod und Verklärung* (1889–90).

Performances of Strauss's early tone poems brought him celebrity. In 1894 he took over from von Bülow as conductor of the Berlin Philharmonic. In the next few years he composed some of his greatest tone poems, *Till Eulenspiegels lustige Streiche* (1895) and *Ein Heldenleben* (1899). *Also sprach Zarathustra* (1896), inspired by a poem by Nietzsche, was to become familiar to a wide audience over half a century later, when it was used as part of the theme music for the science fiction film *2001: A Space Odysssey*.

THE OPERAS

At the end of the 19th century, Strauss also began writing opera. Neither *Guntram* (1892) nor *Feuersnot* (1901) was particularly well received. But the electrifying *Salome* (1905), which was based on a play by the notorious Oscar Wilde, created a sensation. An erotic drama was matched with atmospheric, sensual music, to present the story of the young priestess infatuated with John the Baptist. *Salome* was followed by *Elektra* in 1909, another dark drama based on Sophocles' great ancient tragedy. Then, in 1911, Strauss surprised his audiences yet again with a complete contrast—the sparkling *Der Rosenkavalier*, a heavily ironic romantic opera set in 18th-century Vienna.

As a conductor, Strauss moved to the Berlin Opera in 1898, remaining there until 1918, and then went to the Vienna State Opera (1919–24). His reputation rests mainly on his magnificent tone poems, operas, and songs but he wrote other works, including *Burleske* for piano and orchestra (1886), *Metamorphosen*, for 23 strings (1945), two French horn concertos (1882–83 and 1942), an oboe concerto (1945–46), and a serenade for 13 wind instruments (1881–82). For most of World War II, Strauss lived quietly in Bavaria, where he died on September 8, 1949.

Richard Trombley

SEE ALSO:

LATE ROMANTICISM; OPERA; ORCHESTRAL MUSIC.

FURTHER READING

Gilliam, Bryan. *Richard Strauss and his World* (Princeton, NJ: Princeton University Press, 1992); Kennedy, Michael. *Richard Strauss* (New York: Schirmer Books, 1996).

SUGGESTED LISTENING

Also sprach Zarathustra;
Concerto for Oboe;
Don Quixote; *Four Last Songs*;
Ein Heldenleben;
Metamorphosen;
Der Rosenkavalier; *Salome*;
Till Eulenspiegels lustige Streiche.

IGOR
STRAVINSKY

Igor Stravinsky is one of the greatest and most cosmopolitan figures in 20th-century music. During his long life, his music underwent several profound changes, and his influence on other composers, as well as on artists and choreographers, has been enormous.

Stravinsky was Russian by birth. He was born at Oranienbaum, not far from St. Petersburg, on June 17, 1882. His father, Fyodor, was principal bass singer in the Imperial Opera House in St. Petersburg, and the family lived in an apartment near the canal, which was also convenient for the theater. Stravinsky was the third of four sons. The children were often taken to the opera and ballet, and they also heard their father rehearsing his roles at home. At the age of 11, at a gala opera performance, Stravinsky glimpsed Tchaikovsky only weeks before the famous composer died.

Stravinsky went to school in St. Petersburg, where he started taking piano lessons. This led to later lessons in harmony and counterpoint, and as a teenager Stravinsky became interested in improvisation and composition. After leaving school he studied law at St. Petersburg University, but his heart was never in it. He disovered that the composer Nicolai Rimsky-Korsakov was the father of a fellow-student, and this led to a meeting with the composer, who took an interest in the young musician and agreed to supervise his musical studies. Stravinsky continued his law studies, graduating in 1905. At the same time he was starting to compose, and received invaluable advice and instruction in orchestration from Rimsky-Korsakov. Early in 1906 he married his cousin, Katerina Nossenko.

Stravinsky started composing in earnest, always discussing his work with Rimsky-Korsakov. His Symphony in E flat was performed in private in 1907. Two other early works, the *Scherzo fantastique*, and a dazzling orchestral piece called *Feu d'artifice* or *Fireworks*, were performed at a concert in St. Petersburg and heard by the impresario Sergey Diaghilev. Diaghilev formed his Russian Ballet company, which he was planning to take to France.

"THE FIREBIRD" AND THE BALLETS RUSSES
Diaghilev commissioned Stravinsky to compose a score for his new ballet, *The Firebird*. Stravinsky wrote the music in 1909 and the ballet was staged in Paris in May 1910. It was an immediate success and made the composer famous. In Paris, Stravinsky was surrounded by a galaxy of brilliant dancers, choreographers, artists, and designers. Other composers

Igor Stravinsky at the age of 76, conducting a rehearsal of his work in London in 1958.

active in Paris at the time included Claude DEBUSSY and Maurice RAVEL. It now seemed that Stravinsky's future lay in Paris with Diaghilev's ballet company, so he brought over his wife and children to be with him.

Stravinsky wrote three major ballet scores for Diaghilev at this time, and they remain his most famous and popular works. *The Firebird* itself was inspired by a Russian fairy tale about a fabulous bird which helps the dashing Prince Ivan destroy the kingdom of the evil King Kastchei and rescue a bevy of beautiful maidens. Stravinsky's exciting score still retains much Romantic feeling, though parts of it, notably "King Kastchei's Infernal Dance," strike a highly original note. The music is best known today as an orchestral suite.

Petrushka followed in 1911. Set in a fairground in old St. Petersburg, it centers around the figure of a puppet, Petrushka, who is tormented by his love for a doll and jealous of his puppet rival. Stravinsky's music for *Petrushka* was advanced compared to anything he had written so far; his innovative harmonies and striking instrumental effects announcing the arrival of a brilliant new composer.

"THE RITE OF SPRING"
Then, on May 29, 1913, came the premiere, at the Théâtre des Champs Elysées in Paris, of *The Rite of Spring* (known in French as *Le sacre du printemps*). The setting is the sudden and quite violent arrival of spring in Russia as the composer remembered it, with the ice cracking in the rivers and lakes, and with deep stirrings in the frozen ground. The action centers on Stravinsky's interpretation of the pagan rites and the sacrifice of a young virgin girl connected with the coming of spring. Nothing like either the dancing or the music had ever been seen or heard before. It was the music, especially, with its relentless, explosive rhythms and its shattering harmonies, that provoked the notorious riot in the audience. Years later, the usually matter-of-fact Stravinsky spoke quite mystically about the music. "I heard, and I wrote down what I heard," he said. "I was the vessel through which *Le Sacre* passed." It certainly made him the most notorious composer living and *The Rite of Spring* is regarded as the major work that set 20th-century music ablaze.

World War I, for its duration, put an end to the extravagant productions of Diaghilev's Ballets Russes, and Stravinsky, now living in Switzerland, turned to more modest projects. His witty stage piece, *The Soldier's Tale*, dating from these war years, also heralded the neoclassical postwar period.

NEOCLASSICISM
Neoclassicism was a reaction against the prewar music of such composers as Gustav MAHLER, heavy with emotion and written on a large and complex scale. It was also a reaction to the horrors of the war itself. Stravinsky returned to Paris in 1920, where he shared the generally spare, sometimes satirical, sometimes jazz-inspired spirit of the period with Ravel and the young group of French composers known as "Les Six." His new ballet score for Diaghilev, *Pulcinella,* was based on music by Giovanni Pergolesi and other 18th-century composers, and therefore was almost literally neoclassical in content and style. His Octet for wind instruments (1923) is a fine and disciplined piece of chamber music. The opera-oratorio *Oedipus Rex* (1927), with a libretto by the French writer Jean Cocteau, taken from the classical Greek drama by Sophocles, is stark and severe.

At about this time, Stravinsky underwent a spiritual crisis and rejoined the Russian Orthodox Church. This had an inevitable effect on his music. The Orthodox church retains a traditional and solemn chant directly linked to the Gregorian chant of early Christianity. This can be traced in Stravinsky's sacred choral works of 1926–34.

THE AMERICAN YEARS
During the 1920s and 1930s Stravinsky began forging links with the United States. He wrote his *Symphony of Psalms* as part of the 1930 celebrations for the 50th anniversary of the Boston Symphony Orchestra. This is a setting of three Biblical psalms for chorus and orchestra, and the music manages to sound both marvellously archaic and modern at the same time. He made several tours of the U.S. at this time, conducting his own works.

The late 1930s were a tragic period for Stravinsky, as an outbreak of tuberculosis killed his mother, his wife, and his elder daughter. The shock caused by these tragedies meant that he felt he no longer had any ties with Europe, and in 1939, on the eve of World War II, Stravinsky sailed for America.

The first event of his American years was a series of lectures in 1939 at Harvard University on the poetics of music, later published as *Poétique*

Musicale. He later settled in Hollywood and was married again in 1940 to Vera de Bosset, whom he had met in Paris. He and his new wife then applied for American citizenship. One of the first important works of this time was the Symphony in C (1940), written to mark the 50th anniversary of the Chicago Symphony Orchestra. Stravinsky followed this in 1945 with the *Symphony in Three Movements*, a powerful work with echoes of *The Rite of Spring*; and with his *Ebony Concerto*, written for the jazz clarinetist Woody Herman.

Stravinsky returned to the neoclassical mode with a masterly opera, *The Rake's Progress* (1951), inspired by the paintings of the 18th-century English artist William Hogarth, which Stravinsky had seen in the Chicago Art Institute. The story, which describes the career of a debauched aristocrat who gambles and drinks his way to eventual madness, gave the composer scope for imitating other works, echoing 18th-century sources, and dramatic action. The libretto was written by the poet W. H. Auden. This was Stravinsky's first long operatic score, and he took three years to complete the composition. It had its first performance in Venice in 1951, at the International Festival of Contemporary Music, and has been a popular part of the operatic repertoire ever since. This work can be seen as the culmination of Stravinsky's neoclassical period. While the opera is constructed in a formal framework, the music is exuberant and emotionally expressive.

FLIRTATION WITH SERIALISM

In 1948, Stravinsky met the younger American conductor and scholar Robert Craft, who was to become his assistant and eventual biographer. This association opened up yet another new chapter in Stravinsky's creative life. Craft encouraged him to start composing in the 12-tone or serial style of SCHOENBERG, who was his neighbor in Hollywood. The ballet *Agon* (1957) is one of the major works of this serialist period. Craft also collaborated with Stravinsky in the production of several books, created as interviews with the composer and including parts of his correspondence over the years.

In 1953, Stravinsky met the Welsh poet Dylan Thomas, who was giving a series of poetry readings in America. Stravinsky was impresssed with Thomas's poetry and planned to ask him for a libretto for an opera. Thomas died in New York before the project could get off the ground, and instead Stravinsky composed an elegy, *In Memoriam Dylan Thomas* (1954), which included a setting to music of Thomas's poem, "Do not go gentle into that good night."

Stravinsky was now busy conducting and recording for posterity much of his own music. In 1962, at age 80, he was a guest at the White House, and then paid a long overdue and triumphant return visit to the Soviet Union. He gave three concerts in Moscow and two in Leningrad, and he, de Bosset and Craft were received by Khrushchev in the Kremlin.

Stravinsky died in New York City on April 6, 1971. He was buried, according to his wishes, on the island cemetery of San Michele, near Venice, close to the grave of Diaghilev, the man who first recognized his genius so many years before. Stravinsky's amazing creative journey, from the Late Romantic glitter of *The Firebird* to the austerity of his final compositions, took in every important aspect of 20th-century music over 60 years.

He has been compared with his close contemporary, the artist Pablo Picasso. Both had the chameleon-like ability to adapt their style to changing times while remaining completely themselves. Stravinsky's music, for instance, is always instantly recognizable from its nervous, restless rhythms and its astringent harmonies.

Richard Trombley

SEE ALSO:

BALLET AND MODERN DANCE MUSIC; CHAMBER MUSIC; OPERA; ORCHESTRAL MUSIC; SERIALISM; SIX, LES; VOCAL AND CHORAL MUSIC.

FURTHER READING

Griffiths, Paul. *Stravinsky* (New York: Schirmer Books, 1993); White, Eric Walter. *Stravinsky: A Critical Survey 1882–1946* (Mineola, NY: Dover, 1997).

SUGGESTED LISTENING

Firebird Suite; *Les Noces*; *Petrushka*; *Pulcinella Suite*; *The Rite of Spring*; *Symphony of Psalms*; *Violin Concerto*.

BARBRA STREISAND

Barbra Streisand, singer, songwriter, actress, and movie producer and director, has been one of the most popular and influential entertainers of the late 20th century. Barbara Joan Streisand, born on April 24, 1942, began her musical career at an early age. When someone said her last name sounded "too Jewish," she changed the spelling of her first name.

In 1961, Streisand landed her first job as a Greenwich Village nightclub singer. Then, while headlining at the Blue Angel, she was discovered by Broadway producer David Merrick. He immediately signed her for a supporting role in the musical comedy *I Can Get It for You Wholesale*, which opened in March 1962. Her performance in that show brought her a recording contract with Columbia Records, and her first release, *The Barbra Streisand Album*, became 1963's top-selling album by a female performer. Her second and third albums also both sold very well. By the mid-1960s she had won three Grammy Awards for the best female pop vocalist.

Throughout the decade, she continued her rise to superstardom with national television guest appearances, recordings, Broadway musicals, and eventually films. She opened on Broadway in March 1964 in *Funny Girl*, a musical comedy based on the life of Fanny Brice, and in 1968 she starred in the film version, for which she won her first Oscar. She played the lead in the film version of *Hello Dolly!* which was released in 1969, and in the same year she received an honorary Tony Award as "star of the decade" for her stage work. In the 1970s, Streisand moved more toward film work and recording. Her biggest success was the film *The Way We Were*, the title song from which became her first movie hit. In 1976 she won her second Oscar for the song "Evergreen," from the film *A Star Is Born*.

Streisand continued her dual careers in both the 1980s and the 1990s, releasing movies such as *Yentl*, accompanied by a platinum soundtrack, and the late 1985 album *The Broadway Album*, a collection of songs from Broadway musicals, which won the 1986 Grammy Award for best pop vocal performance.

Although Barbra Streisand rarely performed on the concert stage, few could equal her there.

Throughout her musical career, Streisand has demonstrated mastery of a variety of singing styles. This diversity and her striking vocal technique, with its highly individual use of timbre and vibrato, mark her as one of the outstanding interpreters of popular songs. While Streisand continued her dual acting and singing careers throughout the 1990s, she still shied away from live performances except for very rare or special occasions, such as the 1992 Inauguration of President Bill Clinton.

Judi Gerber

SEE ALSO:
FILM MUSICALS; POPULAR MUSIC.

FURTHER READING
Edwards, Ann. *Streisand: A Biography*
(New York: Little, Brown, 1997);
Spada, James. *Streisand: Her Life*
(New York: Crown Publishers, 1995).

SUGGESTED LISTENING
A Star Is Born;
The Barbra Streisand Album;
The Broadway Album;
Color Me Barbra; *Funny Girl*;
Guilty (with Barry Gibb); *My Name Is Barbra*;
People; *Stoney End*;
The Way We Were; *Yentl*.

CHARLES STROUSE

Charles Strouse is one of the most popular and prolific composers in the American musical theater. His hit musical *Annie* ranks as one of the most loved shows of all time. In his four-decade career, Strouse has written the music for some of Broadway's most successful musicals, including *Bye Bye Birdie*, *Golden Boy*, and *Applause*. According to *New York* magazine theater critic John Simon, Strouse is "a master of songs whose tunefulness is unfussy, endearing, and, once properly heard, unforgettable. And always different."

Born in New York City on June 7, 1928, Strouse studied classical music at the Eastman School of Music in Rochester, New York. Later, he was a pupil of Aaron COPLAND at Tanglewood in Massachusetts, and wrote several pieces for the concert hall, including a string quartet and a symphonic work titled *What Have We to Sing About?*

In the early 1950s, Strouse and the lyricist Lee Adams began contributing songs for off-Broadway revues such as *Shoestring Revue*, *Shoestring '57*, *Kaleidoscope*, and *Catch a Star*, and in 1958, he wrote the pop hit "Born Too Late." *Bye Bye Birdie*, produced in 1960, was Strouse and Adams's first Broadway hit, and was the first Broadway show about the rock'n'roll craze that was sweeping the country at that time. The story was loosely based on Elvis PRESLEY's career, in that the Birdie of the title is a rock singer whose career is about to break when he is drafted into the army. Starring Dick Van Dyke and Chita Rivera, the Tony-award-winning show yielded several memorable songs, including "Put on a Happy Face," "Kids," and "A Lot of Livin' to Do."

Bye Bye Birdie was filmed in 1963 with Van Dyke and Ann-Margret, and was produced for television in an acclaimed 1995 production starring Jason Alexander of *Seinfeld*. (The TV show won Strouse and Adams an Emmy for the song "Let's Settle Down.") Strouse followed *Birdie*'s triumph with *All American* in 1962 ("Once Upon a Time"), *Golden Boy* in 1964 ("Night Song") starring Sammy Davis, Jr., and *Applause* in 1970, based on the classic film, *All About Eve*.

ORPHAN ANNIE GOES ON STAGE

But Strouse's greatest triumph was to come in the mid-1970s when lyricist-director Martin Charnin persuaded him to create a musical based on the legendary comic strip *Little Orphan Annie*. In the musical, Annie is eventually adopted by a rich man after various plots are hatched to get between her and his money. Opening on April 21, 1977, *Annie* immediately captivated Broadway, winning seven Tonys and becoming the third-longest-running show of all time with 2,377 performances—plus innumerable revivals, a 1982 film version, and a 1993 stage sequel called *Annie Warbucks*. The infectious score, which perfected Strouse's genius for matching song to character, featured new Broadway classics such as "It's a Hard-Knock Life," "Easy Street," and the gushingly sentimental anthem to optimism, "Tomorrow."

Even though Strouse's biggest successes came with Adams and Charnin, he also collaborated on several shows (including *Nick and Nora*, *Charlie and Algernon*, and *Rags*) with other acclaimed lyricists, including Sammy Cahn, Alan Jay Lerner, and Stephen Schwartz. He scored the soundtrack for the classic 1967 movie *Bonnie & Clyde* and the 1989 cartoon feature *All Dogs Go to Heaven*. Strouse also wrote "Those Were the Days," the theme song for the groundbreaking 1970s sitcom *All in the Family*. Strouse founded ASCAP's Musical Theater Workshop, and was elected to the Songwriter's Hall of Fame. In 1997, Strouse's wife, the choreographer Barbara Siman, produced *A Lot of Living!*, an off-Broadway revue showcasing 40 of the veteran songwriter's best tunes. Although he is now retired, Strouse still takes an interest in musical theater.

Linnie Messina

SEE ALSO:

FILM MUSIC; FILM MUSICALS; MUSICALS.

FURTHER READING

Charnin, Martin. *Annie: A Theater Memoir* (New York: Dutton, 1977);
Green, Stanley. *The World of Musical Comedy* (New York: A.S. Barnes & Co., 1980).

SUGGESTED LISTENING

Annie; *Applause*; *Bye Bye Birdie*;
Golden Boy; *It's a Bird, It's a Plane, It's Superman*; *Nightingale*.

JULE STYNE

One of Broadway's greatest songwriters, Jule Styne was a prolific composer for film and stage. In just over 30 years he penned more than 1,500 tunes, including the outstanding scores for *Gypsy* and *Funny Girl*, as well as pop standards like "Time After Time," "I've Heard That Song Before," and "It's Magic." And yet the flamboyant and irascible Styne remains, according to English theater critic Kenneth Tynan, "the most persistently underrated of all popular composers."

Born Julius Kerwin Stein in December 1905, in London's working-class area of Bethnal Green, to Ukrainian-Jewish parents, Stein proved to be a musical prodigy, dueting with music hall star Harry Lauder at the tender age of three. Stein emigrated to Chicago with his family in 1913, and by age eight he was performing Haydn and Mozart with the Chicago and Detroit symphony orchestras. Stubby fingers forced him to shorten his concert career and, switching from classics to pop, he wrote his first hit, "Sunday," in 1926. In 1931, he started his own dance band, changing his name to "Styne" to avoid confusion with Jules Stein, the founder of the Music Corporation of America.

After a brief spell in New York, where he split his time between songwriting and teaching singing, he moved to Hollywood in the mid-1930s to work as a vocal coach for Shirley Temple. In 1935 he joined Republic Studios as a staff songwriter, where he was teamed up with lyricist Frank LOESSER. By 1940 he was churning out cowboy tunes for Gene Autry and Roy Rogers at Republic. He later recalled that he "did just about anything they asked me to do ... orchestrations, conducting, playing the piano for [Rogers' horse] Trigger...."

PROFITABLE PARTNERSHIP

During World War II, when Loesser went into the army, Styne was paired with lyricist Sammy Cahn. The pair worked on minor film musicals that produced major jukebox hits, such as "It's Been a Long, Long Time," "The Things We Did Last Summer," and the Academy Award-nominated "I'll Walk Alone." In 1944, they wrote the score for the Frank SINATRA movie *Step Lively*, and began a long, hit-filled relationship with the singer that included "Saturday Night (Is the Loneliest Night of the Week)," "Give Me Five Minutes More," and "Guess I'll Hang My Tears out to Dry." Sinatra also sang Styne's title song to the 1954 movie *Three Coins in the Fountain*, which earned Styne his sole Oscar.

In 1947, Styne, a compulsive gambler, hit the jackpot with his first Broadway musical *High Button Shoes* (featuring "Papa, Won't You Dance With Me?"). For the next two decades, Styne had a nearly unbroken string of smash shows, teaming up with lyricists such as Leo Robin, Betty Comden, Adolph Green, and Stephen SONDHEIM. Among these triumphs were 1949's *Gentlemen Prefer Blondes* ("Diamonds Are a Girl's Best Friend"), 1956's *The Bells Are Ringing* ("Just in Time"), and 1959's *Gypsy* ("Everything's Coming Up Roses"). Comden, one of his collaborators, said of his quixotic, shorthand speech and working methods: "In the first five minutes Jule Styne will have a thousand ideas, 995 of which will be somewhere between surrealistic and Martian, and five of which will be pure gold."

In *Funny Girl* (1964), Styne's most successful musical, he showed off the full range of its young star, Barbra STREISAND, with her signature song "People." The show also produced the hit "Don't Rain on My Parade." Following a string of ambitious failures, Styne returned to top form with 1972's *Sugar* (based on the classic film comedy *Some Like It Hot*) and *Lorelei*, a 1974 sequel to *Gentlemen Prefer Blondes*.

When Jule Styne died on September 20, 1994, in Manhattan, at the age of 88, he left a rich musical legacy typified by what music historian Dwight Blocker Bowers called "the neon-lit brashness and sentimentality that are vital elements of American show business."

Michael R. Ross

SEE ALSO:

FILM MUSIC; FILM MUSICALS; MUSICALS.

FURTHER READING

Taylor, Theodore. *Jule: The Story of Composer Jule Styne* (New York: Random House, 1979).

SUGGESTED LISTENING

Various Artists: *American Songbook Series: Jule Styne*.

SURF MUSIC

Surf music is a style of rock'n'roll that developed in the early 1960s in celebration of the California surfing culture. Using the location, clothes and gear of the sport for its lyrics, surf music underscored the surfing experience. The style is characterized by driving rhythms, a reverberating guitar, close-harmony vocals, and a verse-chorus song form.

In the late 1950s, surf music began as an instrumental sub-genre that emerged from rock'n'roll. One of the earliest examples was Ventures recording "Walk, Don't Run" (1960), in which the conventional tension between melody, beat, and riff is broken. Such instrumental hits quickly moved up the charts, and in coastal towns throughout California instrumental bands performed to the wildly enthusiastic young surfing crowd.

Although many musicians claim to have invented surf music, Dick Dale actually deserves the credit. The frontman of a band called the Deltones, Dale achieved the "surf sound" through staccato picking on a Fender Stratocaster, with heavy use of reverberation accompanied by a pounding rhythm. To Dale, this sound captured the same vibration as riding the surf.

As a result of Dale's popularity, imitators began popping up. Instrumental groups geared their style toward the recognizable surf sound, characterized by pounding drums and frequent Latin touches in rhythm and percussion, while focusing on the reverb or echo of the lead guitar.

Dale and the Deltones, however, remained a local band, and it wasn't until another Southern California group, the BEACH BOYS, hit the scene, that the music gained a national following.

The Beach Boys had formed as part of the instrumental surfing scene. Yet they were innovators in the genre because they added surfing-related lyrics to the music. Band member Brian Wilson began writing songs celebrating not only surfing but also the whole young Californian lifestyle. Soon other acts began emulating the Beach Boys' style and a whole new genre began to develop, using their music as its roots. Another surf group, Jan and Dean,

The Beach Boys epitomized surf music in 1965, but they also went on to outgrow the genre in spectacular fashion.

also made it to the U.S. charts with the song "Surf City," co-written by Wilson and Jan Berry, which became the first surf-oriented No. 1 hit, in 1963.

Several other instrumental surf bands also managed to achieve national hits, notably the Chantays, with "Pipeline" (1963), and the Surfaris, with the best-known surf guitar song of all: "Wipe Out" (1963).

By the mid-1960s the "British invasion" led Californian groups to imitate the English sound, and surf music died out. However, in the early 1980s, a revival of the original surfing sound took place, led by "surf punk" groups such as the Forgotten Rebels, who recorded "Surfin' on Heroin" in 1983.

Judi Gerber

SEE ALSO:
BRITISH BEAT MUSIC; POP MUSIC; ROCK'N'ROLL.

FURTHER READING
Blair, John. *The Illustrated Discography of Surf Music, 1961–1965* (Ann Arbor, MI: Popular Culture Ink, 1995); Wood, Jack. *Surf City: The California Sound* (New York: Friedman/Fairfax Publishers, 1995).

SUGGESTED LISTENING
Beach Boys: *Summer Days (and Summer Nights!)*; *Surfin' Safari*; *Surfing USA*; Jan and Dean: *Dead Man's Curve*; *Surf City*.

DAME JOAN
SUTHERLAND

Joan Sutherland has been universally acknowledged as one of the foremost coloratura sopranos to specialize in the 19th-century Italian and French opera repertoire. Her brilliance of tone and ornamentation is ideally suited to the Italian *bel canto* style (an elegant style associated with 17th–19th century Italian singing). Her emotional commitment in phrasing—occasionally at the expense of intelligibility—along with great technical virtuosity have earned her lasting international acclaim.

Born in Sydney, Australia, on November 7, 1926, Sutherland received her initial musical training in voice and piano from her mother until the age of 19. After receiving recognition in vocal competitions, she began formal training with John and Aida Dickens in Sydney, and for the next two years she performed throughout Australia in concerts and oratorios.

In 1947, at the Lyceum Club in Sydney, Sutherland appeared in her first operatic role in a concert performance of Purcell's *Dido and Aeneas*. Her operatic stage debut came in 1951, when she appeared in the title role in the Sydney Conservatorium production of *Judith*, by Sir Eugene Goossens. In that same year, after winning a prestigious Australian vocal competition, she had enough money to further her career by moving to England.

In London, Sutherland studied with Clive Carey at the Opera School of the Royal College of Music, and made her Covent Garden debut in 1952 as the First Lady in Mozart's *Die Zauberflöte*. Sutherland appeared in a variety of roles with the Covent Garden company, including *Aida* (1954); creating the role of Jenifer in Sir Michael TIPPETT's *The Midsummer Marriage* (1955); as Gilda in Verdi's *Rigoletto* (1957); in the title role of Handel's *Alcina* (1957); and in roles in *Un ballo in maschera*, *Carmen*, *The Ring*, and *Les contes d'Hoffman*.

THE BEL CANTO REPERTOIRE

Sutherland married her long-time accompanist, fellow Australian Richard Bonynge in 1954. Bonynge developed and coached her in the Italian *bel canto* style, which emphasizes floridity (a musical line decorated with many ornaments), beauty of tone throughout the full range of the voice, and ease and clarity in the high register. It was after her performance in the title role in Donizetti's *Lucia di Lammermoor* at Covent Garden in 1959 that she received acclaim as a dramatic coloratura soprano.

Sutherland made her North American debut in 1958 at the Vancouver Festival and her U.S. debut in Dallas in 1960. Her debuts at the Paris Opera (1960), Venice (1960), La Scala in Milan (1961), and the Metropolitan in New York (1961) were all critically acclaimed.

By 1965, Sutherland and Bonynge had formed their own opera company, with Bonynge as artistic director. They performed in Australia during the 1965–66, 1974, and the 1976–86 seasons, earning Sutherland recognition as the greatest Australian singer since Dame Nellie MELBA.

In 1990, Sutherland made her operatic farewell as Marguerite de Valois in the Sydney production of Meyerbeer's *Les Huguenots*. In 1961, she was made a Commander of the Order of the British Empire and, in 1979, was further honored with the title Dame Commander of the Order of the British Empire.

A generous and popular artist, Sutherland could, nevertheless, be "difficult" when she considered the conducting to be unsympathetic or ill-judged. However, during her career, she distinguished herself as an interpreter of the *bel canto* style and a champion of the Italian, French, and Handelian repertoires, bringing opera a renewed popularity.

David Brock

SEE ALSO:
OPERA; VOCAL AND CHORAL MUSIC.

FURTHER READING

Major, Norma. *Joan Sutherland:
The Authorized Biography*
(Boston, MA: Little, Brown 1994);
Sutherland, Joan. *A Prima Donna's Progress:
The Autobiography of Joan Sutherland*
(Washington, D.C.: Regnery Pub., 1997).

SUGGESTED LISTENING

Live from Lincoln Center; *Serate Musicali*;
Bellini: *Beatrice di Tenda*;
Handel: *Alcina*; Meyerbeer: *Les Huguenots*;
Verdi: *I Masnadieri*, *La Traviata*.

SWING

Swing has two meanings in music. It refers to the bouncy, "shuffle" rhythm in jazz and its effect on the music. It also describes the popular jazz form that reached its zenith in the mid-1930s to the early 1940s, and remains a musical favorite. The swing era was the only time in U.S. history when a type of jazz was considered America's popular music, with the bands of Duke ELLINGTON, Harry JAMES, Glenn MILLER, and Benny GOODMAN dominating international popular music markets. Many of the most enduring jazz performers, composers, and compositions came out of the swing era.

THE SHUFFLE RHYTHM

The basis for all swing music is the "shuffle rhythm." Used by modern jazz, Dixieland, Chicago-style and jump blues, and, of course, swing big band music, the shuffle rhythm is based on the shuffle dance step. The rhythm is most easily described as a kind of strong four-in-a-bar feel, with a 12/8 feel overlaid on it. Some musicians take a broader approach to the concept of swing—they feel that any rhythm played loosely and with a sense of "forward motion" could be considered "swinging."

MUSIC FOR DANCING

By the early 1930s, New Orleans and Chicago-style jazz were giving way to swing. Big band swing music was primarily music for dancing. Large and small ensembles led by Duke Ellington, Count BASIE, Benny Goodman, Gene Krupa, Jimmy and Tommy DORSEY, Artie Shaw, Woody Herman, Chick Webb, and Glenn Miller, among others, recorded arrangements that were geared toward creating a big, "swinging" sound. That swinging sound kept crowds of young people dancing in ballrooms such as the Savoy, the Meadowbrook, and the Glen Island Casino.

Radio broadcasts from these popular venues were made live and could be heard across the country; during the early days of network radio, the airwaves were filled with the sounds of big band jazz. The big band sound, performed by jazz "orchestras," is typified by moderate tempo to upbeat swing

Corbis-Bettmann

The legendary jazz drummer Gene Krupa, whose electrifying performances in Benny Goodman's swing band forever raised the status of the drummer.

rhythms played by 10- to 25-piece bands. These orchestras consist of brass and reed instruments, accompanied by a rhythm section of bass, piano, drums, and often guitar or vibraphone. Popular recordings frequently include blues- or boogie-woogie-based musical arrangements and exciting ensemble brass features known as "shout choruses," in which the horns and the rhythm section perform unison riffs that dynamically build in intensity toward the climax of the piece.

This blues-based style was popularized by big bands, most famously Count Basie's. Other swing styles include ballads and vocal numbers in the tradition of the great big band singers, such as Jimmy Rushing, Joe Williams, Frank SINATRA, Billy Eckstine, and Ella FITZGERALD.

THE DIFFERENCE BETWEEN SWING AND BIG BANDS

Although the terms are often used interchangeably, there are some important distinctions, musically speaking, between swing and big bands. "Swing" as a musical style began as dance music, and only later evolved and developed a "concert" repertoire intended for listening only. Groups and artists performing in this style include Duke Ellington, Stan KENTON, the Buddy Rich Big Band, the Thad Jones/Mel Lewis Orchestra, Doc Severinsen, Don Ellis, the Willem Brueker Kollecktife, and Jaco

Pastorius's Word of Mouth big band. On the other hand, many big bands performed "commercial" music (dance music that isn't jazz). These groups were often called "sweet" bands. Examples of "sweet" music included Lawrence Welk, Guy Lombardo, Paul Whiteman, some of Glenn Miller's work, and many of the well-known popular singers of the 1930s through the 1960s, such as Bing CROSBY, Perry Como, Jack Jones, and Steve and Edie Gorme.

SMALL AND SWINGING

Swing does not necessarily have to be performed by large ensembles or big bands. There were several important small groups and even solo performers (such as Benny Goodman's small ensembles, the Nat King COLE Trio, Teddy Wilson, and Art TATUM), as well as mid-sized, blues-oriented bands (such as Louis Jordan's) that helped shape and define the "jump blues" style of swing. B. B. KING is an example of a blues performer who was greatly influenced by the big band format, and who often uses big band arrangements to present his electrified southern blues.

Several big bands and jazz orchestras feature Latin music exclusively. Many of these bands began as dance orchestras, but this style too has developed its own concert music, and has also influenced more modern sounds and styles (such as salsa). A large ensemble that plays jazz, and is exclusively dedicated to Latin style music, is the Tito PUENTE Orchestra.

RISE OF THE ARRANGER

Musicians such as guitarist and banjoist Elmer Snowden (the original bandleader of what became the Duke Ellington Orchestra) had experimented with larger ensembles as early as the 1920s, and by the mid-1930s the big band format was firmly entrenched in jazz and popular music. This explosion of larger groups helped to establish the importance of the arranger.

An "arranger" in jazz is someone who helps bring a song or piece to life through the creative use of musical materials and instrumentation.

Written arrangements had not been necessary with smaller combos, but with the advent of big bands they became essential. The number of tunes in a group's repertoire, and the accompanying written music, became known as that band's "book" (a term that is still used for a musical group's repertoire). Jazz arrangers were important in defining the big band/swing sound, and several arrangers helped create many memorable hits. Duke Ellington, often in collaboration with Billy Strayhorn, was the most important jazz arranger, and he had many hits, including "Cotton Tail" and "Moon Mist."

Over the years, several conventions or standard practices developed in jazz arranging—the use of "kicks" and "fills" (drummers punctuating ensemble passages and shout choruses, filling in the spaces between these ensemble sections with rhythmic "fills" on the drums), block voicing (harmonized melody spread across the ensemble), "antiphonal" (call and response), and alternating sections where saxes are featured over a brass accompaniment, or where brass instruments are featured over sax accompaniment.

Regional styles developed as well. These styles ranged from the "Kansas City" sound (Count Basie and "Big Jay" McShann), an "East Coast" sound (Duke Ellington, Cab Calloway, and the groups for which Fletcher HENDERSON arranged) and much later, with the development of "cool jazz," there was a "West Coast" sound in which Gerry MULLIGAN was instrumental.

Big band music continues to draw audiences to both the concert arena and the ballroom. Many of the important groups are still touring (often under the direction of former band members who have stepped up to lead after the retirement or death of the founder). And, movies such as the early 1990s release *Swing Kids* draw younger listeners to the music.

The music of the swing era and the big band style remain viable as entertainment and as part of the serious jazz repertoire.

Gregg Juke

SEE ALSO:

ARRANGERS; BIG BAND JAZZ; BLUES; BOOGIE-WOOGIE; JAZZ; LATIN JAZZ; NEW ORLEANS JAZZ/DIXIELAND; SALSA.

FURTHER READING

Koerner, Julie. *Swing Kings* (New York: Friedman/Fairfax Publishers, 1994); Schuller, Gunther. *The Swing Era: The Development of Jazz, 1930–1945* (New York: Oxford University Press, 1989).

SUGGESTED LISTENING

Count Basie: *Count Basie and His Orchestra*; Gene Krupa: *Leave Us Leap*; Paul Whiteman: *Paper Moon*.

KAROL SZYMANOWSKI

The Polish composer Karol Szymanowski wrote songs, piano music, operas, and ballet music that express the character of his native land perhaps even more poignantly than his better known predecessor, Frédéric Chopin.

Szymanowski was born on October 6, 1882, in the town of Tymoszówka in the Ukraine, a part of the Russian Empire that had belonged to the ancient kingdom of Poland. The Szymanowskis were landholders, and Polish rather than Russian. The family was musical: his sister was an opera singer and his brother was a pianist and composer. His uncle, Gustav Neuhaus, ran a music school, where Szymanowski studied from the age of ten. Otherwise, he was educated at home, since he was lame following a childhood accident. In Vienna, at the age of 13, he heard the music of Richard Wagner, and this, together with the ideas of the German philosopher Nietzsche, influenced his music until the 1920s.

Szymanowski composed piano preludes from the age of 14. Realizing his son was exceptionally talented, Szymanowski's father sent the young composer to Warsaw in 1901, where he studied counterpoint and composition under the Polish composer Zygmunt Nosowski. He joined with some of Nosowski's other students to form a group dedicated to composing music with a recognizably Polish character. They used Polish forms such as the polonaise and the mazurka, collected Polish folk songs, and infused Polish themes into their work. With help from a rich patron, Prince Wladyslaw Ludomirski, they set up the Young Polish Composers' publishing company in Berlin for their own music. Szymanowski's first published work appeared in 1906, a set of nine piano preludes called Opus 1.

EXOTIC INFLUENCES

Before World War I, Szymanowski was able to travel to Austria, Italy, and North Africa, where he heard the calls to worship of the Islamic muezzins and worked them into his songs. On his travels he also saw STRAVINSKY's *Firebird* and *Petrushka*, and met

Stravinsky himself in London. In 1911, he met and became friends with the young pianist, Artur RUBINSTEIN, who was impressed with his piano compositions and started playing them in concerts throughout the world.

The outbreak of World War I put an end to his travels. He was ineligible for service because of his disability, so he was able to devote himself to composition. This period saw the beginnings of the development of his own individual style, as Szymanowski's early enthusiasm for Wagner gave way to an interest in the Impressionism of DEBUSSY and to specifically Polish elements.

When his home was burned in 1917 after the Russian Revolution, Szymanowski and his family escaped to Elisavetgrad on the Russian border, and when that town was seized by the Austrians, they moved once more to Warsaw. After the liberation of Poland in 1919, Szymanowski's aim was to write specifically Polish music that would restore a sense of nationalism. His *Stabat mater* (1926) combined medieval church music with Polish folk material, while the *Kurpie songs* (1928) echoed the music of the Kurpie plainsmen. His ballet *Harnasie* was inspired by the folk songs of the Tatra highlanders— a rich resource for his music. Szymanowski also directed his energies to improving Polish musical education and encouraging young composers.

In 1935 *Harnasie* opened in Prague to great acclaim. However, Szymanowski's health was declining (he had tuberculosis) and the fact that he had to give concerts to support himself and his sister Stasia did not help. He died in Cannes on March 29, 1937.

Alan Blackwood

SEE ALSO:

CHAMBER MUSIC; OPERA; VOCAL AND CHORAL MUSIC.

FURTHER READING
Chylinska, Teresa, trans. John Glowacki.
Karol Szymanowski: His Life and Works
(Los Angeles, CA: University of Southern California, 1993);
Samson, Jim. *The Music of Szymanowski*
(New York: Taplinger, 1981).

SUGGESTED LISTENING
Harnasie; *King Roger*; *Stabat mater*;
Symphony No. 3; Violin Concerto No. 1.

TAKE 6

The critically acclaimed a cappella gospel sextet Take 6, with their jazz-based arrangements, have appeared on practically every American talk show, lent their voices for numerous television commercials, sung on TV sit-coms (including the theme song "Like the Whole World's Watching" for *Murphy Brown*), and appeared with myriad recording artists, both secular and sacred. They paved the way for a number of other black male vocal groups in the 1990s.

Take 6 had a modest beginning in the early 1980s. They were formed by tenor Claude McKnight at Oakwood College (a Seventh Day Adventist school) in Huntsville, Alabama, initially as a jazzed-up barbershop quartet called Alliance. The other members were David Thomas (tenor), Alvin Chea (bass), and Cedric Dent (baritone). They were joined by Mark Kibble, another tenor, after he heard them singing in a bathroom and joined in with his own improvisation.

Kibble became the group's main arranger, and was responsible for expanding their sound from barbershop to big band, using their voices to imitate instruments. Kibble also introduced the sixth member, tenor Mervyn Warren.

DEBUT ALBUM

They signed to Reprise in 1987, changing their name the same year to Take 6. Their debut album, *Take 6,* contained a cappella jazz arrangements of spirituals and early gospel numbers, and three songs composed by Kibble and Warren. It was a huge success, sold over a million copies and won the group two Grammys.

The group toured with Al Jarreau and contributed to Quincy JONES's project *Back on the Block,* before recording their second album, *So Much 2 Say,* released in September 1990. Although primarily a jazz project, it featured sampling and special effects, hip-hop and Latin rhythms, and instrumentation for the first time (everyone in Take 6 plays an instrument). On those tracks with no instrumentation, all sounds were vocally or anatomically produced, reminding one of jazz singer Bobby McFerrin, and adding a level of excitement not heard before in gospel jazz. Like the first album, this one also went gold and won a Grammy.

In 1990, Take 6 collaborated with k.d. lang on the song "Ridin' the Rails" for the film *Dick Tracy.* The album *So Much 2 Say* was followed by *He Is Christmas* (1991), a mix of traditional Christmas carols and jazz arrangements, primarily in a cappella style. This too—almost predictably—won a Grammy.

Take 6 contributed six songs to Johnny Mathis's *Better Together* (1991). Most notable on this album was the rendition of "In the Still of the Night," with Mathis singing lead and Take 6 the base of the a cappella harmonies. Warren left the group during 1991 and was replaced by Kibble's brother Joel.

The next year Take 6 contributed an a cappella performance of the jazz standard "I'm Always Chasing Rainbows" for the soundtrack to the film *Glengarry Glen Ross* (1992). In 1992 they also participated in the production of *Handel's Messiah: A Soulful Celebration.* Produced by Mervyn Warren, this album reworked the Christmas part of *Messiah,* including the "Hallelujah Chorus." Take 6, with Stevie WONDER, sang "O Thou That Tellest Good Tidings to Zion."

CHANGE OF STYLE

Unlike their previous album releases, which had been mainly a cappella, Take 6 turned a corner with *Join the Band* (1994). This featured artists such as Ray CHARLES, Stevie Wonder, Queen Latifah, and Herbie HANCOCK. The follow-up, *Brothers* (1996), was their first album to have no a cappella tracks at all.

Although they continue to stretch beyond their a cappella origins, Take 6 take pains to maintain their musical and religious integrity: all members are devout Christians and evaluate all lyrics before agreeing to perform any song on their own recordings or with others. It is this commitment to high ideals and musical detail that endears them to the world.

Donna Cox

SEE ALSO:

FILM MUSIC; GOSPEL; JAZZ.

FURTHER READING
Young, Alan. *Woke Me Up This Morning:*
Black Gospel Singers and the Gospel Life
(Jackson, MS: University Press of Mississippi, 1997).

SUGGESTED LISTENING
Brothers; *Join the Band*; *So Much 2 Say*; *Take 6.*

TORU
TAKEMITSU

Takemitsu's compositions bridge the gap between East and West. He was first inspired by the music of the West, but he later embraced his Japanese musical heritage, ultimately producing music that was a synthesis of both. In his chamber works, the contemplative and wandering tones of the *shakuhachi*, the traditional Japanese flute, play a central role, and it is this sound that Western listeners most often associate with Takemitsu's work.

Takemitsu was born in Tokyo on October 8, 1930, but spent his childhood in China, returning to Japan in 1937 to attend school until he was drafted in 1944. In 1948, he had 18 composition lessons with Yosuji Kiyose, but has otherwise been self-taught in music. In 1951, he formed an experimental workshop for music and other arts, the Jikken Kobo, with a group of other young musicians and artists. His first compositions were for piano, and afterward he turned to experimenting with electronic media and prerecorded tapes. His composition of 1960, *Mizu no kyoku* (Water Music), consisted of recorded water sounds.

At this time, the composer was mostly interested in Western avant-garde techniques. He employed graphic notation (non-conventional music notation used to facilitate improvisation) in some compositions, and his *Textures* for orchestra was named the best work at the 1965 ISCM festival (International Society for Contemporary Music).

TAKEMITSU MEETS CAGE

In other ways, however, Takemitsu's work owes very little technically to Western tradition. He does not use tonality or metrical regularity to give structure to his compositions, but appears to be concerned chiefly with the dialogue between sound and silence. In this context, it is not surprising that John CAGE, whom Takemitsu met in 1964, became a friend, and that Takemitsu borrowed elements from Cage's theory. From him, Takemitsu adopted the prepared piano and the placement of sounds in space as an element of composition, particularly in *Dorian Horizon,* which Aaron COPLAND conducted in San Francisco in 1967.

Ironically, it was probably Cage, with his eclectic interests in Zen and Eastern philosophy, who stimulated Takemitsu's rediscovery of traditional Japanese instruments and style. Takemitsu had used the Japanese lute, the *biwa,* in his score for the film *Seppuku* in 1962, but later began to use the *shakuhachi,* and the lute in many of his works. *Shuteika* (In an Autumn Garden) written in 1973, is for the traditional Japanese *gagaku,* or court music, ensemble. In addition, some of Takemitsu's works have a mathematical basis. For example, the "pentagonal garden" of *A Flock Descends into the Pentagonal Garden* is derived from the intervals of the pentatonic scale (thirds and seconds) that Takemitsu worked into a "magic square."

Takemitsu had considerable popular success, composing the music for 90 films, including Akira Kurosawa's *Ran.* The ecological group Greenpeace also commissioned his *Toward the Sea* (1981) for their Save the Whales campaign.

Most of Takemitsu's extensive writings have not been translated, but his *Confronting Silence* contains much of the theoretical underpinnings for his major works. He has lectured at Harvard, Yale, and the University of California at San Diego. In 1973, Takemitsu founded Music Today, which sponsors concerts of contemporary music annually in Tokyo. The New York Philharmonic commissioned the piece *November Steps* in 1975, and in 1989 a series of concerts was held at Columbia University in Takemitsu's honor. Takemitsu died in 1996, but the bridge he built between Japanese and Western music still survives.

Jane Prendergast

SEE ALSO:
CHAMBER MUSIC; FILM MUSIC; ORCHESTRAL MUSIC; VOCAL AND CHORAL MUSIC.

FURTHER READING
Ohtake, Noriko. *Creative Sources for the Music of Toru Takemitsu* (Brookfield, VT: Ashgate, 1993); Takemitsu, Toru. *Confronting Silence* (Berkeley, CA: Fallen Leaf Press, 1995).

SUGGESTED LISTENING
All in Twilight; Complete Solo Piano Music; A Flock Descends into the Pentagonal Garden; Rain Tree; Toward the Sea.

TAMPA RED

Tampa Red was an essential part of the Chicago blues scene during its early years. The legacy of this redheaded guitarist includes both an extensive library of recordings and a long list of musicians who were profoundly influenced by his slide-guitar and single-string solo style, including Big Bill BROONZY and Robert Nighthawk. He helped to bridge the gap between rural and urban blues in the 1930s.

He was born Hudson Woodbridge, probably on Christmas Day in 1900 or 1901 (but perhaps as late as 1904), in Smithville, Georgia. He grew up in Tampa, Florida, and that and the fact that he had red hair gave him his nickname. By the time he moved to Chicago in the mid-1920s, he had mastered the slide guitar and earned the nickname "The Guitar Wizard." He initially played street corners and a few clubs, but his big break came when he was asked to play as a sideman to Ma RAINEY. He met Thomas A. DORSEY in the process, and they soon won local fame on the black theater circuit.

PLAYING HOKUM

Tampa Red and "Georgia Tom," as Dorsey was known, specialized in jivey and risqué party music called "hokum." Their bawdy first recording, "It's Tight Like That (1928)," was one of the biggest-selling pre-war blues records. It encouraged numerous imitators, and initiated what became known as "the hokum sound." This was characterized by light, airy melodies with sentimental or humorous lyrics, often relying on double-meaning wordplay. Tampa Red and Georgia Tom even called themselves the Hokum Boys for a time, performing extensively in Chicago and Memphis. They kept recording until Dorsey became disillusioned with blues and turned instead to gospel in 1932.

Hokum, although it propelled Tampa Red into the limelight, was short-lived. Tampa followed it with sexy blues ballads such as "Sugar Mama Blues No.1." This he played in E, with his guitar tuned down a semitone, which showcased his ability to play backward finger-to-thumb rolls with his right hand and create sound effects using a bottleneck (sliding a metal cylinder down the strings). "Nobody in the world can do that, because there's only one Tampa Red, and when he's

dead, that's all, brother," said Big Bill Broonzy. Broonzy also revealed that Tampa Red was the first bottleneck player he saw, and that Tampa was also one of the earliest blues musicians to record with an electric guitar. Broonzy was one of many whose first Chicago stop was Tampa Red's house. Tampa Red's wife, Frances, ran their home as a blues lodging house in the 1930s and 1940s, with some performers living there, others using it for rehearsals, and almost all asking Tampa Red for advice. Among those who passed through were Memphis SLIM, Sonny Boy WILLIAMSON, Big Joe Williams, and Major "Maceo" Merriweather.

RECORDING HIGHLIGHTS

Tampa Red recorded more than 200 sides for a variety of companies, but his greatest success came with RCA Bluebird from 1934 to 1953. His 1938 "Rock It in Rhythm" mixed swing and boogie in a way that hinted at rock'n'roll. In "Jitter Jump" and "I Wanted to Swing" (both 1941), he showed off jazz chord voicings that were well ahead of his time. By the 1940s, blues music was changing, with electrified and powerful Mississippi Delta musicians taking charge. However, they still looked to Tampa Red for inspiration: Elmore James had a major hit when "Things 'Bout Coming My Way" was revamped into "When Things Go Wrong With You (It Hurts Me Too)," and B. B. KING, Robert Nighthawk, Fats DOMINO, Freddie KING, and LITTLE WALTER all turned his songs into hits.

After his wife died in 1953, Tampa developed an alcohol problem, which took its toll on his music. He did little recording during the 50s, but returned with two albums for the Prestige-Bluesville label in 1960. He died in poverty on March 9, 1981, the same year he was inducted into the Blues Foundation's Hall of Fame.

Stan Hieronymus

SEE ALSO:
BLUES; ROCK'N'ROLL.

FURTHER READING
Davis, Francis. *The History of the Blues*
(New York: Hyperion, 1995).

SUGGESTED LISTENING
Bottleneck Guitar 1928–1937; *Don't Tampa with the Blues*; *It Hurts Me Too: The Essential Recordings*; *Tampa Red: Guitar Wizard*.

TANGO

Tango primarily describes the national dance of Argentina, but it is also the term for an elegant and sensual song and dance music. It became internationally popular in the 1910s and a variety of styles appeared, but the basis of them all remains the *tango argentino*, Argentina's premier musical export.

The roots of tango lie in the 19th-century slums of Buenos Aires. Rural Argentines had their *milonga*—the music of the gaucho—but in the cities they joined the immigrant population of Europeans and blacks in a musical mix. The city's outskirts became an urban laboratory of *milonga, muñeira*, flamenco, Cuban habanera, Italian folk, and African percussion.

Tango music was first played on guitar, violin, and flute, but the arrival of the *bandoneón* (a boxy button accordion from Germany) completed the classic tango orchestra. The music is played in 4/4 time, usually in minor mode, with syncopated rhythms. Integral vulgar lyrics and sexually suggestive steps meant that it thrived in bars and brothels. In a milieu of violence, brawls, and male chauvinism, men choreographed steps for a dance in which the woman represented Argentina, and the man, the newly arrived immigrant.

Tango became the premier music of the working class and was denounced as vulgar by others. Much as rock'n'roll would be banned in certain U.S. households, so tango was barred from aristocratic Argentine homes. But in Europe it was all the rage, and was danced in the chic salons of Paris; finally, Argentines of all classes had to accept it.

The 1920s and 1930s took the music from brothels and barrooms to theaters and cabarets, and a golden age began. The artist credited with transforming tango into a song style for all classes was Carlos Gardel, whose voice and demeanor oozed passion, arrogance, machismo, and elegance—the very essence of tango. With nearly 900 songs recorded before his death in a plane crash in 1935, Gardel is tango's patron saint.

Tango was at its height in the 1940s, adopted by bandleaders like Anibal Troilo, Osvaldo Pugliese, and Juan D'Arienzo, whose 1937 recording of "La cumparsita" is perhaps the most popular tango ever.

Rosita and Ramon demonstrating the tango at the club El Patio in New York City, in 1931.

Astor Piazzolla is tango's modern voice. His *tango nuevo* (new tango) has transformed dance music into serious listening. While preserving the essence of tango, he toyed with jazz and recorded with groups such as the Kronos Quartet. Piazzolla won world acclaim in the 1980s and played well into the 1990s.

Tango's golden era has passed, and rock and jazz now run through its veins, but Argentine tango still is popular at home and abroad.

Brett Allan King

SEE ALSO:
DANCE MUSIC; LATIN AMERICA.

FURTHER READING

Collier, Simon. *Tango: The Dance, the Song, the Story* (New York: Thames and Hudson, 1995); Munoz, Isabel, and Evelyne Pieiller. *Tango* (New York: Stewart, Tabori & Chang, 1997).

SUGGESTED LISTENING

Carlos Gardel: *The Best of Carlos Gardel*; Astor Piazzolla: *Tango: Zero Hour*.

ART TATUM

Considered by many to be the greatest pianist in the history of jazz, Art Tatum's astonishing talent belied the fact that he was nearly blind. Tatum was one of the true innovators of piano music: he redefined the musical genres of stride, swing, and boogie-woogie through his reworkings of piano standards, which in turn became classics in their own right. Tatum was the most technically advanced piano player of his generation, and pianists today still measure their work using Tatum's style as a yardstick.

Arthur Tatum was born on October 13, 1909, in Toledo, Ohio. Blind in one eye from birth, and only partially sighted in the other, he nevertheless studied piano from early childhood and learned to read music. He received some formal education at the Toledo School of Music, but he was mainly self-taught. By his mid-teens, he was playing professionally in Toledo and Cleveland. Tatum had his own radio show in the late 1920s and was the regular pianist for singer Adelaide Hall in New York and toured with her in the early 1930s.

STYLE AND INFLUENCE

Tatum signed with Decca Records and recorded his first solo work in 1933. His unique solo style often featured breathtaking runs interspersed with striking single notes and unexpected chords. While Tatum cited artists such as Earl HINES, James P. Johnson, Fats WALLER, and Duke ELLINGTON as influences, his music was quite unlike that of any artist of the day. The complexity of his music and the sheer speed at which he could play notes on the piano led many to wonder in later years where Tatum's inspiration originated. As is often the case with visionaries, Tatum's achievement on the piano was so far ahead of its time that there were those who disdained him because he "played too many notes," referring to his uncanny ability to play difficult, complex lines with both hands.

While Tatum was not a composer, his versions of songs such as "Tiger Rag" clearly illustrated not only tremendous speed and accuracy—as if he were trying to impress and intimidate would-be competitors—but

also an approach to harmonies never taken before. This innovation and ability applied to the repertory standards gave them a fresh feel that appealed to the new generation of swing and bop musicians, who were searching for something against the grain of established jazz.

CAREER HIGHLIGHTS

Throughout the 1930s, Tatum spent periods working in Cleveland, Chicago, New York, and Los Angeles, and also traveled throughout the U.K. in 1938. Although continuing to work principally as a soloist, he led the Art Tatum Trio from 1943 to 1945, accompanied by bassist Slam Stewart and Tiny Grimes on guitar (later guitarist Everett Barksdale replaced Grimes). In 1947, Tatum appeard in the film *The Fabulous Dorseys*. In the early 1950s, he recorded extensively for legendary jazz producer Norman GRANZ, including a marathon series of tracks—120 in one year. Granz teamed Tatum up with artists such as Lionel Hampton, Barny Kessel, Buddy Rich, Ben WEBSTER, and Benny CARTER.

Tatum's final recording, *Art Tatum in Person* (1956), was made shortly before his death at the age of 47 from uremia associated with severe kidney disease. While his death in 1956 was premature, his influence on subsequent generations of pianists was profound and can still be experienced today through their music.

James Tuverson

SEE ALSO:
BEBOP; BOOGIE-WOOGIE; JAZZ; SWING.

FURTHER READING
Green, Benny. *The Reluctant Art: Five Studies in the Growth of Jazz* (New York: Da Capo Press, 1991); Laubich, Arnold, and Ray Spencer. *Art Tatum, a Guide to His Recorded Music* (Metuchen, NJ: Scarecrow, 1982); Lester, James. *Too Marvellous for Words: The Life and Genius of Art Tatum* (New York: Oxford University Press, 1994).

SUGGESTED LISTENING
20th-Century Piano Genius;
Best of Art Tatum;
Classic Early Solos, 1934–37;
Presenting the Art Tatum Trio.

SONNY
TERRY
& BROWNIE McGHEE

Sonny Terry and Brownie McGhee helped introduce the Piedmont blues style to the white New
York City folk-crowd in the 1940s, then to the rest of
the United States during the folk music revival of the
1950s and 1960s, and after that, to the world. They
formed one of the most enduring partnerships in
blues, playing together for more than 30 years.

Terry was born Saunders Terrell in October 1911,
in Greensboro, North Carolina. He lost the sight of
both his eyes in separate childhood accidents.
Devoting himself to music, he became a blues
harmonica player, and performed on street corners.
Around 1934, he met Blind Boy Fuller, a popular and
influential blues guitarist. He played with Fuller often
in the next few years and accompanied him to New
York City in 1937 for a recording session. In 1938,
Terry played in John Hammond's legendary *From
Spirituals to Swing* concert at Carnegie Hall, creating
a sensation with his interwoven harmonica playing
and singing (characterized by a distinctive falsetto
whoop). He met Brownie McGhee shortly after,
although they did not become permanent partners
until McGhee moved to New York in 1942.

Brownie McGhee was born Walter Brown McGhee
in November 1915, in Knoxville, Tennessee.
Childhood polio left him crippled and frequently
housebound, and he continued to walk with a limp
after an operation. He learned guitar from his father,
and was playing in church before the age of ten. By
his early teens, he was performing in medicine
shows, minstrel troupes, and carnivals. Influenced by
Lonnie JOHNSON and Blind Boy Fuller, he soon made
his mark playing blues. He even recorded under the
name Blind Boy Fuller No. 2, after Fuller died of
blood poisoning in 1941.

STORMY PARTNERSHIP

It was talent scout J. B. Long, also Fuller's mentor,
who first put Terry and McGhee together. Terry and
McGhee both lived with LEADBELLY during their early
years in New York, and soon began performing
before the same liberal audiences as Leadbelly, Pete
Seeger, Woody GUTHRIE and others, playing acoustic
blues in the old style. They also made several recordings for the Library of Congress, and closely associated themselves with the folk-blues movement. For
many years they toured extensively, playing clubs,
festivals, and concerts, becoming perhaps the best-
known blues artists of the era.

They recorded mostly rhythm and blues on black
labels until the late 1950s, performing sometimes as a
duo, sometimes as sidemen for other performers, and
sometimes with sidemen of their own. McGhee had
two big hits, "Baseball Boogie" in 1946 and "My Fault"
in 1948. They also began careers in theater, landing
parts on Broadway in *Finian's Rainbow* in the 1940s,
and in *Cat on a Hot Tin Roof* in the 1950s. McGhee
later appeared in movies and on television shows.

FOLK REVIVAL

McGhee's fingerpicked guitar-playing in a rocking,
rhythmic-melodic style, and Terry's "whooping"
harmonica defined the blues of the Piedmont area of
the Southeast U.S. They recorded often for a half
dozen labels, then became fixtures at folk and blues
festivals around the world.

Despite their long association, they were not the
closest of friends. Their often stormy relationship—
occasionally involving on-stage bickering—ended in
the 1970s. They continued to perform individually into
the 1980s, with Terry recording the album *Whoopin'*
with Johnny Winter and Willie DIXON on the Alligator
label. Terry died on March 12, 1986, the same year he
was inducted into the Blues Foundation's Hall of
Fame. McGhee died, on the brink of making a
comeback, on February 16, 1996.

Stan Hieronymus

SEE ALSO:
BLUES; FOLK MUSIC.

FURTHER READING
Davis, Francis. *The History of the Blues*
(New York: Hyperion, 1995).

SUGGESTED LISTENING
Brownie McGhee and Sonny Terry Sing;
The Folkway Years, 1944–1963;
Toughest Terry and Baddest Brownie.

SISTER ROSETTA
THARPE

Rosetta Tharpe was a musical enigma: both her singing and guitar playing defied conventional categories.

Born Rosetta Nubin in Cotton Plant, Arkansas, on March 20, 1915, "Sister" Rosetta Tharpe was playing the guitar by the age of four, and at six she was confidently singing for huge audiences. While she was clearly a talented singer, it was her ability to play the guitar that propelled her forward. Her mother, evangelist Katie Bell Nubin, played the mandolin while singing gospel songs. Together Katie Bell and little Rosetta preached and sang their way through the Southern states, eventually settling in Chicago in the late 1920s.

Rosetta was drawn to the ecstatic religious practices of the evangelical Sanctified Church and was active in its ministry. However, she was also impressed by the blues singers she heard in Arkansas and the jazz that was so prevalent in the Chicago area. She often performed in multi-act concerts with blues, jazz and folk musicians, and became further entrenched in the runs, riffs, and melodic structures associated with these genres. In 1934 Rosetta married pastor Wilbur Thorpe—he later changed the spelling to Tharpe—and moved to New York. She made a demonstration tape for Decca Records in mid-1938 which was well received by the producers. However, they felt she would have greater success potential if her songs were less "churchy." Rosetta agreed to experiment with her style. The result was the release of *Rock Me* (1938), on which, in addition to her own guitar playing, Tharpe was accompanied by the Lucky Millinder jazz orchestra. In December 1938 Tharpe appeared in John Hammond's extravanganza of African-American music, *From Spirituals to Swing*, at New York's Carnegie Hall, where she sang with the swing orchestras of Cab Calloway, Benny GOODMAN and Count BASIE.

Rosetta's success with *Rock Me* did not endear her to the Sanctified Church congregation that she so loved. The use of a jazz orchestra caused such an uproar in the staunch community that Rosetta persuaded Decca to allow her to record with just her guitar. They compromised by adding piano, bass and drum to her guitar. Thus began a fruitful seven-year collaboration between Tharpe and boogie-woogie pianist Samuel Blythe Price. Despite the compromises she had made for their sake, Tharpe was still not fully embraced by the church community. Her guitar technique was very blues-influenced, her singing jazz-inflected, and her stage decorum more reminiscent of a nightclub than a church service. These all combined to increase her popularity with the non-church listener, however. From 1947 to 1952, Decca paired Rosetta with Marie Knight and the two enjoyed much commercial success. Their relationship ended when Rosetta married Russell Morrison, who wanted her to go solo again. Rosetta died in Philadelphia in 1973 after a debilitating stroke.

Donna Cox

SEE ALSO:

BLUES; FOLK MUSIC; GOSPEL; JAZZ.

FURTHER READING
Heilbut, Anthony. *The Gospel Sounds*
(New York: Limelight, 1997).

SUGGESTED LISTENING
The Best of Sister Rosetta Tharpe;
Gospel Train Vol. 2: Sister Rosetta Tharpe.

VIRGIL
THOMSON

Virgil Thomson, born in Kansas City, Missouri, on November 25, 1896, was known for his sharp intellect and wide-ranging interests in music, which manifested themselves in his work as a composer and critic. Thomson drew upon musical elements such as folk songs, hymns, and dance music that he heard in his boyhood, to develop his individual style of composition.

As a young child, Thomson took occasional piano lessons and later studied the organ. When he was 12 he began working as a pianist in movie theaters, improvising music for the various kinds of action on the screen. Thomson claimed that he always felt at home in the theater, whether backstage or in the audience. During these years he also began playing the organ for various churches in Kansas City.

In 1917, he enlisted in the army, but World War I ended before he could be sent overseas. Thomson then moved to Boston, where he studied at Harvard University. He also took full advantage of that city's musical environment. At Harvard, in the fall of 1919, he began studies with the conductor Archibald T. Davison, and the composer Edward Burlingame Hill.

TRAINING IN PARIS

In 1921, Thomson received the John Knowles Paine Fellowship for travel, and decided to use it for a year of study in Paris. While there, Thomson studied organ and counterpoint with Nadia BOULANGER, and met many of the leaders of music and letters, including MILHAUD, POULENC, Auric, Honegger, SATIE, the poet Cocteau, the novelist Radiguet, and Picasso. He also sent back reviews to the *Boston Transcript* which marked the beginning of his career as a music critic. In only a few short months he submitted articles on concerts of music by Milhaud, Berlioz, DEBUSSY, SCHOENBERG, and, perhaps most importantly, a review of a concert conducted by Sergey KOUSSEVITZKY, which helped in Koussevitzky's eventual appointment as conductor of the Boston Symphony Orchestra. Thomson returned to Boston to complete his studies at Harvard, spent a year in

New York, and then returned to Paris, where he stayed from 1925 to 1940. Perhaps most significant during this second sojourn in Paris was Thomson's meeting and working with the writer Gertrude Stein. Their collaboration resulted in two operas, *Four Saints in Three Acts*, composed while they were both in Paris, and *The Mother of Us All*, composed after Thomson had returned to America. In these two works, Thomson used a variety of sources, quoting from Baptist hymns, Gregorian chant, and popular songs, setting them in traditional harmonic language with only occasional dissonance employed. In the late 1930s, Thomson composed the scores for two documentary films, *The Plow that Broke the Plains* and *The River*. Both of these works use folk songs, cowboy tunes, and hymn tunes as structural melodic material.

In 1940, Thomson returned to the United States, where he became music critic for the *New York Herald Tribune*. His articles strongly expressed his personal opinions on music and culture, and spread knowledge of both "new music" and American music to a general readership. During these years he also continued to compose works including the film score for *Louisiana Story*, for which he received a Pulitzer Prize, an opera entitled *Lord Byron*, and works for chorus, string quartet, solo voice, and orchestra.

Virgil Thomson died in 1989. His compositions and writings were personal, direct, not overstated, and accessible to a wide audience.

Michael Lamkin

SEE ALSO:
FILM MUSIC; OPERA; ORCHESTRAL MUSIC; SIX, LES.

FURTHER READING

Thomson, Virgil. *Music with Words:
A Composer's View*
(New Haven, CT: Yale University Press, 1989);
Thomson, Virgil. *The State of Music*
(Westport, CT: Greenwood Press, 1974);
Tommasini, Anthony. *Virgil Thomson:
Composer on the Aisle*
(New York: W. W. Norton, 1997).

SUGGESTED LISTENING

Filling Station; *Four Saints in
Three Acts*; *Lord Byron*; *The Mother of Us All*;
Symphony on a Hymn Tune*.

TIN PAN ALLEY

In the 1860s sheet music for songs was in great demand. Before the era of television or radio, families made their own entertainment at home in the evenings, often singing around the piano, usually played by Mom. Popular songs for family singing were Irish ballads like "When You Were Sweet Sixteen," and melodramatic pieces such as "The Lost Chord." One of the most popular songs of all was the tearjerker "After the Ball." The sheet music for this 1892 ballad sold 10 million copies, and fortunately for the composer, Charles K. Harris, he had published the song himself.

Since there was good money to be made from song publishing, New York publishers conducted surveys to discover the public's tastes, and then commissioned songwriters to fill that need. Audiences across the country would hear the song sung at their local vaudeville theater, and would then go and buy the sheet music to try it out at home.

The songwriting factories on New York's 28th Street—Tin Pan Alley—where many songwriters sold their first songs.

Archive Photos/G.D. Hackett

ORIGIN OF TIN PAN ALLEY

By 1900, several important publishers were based on Manhattan's 28th Street. The cramped offices were partitioned into cubicles with pianos so that the composers and song-pluggers could write and sell their work. There was no air-conditioning, so the windows would be open in summer. A journalist, Monroe H. Rosenfeld, likened the discordant sounds of these well-worn pianos to "tin pans beating." And so Tin Pan Alley was named—although by the 1920s it had moved closer to Broadway, on 42nd Street.

Once a song was written it had to be sold, and this was the job of the song-plugger. The best way to get it heard by the buying public was to persuade a big-name artist to sing it in vaudeville. One of the biggest names was Al JOLSON, and his greatest hits— "Swanee," "Sonny Boy," and "California, Here I Come"—are sung and whistled even today.

Many songwriters received a one-time payment for their songs—it was the publishers who made the most money. So it made sense for a good songwriter

to become a publisher himself. As well as Charles K. Harris, other songwriter-publishers were Harry von Tilzer, who wrote "Wait Till the Sun Shines, Nellie" and "A Bird in a Gilded Cage"; and Kerry Mills, composer of "Meet Me in St. Louis, Louis."

Another problem for both songwriters and publishers was the difficulty of getting a royalty payment when their songs were performed in public. In the early years of the 20th century, the composer Victor Herbert successfully sued a New York restaurant for playing his music without payment. Following the Court's decision in his favor, the American Society of Composers, Authors, and Publishers (ASCAP) was founded in 1914 to protect performing rights. ASCAP was then able to license and collect fees from thousands of restaurants and theaters.

THE ADVENT OF RECORDED SOUND

The coming of recorded sound in the early part of the 20th century changed the music scene radically. By the late 1920s, sales of records were outstripping those of sheet music, and movies were on the horizon. The first "talkie," *The Jazz Singer*, featured Al Jolson, who then requested a ballad "that will make people cry" for his second film, *The Singing Fool*. The songwriters wrote "Sonny Boy" as a practical joke, but Jolson took the ultra-corny song seriously, and it sold a million records as well as a million copies of sheet music.

Between the wars, Tin Pan Alley was dominated by several brilliant composers. Irving BERLIN, a Russian immigrant who became the all-American songwriter, wrote a stream of hits for over 50 years, starting with "Alexander's Ragtime Band" in 1911. He also became a publisher in the 1920s, and began buying back his own songs. Hits included "Blue Skies" (from *The Jazz Singer*), "Always," and "White Christmas."

George GERSHWIN was a superbly gifted pianist and arranger who could dazzle with a myriad of styles. He also wrote a stream of hits, including "Swanee," "The Man I Love," and "Embraceable You." Cole PORTER's witty, intelligent lyrics can be heard in "You're the Top," "Just One of Those Things," and "'I Get a Kick Out of You."

A BRITISH VERSION OF TIN PAN ALLEY

In 1911 the publisher Lawrence Wright bought a shop on Denmark Street, just off London's Charing Cross Road; soon he had acquired and leased the whole block, which also became known as Tin Pan Alley. His hits from the British song factory include "Among My Souvenirs," written under the pseudonym Horatio Nicholls, and "Don't Go Down the Mine, Daddy," which he bought from a street musician for 5 pounds following a pit disaster and then sold a million copies of it. In 1922, he founded the paper *Melody Maker,* devoted to popular music.

Noel COWARD challenged American supremacy with love songs such as "Someday I'll Find You" and "I'll See You Again," while also writing satirical lyrics about the British Establishment in songs such as "The Stately Homes of England" and "Mad Dogs and Englishmen." Jimmy Kennedy kept the song-pluggers busy with "Red Sails In the Sunset," "South of the Border," and "These Foolish Things," plus "The Teddy Bears' Picnic."

BRILL BUILDING

The heyday of Tin Pan Alley was over by World War II. The 1940s and 1950s were the era of the great musicals. RODGERS and HAMMERSTEIN struck gold with *Oklahoma!* and *Carousel*, while *South Pacific*, in

1949, coincided with the birth of the LP. The 1950s saw hit musicals such as *The King and I, Guys and Dolls, My Fair Lady, The Sound of Music,* and *West Side Story*, all packed with memorable singles. Whenever an artist recorded a song, a new orchestration was required, and this provided plenty of work for arrangers and orchestrators who had learned their trade in Tin Pan Alley.

In the 1960s, the need for quality songs that reflected teenage interests was satisfied by former Tin Pan Alley songwriters Al Nevins and Don Kirshner, who formed Aldon Music, one of many publishers based in New York's Brill Building. Many of the Brill Building songwriters were good performers themselves. The most sophisticated Brill Building partnership was that of Burt BACHARACH and Hal David, whose hits included "Magic Moments," "Anyone Who Had a Heart," and "Raindrops Keep Falling on My Head."

However, the market for songwriters was disappearing. The singers of the early 1970s, such as Elton JOHN and James Taylor, wrote their own material. Nowadays, the record and the accompanying video are more important than the song itself, and very few of today's chart songs are recorded by other performers. The market for sheet music has declined.

The golden age of Tin Pan Alley, with its system of songwriters, was responsible for producing many classic popular songs of enduring quality, which sold millions of copies of sheet music, which remain the standard repertoire of club and cabaret singers.

Spencer Leigh

SEE ALSO:

ARRANGERS; FILM MUSICALS; MUSICALS; POPULAR MUSIC; SINGER-SONGWRITERS.

FURTHER READING
Furia, Philip. *The Poets of Tin Pan Alley: A History of America's Greatest Lyricists* (New York: Oxford University Press, 1990).

SUGGESTED LISTENING
Burt Bacharach: *Burt Bacharach's Greatest Hits*; Irving Berlin: *Annie Get Your Gun*; *Call Me Madam* (soundtracks); Noel Coward: *Noel Coward Live in Las Vegas*; George Gershwin: *Porgy and Bess*; Al Jolson: *The Best of Al Jolson*; Cole Porter: *Kiss Me Kate*; *Silk Stockings* (soundtracks).

SIR MICHAEL TIPPETT

Michael Tippett was among those 20th-century composers who saw their work in a social context, always alive to the social and philosophical issues of the day. In his compositions, blues and spirituals can be found side by side with the extended dissonances of the atonal 20th-century idiom.

Tippett was born in London on January 2, 1905, the child of a lawyer and a nurse. His mother was an active suffragette, and perhaps it is from her that he acquired the social activisim that marked many of his works. Residence on the continent gave him fluency in French, Italian, and German as a child. Tippett attended the Fettes School in Edinburgh, and in 1923 entered the Royal College of Music as a student of composition, conducting, and piano. At the college, Tippett familiarized himself with the scores of Palestrina and other 16th-century composers, and some of his compositions echo the unmetered fluency of early music. In addition, he studied counterpoint with R. O. Morris for over a year, supporting himself by teaching French and only able to compose in his leisure time. A concert of his early compositions was given in Oxford in 1930, and his first string quartet was published in 1935.

MOURNING THE HOLOCAUST

In the 1930s, Tippett worked with the unemployed in the north of England, composing for them a short opera, *Robin Hood*. In 1940, he became director of music at Morley College, London, where Gustav HOLST had taught three decades earlier. Tippett remained in the post until 1951. During World War II, he served a three-month jail term as a conscientious objector. The revelation of the destruction of European Jewry affected Tippett deeply, and he adapted his oratorio, *A Child of Our Time*, to tell their story. The score was enthusiastically received at its first performance in 1944.

The success of *A Child of Our Time* gave Tippett the impetus to compose four more operas, the first of which, *The Midsummer Marriage*, was performed at Covent Garden in 1955. His other operas are *King Priam* (1962);

The Knot Garden (1970), and *The Ice Break* (1977). The last opera depicts American race relations, using riot scenes and a broad mix of musical references including the blues. All these operas had libretti written by Tippett himself. His operas moved in great strides of experimentalism—*King Priam* is based on the Greek epic, the *Iliad*, and the score has something of the impersonal grandeur of Greek tragedy. In *The Knot Garden,* Tippett moved to a contemporary scenario, dealing with a web of complex human relationships although without a conventional plot.

Other works include a piano concerto, four piano sonatas, five string quartets and four symphonies, plus the well-known *Fantasia Concertante on a Theme of Corelli*. Tippett set to music the words of modern poets—*Crown of the Year* (1958) was a choral setting of a poem by his friend Christopher Fry, and he used the poetry of W. B. Yeats in *Music for Words Perhaps* (1960) for speaker and chamber ensemble, and in *Byzantium* (1989) for soprano and instruments.

During the 1960s, Tippett served as director of the Bath Festival in England, taught in the United States at Aspen in 1965, and was knighted by the Queen in 1966. His last major work, the oratorio *The Mask of Time*, premiered in 1983. Tippett was always an active and articulate figure in music education, and a proponent of the broader implications of music in people's lives. He wrote a number of books including *Moving into Aquarius,* which embodied his philosophy of the New Age. Tippett died on January 8, 1998.

Jane Prendergast

SEE ALSO:

CHAMBER MUSIC; OPERA; ORCHESTRAL MUSIC; VOCAL AND CHORAL MUSIC.

FURTHER READING

Kemp, Ian. *Tippett, The Composer and His Music* (New York: Da Capo Press, 1984); Tippett, Michael, and Meirion Bowen, ed. *Tippett on Music* (New York: Oxford University Press, 1995).

SUGGESTED LISTENING

A Child of Our Time; *The Blue Guitar*; Five String Quartets; *King Priam*; Symphony No. 4; Triple Concerto for Violin, Viola, and Cello.

MEL
TORMÉ

Throughout most of his long career, Mel Tormé has been known as "the Velvet Fog." The singer himself never cared much for the nickname, coined for him by radio DJs, but it does give a sense of the uniquely mellow and almost misty quality of his voice. In addition to his vocal talents, Tormé is also a highly accomplished songwriter, pianist, drummer, actor, and author.

Melvin Howard Tormé was born in Chicago on September 13, 1925. By the age of four he was singing on the radio, and by nine he had performed in several radio soap operas. His increasing interest in singing led to a stint from 1942 to 1943 as a vocalist with a band directed by Chico Marx of the Marx Brothers.

THE MEL-TONES

In 1943, Tormé appeared in the movie *Higher and Higher* (in which another illustrious crooner named Frank SINATRA made his starring debut), and formed one of the finest pop vocal groups of the decade, the Mel-Tones. The group recorded with band singer Eugenie Baird ("I Fall in Love Too Easily," 1945), Artie Shaw's orchestra ("I Got the Sun in the Morning," 1946), Bing CROSBY ("Day by Day," 1946), and under their own name ("It's Dreamtime," 1947).

Tormé went solo in 1947, recording several hits for Capitol between 1949 and 1952, including "Careless Hands" (which reached No. 1 in 1949); "Bewitched" (backed by a band led by Stan KENTON), and "The Old Master Painter" (a duet with his regular singing partner Peggy LEE) in 1950. From the early 1950s Tormé was noted less for singles and more for his albums, especially live LPs such as *Mel Tormé at the Crescendo* (1954), which included his sped-up rendition of Richard RODGERS and Lorenz Hart's "Mountain Greenery."

In his later career, Tormé recorded for several labels, producing albums such as *Right Now* (1966), *Raindrops Keep Falling on My Head* (1970), and *An Evening with George Shearing and Mel Tormé* (1982), for which the singer won a Grammy Award as best

male jazz singer. Tormé often collaborated with his close friend Shearing, whom he described as "mercurial, with the most delicate pianistic touch on this planet."

The vocalist also made albums with several other top jazz musicians, including drummer Buddy Rich and saxophonist Gerry MULLIGAN. However, the only Top 40 pop single of Tormé's later career was "Comin' Home, Baby" (1962).

Tormé also wrote hundreds of songs (both words and music), notably "Lament to Love," "Born to Be Blue," "County Fair" and, above all, "The Christmas Song" (the 1946 Nat King COLE hit that begins "Chestnuts roasting on an open fire"), one of many tunes he composed with Robert Wells Levinson. Tormé's critically acclaimed books include *My Singing Teachers*, a tribute to artists who were his influences, *The Other Side of the Rainbow*, an account of his TV experiences with Judy GARLAND, and *It Wasn't All Velvet: An Autobiography*.

STAGE AND SCREEN

As an actor, Tormé was nominated for an Emmy for his supporting role in the 1956 Playhouse 90 production, *The Comedian*. In the 1990s Tormé not only carried on performing but also gained new, generation-crossing recognition, appearing on several popular TV sitcoms and becoming the subject of a four-CD box set spanning his career. Though weakened by heart problems, he remains one of pop music and jazz's most admired elder statesmen.

Michael R. Ross

SEE ALSO:

JAZZ; POPULAR MUSIC.

FURTHER READING
Friedwald, Will. *Jazz Singing*
(New York: Da Capo Press, 1996);
Tormé, Mel. *It Wasn't All Velvet: An Autobiography*
(New York: Viking, 1988);
Tormé, Mel. *My Singing Teachers*
(New York: Oxford University Press, 1994).

SUGGESTED LISTENING
An Evening with George Shearing and Mel Tormé;
The Mel Tormé Collection;
Mel Tormé Swings Schubert Alley.

ARTURO TOSCANINI

Arturo Toscanini was one of the great virtuoso conductors of the first half of the 20th century. His musical ear and phenomenal memory let him continue performing well into his 80s, despite failing eyesight.

Toscanini was born March 25, 1867, the sickly child of poor, working-class parents in Parma, Italy. At the age of nine, Toscanini was sent to boarding school at the Parma Conservatory of Music. Although he studied cello and composition at the conservatory, he spent hours scrutinizing and memorizing musical scores—study that was to pay dividends later in life.

FEAT OF MEMORY

Toscanini's knowledge and dedication led to an unexpected first conducting experience in 1886. He was in Rio de Janeiro as principal cellist with an Italian touring company. The singers refused to perform under an incompetent conductor, and the 19-year-old Toscanini was called to conduct. He gave a brilliant performance of Verdi's *Aida* entirely from memory.

As a result, Toscanini was engaged to conduct Catalini's new opera, *Edmea*, and his conducting career was soon well established. In 1892, he gave the premiere of Leoncavallo's opera, *I Pagliacci*, in Milan. In his 1895–96 season at Turin, he conducted the first Italian performance of Wagner's *Gotterdämmerung*, and the premiere of Puccini's *La bohème*.

In 1898, a call came from La Scala, in Milan, Italy. La Scala was at a low point, with undisciplined singing and poor playing marring the operatic productions. Toscanini made the singers stick to the score, refused to allow encores that disrupted the drama, and greatly improved the quality of the orchestral playing.

He also had the good fortune to work with two magnificent singers—the Russian bass Fyodor CHALIAPIN, and the Italian tenor Enrico CARUSO—and within a few years had returned La Scala to the pinnacle of world opera.

Toscanini was renowned for his attention to details, such as the intensity of the house lights, and asked ladies to remove their hats during performances. In 1902 he caused an uproar when he refused to allow an encore in one of Verdi's operas. As a result, he stormed out of La Scala and spent much of the next four seasons in Buenos Aires.

As much of Europe became prey to Fascism in the 1930s, Toscanini gradually ceased to conduct in Italy, Germany and Austria. This ended his association with Germany's Bayreuth festival and Austria's Salzburg Festival, where he had conducted Beethoven's *Fidelio*, and Verdi's *Falstaff*.

ABANDONING EUROPE

Toscanini now concentrated exclusively on the U.S. until the end of World War II. He had already enjoyed great success at the Metropolitan Opera in New York between 1908 and 1915, and since 1928 had spent much time there as principal conductor of the New York Philharmonic. Such was his fame that in 1937 the National Broadcasting Company (NBC) created an orchestra of top players especially for him (the NBC Symphony Orchestra). His recordings of Beethoven's symphonies with this orchestra became legendary.

Although Beethoven, Brahms, DEBUSSY, Verdi, and Wagner made up his core repertoire, Toscanini was also well known for his performances of Mozart and Richard STRAUSS among others, and for his encouragement of the American composer Samuel BARBER. He died in New York just before his 90th birthday, on January 16, 1957.

Toscanini became the first modern maestro: his dominating character, masterful conducting, and personal charisma extracted electrifying performances from his orchestras, creating a unique sound that, in many ways, revolutionized orchestral music.

Michael Lamkin

SEE ALSO:

OPERA; ORCHESTRAL MUSIC.

FURTHER READING

Haggin, B. H. *Conversations with Arturo Toscanini: Contemporary Recollections of the Maestro* (New York: Da Capo Press, 1989); Sachs, Harvey. *Toscanini* (Rocklin, CA: Prima Publishing, 1995).

SUGGESTED LISTENING

Beethoven: Symphony No. 7; Brahms: Symphonies; Debussy: *La Mer*; Puccini: *La bohème*; Verdi: *Otello*.

MERLE
TRAVIS

O ne of the greatest guitarists in the history of country music, Merle Travis was also a prolific and original songwriter. He started out on the acoustic guitar and developed the technique that is named after him, and he is also credited with inventing the idea for the solid-body electric guitar that was developed for him by Leo Fender.

Travis was born in Muhlenberg County, Kentucky, on November 29, 1917. His father was a tobacco farmer but, when Merle was four years old, he moved to work in the Kentucky coal mines. Travis's father taught him the rudiments of the mountain banjo, and later his brother made a guitar for him. Under the tutelage of local coal-mining musicians Mose Rager and Ike Everly (father of the famous EVERLY BROTHERS), Travis learned the two-finger picking style on the guitar.

FAME OVER THE RADIO

After finishing grade school, Travis began his career in earnest playing at square dances, and then joined the Knox County Knockabouts, playing live music on radio station WBGF in Evansville, Indiana. After a stint with the Tennessee Tomcats, Travis joined Clayton McMichen's renowned Georgia Wildcats, and eventually landed at Cincinnati's WLW as a member of the Drifting Pioneers. He was then reaching much wider audiences through the *National Barn Dance* and *Plantation Party* radio programs.

Travis also worked with the gospel quartet, the Brown's Ferry Four, which included Grandpa Jones and the Delmore Brothers. The group became important cast members on Cincinnati's *Boone County Jamboree* (later renamed *Midwestern Hayride*), and recorded various projects for King Records.

In the years following his service in the U.S. Marines in World War II, Travis perfected his innovative style of guitar picking—one that would become widely imitated and credited as "Travis picking." His technique involved damping the bass strings with the palm of the hand, then picking them with the thumb, and playing the melody on the higher strings with one or two fingers. At this time, he is also said to have

invented the solid-body electric guitar, now a standard instrument in most country and rock bands. Travis returned to WLW briefly, then in 1946 relocated to southern California to do session work and record for Capitol Records. His solo and duet recordings during his 23 years with Capitol included several of his biggest hits, including "Divorce Me C.O.D.," "So Round, So Firm, So Fully Packed," "Smoke, Smoke, Smoke (That Cigarette)," "Dark as a Dungeon," the very famous "Sixteen Tons" and the "Nine Pound Hammer." This was the period when Travis was using material from his coal-mining background to write folk songs about the lives of the miners.

In 1954, Travis played a young GI in the movie *From Here to Eternity*, singing "Re-Enlistment Blues," and in 1955, with Hank Thompson, had a country hit with a reworking of the CARTER FAMILY's "Wildwood Flower." With the ensuing folk music revival, Travis rode another wave of popularity in the late 1950s, as his tradition-rooted mountain ballads and guitar wizardry were re-discovered by college students and festival audiences around the world.

Travis took part in Nitty Gritty Dirt Band's monumental 1971 album celebrating country music, *Will the Circle Be Unbroken?* His duet recording with Chet ATKINS produced a Grammy for best country instrumental performance. In 1977, he was inducted into the Country Music Hall of Fame. Travis died in Oklahoma in 1983.

The music of Merle Travis had a profound impact on the next generation of country guitar pickers, including Atkins and Johnny Watson, and his influence still lives on for country music guitar players.

Todd Denton

SEE ALSO:
COUNTRY; FOLK MUSIC.

FURTHER READING
Eatherly, Pat Travis. *In Search of My Father*
(Nashville, TN: Broadman Press, 1987);
Eremo, Judie, ed. *Country Musicians: From the Editors of Guitar Player, Keyboard and Frets Magazines*
(Cupertino, CA: Grove Press, 1987).

SUGGESTED LISTENING
Country Guitar Thunder; *Folk Songs of the Hills*;
Guitar Retrospective; *Walkin' the Strings*.

ERNEST TUBB

Country music veteran Ernest Tubb makes a surprise appearance at singer Loretta Lynn's show at the Riviera Hotel in Las Vegas, July 1981.

A tremendous innovator in country music as well as a great stylist, Ernest Tubb had a warm, slightly flat baritone voice that made him one of country's best-loved and most enduring performers.

Ernest Dale Tubb was born on February 9, 1914, in Ellis County, Texas, to a cotton-farming family. In 1928, Tubb was enthralled by a record of country music pioneer Jimmie RODGERS, and made it his life's mission to follow in Rodgers' footsteps. Tubb took up guitar in 1933, just months before his hero succumbed to tuberculosis. On a whim, Tubb contacted Rodgers' widow Carrie, who struck up a friendship with Tubb and offered to assist him with his career. She loaned him one of her late husband's guitars and championed the aspiring Tubb to RCA, who gave him a recording contract in 1936. Unfortunately, Tubb's records flopped and RCA dropped him. He lost his ability to yodel like Rodgers after having his tonsils removed in 1939.

In 1940, Tubb secured a contract with Decca, starting an association with the label that was to last nearly 40 years. He developed his own country style on his early Decca recordings. Aside from his distinctive voice, Tubb's records featured both steel and electric guitar, ushering in the harder-edged sound of honky-tonk. The new style immediately proved popular—Tubb's 1941 recording "Walking the Floor Over You" sold over a million copies and turned him into a country star. In 1943, Tubb and his band, the Texas Troubadours, made their *Grand Ole Opry* debut, daring to introduce electric instruments on the hallowed stage of Nashville's Ryman Auditorium. Tubb's other business venture, the Ernest Tubb Record Shop, opened in Nashville in 1947, and became the site of WSM's post-Opry *Midnight Jamboree* radio show, hosted by Tubb himself. Along with Roy ACUFF, Tubb was one of the biggest stars of the 1940s country boom, scoring hits with "Rainbow at Midnight," "It's Been So Long Darling," and "Blue Christmas."

Although he never again reached the commercial heights he enjoyed in the 1940s and 1950s, Ernest Tubb remained one of country music's most popular personalities throughout the rest of his life. In the 1960s, he hosted a network television show and recorded a series of duets with the up-and-coming female country star Loretta LYNN. Tubb maintained a rigorous touring schedule, playing nearly 300 dates a year through the late 1970s, until emphysema forced him to retire in 1982. He died on September 6, 1984, in Nashville.

While never a classically "good" singer by any stretch of the imagination, the rough-hewn sincerity of Tubb's delivery outweighed the need for perfect pitch, at least as far as his fans were concerned. The man who began his career as a Jimmie Rodgers imitator eventually became a powerful influence in his own right: many later country singers, especially Red Foley, Lefty Frizell, and Junior Brown, have acknowledged that they owe a stylistic debt to the man they lovingly called "E. T."

Greg Bower

SEE ALSO:
COUNTRY.

FURTHER READING

Pugh, Ronnie. *Ernest Tubb: The Texas Troubadour* (Durham, NC: Duke University Press, 1996).

SUGGESTED LISTENING

The Country Music Hall of Fame;
The Legendary Ernest Tubb and Friends.

RICHARD
TUCKER

Richard Tucker inherited the mantle of Enrico Caruso as leading tenor at the Metropolitan Opera in New York, where, from 1945 to 1975, he appeared in 499 performances at the house (and an additional 225 on tour), in 30 roles. One of the most popular tenors of his time, it is appropriate that Tucker gained the nickname "America's Caruso."

The future lyric tenor was born Reuben Ticker in New York City on August 28, 1913. His parents were Jews who had emigrated from Eastern Europe, and Tucker remained conscious of his Jewish heritage throughout his life. As an opera singer, he might be given the role of a monk, but he refused to wear a crucifix. He sang only once in a Christian church—at St. Patrick's Cathedral, in New York City—for the funeral of Robert Kennedy.

Tucker's earliest singing experience was as a boy alto in the synagogue choir. Later he entertained at weddings and bar mitzvahs, which, along with work as a tailor in a furrier's business, helped him to finance his vocal studies with Paul Althouse.

OPERA DEBUT

In 1943 Tucker became the cantor of the Brooklyn Jewish Center, with a congregation of 2,000, and that same year made his operatic debut with the Salmaggi Opera, a small company in New York. He entered the Metropolitan Opera auditions but did not do well. Nonetheless, his teacher persuaded Edward Johnson, the general director of the Metropolitan, to attend services at the Jewish Center in order to hear the cantor sing, and a contract was issued, enabling Tucker to make his Metropolitan Opera debut in 1945 as Enzio in Ponchielli's *La Gioconda.*

Even after his operatic career was assured, Tucker continued to act as an ordained cantor, and in fact recorded the Passover Service. The tenor achieved widespread fame in North America in the 1940s through his radio exposure on the program *Chicago Theater of the Air*. Tucker's European debut in 1947 coincided with that of Maria CALLAS when they sang together in *La Gioconda* in Verona.

At this time, Tucker's voice was what is called *lirico spinto* (an incisive lyric voice), and he soon added the demanding roles of Rodolfo in Puccini's *La bohème*, and Don José in Bizet's *Carmen* to his repertoire. He hesitated before tackling any Mozart roles, but was successful in *Così fan tutte*.

PRACTICAL JOKES

Despite his excellent singing voice and powerful range, Tucker's acting was often criticized for being too melodramatic and overstated. Also while onstage, although dependable and easy to work with, Tucker became well known for carrying out pranks. Once during a performance at the Metropolitan, Tucker handed baritone Robert Merrill a casket with a nude picture inside. Similar jokes were not uncommon during Tucker's performances.

As he aged, Tucker's voice tended more to the dramatic, and he sang in Saint-Saëns' *Samson* and as Calaf in Puccini's *Turandot*. Only weeks before his death he appeared in Leoncavallo's dramatic *I Pagliacci*. He had campaigned for the reintroduction of Halévy's *La juive* into the Met's repertoire, but as he readied himself to perform in Michigan, he died of a heart attack on January 8, 1975.

Tucker sang at La Scala from 1961, and in Vienna and Covent Garden from 1958. However, he was so closely identified with the Metropolitan Opera that his funeral was held onstage at the opera house. The Richard Tucker Foundation set up in his memory awards $20,000 annually to further the career of a promising young singer.

Jane Prendergast

SEE ALSO:

OPERA; VOCAL AND CHORAL MUSIC.

FURTHER READING
Breslin, Herbert H. ed. *The Tenors*
(New York: Macmillan, 1974);
Drake, James A. *Richard Tucker:
A Biography*
(New York: Dutton, 1984).

SUGGESTED LISTENING
Tucker at the Met (Donizetti, Verdi,
Ponchielli, Puccini); Puccini: *La bohème*;
Verdi: *La Forza del Destino*; *Il Trovatore*.

SOPHIE
TUCKER

During her 60-year singing career, Sophie Tucker, nicknamed "the last of the red hot mamas," established herself as one of the great entertainers of the century. With her raucous singing style, she triumphed in every arena she entered, from theater, film, and cabaret, to records, radio, and television. Whether she was belting out "hot" tunes such as "After You're Gone" or ethnic tearjerkers like "My Yiddishe Mommie," Tucker was a larger-than-life performer who made audiences laugh and weep. Exulting in her flamboyant image, she would appear on nightclub stages in 24-carat-gold gowns, mink coats, and diamond headdresses. She was perhaps the biggest recording star of the vaudeville era.

Born Sophie Kalish in Poland in January 1884, to Jewish parents fleeing Russia, she came to America when she was three. The young Sophie sang in her parents' restaurant in Hartford, Connecticut, between cooking and waitressing duties. At age 16, she married Louis Tuck and expanded his name when she left him to pursue a career in New York (with her young son now in the care of her parents).

In 1905, Sophie Tucker won an amateur singing contest and took a $15-a-week job performing in a German beer hall. Plump and plain (but blessed with a stage presence once compared to "a battleship with a voice like 70 trombones"), she was forced to perform in blackface at Tony Pastor's Music Hall. Tucker was an immediate success on the vaudeville circuit, but then dropped this racist style when her costumes and makeup failed to show up one night—and was a smash in her own right. She began calling herself a ragtime singer, and got her first real taste of stardom as a featured act in the 1909 *Ziegfeld Follies*.

In 1910, she made her first recording for Edison— "That Loving Rag." Her first reaction to her recorded voice was, "My God, I sound like a foghorn!" Sophie's maid convinced her to hear a new tune by the African-American songwriter and vaudevillian Shelton Brooks. The tune was "Some of These Days," and it became her theme song. She recorded it in 1911 and on numerous subsequent occasions, including a 1926 version with the Ted Lewis band, which sold a million copies. "I've turned it inside out, singing it in every way imaginable," she wrote in her autobiography, "as a dramatic song, as a novelty number, as a sentimental ballad, and always audiences have loved it and asked for it." Another Shelton Brooks number closely associated with Sophie Tucker was "Darktown Strutters Ball."

She formed a jazz band called Sophie Tucker and Her Five Kings of Syncopation, but disbanded it to star in musical revues such as *Shubert Gaieties* (1919) and *Earl Carroll Vanities* (1924). She remained associated with ragtime through the 1920s, with recordings such as "International Rag" and "Bugle Call Rag." In the 1927 show *La Maire's Affairs*, Tucker sang the classic "When the Red Red Robin Goes Bob Bob Bobbin' Along." She had another million-copy seller in 1928, with "My Yiddishe Mommie," on which she was supported by Ted Shapiro, her accompanist of 46 years.

Sophie Tucker was always at her best in live performance, being just as at home with jazz, blues, swing, and schmaltzy ballads as she was with ragtime. With the demise of vaudeville in the 1930s, Tucker spent more time in cabaret. She appeared in several unremarkable Hollywood musicals, including 1929's *Honky Tonk*, and also starred on Broadway in the 1937 Cole PORTER musical, *Leave It to Me*.

As Tucker got older, she continued to perform across America and in Europe, mocking the aging process with spicy specialty numbers such as "Life Begins at 40" and "I'm Having More Fun Since I'm 60." The last of the red hot mamas died in February 1966, at the age of 82, in New York City.

Michael R. Ross

SEE ALSO:

CABARET MUSIC; FILM MUSICALS; MUSICALS.

FURTHER READING
Segal, Harold. *Turn-of-the-Century Cabaret* (New York: Schirmer Books, 1996); Tucker, Sophie. *Some of These Days* (Garden City, NY: Doubleday, Doran, 1945).

SUGGESTED LISTENING
I'm the Last of the Red Hot Mamas; *Jazz Age Hot Mama: 1922–1929*; *Some of These Days*.

TINA
TURNER

Legendary for her tireless live performances, Tina Turner has a strong, soaring voice with a raw edge—the epitome of the soul/blues singer. Though possessing a wide vocal range, her most passionate work is sung in the lower register. While she could be described as a "shouter" in the rhythm and blues (R&B) tradition, she is also a superb performer of slow emotional numbers.

She was born Annie Mae Bullock in Nutbush, Tennessee, on November 26, 1938. As a child she sang gospel in her family's church choir, and appeared in talent shows. She moved to St. Louis with her mother and sister in the 1950s, where she met guitarist and vocalist Ike Turner of The Kings of Rhythm. She joined The Kings as backing singer, and soon became the core of the group, marrying Turner in 1958. Her first recording was the song "Box Top" (1958), and she first sang lead vocals on "A Fool in Love" (1960), which became the group's first million-copy hit. For the release of that record, Ike changed her name to Tina.

In 1962, The Kings of Rhythm became the Ike and Tina Turner Revue. With nine musicians and three female backing singers, the Revue became a major soul band. Unfortunately, their critically acclaimed album *River Deep, Mountain High* (1966) failed to create interest with the U.S. listening public, although it reached No. 3 on the U.K. charts. As a result, they were given a slot as the warm-up act on the ROLLING STONES' 1966 British tour, which won them many fans. They were also the opening act for the Stones' U.S. tour in 1969. In the 1970s, the Turners continued recording and touring, releasing a successful version of Creedence Clearwater Revival's "Proud Mary" in 1971. The autobiographical song "Nutbush City Limits" (1973), written by Tina, brought them widespread international success. Tina Turner also enjoyed critical acclaim for her performance as the Acid Queen in Ken Russell's film version of THE WHO's rock-opera *Tommy* (1975).

Tina and Ike fought frequently over his womanizing, and their relationship deteriorated as he fell into the grip of drugs. On stage and in the studio, he was a musical martinet, rarely allowing her to expand as an artist. After several suicide attempts, Tina eventually left Ike and the Revue at the beginning of a tour in 1976, sneaking out of a motel room with only the clothes she was wearing and the money in her pocket (36 cents). She also relinquished all legal rights to the songs she had recorded with Ike.

DRAMATIC COMEBACK

After appearing with various artists such as Rod Stewart and the Stones, Tina Turner began to reestablish her career. In 1982, she enjoyed enormous success in Europe with Al Green's song "Let's Stay Together." She signed with Capitol Records in 1984 and released the album *Private Dancer*, which reached the No. 3 slot in the U.S. album charts and produced three Top 10 singles: "Better Be Good to Me" (1984, No. 5), "What's Love Got to Do with It?" (1984, No. 1), and "Private Dancer" (1985, No. 7). Turner earned three Grammys in 1984 for best pop single ("Private Dancer"), best rock performance ("Better Be Good to Me"), and album of the year. In 1985, she starred in the film *Mad Max: Beyond Thunderdome*. Her 1986 autobiography *I, Tina* was a best-seller, and was later made into the movie *What's Love Got to Do with It?* (1993), although she condemned it as inaccurate.

To promote her 1986 album *Break Every Rule*, Turner toured for 14 months, performing 230 concerts. It paid off: the album went platinum and "Typical Male" was a No. 2 hit. In 1989, she released the album *Foreign Affair*, her first in three years. She sang the title theme for the 1995 James Bond film *Goldeneye,* and in 1996 released the album *Wildest Dreams*. Tina Turner has built up an enormous and devoted fan-base for her gutsy songs and performance style.

Steve Valdez

SEE ALSO:

FILM MUSIC; GOSPEL; ROCK MUSIC; ROCK'N'ROLL; SOUL.

FURTHER READING
Gaar, G. *She's A Rebel* (Seattle, WA: Seal Press, 1992);
Turner, Tina, and Kurt Loder. *I, Tina*
(New York: Avon, 1986).

SUGGESTED LISTENING
Break Every Rule; *Ike and Tina Turner Revue Live*;
Private Dancer; *River Deep, Mountain High*;
Simply the Best; *Wildest Dreams*.

McCoy
TYNER

A unique jazz pianist unsurpassed in musical fire, style, and overall sound, McCoy Tyner has enjoyed a long and successful career in both supporting roles and as a soloist, bandleader, and composer. His creative and extraordinary tenure with the John COLTRANE Quartet from 1960 to 1965 (with bandmates Coltrane, Jimmy Garrison, and Elvin JONES) earned Tyner the position of venerated master and a place in the annals of jazz history.

McCoy Tyner was born in Philadelphia on December 11, 1938, and studied piano from an early age through his college years. He first gained serious attention as a member of Art Farmer and Benny Golson's Jazztet in the late 1950s, but by 1960 he had received and accepted an offer to join the new John Coltrane group. Over the next five years, saxophonist Coltrane, Tyner, drummer Elvin Jones, and bassist Jimmy Garrison set about redefining jazz. In helping to establish and expand upon the ideas of Miles DAVIS's modal jazz and Ornette COLEMAN's free jazz experiments, they created several classic recordings, including "My Favorite Things," "A Love Supreme," "Africa Brass," and "Sun Ship."

It was during this period that Tyner developed many of his unique abilities—interesting, open chord-voicings, a departure from traditional jazz harmony necessitated by Coltrane's focus on modal playing, an aggressive but controlled rhythmic style, and most of all, endurance. Live and on record, the Coltrane Quartet often improvised on pieces that lasted 20 or 30 minutes each. The muscular propulsion of Garrison and Jones, and the Coltrane penchant for long exploratory solos, demanded similar stamina from Tyner.

Tyner left Coltrane in 1965, and after some lean years embarked on a solo career that has included releases on the Impulse, Blue Note, Milestone, and Elektra labels. Tyner has recorded and performed with Jackie McLean, Arthur Blythe, Ron Carter, and Joe HENDERSON, among others, and has helped initiate or propel the careers of John Blake, Joony Booth, and Alphonse Mouzon.

David Redfern/Redferns

"Elder statesman of jazz" McCoy Tyner remains an exciting, creative contributor to the modern jazz scene.

By continuing the experimental direction set by the Coltrane Quartet, Tyner allows the jazz public to hear and evaluate these experiments. His own compositions, which include "Blues on the Corner," "Land of the Lonely," and "Desert Cry," are informed by the dynamism of his playing, and by the African, European, and Oriental music traditions that influence his music. Through it all, he remains steadfastly a hard-swinging modern jazz pianist thoroughly grounded in the hard bop tradition.

Gregg Juke

SEE ALSO:
FREE JAZZ; JAZZ; MODAL JAZZ.

FURTHER READING

Feather, Leonard. *The Passion for Jazz* (New York: Da Capo Press, 1990); Lyons, Len. *The Great Jazz Pianists* (New York: Da Capo Press, 1983).

SUGGESTED LISTENING

Enlightenment; *Inception*; *The Real McCoy*; *Sahara*; John Coltrane: *Impressions*; *A Love Supreme*.

U2

A rock group with a social conscience and a spiritual message can still be immensely popular and produce great music—especially if it has a powerful beat. The group U2 proves the theory.

Hailed by *Rolling Stone* magazine as "one of the most adventurous and groundbreaking acts in pop music," the Irish ensemble features a big, soaring sound, highlighted by their singer Bono's intense, often sensuous vocals, and the Edge's reverb-laden guitar style. The blending of this powerful wall of sound with Bono's starkly poetic lyrics has created a catalog of classics (including "Where the Streets Have No Name" and "Desire") which made U2 the most commercially successful rock band of the 1980s.

HIGH SCHOOL BOND

U2 was assembled in 1978 while its members were still students at Dublin's Mount Temple High School. Made up of singer-lyricist Bono (b. Paul Hewson, May 10, 1960), guitarist the Edge (b. Dave Evans, August 8, 1961), bassist Adam Clayton (b. March 15, 1960), and drummer Larry Mullen, Jr. (b. October 31, 1961) the band started their musical career playing other people's songs at small, local clubs. They were first called Feedback and later the Hype, before settling on U2.

In 1980, U2 signed with the Island record label, and released its debut album *Boy*, which is full of fierce energy and teenage angst. The group manifested its spiritual side on the 1981 album *October*, with the Christian symbolism most evident in the songs "Gloria" and "Rejoice." With the 1983 album *War*, the band went from being a successful Irish band to world superstardom. Revealing the group's political consciousness, the album featured the song "Sunday Bloody Sunday," a rock anthem that dealt with the troubles in Northern Ireland. The title refers to the day in January 1972, when 13 Catholic protesters were shot dead by British paratroopers. Another song, "The Unforgettable Fire" (1984), further documented the band's devotion to social justice. "(Pride) In the Name of Love" was dedicated to the civil rights leader Martin Luther King. The band made

a memorable appearance at the 1985 Live Aid charity concert, and later that year Bono appeared as one of the Artists Against Apartheid on the "Sun City" single. But the critical and commercial success of their 1987 album *The Joshua Tree*, with its two No. 1 hits, "With or Without You" and "I Still Haven't Found What I'm Looking For," elevated the band into the pantheon of rock legends. Ranked by *Rolling Stone* as the third best album of the 1980s, *Joshua Tree* won two Grammys, including album of the year.

Rattle & Hum, a 1988 "rockumentary" of the band's U.S. tour, yielded two hit singles, "Desire" and "Angel of Harlem." However, the accompanying album was met with, at best, indifference from critics. *Achtung Baby* (1991), notable for "Mysterious Ways" and "One," showed U2 undergoing a stylistic change to a more dance-oriented sound and more intimate love songs.

FAMOUS FRIENDS

Johnny CASH made a memorable guest appearance, singing "The Wanderer" on the 1993 album *Zooropa*, which Bono hailed as his favorite U2 track—even though his voice was not on it. However, Bono did appear with Frank SINATRA on his 1993 album *Duets*, singing a gender-bending "I've Got You Under My Skin." The 1995 single "Hold Me, Thrill Me, Kiss Me, Kill Me" heard in the film *Batman Forever*, signaled a continuing interest in experimenting with many musical genres, as did the album *Pop* (1997), with its innovative blend of funk, house and rock.

Michael R. Ross

SEE ALSO:

ROCK FESTIVALS; ROCK MUSIC.

FURTHER READING
Carter, Alan. *U2: The Road to Pop*
(Boston: Faber and Faber, 1997);
Flanagan, Bill. *U2 at the End of the World*
(New York: Delacorte Press, 1995);
Stokes, Niall. *Into the Heart:*
The Stories Behind Every U2 Song
(New York: Thunder's Mouth Press, 1998).

SUGGESTED LISTENING
Achtung Baby; *The Joshua Tree*; *Pop*;
Under a Blood Red Sky; *The Unforgettable Fire*;
War; *Zooropa*.

RUDY
VALLEE

Wavy-haired Rudy Vallee was the first star—and arguably the father—of the relaxed, intimate singing style known as "crooning." With his trademark megaphone, which he used to amplify his thin, nasal voice, Vallee became one of the most popular performers of the late-1920s and 1930s, with hits such as "My Time Is Your Time" and "I'm Just a Vagabond Lover." He admitted, rather candidly, "I never had much of a voice ... one reason for the success was that I was the first articulate singer—people could understand the words." Known as the "Heigh-ho" man, after his catchphrase, Vallee was one of the earliest artists to generate mass hysteria among his fans. He also established a second career as a Hollywood actor.

Born in July 1901, in Island Pond, Vermont, Hubert Prior Vallee was the son of a pharmacist. He learned to play the saxophone as a teenager by imitating his idol Rudy Wiedhoft. Later, he took the name "Rudy" himself, both in tribute to Wiedhoft and also to play on the romantic image of silent-screen star Rudolph Valentino. Vallee made his professional debut in 1920 with a theater orchestra in Portland, Maine, and played throughout his college years with various bands at the University of Maine and at Yale. Starting in 1924, he took a year off from school to play sax in London with the Savoy Havanna Band.

In 1928, after graduating, Vallee organized a society band, the Yale Collegians, which was soon performing at New York's chic Heigh-Ho Club. After rich Yale alumni complained that the bandmembers didn't resemble Yale men, the orchestra was rechristened the Connecticut Yankees. The orchestra became an immediate sensation with its blend of college and dance tunes, spotlighting Vallee's genteel crooning and sax playing. In 1929, Vallee was hired to star on radio's first variety show, *The Fleishmann Hour*, and quickly became one of the biggest stars in show business. His sweet, sentimental style was perfectly suited to the new medium, and his catch-phrase "Heigh-ho everybody" became as famous as his megaphone. Many of Vallee's biggest hits were introduced on the show, including "Goodnight, Sweetheart," "Sweet Lorraine," "The Stein Song," and Yale University's "The Whiffenpoof Song." The song "I'm Just a Vagabond Lover," featured in his 1929 movie debut *Glorifying the American Girl*, provided the title for Vallee's first starring feature film later that year. Another 1929 hit was "My Time Is Your Time," which was the theme to his long-running radio show. Vallee grew so successful during this period that he founded his own talent agency and a music publishing company.

Vallee moved to Broadway and appeared in the 1931 and 1936 editions of *George White's Scandals*, and the 1934 screen version. However, his star was beginning to fade with the emergence of a new breed of natural-sounding crooners like Bing CROSBY and Frank SINATRA. During World War II, Vallee led the California Coastguard Orchestra, and his film career switched to comedy, with hilarious performances in the classic Preston Sturges films *The Palm Beach Story* (1942) and *Mad Wednesday* (1947).

In 1962, Vallee starred as a stuffed-shirt industrialist in Frank LOESSER's hit musical *How to Succeed in Business Without Really Trying*, and reprised the role in the 1967 movie version of the show. The New Vaudeville Band's 1966 novelty hit "Winchester Cathedral" was a tribute to Vallee's style (complete with megaphone), and the aging crooner repaid the compliment by recording the song during a failed comeback attempt.

Vallee made his last feature film in 1976, and performed his one-man show right up until his death from a heart attack in Los Angeles, California, in July 1986, at the age of 84.

Michael R. Ross

SEE ALSO:

FILM MUSICALS; MUSICALS; POPULAR MUSIC.

FURTHER READING

Vallee, Eleanor, and Jill Amadio. *My Vagabond Lover: An Intimate Biography of Rudy Vallee* (Dallas, TX: Taylor Publishing, 1996); Vallee, Rudy. *Let the Chips Fall* (Harrisburg, PA: Stackpole Books, 1975).

SUGGESTED LISTENING

How to Succeed in Business Without Really Trying; *I'm Just a Vagabond Lover*; *Rudy Vallee and His Connecticut Yankees*; *Sing for Your Supper*.

EDGARD VARÈSE

Edgard Varèse's ground-breaking atonal pieces made much use of unpitched percussion, complex rhythms, and unconventional instruments to produce his "organized sound," as he called his music. He was one of the first to use a tape recorder in music, producing early electronic pieces. Although his total output was quite small, his influence on 20th-century music was enormous.

Varèse was born in Paris on December 22, 1883. He studied under Vincent d'Indy and Albert ROUSSEL at the Schola Cantorum in Paris, and later with Charles Widor at the Paris Conservatory. For a few months, Varèse lived in Germany, where he met Busoni, the Italian composer who had settled in Berlin. Although Busoni had a slight influence on him, Varèse's main inspiration was the 12th-century composer Perotin. In 1915, Varèse moved to the U.S.

The music from his early period, most of which is now lost or destroyed, was of a Romantic or Impressionist nature. It included the *Rhapsodie romane* (1905), *Les Cycles du Nord* (1914), *Oedipus und die Sphinx* (1910–14), and the symphonic poem *Bourgogne* (1908), which Varèse himself destroyed in the early 1960s.

EXPONENT OF THE NEW MUSIC

During the 1920s, Varèse was one of the most active composers in the United States, organizing concerts of "new music," both American and European, in New York and elsewhere. The works from this second period use fairly small wind and percussion ensembles (he disliked strings). Varèse also introduced extra percussion, employing the instruments as much for timbre as for rhythm, and "noise instruments" such as sirens. Important pieces from this period were *Amériques*, for orchestra and siren (1917–21); *Hyperprism*, a short work for wind, percussion, and siren (1922–23); *Octandre*, for wind, brass, and double bass (1923); and *Intégrales*, for chamber orchestra and percussion (1924–25). *Arcana* (1925–27) was written for a large orchestra. In 1928, Varèse returned to Paris for an extended period. Here he became increasingly interested in the need for and potential of electronic instruments, and this period produced some of his most innovative music. *Ionisation* (1931), scored for 41 percussion instruments and two sirens, is almost entirely unpitched. *Ecuatorial* (1934) was written for voice, brass, organ, percussion, and two theremins or ondes martenot (early electronic instruments); and *Density 21.5* (1935) was composed for solo flute.

FOUND SOUNDS

Varèse wrote very little during the next 18 years. Then, in 1953, someone gave him a tape recorder, and this enabled him to record and cut in the "found sounds" (everyday sounds from the world around) that he used in *Déserts* (1954), which was scored for wind, percussion, and tape. This was followed by *Poème électronique*, a piece of pure *musique concrète* (using natural sound sources) for a three-track tape. This piece was constructed of both electronically generated and manipulated sounds in the Philips electronic laboratories at Eindhoven in the Netherlands. It was played through 400 loudspeakers inside the Philips Pavilion, designed by the architect Le Corbusier, at the World's Fair in Brussels in 1958.

Back in the U.S. Varèse began to receive recognition for his work, which was recorded and also performed live. He became interested in the themes of night and death, and worked intermittently on a new project, *Nocturnal*, which was performed incomplete at a concert in 1961. It was still unfinished at the time of Varèse's death on November 6, 1965.

Richard Trombley

SEE ALSO:

AMPLIFICATION; ELECTRONIC MUSIC.

FURTHER READING

Bernard, Jonathan W. *The Music of Edgard Varèse* (New Haven, CT: Yale University Press, 1987); Quellette, Fernand, trans. Derek Coltman. *Edgard Varèse* (New York: Da Capo Press, 1981).

SUGGESTED LISTENING

Amériques; *Density 21.5*; *Déserts*; *Ecuatorial*; *Intégrales*; *Ionisation*; *Nocturnal*; *Poème électronique*.

SARAH VAUGHAN

Her rich contralto voice, combined with an impeccable pitch and spellbinding style, made Sarah Vaughan an artist of considerable importance in jazz and pop music. With more than 1,000 records and nearly 100 albums to her credit, Vaughan was, according to critic Gary Giddins, "jazz's greatest virtuoso singer."

Born in Newark, New Jersey, on March 27, 1924, Sarah Lois Vaughan began studying the piano and organ when she was seven. Her mother, a laundress, played piano and sang in a local church choir. By age 12, Sarah was a featured soloist in the choir and also its organist. In 1942, she entered the Amateur Night at the Apollo talent contest, winning the first prize of ten dollars and a week's engagement at the legendary Harlem Theater. The great African-American singer Billy Eckstine, who performed with the Earl Hines Orchestra, heard Sarah and urged Hines to hire her.

When Eckstine launched his own orchestra in 1944, Sarah joined the new ensemble, which featured future jazz luminaries such as Charlie PARKER, Dizzy GILLESPIE, and Miles DAVIS. During this time, Vaughan cut her first records, including a legendary version of "Lover Man" with Parker and Gillespie, and signed as a solo artist with Musicraft Records in 1945.

Trumpeter George Treadwell, Vaughan's first husband, became a Svengali-like manager who molded her image from that of an ugly ducking to a glamorous star. Between 1945 and 1954, which included a four-year stint with the major Columbia label, she became one of modern jazz's top singers and earned the nickname "the Divine One."

In 1954, Vaughan launched two simultaneous careers—as a pop hitmaker for Mercury Records and a jazz artist for its EmArcy subsidiary. She cut several pop hits such as "Misty," "Tenderly," the million-selling "Broken-Hearted Melody," several albums of show music (most notably a duet LP of Irving BERLIN songs with Eckstine), and several small-group jazz sides with Clifford BROWN and Cannonball ADDERLEY. In the first half of the 1960s, she recorded for Roulette, Mercury, and Columbia before taking a five-year break.

Sarah Vaughan performing at the 1985 Newport Jazz Festival—she also appeared at the first event in 1954.

UPI/Corbis

Vaughan returned to music in the early 1970s with a new maturity and a deeper range (the result perhaps of chain-smoking). During this period she recorded some of her best work for producer Norman GRANZ's Pablo label, backed by everything from small ensembles and strings to big bands and Brazilian rhythm sections. Even though she became increasingly ill in the 1980s, she still performed at concerts and recorded frequently—including a 1985 concept album based on poems by Pope John Paul II. Vaughan died at her home in Hidden Hills, California, on April 3, 1990.

Michael R. Ross

SEE ALSO:
JAZZ; POPULAR MUSIC.

FURTHER READING
Friedwald, Will. *Jazz Singing*
(New York: C. Scribner's Sons, 1990);
Gourse, Leslie. *Sassy: The Life of Sarah Vaughan*
(New York: C. Scribner's Sons, 1993).

SUGGESTED LISTENING
16 Most Requested Songs; Sarah Sings Soulfully;
Sarah Vaughan and Clifford Brown;
Sarah Vaughan: Golden Hits;
Verve Jazz Masters: Sarah Vaughan.

RALPH
VAUGHAN
WILLIAMS

The English composer Ralph Vaughan Williams transformed the simple elements of folk song and hymn into a glorious outpouring of musical compositions for solo voice, mixed chorus, and symphony orchestra. But he also incorporated a wide-ranging humanism in his use of texts by John Bunyan, Shakespeare, and Walt Whitman, and in his explorations of the themes of war and heroism.

In contrast to many of his contemporaries in music, Vaughan Williams led a quiet life. He was born on October 12, 1872, the son of a church rector, in Gloucestershire. In 1887, he was sent to Charterhouse school, where several of his compositions were performed, and in 1890 he entered the Royal College of Music in London, as a student of composition and organ. He took a Bachelor of Music degree in 1894, and an Arts degree from Trinity College in 1895. That year, he married Adeline Fischer and returned to the Royal College of Music to work towards a doctorate in music, supporting himself as an organist in South Lambeth Church. He studied in Berlin with the composer Max Bruch, and in 1908 began composition lessons in Paris with Maurice RAVEL. Although Vaughan Williams returned to England after three months, his correspondence with Ravel, who admired his work, continued for many years.

In 1904, Vaughan Williams was given the job of editing the new *English Hymnal*. This collection of hymns was the composer's first exercise in setting words to music for popular use, and many of the musical settings are fresh, miniature art forms. In addition, he spent time in Norfolk, England, together with his life-long friend Gustav HOLST, recording over 800 British folk songs. These tunes were to emerge years later in the incidental music for the play *The Merry Wives of Windsor* (1908), as well as in his operas *Sir John in Love* (1929) and *Hugh the Drover* (1924). Several of Vaughan Williams's most enduring works were written in 1910, including the choral *Sea Symphony*, which was performed that year at the Leeds Festival, and the *Fantasia on a Theme of Thomas Tallis*. However, his first great success was *A London Symphony*, which premiered in 1914.

During World War I, Williams served in Macedonia and France. After demobilization, he became professor of composition at the Royal College of Music, and the conductor of the Bach Choir from 1920 to 1926. During this time he wrote the *Pastoral Symphony* (1921), which looked for serenity after the war, and the choral *Sancta Civitas* (1925), an exploration of man's soul, with texts from the book of Revelation.

He visited the United States for the first time during the Norfolk Festival (Connecticut) in 1923. The following year, he finished his opera, *Hugh the Drover*, and the song cycle, *On Wenlock Edge*. Vaughan Williams returned to the U.S. to lecture at Bryn Mawr in 1932, and at Cornell in 1954.

The gathering threat of World War II in Europe inspired Williams' tremendous choral masterpiece *Dona Nobis Pacem* (1936), to which Walt Whitman contributed the text. His work for German refugees resulted in his music being banned by Nazi Germany. During the war, Vaughan Williams, entering his 70s, threw himself into war work with unabated energy.

Adeline, his wife of 54 years, died in 1951, and in 1953 he married Ursula Wood, an old family friend. He wrote the last five of his nine symphonies, the seventh of which was the *Sinfonia antarctica*, originally a score for the film *Scott of the Antarctic* (1948), and a large number of vocal and instrumental pieces. He died on August 26, 1958, leaving behind a rich body of work.

Jane Prendergast

SEE ALSO:
ORCHESTRAL MUSIC; VOCAL AND CHORAL MUSIC.

FURTHER READING
Vaughan Williams, Ursula. *RVW*
(New York: Oxford University Press, 1984);
Vaughan Williams, Ursula, and Imogen Holst, eds.
*Ralph Vaughan Williams and Gustav Holst:
Correspondence* (Westport, CT: Greenwood Press, 1980).

SUGGESTED LISTENING
Dona Nobis Pacem; *Lark Ascending*;
Sea Songs; *A Sea Symphony*; *Serenade to Music*;
Sinfonia Antarctica; Symphony No. 5.

CAETANO VELOSO

Caetano Veloso has been at the forefront of Brazilian music since the early 1960s. As well as producing innovative music, Veloso is also one of the most respected poets in the Portuguese language, and he was one of the prime creators of an inventive wave of Brazilian pop known as *tropicalismo* (tropicalism).

In the early 1960s, in college in Bahia, Veloso was exposed to rock music and linked up with another young singer/guitarist, Gilberto Gil. Both men moved to the south, Veloso to chaperone his teenaged sister, Maria Bethânia, who had been cast in "a left-wing play based in popular music" in Rio. With an expanding book of his own poetically engaging songs, Veloso recorded his debut album with Gal Costa, another Bahia expatriate, in 1967, while Gil appeared on singer Elis Regina's television program, originating in Sao Paulo. They produced music that was a mix of volatile Brazilian music with foreign rock influences. "We wanted to put lots of things together," recalls Veloso, "so we came up with British neo-rock-and-roll, that is BEATLES and ROLLING STONES, plus Argentinian tango, plus really traditional Brazilian things, and bad taste whorehouse music from Brazil and Mexico and Cuba."

TROPICALISMO EMERGES

From this melting pot Veloso pioneered the new musical movement, *tropicalismo*. The movement was a rebellious reaction against the censorship of song lyrics and the suppression of artistic expression that the military dictatorship imposed with an Institutional Act in 1964. The music appealed to a certain element at the country's newly established televised International Song Festivals. Veloso's resulting song "Tropicália" successfully mixed Brazilian music with Western rock, and the song was adopted as the movement's anthem. Another of his most successful songs, "Alegria, Alegria," was later adopted as the theme tune during demonstrations that culminated in the impeachment of President Fernando Collor.

The term *tropicalismo* was picked up by journalists, and in 1967, the legendary label came to cover electrifying experiments in visual art and theater, as well as in music, although in music the term proved longer-lived. *Tropicalismo* shocked those at either end of Brazil's turbulent political spectrum: the leftists resented the importation of foreign "capitalist" elements, and the right-wing militarists, on the verge of assuming complete control of the country, were suspicious of Veloso's and Gil's mocking and mysterious lyrics. Without warning, the pair were arrested and their heads shaven. Then they were imprisoned for an extended period, and finally forced to leave Brazil.

They turned their exile to good purpose, using a long stay in London to jam with PINK FLOYD and YES, and to compose their own increasingly sophisticated rock material, some of which made its way back home. As high-profile political refugees, the pair began to be viewed as heroes by their former leftist detractors. They came back to Brazil in 1971 (though the military retained power there until 1985), recorded "Doces Barbaros" ("Sweet Barbarians") with Bethânia and Costa in 1976, and a year later visited Nigeria to absorb West African music.

Tropicalismo, like some of its contemporary psychedelic music in the U.S. and Britain, somehow avoided aging through the next few decades, despite the dispersion of the movement itself. While Gil and Costa became attached to more commercially viable forms of music, Veloso continued his output of exciting eccentric amalgamations with visually evocative lyrics, never losing his idiosyncratic guitar style or his sense of humor. He and Gil shared a long-delayed reunion with their fans at home and abroad in the form of 1994's *Tropicalia 2* album and subsequent world tour, followed by Veloso's recording and tour showcasing other styles of Latin American music.

Jeff Kaliss

SEE ALSO:
BRAZIL; CUBA; JOBIM, ANTONIO CARLOS; MEXICO; TANGO.

FURTHER READING
McGowan, Chris. *The Brazilian Sound: Samba, Bossa Nova, and the Popular Music of Brazil* (New York: Billboard Books, 1991).

SUGGESTED LISTENING
Brazilian Collection; Caetano Veloso; Fina Estampa; Mi Historia; Tropicalia 2.

THE VELVET UNDERGROUND

For a band that never had a hit single while performing as a unit between 1965 and 1970, the Velvet Underground (VU) had an almost mythic influence on subsequent rock artists, from 1970s singers such as David BOWIE and Patti Smith, to 1990s grunge rockers like Sonic Youth. The main creative architects of the VU's dark, confrontational sound were Lou Reed and John Cale, who met at Syracuse University.

After graduating, Reed (b. March 2, 1942) became a staff songwriter at Long Island's Pickwick Records. Cale (b. December 4, 1940) had studied classical music in Britain before winning a scholarship to the U.S. Teaming up with guitarist Sterling Morrison (1942–95), Reed and Cale played local clubs as the Warlocks and the Falling Spikes. After replacing their drummer with Maureen (Mo) Tucker (b. 1945), they renamed themselves The Velvet Underground and became pop artist Andy Warhol's house band. Warhol added Nico (b. October 16, 1938), a German singer with a Dietrich-like voice, to the mix and booked the VU for his 1966 psychedelic show, the Exploding Plastic Inevitable. The group's 1967 debut album, *The Velvet Underground and Nico*, with its famous peelable-banana cover, was produced by Warhol. Riddled with discordant rhythms and screeching feedback, this now-landmark album of dark city life—made up of powerful songs about drugs and sex—was a resounding commercial flop.

A SPLIT IN THE BAND

After Warhol lost interest, taking his financial support with him, and Nico was fired, the Velvets released an equally unsuccessful second album, *White Light/White Heat* (1968). Internal dissension escalated until Reed fired Cale and replaced him with bassist Doug Yule. A third album, 1969's *The Velvet Underground*, had a hauntingly gentle sound and an odd mix of songs about nihilism, Jesus, and adultery. Although dropped by their record label, the band recorded *Loaded* (Atlantic, 1970), a near-perfect rock album filled with classics like "Sweet Jane" and "Rock and Roll." Ironically, Reed quit and the group split up just as the VU seemed poised for commercial success.

In the late 1970s and through the 1980s, the band gradually acquired legendary status. In 1993, the original Velvets regrouped for a highly successful tour and live album. But after Morrison died of cancer in Poughkeepsie, New York, on August 30, 1995, Reed decided that was the end of the Velvet Underground. Tucker, however, keeps the VU's legacy alive with a series of offbeat solo albums.

Michael R. Ross

SEE ALSO:
GRUNGE; PUNK ROCK; ROCK MUSIC.

The Velvet Underground—Sterling Morrison (left), Lou Reed, John Cale, and Mo Tucker—are now viewed as one of the most influential and innovative bands of the 1960s.

Glenn A. Baker Archives/Redferns

FURTHER READING
Bockris, Victor, and Gerald Malanga.
Up-Tight: The Story of the Velvet Underground
(New York: Omnibus Press, 1995);
Reed, Lou. *Between Thought and Expression*
(New York: Hyperion Books, 1991);
Zak, Albin, III. *The Velvet Underground Companion*
(New York: Schirmer Books, 1997).

SUGGESTED LISTENING
Loaded; *Peel Slowly and See* (5-CD set);
The Velvet Underground; *The Velvet Underground and Nico*; *White Light, White Heat*;
Lou Reed: *Between Thought and Expression*.

VENEZUELA

Like the music of most Latin American countries, Venezuelan music is a rich amalgam of indigenous sounds that centuries ago were heavily influenced by musical imports from Europe and Africa.

Prior to colonization in the 16th century, Venezuelan music appears to have been primarily ceremonial, including songs for hunting, healing, and other specific purposes. With colonization, Catholic priests from Spain taught European music to the indigenous people in their own Carib language. Many years later, the displacement of African slaves brought music mostly from the Congo to the coastal regions of Venezuela. The best example of this African influence is the *baile de tambor*, a dance performed with drumming at religious ceremonies.

The European influence continued to be felt in the early 20th century, and native composers were inspired by RAVEL, DEBUSSY, and other European masters. Notable Venezuelan composers in the classical ilk included Vicente Emilio Sojo, who founded the Venezuela Symphony Orchestra.

MODERN-DAY VENEZUELAN MUSIC

Popular music in modern Venezuela includes the dances and vocal styles *boleros*, *valses*, *cumbia*, *comparsas*, *zarzuela*, and *joropo*—the national dance which has also come to mean a music that has creole characteristics. These different types of music are played on instruments similar to those found throughout Latin America and, like much of the music, were brought in from Spain and Africa, or via other Latin American countries. These include stringed instruments, such as violins, mandolins, guitars, and harps, and a wide variety of percussion instruments.

Traditional folk music is still played, but rock too has its place. Performers include Altazor, who played folk music, including the traditional *joropo*; Soledad Bravo, who sang songs of social protest; and Maria Rodriguez, an Afro-Venezuelan singer of *comparsas* and *joropos* who was known as "La Tremenda."

The *llanera*, or music from the plains, is perhaps the most identifiable music style. It is sometimes called *musica criolla* and is akin to country music.

Among the most well-known *llanera* singers is Simon Diaz. Other musicians who perform this and hybridized forms of the *llanera* include Reynaldo Armas, Reyna Lucero, Freddy Salcedo, La Manga E'Coleo, La Misma Gente, and Un Solo Pueblo.

In the 1940s and 1950s dance music became popular, particularly that imported from Dominica. Popular groups who include mambo, cumbia, merengue, and soca in their repertoire are Billo's Caracas Boys, Los Melodicos, and the Porfi Jimenez Orquesta.

In the early 1970s, salsa was perceived to be the music of the lower classes, but the mid-1970s saw a change in attitudes. Salsa's popularity surged. With artists such as Oscar D'LEÓN coming into their own, sales of salsa in Venezuela in the mid-1970s were greater during this period than in New York and Puerto Rico combined.

Then, too, there are pop artists such as Ricardo Montaner, a singer-songwriter who had success on the *Billboard* magazine Latin charts. His 1988 album *Montaner 2* established him as a Latin American balladeer. Venezuelan rock musicians include Yordano and the group Daiquiri.

As is the case throughout Latin America, continuing experimentation in Venezuela is fusing musical styles into new combinations without losing the essence of its diverse musical history.

Linda Dailey Paulson

SEE ALSO:
BRAZIL; CARIBBEAN; LATIN AMERICA; SALSA.

FURTHER READING
Girard, Sharon. *Funeral Music and Customs in Venezuela* (Tempe, AZ: Center for Latin American Studies, Arizona State University, 1980); Olsen, Dale A. *Music of the Warao of Venezuela: Song People of the Rain Forest* (Gainesville, FL: University Press of Florida, 1996).

SUGGESTED LISTENING
Altazor Altazor; *La Dimension Latina Exitos de La Dimension Latina*; *Harps of Venezuela*; *Maria Rodriguez Songs from Venezuela*; *Oscar D'León La Salsa Soy Yo*; *Ricardo Montaner Montaner 2*; *Ricardo Montaner Un Manana Y Un Camino*; *Soledad Bravo Cantos Revolucionarios de America Latina*.

HEITOR VILLA-LOBOS

South America's leading 20th-century composer, Heitor Villa-Lobos, was born in Rio de Janeiro, Brazil, on March 5, 1887. He received his early musical education from his father, who taught him to play the cello. Villa-Lobos later studied the cello at music college and became proficient on the guitar—these two instruments feature largely in his compositions.

Although Villa-Lobos' father intended his son to train for a career in the medical profession, the young composer was far more interested in exploring the popular music of Brazil and other countries. In 1905, and again in 1912, he made extensive field trips throughout Brazil collecting native folk songs. In between, he attended the National Institute of Music, but could never harness his lively temperament to the disciplines of harmony and composition.

Later, Villa-Lobos received his introduction to 20th-century French music (in particular, that of Les Six) through his friendship with Darius MILHAUD, who was the French cultural attaché to Brazil from 1916 to 1918. At around this time, he also met the pianist Artur RUBINSTEIN, who became a champion of his music. From 1923 to 1930, Villa-Lobos traveled widely in Europe, including London, Vienna, Berlin, Lisbon, and Paris, where his works received their strongest support. He was also introduced to African music while visiting Dakar in Senegal.

BRAZIL'S MUSICAL ICON

In 1930, Villa-Lobos was appointed director of music education in São Paulo, Brazil, and in 1932 he became superintendent of music and art education in Rio de Janeiro. He established a conservatory in Rio de Janeiro that became the center for instrumental teaching in Brazil, but his chief interest remained his mission to bring Brazilian folk music into the schools. In 1944, he visited the United States, conducting his own music in New York, Boston, and Los Angeles, and in 1949 he returned to Europe, but Rio remained his home.

Villa-Lobos was largely self-taught, following on from his father's early encouragement, and this allowed him a large measure of creative freedom. His musical style draws on a wide range of influences, notably Brazilian folk song, but also the music of Les Six, Impressionism, and jazz. He was never a mere copyist, however. Being stimulated by the folk tradition of his country, he could write in its style without ever plagiarizing.

A prolific writer, Villa-Lobos was credited with more than 2,000 compositions. His work tended to be uneven in quality, but his best work has a freshness and energy that celebrates the vigor of his country.

In addition to being a composer, Villa-Lobos was also a virtuoso performer on the guitar and wrote many pieces for it, including Etudes (1929), Preludes (1940), and a Concerto for Guitar and Orchestra (1952). For mixed ensembles, he wrote nine important works called *Bachianas Brasileiras*, the name echoing the affinity he felt for the music of J. S. Bach. No. 1 for eight cellos (1930), and No. 5 for soprano and eight cellos (1938–45) are the best known. Inspiration came from meeting Les Six and Erik SATIE in the 1920s, and resulted in a synthesis of Baroque and Brazilian music.

Villa-Lobos wrote a series of works for mixed ensembles called *Chôros*. Of interest are No. 13, for two orchestras and band, and No. 14, for orchestra, band, and chorus. Among the most impressive of his other works are his 1928 Woodwind Quintet, the song cycle *Serestas* (1925), and the 1939 piano piece, *The New York Skyline Melody*, written for the New York World's Fair.

When Villa-Lobos died in Rio on November 17, 1959, his funeral was attended by the president and other national dignitaries—a tribute to his stature in his native land.

Richard Trombley

SEE ALSO:

FOLK MUSIC; IMPRESSIONISM IN MUSIC; SIX, LES; VOCAL AND CHORAL MUSIC.

FURTHER READING

Tarasti, Eero. *Heitor Villa-Lobos: The Life and Works, 1887–1959* (Jefferson, NC: McFarland, 1995); Wright, Simon. *Villa-Lobos* (New York: Oxford University Press, 1992).

SUGGESTED LISTENING

Bachianas brasileiras; *Chôros*; Guitar Concerto; *Hommage à Chopin*; *Momoprecoce*; *Suite populaire brésilienne*.

VOCAL AND CHORAL MUSIC

Although most modern choral music has been written for the concert hall rather than the cathedral, the traditional bond between the choir and spiritual expression is still strong. By contrast, solo vocal music has moved farther away from its traditional theme of romantic love. Nonetheless, both types of vocal writing have been subject to all the international experiments of modernism.

MUSIC FOR VOICE IN EUROPE

As the century dawned, the musical scene in central Europe was dominated by the heritage of Richard Wagner, which brought not only an increased harmonic freedom but also a heroic scale. One devotee of this music was Gustav MAHLER, whose second, third, and eighth symphonies used choruses and massive orchestral forces. *Das Lied von der Erde*, for solo voices and orchestra, and the *Kindertotenlieder* are also massive in scale, unlike the earlier *lied* (Romantic art song) tradition of finely crafted smaller works.

Scarcely less massive was Arnold SCHOENBERG's *Gurrelieder* (1901), a setting of poems by Jens Peter Jacobsen for soloists, chorus, and 400 musicians. His *Pierrot Lunaire* (1912) for speaking voice and chamber ensemble was an experiment in *sprechstimme*—a form of delivery halfway between speaking and singing—to uncanny effect. Schoenberg returned to choral writing toward the end of his life with the eight-minute cantata, *A Survivor from Warsaw* (1945) for narrator, chorus, and orchestra, which employs his 12-tone technique.

FROM POETRY, FOLK SONGS AND LYRICS

In England, Frederick DELIUS and Edward ELGAR wrote in the Romantic tradition. Elgar ushered in the century with the oratorio *The Dream of Gerontius* (1900), a work deeply influenced by the harmonies of Wagner's *Parsifal*. Delius also owed the flowing quality of his music with its short phrases (motifs) and chromaticism to Wagner. His choral works include *Sea Drift* (1904), based on Whitman's poetry, and *A Mass of Life* (1905).

Whitman's poetry supplied the greater part of the text of Ralph VAUGHAN WILLIAMS' cantata, *Dona Nobis Pacem* (1936) and *A Sea Symphony* (1910). Vaughan Williams wrote many choral pieces: *Hodie* (1954), a Christmas cantata, and the Mass in G Minor (1922). He was also passionately interested in English folk song and used folk lyrics and melodies in many song settings.

Benjamin BRITTEN too was interested in using folk songs, and his *Serenade for Tenor, Horn, and Strings* uses the eerie medieval "Lyke Wake Dirge" ballad to striking effect. He wrote many choral works: his *Ceremony of Carols* (1942) for trebles and harp is consciously medieval in flavor though modern in harmony, drawing on chant, canon, and chorale. *Rejoice in the Lamb* (1943) transmutes the libretto, taken from the journal of a mad poet, into a work of radiant devotion. His *War Requiem* (1962) combines Wilfred Owen's poems with the Latin requiem mass.

William WALTON's cantata *Belshazzar's Feast* (1931) is a highly dramatic work. While the harmonic elements are relatively simple, the orchestration is stunning, with antiphonal brass choirs, augmented percussion (including gong, anvil, xylophone, and castanets) and a shout of horror by the chorus on the word "slain." The song tradition in England continued with cycles written by Ivor Gurney, Gerald Finzi, Peter Warlock, and John Ireland taking their texts from the works of major English poets. In France, Claude DEBUSSY also wrote song cycles with texts from major poets. His short *Trois chansons de Charles d'Orléans* (1908) for chorus a capella shows the full development of his unique style, which has been called Impressionism.

LES SIX

Later, the group of iconoclastic French composers known as Les Six aspired to write music of elegance and clarity, free from what they regarded as the ambiguities of chromatic harmonies and the imagery of Impressionism. They took their rhythmic inspiration from jazz. The two members of Les Six who wrote choral music in any quantity were Francis POULENC and Arthur Honegger. Honegger's best known choral work is *Le roi David* (1921) for narrator, soloists, and mixed chorus. Poulenc contributed several choral works, among them his *Stabat mater* (1951) for unaccompanied chorus and the *Gloria* (1959) for chorus and orchestra. Maurice RAVEL wrote much exquisite vocal music, and Gabriel FAURÉ and Henri Duparc were best known for their songs: Fauré's later settings combined a boldness of vocal line with rich polyphonic accompaniments. Olivier MESSIAEN also wrote choral works, including *Cinq rechants* (1949) for a small choir and *La Transfiguration de Notre Seigneur* (1969) for a choir of 100 voices. He wrote few solo songs, but *Poèmes pour Mi* (1936) for voice and piano shows stylistic features of his longer works, such as his use of rhythmic complexity, and idiosyncratic modes.

THE RUSSIAN TRADITION

After the Russian Revolution of 1917, church choral music was no longer in demand. However, the film industry needed music, and in 1938 Sergey PROKOFIEV wrote a score for Eisenstein's film *Alexander Nevsky*, in which he used the sounds of Russian church choral music. He later abstracted a choral cantata from this score.

Igor STRAVINSKY'S greatest choral work is the *Symphony of Psalms* (1930), in which modal harmonies and striking modulations do not impede the strict fugal writing of the last two movements. He used serialist technique later in solo songs such as *Three Shakespeare Songs* (1953) and *In Memoriam Dylan Thomas* (1954). Dmitry SHOSTAKOVICH also wrote choral works and songs, and his Symphony No. 14 uses texts by poets, including Lorca and Rilke, to produce a prolonged meditation on death.

THE U.S.A.

Many American composers have written minor but still performed choral works, including Howard Hanson, William Schuman, and Daniel Pinkham, who composed the short but brilliant *Christmas Cantata* (1957). Charles IVES wrote many choral pieces and songs in his vast output. His earlier choral works are primarily psalm settings, but he later set political protest songs and songs by many poets, including Whittier, Emerson, and Whitman.

Aaron COPLAND'S vocal music is best represented by his settings of the *12 Poems of Emily Dickinson* and his two collections of *Old American Songs*.

Samuel BARBER'S collection of *Hermit Songs* uses early Irish Christian texts; later, he set the words of the Agnus Dei to his famous Adagio for Strings.

Ned Rorem has set a vast selection of poets' work in songs, from the psalms of King David to the poems of Elizabeth Bishop. However, the most popular choral work from the U.S. is undoubtedly *Chichester Psalms* (1965) by Leonard BERNSTEIN.

THE AVANT-GARDE

The serialists did not write much for chorus: Schoenberg's choral piece, *Gurrelieder*, predated his serial period. Of his followers, Anton WEBERN, Ernst Krenek, and Frank Martin wrote for chorus. Martin is notable for a setting of the Tristan and Isolde story in *Le vin herbé* (1941). Pierre BOULEZ' work for soprano and orchestra *Pli selon pli* (1962), a setting of texts by Mallarmé, shows him moving from a strict serialism to a new expressive freedom. Luciano Berio experimented with electronic manipulation of spoken text in *Omaggio a Joyce* (1958), and different techniques of vocal delivery in *Circles* (1960) for voice, harp and percussion. In America, Milton Babbitt's song cycle *Du* (1951) reflected his mathematician's approach. The advent of electronic music in the 1950s opened new avenues. Karlheinz STOCKHAUSEN's *Stimmung* (1970) is for six voices with electronic feedback. The Polish composer Krzystof PENDERECKI wrote many liturgical choral works; a *Stabat mater*, *Te Deum*, and *Requiem Mass*. In Warsaw on March 16, 1997, he conducted his cantata to mark Jerusalem's 3,000th anniversary.

Vocal and choral music composition continue to keep pace with the times, using techniques and interpretations to express contemporary sentiments.

Jane Prendergast

SEE ALSO:
CHAMBER MUSIC; ELECTRONIC MUSIC; LATE ROMANTICISM.

FURTHER READING
Coroniti, Joseph. *Poetry as Text in Twentieth-Century Vocal Music: From Stravinsky to Reich* (Lewiston, NY: E. Mellen Press, 1992); Garretson, Robert L. *Choral Music: History, Style, and Performance Practice* (Englewood Cliffs, NJ: Prentice Hall, 1993).

SUGGESTED LISTENING
Bernstein: *Chichester Psalms*; Boulez: *Pli selon pli*; Britten: *A Ceremony of Carols*; Delius: *A Mass of Life*; Fauré: Songs; Lutoslawski: *Les Espaces*; Mahler: Symphony No. 8 (*Symphony of a Thousand*); Penderecki: *St Luke Passion*; Rorem: *Poems of Love and the Rain*; Schoenberg: *Pierrot lunaire*; *A Survivor from Warsaw*; Stravinsky: *Symphony of Psalms*; Vaughan Williams: *Dona Nobis Pacem*; *On Wenlock Edge*; Walton: *Belshazzar's Feast*.

T-BONE
WALKER

The guitarist T-Bone Walker was a pivotal character in the story of the blues. In his youth he helped Blind Lemon JEFFERSON in street performances, and he was one of the first blues artists to play the electric guitar. He was a dynamic performer and excellent songwriter, and his influence is evident in the recordings of B. B. KING, Jimi HENDRIX, Albert KING, Buddy GUY, Eric Clapton, and Stevie Ray Vaughan.

Aaron Thibeaux Walker was born on May 28, 1910, in Linden, Texas, and grew up in Dallas. His mother, stepfather, and virtually all his uncles played guitar. Walker himself took up the instrument when he was 13, and also became proficient on the ukelele, banjo, violin, mandolin, and piano. In the early 1920s, he helped lead Blind Lemon Jefferson, a friend of his family, around the streets of Dallas, often collecting his money for him. By the mid-1920s, Walker was good enough at the guitar himself to make a living traveling with a medicine show and various carnivals. He cut two songs for Columbia in 1929, under the name Oak Cliff T-Bone, but they did not sell. After a stint playing with Texas bands, he moved to California in 1934. Five years later, Walker attracted attention after joining Les Hite's Cotton Club Orchestra, winning praise for his strong, virile singing, his songwriting, and his work on the guitar.

Walker had begun experimenting with the electric guitar as early as 1934, and he first recorded with it in 1939. The classic single "T-Bone Blues" was cut the same year, and after its success Walker set out on his own. His combination of single-string melodic work and arpeggio became the backbone of the electric blues guitar style. During this period he wrote many songs that were to become standards, including the one for which he is best known, "Call It Stormy Monday" (1947). As well as being an accomplished musician, Walker was also a great showman, playing the guitar behind his back and between his legs.

In the 1950s, Walker recorded for Imperial and Atlantic, and while he was not able to match his hits from the 1940s, he remained a popular touring attraction. His album *T-Bone Blues* for Atlantic, released in

A highly charismatic performer, T-Bone Walker was one of the first blues artists to popularize the electric guitar.

1960, found him a whole new audience when jazz enthusiasts and white folk fans embraced his work. Walker remained in demand at jazz and folk clubs around the world throughout the 1960s and early 1970s, before he was sidelined by ill health. He died of pneumonia on March 16, 1975.

"I can still hear T-Bone in my mind today, from that first record I heard, 'Stormy Monday,'" B. B. King once said. "He was the first electric guitar player I heard on record. He made me so that I knew I just had to go out and get an electric guitar."

Stan Hieronymus

SEE ALSO:
BLUES.

FURTHER READING

Dance, Helen Oakley. *Stormy Monday: The T-Bone Walker Story* (Baton Rouge, LA: Louisiana State University Press, 1987).

SUGGESTED LISTENING

The Complete Recordings of T-Bone Walker, 1940–1954.

FATS WALLER

Fats Waller was one of the greatest of jazz pianists and one of the first to introduce the organ to jazz ensembles. He was also a consummate showman with an irrepressible sense of fun. Compositions such as "Ain't Misbehavin'," "Honeysuckle Rose," and the *London Suite* inspired generations of jazz musicians.

Thomas Wright Waller was born May 21, 1904, in New York. His mother was an organist and pianist and his father a Harlem Baptist lay preacher. At age six, he started playing piano in his school orchestra. After the death of his mother when he was 14, he moved in with the family of pianist Russell Brooks. He took classical lessons from Leopold Godowsky and from Carl Bohm at the Juilliard School of Music, but also became the protégé of blues pianist James P. Johnson.

At 15, Waller got the job of playing the Wurlitzer organ at the Lincoln Theater. Soon after he was playing in nightclubs, and by age 18 had cut his first record, "Birmingham Blues"/"Muscle Shoals Blues." He then played piano and organ at parties, clubs, and theaters, and backed blues vocalists including Bessie SMITH. In 1923, he made his first radio broadcast and was thereafter heard regularly on radio, with programs like *Fats Waller's Rhythm Club*. He also collaborated with lyricist Andy Razaf on three Broadway shows: *Keep Shufflin'* in 1928, and *Load of Coal* and *Hot Chocolates* in 1929. It was this last show that included the famous "Ain't Misbehavin'," sung first by Cab Calloway and then by Louis ARMSTRONG.

Waller began with Victor Records in 1926, recording his own compositions such as "Smashing Thirds" and "Handful of Keys" on solo piano. These recordings show Waller's magisterial "stride" technique. A large man with a light touch, he used a powerful left hand to play a rapid-fire stream of octaves and tenths. With an exclusive contract in 1934, Fats Waller formed a group, "Fats Waller and His Rhythm," which scored a long list of hits with "The Joint Is Jumpin'" and "I'm Gonna Sit Right Down and Write Myself a Letter."

Onstage, Waller was a spectacle. His comical demeanor and clever vocals infused whatever he played, and he was a master at subverting the racist lyrics that were forced on him. "Stupid or mediocre songs—he recorded hundreds—are sent up by various means," said the *New Republic* magazine. "Sarcastic or falsetto delivery … heavy sighs, mock-gospel-meeting exhortations … and outrageous sound effects."

Showmanship aside, he was an amazing pianist. Giving a swing sensibility to the Hammond and pipe organs—a staccato right hand accompanied by fancy pedal work and creative changes of registration—he turned them into jazz instruments.

Apart from concerts, recordings, and radio, Waller appeared in films such as *Hooray for Love!* (1935) and *King of Burlesque* (1936), and the musical *Stormy Weather* (1943), which starred Lena HORNE.

In 1938, Waller made a tour of Europe, distinguishing himself again by being probably the only jazz musician to play the organ in Notre Dame Cathedral in Paris. On a second tour the next year, he recorded the *London Suite*, a series of six related pieces for solo piano, but returned home on the outbreak of World War II. His health began to deteriorate around this time. He had always been overweight, and ate and drank to excess all his life. Coupled with this, the stress of his personal life and a grueling tour schedule took their toll. After becoming ill at a Hollywood concert, Waller died of pneumonia on the train back to New York on December 15, 1943.

Although the public remembers him mainly for his humor, Waller's piano style had an enormous influence on Count BASIE, Thelonious MONK, and the whole next generation of jazz pianists.

Brett Allan King

SEE ALSO:
BLUES; BOOGIE-WOOGIE; JAZZ.

FURTHER READING
Kirkeby, W. T., ed. *Ain't Misbehavin':
The Story of Fats Waller*
(New York: Da Capo Press, 1975);
Shipton, Alyn. *Fats Waller: His Life and Times*
(New York: Universe Books, 1988).

SUGGESTED LISTENING
Ain't Misbehavin'; *Fats Waller at
the Organ*; *London Suite*;
Souvenirs of Hot Chocolate.

BRUNO WALTER

Bruno Walter was an important conductor whose career spanned almost 70 years. Renowned for his interpretations of Mozart and MAHLER, he was remarkable for his warm yet demanding rehearsal methods and his relaxed manner.

Born Bruno Walter Schlesinger on September 15, 1876, in Berlin, the son of a Jewish shopkeeper, Walter demonstrated his musical aptitude at an early age. He began playing the piano at age 4, and at age 8 was enrolled in the Stern Conservatory in Berlin. After witnessing a performance conducted by Hans Guido von Bülow in 1889, Walter decided to pursue a career as a conductor instead of as a pianist. He made his conducting debut at the age of 17 in Cologne, with a performance of Lortzing's opera, *Der Waffensmied*. Walter's talent was immediately appreciated, and in the following year he was appointed as a coach at the Hamburg Opera, where he met and worked with Gustav MAHLER. The two enjoyed a close friendship, which lasted until Mahler's death in 1911. It was Mahler who advised Walter to drop his family name Schlesinger, a change that became official when Walter was granted Austrian citizenship. Mahler appointed Walter assistant conductor and chorus master, and in 1901, Walter joined Mahler in Vienna as his assistant at the Vienna Court Opera.

It was Walter who was to conduct the first performances of Mahler's *Das Lied von der Erde* in Munich shortly after the composer's death, and his Symphony No. 9 the next year. He also championed the work of Hans Pfitzner, and gave the first performances of his music drama *Palestrina*. Walter conducted at the Vienna Court Opera until 1912. From 1913 to 1922, he was music director of the Munich Royal Opera, succeeding Felix Mottl. After leaving Munich, his guest conducting appearances continued to multiply, and on February 15, 1923, he made his American debut as guest conductor of the New York Symphony Orchestra.

In 1925, Walter returned to Berlin as director of the Berlin Civic Opera at Charlottenburg. That same year saw the beginning of Walter's long and fruitful association with the festival in Salzburg. In 1929, Walter left Berlin to assume the direction of the Gewandhaus concerts in Leipzig, a post that had previously been held by Wilhelm FURTWÄNGLER.

After the Nazis came to power in Germany, Walter's contract in Leipzig was terminated. On August 3, 1933, the day the Nazi government issued a decree forbidding him to work, he conducted a performance of Beethoven's Symphony No. 8 in Salzburg, following which the emotional audience showered him with roses. When the Nazis annexed Austria in 1938, Walter had to resign his position with the Vienna Opera and leave Austria. He went to France and, in 1939, to America. He established his residence in California and eventually became a U.S. citizen.

The Metropolitan Opera engaged Walter as a guest conductor, where his first performance, on February 14, 1941, of Beethoven's *Fidelio*, earned him 13 curtain calls. Walter conducted extensively in the United States, with orchestras such as the Los Angeles Philharmonic, the New York Philharmonic, the NBC Symphony, and the Philadelphia Orchestra. After 1947, he visited Europe often to conduct, and in the last years of his life he spent time recording some of his favorite works in California with the Columbia Symphony Orchestra.

His awards and accolades include honorary degrees from UCLA, USC, and the University of Edinburgh, and the Grand Cross with Star of the Order of Merit from the Federal Republic of Germany. His greatest role was in his unswerving devotion to the music of Mahler and his recordings of Mahler's work. Bruno Walter died at his home in Beverly Hills on February 17, 1962.

Douglas Dunston

SEE ALSO:
ORCHESTRAL MUSIC.

FURTHER READING

Chesterman, Robert. *Conversations with Conductors: Bruno Walter, Sir Adrian Boult, Leonard Bernstein, Ernest Ansermet, Otto Klemperer, Leopold Stokowski* (Totowa, NJ: Rowman and Littlefield, 1976); Walter, Bruno. *Theme and Variations: An Autobiography* (Westport, CT: Greenwood Press, 1981).

SUGGESTED LISTENING

Beethoven: *Fidelio*; Brahms: Symphonies Nos. 3 and 4; Mahler: Symphony No. 5; Mozart: Symphonies Nos. 36 and 38.

SIR WILLIAM ── WALTON

Sir William Walton, whose music included film scores and operas as well as colorful orchestral music.

The works of Sir William Walton have enjoyed both commercial and critical success. At least two major works, *Façade* and *Belshazzar's Feast,* have found enduring popularity with concert audiences, and he has reached a wider audience with his scores for the Shakespeare films of Laurence Olivier.

Walton was born on March 29, 1902, in Oldham, Lancashire. Both of his parents were singing teachers, and his father was a church choirmaster. At age nine, Walton passed the entrance audition for the Christ Church Cathedral School in Oxford, where he remained for the following six years. He excelled at sports, but did not exhibit any prowess in instrumental playing. Instead, he composed music from the age of 11. At only 16 years of age, he became an undergraduate at Christ Church College, Oxford, where he specialized in music history. His compositions there were much admired by a fellow student, Sacheverell Sitwell, whose family gave Walton an allowance and invited him to live with them after Oxford in 1919.

Walton's *Façade*, a setting of Edith Sitwell's poetry made in 1922, with the words recited offstage through a Sengerphone (a kind of megaphone), won him admiration from the many prominent musicians he met through the Sitwells' artistic circle. Among these were Sir Thomas BEECHAM, who suggested that he write a concerto for the violist Lionel Tertis. Tertis rejected the Viola Concerto, so it was given its first performance by Paul HINDEMITH, and the rapturous reception given to the piece established Walton as a major composer.

Walton's success continued with the Symphony No. 1 (1935) and a concerto commissioned by violinist Jascha HEIFETZ in 1937. In 1935, he wrote his first film score to *Escape Me Never,* produced by Herbert Wilcox. This was followed by the Olivier versions of *Henry V, Richard III, As You Like It,* and *Hamlet.* The music for *Henry V* was later made into an orchestral suite.

During World War II, Walton composed music for propaganda films, and also drove an ambulance. The lyrical Sonata for Violin and Piano was written for Yehudi MENUHIN and Louis Kentner. He composed Queen Elizabeth II's coronation march (in 1953) as he had done for her father George VI (in 1937). He wrote many pieces for choir and orchestra during his career, including the wildly exciting *Belshazzar's Feast,* with its emphasis on brass instruments, and a *Te Deum* that was sung in Westminster Abbey in 1953. In 1954, he wrote the opera *Troilus and Cressida* for Elisabeth SCHWARZKOPF. His last major composition was a cello Passacaglia for Mstislav ROSTROPOVICH in 1982. Walton died on March 8, 1983 in Ischia, Italy.

Jane Prendergast

SEE ALSO:

FILM MUSIC; ORCHESTRAL MUSIC; VOCAL AND CHORAL MUSIC.

FURTHER READING
Smith, Carolyn J. *William Walton: A Bio-bibliography* (New York: Greenwood Press, 1988);
Walton, Susana. *William Walton: Behind the Façade* (New York: Oxford University Press, 1989).

SUGGESTED LISTENING
Belshazzar's Feast; *Coronation March*; *Façade*; *Henry V Suite*; Symphony No. 1; *Troilus and Cressida*; Viola Concerto.

Hulton-Deutsch Collection/Corbis

DINAH
WASHINGTON

Dinah Washington lived fast, died young, and left an indelible mark, especially on the music that became known as soul. With a huge, powerful voice and a style that could be alternately earthy and ethereal, Washington was a music legend conquering jazz, gospel, rhythm and blues, and pop. She earned a reputation as one of the premier singers of her time—and the well-deserved nickname, "Queen of the Blues." The jazz historian Leonard Feather called her "a unique interpreter of pop songs, a great blues singer, and a performer with complete savoir faire."

Born Ruth Lee Jones on August 8, 1924, in Tuscaloosa, Alabama, she learned how to sing and play piano from her mother, a church pianist and choir leader. When Ruth was three, her family moved to the southside of Chicago, and by the age of ten, she was giving piano recitals and singing in the St. Luke's Baptist Church choir. At 15, she won an amateur contest at the Regal Theater, and began her professional career in 1940 as part of a female gospel group, the Sallie Martin Colored Ladies Quartet. But Ruth was more interested in sinning than in being a saint. In 1941, she switched to singing in Chicago nightclubs and changed her name to Dinah Washington—"Dinah" after singer Dinah Shore, and "Washington" after the first president.

QUEEN OF THE JUKEBOXES

In 1943, vibraphonist Lionel Hampton spotted Washington's talent and hired her as his band's vocalist. She was to stay with Hampton for three years, recording hits such as "Evil Gal Blues" and "Salty Papa Blues." When Washington went solo in the mid-1940s, she became the queen of African-American jukeboxes with Bessie SMITH-influenced blues and novelty tunes like "Chewin' Woman Blues" and "Me Voot Is Boot." In 1946, Dinah joined the newly formed Mercury label and produced a string of rhythm-and-blues hits, including "A Slick Chick (On the Mellow Side)" (1946), "Good Daddy Blues" (1949), and "Trouble in Mind" (1952), as well as jam sessions with modern jazz masters Clifford BROWN and Max ROACH.

In the 1950s, Washington crossed over from rhythm and blues to pop music, releasing several classic albums and achieving her first—and only—Top-10 pop hit with "What a Diff'rence a Day Makes" (1959). The record sold a million copies, won a Grammy, and established Dinah's main repertoire for the rest of her short-lived career. From this record on, Washington's output consisted largely of sentimental ballads with lush string accompaniment. Typical of these were "Unforgettable" (1961) and "September in the Rain" (1961), originally hits for Nat King COLE and Guy LOMBARDO respectively. During this period, Washington also duetted with Eddie Chamblee—one of her seven husbands.

Washington quit the music business in 1962 and opened a restaurant in Detroit. She was a hands-on owner, manning the cash register, supervising the staff, and even locking up at night. In 1963, she returned to recording with Roulette Records and that year recorded eight albums—a feat only slightly diminished by the fact that she never rehearsed and performed only one take of each song.

Washington was well-known for her heavy use of alcohol and drugs, and on December 14, 1963, her wild lifestyle caught up with her. Accidentally overdosing on a mixture of diet pills and alcohol, the singer died in her sleep at the age of 39. Thirty years later, the "Queen of the Blues" was posthumously inducted into the Rock and Roll Hall of Fame, universally recognized as one of the most talented and versatile singers of her generation.

Michael R. Ross

SEE ALSO:
BLUES; GOSPEL; SOUL.

FURTHER READING
Haskins, James. *Queen of the Blues: A Biography of Dinah Washington*
(New York: W. Morrow, 1987);
Hemming, Roy, and David Hajdu, *Discovering Great Singers of Classic Pop*
(New York: Newmarket Press, 1991).

SUGGESTED LISTENING
The Bessie Smith Songbook;
Complete on Mercury, Vols. 1–7; *Dinah Jams*;
First Issue: The Dinah Washington Story.

MUDDY WATERS

There have been many great blues guitarists, but Muddy Waters stands alone as a musician who, with his talented band, created a distinctive style that came to be called the "Chicago blues." Waters turned what had been a regional form of expression, traditional Delta blues, into an internationally respected popular music.

Born on April 4, 1915, in Rolling Fork, Mississippi, McKinley Morganfield got his nickname as a child because he liked to play in a muddy creek. Waters played the Jew's-harp and harmonica before buying his first guitar for $2.50 when he was 17. His early influences included Son HOUSE and Robert JOHNSON, and he became a talented slide guitarist.

Waters was working as a sharecropper on a plantation at Stovall, Mississippi, in 1941, when folk historian Alan LOMAX visited and recorded him. Lomax returned the next year and recorded more songs, feeding Waters' musical ambition.

MUSICAL BEGINNINGS

In 1943, Waters moved to Chicago, where he found work at a paper factory and began to play at house parties. He bought an electric guitar and soon became a sideman for established musicians. Waters recorded several times for the Aristocrat, later Chess, label before scoring his first hit, "I Can't Be Satisfied," in 1948. He dominated the national rhythm and blues charts in the 1950s with hits that have become standards, including "I Just Want to Make Love to You," "Rollin' Stone," "Honey Bee," "She Moves Me," "Hoochie Coochie Man," "Got My Mojo Working," "Mannish Boy," and many others.

The Muddy Waters Band was formed in 1951 and featured some of the finest musicians in the blues, many of whom became well known in their own right. They included harmonica players LITTLE WALTER, Junior Wells, and James Cotton; pianists Sunnyland Slim and Otis SPANN; guitarists Jimmy Rogers and Pat Hare; bassists Ernest "Big" Crawford and Willie DIXON (who wrote some of Waters' biggest hits); and drummers Elgin Evans and Fred Below.

Waters electrified the country blues, incorporating traditional themes such as sexuality, homesickness, and superstition into a sophisticated sound. His songs reflected the alienation and anxiety of many urban African-Americans of the time, while the country themes appealed to their longing for home. The acoustic sound he had learned in the Mississippi Delta was featured in his guitar playing as single-note slide phrases. Enhanced by a slow, solid beat he played sparely, stripping a tune to its essentials and creating a palpable tension. He used amplification to turn the music into something physical and ferocious. The guitar playing was complemented by his rough, barrel-chested voice, which was at times boastful, menacing, brooding, or celebratory.

INSPIRATION TO ROCK

A recording of the Muddy Waters Band's outstanding performance at the 1960 Newport Jazz Festival proved influential in Great Britain, and by Waters' second British tour in 1963, he had a substantial international audience. When musicians such as the ROLLING STONES (named after one of his hits) began covering his songs, white American music fans began to listen, and Waters became a star back home. Waters spent much of the 1970s on the U.S. college and festival circuits, until his band split up in 1980. The other members of the band later performed as the Legendary Blues Band.

Muddy Waters made several records for Blue Sky in the late 1970s and early 1980s, and continued to enjoy a successful career until his death in Chicago on April 30, 1983.

Daria Labinsky

SEE ALSO:
BLUES; JAZZ; ROCK MUSIC.

FURTHER READING
Palmer, Robert. *Deep Blues*
(New York: Penguin Books, 1981);
Rooney, James. *Bossmen: Bill Monroe and Muddy Waters* (New York: Da Capo, 1991).

SUGGESTED LISTENING
Best of Muddy Waters; *The Chess Box*;
Muddy Waters at Newport;
The Real Folk Blues.

FRANZ WAXMAN

Franz Waxman, one of Hollywood's most distinguished composers, was born in Königshütte, Germany (later Chorzow, Poland), on December 24, 1906. While a student at the Music Academy in Dresden and later at the Conservatory of Music in Berlin, he supported his education by playing the piano in bars and restaurants. At the age of 24, he began to orchestrate and compose film music. His first major assignment was orchestrating and conducting Frederick Hollander's score for the film *The Blue Angel* in 1930.

In the early 1930s, Waxman moved to Paris because of the increasingly anti-Semitic climate in Germany, and here wrote the score for Fritz Lang's film *Liliom* (1933). In 1935, Waxman moved to Hollywood, as Lang had done shortly before him.

In America, he became a member of the group of European composers who migrated to Hollywood at this time to escape oppression in Europe. They included Max STEINER, Dimitri Tiomkin, Erich Korngold, Alfred NEWMAN, Miklós Rózsa, and Hugo Friedhofer. Most of them were classically trained, but proved comfortable with lighter forms, especially operetta and music for the theater. They had in common a post-Romantic musical vocabulary involving large orchestras, an adherence to tonality, and a strong sense of melody. Their music was highly programmatic, often making use of the Wagnerian leitmotiv, in which each character, place and dramatic situation is given its own particular musical idea, such as a melodic strand.

SENTIMENTAL MUSIC

The music of these composers was often sentimental, at a time when giants such as Igor STRAVINSKY, Arnold SCHOENBERG, and Charles IVES were moving in the opposite direction. For this reason, the musical establishment found it hard to accept their work as anything more than a commercial rehash of late 19th-century models. Nevertheless, these composers did succeed in establishing the manner of writing for film that became the foundation for succeeding generations to emulate and build on. As younger composers started to explore later contemporary styles of musical composition, they never totally abandoned the basic principles laid down by Waxman and his generation.

Waxman's first Hollywood score was for *The Bride of Frankenstein* (1935), after which he was given a two-year contract with Universal Studios, followed by a seven-year contract with MGM. He composed the music for the third film version of *Dr. Jekyll and Mr. Hyde*, starring Spencer Tracy. In a very different vein, Waxman scored two classic comedies featuring Katharine Hepburn, *The Philadelphia Story* (1940) and *Woman of the Year* (1942). Waxman left MGM in 1943 and began working for Warner Bros. Waxman won Academy Awards for his scores for *Sunset Boulevard* (1950) and *A Place in the Sun* (1951), as well as receiving numerous other Oscar nominations.

WORKING WITH HITCHCOCK

Waxman collaborated with Alfred Hitchcock on four movies: *Rebecca* (1940), *Suspicion* (1941), *The Paradine Case* (1948), and *Rear Window* (1954). His score for *Rebecca* is a good example of his typical style. It is 19th-century in inspiration, is based on a rich orchestration, makes use of leitmotiv, and although it may seem very sentimental at times, it is invariably skillful in its support of the drama.

In 1947, Waxman founded the Los Angeles Music Festival, dedicated to popularizing contemporary classical music, and he remained its director until 1966. His non-film compositions included *Elegy for Strings*. Waxman died on February 24, 1967.

Richard Trombley

SEE ALSO:

FILM MUSIC; LATE ROMANTICISM.

FURTHER READING
Brown, Royal S. *Overtones and Undertones* (Berkeley, CA: University of California Press, 1994); Gorbman, Claudia. *Unheard Melodies* (Bloomington, IN: Indiana University Press, 1987); Prendergast, Roy. *Film Music, A Neglected Art* (New York: W. W. Norton, 1977).

SUGGESTED LISTENING
Legends of Hollywood: Franz Waxman, Vols. 1–3; *Rebecca*; *The Silver Chalice*.

THE WEAVERS

The Weavers were one of the most influential folk groups of the 1950s and are remembered by many as the epitome of the protest era. Their songs form the link between old-style folk music and the folk/protest music that gave rock its intellectual and philosophical underpinning. The original Weavers were Pete Seeger, Lee Hays, Fred Hellerman, and Ronnie Gilbert. Seeger and Hays had formed the legendary Almanac Singers with Woody GUTHRIE and Millard Lampell in the early 1940s. The quartet included a baritone, a bass, an alto, and Seeger, who described himself as a "split-tenor." Their formula was to create a harmonious sound that commanded listeners to join in, focusing on content rather than vocal effects.

Their first big break came in 1949, at the Village Vanguard in New York, when poet Carl Sandburg saw them and wrote: "When I hear America singing, the Weavers are there." Soon the club was packed and the band had a contract with Decca. "Tzena, Tzena," an Israeli soldier's tune, was their first recording, and within weeks of release in April 1950 it was a hit. Next, DJs began playing the flip side, "Goodnight, Irene." Though the Weavers did not include some of LEADBELLY's more controversial lyrics, singing the music of a black ex-convict was an affirmation of the group's political leanings. "Goodnight, Irene" stayed No. 1 for 13 weeks and sold 2 million copies, while "Tzena" rose to No. 2. The group had ten more hits by early 1952, including "Kisses Sweeter Than Wine," "So Long (It's Been Good to Know You)," and the East African "Wimoweh."

The Weavers' early years as a group were turbulent, as they battled with the rising tide of McCarthyism, and fear of anti-Communist violence prevented the progressives who made up their audience from gathering in public. Finally, in 1952, Seeger was blacklisted and ordered to appear before the House Un-American Activities Committee. This put a temporary halt to the group, but by this time their albums had all reached the charts and many songs had become standards.

Emilio Rodriguez/Pictorial

Pete Seeger, the Weaver's leading light and a symbolic figure for the politically aware folk music movement.

In 1955, the group formed again at the instigation of their manager, Harold Leventhal. New York's Town Hall refused to accept a booking, and instead they performed at Carnegie Hall to tremendous acclaim. They continued to play together until 1964, although Seeger left the group in 1957 and was replaced by several different performers over the years. The group gathered for a final reunion concert at Carnegie Hall in 1980, with Lee Hays singing from a wheelchair. This concert was the centerpiece of a TV documentary on the Weavers, appropriately titled *Wasn't That a Time!*

Stan Hieronymus

SEE ALSO:

DYLAN, BOB; FOLK MUSIC; FOLK ROCK.

FURTHER READING

Harris, Craig. *The New Folk Music*
(Crown Point, IN: White Cliffs Media Co., 1991);
Seeger, Pete, and Bob Reisner.
Everybody Says Freedom: A History of the Civil Rights Movement in Songs and Pictures
(New York: W. W. Norton, 1989).

SUGGESTED LISTENING

Best of the Weavers; *Kisses Sweeter Than Wine*; *Wasn't That a Time!*; *The Weavers at Carnegie Hall.*

ANTON WEBERN

Anton Webern earned a living as a conductor, while writing music according to the strict dictates of serialism that were to influence a whole generation of composers.

Although it was Arnold SCHOENBERG who formulated the rules of 12-note serial composition around 1920, it was in the precisely focused works of his Austrian disciple, Anton Webern, that a generation of European serial composers found their main inspiration. Among those who were profoundly influenced by the music of Webern were Karlheinz STOCKHAUSEN and Pierre BOULEZ.

Anton Webern was born in Vienna on December 3, 1883. His father was a mining engineer and landholder, and his mother was an amateur pianist who gave Webern his first lessons on the piano. When Webern was three, the family moved to Graz, and then in 1894 to Klagenfurt, where Webern started formal lessons in piano and the cello. The summers were spent on the family estate in Carinthia. Here Webern and his cousin Ernst enjoyed walking in the mountains, looking for rocks and wild flowers, and these walks instilled in Webern a love of the countryside that lasted throughout his life.

In Klagenfurt, Webern attended the high school, and also played the cello in a community orchestra. His first musical composition—for cello and piano—was written in 1899.

STUDYING WITH SCHOENBERG

In 1902, the young Webern enrolled in the University of Vienna to study musicology. He also took lessons in harmony and counterpoint while continuing with his instrumental studies on cello and piano. In 1904 (the year he received his doctorate in musicology), he joined the private classes in composition being given in Vienna by the young Arnold Schoenberg; another member of the class was Alban BERG.

The following four years were crucial for Webern. Although his teacher Schoenberg had yet to arrive at his theory of serial composition, he was already moving away from tonality and this inevitably influenced his pupils. Other major influences at this time were Richard Wagner, a towering figure in the musical world who had died only 20 years earlier, and Gustav MAHLER, who was musical director at the

Vienna Opera House. Between 1904 and 1908, Webern wrote over 100 pieces. His string quartet of 1905 was heavily influenced by Schoenberg, while a set of five songs written between 1906 and 1908 show him trying to move away from tonality. His studies with Schoenberg culminated in a "graduation" piece for orchestra, *Passacaglia*, which Webern labeled his Opus 1.

Although Webern had had no formal training as a conductor, he now embarked on a conducting career. Fortunately, he was supported by an allowance from his father, because many of his attempts to find work as a conductor were frustrated, in part because musicians found his rehearsals too detailed and demanding. A position as chorusmaster and assistant conductor at Bad Ischl ended after only a few months because Webern was impatient with the operettas and other light works that the spa visitors wanted to hear. Subsequent periods of employment in Innsbruck and Bad Teplitz lasted not much longer.

It was during this period, in 1909, that Webern composed his short Five Movements for string quartet and Six Pieces for orchestra.

Webern ceased to be Schoenberg's pupil in 1908, but he was to remain his friend and devoted protégé for many years. At the outbreak of World War I in 1914, Webern enlisted and underwent military training. However, the conductor Alexander Zemlinsky used his influence to have Webern discharged from his military service and procured for him the conductorship of the Deutscher Landestheater in Prague. Nevertheless, Webern re-enlisted because Schoenberg had been drafted. After the war, Webern left a post in Czechoslovakia to follow Schoenberg to Mödling, a suburb of Vienna. Webern was to live there for the rest of his life.

During the war and afterwards, Webern continued to write songs and short pieces all characterized by their atonality, brevity, and stark textures.

After the end of World War I, Webern's conducting career took a turn for the better. He became musical director of the Vienna Workers' Symphony orchestra and chorus (sponsored by the Social Democratic Party), and embarked on a series of concerts aimed at bringing the classics to the people (although he also took the opportunity to introduce them to some new music, including his own).

ADOPTING THE CONCEPT OF SERIALISM

By the early 1920s, Schoenberg had formulated his ideas on the use of the 12-tone series as the basis of composition. To some extent, Webern had been moving in the same direction independently, and he seized on the concept of the tone-row eagerly. His first serial composition, the piano piece *Kinderstück* (1924), was a straightforward demonstration of the idea of serialism, with the tone-row repeated without alteration. In a series of songs that he wrote in 1924 and 1925, he experimented with different ways of exploiting the tone-row. From this time on, all Webern's music was composed serially.

In 1927, he completed a longer serial piece (it lasted all of eight minutes). This was the String Trio, Opus 20, which had two movements. This was followed by his Symphony Op. 21, in 1928, which again had two movements. A noticeable feature of this work was its symmetry, an element that was to become even more pronounced in the works that followed.

Webern was at last achieving recognition as a conductor. Austrian radio gave him regular conducting work, and in 1929 he toured some of the major cities in Germany as visiting conductor before going on to appear in London. In Vienna he had some teaching work, and he delivered two series of lectures on 12-note composition and the new music.

By 1936, the Social Democratic Party was outlawed, and Webern's income from conducting evaporated. Schoenberg (who was Jewish) had fled to America, but Webern remained in Austria. His regular radio program ended after an injudicious broadcast of the music of Mendelssohn, who was Jewish. Webern was able to travel to Barcelona to rehearse Berg's Violin Concerto, and to England to conduct the BBC Orchestra. The American pianist Edward Steuermann premiered Webern's Piano Variations in 1936, followed by *Das Augenlicht* in 1938, and the Cantata No. 1 in 1939.

In 1926, Webern had met the poet Hildegard Jone, whose work struck a deep chord with him, expressing as it did the idea that the order and symmetry of nature paralleled the divine order. From then on, all his choral works were based on texts by Jone. His second cantata, which was completed in 1943, was to be his longest work, lasting just over ten minutes.

During most of World War II, Webern lived quietly at his home in Mödling. Toward the end of the war, he and his wife went to stay with their daughter near Salzburg. On September 15, 1945, Webern was accidentally shot and killed by American occupation military police. He left behind a body of work with a total performance time of about four hours.

Jane Prendergast

SEE ALSO:

CHAMBER MUSIC; ORCHESTRAL MUSIC; SERIALISM; VOCAL AND CHORAL MUSIC.

FURTHER READING

Bailey, K. *The Twelve-Note Music of Anton Webern* (New York: Cambridge University Press, 1991); Moldenhauer, H. and R. *Anton von Webern* (New York: Alfred A. Knopf, 1978); Webern, Anton. *The Path to the New Music* (Bryn Mawr, PA: Presser, 1963)

SUGGESTED LISTENING

Cantata No. 1; Five Movements; *Passacaglia*; Piano Variations; Six Bagatelles; Symphony Op. 21.

BEN WEBSTER

T enor saxophonist Ben Webster is one of those giants of classic jazz whose sound has never become dated. With his tough, growling approach to swing, and seductive, almost crooning ballad playing, Webster remained a force on the jazz scene from the 1930s through the 1950s. His warm, big-toned sax was always inspired and inspiring, whether as a soloist in Duke ELLINGTON's celebrated reed section or in his own intimate sessions as a small-group leader. "Apart from Coleman HAWKINS and Lester YOUNG," Mark C. Gridley wrote in *Jazz Styles*, "Ben Webster was the most influential tenor saxophonist of the swing era."

Benjamin Francis Love Webster was born in Kansas City, Missouri, on March 27, 1909. As a child he learned violin, and then studied music at Wilberforce University in the mid-1920s. Legendary boogie-woogie pianist Pete Johnson, a neighbor, taught him how to play the blues. Soon Webster could be found accompanying silent movies in a theater in Amarillo, Texas, and playing boogie piano with various Southwestern bands.

After learning the rudiments of sax, Webster refined his skills in the Young Family Band (led by the father of tenor sax, the great Lester Young) in the early 1930s. Switching permanently to sax, he worked with many influential jazz outfits, such as Bennie Moten's (he was featured soloist on Moten's classic *Moten's Swing*) and Andy Kirk's, before moving to New York in 1934 to replace his idol Coleman Hawkins in the famed Fletcher HENDERSON band.

THE ELLINGTON YEARS

After leaving Henderson in the mid-1930s, Webster played freelance with several major New York swing bands (including Benny CARTER's and Cab Calloway's, along with brief stints with Duke Ellington's Orchestra in 1935 and 1936). In January 1940, he became a full-time member of the Ellington ensemble. "I got my college degree in music from playing with Fletcher Henderson," said Webster, "And my Ph.D. from Duke."

Joining Johnny HODGES (alto sax) and Harry Carney (baritone sax) in the Ellington reed section, Webster became Ellington's first major tenor sax soloist. For the next three years, he produced several masterpieces with Ellington, including "Perdido," "All Too Soon," "Blue Serge," and "Just a-Settin' and a-Rockin.'" Webster's swinging "Cotton Tail" solo (based on GERSHWIN's "I Got Rhythm") is one of the most celebrated improvisations in all jazz. According to critic Mark Tucker, "He brought great power and drive to fast tunes and a romantic, smoldering tenderness to ballads." He finally left the orchestra in 1943 after a spat with Ellington, who didn't like his saxophone player playing piano with the band.

TENDER BALLADEER

After working with several bands, including those of Red Allen and Stuff Smith, he fronted his own ensembles on Swing Street in New York City before rejoining Ellington in 1948 for another year. In the early-1950s, Webster became a member of Norman GRANZ's Jazz at the Philharmonic. He produced several small band sessions in the 1950s and 1960s (his lush and soulful ballad sessions are especially memorable), and worked extensively as a studio musician backing singers such as Billie HOLIDAY and Ella FITZGERALD.

Webster decided to relocate permanently to Copenhagen, Denmark, in 1964, and the legendary saxophonist spent the next decade playing European clubs and festivals. He died in Amsterdam, Holland, on September 20, 1973.

Michael R. Ross

SEE ALSO:

BIG BAND JAZZ; BOOGIE-WOOGIE; JAZZ; SWING.

FURTHER READING

Balliett, Whitney. *New York Notes: A Journal of Jazz in the Seventies* (New York: Da Capo Press, 1977); Stewart, Rex. *Jazz Masters of the Thirties* (New York: Da Capo Press, 1982).

SUGGESTED LISTENING

Duke Ellington: *The Blanton-Webster Band*; Ben Webster: *Ben Webster & Associates*; *Soulville*.

KURT WEILL

Kurt Weill's music is respected by theater audiences and musicians alike. His operas, *The Rise and Fall of the City of Mahagonny* and *Threepenny Opera* are revived regularly throughout the world, and his songs are sung in films, cabarets and recital halls. Weill inherited aspects of the German *lied* (song) tradition and married these to the cabaret style to produce a music uniquely his own, in which his ironic lyricism is the perfect setting for texts such as "Mack the Knife" and "My Ship."

Kurt Julian Weill was born on March 2, 1900, in Dessau, Germany, the son of the chief cantor of the synagogue. Kurt Weill studied piano as a child, and wrote piano pieces and songs from his early teens. At 15, he became a pupil of Albert Bing, director of the Dessau Opera House, and in 1918 entered the Berlin Hochschule für Musik. Although Weill did well, he left after only a year to return to Dessau as Hans Knappertsbusch's rehearsal pianist at the Opera House. Just one year later, he was hired as conductor of a new opera company at Lüdenscheid.

However, Feruccio Busoni had begun teaching a master class in composition at the Berlin Academy, and Weill left his job and became Busoni's student, with a scholarship for full tuition. Weill identified with the poor and his Symphony No. 1 (1921) was subtitled *Workers, Peasants and Soldiers—A People's Awakening to God*. A ballet for children, *Die Zaubernacht* (The Magic Night) and a string quartet followed. Among the dancers auditioning for *Zaubernacht* was the Austrian ballerina Lotte Lenya, whom Weill later married.

Weill then worked as a music critic on German radio and taught composition. Among his students were the conductor Maurice Abravanel and the pianist Claudio ARRAU. He wrote a violin concerto for Joseph Szigeti to be played with band. His first opera, *Der Protagonist*, with a libretto by the playwright Georg Kaiser, was an instant success at the Dresden State Opera and led to a commission for another chamber opera from Paul HINDEMITH for the Baden-Baden Festival.

WEILL MEETS BRECHT

This commission was the beginning of Weill's collaboration with the playwright, Bertolt Brecht, which produced, in the first place, the *Mahagonny*

Kurt Weill (left), composer of many operas and Broadway musicals, with the playwright, Maxwell Anderson.

Songspiel, a setting of poems by Brecht which later became the full-scale opera, *The Rise and Fall of the City of Mahagonny*, in 1930. The partnership, in fact, lasted only three years but it produced the works for which Weill is best remembered. *The Threepenny Opera* had its premiere in Berlin in 1928 to tremendous acclaim, with Lotte Lenya playing the part of the prostitute Jenny. *The Threepenny Opera* was a reworking of *The Beggar's Opera,* written in the 18th century by John Gay in reaction against the heroic operas of Handel.

Brecht and Weill used the subject matter of the seedy underworld of London to comment on the pretensions and dangers of right-wing political parties, including the Nazi party, in Germany. Weill's music uses the deprecatory ironies of cabaret music to simultaneously seduce and repel the audience. The Weill-Brecht team also wrote the 1928 *Berlin Requiem*, a cantata for radio, *The Lindbergh Flight*, as well as *Happy End*, whose first performance ended in a riot after Frau Brecht took the stage to read a political text by her husband. In contrast to *The Threepenny Opera,* which was designated a "musical play," *Mahagonny* (1930) developed into a full-scale opera. The piece took as its theme greed, anarchy, and immorality and was set in some unspecified part of the American West. Its first performance in Leipzig was aborted by Nazi-inspired riots.

Weill felt that his music was becoming subservient to Brecht's politics, so they went their separate ways after 1930. In 1932, Weill composed incidental music to Kaiser's play *Der Silbersee*. However, although his music was now eagerly sought after in opera houses all over Europe, it became clear that, in Germany itself, the composer was about to be banned, if not in physical danger, as the Nazi party took power. Weill emigrated to Paris on March 21, 1933. After the Anschluss in 1938 (Germany's seizure of power in Austria), his scores at Universal Editions in Vienna were destroyed. In France, he briefly resumed a collaboration with Brecht which resulted in the sung ballet, *The Seven Deadly Sins.*

AMERICAN YEARS

Weill went to New York in 1935 to conduct the score he had written for *The Eternal Way*, Franz Werfel's seven-hour epic on the history of the Jewish people. The funding of this enormous work ran into difficulties and, while he was waiting, Weill worked with Paul Green on the anti-war protest *Johnny Johnson.* Both *The Eternal Road* (as it was eventually known) and *Johnny Johnson* were flops, but Weill nevertheless felt that his future lay on Broadway, and in 1937 he applied for American citizenship. In his later years, Weill repudiated any interest in "serious" music, in the sense of music written for an elite audience. However, he failed to realize how little Broadway audiences cared about his committed social criticism. In those war years and after, theater audiences needed to be amused and to forget the realities of war and poverty.

In 1938, he worked with Maxwell Anderson on the political satire, *Knickerbocker Holiday,* which had a moderate success. Then, in 1940, he collaborated with Ira Gershwin and Moss Hart on *Lady in the Dark,* which was made into a film starring Ginger Rodgers and Ray Milland. Next came the Perelman/Nash *One Touch of Venus*, and then Elmer Rice's *Street Scene* (1946). Weill had seen this play about life in a tenement block in New York while he was still in Germany. It was a subject after his own heart, a hopeless depiction of poverty and addiction, culminating in murder. The composer managed to woo his audience with a mixture of grim realism and humor, and the opera ran for 21 weeks in New York's Adelphi Theater. Weill's last work was a collaboration with Alan Jay Lerner on *Love Life* (1948), an ironically titled look at the state of marriage in modern America. Weill died on April 3, 1950.

Jane Prendergast

SEE ALSO:

CABARET MUSIC; MUSICALS; OPERA.

FURTHER READING

Jarman, Douglas. *Kurt Weill, An Illustrated Biography* (Bloomington, IN: Indiana University Press, 1982); Symonette, L. and K.H. Kowalke, eds. *Speak Low: Letters of Kurt Weill and Lotte Lenya* (Berkeley, CA: University of California Press, 1996).

SUGGESTED LISTENING

Happy End; *Lady in the Dark*; *The Rise and Fall of the City of Mahagonny*; *The Seven Deadly Sins*; Symphony No. 1; *The Threepenny Opera*; Violin Concerto.

PAUL WHITEMAN

During his heyday in the 1920s, Paul Whiteman conducted a publicity campaign to be crowned the "king of jazz." The title did not fit the man in terms of influence or invention—Louis ARMSTRONG and Duke ELLINGTON among others, had a much stronger claim. However, he was not the figure of derision that is so often portrayed. At a time when the color lines were hard and fast, Whiteman's orchestra was the leading white ensemble, both in terms of musicianship and in popularity.

Whiteman was born in Denver, Colorado, on March 28, 1890, the son of the musical director for the city's schools. He was given his first viola at age seven, and eventually played with the Denver Symphony Orchestra and several Bay Area ensembles after moving to San Francisco in 1911. He developed a strong interest in popular music and, through frequent visits to local saloons, became acquainted with jazz. As he wrote in his 1926 autobiography, jazz "hit me hard … rhythmic, catching as the smallpox and spirit-lifting." He got his first opportunity to lead a band while serving in the navy during World War I.

THE PAUL WHITEMAN ORCHESTRA

After the war he settled in New York City, where he organized the Paul Whiteman Orchestra (originally the Ambassador Orchestra), soon to be America's dominant pop-jazz band. A glance at the line-up of the orchestra reveals legendary names such as cornetist Bix BEIDERBECKE, saxophonist Frankie Trumbauer, trumpeter Henry Busse, guitarist Eddie Lang, violinist Joe Venuti, and singers Bing CROSBY and Mildred Bailey. Whiteman's arrangers—including the great Bill Challis—were also among the best in the business. Unsurprisingly, this gathering of talent produced a string of hits—from the breakthrough 1920 single "Whispering" to late 1920s releases such as "Coquette" and "That's My Weakness Now."

Besides issuing some of the most popular instrumental and vocal recordings of the 1920s, Whiteman also made musical history on February 12, 1924, when he produced the groundbreaking, multi-genre concert *Experiment in Modern Music*. The high-spot of this concert was the composer George GERSHWIN playing his own *Rhapsody in Blue*—a work specially commissioned for the event. Whiteman made jazz popular, if not respectable. It was his concept of the big band show, immortalized by the 1930 film, *King of Jazz*, that prevailed for years to come.

Many critics have dismissed Whiteman's music. His orchestra's output has often been seen as simplified and corny. However, many of the late 1920s recordings, especially numbers featuring Crosby and Beiderbecke, and those with the Rhythm Boys (a vocal trio consisting of Crosby, Al Rinker, and Harry Barris), still sound fresh and exciting today.

KING OF THE JAZZ ERA

Whiteman provided a platform for some of the greatest performers of his time. As Joe Venuti said: "Don't ever make fun of Paul Whiteman. He took pride in having the finest musicians in the world and paid the highest salaries ever paid." Whiteman was more than fair to his bandsmen, keeping a place in the orchestra for Bix Beiderbecke during his many illnesses, dealing with difficult behavior from performers like Venuti, and releasing artists if they were offered something better.

During the 1930s Whiteman continued to lead successful orchestras. Then in 1944, he gave up regular bandleading and became the longstanding musical director of ABC radio.

Paul Whiteman died of heart failure on December 29, 1967 in Doylestown, Pennsylvania. Few musical legends are more deserving of re-evaluation than this imaginative conductor and talent-spotter who was, if not the "king of jazz," at least king of the jazz era.

Terry Atkinson

SEE ALSO:
BIG BAND JAZZ; JAZZ; POPULAR MUSIC.

FURTHER READING

DeLong, Thomas. *Pops: Paul Whiteman, King of Jazz* (Piscataway, NJ: New Wind Publishing, 1983).

SUGGESTED LISTENING

Paul Whiteman: Featuring Bix Beiderbecke; *Paul Whiteman: Victor Masters*.

THE
WHO

The Who were one of the most energetic of the British beat groups: fans came to expect exhibitions of explosive violence at their live performances, and it was this element of performance art that made the band an ideal subject for films.

The Who, formed in 1964, were four young men from the poorer parts of London: guitarist Pete Townshend (b. May 1945), vocalist Roger Daltrey (b. May 1944), drummer Keith Moon (b. August 1947, d. September 1978), and bassist John Entwistle (b. October 1944). Rage on stage was an integral part of their live performances, and Townshend would end a concert with the ritual smashing of his guitar, while Moon would send his drum kit toppling over.

The band made a series of exciting, pithy singles, often with adolescent antiheroes as their subject, including "My Generation" (1965). Their first big success came in 1969 with their concept album, *Tommy*, which is widely regarded as being the first rock opera. This tale of a deaf, dumb, and blind kid with an unusual talent for pinball brought them long-awaited chart success in the U.S., peaking at No. 4. Another rock opera, *Quadrophenia*, was to follow in 1973. This was based on the adventures of a group of mods—a British youth subculture of the 1960s, for whom The Who had been heroes.

The album *Live at Leeds* (1970) captured the group at its incandescent best, and songs from *Who's Next* (1971) reached the U.K. Top 10. "Won't Get Fooled Again," a track from that album, is eight-and-a-half minutes of stirring music, with Daltrey's passionate singing deployed to its best effect. In the song Townshend summed up the failure of the 1960s hippie movement in the line: "Meet the new boss/Same as the old boss," which Daltrey roared out over a tumultuous background of crashing instrumentation to provide an awesome climax to the song.

In the late 1970s, the group's energies were dissipated by their separate solo work, although *Tommy* was made into a film, directed by the eccentric Ken Russell, in 1975. In 1978, Moon—who had enjoyed a reputation for being "the bad boy of rock" by trashing hotel rooms and driving cars into swimming pools—finally destroyed himself with an overdose of drugs that had been prescribed to fight his alcoholism. He was replaced by Kenny Jones (b. September 1948), formerly of the Small Faces. In 1983, the group officially disbanded, although they occasionally reformed for concert appearances.

The Clash, SEX PISTOLS, and the Britpop bands were among the many to find The Who's brand of no-frills rock inspiring. In the 1990s, *Tommy* was successfully revived in London's West End, and on Broadway.

Graham McColl

SEE ALSO:
BRITISH BEAT MUSIC; PUNK ROCK; ROCK MUSIC.

Corbis-Bettmann/UPI

The Who: (from left) Keith Moon, Pete Townshend, Roger Daltrey, and John Entwistle.

FURTHER READING
Butler, Dougal. *Full Moon* (New York: Quill Books, 1982); Kamin, Philip, and Peter Goddard. *The Who: The Farewell Tour* (New York: Beaufort Books, 1983); Swenson, John. *The Who: Britain's Greatest Rock Group* (New York: Tempo, 1979).

SUGGESTED LISTENING
Live at Leeds; *My Generation: The Very Best of The Who*; *Quadrophenia*; *Tommy*; *Who's Next*.

HANK
WILLIAMS

Few figures in country music can claim a legacy to match that of Hank Williams. His musical contribution and legendary life—and death—have consecrated Williams as country's preeminent artist. The original role-model for the rock'n'roll myth, Williams lived fast and died young, singing of the overwhelming joy and inconsolable sorrow of his personal life. He sang with a voice limited in range but strong in expression, breaking into tremolo effects and yodels that perfectly embodied the emotions expressed in his songs.

Hiram Williams was born September 17, 1923, in rural Georgiana, Alabama, suffering from a spinal defect that would torment him throughout his short life. His father was confined to a veterans' hospital, leaving Hank's mother, Lilly, with the impoverished family. She gave Hank a cheap guitar when he was seven, and local bluesman Rufe "Tee-tot" Payne taught him to play. Other early influences were the gospel music of local churches and the country music he heard on the radio. By his early 20s, he was playing regularly on the Alabama dance-hall circuit.

SOURCE OF HIS INSPIRATION

In December 1944, Hank married the feisty Audrey Sheppard. Their tumultuous marriage provided material for many of Williams' songs, defining modern country music's "can't-live-with-'em-can't-live-without-'em" vision of male–female relationships.

Williams moved to Nashville, Tennessee, in 1946 in pursuit of a recording contract. Audrey arranged a meeting with Fred Rose of the newly formed Acuff-Rose Publishing. Rose was taken with the young singer, getting Williams signed to MGM, and becoming his mentor and songwriting partner. Williams had a hit with "Move It on Over" in 1947, and joined the *Louisiana Hayride* radio show a year later. He then had a major hit with a revival of Emmet Miller's minstrel number "Lovesick Blues." When he performed the song at his debut at Nashville's Grand Ole Opry in June 1949, the crowd called him back for six encores, and Williams had become a star. Soon

Williams was churning out the country hits that would become standards: "I'm So Lonesome I Could Cry," "You're Cheatin' Heart," "Hey, Good Lookin'," "Cold, Cold Heart," "I Can't Help It (If I'm Still in Love with You)," "I'll Never Get Out of This World Alive," and many more. Pop crooners such as Tony BENNETT, Pat Boone, and Jo Stafford went on to score hits with Williams' material.

As his fame increased, Williams' personal life spiraled out of control. His mercurial personality and constant physical pain led to binges of alcohol and painkillers, and his erratic, often violent, behavior became the stuff of legend around Nashville. He trashed hotel rooms and fell off stages, aggravating his back injury further and sending him in search of stronger relief. Then, in 1952, Williams suffered a series of personal and professional disasters. He was fired from the Opry, Audrey divorced him, and his backing band quit. His life became one long bender, barely slowed by a hasty wedding to Billie Jean Jones in October of the same year. On New Year's Day in 1953, Hank lay on the back seat of a Cadillac, en route to a show in Ohio. When his driver checked on him in Oak Hill, West Virginia, he found the 29-year-old Williams dead, killed by a lethal combination of pills and booze. Legend has it that the lyrics for a new song were in his hand.

Like his life, Williams's legend is a messy thing. His songs, however, are simply written country laments, wrought with humor and heartache. They still resonate with an undeniable power, offering a window into the soul of their troubled creator and inspiring countless musicians and songwriters in many genres. Nearly fifty years after his death, Williams's work pervades American country music.

Greg Bower

SEE ALSO:

COUNTRY; GOSPEL; ROCK'N'ROLL; SINGER-SONGWRITERS.

FURTHER READING
Escott, Colin, et al. *Hank Williams: The Biography* (Boston, MA: Little, Brown & Co., 1994).

SUGGESTED LISTENING
Moanin' The Blues; *Live at the Grand Ole Opry*; *The Original Singles Collection*.

JOHN
WILLIAMS

The music of John Williams is probably known to more Americans than that of any other composer. Over the last three decades of the 20th century, his scores for major Hollywood films have been heard by millions. Themes from these movies have taken on a life of their own, and it is possible that they will survive the films for which they were originally written. Also, Williams had crossed over into classical music and this work has been well received by serious musicians.

Williams was born at the height of the Great Depression, on February 8, 1932, in Flushing, New York. His father was a professional percussionist, and Williams studied piano from the age of six—later learning bassoon, cello, clarinet, trombone, and trumpet. At eight, he taught himself orchestration using Rimsky-Korsakov's treatise on the subject as his textbook.

In 1948, Williams moved to California and studied at the University of California at Los Angeles. There he continued learning orchestration, and took lessons in composition from Mario Castelnuovo-Tedesco.

Williams joined the U.S. air force during the Korean War, and spent his time conducting and arranging music for military bands. After the war he used his GI benefits to good effect, attending the Juilliard School, where he studied for a year in the prestigious studio of Rhosina Lhevinne. In the evenings he played jazz piano in clubs in order to support himself.

MUSIC FOR THE MOVIES

In 1956, Williams found work as a pianist with the 20th Century Fox Studio Orchestra. He soon began to write scores for television shows, producing 30 minutes of music every week.

In 1960, Williams wrote his first film score for *Because They're Young*. During the 1960s his work was nominated for several Academy Awards, and he finally won his first Oscar for the 1971 film of *Fiddler on the Roof*. During this period he wrote some of his greatest and most successful scores for films such as *The Reivers, Jane Eyre,* and *Images,* and arranged and conducted the music for *Goodbye Mr. Chips*.

The mid-1970s could be characterized as Williams' disaster-movie period. He wrote the film scores for several big budget disaster epics including *The Poseidon Adventure,* and *The Towering Inferno.* In 1975, a highly successful collaboration began with film director Steven Spielberg, when Williams wrote the score for *Jaws.* The famous two-note theme from this movie earned him his second Oscar. After the *Jaws* theme, Williams wrote his famous music for George Lucas' phenomenally successful *Star Wars* trilogy.

In the late 1970s he scored blockbusters such as *Superman.* During the 1980s, Williams continued his association with Steven Spielberg, for whom he scored *E.T.,* and *Close Encounters of the Third Kind,* as well as the "Indiana Jones" series. His success continued with the films *The Accidental Tourist, Home Alone, Jurassic Park,* again with Spielberg, in 1993, and its sequel *The Lost World* in 1997. He also wrote extensively for TV, notably for NBC news programs and for BBC dramas.

Williams' work was conservative, and would not have sounded out of place scoring films produced 20 years earlier. He eschewed innovations such as rock or rap, and his themes tended to be memorable and easily hummed, as they were built around short motifs that he quoted in simple variations throughout the film.

In 1980, Williams succeeded Arthur FIEDLER as conductor of the Boston Pops Orchestra. He began to devote himself to composing music independent of film. Since 1980, Williams has written two symphonies, a large body of chamber music and concertos for bassoon, clarinet, flute, and violin. He has also been artist in residence at the Tanglewood Music Center begun by Sergey KOUSSEVITZKY.

Jane Prendergast

SEE ALSO:
FILM MUSIC; JARRE, MAURICE; MANCINI, HENRY.

FURTHER READING
Darby, William, and Jack Du Bers.
American Film Music
(Jefferson, NC: McFarland & Co., 1990).

SUGGESTED LISTENING
Close Encounters of the Third Kind;
E.T.; *Fiddler on the Roof*; *Jaws*; *Jurassic Park*;
The Poseidon Adventure;
Star Wars; *The Towering Inferno*.

JOHN WILLIAMS

If Andrés SEGOVIA was the 20th century's king of the classical guitar, then John Williams was surely his worthy successor. In fact, it was Segovia himself who called Williams "a prince of the guitar."

John Williams was born on April 24, 1941, in Melbourne, Australia. His father, Leonard Williams, was a British guitarist of great ability. The young Williams was taught the classical guitar by his father from age seven, and after the family had returned to England in 1952, he performed at the Conway Hall, in London. His precocious talent earned him a scholarship to the Accademia Musicale Chigiana, in Siena, where he studied with Segovia during three summers. Between 1956 and 1959, he studied piano and music theory at London's Royal College of Music.

In 1958, Williams made his official debut at the Wigmore Hall in London, followed by performances in Paris and Madrid. One year later, he released his first two recordings. He toured Russia in 1962 and the United States and Japan in 1963, going on to perform throughout the world over the following decade. In the mid-1970s, he formed a duo with fellow guitarist Julian Bream, which resulted in several tours and three recordings. From 1960 to 1973, he also found time to be professor of the guitar at the Royal College of Music and served as Segovia's deputy at Santiago de Compostela in Spain in 1961 and 1962.

BEYOND CLASSICAL MUSIC

As he pursued his own musical vision, Williams began to challenge the demands and constraints placed on the classical performing artist. He toured less and traded traditional concert garb for more colorful and casual attire. In 1970, Williams scored an unexpected chart success with his album *John Williams Plays Spanish Music*. This popular success continued with his recording of RODRIGO's *Concierto de Aranjuez*. However, the comparative failure of the album *Cavatina* led to Williams moving further away from the traditional classical guitar canon. Segovia hated the electric guitar and popular guitar music, but Williams embraced it. During the late 1970s, he formed the classical-rock group Sky and performed with them on electric guitar. Sky was hugely successful, producing million-selling records and sell-out world tours. However, the pressure of touring was one of the reasons Williams left the group in 1984. On his own again, he continued to broaden his musical horizons, his interest in musical styles running the gamut from classical to folk, jazz, pop, and non-Western idioms.

In the classical arena, Williams commissioned guitar concertos from composers such as Stephen Dodgson, André PREVIN, Richard Harvey, and Steve Gray. He also worked with composers from his native Australia, including Phillip Houghton, Peter Sculthorpe, and Nigel Westlake, to produce guitar works that captured the spirit of his homeland.

EASTERN INFLUENCES

Williams' exploration of jazz led to collaborations with singer Cleo Laine and guitarist Joe Pass. His interest in non-Western musical forms resulted in the first complete disc devoted to the guitar works of Japanese composer Toru TAKEMITSU. By crossing and blurring these musical boundaries, Williams created a bigger and richer landscape for the classical guitar.

Many musicians and aficionados consider Williams to be the most technically proficient classical guitarist who has ever lived. His technique is strong and economical and, over time, his musical expressiveness has grown even more sublime. As a result, Williams conveys to an audience the essence of a composer's intentions, unconstrained by the technical limitations of the classical guitar.

Jim Tosone

SEE ALSO:
FOLK MUSIC; JAZZ.

FURTHER READING
Gregory, Hugh. *One Thousand Great Guitarists* (San Francisco, CA: GPI Books, 1994).

SUGGESTED LISTENING
From Australia;
Masterpieces: The Very Best of Sky;
Bach: *Lute Suites*;
Rodrigo: *Concierto de Aranjuez*;
Takemitsu: *To the Edge of a Dream*.

TONY
WILLIAMS

Tony Williams belongs to a select category of jazz percussionists. As a drummer he made his mark in terms of technique, sound, and style, establishing himself as one of the jazz greats, alongside players such as Art BLAKEY and Elvin JONES. His furious yet sensitive brand of creative accompaniment is studied and emulated by young drummers around the world.

Born in Chicago, Illinois, on December 12, 1945, Williams' family moved to the Boston area while he was still very young. He was given his first drumset at age eight and later studied with renowned jazz drummer Alan Dawson. He soon found employment with Sam Rivers and Jackie McLean, and this led to an invitation to join the Miles DAVIS Quintet when he was still only 17.

The original line-up consisted of Miles Davis on trumpet, Williams on drums, Herbie HANCOCK on piano, Ron Carter on bass, and George Coleman on tenor sax. After Coleman had been replaced by the more adventurous Wayne SHORTER, the young, creative band exploded with new sounds and ideas. The rhythm section—Carter, Hancock, and Williams—is widely regarded as one of the greatest of all time.

The musical concept changed from a straight hard bop feel to a rhythmically looser and more harmonically complex sound. Williams, Hancock, Carter, and Shorter were greatly influenced by the avant-garde musical ideas of the time, but they filtered these new sounds and fitted them neatly into the mold of Miles Davis's music. This led to the development of a new style in jazz, and the group made their improvisation concepts more accessible to the general listening public. The quintet played originals but also found ways to refresh the old jazz standards.

Williams recorded several landmark albums with the Davis group, including *Miles Smiles* and *In a Silent Way*. He also performed on a number of historic Blue Note recordings by Eric DOLPHY, Herbie Hancock, Wayne Shorter, and Jackie McLean.

In 1968, Williams left the Miles Davis group to pursue a career as a bandleader—and once again his direction was groundbreaking. At this time, the new genre of jazz rock was yet unnamed, and his new group—Tony Williams' Lifetime—proved to be extremely influential in defining this new style.

Through the 1970s and early 1980s, Williams recorded jazz rock albums, performed on the recordings of others, and toured with a reformed version of the Miles Davis group called V.S.O.P. The new group included Carter, Hancock, and Williams, with trumpeter Freddie HUBBARD standing in for Davis.

In 1985 Tony Williams signed a deal with Blue Note, and released a series of successful recordings, including *Foreign Intrigue*, and *Believe It!* His last release as a bandleader, *Wilderness*, came out just before his death.

A SINGULAR TECHNIQUE

Williams' drumming style was marked by his loose yet unwavering time feel, his creative use of the ride cymbal, and a penchant for playing the hi-hat on all four beats of the bar, or even constant eighth notes rather than the traditional second and fourth beats. His technique with sticks and brushes was both light and dramatic, and he amazed listeners with his ability to play at astonishingly fast tempos. He was able to do much more than keep time. He extended the possibilities of jazz drumming by freeing himself to leave spaces, imply the beat, and produce counter-rhythms and polyrhythms.

Tony Williams died on February 23, 1997, following a heart attack after minor surgery. He was only 51. His forward thinking approach embodied the spirit of jazz and was evident throughout his career. His original style and openness to new ideas has had a continuing influence on jazz percussion.

Gregg Juke

SEE ALSO:

FREE JAZZ; HARD BOP; JAZZ; JAZZ ROCK; JONES, ELVIN; MCLAUGHLIN, JOHN.

FURTHER READING

Taylor, Arthur, ed. *Notes and Tones: Musician-to-Musician Interviews* (New York: Da Capo Press, 1993).

SUGGESTED LISTENING

Emergency!; *Foreign Intrigue*; *Lifetime*; *Wilderness*; Miles Davis: *E.S.P.*; *Miles Smiles*; *In a Silent Way*; Herbie Hancock: *Maiden Voyage*.

SONNY BOY
WILLIAMSON

Despite a career that was tragically cut short, John Lee "Sonny Boy" Williamson was one of the most influential harmonica players in the history of the blues. In his hands, the harmonica became a lead instrument, a major voice of the urban blues. He set the standards of technical and emotional perfection for blues harmonica that still persist today. Before Williamson, the "harp" (harmonica) had been used mainly for novelty value and light jug band riffs, but his talent turned it into an integral part of the early Chicago blues sound. After his death it fell to LITTLE WALTER to complete the harmonica's transition into the postwar electric blues sound.

Born on March 30, 1914, in Jackson, Tennessee, Williamson was a self-taught musician. In his teens he drifted around the South and performed in the Memphis area, associating with musicians such as Sleepy Joe Estes. He moved to Chicago in 1934 and became a popular session musician. Three years later he signed with the Bluebird subsidiary of Victor Records. The tracks he cut during this period still retain the plaintive sound of Estes's music.

DISTINCTIVE STYLE

Williamson's unique playing style quickly distinguished him from the generation of harmonica players that preceded him, and he greatly expanded what the instrument could do. He played his harmonica cross-tuned—with the key of the harmonica a fourth above that of the music. Thus, if the tune was in the key of D, Williamson would play a G harmonica. This allowed him to "draw" most notes and "bend" them more easily, producing flattened "blue" notes. Williamson would use his tongue, breath, and lips to create different sounds. By fluttering his fingers and moving his hand over the harmonica, he could "open" and "close" it, just like a trumpeter would do with a mute. Williamson perfected the use of the harmonica as a second voice, trading vocal lines back and forth with harmonica lines to produce a continuous line of melody. A slight speech impediment known as slow tongue caused him to extend his vowels and thicken the consonants, producing a laid-back, slurring style that was to be widely imitated.

Williamson recorded around 120 sides for Bluebird. He established the idea of using the harmonica as a solo instrument at his first session in 1937, when he was accompanied by Delta guitarists Robert Nighthawk and Big Joe Williams. At this session Williamson cut his biggest hit, "Good Morning, Little Schoolgirl," which has since been covered (performed) many times by blues, rhythm-and-blues, and rock musicians.

While most of his first recordings were rooted in the country sound, Williamson soon began recording with small combos and incorporating elements of swing. His work became heavily rhythmic while still retaining a downhome sound. Among his many hits were "Bluebird Blues" and "Early in the Morning." Williamson wrote many of his own songs and performed with Chicago's top stars and sidemen, including Muddy WATERS, Eddie Boyd, Big Bill BROONZY, TAMPA RED, and Sunnyland Slim.

VIOLENT END

Williamson died on June 1, 1948, at the age of 34, when muggers stabbed him to death with an ice pick while he was heading home from a gig. He was one of the most popular and respected personalities on the Chicago circuit and exerted a profound influence on more than one generation of harmonica players, including Walter Horton, Drifting Slim, Junior Wells and Billy Boy Arnold. Many of his songs have gone on to become blues standards.

Daria Labinsky

SEE ALSO:
BLUES; ROCK MUSIC.

FURTHER READING

Cohn, Lawrence. *Nothing But the Blues: the Music and the Musicians* (New York: Abbeville Press, 1993); Palmer, Robert. *Deep Blues.* (New York: Penguin Books, 1981).

SUGGESTED LISTENING

The Complete Recorded Works Vols. 1–5; *Sugar Mama; Throw A Boogie Woogie* (with Big Joe Williams).

BOB
WILLS

For 60 years Bob Wills made his kind of country music, and though he became ill and unfashionable, the desire to make music never left him.

Wills was born near Kosse, Texas, on March 6, 1905. His father was a fiddler who taught the young Wills to play mandolin so that he could accompany him at ranch dances. Playing with his father introduced Wills to new styles of music, featuring guitars and trumpets, that inspired him to take up the fiddle himself.

He played with his family and other bands throughout his teens, until the crop failure of 1927 spurred Wills to move to Fort Worth and take up music full-time. With singer Milton Brown, Wills appeared on radio as the Wills Fiddle Band. The show was popular and brought in sponsors and a new name—the Light Crust Doughboys. By 1932, their program was being broadcast all over the Southwest. However, Wills' drinking and differences of opinion with the sponsor ended the Doughboys career only a year later. Wills moved around, ending up in Tulsa, Oklahoma, where he formed a new band, the Texas Playboys. In 1935, Wills got a record deal with the American Recording Company—later to become Columbia Records—and the Playboys made their first studio recordings. Wills stayed in Tulsa throughout the late 1930s and the band continued to evolve. By 1940, when Wills recorded "New San Antonio Rose," he had 18 musicians—more than the big bands of contemporaries Glenn MILLER and Benny GOODMAN. The late 1930s and early 1940s were the high point of Wills's career. He was now one of the biggest-selling recording artists in the U.S., and able to run two live bands.

Wills was unique in the musical integration he achieved with his bands and in the wide range of styles that were encompassed by the phrase "Western swing" that best describes his music. His habits of uttering high-pitched shouts during numbers and talking to his musicians reflected the two great influences on his music—the former a remnant of his days playing at ranch dances, the latter picked up from the African-American musicians he associated with in his youth.

Throughout the late 1940s and 1950s, Wills kept recording and performing but the new Playboys never achieved their past success. In 1968 Wills was elected to the Country Music Hall of Fame, but by the 1970s, Western swing was all but dead. In 1973, although illness had forced him to stop playing, he assembled a group of musicians for a greatest hits collection. After the first night of recording, Wills had a stroke and remained in a coma until his death in 1975.

Renee Jinks

SEE ALSO:
COUNTRY.

UPI/Corbis-Bettmann

Country music violinist Bob Wills gives an impromptu performance in his Hollywood home in 1944.

FURTHER READING
Wills, Rosetta. *The King of Western Swing: Bob Wills Remembered* (New York: Billboard Books, 1998); Wolfe, Charles. *The Devil's Box: Masters of Southern Fiddling* (Nashville, TN: Vanderbilt University Press, 1997).

SUGGESTED LISTENING
The Best of Bob Wills; *The Essential Bob Wills*; *Tiffany Transcriptions* Vols. 1–10.

STEVIE WONDER

A gifted musician, innovative composer, and spiritually inspired songwriter, Stevie Wonder is one of popular music's brightest lights. With his best material, Wonder represents the high point of the union of pop and rhythm and blues (R&B).

Wonder was born Steveland Judkins on May 13, 1950, in Saginaw, Michigan (he later changed his last name to Morris, his mother's maiden name). Soon after birth, he was placed in an incubator and given too much oxygen, leaving him permanently blind.

But young Stevie mastered piano, harmonica, and drums, and joined a church choir—all by the age of nine. In 1961, a member of the Miracles, a talented R&B group, suggested he audition for MOTOWN. It was Motown who changed Steveland Morris into "Little Stevie Wonder."

PRECOCIOUS TALENT

Wonder soon became a fixture at Motown's studio, making recordings that showcased his talent as a multi-instrumentalist. In 1963, an exuberant live recording "Fingertips (Part 2)" became a No. 1 hit and Motown began marketing the "12-year-old genius" as the new RAY CHARLES. For all his talent, the young Wonder had little musical direction to call his own.

As Wonder grew older and the novelty of youth wore off, he began to assert himself as a songwriter, cowriting his hits "Uptight (Everything's Alright)" and "Signed, Sealed, Delivered, I'm Yours." With the break up of the Holland-Dozier-Holland songwriting team, Wonder's skill as a composer became vital to Motown's continued success. As well as providing his own material, Wonder cowrote "Tears of a Clown" with Smokey Robinson and "It's a Shame"—a hit for the Spinners.

In 1971, Wonder renegotiated his Motown contract, offering two finished, self-produced, self-written albums as leverage to obtain the complete artistic freedom enjoyed by other stars. Motown conceded, and the resulting albums, *Where I'm Coming From* and *Music of My Mind,* announced Wonder's arrival as a mature artist. A consummate tonal painter, Wonder also used these albums to demonstrate how the synthesizer could be used as a legitimate instrument in R&B and pop. His 1972 album *Talking Book* produced two huge hits—the strikingly original "Superstition" (written originally for rock guitarist Jeff Beck) and "You Are the Sunshine of My Life." These successes earned him a spot as an opening act for the ROLLING STONES.

ISN'T HE LOVELY?

Wonder became one of pop music's biggest stars, selling millions of copies and winning Grammys for *Innervisions* (featuring the hits "Living for the City" and "Higher Ground") and *Fulfillingness' First Finale.* The critical and commercial high point of Wonder's career was the sprawling 1976 masterpiece, *Songs in the Key of Life,* a double album that featured, among others, "Isn't She Lovely," "I Wish," and the ebullient "Sir Duke." Despite its high retail price, it raced to the top of the charts.

Wonder took three years to record his next album, *Journey Through the Secret Life of Plants,* a mostly instrumental affair that confused listeners and sold poorly. Wonder scored hits, however, with 1980's *Hotter Than July* ("Masterblaster (Jammin')") and the 1984 soundtrack to *The Woman in Red* (featuring "I Just Called to Say I Love You"). He became a high-profile activist in the successful campaign to establish Martin Luther King's birthday as a national holiday—refusing to issue the single "Happy Birthday" in the U.S. until a majority of states recognized the holiday. However, his commercial career never regained its mid-1970s momentum. Wonder remained active musically in the 1980s and 1990s, albeit recording less frequently than he did in the 1970s.

Greg Bower

SEE ALSO:

GAYE, MARVIN; JACKSON, MICHAEL; ROSS, DIANA.

FURTHER READING

George, Nelson. *Where Did Our Love Go?: The Rise & Fall of the Motown Sound* (New York: St. Martin's Press, 1987).

SUGGESTED LISTENING

Innervisions; Songs in the Key of Life; Stevie Wonder's Original Musiquarium I; Talking Book.

TAMMY
WYNETTE

Tammy Wynette blazed a trail for successive generations of women country singers. Equally strong and feminine, Wynette was a popular recording artist and live performer from the late 1960s until her death in 1998. Her songs faithfully and often literally reflected her life: poverty, marriage, divorce, illness, and addiction are all featured in her lyrics.

Born Virginia Wynette Pugh on May 5, 1942, in Itawamba County, Mississippi, Wynette was brought up by her cotton-farming grandparents. Her father died when she was an infant, and her mother took a wartime factory job. Her father had been a musician and Wynette began learning to play the instruments he had left, including accordion, guitar, and piano.

Hard work, gospel music, and Pentecostalism shaped Wynette's life. She worked in the cotton fields as a child, then dropped out of high school to marry Euple Byrd at age 17 and soon had three daughters. She worked as a hairdresser to pay the family's bills.

HER FIRST HIT

She left Byrd to pursue her singing career and, on a 1966 trip to Nashville, met the record-producer Billy Sherrill. He signed her to a recording contract and changed Wynette Byrd to Tammy Wynette. Her first hit, recorded in 1966, was "Apartment No. 9." She recorded 16 consecutive No. 1 hits through the 1960s, including the ballad "Stand by Your Man" (1968), co-written with Sherrill. It became the best-selling single by a woman in country music and a country standard.

Meanwhile, her life was providing more material for her songs: after a brief marriage to guitarist Don Chapel, she eloped with the country singer George Jones. The marriage lasted from 1969 to 1975, with Jones gradually sinking into alcoholism. The pair, whose relationship became tabloid fodder, had one daughter and frequently recorded together. One song, "The Ceremony," sets the marriage vows to music.

After romantic liaisons with celebrities including Burt Reynolds and Larry Gatlin, and a 44-day marriage to a realtor, Michael Tomlin, her final marriage of 20 years was to George Richey, her manager since 1981.

Wynette's solo career was at its peak through the 1970s and she dominated the country music charts in that decade. Her many hit singles included "Your Good Girl's Gonna Go Bad," "D.I.V.O.R.C.E," and "Dear Daughters."

Professionally, she was matched repeatedly with top country and pop singers. Known best for her collaborations with Jones, she also recorded with Emmylou HARRIS, Vince Gill, STING, Wayne Newton, Randy Travis, and Tom Petty. She also recorded and wrote with Loretta LYNN and Dolly PARTON.

Wynette continued as a solo artist through the 1980s and 1990s. In her final years she reportedly felt "abandoned by Nashville," and recorded with younger pop singers such as Elvis Costello and Melissa Etheridge. One of her last chart-toppers was as a guest vocalist with The KLF on their dance hit "Justified and Ancient," which became an international No. 1.

During her career she sold more than 30 million records, 39 singles of which were Top 10 country hits. Her awards included three Country Music Association Awards and she was named a living legend by TNN/Music City News in 1991.

Wynette died in her sleep on April 6, 1998, after developing a blood clot in her lung. A week before Wynette's death, "Stand by Your Man" was re-released to mark its 30th anniversary. Her autobiography of the same title had been made into a film in 1981.

Linda Dailey Paulson

SEE ALSO:

COUNTRY; POPULAR MUSIC.

FURTHER READING

Bufwack, M. A. and R. K. Oermann. *Finding Her Voice: The Illustrated History of Women in Country Music* (New York: Henry Holt, 1995); Wynette, Tammy, with Joan Drew. *Stand by Your Man* (New York: Simon and Schuster, 1979).

SUGGESTED LISTENING

D.I.V.O.R.C.E; *Higher Ground*; *Kids Say the Darnedest Things*; *Stand by Your Man*; *Take Me to Your World*; With George Jones: *We Love to Sing About Jesus*; With Dolly Parton and Loretta Lynn: *Honky Tonk Angels*.

IANNIS XENAKIS

The music of Iannis Xenakis employs various mathematical theories, such as set theory and probability calculus, to give it a logical structure. Xenakis was both an architect and a composer, and his use of mathematics in music is analogous to its use in architecture in that it is used to "build" the music, although often this is not obvious to the listener.

Xenakis was born to Greek parents in Braïla, Romania, on May 29, 1922. His mother was an amateur pianist who died when the composer was only five years old. At age ten, Xenakis was sent to a boarding school on the Greek island of Spetzai, where he became interested in music, mathematics, and classical literature. In 1938, he went to Athens to the Polytechnic Institute to study engineering, but continued to study piano and music theory with Aristotle Kondurov. Xenakis' studies were interrupted by World War II. During the occupation, he joined the resistance, becoming a member of the left-wing Army of Liberation and was repeatedly imprisoned.

After the war, violent resistance to the right-wing government continued, and Xenakis lost an eye and his jawbone was broken by shrapnel. Despite this, he managed to earn his engineering degree in 1945. By 1947, his continuing involvement in the nationalist movement had led to a death sentence. He was smuggled into Paris on a forged passport, where he found work with the architect Le Corbusier. Xenakis then settled in France and took French citizenship.

Xenakis took his scores to the Paris Conservatory and studied with Olivier MESSIAEN until 1962. However, Messiaen encouraged Xenakis to go his own way, and the composer remained an isolated figure experimenting with his sound structures. One of his first experiments was in the use of the Fibonacci series, which Le Corbusier used as a design principle in architecture. The sequence, in which each number is the sum of the two previous (0, 1, 1, 2, 3, 5, 8, 13, 21, 34, etc.) gave Xenakis the form of his composition, *Metastasis* (1953), a memoir of the resistance, in which the durations of the sections were based on a Fibonacci series. It was performed at the Donaueschingen Festival of contemporary music in Germany in 1955. At about this time, Xenakis joined the Groupe de Recherche de Musique Concrète in Paris, and began to work with electronic tape. As a codesigner of the Philips Pavilion for the Brussels World Fair, he was able to broadcast his electronic music through 400 loudspeakers as an integral design element.

In 1954, Xenakis introduced the idea of stochastic music as a strategy to combat what he saw as the disconnectedness of contemporary music. He grouped his music into sound masses that he called clouds and galaxies, and then applied probability theory to chart the movement of the masses. The result was *Pithoprakta* ("actions through probability"). Stochastic elements were combined with game theory in *Duel* (1959) for two small orchestras, in which the two conductors have to respond to each other's moves as in a game.

Another mathematical theory that Xenakis used was set theory, in *Herma* (1963). Set theory is another way of dealing with elements as groups (sets) that can include or exclude other sets. In *Herma*, the notes of the piano keyboard are organized into sets that can then be manipulated.

In 1961, Bruno Maderna conducted Xenakis' *Stratégie* at the 1961 Venice Biennial, and in May 1965 there was a Xenakis Festival in Paris.

Xenakis continued to compose throughout the 1980s and 1990s, and taught at the School for Mathematical Music in Paris, which he had founded in 1966. Earlier, he had taught at Indiana University and also founded a center for musical mathematics there.

Jane Prendergast

SEE ALSO:

ALEATORY MUSIC; BOULEZ, PIERRE; CHAMBER MUSIC; ELECTRONIC MUSIC; ORCHESTRAL MUSIC; VARÈSE, EDGARD.

FURTHER READING

Bois, Mario. *Iannis Xenakis: The Man and His Music* (Westport, CT: Greenwood Press, 1980); Xenakis, Iannis. *Formalized Music* (Bloomington, IN: Indiana University Press, 1971).

SUGGESTED LISTENING

Antikhthon; *Metastasis*; *Nomos gamma*; *Orient-Occident*; *Psappha*.

YES

The definitive progressive rock band, British group Yes specialized in multilayered harmonies and extended themes. They took rock music almost as far as it was possible for it to go from its basic roots—too far for some, who considered Yes's neoclassical pretensions overblown and irrelevant. Although unwittingly, bands like Yes contributed to the birth of the punk rock movement.

Formed in 1968, Yes originally included vocalist Jon Anderson (b. October 1944), guitarist Peter Banks (b. July 1947), keyboards player Tony Kaye (b. January 1946), bass guitarist Chris Squire (b. March 1948), and drummer Bill Bruford (b. May 1948).

One of their first engagements was to open for CREAM at their farewell concert at London's Albert Hall in November 1968. In 1970, Banks was replaced by Steve Howe (b. April 1947), and the following year their third album, *The Yes Album*, made the Top 10 in Britain. Within months, Kaye had left. He was replaced by Rick Wakeman (b. May 1949), a keyboards player given to colorful instrumental (and sartorial) flourishes.

Science-fiction imagery was a mainstay of the Yes repertoire and *Fragile*, released in late 1971, was the first of a series of albums to feature Roger Dean's futuristic, science-fiction artwork on the sleeve. It reached No. 4 in the U.S. and No. 7 in Britain. Another departure followed in 1972, with Bruford heading off to form the band King Crimson. He was replaced by former Plastic Ono Band drummer Alan White (b. June 1949), shortly before the release of *Close to the Edge*, which made No. 3 on the U.S. album chart and No. 4 in Britain. *Tales from Topographic Oceans* (1974) was their first No. 1 album in the U.K., and made No. 6 in the U.S.A. double album, it contained just four tracks. In the middle of that year, Wakeman left to concentrate on a solo career. He was replaced on keyboards by Patrick Moraz (b. June 1948).

Yes success continued in late 1974 with the album *Relayer*. The whole of side one consisted of one extended work "The Gates of Delirium," based on Russian author Leo Tolstoy's novel *War and Peace*. Progressive rock had moved closer and closer to classical music, but on *Going for the One* (1977), Yes adopted a more streamlined rock format. Wakeman was back in place of Moraz for that album—a British No. 1—and 1978's *Tormato*.

Wakeman left again in 1980 along with Anderson, who was by then enjoying success by collaborating with Greek keyboard player Vangelis. Vocalist-guitarist Trevor Horn and keyboard player Geoff Downes were drafted in from lightweight pop act Buggles for the album *Drama*, which made No. 2 in Britain in 1980. The following year Yes split up, but reformed in 1983 with the line-up of Squire, White, Anderson, and Kaye, along with a new guitarist Trevor Rabin (b. January 1954). With Horn as producer, "Owner of a Lonely Heart," a lively rocker, was a No. 1 single in the U.S., while *90125*, its parent album, made No. 5. Although *Big Generator* (1987) was similarly successful, the rest of the decade was less so—during which time individual members became embroiled in a legal battle over ownership of the name Yes. This reached such a low point that another album was released in 1989 entitled *Anderson, Bruford, Wakeman, and Howe*, as they now were legally forbidden to use the name.

Yes enjoyed a revival, and a reconciliation, in 1991 with a world tour and the aptly-named album *Union*. This time the line-up featured Howe, Kaye, Anderson, Squire, White, Rabin, Bruford, and Wakeman. However, the subsequent album, 1994's *Talk*, returned to the personnel featured on *90125*.

It is the version of Yes from the early 1970s that will be most fondly remembered by their fans. Their series of albums from that time remain classic examples of the progressive rock genre.

Graham McColl

SEE ALSO:

GENESIS; PINK FLOYD; PROGRESSIVE ROCK; PUNK ROCK.

FURTHER READING

Martin, Bill. *Music of Yes: Structure and Vision in Progressive Rock* (Chicago, IL: Open Court, 1996); Morse, Tim. *Yesstories: Yes in Their Own Words* (New York: St. Martin's Press, 1996).

SUGGESTED LISTENING

Close to the Edge; Fragile; Highlights: The Very Best of Yes; Tales from Topographic Oceans; Talk; Union; The Yes Album.

LESTER
YOUNG

Lester Young was one of the most individualistic jazz improvisers, and one of the great tenor saxophonists. Influenced by cornetist Bix BEIDERBECKE and saxophonist Frankie Trumbauer, Young developed a cool style of playing at a time when Coleman HAWKINS' large tone and prominent vibrato was the norm. When most improvisers followed the standard two- and four-bar phrases of a popular song, Young would play against such phrasing in subtle and oblique ways. His fertile imagination allowed him to improvise a number of choruses without repeating his ideas.

Young was born on August 27, 1909, into a musical family, and studied several instruments from an early age. In the late 1920s he began playing with various groups. After 1933 his easy, flowing style of improvisation gained greater attention when he bested the reigning master of the tenor saxophone, Coleman Hawkins, in a jam session in Kansas City. He joined Count BASIE's band in 1934, a perfect association that matched Young's unique style with the smooth, relaxed swing of the Basie rhythm section.

BACK TO BASIE

After a few months with Basie, Young joined Fletcher HENDERSON's orchestra and encountered a very different reaction. Friends and bandmembers tried to get Young to change his style to produce a bigger sound, closer to the hot jazz popularized by Hawkins. It was with relief that Young returned to Basie two years later. Basie encouraged an amicable rivalry between Young and Herschel Evans, a talented follower of Hawkins. In this forum Young was able to play the sort of music he had been suppressing for so long. This was Young's happiest period. It was around this time he gained the nickname "The President" (or "Pres"), and with the Basie orchestra he set out to enjoy life; indulging in practical jokes, nicknaming the other members of the band, and even becoming the star pitcher for the Count Basie softball team.

Young had just completed a short film, *Jammin' the Blues* (nominated for an Academy Award in 1945) when he was drafted into the army. He was a sensitive person, ill-suited to the harshness of military life, and was dishonorably discharged (charged with drug and alcohol use). The experience changed his life, leaving deep emotional scars.

Young continued to perform throughout most of the 1950s, although some critics noted a decline in his playing that paralleled the decline in his health. There were now new challenges to face. Bebop was the current trend and new players were using Young's ideas to achieve fame and success at his expense. One of the problems facing Young was his incompatibility with the new players.

LATE BUT SHINING MOMENTS

A notable exception to the general decline is Young's performance on the 1957 CBS television program *The Sound of Jazz*. This program featured the song "Fine and Mellow," written and sung by Billie HOLIDAY, with many other jazz greats. Gunther Schuller considered Young's single chorus on "Fine and Mellow" to be a perfect distillation of Young's style and career, and one of the most moving performances in all of jazz.

Young died of a heart attack on March 15, 1959, yet his influence outlasted him. His phrasing and creativity can be heard in the alto-sax work of Charlie PARKER, and his cool style—laid-back and light-toned—provided the first alternative to the heavy tenor sax vocabulary laid out by Coleman Hawkins.

Paul Rinzler

SEE ALSO:
BEBOP; BIG BAND JAZZ; COOL JAZZ; GILLESPIE, DIZZY.

FURTHER READING
Büchmann-Møller, Frank.
You Just Fight for Your Life: The Story of Lester Young
(New York: Greenwood Press, 1990);
Büchmann-Møller, Frank.
You Just Got to Be Original, Man
(New York: Greenwood Press, 1990);
Porter, Lewis, ed.
A Lester Young Reader
(Washington, D.C.: Smithsonian Institution Press, 1991).

SUGGESTED LISTENING
The Lester Young Story;
Pres Conferences;
Pres and Teddy and Oscar.

FRANK ZAPPA

E ven after his premature death, Frank Zappa continues to be identified as an cult hero. A prolific composer, he made standard rock albums as well as experimental music—all critically acclaimed.

Francis Vincent Zappa was born in Baltimore to second-generation Greek parents on December 21, 1940. As a teenager, he played drums and guitar in local bands. He collected rock'n'roll, rhythm-and-blues (R&B), and doo-wop records, and recordings of compositions by contemporary classical composers.

In 1964, Zappa joined the Soul Giants, who became the Mothers; in 1966 they released their first album, *Freak Out!* as the Mothers of Invention. Some of Zappa's early songs, such as "Help, I'm a Rock," utilize *sprechstimme*, a non-pitched vocal style that predates rap. He often used the Edgard VARÈSE-influenced technique of quickly alternating between short musical phrases in sharply contrasting styles. Other pieces reveal his interest in complex rhythmic meters of jazz.

On his own label, Zappa helped record other performers, such as Alice Cooper and Captain Beefheart. Zappa's first solo album, *Hot Rats* (1969), featured his virtuosic guitar playing. In 1970, when he completed the score for his cult film *200 Motels*, his live soundtrack was accompanied by Zubin MEHTA and the Los Angeles Philharmonic.

The 1970s brought accidents, lawsuits, and legal battles, and the band's equipment was destroyed in a fire at Montreux. That same year, 1971, Zappa was seriously injured after being pushed off the stage during a concert in London. His concerts were banned because of obscenity, and a lawsuit was filed protesting one of his songs. He made his final albums with the Mothers, *Live at the Fillmore East* and *Just Another Band from LA*, in 1971 and 1972.

After the group disbanded, Zappa focused on his own projects. "Don't Eat the Yellow Snow" became his first hit single in 1973, and his next was "Valley Girls" in 1982, with his daughter Moon Unit. His successful album *Shut Up 'n Play Yer Guitar* was released in 1981. Zappa's perfectionism led to a high turnover of session musicians, and he turned to the

Corbis-Bettmann

Frank Zappa in 1968: a renegade at the cutting edge of a generation's musical and anti-establishment strivings.

Synclavier, a multi-track synthesizer, to give him total control of composition and performance. His Synclavier-generated album *Jazz From Hell* won him a Grammy Award in 1987.

In 1982, Zappa produced a concert in New York featuring the music of Varèse. In 1984, Pierre BOULEZ conducted Zappa's works on the album *The Perfect Stranger*. During the late 1980s, Zappa remastered performances from the 1960s, releasing them in the series *You Can't Do That on Stage Anymore*, and also wrote his autobiography, *The Real Frank Zappa Book*. In 1991, however, Zappa was diagnosed as having cancer. He died of the disease on December 4, 1993.

A serious composer, Zappa nevertheless maintained a sense of humor. He has been called "rock music's closest equivalent to the legacy of Duke ELLINGTON."

Timothy Kloth

SEE ALSO:

DOO-WOP; ROCK MUSIC.

FURTHER READING

Kostelanetz, Richard, ed. *The Frank Zappa Companion* (New York: Schirmer Books, 1997);
Lennon, Nigey. *Being Frank: My Time with Frank Zappa* (Los Angeles, CA: California Classic Books, 1995).

SUGGESTED LISTENING

200 Motels; *Frank Zappa Meets the Mothers of Prevention*; *Freak Out!*; *Hot Rats*; *Mothermania*.

ZOUK

A style of highly rhythmic dance music, zouk has its roots in both traditional styles of music and high-tech recording and amplification processes. Created in the late 1970s in Guadeloupe and Martinique, the islands of the French Antilles in the West Indies, it is a Caribbean style that owes much to the music that West African slaves brought with them to the Caribbean.

The word "zouk" is old Creole slang for party, but also refers to the sound systems that cadence (Antillean pop music) was played on in the 1960s. Zouk integrates dance music with lyrics sung almost exclusively in French or the Creole dialect of French. While zouk had many fans in the French-speaking islands of the Antilles, it was not until the heavy-metal guitarist Jacob Desvarieux took up residence in Paris and formed his band Kassav with Pierre Decimus, that the style began to be known outside the islands.

Desvarieux had spent only a limited amount of time in the French Antilles, but most of the members of Kassav were Guadeloupean musicians living in Paris, and their new exciting style of playing made an immediate impact. Desvarieux's rock input may also have helped to make the rhythms of zouk popular in Europe and the West.

Zouk draws from the rich musical heritage of many nations, and blends African styles, Caribbean pop, and American funk. In its highly rhythmic, loping beat can be heard *gwo ka,* the drum and voice music of Guadeloupe, and *chouval bwa*, the percussive style of Martinique. Added to this was the biguine, Martinique's mellow jazz style, and cadence, the pop style that developed in the French Antilles in the 1950s and 1960s. Drawing from so many influences, it is not surprising that zouk can range from highly percussive, driving dance music to slow ballads that resemble cabaret singing.

THE VERSATILITY OF ZOUK

One of the defining elements of zouk is the creation of "space" in the music by avoiding an overwhelming density of simultaneous musical parts. This means that musicians leave "holes" in the music into which lyrics, electronic samples, and instrument solos can be inserted. These holes let zouk artists incorporate styles from African worldbeat to American blues and rap.

One highly popular band playing zouk is the Zouk Allstars. The zouk group centers around Dominique Gengoul, Jean-Luc Alger, Frederic Caracas, and Charles Maurinier, each of whom has made an indelible mark on zouk music. To call them prolific is a gross understatement; pick up any ten zouk albums, and it is likely that one or more of their names will appear on at least seven as either producers or instrumentalists.

ZOUK MACHINE

Zouk Machine, formed by Jocelyn Beroard from Kassav, incorporates many American rhythm-and-blues elements into its music. Its trio of three women singers from Guadeloupe have made the band extremely popular in both Paris and the Antilles. One of the trio, Joelle Ursull, made one of France's top-selling pop records, "Black French." Because Zouk Machine "Americanized" the zouk sound, even singing some lyrics in English, it was thought in the late 1980s that it would be the band to bring zouk to a worldwide (especially U.S.) audience. Unfortunately, this did not prove to be the case.

Zouk records usually come out twice a year in the Antilles, timed either for summer vacation or for the Christmas holidays leading into Carnival. Most recordings are done in Paris, although there are small studios in Guadeloupe and Martinique that also release zouk albums. Most releases from zouk artists are treated to only one pressing by record producers, so that recordings become hard to find after their initial release.

James Tuverson

SEE ALSO:

CARIBBEAN; DANCE MUSIC; FUNK; ROCK MUSIC; SALSA.

FURTHER READING
Guilbault, Jocelyne, with Gage Averill, Edouard Benoit, and Gregory Rabess.
Zouk: World Music in the West Indies
(Chicago, IL: University of Chicago Press, 1993).

SUGGESTED LISTENING
Zouk Allstars: *Top Niveau*;
Zouk Love: *Le Meilleur Du Zouk Love*;
Zouk Machine: *Kreol.*

BIOGRAPHICAL DIGEST

Words or names that appear in SMALL CAPITALS refer to articles in the main part of the encyclopedia.

ABRAMS, Muhal Richard (1930-) *Jazz musician, composer, and administrator* Based in Chicago and later in New York, Abrams wrote arrangements for saxophonist King Fleming and played with MJT+3, Miles DAVIS, and Max ROACH. He started the Experimental Band (1961) and the Association for the Advancement of Creative Musicians (1965). His work reflected interests in many fields such as FREE JAZZ and stride piano.

ACCARDO, Salvatore (1941-) *Violinist* Born in Turin, Accardo studied in Naples and Siena. His international reputation is based on technical brilliance and interpretations in a repertoire ranging from Bach to contemporary music.

AC/DC *Rock band* Formed in Australia in 1973, AC/DC play an energetic brand of HEAVY METAL that gave them a worldwide following in the mid-1970s. Their stage attire—especially the British schoolboy caps, ties, and shorts worn by guitarist Angus Young—were utterly distinctive.

ACE, Johnny (1929-54) *R&B singer and pianist* Formed the Beale Streeters with Bobby "Blue" Bland in the late 1940s. Ace topped the R&B charts with "My Song" in 1952 and "Pledging My Love" in 1955. He died in a Russian roulette game.

ADAMS, Bryan (1959-) *Rock musician* Canadian singer and guitarist Adams formed his first group in Vancouver in 1976. His first international success came in 1981. His muscular singing made him a staple of 1980s stadium rock. His 1991 single "(Everything I Do) I Do It for You," used in the soundtrack to the movie *Robin Hood, Prince of Thieves* stayed at No.1 on the U.K. charts for 15 weeks.

ADAMS, John (1947-) *Composer* U.S.-born Adams originally wrote ELECTRONIC MUSIC, but under the influence of Steve REICH he began experimenting with MINIMALISM. *Shaker Loops* (for string orchestra) was followed by the operas *Nixon in China* (1987) and *The Death of Klinghoffer* (1989).

ADAMS, Johnny (1932-) *Gospel singer* Known as "The Tan Nightingale" in his native New Orleans, Adams sang in GOSPEL groups and later had hits with "Losing Battle," "Release Me," and "I Can't Be All Bad." The LP *From the Heart* (1983) demonstrates high quality singing in a variety of styles.

ADDERLEY, Nat (1931-) *Jazz musician* Brother of the more celebrated Cannonball ADDERLEY, Nat played cornet and trumpet (often in his brother's bands) in a HARD-BOP style. He modeled himself on Miles DAVIS.

ADE, King Sunny (1946-) *Juju singer and guitarist* Nigerian-born Ade learned his music playing in various HIGHLIFE bands in Nigeria during the 1960s. In 1982, Island Records signed him up to replace the recently deceased Bob MARLEY in their artists' roster, and he enjoyed critical acclaim and commercial success with the albums *Juju Music* (1982) and *Synchro System* (1984).

ADLER, Larry (1914-) *Instrumentalist* U.S. harmonica virtuoso Adler gained recognition for the instrument in classical music circles. He was the dedicatee of many concertos including works by MILHAUD and VAUGHAN WILLIAMS.

AEROSMITH *Rock band* Formed in the U.S. in 1970 by Steven Tyler and Joe Perry, Aerosmith became a highly successful hard-rock outfit in the mold of LED ZEPPELIN and the ROLLING STONES. Their most popular song, "Walk This Way," appeared on the million-selling album *Toys in the Attic* (1975).

AKIYOSHI, Toshiko (1929-) *Jazz musician, bandleader, and arranger* Discovered in Japan by American musicians, notably Oscar Peterson, Akiyoshi, a pianist, ran a successful big band from 1973 with her tenor sax-playing husband, Lew Tabakin.

ALEXANDER, Alger "Texas" (1880-1955) *Blues singer* Alexander made many records before being imprisoned for murder in the late 1940s. He sang with his cousin Sam Lightnin' HOPKINS on the street and on buses in Houston. His style was based on work songs and field hollers.

ALLEN, Fulton "Blind Boy Fuller" (1909-41) *Blues singer and guitarist* Allen typified the Piedmont style of BLUES. He regularly played with the harmonica virtuoso Sonny TERRY on songs such as "Pistol Slapper Blues" and "Want Some of Your Pie."

ALLEN, Henry "Red" (1908-67) *Jazz musician* After learning trumpet in New Orleans, Red Allen, initially a Louis ARMSTRONG follower, came to prominence with Luis Russell's band in New York in 1929. He was equally at home in big band SWING and small group settings. In the 1950s Allen became a popular mainstream player.

ALLEN, Thomas (1944-) *Opera singer* British born Allen studied in London and joined the Welsh National Opera in 1969. A baritone with an international OPERA and concert career, he is best known for interpretations of the roles of Mozart's Papageno, Almaviva, Don Giovanni, and Don Alfonso. He was also known for his song recitals.

ALLMAN BROTHERS, The *Rock band* Formed in 1968, the Allman Brothers' early albums included *The Allman Brothers Band* (1969) and *The Allman Brothers Band at Fillmore East* (1971). Fronted by brothers Duane and Gregg—whose guitar playing gave the band their distinctive sound—their brand of Southern blues rock was particularly infectious in concert. Their most commercially successful album was *Brothers and Sisters* (1973).

AMERICA *Country rock band* Formed in London in 1970, U.S.-based America made several hit albums during the 1970s. Their FOLK ROCK style is epitomized in the song "Muskrat Love" on the album *Hat Trick* (1973). They had worldwide chart success with the single "Horse with No Name" (1972).

AMMONS, Albert (1907-49) *Jazz musician* Before forming his own band, the Rhythm Kings in 1934, Ammons played piano with various Chicago bands. He recorded "Boogie Woogie Stomp" in 1936, and became identified with BOOGIE-WOOGIE playing. In 1938 he moved to New York where he made a series of popular recordings.

AMMONS, Gene (1925-74) *Jazz musician and bandleader* Gene was the son of Albert Ammons. He was the principal tenor saxophonist and soloist in Billy Eckstine's big band. After playing in Woody Herman's big band he became associated with a fusion of BEBOP and GOSPEL styles.

AMOS, Tori (1963-) *Rock singer-songwriter* Amos began recording in 1987, but in 1992 her breakthrough came with the album *Little Earthquakes*, which was a huge hit. Her success is based on her songwriting, but she is also an accomplished pianist and performer. Her second album, *Under the Pink* (1994), became a million-seller and spawned her most successful single, "Cornflake Girl."

ANDERSON, John (1954-) *Country singer* Anderson's career as a singer in 1950s honky-tonk style achieved success in the 1970s and 1980s with hits such as "I've Got a Feelin'," "Your Lying Blue Eyes," and "I'm Just an Old Chunk of Coal." He also had hits with albums such as *Tokyo, Oklahoma,* and *Blue Skies Again* in the 1980s.

ANDERSON, Laurie (1947-) *Composer* New York-based Anderson studied as a painter and sculptor, writing her first music in 1972. She had a hit in the U.K. pop charts in 1981 with "O Superman." She composed for mixed-media, and developed her own electronic instruments and a unique style of playing them.

ANDRÉ, Maurice (1933-) *Trumpeter* André studied music at the Paris Conservatory before playing in various Parisian orchestras. His brilliant solo career began in the 1960s. He is best known for work in the baroque repertory. Many composers have written for him.

ANDREWS, Julie (1935-) *Singer and actress* Julie Andrews is best known for her performances in FILM MUSICALS such as *Mary Poppins* and *The Sound of Music*—one of the biggest selling soundtrack albums ever (both 1965). She also sang on the original recording of the stage version of *My Fair Lady.*

ANIMALS, The *R&B band* Formed in England in 1962, the Animals rivaled the ROLLING STONES for chart success. They split up in 1968, reforming several times. Their best-known song and biggest hit was "The House of the Rising Sun" (1964). Singer Eric Burdon also had a successful solo career.

ANKA, Paul (1941-) *Songwriter* Canadian-born Paul Anka had success as a singer and actor, but was best known as a songwriter, writing hugely successful songs in the 1950s and 1960s, including "My Way" and "She's a Lady" for artists such as Buddy HOLLY, Donny Osmond, Frank SINATRA, and Tom JONES.

ANTHRAX *Rock band* Formed in New York in 1982, Anthrax was a hard core thrash metal band. Their live shows attracted a large following and they had chart success during the mid-1980s with "I'm the Man" and "Attack of the Killer B's."

ARDOIN, Amadé (c.1900-c.1930) *Accordionist and singer* Ardoin's songs combined BLUES and CAJUN styles with African songs and traditional French material. It was rare in those days for a black player to play white music, but he was a popular live performer in Louisiana. He recorded mainly during the mid-1920s.

ARMATRADING, Joan (1950-) *Rock singer-songwriter* Born in the West Indies, Armatrading moved to Birmingham, England in 1956. A prolific writer, she rose to prominence in the 1970s during the era of SINGER-SONGWRITERS. Her biggest hit was "Love and Affection" (1976).

ARMSTRONG, Karan (1941-) *Opera singer* American-born soprano Karan Armstrong made her debut with the San Francisco Opera in 1966. She achieved success in the U.S. and Europe with a repertoire ranging from Mozart and Wagner to contemporary music.

ARMSTRONG, Lil (1898-1971) *Jazz pianist, singer, and composer* Armstrong (née Hardin) was born in Memphis and moved to Chicago where she fronted her own band. There she met Louis ARMSTRONG, whom she married in 1924. Her encouragement contributed much to the development of his career. After divorcing him in 1938 she became a session pianist for Decca Records.

ARNOLD, Eddy (1918-) *Country singer* Billed as "The Tennessee Plowboy," Arnold made his radio debut in 1936 and began having hits in 1946, including "Texarkana Baby" and "A Heart Full of Love." He had his own TV series *Eddie Arnold Time* in the 1950s and was elected to the Country Music Hall of Fame in 1966.

ARNOLD, James "Kokomo" (1901-68) *Blues singer and guitarist* Born in Texas, Arnold first recorded in Memphis in 1930 under the name "Gitfiddle Jim." Though commercially unsuccessful, the record revealed a unique slide guitar and vocal sound. He later recorded successfully in Chicago and New York and made a low-key comeback in 1962.

ARNOLD, P.P. (1946-) *Rock singer* Arnold was a member of Ike and Tina TURNER's backing group before she had a U.K. Top 20 hit with "The First Cut Is the Deepest" in 1967. Since then she has become a renowned session singer, recorded several albums of her own, and appeared in the musicals *Jesus Christ Superstar* and *Starlight Express.*

ARRESTED DEVELOPMENT *Hip-hop/rap band* Arrested Development plays a blend of RAP and black country music. Their first album, *3 Years, 5 Months and 2 Days in the Life of* (1992) brought two Grammy awards and chart success with the Top 10 hit "Tennessee." Their second, *Zingalamaduni* (1994) received critical praise but achieved smaller sales.

ASTAIRE, Fred (1899-1987) *Dancer and singer* Astaire sang and danced in some of the most important FILM MUSICALS of all time, notably *Top Hat* and *Shall We Dance?,* in both of which he was paired with Ginger Rogers. His singing inspired many songs by BERLIN, KERN, GERSHWIN, and PORTER.

ASWAD *Reggae band* Formed in 1975 in the U.K., Aswad was originally a REGGAE act, moving to a lightweight FUNK style in the 1980s. Essentially a live band, they had chart success with "Chasing the Breeze" (1984) and "Don't Turn Around" (1988).

ATHERTON, David (1944-) *Conductor* Atherton was born in Blackpool, England, and studied at Cambridge University. He is chiefly noted for his performances of modern music and for his association with the London Sinfonietta. He worked extensively at London's Covent Garden Opera House. He retired in 1973.

AUTRY, Gene (1907-98) *Popular music singer* Born in Texas, Autry was the son of a baptist minister. In the early 1930s he recorded "That Silver Haired Daddy of Mine" which sold 30,000 copies in three months. He achieved moderate success as an actor before enlisting during World War II. Although most famous as a singer of cowboy songs, his postwar hits included "Rudolf the Red-Nosed Reindeer" and "Frosty the Snow Man." During the 1950s and 1960s he became a very successful businessman in TV and radio.

AVALON, Frankie (1939-) *Pop singer* Avalon had chart success in 1959 with the singles "Venus" and "Why," and quickly established himself as a teen idol. He went on to make many successful films, including a cameo appearance in *Grease* in 1978.

AVERAGE WHITE BAND, The *Soul band* Formed in Scotland in 1973, A.W.B. had considerable success with their LP *AWB,* usually known as the "White Album." Their tight FUNK music was well suited to live shows. Their single "Pick Up the Pieces" was a No.1 hit.

AYERS, Roy (1940-) *Jazz and funk vibraphonist* Ayers played with JAZZ artists such as Chico Hamilton and Herbie Mann, before forming his own group, Ubiquity in 1970. Sometimes featuring Herbie HANCOCK, George Benson, and Billy Cobham, this band enjoyed some commercial success and helped to popularize crossover JAZZ-FUNK music.

AYLER, Albert (1936-70) *Jazz musician* Renowned for his revolutionary use of pure sound elements, Ayler, a tenor sax player, was a critical factor in the development of FREE JAZZ in the 1960s and had great influence on the recordings of John COLTRANE.

B-52s, The *Rock band* Formed in Athens, Georgia, in 1976, the band quickly gained a following on the U.S. college circuit. A heady mix of 1950s ROCK'N'ROLL and punky rhythms, their first single "Rock Lobster" sold well in the U.K. Hit albums followed in the early 1980s and the band earned a good reputation on both sides of the Atlantic as a live act. In 1989 they had their biggest success with the huge hit single "Love Shack."

BABBITT, Milton (1916-) *Composer* Born in Philadelphia, Babbit moved to Princeton in 1938 to teach and to study with Roger Sessions. He developed a style of 12-note composition after the manner of WEBERN and SCHOENBERG. In the 1960s he applied serial techniques to rhythm and began composing for the RCA synthesizer. Works composed for it include *Ensembles for Synthesizer* (1964).

BACKHAUS, Wilhelm (1884-1969) *Pianist* Backhaus studied in Leipzig, Germany, until 1899, and subsequently with d'Albert in Frankfurt before beginning an international career. In playing Beethoven and the Romantic repertoire his clarity of style and structural sense was widely admired.

BAILEY, Buster (1902-67) *Jazz musician* Bailey played clarinet in a number of bands from 1919. He worked with Erskine Tate in Chicago and later with Fletcher HENDERSON in New York. From 1965 to 1967 he played in Louis ARMSTRONG's All Stars.

BAILEY, Mildred (1907-51) *Jazz musician* Bailey began her career as a cinema pianist and radio performer on the West Coast. A skilled scat singer, she was the first white singer to capture the style of black contemporaries such as Billie HOLIDAY.

BAKER, Dame Janet (1933-) *Opera singer* Dame Janet's richly expressive mezzo-soprano has been heard in a repertory ranging from Baroque to contemporary, in OPERA, concert, and recital. Benjamin BRITTEN wrote works especially for her.

BAKER, Lavern (1929-) *R&B singer* Baker, born in Chicago, was spotted performing by bandleader Fletcher HENDERSON. She signed up for OKeh Records at age 17. A major contract with Atlantic Records saw her achieve eight Top 10 hits in the 1955–65 period, including the million-selling "Tweedle Dee" and her most famous recording "Cee Cee Rider." Influential in the black music scene of the early 1960s, her music did not blend well with the new-style SOUL coming out of Detroit and Memphis toward the end of the decade.

BAMBAATAA, Afrika (1960-) *Rap singer* Bambaataa was the most important hip-hop DJ in New York in 1980. He began recording in 1982, and made several highly influential RAP albums, often mixing disparate beats. Bambaataa has collaborated with artists as diverse as James BROWN, and the SEX PISTOLS' John Lydon.

BAND, The *Rock band* Formed in Woodstock, New York, in 1967, the Band became one of the seminal groups of America in the 1970s. Using traditional FOLK tunes and new material, they created a unique sound. They recorded and played extensively with Bob DYLAN. Their final concert in 1976 was recorded and filmed by Martin Scorsese and released as *The Last Waltz.*

BAND AID *Rock band* In 1984 Bob Geldof brought together rock and pop artists, forming a group called Band Aid to record the single "Do They Know It's Christmas?" to raise money for the starving people of Ethiopia. The following year a concert, "Live Aid," was broadcast worldwide using the same artists.

BARBER, Chris (1930-) *Jazz musician* As a trombonist and bandleader, Barber led the British JAZZ boom of the 1950s. As fashions changed with the arrival of the BEATLES in 1962, Barber was flexible enough to cope. His band remains one of the most popular of its kind.

BARBIERI, Gato (1934-) *Jazz musician* The Argentine tenor sax player and composer achieved international recognition for music that mixed European and American JAZZ techniques with South American rhythms and ROCK. He composed and played on the soundtrack of the film *Last Tango in Paris* in 1972.

BARBIROLLI, Sir John (1899-1970) *Conductor* Barbirolli studied the cello in London before turning to conducting in the late 1920s. He succeeded TOSCANINI at the New York Philharmonic, but returned to England in 1943 to work with the Hallé Orchestra. A great MAHLER interpreter, he also conducted first performances of VAUGHAN WILLIAMS and BRITTEN.

BARE, Bobby (1935-) *Country singer* A prolific songwriter, Bare had over 50 COUNTRY hits during the early 1960s, including the ballads "Have I Stayed Away Too Long?" and "Streets of Baltimore."

BARKER, Danny (1909-) *Jazz musician* American guitarist, banjoist, singer, and composer, Barker recorded prolifically, particularly with his wife, Blue Lu Barker, and Henry "Red" Allen. He worked with several big bands in the 1930s and 1940s, including Cab Calloway's. Barker was also interested in the study of JAZZ, and played a big part in the 1950s revival of NEW ORLEANS JAZZ through a series of radio programs called "This Is Jazz."

BARNES, J.J. (1943-) *Soul singer* Formerly a member of the Halo Gospel Singers, Barnes left his native Detroit in the late 1960s and joined the British Northern Soul scene. His style closely resembles that of Marvin GAYE.

BARNET, Charlie (1913-) *Jazz musician* Barnet was a popular saxophonist and bandleader of the SWING period. He had a major hit with "Cherokee" in 1939.

BARRETT, Syd (1946-) *Pop songwriter and guitarist* A founder member of PINK FLOYD in 1965, Barrett stayed with the group until 1968, writing songs such as "Arnold Layne" and "See Emily Play." A reclusive character, he made several solo albums during the 1970s. Barrett is the subject of the Pink Floyd song, "Shine on You Crazy Diamond."

BARRY, John (1933-) *Composer* British-born, Barry wrote songs for Adam Faith and Matt Monro in the 1960s. He provided music for James Bond films, including the "James Bond Theme," and went on to become one of the world's leading composers of FILM MUSIC during the 1970s and 1980s.

BARSTOW, Josephine (1940-) *Opera singer* Barstow joined Sadler's Wells OPERA in the U.K. in 1967 and went on to work with all the major opera companies. An exceptional singing actress, her repertory included the soprano roles of Mozart, JANÁCEK, Verdi, Richard STRAUSS, and TIPPETT.

BASSEY, Shirley (1937-) *Pop singer* In a career spanning over 40 years, Shirley Bassey has had U.K. chart successes, sung title tracks for three James Bond films, and performed regularly at major concert halls throughout the world. Armed with a huge voice and a personality to match, Bassey is a leading star in the world of CABARET MUSIC.

BATE, Jennifer (1944-) *Organist and composer* British-born, Bate studied early music with Dolmetsch and composition with Eric Thiman. She is also closely associated with Olivier MESSIAEN, whose complete organ works she recorded.

BATTLE, Kathleen (1948-) *Opera singer* Battle made her debut in her native U.S. in 1972. An international star, her repertoire includes soprano roles ranging from Mozart to coloratura, such as Zerbinetta and Adina. She is also renowned for her recitals and recordings of early music, such as songs by John Dowland.

BEASTIE BOYS, The *Rap group* From New York, the Beastie Boys were the first of the 1980s crossover white RAP bands. They attracted a following with their raucous, rebellious style. Their albums include *Licensed to Ill* (1986) and *Hello Nasty* (1998).

BECHET, Sidney (1897-1959) *Jazz musician* Born in New Orleans, Bechet was one of the earliest JAZZ virtuosi. Playing clarinet and soprano sax, he made some classic recordings with Louis ARMSTRONG in the mid-1920s in a group called Clarence Williams' Blue Five.

BECK (1971-) *Rock guitarist* Los Angeles-born Beck Hansen played a self-styled PUNK ROCK/FOLK MUSIC, influenced by a whole range of styles. His first single "MTV Makes Me Want to Smoke Crack" was followed by "Loser," which was adopted by MTV as an anthem for a generation. His album *Odelay* (1996) received critical acclaim and achieved massive sales in the U.S. and the U.K.

BECK, Jeff (1944-) *Rock guitarist* Beck replaced Eric Clapton in the Yardbirds in 1964. He was one of the first great ROCK guitarists. His style, mixed rock, JAZZ, and BLUES licks and earned him great respect but little success. However, the album *Truth* (1968) was a hit in the U.S.

BEE GEES, The *Pop group* Formed as a child band by brothers Maurice, Robin, and Barry Gibb in 1955, the Bee Gees had decades of success. The striking harmony of their voices earned them a U.K No.1 hit with "(The Lights Went Out In) Massachusetts" in 1967. Mega stardom arrived in 1977 when they wrote and sang the soundtrack to the film *Saturday Night Fever,* which sold more than 30 million copies. They continued to sell millions of singles and CDs in the 1990s.

BENJAMIN, George (1960-) *Composer* British-born Benjamin studied with Olivier MESSIAEN in Paris and later Alexander Goehr in Cambridge. His orchestral work *Ringed by the Flat Horizon* brought him to international prominence in 1980.

BENTON, Brook (1931-88) *Soul singer* From a GOSPEL music background, Benton developed a versatile warm SOUL singing style. He had great commercial success in the 1950s and 1960s. His biggest hit as a singer, "Rainy Night in Georgia" (1970) was his last.

BERBERIAN, Cathy (1925-83) *Classical singer* American-born Berberian's singing talent was ideal for the works of avant-garde composers such as John CAGE and Luciano Berio, whom she married in 1950. Berio wrote *Sequenza III* and *Visage*, among other pieces, especially for her.

BERGANZA, Teresa (1935-) *Opera singer* After studying in her native Madrid, Berganza sang in Europe before making her U.S. debut in Dallas in 1958. As a mezzo-soprano she was particularly noted for her Carmen and Rossini roles, and for her work with the Spanish composer Manuel de FALLA.

BERGMAN, Erik (1911-) *Composer* Bergman studied, worked, and taught in his native Finland. His compositional approach, often of VOCAL AND CHORAL MUSIC, moved from a tonal style in his earlier work, through 12-note technique, and later on to a freer idiom using ALEATORY MUSIC.

BERIGAN, Bunny (1908-42) *Jazz musician* Berigan was a trumpeter and bandleader during the 1930s, showing the influence of Louis ARMSTRONG in his playing and Bix BEIDERBECKE in his musical ideas. He started to lead his own bands in 1935. Best heard on his version of "I Can't Get Started" and Tommy DORSEY's version of "Marie" (both 1937).

BERIO, Luciano (1925-) *Composer* Berio studied piano with his father. He graduated in composition from Milan in 1950. His early work featured 12-note SERIALISM and ELECTRONIC MUSIC techniques. He remained at the forefront of new music, whether dramatic, orchestral, or vocal, and established himself as the most important Italian composer, conductor, and teacher in the 1960s and 1970s. He is well known for his sequenzas, a series of solo pieces for all the main instruments. He collaborated with writer Italo Calvino on two operas, *La Vera Storia* (1982) and *Un Re In Ascolto* (1984).

BERRY, Chu (1908-41) *Jazz musician* As a tenor sax player in the 1930s, Berry used a soft, heavy tone based on the arpeggiated style of Coleman HAWKINS. He excelled in ballad playing and featured as a soloist in the big bands of Cab Calloway and Fletcher HENDERSON.

BIGARD, Barney (1906-80) *Jazz clarinetist* One of the most celebrated clarinet players in JAZZ, Bigard played in Duke ELLINGTON's band in New York for many years during the 1930s. In 1945 he joined Louis ARMSTRONG's All Stars, and became an integral part of the band.

BIRTWISTLE, Harrison (1934-) *Composer* Birtwistle's very early compositions showed the influence of VARÈSE and STRAVINSKY. Regarded as one of the more serious British composers, his output included several major orchestral works, such as *The Triumph of Time* (1970), and the operas *Punch and Judy* (1968), *The Mask of Orpheus* (1984), and *Gawain* (1990).

BISHOP-KOVACEVICH, Stephen (1940-) *Classical pianist* Born in Los Angeles of Yugoslav parentage, Bishop-Kovacevich made his U.S. concert debut in 1961. He is noted for his interpretations of Beethoven and contemporary music.

BJÖRK (1966-) *Rock singer* Iceland-born Björk achieved some success as a member of the Sugarcubes, until they split in 1992. Her striking voice and unusual singing style were put to good effect on her first solo album *Debut* (1993), which sold over 2 million copies worldwide, establishing her as one of the most original artists on the ROCK scene.

BJÖRLING, Jussi (1911-60) *Opera singer* Swedish-born Björling began his career with the Royal Swedish Opera, and went on to achieve an international reputation in tenor roles singing PUCCINI and Verdi.

BLACK SABBATH *Rock group* Formed in 1969 by Tony Iommi and Ozzy Osbourne, Black Sabbath formed part of the first wave of HEAVY METAL bands. Their first four albums, *Black Sabbath* and *Paranoid* (both 1970), *Master of Reality* (1971), and *Volume IV* (1972) are all regarded as classics.

BLACK UHURU *Reggae band* Formed in Jamaica in the early 1970s, Black Uhuru achieved international status with several well-received albums such as *Love Crisis* (1977), *Red* (1981), and *Anthem* (1984). Originally a traditional vocal trio, Ducky Simpson, Michael Rose, and Puma Jones were backed by the heavyweight rhythm section of Sly Dunbar and Robbie Shakespeare for their best work.

BLACKMORE, Ritchie (1945-) *Rock guitarist* Blackmore played HEAVY METAL guitar in several bands during the 1970s and 1980s. Most famous for his work with Deep Purple, Blackmore remained one of the world's greatest guitar heroes.

BLACKWELL, Francis "Scrapper" (1903-62) *Blues Musician* Blackwell was a self-taught BLUES singer, guitarist, and pianist. He recorded as a soloist, and with Leroy Carr during the late 1920s and early 1930s. He was shot dead in Indianapolis in 1962.

BLAKE, Arthur "Blind" (1890-1933) *Blues musician* Florida-born Blake was one of the best prewar BLUES guitarists. His finest work was recorded in Chicago during the 1920s. As well as his own songs, such as "West Coast Blues" and "Blind Arthur's Breakdown," he can also be heard playing with artists such as Ma RAINEY.

BLAKE, Eubie (1883-1983) *Jazz musician* Born in Baltimore, pianist and bandleader Blake was also a composer, writing a Broadway show, *Shufflin' Along* (1921), and several ragtime piano hits. His most famous song, "I'm Just Wild About Harry" (1921) was used by Harry S. Truman during the 1948 presidential campaign, which sparked a revival of interest in Blake's career.

BLAND, Bobby "Blue" (1930–) *Jazz musician* Tennessee-born Bland began his career singing GOSPEL. He developed his unique vocal style on Beale Street in Memphis. Turning more toward R&B during the 1950s and 1960s, he had several hits including "Little Boy Blue" and "Turn on Your Love Light."

BLANTON, Jimmy (1918-42) *Jazz musician* Born in Chattanooga, Blanton was a bass player discovered by Duke ELLINGTON. His technique and fluency were used to best effect by Ellington, who featured him playing solo passages and melodic bass lines.

BLEY, Carla (1938–) *Jazz musician, composer, and arranger* After a musical childhood, Bley came to prominence as a composer in 1964 when she founded the Jazz Composers' Orchestra playing FREE JAZZ. She married the pianist Paul Bley in 1957. A prolific writer, her output of albums and concerts is prodigious.

BLEY, Paul (1932–) *Jazz musician and composer* Canadian born Bley was part of the avant-garde movement in New York during the 1960s. Playing with artists such as Charles MINGUS, Ornette COLEMAN, Don Cherry, and Sonny ROLLINS, Bley became one of the leading jazz pianists and experimentalists of the era.

BLONDIE *Rock band* Formed in New York in 1974, Blondie were at the forefront of the NEW WAVE of the late 1970s. Fronted by singer Debbie Harry, the band had several chart successes, such as "Heart of Glass" (1979), "Call Me" (1980), "The Tide Is High" (1980), and "Rapture" (1981) that all reached No.1.

BLOOD, SWEAT AND TEARS *Jazz rock band* Formed by Al Kooper in 1968, BS&T, as they became known, were the leading exponents of JAZZ-ROCK. Kooper left in 1969 and vocalist David Clayton Thomas joined the band.

They were immediately successful. Best heard on their eponymous 1969 album, they also had several hit singles, notably "You Make Me So Very Happy" (1969). They disbanded in 1980 after several more albums.

BLOOMFIELD, Mike (1944-81) *Rock musician* Bloomfield was a Chicago-born guitarist following in the tradition of the Chicago BLUES greats. His work often crossed over into ROCK MUSIC. He recorded several albums of his own, but is most famous for his guitar work on Bob DYLAN's "Like a Rolling Stone."

BLUE OYSTER CULT *Rock band* Formed in 1969 in Long Island, New York, Blue Oyster Cult played what was dubbed "intelligent HEAVY METAL." Releasing several albums during the 1970s and 1980s, they achieved worldwide recognition with the single "Don't Fear the Reaper" from their 1975 album *Agents of Fortune.*

BLUR *Rock band* Formed in the U.K. in 1990, Blur described themselves as the quintessential English band of the 1990s. Their brand of guitar pop struck a chord in an era of techno sounds. Their album *Parklife* (1994) established the band as one of the leaders of the BRITPOP boom. Led by singer Damon Albarn and guitarist Graham Coxon, Blur are the only credible rivals to Oasis on the 1990s U.K. rock scene.

BOLAN, Marc (1947-77) *Pop singer* Bolan formed Tyrannosaurus Rex with percussionist Steve "Peregrine" Took in the late 1960s. A change of name, to T.Rex, in the early 1970s launched Bolan into the teenybop market. A string of huge hits, such as "Hot Love," "Get It On," and "Metal Guru" followed. Bolan was killed in an auto accident in 1977.

BON JOVI *Rock group* Formed in New Jersey in 1983, Bon Jovi had the biggest-selling ROCK album of 1987 with *Slippery When Wet.* Their brand of hard rock, allied to singer and guitarist Jon Bon Jovi's good looks, enabled the band to become one of the top rock acts of the mid-1980s. They continued to record and tour with some success in the 1990s, particularly in the U.S. and the U.K.

BONYNGE, Richard (1930–) *Conductor* Australian-born Bonynge was influential in the career of singer Joan SUTHERLAND, whom he married in 1954. They were heard together chiefly in the bel canto repertoire of 17th- and 18th-century Italian opera.

BOOKER T. & THE MGs *Soul band* Booker T. & the MGs were the house band for Stax Records in Memphis during its heyday in the 1960s and early 1970s. They recorded with many Stax artists, such as Wilson Pickett, Otis REDDING, Sam & Dave, and Eddie Floyd. They also had several hits of their own, such as "Green Onions" (1962) and "Time Is Tight" (1969). Booker T. himself co-wrote many classic soul songs such as "Knock On Wood," "Dock of the Bay," and "In the Midnight Hour."

BOSKOVSKY, Willi (1909–) *Violinist and conductor* Boskovsky studied in his native Vienna and joined the Vienna Philharmonic in 1932. His most famous recording is of *Die Fledermaus* by Richard STRAUSS.

BOSTIC, Earl (1913-65) *Jazz musician* Bostic was a distinguished alto saxophonist and arranger. He played with several New York bands in the late 1930s and early 1940s, including Lionel Hampton's. His technical mastery of the sax encouraged him to front his own groups. His biggest success was with a recording entitled "Flamingo" (1951).

BOULT, Sir Adrian (1889-1983) *Conductor* Born in Chester, England, Boult was always a champion of British composers, particularly Edward ELGAR and Ralph VAUGHAN WILLIAMS. In a long and distinguished career, he conducted almost all the leading British orchestras as well as several in the U.S. and Europe.

BOWIE, Lester (1941–) *Jazz musician and composer* Trumpeter Bowie grew up in St. Louis. Married to R&B singer Fontella Bass, he moved to Chicago in 1966. A founder member of the influential Art Ensemble of Chicago, Bowie remains one of the leading players of jazz trumpet recording in the 1990s with his 10-piece band Brass Fantasy.

BOWMAN, James (1941-) *Singer* James Bowman's career as a countertenor encompassed the baroque repertoire as well as more contemporary music. His powerful voice and good acting skills prompted composers such as BRITTEN, TIPPETT, and Maxwell Davies, to write pieces specifically for him.

BOYZ II MEN *Soul band* Formed in 1990 in Philadelphia, this close harmony group has had huge success with several smooth SOUL albums, the second of which, produced by Puff Daddy, sold over 8 million copies.

BRAIN, Dennis (1921-57) *Horn player* Born in the U.K., Brain was principal horn player with the Royal Philharmonic Orchestra from 1946, and went on to work mainly as a soloist. His repertory included the Mozart and Strauss concertos and the BRITTEN Serenade, which was written specifically for him. Brain died in a car accident at age 36.

BRAXTON, Anthony (1945-) *Jazz musician* Braxton is an alto saxophonist, contrabassist, clarinetist, and composer. In 1968 he released the historic double album *For Alto*, which featured unaccompanied saxophone. Technically gifted, Braxton, who played with Chick COREA and Ornette COLEMAN, is renowned for improvisation in an essentially FREE JAZZ idiom.

BREAM, Julian (1933-) *Guitarist and lutenist* Bream made his London debut in 1950. One of the most popular classical guitarists, he played a wide repertoire, from British music of the Elizabethan period to music written specially for him by composers such as BRITTEN, WALTON, and HENZE. Bream was largely responsible for the revival of lute playing in the U.K. in the 1970s.

BRECKER, Michael (1949-) *Jazz musician* An accomplished tenor sax player, Brecker formed the JAZZ ROCK band, the Brecker Brothers, with brother Randy in the mid-1970s. His stature as one of the most original players was enhanced by solo projects and touring as a soloist with Paul Simon in 1990.

BRECKER, Randy (1945-) *Jazz musician* Brecker played trumpet and flugelhorn for the JAZZ ROCK band Blood, Sweat and Tears in the late 1960s. He featured in the Brecker Brothers with brother Michael, as well as with other JAZZ and ROCK artists, such as Art BLAKEY, Stevie WONDER, Johnny and Edgar Winter, and Larry Coryell's Eleventh House.

BRICE, Fanny (1891-1951) *Singer and Actress* Brice took part in *Ziegfeld Follies* of 1910 and other Broadway MUSICALS. Remembered particularly for singing comic songs with a Yiddish accent, she was also associated with ballads such as "Second-Hand Rose" and "My Man" (both 1921). The 1960s musical *Funny Girl* was the fictionalized story of her life.

BROOKMEYER, Bob (1929-) *Jazz musician* Brookmeyer, a Kansas-born valve-trombonist, pianist, and arranger, played with Stan GETZ and Gerry MULLIGAN during the 1950s. He is the most important player since Juan Tizol to have based his career on the valve trombone.

BROOKS, Garth (1962-) *Country singer* In 1996 Oklahoma-born Brooks became the biggest-selling solo artist in the world. The honky-tonk style of his first album, *Garth Brooks* (1989), developed through the years, giving way to a soft rock approach. Brooks revolutionized COUNTRY music by making it more popular and appealing.

BRÖTZMANN, Peter (1941-) *Jazz musician* Brötzmann was a self-taught German tenor saxophonist. He played FREE JAZZ during the 1960s, then graduated to abstraction. During his career, he played with all the major European improvisers, such as Carla Bley, Michael Mantler, and Don Cherry.

BROWN, Clarence "Gatemouth" (1924-) *Blues musician* A great all-round entertainer, Brown was a singer, guitarist, and fiddler, who also played the drums, bass, and harmonica in BLUES and bluegrass styles. A classic Texas blues guitarist, his recording career, which started in the late 1940s, continued into the 1980s.

BROWN, Dennis (1957-) *Reggae singer* Albums such as *Joseph's Coat of Many Colours* (1979) and *Spellbound* (1980), recorded with Joe Gibbs and Errol Thompson, gave Brown the title "The Crown Prince of Reggae." His biggest hit came in 1979 with the single "Money in My Pocket."

BROWN, Milton (1903-36) *Country singer* In his short career, Texas-born vocalist Brown, together with fiddler Bob WILLS, created what subsequently became known as Western SWING music.

BROWN, Roy (1925-81) *R&B singer* Brown recorded his own song "Good Rockin' Tonight" in 1947, a tune later recorded by Elvis PRESLEY. His style of GOSPEL/SOUL singing earned him a number of hits in the 1950s before joining the Johnny Otis Review at the end of the 1960s.

BRUCE, Jack (1943-) *Jazz and rock musician* Scottish bass player, Bruce played with Eric Clapton and Ginger Baker in the BLUES and ROCK group CREAM, formed in 1966. After they disbanded he joined Tony WILLIAMS' Lifetime. Bruce continued to change between rock and JAZZ bands and found it difficult to maintain an audience for his music.

BUCKLEY, Tim (1947-75) *Singer-songwriter* After an apprenticeship in the folk clubs of Los Angeles, Buckley recorded his first album *Tim Buckley* in 1966. His huge voice and intimate songs earned him critical acclaim. He continued to write and record throughout the 1960s and early 1970s, his biggest success came with the album *Greetings from LA* (1972). Buckley died from a drug overdose in Washington, D.C. in 1975.

BURKE, Solomon (1936-) *Soul singer* Burke, an ordained minister, was one of the most successful SOUL singers of the 1960s. As well as having a distinguished solo career, he worked with the ROLLING STONES and Otis REDDING. His biggest hits came during the mid-1960s, with songs such as "Everybody Needs Somebody to Love," "Goodbye Baby (Baby Goodbye)" (both 1964), and "Got to Get You Off My Mind" (1965).

BURRELL, Kenny (1931-) *Jazz musician* Detroit-born guitarist Burrell worked with Dizzie GILLESPIE, Oscar Peterson, Stan GETZ, and Billie HOLIDAY. He played in a BEBOP style, and his melodic approach marked his considerable virtuosity.

BUSH *Rock band* Bush, formed in London in 1992, got their breakthrough when a Los Angeles radio station, KROQ, began plugging the song "Everything Zen." Their debut album, *Sixteen Stone* (1995), sold a million copies, and the band became arena favorites for a time.

BUSH, Alan (1900-) *Composer* U.K.-born Bush studied music and the piano in London and in Berlin. His belief in communism greatly influenced his work and the way his work was received, particularly in the U.K. He wrote a number of operas on political subjects such as *Wat Tyler* in 1951 and *The Sugar Reapers* in 1962. He also composed orchestral pieces and chamber music.

BUSH, Kate (1958-) *Pop singer* Discovered in the U.K. in the 1970s by PINK FLOYD's Dave Gilmour, Bush had a massive hit with her first single "Wuthering Heights" (1978). Her brand of theatrical songwriting and performing earned her critical acclaim and commercial success throughout the 1980s, with albums such as *The Dreaming* (1982), *Hounds of Love* (1985), and *The Sensual World* (1989).

BUSONI, Ferruccio (1866-1924) *Composer and pianist* Of German/Italian parentage, Busoni lived in Austria and Germany. A child prodigy, his early works were composed mainly for piano or chamber ensembles. His later work included operas such as his own interpretation of *Turandot* (1917) and *Doktor Faust* (1924).

BUSTER, Prince (1938-) *Ska singer* Originally a bouncer for Sir Coxone's Sound System in Kingston, Jamaica, Buster started his own Voice of the People Sound System in the early 1960s. His first recordings, such as "Al Capone" and "Madness," were hugely popular in Jamaica and in the U.K., where ska music was

fashionable with both black and white people. The songs remained popular during the 1980s and 1990s and became jukebox favorites.

BUTLER, Jerry (1939-) *Soul singer* Mississippi-born Butler moved to Chicago in the mid-1950s to join the city's GOSPEL circuit. He formed the Impressions in 1958 and hit the big time when they were joined by guitarist Curtis Mayfield. They had chart success with songs such as "Find Another Girl" and "I'm a Telling You" (both 1961). Butler and Mayfield parted company in 1966 and both went on with solo careers.

BUTTERFIELD, Paul (1942-87) *Blues musician* Butterfield was a white harmonica player following the tradition of great black BLUES players. As leader of the Paul Butterfield Blues Band, he was highly influential. He is also remembered for assisting Bob DYLAN to embrace electric music. Butterfield's style is best heard on his 1966 album *East-West.*

BUZZCOCKS, The *Rock band* Formed in Manchester, England, in 1976, the Buzzcocks were one of the leading PUNK ROCK bands. Playing a high energy style, they are best remembered for songs such as "What Do I Get," and "Ever Fallen in Love (With Someone You Shouldn't've)." They made several albums and influenced British music of the 1980s.

BYARD, Jackie (1922-) *Jazz musician* Massachusetts-born Byard played trumpet, piano, guitar, drums, and tenor saxophone. He appeared with Earl Bostic, Herb Pomeroy, and Maynard Ferguson in the 1940s and 1950s. As a soloist in the 1960s he specialized in the piano and led several of his own big bands.

BYAS, Don (1912-72) *Jazz musician* Netherlands-born tenor saxophonist Byas succeeded Lester YOUNG in Count BASIE's orchestra in 1941. He later played in his own bands, as well as with Dizzie GILLESPIE and Duke ELLINGTON. He was the prime tenor player of his time. In 1946 he moved to Paris and became a local jazz superstar. Byas was heavily influence by Coleman HAWKINS

BYRD, Donald (1932-) *Jazz musician* Trumpeter and flugelhorn player Byrd was also a distinguished teacher. One of the finest trumpeters in the HARD BOP style, he is best heard with Red Garland on "They Can't Take That Away from Me" (1957). In 1973 he released a jazz-soul crossover album *Black Byrd,* which became a worldwide hit.

BYRDS, The *Rock band* Growing out of the U.S. FOLK ROCK scene of the early 1960s, The Byrds added the political concerns of FOLK MUSIC to the popular beat style of British groups of the time. Abandoning folk styling for amplifiers in 1964, founder members Roger McGuinn, David Crosby, and Gene Clark joined up with Chris Hillman to form the Beefeaters. Renamed the Byrds, the group's electric remake of the Bob DYLAN original "Mr. Tambourine Man" topped the charts in 1965. David Crosby later became a founding member of the group Crosby, Stills and Nash.

CABALLÉ, Montserrat (1933-) *Opera singer* Soprano Caballé was born and educated in Spain. Engagements in Basle and Bremen led to work at Vienna, New York, La Scala in Milan, and London's Covent Garden, where she sang Verdi's Violetta in 1972. She is best known for her interpretations of Verdi, Donizetti, and PUCCINI.

CALE, J.J. (1938-) *Rock guitarist* With a background in Western SWING and ROCK'N'ROLL, guitarist Cale's big break came in 1970 when Eric Clapton recorded his song "After Midnight." Cale's low-key vocal style characterized all his albums, which enjoyed critical acclaim and commercial success throughout the 1980s.

CALLOWAY, Cab (1907-94) *Jazz singer and bandleader* Once a small-time singer and drummer on the Chicago club circuit, Calloway was recommended to the Savoy club by Louis ARMSTRONG. His over-the-top conducting and singing got him noticed and he was transferred to the Cotton Club. He has come to symbolize the big band era, and success with the song "Minnie the Moocher" ensured that he has remained one of the biggest names in big band SWING.

CAMPBELL, Glen (1936-) *Country singer* Campbell came from a musical family. At the end of the 1950s he moved from Arkansas to Los Angeles and became a session musician. A solo career started in 1967 with the hit single "Gentle on My Mind." Campbell hit the big time with three hits cowritten with Jim Webb: "By the Time I Get to Phoenix," "Wichita Lineman," and "Galveston." Campbell's career was further enhanced by short-lived but memorable membership of the BEACH BOYS in the 1960s and an appearance in the film *True Grit* starring with John Wayne.

CAN *Rock band* Formed in Germany in 1968 by Holger Czukay and Irmin Schmidt, two modern music students, Can evolved into an important band in contemporary music. Several albums, such as *Tago Mago* (1971), *Future Days* (1973), and *Landed* (1975) are regarded as classics of their time.

CANNON, Gus (1883-1979) *Blues musician* Born in Mississippi, Cannon was a fiddler, guitarist, and pianist. But his major instrument was the banjo. Music historians often claim that Cannon filled the gap between pre-blues African-American FOLK MUSIC and the BLUES.

CAPTAIN BEEFHEART (1941-) *Rock musician and songwriter* Captain Beefheart was a genuine maverick on the ROCK MUSIC scene. His various Magic Bands have always shown musical virtuosity to match Beefheart's incredible vocal range. The album *Trout Mask Replica* (1969) was a classic of the psychedelic 1960s. His last album *Ice Cream for Crow* (1982) was well received, but after that he concentrated on his oil painting, which he pursues under his real name, Don Van Vliet.

CARDEW, Cornelius (1936-81) *Composer* British-born Cardew studied in London, England, and in Cologne, Germany, where he became STOCKHAUSEN's assistant. A leading exponent of experimental music, he involved himself with improvisation groups and avant-garde musicians such as John CAGE, and David Tudor.

CARPENTER, Mary-Chapin (1958-) *Country singer* Princeton-born Carpenter did the rounds of the Washington folk clubs for several years. A 1992 hit with the song "I Feel Lucky" brought her national recognition. She continued to produce new vibrant songs for a genre that some felt was beginning to go stale, and her success continued in the 1990s.

CARPENTERS, The *Pop group* Brother and sister, Richard and Karen Carpenter began performing in the 1960s. A&M Records president, Herb ALPERT, heard a demo tape, and signed them in 1968. A string of worldwide hits followed: "Ticket to Ride," "Close to You," "We've Only Just Begun." The hits continued until the mid-1970s when they both encountered health problems. Tragically, Karen died in 1983 as a result of complications associated with anorexia nervosa.

CARR, Leroy (1905-35) *Blues musician* A Tennessee-born pianist and singer, Carr recorded his own compositions such as "Midnight Hour Blues" and "How Long, How Long Blues" in the mid-1920s. His vocal style was highly influential, for example, on artists such as Champion Jack Dupree and Otis SPANN.

CARRERAS, José (1946-) *Opera singer* After studying in his native Spain, Carreras achieved international success during the 1970s as a lyric tenor in the romantic repertory of Verdi and PUCCINI. He became known universally as one of the Three Tenors for his concert performances with Placido DOMINGO and Luciano PAVAROTTI.

CARS, The *Rock band* Formed in Boston, in 1977, the Cars had huge success as a NEW WAVE band with songs such as "My Best Friend's Girl" (1978) and "Drive" (1984). They broke up in the late 1980s, having made 6 albums.

CARTER, Bettie (1930-) *Jazz musician* Carter grew up in Detroit. During the late 1940s and early 1950s she sang with artists such as Charlie PARKER and Lionel Hampton. Always at the forefront of her genre, Carter's instrumental vocal style inspired others. She continued to record and innovate until the 1990s.

CASH, Rosanne (1955-) *Country singer* Daughter of Johnny CASH, Rosanne originally trained as an actress, but worked on her father's roadshow at the same time. In 1979 she secured a recording contract and married Nashville producer Rodney Crowell. Solo albums followed and Cash gradually made her way up the COUNTRY popularity charts. She had a decade of musical success before turning her attentions to writing.

CAVE, Nick (1957-) *Rock singer* Australian-born Cave was always an enigmatic figure in the ROCK MUSIC world. His first band, the Birthday Party, split up in 1983. He embarked on a solo career with a new band, the Bad Seeds, in 1984. Critically acclaimed, Cave's blend of literary allusions, and his obsession with murder and violence, made him a compulsive performer. He is best heard on the albums *Your Funeral, My Trial* (1986), *Murder Ballads* (1996), and *The Boatman's Call* (1997).

CELIBIDACHE, Sergei (1912-97) *Conductor* Born in Romania, Celibidache studied in Berlin, Germany, and became principal conductor of the Berlin Philharmonic Orchestra in 1945. He worked widely in Europe and in the U.S., teaching and conducting, and gaining a particular reputation for Russian music. Celibidache was legendary for his work in performance, and was regarded by many as capable of achieving near perfection.

CHECKER, Chubby (1941-) *R&B singer* Checker achieved national fame in 1960 with "The Twist," and international recognition with "Let's Twist Again" in 1961, which peaked with the twist dance craze. His success, though short-lived in years, yielded 32 hits in six years.

CHER (1946-) *Pop singer* Californian-born Cher first achieved success with her husband Sonny Bono (1935–98) as Sonny and Cher with the song "I Got You Babe" (1965). They met while working as session singers for Phil SPECTOR. A solo career yielded many hits during the 1970s and 1980s. Cher is also a successful film actress.

CHERKASSKY, Shura (1911-97) *Pianist* Russian-born American pianist Cherkassky made his debut at age 11 in Baltimore in 1922. In the postwar period, he established an international reputation in the romantic repertoire. His recordings of Russian music, particularly Tchaikovsky and RACHMANINOV, are world renowned.

CHERRY, Don (1936-) *Jazz trumpeter and bandleader* Cherry began playing trumpet with Ornette COLEMAN in 1959. He worked with all the great FREE JAZZ players during the 1960s. An interest in ethnic music developed during the 1970s. Cherry felt himself to be a "world musician," and used his influence to educate people throughout the world.

CHI-LITES, The *Soul band* Formed in Chicago in 1960, their first U.S. hit was "(For God's Sake) Give More Power to the People" (1971). However, further hits, such as "Have You Seen Her" (1971) and "Homely Girl" (1974), were renowned for their sentimental falsetto vocals, giving the band a pop tag.

CHIC *Soul band* Formed in New York in 1976 by Nile Rogers and Bernie Edwards, Chic became one of the key bands of the DISCO generation. Their up-tempo basslines and high energy dance tunes appealed to SOUL, ROCK and POP MUSIC fans. The single "Dance (Yowsah, Yowsah, Yowsah)" (1977) sold a million copies in its first month. "Le Freak" (1978) and "Good Times" (1979) were also huge successes. The group disbanded in 1983, but Edwards and Rogers went on to have successful careers as producers during the 1980s.

CHICAGO *Rock band* Formed in Chicago in 1966 as the Chicago Transit Authority, Chicago played brass rock in the mold of Blood, Sweat and Tears. Mainly an albums band, they did have a few hit singles during the early 1970s, such as "25 or 6 to 4" (1970). From the mid-1970s they produced more pop-oriented music and achieved huge success with songs such as "If You Leave Me Now" (1976) and "Hard to Say I'm Sorry" (1982). They released their last album in 1989.

CHIEFTAINS, The *Folk group* Formed in the late 1950s, the Chieftains became one of the leading exponents of traditional Irish music. Praised by leading musicians such as Eric Clapton and Mick Jagger, success with film soundtracks like *Barry Lyndon* (1975), and collaborations such as the 1988 album *Irish Heartbeat* with Van MORRISON kept the Chieftains in the public eye well into the 1990s.

CHIFFONS, The *Soul group* Formed in New York in the early 1960s, this all-girl group were best remembered for their hits "He's So Fine," "One Fine Day" (both 1963), and "Sweet Talkin' Guy" (1966).

CHRISTIE, William (1944-) *Harpsicordist and conductor* U.S.-born Christie founded *Les Arts Florissants*, a group specializing in Italian and French baroque music. He achieved critical acclaim in the 1990s for his performances of baroque OPERA.

CHRISTOFF, Boris (1918-94) *Opera singer* Born in Bulgaria, Christoff made his London debut in 1949 at Covent Garden. His remarkable bass voice and stage presence made him ideal for Boris Gudunov and other great 19th-century roles.

CHUNG, Kyung-Wha (1948-) *Violinist* Korean-born Chung studied in New York before debuting there and in London, establishing herself as an international soloist. She often appears with her sister, cellist Myung-Wha (1944-), and her brother, pianist Myung-Whun (1953-).

CLAPTON, Eric (1945-) *Rock guitarist* Regarded as one of the world's greatest guitarists, Clapton learned BLUES guitar at age 14. Membership of bands such as the Yardbirds, John Mayall's Bluesbreakers, CREAM, Blind Faith, and Derek and the Dominoes, with whom he recorded "Layla," perhaps his most famous song, prepared him for a massive solo career. Drug problems aside, Clapton has continued to release high-quality, commercially successful albums. He is regarded as the finest white blues guitarist. He is best heard on the albums *461 Ocean Boulevard* (1974) and *August* (1986).

CLARKE, Kenny (1914-85) *Jazz drummer and bandleader* Clarke is regarded as the originator of BEBOP drumming. Born in Pittsburgh, his career included playing with all the greats from Dizzy GILLESPIE and Charlie PARKER to Miles DAVIS and Dexter GORDON. Clarke was also a founder member of the MODERN JAZZ QUARTET.

CLARKE, Stanley (1951-) *Jazz musician* A highly talented bass player, Clarke first came to prominence in the 1970s with Chic COREA's band Return to Forever. Technically brilliant, Clarke was able to produce music that crossed over from JAZZ to SOUL and ROCK MUSIC. He made a series of albums in the 1980s with pianist George Duke.

CLASH, The *Punk rock band* Formed in London in 1976, the Clash were one of the spearheads of the PUNK ROCK movement. Playing high-powered ROCK MUSIC, they projected a genuine rebellious image while not pandering to record business hyperbole. Best heard on their albums *The Clash* (1977) and *London Calling* (1979) they developed into a competent band, incorporating REGGAE and dance rhythms into their music. Their most commercially successful album, *Combat Rock* (1982), saw them score heavily with American rock fans. They disbanded in 1986 and resisted the temptation to make a comeback.

CLAYTON, Buck (1911-) *Jazz trumpeter and arranger* A central figure in mainstream JAZZ, Clayton played with Count BASIE in the 1930s, accompanied Billie HOLIDAY, and appeared with Benny GOODMAN in the film *The Benny Goodman Story* (1955). In the 1960s he toured Europe annually, often playing with Humphrey Lyttleton.

CLEMENT, Jack (1931-) *Country songwriter and guitarist* In the late 1960s and early 1970s Clement wrote, produced, or played on records by artists such as Jerry Lee LEWIS—for whom he produced "Whole Lotta Shakin' Goin' On"—Johnny CASH—he produced "Ring of Fire"—and Roy Orbison. More recently he produced tracks recorded at Sun Studios in Memphis for the rock band U2.

CLIFF, Jimmy (1948-) *Reggae singer-songwriter* Cliff did much to popularize REGGAE music in the era before Bob MARLEY. He had his first hit with "Wonderful World, Beautiful People" in 1969. In 1972 he appeared in the film *The Harder They Come.* Both the film and its accompanying soundtrack were a huge success, making Cliff Jamaica's hottest export.

CLIFTON, Bill (1931-) *Country musician* Singer, guitarist, and autoharp player Clifton formed a bluegrass group, the Dixie Mountain Boys, in 1953. His music bridged the gap between bluegrass music and urban FOLK, bringing traditional American music to new audiences.

CLOONEY, Rosemary (1928-) *Popular singer* Clooney was one of the most popular female singers in the early 1950s. Hits with songs such as "Half As Much" (1952), "This Ole House," and her biggest hit "Mambo Italiano" (both 1954) maintained her popularity and high profile. She began an acting career, but apart from an appearance with Bing CROSBY in *White Christmas* (1953), she had little success.

COASTERS, The *R&B band* Originally called the Robins, the Coasters were the creation of the songwriting team of LEIBER & STOLLER. Their biggest hits came with the songs "Yakety Yak" (1958) and "Poison Ivy" (1959).

COBHAM, Billy (1944-) *Jazz drummer* Born into a musical family, Cobham learned to play JAZZ when very young. He joined the Horace SILVER band in 1968, then formed Dreams with the Brecker Brothers. In the early 1970s he played with Miles DAVIS and John McLAUGHLIN's Mahavishnu Orchestra and then, as leader, released the album *Spectrum,* later regarded as a classic JAZZ ROCK record.

COCHRAN, Eddie (1938-60) *Rock'n'roll singer and guitarist* American-born Cochran was one of the great 1950s ROCK'N'ROLL stars. He wrote and recorded some classic teenage songs, such as "Summertime Blues" (1958) and "C'mon Everybody" (1959). Cochran was killed in a road accident in the U.K. in 1960 on the way to give a performance.

COCKER, Joe (1944-) *Rock singer* A white British singer with a black voice, Cocker won American attention for his legendary performance at the Woodstock festival in 1969. However, his greatest hit came singing a duet with Jennifer Warnes, called "Up Where We Belong," the theme song to the film *An Officer and a Gentleman* (1982).

COHEN, Leonard (1934-) *Rock singer-songwriter* U.S. born Cohen was a poet in the 1950s, reciting his verses to a JAZZ accompaniment. He started to write songs in the 1960s, releasing his first and most successful album *Songs of Leonard Cohen* in 1968. Further albums followed, mostly in the same low-key, melancholy, acoustic style.

COLE, Cozy (1906-81) *Jazz drummer* A classic JAZZ drummer, Cole worked with Jelly Roll MORTON in the 1930s. He became famous while playing with Cab Calloway's band in the late 1930s, and continued at the top with Louis ARMSTRONG's All Stars until the mid-1950s.

COLLINS, Albert (1932-) *Blues guitarist* Collins learned his trade on the 1950s BLUES club circuit in Texas. Always popular with white audiences, Collins moved into the big time supported by George Thorogood and Robert Cray. A superb guitarist, Collins remains one of the most famous blues artists in the world in the 1990s.

COLLINS, Bootsy (1951-) *Funk bass guitarist* Collins found fame as part of James Brown's JBs in the early 1970s. His striking bass technique was regarded as defining FUNK music. A meeting with George Clinton led to a partnership that included the bands Funkadelic and Parliament. Collins had other solo projects, notably Bootsy's Rubber Band, all of them exploring the limits of SOUL and funk music.

COMMODORES, The *Soul group* Formed in 1968 the Commodores signed with MOTOWN in 1972 and supported the Jackson 5 on tour. By 1975 they had a reputation as a soft SOUL band, and songs like "Easy" (1977) and "Three Times a Lady" (1978), both written by Lionel Richie, achieved massive sales.

COMO, Perry (1912-) *Pop singer* Como was a ballad singer with a warm baritone voice. Singing mostly ballads or novelty songs, he delighted audiences with a relaxed style, selling over 60 million records between the 1930s and the 1990s. His biggest hits were "Hot Diggity (Dog Ziggity Boom)" (1956) and "Round and Round" (1957). His weekly TV show *Music Hall* ran, with tremendous popularity, from 1955–63.

COOPER, Alice (1948-) *Rock singer* Born Vincent Furnier, Cooper became popular in the 1970s with hit singles and spectacular concert appearances that featured gallows, "dead" babies, and live snakes. His breakthrough came in 1972 with "School's Out." Other hit singles and albums followed, and Cooper retained his position as a cult hero.

CORIGLIANO, John (1938-) *Composer* New York-born Corigliano studied with Giannini and Creston. His works include the electric rock opera, *The Naked Carmen,* the opera *A Figaro For Antonio,* instrumental and vocal music, and film scores.

CORTOT, Alfred (1877-1962) *Pianist and conductor* Cortot studied with Decombes, one of Chopin's last pupils. As a leading figure in French music in the early 1900s, he also conducted early French performances of Wagner and promoted the music of young French composers.

CORYELL, Larry (1943-) *Jazz rock guitarist and bandleader* A virtuoso guitarist, Coryell has never really found his metier. In the early 1970s he played with John McLAUGHLIN and Billy Cobham, but did not form his own band, Eleventh House, until 1972. Despite being able to highlight his playing, they disbanded shortly afterwards, and Coryell stopped playing the electric guitar. He returned to it in the 1980s.

COSTELLO, Elvis (1955-) *Rock singer* The self-styled "angry young man" of the U.K. PUNK scene of the late 1970s, Costello had a string of hits with songs such as "Watching the Detectives" (1977) and "Oliver's Army" (1979). His status as a serious musician and songwriter was enhanced with a series of successful albums such as *King of America* (1986) and *Brutal Youth* (1994).

Cox, Ida (1896-1967) *Blues singer* A classic BLUES artist of the 1920s, Cox personified the new liberated spirit of African-American blueswomen. She was renowned for writing and singing songs, such as "Wild Women Don't Have the Blues" and "Last Mile Blues," about contemporary issues.

Craft, Robert (1923-) *Conductor and writer* Craft's principal interests were early and contemporary music. From 1948 he was closely associated with STRAVINSKY, with whom he shared concerts and the writing of several books. He also recorded extensively with Canadian pianist Glenn GOULD. Apart from this work, Craft wrote extensively on music, both as a critic and an essayist.

Crawford, Randy (1952-) *Jazz and soul singer* Starting out as a jazz singer, Crawford first achieved fame as the singer on the Crusaders' hit "Street Life" (1979). Further solo hits with "One Day I'll Fly Away" (1980) and "You Might Need Somebody" (1981) followed, but Crawford's work with the Crusaders remained her most successful.

Crayton, Connie Curtis "Pee Wee" (1914-85) *Blues musician* Crayton played jazz-influenced BLUES guitar, and helped shape the West Coast blues sound. He played and recorded in the mid-1940s with Ivory Joe Hunter. During the 1950s he worked with a whole range of artists such as Clarence "Gatemouth" Brown, Big Joe Turner, and Johnny Otis.

Creedence Clearwater Revival *Rock group* Formed in California in 1967, Creedence became one of the most successful American ROCK groups of the early 1970s. Led by guitarist John Fogerty, their brand of Southern swamp rock took the band to mega stardom. Starting with the hit singles "Proud Mary" and "Bad Moon Rising" (both 1969), their success culminated in the classic album *Cosmo's Factory* (1970). They disbanded in 1972 but continued to sell greatest hits albums.

Crosby, Stills and Nash *Rock group* Formed in 1968 by David Crosby of the Byrds, Stephen Stills from Buffalo Springfield, and Graham Nash of British group the Hollies, CSN were an instant hit. The eponymous first album, released in 1969, sold well and their appearance at the Woodstock festival confirmed their popularity. Joined at various times by Neil Young, the band peaked in 1970 with the album *Déjà Vu.*

Crow, Sheryl (1962-) *Rock singer* Born into a musical family, Crow was writing songs at age 14. She got a job as a backing singer on Michael JACKSON's world tour in 1988, and more work soon followed. A deal with A&M Records in 1992 allowed her to record her first solo album. The resulting *Tuesday Night Music Club* (1993) was an enormous success, with the single "All I Wanna Do" turning her into a worldwide star. She released *The Globe Sessions* in 1998.

Crowell, Rodney (1950-) *Country singer-songwriter* One of the leading lights in Nashville during the 1970s, Crowell wrote songs for, and produced artists such as Emmylou HARRIS, Rosanne Cash, Waylon JENNINGS, Guy Clark, and George Jones. Once a member of Harris's Hot Band, Crowell's career went from strength to strength, with a set of solo albums and strong songs from 1978 well into the 1990s.

Crudup, Arthur "Big Boy" (1905-74) *Blues singer and guitarist* Mississippi-born Crudup was one of the first BLUES artists to record using an electric guitar in the late 1940s. An important influence on Elvis PRESLEY, who recorded some of his songs including the classic "That's All Right, Mama," Crudup remained a popular performer into the 1960s.

Crumb, George (1929-) *Composer* Born in Charleston, West Virginia, Crumb studied music at the University of Michigan. His music is characterized by use of numerology, quotations, and unconventional instruments. He composed many vocal pieces using verse by Spanish poet García Lorca. His work was principally influenced by DEBUSSY, MAHLER, and BARTÓK.

Curtis, King (1934-71) *R&B-jazz tenor saxophonist and bandleader* Initially a jazz musician, Curtis became famous after moving to New York in the early 1950s. He worked as a session musician backing artists such as Buddy HOLLY and Eric Clapton, often playing a featured sax solo. He was Aretha FRANKLIN's musical director during the early 1960s. He was murdered in New York in 1971 at the peak of his career. He is best heard on his 1960 album *The New Scene of King Curtis.*

Curzon, Sir Clifford (1907-82) *Pianist* Curzon made his London debut under Sir Henry Wood in 1923. He studied with Schnabel and toured widely in Europe and the U.S., earning critical acclaim in particular for his playing of Schubert and Mozart.

Cypress Hill *Rap group* Coming from Los Angeles, and representing the new-wave of RAP, Cyprus Hill made two albums in the early 1990s. The single "Black Sunday" (1993) went to the top of the charts and helped the band find a new audience. Advocates of a legalize marijuana campaign, Cypress Hill continued to score big hits with black and white audiences alike.

Dameron, Tadd (1917-65) *Composer, arranger, bandleader, and pianist* At his peak Dameron wrote arrangements for Dizzie GILLESPIE's big band between 1945–47, and played with Miles DAVIS at the Paris Jazz Fair of 1949. He had a varied career and played both SWING and BEBOP. His best work includes "Good Bait," "Our Delight," and "Hot House," recorded with Dizzie Gillespie and Charlie PARKER.

Dart, Thurston (1921-71) *Harpsicordist and musicologist* Dart taught at Cambridge University in the U.K. before founding the music faculty at King's College, London. Both performer and teacher, Dart specialized in the music of J.S. Bach, keyboard and consort music of the 16th, 17th, and 18th centuries, and in the life and music of the composer John Bull. He also gave frequent recitals on the harpsichord, clavichord, and organ.

DAVIES, Sir Peter Maxwell (1934-) *Composer* The roots of Davies' compositional style were in early English music and in the music of composers BOULEZ and STOCKHAUSEN. He wrote instrumental music, orchestral music, and several operas including *The Martyrdom of St. Magnus* (1977) and *The Lighthouse* (1980).

DAVIS, Andrew (1944-) *Conductor* Originally an organist, Davis was associated with the BBC Symphony Orchestra and the Glyndebourne Festival between the 1970s and 1990s. He has also been musical director of the Toronto Symphony Orchestra. An expressive conductor, Davis is particularly admired for his recording of SHOSTAKOVICH'S Symphony No.10 with the London Philharmonic Orchestra.

DAVIS, Sir Colin (1927-) *Conductor* Sir Colin Davis conducted OPERA and symphonic music all over the world between the 1950s and the 1990s. He was musical director at Covent Garden, London, from 1971–86. His style revealed an emotional connection to certain composers rather than all-round excellence. He is particularly associated with Berlioz, STRAVINSKY, and TIPPETT.

DAVIS, Rev. Gary (1896-1972) *Blues musician* Davis played harmonica, guitar, and banjo as well as singing GOSPEL and rural BLUES. His finger picking technique and his gravelly voice produced music with great vitality. Davis moved from Durham, North Carolina, to New York in 1945, and took his place at the center of a lively FOLK MUSIC scene.

DAVIS, Jimmie (1902-) *Country singer* Imitating Jimmie RODGERS' yodeling style, Davis was a fine COUNTRY singer with hits such as "You Are My Sunshine" (1939), and "There's a New Moon Over My Shoulder" (1945). Alternating between music and politics, Davis gradually turned to GOSPEL singing during the 1950s.

DAVIS, Sammy, Jr. (1925-90) *Popular singer and dancer* Primarily a vaudeville entertainer, Davis spent a lifetime singing, dancing, and acting. He had several hit songs during the postwar years, also appearing in films and Broadway shows. His biggest hit and only No.1 was with the song "Candy Man" (1972) from the film *Willy Wonka and the Chocolate Factory.*

DAVIS, Skeeter (1931-) *Country singer* A prime mover in the 1960s Nashville music scene, Davis had several COUNTRY and POP hits. "The End of the World" and "I Can't Stay Mad At You" (both 1963) were her most popular releases. During the 1970s and 1980s she turned increasingly to GOSPEL and religious music.

DAVIS, Spencer (1941-) *R&B singer and guitarist* Originally a member of the Rhythm and Blues Quartet performing BLUES material, U.K.-born Davis and vocalist Steve Winwood formed the Spencer Davis Group. Signed to Island Records in 1965, they had two big hits with "Keep on Running" (1966) and "Gimme Some Lovin'" the following year. Winwood left in 1967 and Davis carried on without him.

DAVIS, Tyrone (1938-) *Soul singer* One of the lesser known SOUL artists, Davis started recording in the late 1960s. His voice, similar to artists like Bobby "Blue" Bland and Z.Z. Hill, was perfectly suited to soft soul music. He featured in the charts consistently during the 1970s and 1980s.

DE LA SOUL *Rap group* Formed in New York in 1987, De La Soul presented their own vision of hip-hop. Their first album, *3 Feet High and Rising,* was a sunny light-hearted record, decidedly un-macho in its sound. Accusations of selling out influenced the band to return to its black roots. Other albums, such as *De La Soul Is Dead* (1991) and *Buhloone Mindstate* (1993), were darker and more violent in tone and subject matter.

DE PEYER, Gervase (1926-) *Classical clarinetist* Born in the U.K. De Peyer was principal clarinet in the London Symphony Orchestra and a founder member of the Melos Ensemble. He gave first performances of concertos by Sebastian Forbes, Joseph Horovitz, and Thea Musgrave.

DEAD KENNEDYS *Punk rock band* Formed in San Francisco in 1978, the Dead Kennedys earned notoriety for their hardcore PUNK music and their politics. Songs like "California Über Alles," "Holiday in Cambodia," and "Kill the Poor" showed the band at their angry best. Toward the end of the 1980s, police harassment, and the increasingly right-wing nature of American politics, persuaded singer Jello Biafra to disband the group.

DEEP PURPLE *Rock group* Formed in 1968 Deep Purple were HEAVY METAL pioneers. With the album *Deep Purple in Rock* (1970) they played heavy rock at its finest. Featuring the guitar work of Richie Blackmore, the organ playing of Jon Lord, and the aggressive drumming of Ian Paice, Deep Purple went on to make other classic albums and singles. The best of these was "Smoke on the Water" (1972), now regarded as a heavy metal classic.

DEF LEPPARD *Heavy metal band* Formed in 1977 in Sheffield, England, Def Leppard released their first album in 1980. In 1983 their third album *Pyromania* became an instant HEAVY METAL classic, selling over 7 million copies. Despite a car accident—which left drummer Rick Allen with one arm—drug, and alcohol problems, Def Leppard continued to make strong albums that sold millions of copies throughout the world.

DEKKER, Desmond (1942-) *Reggae singer* A hugely successful artist in his native Jamaica in the mid- to late 1960s, Dekker made the charts in 1966 with the song "007 (Shanty Town)." In 1969 he released "Israelites," which was the first REGGAE record to achieve massive worldwide success. He remained reggae's most famous artist until the arrival of Bob MARLEY.

DEL MAR, Norman (1919-) *Composer and writer* British-born, Del Mar was originally a horn player. He later became a conductor, admired particularly for his work with the music of MAHLER, Busoni, and Richard STRAUSS. A respected writer on music, his finest literary work—a three-volume study of Richard Strauss—was published between 1962–72.

DEL TREDICI, David (1937-) *Composer* American Del Tredici's compositional style combined SERIALISM and EXPRESSIONISM. Active during the late 1960s and early 1970s, he set several James Joyce texts to music and based a large scale work on *Alice in Wonderland*.

DELLER, Alfred (1912-79) *Opera singer* English countertenor Deller began his full-time career in 1947. Renowned for the smoothness of his singing, unusual in a high male voice, Deller's finest moment was in having BRITTEN write the part of Oberon in *A Midsummer Night's Dream* for him in 1960.

DENISOV, Edison (1929-) *Composer* Soviet composer Denisov studied in Moscow and became interested in Russian FOLK MUSIC. In the 1960s he worked with ELECTRONIC MUSIC and made more use of the newest developments in composition, such as SERIALISM, unconventional instrumental techniques, and percussive use of wind and strings.

DENVER, John (1942-97) *Country singer* Having written the song "Leaving on a Jet Plane," a hit for Peter, Paul and Mary, Denver embarked on a solo career and emerged as a major figure in the 1970s, singing, and playing guitar and banjo. Hits with songs such as "Take Me Home, Country Roads" (1973) and "Annie's Song" (1978), both of which were million sellers, kept Denver in the public eye. He died when his plane crashed into the Pacific Ocean.

DE PARIS, Sidney (1905-67) *Jazz trumpeter* Sidney played with brother Wilbur in the early part of his career. He worked with Jelly Roll MORTON and Sidney Bechet in 1939–40 before rejoining his trombonist brother in their own traditional JAZZ band.

DEPECHE MODE *Rock group* Formed in 1980 in England, Depeche Mode started out as a synth-pop band, playing light cheery songs. A string of hit singles followed, despite the fact that the music got darker and more serious. In 1987 their album *Music for the Masses* found them a new

audience in the U.S., and further albums, such as *Violator* (1990) and *Songs of Faith and Devotion* (1993), turned them into a stadium act.

DESMOND, Paul (1924-77) *Jazz saxophonist* Desmond joined the Dave BRUBECK quartet in 1951, and stayed with the band for 16 years. He played alto sax in the smooth tradition begun by Lester YOUNG and Benny CARTER. He also recorded with Gerry MULLIGAN and guitarist Jim Hall.

DETROIT SPINNERS *Soul group* Formed in 1961, and signed to MOTOWN in 1963, the Detroit Spinners did not score their first major hit until 1970, when Stevie WONDER's "It's A Shame" hit the charts. A move to Atlantic Records in 1971 was followed by a number of singles, including their Dionne Warwick collaboration "Then Came You" (1973) and "Working My Way Back to You Girl" (1977).

DIAMOND, Neil (1941-) *Pop singer* Diamond's initial success was as a songwriter. He wrote "I'm a Believer" and "A Little Bit Me, A Little Bit You" for the Monkees in the late 1960s. His solo career took off in the early 1970s with a series of hit singles, such as "Cracklin' Rose" and "Sweet Caroline." Diamond went on to become one of the most commercially successful singers in the U.S.

DICKENSON, Vic (1906-84) *Jazz trombonist* Dickenson had no formal music training. He played with Claude Hopkins and Eddie Heywood during the 1930s and 40s. One of the most respected of jazz musicians, Dickenson had an amazing memory for tunes. He is best heard on *Vic Dickenson Septet* (1953), a recording regarded as the beginning of mainstream jazz.

DIETRICH, Marlene (1901-92) *Singer and actress* German-born, Dietrich's heavily accented semi-spoken style of singing brought her a career as a film star. In her first U.S. film *The Blue Angel* (1930) she sang "Falling in Love Again," which became her theme song. She became a U.S. citizen before World War II and sang "Lilli Marlene" as part of the war effort. She became a much sought-after CABARET star during the 1950s and 1960s.

DIMEOLA, Al (1954-) *Jazz-rock guitarist* Inspired by ROCK MUSIC, DiMeola became one of the world's most famous JAZZ guitarists. In 1974 he joined Chick COREA's Return to Forever and then John MCLAUGHLIN's band. After that he led his own band, the Al DiMeola Project. A virtuoso player, he was happy playing both acoustic and electric guitars.

DINOSAUR JR. *Rock group* Formed in Massachusetts in 1984, Dinosaur Jr. joined bands like Sonic Youth on the new GRUNGE scene. Their single "Freak Scene" (1988) became an anthem for the movement. Led by J. Mascis, the band's finest work is heard on their 1988 album *Bug*.

DODDS, Baby (1898-1959) *Jazz drummer* Dodds was a major figure in NEW ORLEANS JAZZ drumming, emphasizing a more liberated style of playing during the 1920s. In a long career he played with Louis ARMSTRONG and Jelly Roll MORTON, and later with Sydney Bechet and Mezz Mezzrow.

DODDS, Johnny (1892-1940) *Jazz clarinetist* Older brother of Baby Dodds, Johnny began playing JAZZ in riverboat bands before moving to Chicago to join King Oliver's Creole Jazz Band. Like Baby, he worked with Louis ARMSTRONG, Jelly Roll MORTON, and Sydney Bechet.

DOHNÁNYI, Christoph von (1929-) *Conductor* Born in Berlin, of Hungarian descent, Dohnányi is the grandson of composer Ernst. He had appointments with major OPERA houses and symphony orchestras all over the world between 1950–1975, in particular the Cleveland Symphony Orchestra. He conducted much modern music, and is widely admired for his interpretation of SCHOENBERG.

DOHNÁNYI, Ernst von (1877-1960) *Composer and pianist* Dohnányi was born in Hungary as Erno Dohnányi. During the early 1920s he led a revival of interest in local music, which included BARTÓK, KODÁLY, and Weiner. His international reputation grew after World War II, when he settled in Florida. He was grandfather of conductor Christoph.

DOLMETSCH, Eugène (1858-1940) *Instrument maker and early music expert* Born into a musical family, Dolmetsch earned a reputation for restoring and making early instruments, in particular recorders. His enthusiasm for the subject led him to perform early music regularly and to write widely about the subject. During a period when early music was largely ignored, Dolmetsch was instrumental in bringing it back into vogue.

DONEGAN, Lonnie (1931-) *Rock singer* The most famous skiffle musician in the U.K., Donegan was originally a jazz guitarist with Ken Colyer and Chris Barber. His version of LEADBELLY's "Rock Island Line" was a hit in the mid-1950s. He followed this with 30 more hits from 1956–62, including "My Old Man's a Dustman" (1960).

DONOVAN (1946-) *Folk singer* Once hailed as the U.K.'s answer to DYLAN, Donovan had several hit songs during the mid-1960s, with tunes such as "Catch the Wind," "Sunshine Superman," and "Mellow Yellow." Of his later work, the album *Cosmic Wheels* (1973) was his most successful, although he enjoyed a brief revival in the 1990s as a guest on tour with the British indie band Happy Mondays.

DOORS, The *Rock group* Formed in 1965, the Doors remain one of the seminal groups in ROCK history. Led by their singer, Jim Morrison, the band inspired love from their fans and hate from the establishment. Hit singles, such as "Light My Fire," "When the Music's Over" (both 1967), and "Hello I Love You" (1968), featured on hit albums such as *Strange Days* (1967) and *Morrison Hotel* (1970). As success took hold, Morrison's drug use and subsequent behavior caused uproar. He died of a drug overdose in Paris, just before the release of the classic *LA Woman* (1971).

DORATI, Antal (1906-88) *Conductor* Hungarian-born Dorati worked extensively in Europe and the U.S., in particular with the Dallas Symphony Orchestra and the BBC Symphony Orchestra. He was strongly associated with the music of Haydn, all of whose symphonies he recorded, and with BARTÓK.

DORHAM, Kenny (1924-72) *Jazz trumpeter* One of the first BEBOP trumpeters, Dorham played with Dizzy GILLESPIE, Billy Eckstine, and Charlie PARKER during the late 1940s and early 1950s. During the 1960s he often led his own groups, but his best work was reserved when he played with others, such as Tadd Dameron, John COLTRANE, and Sonny ROLLINS.

DORSEY, Jimmy (1904-57) *Jazz musician* Dorsey played clarinet and saxophone, coleading bands with his brother Tommy DORSEY. In 1934 they formed the Dorsey Brothers Orchestra. A competent musician, Dorsey's success was often based on his fine choice of vocalist.

DORSEY, Lee (1924-86) *R&B singer* Born in New Orleans, a boxer turned singer, Dorsey had a series of hits during the 1960s. Best heard on tracks like "Ride Your Pony" (1965), "Working in the Coal Mine" (1966), and "Yes We Can" (1969), Dorsey worked mainly with Allen Toussaint.

DR. JOHN (1941-) *R&B singer* Dr. John, real name Malcolm Rebennack, was brought up in New Orleans on Creole music and the piano playing of Professor Longhair. His style brings together elements of JAZZ, ROCK'N'ROLL and FUNK, accompanied by voodoo-inspired mystery. Songs like "Walk on Gilded Splinters" (1968), "Iko Iko" (1972), and "Right Place Wrong Time" (1973) have brought him considerable commercial success to go along with critical acclaim.

DRAKE, Nick (1948-74) *Folksinger-songwriter* A cult figure since his early death, Drake released his first album *Five Leaves Left* (1969) at age 21. Painfully shy, Drake was unable to tour to support the record. A second album, *Bryter Later* (1970), was followed by a third *Pink Moon* (1972). Although critically acclaimed, the records did not sell and Drake went into a depression from which he never recovered. He died, by accident, of an overdose of an anti-depressant. Drake's beautiful songs, his intimate voice, and his clear, melodic guitar style ensured that while he was gone his work would live on.

DU PRÉ, Jacqueline (1945-87) *Cellist* Du Pré launched a successful solo career at her London debut in 1961. She was immediately acclaimed for her natural talent. In 1967 she married the pianist and conductor Daniel BARENBOIM. Her career was cut short in 1973 when she was diagnosed as suffering from multiple sclerosis. She was renowned for her work on the concertos of Sir Edward ELGAR and Robert Schumann.

DUPRÉ, Marcel (1886-1971) *Composer and organist* Born in Rouen, France, Dupré studied in Paris with Vierne and Widor. Widely active as a recital organist, he gave over 1,900 concerts between 1939–53. His compositions were mostly symphonic, often in the form of religious poems set to music. He remained the organist at St. Sulpice in Paris from 1934 until his death in 1971.

DUPREE, Champion Jack (1910-92) *Blues singer and pianist* Raised as an orphan in New Orleans, Dupree learned the piano and worked the bars of the French Quarter. He turned to boxing for a while in the 1930s, but returned to music after World War II, working with Brownie McGee (see Sonny TERRY &), Eric Clapton, and John Mayall. Never a musical expert, Dupree recorded and played enough to keep him in comfort.

DURANTE, Jimmy (1893-1980) *Comedian and singer* A showbiz personality since 1914, Durante sung, played, and acted his way though clubs, stage shows, and films. Originally a honky tonk piano player, he had a number of hit songs to his name, "Inka Dinka Do" and "The Man Who Found the Lost Chord" being the best remembered.

DURHAM, Eddie (1906-87) *Jazz musician* Multi-talented instrumentalist and arranger, Durham made early electric guitar recordings with Count BASIE and the Kansas City Six in the late 1930s, he also played the trombone. He wrote for Artie Shaw and Glenn MILLER during the 1940s and even led his own all-women group. An influential figure in the development of JAZZ guitar, Durham has been neglected by history.

DURUFLÉ, Maurice (1902–86) *Composer and organist* Duruflé studied in Paris with DUKAS and Gigout. He was appointed organist of St. Etienne-du-Mont in 1930. Although Duruflé was not a prolific composer, his *Requiem* of 1947 achieved wide popularity.

DUTILLEUX, Henri (1916–) *Composer* Dutilleux's early works showed the influence of RAVEL and DEBUSSY. But after World War II he developed a highly original idiom in his orchestral work, chamber music, and songs. He wrote a modest number of works, but they were widely acclaimed for their craftsmanship.

EAGLIN, Ford "Snooks" (1936–) *Blues singer and guitarist* From a New Orleans Baptist background, Eaglin developed a country blues style. By the time he was 20, he had written the R&B classic "Lucille" for LITTLE RICHARD. He was popular locally during the 1960s, often accompanying Professor Longhair. During the 1970s and 1980s, he continued to record in a variety of styles such as R&B, POP, and BLUES.

EARTH, WIND AND FIRE *Soul group* Formed in the 1960s by Maurice White, Earth, Wind and Fire blended SOUL and JAZZ with huge commercial success. They had a string of hits, such as "Shining Star" (1975), "Got to Get You into My Life" (1978), and "Boogie Wonderland" (1979). They made 11 million-selling albums during the 1970s, also earning a reputation with their spectacular live shows.

EBEN, Petr (1929–) *Composer and pianist* Czech-born Eben wrote vocal, instrumental, and organ music. His work showed the fusion of the Renaissance and contemporary ideas, which emphasized the continuity and extension of tradition. His best-known works were a series of "6 Love Songs" (1951), and his choral work *Apologia Sokrates* (1961–67), which gained him international recognition.

ECHO AND THE BUNNYMEN *Rock group* Formed in Liverpool in 1978, Echo and the Bunnymen caught the end of the NEW WAVE. Their popularity grew during the early 1980s, peaking in 1984 with songs such as "The Cutter" and "The Killing Moon." Led from the start by frontman and singer Ian McCulloch, the Bunnymen continued to make music until well into the 1990s.

ECKSTINE, Billy (1914–93) *Jazz singer, musician, and bandleader* After chosing to be a singer rather than a football player, Eckstine joined the Earl Hines band in Chicago in the early 1930s. With Hines, he learned the trumpet and the trombone. In the early 1940s he started his own band which, over the years, featured musicians such as Dizzy GILLESPIE, Charlie PARKER, Miles DAVIS, Art BLAKEY, and Sarah VAUGHAN.

EDDY, Duane (1938–) *Rock guitarist* Inventor of the legendary "twang" style of guitar playing, Eddy had several hits in 1959 and 1960, including "Rebel 'Rouser," "Because They're Young," "Peter Gunn," and "(Dance with the) Guitar Man." Playing mainly instrumentals, Eddy remains the all-time No.1 ROCK'N'ROLL instrumentalist.

EDDY, Nelson (1901–67) *Singer and actor* Nelson Eddy sang OPERETTAS and OPERA during the early 1920s. In 1935, the film company MGM put him together with singer Jeanette MacDonald, and their popularity was immediate. During the late 1930s and early 1940s they sang and starred in several FILM MUSICALS, such as *Naughty Marietta* (1935), *San Francisco* (1936), and *Maytime* (1937).

EDISON, Harry "Sweets" (1915–) *Jazz trumpeter* Heavily influenced by Louis ARMSTRONG, Edison became a stalwart soloist with Count BASIE during the 1940s. He later led his own groups and worked with saxophonist Eddie "Lockjaw" Davis, developing a distinctive and unique sound.

EDWARDS, Cliff "Ukelele Ike" (1895–1972) *Jazz singer* Popular in the 1920s as a singer and a ukelele player in Broadway shows such as *Lady Be Good* (1924), and *Ziegfeld Follies* (1927). He recorded with jazzmen such as Miff Mole and Jimmy Dorsey. He is perhaps most famous as the voice of Jiminy Cricket in Disney's *Pinocchio* (1940).

EGK, Werner (1901–83) *Composer* German-born Egk studied with Carl Orff and conducted at the Berlin Staatsoper. He wrote several OPERAS in an angular, dissonant style recalling STRAVINSKY. He also wrote for the theater and was specially commissioned to write for the 1936 Olympics.

ELECTRIC LIGHT ORCHESTRA *Rock group* Formed in 1970 from the remnants of the Move, ELO went on to score huge hits on both sides of the Atlantic. Led by guitarist Jeff Lynne and drummer Bev Bevan they had 15 Top 20 entries between 1976 and 1981, including "Livin' Thing" (1976), "Mr. Blue Sky" (1978), and "Don't Bring Me Down" (1979). They disbanded in 1991.

ELLIS, Vivian (1903–) *Composer* Born in London, Ellis was a prolific composer of OPERETTAS for the popular theater in the 1930s. His most famous work was the 1947 hit *Bless the Bride*.

EMERSON LAKE AND PALMER *Rock group* Formed in 1970 by ex-members of the Nice, King Crimson and Atomic Rooster, "supergroup" ELP were highly successful with a classically influenced brand of ROCK MUSIC. Their version of Mussorgsky's *Pictures at an Exhibtion*, their album *Tarkus* (both 1971) and their dramatic interpretation of COPLAND's "Fanfare for the Common Man" (1977) established them as one of the biggest grossing bands in rock. Their star waned, however, with the advent of PUNK and NEW WAVE music at the end of the 1970s.

ENO, Brian (1948–) *Rock musician* After dabbling with music at school, Eno met saxophonist Andy Mackay in 1971 and was invited to join Roxy Music as "musical advisor." They were immediately successful. However, the mix in the band was not, and Eno left in 1973. Eno went on to have a successful recording career both as a solo artist and in collaboration with artists such as David BOWIE and David Byrne, but was also known for his production work, particularly on U2's *The Unforgettable Fire, The Joshua Tree,* and *Achtung Baby.*

ERIK B. AND RAKIM *Rap duo* Eric B. and Rakim met in New York in 1985. Their 1987 album *Paid in Full*, owing much to James BROWN and Bobby Byrd, became one of the first classic RAP/hip-hop records. In turn they were highly influential on West Coast rap.

ESTES, "Sleepy" John (1899-1977) *Blues singer and guitarist* Estes began his recording career in 1929 and was still recording in the 1960s. A country blues singer in the field holler tradition, he is best heard on songs like "Milk Cow Blues" (1930), and "Floating Bridge" (1938). His best-selling album *Broke and Hungry* (1963) featured the legendary Mike Bloomfield on guitar.

EVANS, Sir Geraint (1922-92) *Opera singer* Welsh-born Evans made his debut at London's Covent Garden in 1948. In an international career spanning three decades he achieved recognition for character baritone roles in the comic tradition including Falstaff and Beckmesser. His recordings remain a major influence on younger generations of singers.

EVANS, Gil (1912-88) *Jazz pianist, arranger, and composer* Evans was inspired during the 1920s and 1930s to compose JAZZ after listening to LOUIS ARMSTRONG. At the end of the 1940s Evans worked as an arranger with Miles DAVIS in a band that originated the "cool" school of jazz. Two of the band's best pieces, "Boplicity" and "Moondreams" were scored by Evans. But his greatest work was as a writer and arranger on three orchestral albums released in the late 1950s. *Miles Ahead*, *Porgy and Bess*, and *Sketches of Spain*, all featured Miles Davis and are often cited as the finest orchestral pieces of modern jazz. Evans also played piano, but he only began playing professionally at age 40.

EVANS, Herschel (1909-39) *Jazz tenor saxophonist* New York-born Evans played with Lionel Hampton and Buck Clayton in the early 1930s. In 1936 he joined Count BASIE's Orchestra. With Lester YOUNG, Evans established the tradition of "battling" tenor saxophones as each traded licks with each other. He died of edema at age 30.

EWING, Maria (1950-) *Opera singer* Born in the U.S., Ewing, a mezzo-soprano, made her Met debut in New York in 1976. She performed with principal opera companies in the U.S. and Europe and worked as a concert soloist and in recital. She is closely associated with Bizet's Carmen and STRAUSS's Salome.

FACES, The *Rock group* Formed in 1969 after the break-up of the Small Faces, the Faces, which included Rod Stewart on vocals, had some success as a band. But they only took off after Rod Stewart had a huge solo hit with "Maggie May" (1971) after which the band effectively became Stewart's backing band. They had success with albums like *A Nod's As Good As a Wink...To a Blind Horse* (1971) and *Ooh La La* (1973), as well as several hit singles. The band broke up when Stewart left in 1975.

FAIRPORT CONVENTION *Folk group* Formed in 1967, this British folk group made their debut album featuring Joni MITCHELL in 1968. By the 1990s the group had become as important as the musical genre they championed. The intervening years saw several line-ups, featuring, at one time or another: Iain Matthews, Sandy Denny, Richard Thompson, Dave Swarbrick, and Dave Mattacks, among others. This seminal folk group is best heard on the albums *What We Did on Our Holidays*, *Unhalfbricking*, and *Liege and Lief* (all 1969).

FALL, THE *Rock group* Formed in 1977 in Manchester, England, the Fall were fronted by the uncompromising Mark E. Smith. Their music, full of choppy guitar riffs and hard-edged lyrics, was critically acclaimed and achieved some commercial success. Their best work is heard on the albums *Live at the Witch Trials* (1979), *Hex Education Hour* (1982), and *Peverted by Language* (1983).

FARLOW, Tal (1921-98) *Jazz guitarist* Farlow played in the early BEBOP style with vibraphonist Red Norvo in the 1950s, and later with Charles MINGUS. He was an innovative and highly individual improviser, whose playing became more lyrical as his career developed.

FARMER, Art (1928-) *Jazz flugelhorn player and trumpeter* Farmer played in the West Coast big bands of Benny CARTER and Lionel Hampton in the late 1940s. He formed Jazztet with Benny Golson in 1959, and later started his own big bands with which he toured around the world.

FEATHER, Leonard (1914-) *Jazz composer and arranger* British-born Feather moved to the U.S. in 1935, where he became one of the most widely read JAZZ journalists. He also wrote and arranged for his favorite artists, such as Count BASIE and George Shearing.

FELDMAN, Morton (1926-87) *Composer* Closely associated with John CAGE and American abstract Impressionist painters of the 1950s, Feldman's best-known works are *The Viola in My Life* (1970) and *The Rothko Chapel* (1971–72). Extremely demanding to play, Feldman's music was renowned for its experimental nature.

FELICIANO, Jose (1945-) *Pop guitarist* One of the most popular performers in the Spanish-speaking world, Feliciano had a dual career in the English language and in Spanish. In English, he had his biggest hit with a version of the Doors' song "Light My Fire" (1968). In South America, he recorded albums in Argentina, Mexico, and Venezuela, and at one time, he had a TV show syndicated throughout the continent.

FERGUSON, Maynard (1928-) *Jazz musician* Canadian-born Ferguson found fame with Stan KENTON in 1950. A skilled musician, his music was always up-tempo and exciting. He is best heard on albums such as *The Birdland Dreamband* (1956) and *Two's Company* (1961).

FERNEYHOUGH, Brian (1943-) *Composer* English-born, Ferneyhough's style is a highly complex continuation of the 1950s avant-garde. Initially influenced by STOCKHAUSEN and WEBERN, Ferneyhough's work made him one of the most significant composers in Europe and America. Representative works include *Transit* (1972–75) and *La terre est un homme* (1976–79).

FERRIER, Kathleen (1912-53) *Opera singer* Ferrier, a British contralto, gave concert performances in Europe and the U.S. during the 1940s. She was widely admired for her warm and firm voice, and for her interpretations of Handel, Bach, Gluck, and MAHLER. BRITTEN's Second Canticle was composed for her.

FINZI, Gerald (1901-56) *Composer* An English composer, Finzi wrote in a pastoral style. His most renowned work was with the poems of Thomas Hardy, but his piece *Dies natalis* (1926) is also regarded as a minor masterpiece of English music.

FISCHER, Annie (1914-) *Pianist* A pupil of Ernst von Dohnányi, Hungarian-born Fischer began a career in the 1920s. She was praised not only for her technique, but also for her interpretative skills. She had a large repertoire including Bach, BARTÓK, Chopin, Mozart, and Liszt.

FLACK, Roberta (1939-) *Soul singer* Discovered singing in a Washington jazz club, Flack released two albums to critical acclaim in the late 1960s. She had an international hit with the Ewan MacColl song "The First Time Ever I Saw Your Face" (1972). Other hits followed, such as "Killing Me Softly with His Song" (1973), and "Tonight I Celebrate My Love" (1983) with Peabo Bryson.

FLANAGAN, Tommy (1930-) *Jazz pianist* Flanagan's mastery of JAZZ piano meant that he was much in demand as an accompanist for singers such as Ella FITZGERALD and Tony BENNETT during the 1960s and 1970s. He also fronted several bands of his own, demonstrating his refined approach to BEBOP piano playing.

FLATT, Lester (1914-79) *Country singer* Flatt was one half of the bluegrass and COUNTRY music duo Flatt and Scruggs. With his guitar and Scruggs' banjo, the pair went on a 20-year crusade taking American traditional music around the country.

FLEETWOOD MAC *Rock group* Formed in 1967 as a BLUES band by Peter Green and Mick Fleetwood from John Mayall's Bluesbreakers,

Fleetwood Mac is one of the premier bands in British rock history. Early success with albums and singles sent the band on several U.S. tours, and it was there that the group had most success. Their album *Rumours*, released in 1977, sold 25 million copies, making it the second biggest-selling album ever.

FLYING BURRITO BROTHERS *Country rock group* Formed in 1968 by Gram Parsons and Chris Hillman from the Byrds, the Flying Burritos released the album *The Gilded Palace of Sin* in 1969. The album featured some songs by Parsons. This seminal COUNTRY album was not matched again during the band's career, despite several albums and regular tours.

FOO FIGHTERS, The *Rock group* The brainchild of Dave Grohl, drummer with NIRVANA, the Foo Fighters burst onto the ROCK scene in 1995 with their first eponymous album. Its hardcore tunes were an immediate success, proving to Grohl and to Kurt Cobain fans that there was life after Nirvana.

FORD, Tennessee Ernie (1919-91) *Country singer* Ford combined a career singing COUNTRY and GOSPEL with great success. Originally a DJ in California, where he adopted the name "Tennessee", he signed for Capitol Records in 1949. "Shotgun Boogie" (1950) was the first of many gold records. He is best heard on the album *Country Hits—Feelin' Blue* (1964).

FOREIGNER *Rock group* Foreigner, formed in 1976, epitomized the late 1970s ROCK sound, the so called "adult oriented rock." They had several worldwide hits, such as "Cold As Ice" (1977), "Waiting For a Girl Like You," and "I Want to Know What Love Is" (both 1981).

FORREST, Helen (1918-) *Jazz singer* Forrest's career began in 1938 when she replaced Billie HOLIDAY in Artie Shaw's band. One of the best white singers of the SWING era, she had her greatest hit with Harry JAMES and the song "I Had the Craziest Dream" (1943). During a long career she also sang with Benny GOODMAN and Tommy DORSEY, and made an album *Now and Forever* as recently as 1983.

FOSTER, Frank (1928-) *Jazz musician and writer/arranger* After learning his trade playing sax and arranging music with Count BASIE and Thelonious MONK in the 1950s and early 1960s, Foster went on to write for Sarah VAUGHAN and Frank SINATRA. He is most associated with the JAZZ standard "Shiny Stockings."

FOU TS'ONG (1934-) *Classical pianist* British pianist, but born in China, Fou Ts'ong made debuts in his native China and in London in the 1950s. His delicate, expressive style was particularly suited to Mozart, Chopin, and DEBUSSY.

FOUR TOPS, The *Soul group* With their roots in the Chicago jazz scene, the Four Tops—led by Levi Stubbs—started as backing singers at MOTOWN. After teaming up with the songwriters, Holland, Dozier, Holland, the band's fortunes changed. Hits such as "It's the Same Old Song" (1965), "Reach Out and I'll Be There" (1966), and "Bernadette" (1967) followed, and they continued at the top until the end of the 1960s.

FOURNIER, Pierre (1906-86) *Cellist* French-born Fournier was originally a pianist, but after an attack of polio he took up the cello. Trained in Paris, he developed a unique style across a wide repertoire, including Martin, MARTINU, and POULENC.

FRAMPTON, Peter (1950-) *Rock guitarist* Frampton sang in 1960s groups the Herd and Humble Pie. His subsequent solo career took an upturn in 1976 when, after several years of touring, his album *Frampton Comes Alive* sold 15 million copies—and became the biggest-selling live album ever. His follow-up, *I'm in You*, also did well, but the NEW WAVE of the late 1970s swept him away as quickly as he had arrived.

FRANCIS, Connie (1938-) *Pop singer* Francis was the best-selling female recording artist of the 1950s, with songs such as "Who's Sorry Now," "My Happiness" (both 1958), and "Lipstick on Your Collar" (1959). She also had an acting career and starred in several FILM MUSICALS between 1961 and 1965.

FRANKIE GOES TO HOLLYWOOD *Rock group* Formed in 1980, Frankie Goes to Hollywood created controversial headlines for their behavior as well as their music. They had several hits in a short career, including "Relax" (1983), "Two Tribes," and "The Power of Love" (both 1984).

FREDDIE AND THE DREAMERS *Pop group* Formed in the U.K. in 1961, their biggest hits included "I'm Telling You Now," and "You Were Made For Me" (both 1965). They formed part of the English "Beat Invasion" of the U.S. during the mid-1960s, often touring in a package with several other groups.

FREE *Rock group* Free were formed in 1968, in the midst of a British BLUES boom. Their first album *Tons of Sobs* was released in 1969 and established their reputation. Best known for the single "All Right Now" (1970), their unique BLUES-ROCK music is best heard on the album *Fire and Water* (also 1970).

FRÉMAUX, Louis (1921-) *Conductor* As its musical director between 1956–66, French-born Frémaux made a number of highly successful recordings with the Monte Carlo Orchestra. He also held musical directorships in Lyon, Birmingham, and Sydney.

FRICK, Gottlob (1906-) *Opera singer* German bass Frick began his career in Coburg and Dresden, where he worked until 1952. He then established himself as a Wagnerian bass of international standing. Armed with a large, rich voice, Frick continued to sing around the world until he retired in 1970.

FRICKER, Peter Racine (1920-) *Composer* English-born Fricker's early works, which came in the years immediately following World War II, showed the influence of BARTÓK and SCHOENBERG. Predominantly instrumental, the music was in stark contrast to the folk-song-style music popularized during the war years.

FRIPP, Robert (1946-) *Rock guitarist* A legendary guitar player, Fripp's first and most enduring band was King Crimson. But his most famous record-ings are collaborations with Brian Eno: *No Pussyfooting* (1972) and *Another Green World* (1975); and with David BOWIE, *Heroes* (1977). Not one to pander to commercial demands, Fripp's music continued to develop into the 1990s.

FRISELL, Bill (1951-) *Jazz guitarist* Frisell's guitar playing showed the influence of Wes Montgomery and Jimi HENDRIX. One of the younger breed of JAZZ guitar players, he explored uncharted territory in terms of electric guitar sound.

FRIZELL, Lefty (1928-) *Country singer-songwriter* At the height of his popularity in the 1950s, Frizell had a string of COUNTRY hits, such as "If You've Got the Money, I've Got the Time" and "I Love You A Thousand Ways" (both 1950). A prolific songwriter, Frizell left his legacy on the country-music scene, a big influence on Merle HAGGARD, Randy Travis, and George Strait.

FUGAZI *Rock band* Hailing from Washington, D.C., Fugazi were a hardcore band with an abrasive style. Best heard on the album *Repeater* (1990), the band were most famous for their live shows, attracting a substantial following despite shunning mainstream publicity.

FULSON, Lowell (1921-) *Blues guitarist and singer* Influenced as a youth by COUNTRY and GOSPEL music, Fulson joined Alger Alexander's BLUES band in 1940. His solo career began in 1946, and had several hits on the R&B charts, such as "Reconsider Baby" and "Tramp." His career began to fade in the 1960s as black music moved away from the blues.

FUNKADELIC *Funk band* Centering on George Clinton, Funkadelic started in Detroit in 1969 as a psychedelic SOUL band. The music developed fast, incorporating soul, ROCK, R&B, and JAZZ, emerging with an original FUNK sound. The band's line-up changed regularly, and at one time or another featured Bootsy Collins, Maceo Parker, and Fred Wesley. The band's seminal funk groove sound is best heard on *Maggot Brain* (1970) and their biggest hit "One Nation Under a Groove" (1978).

GABRIEL, Peter (1950-) *Rock musician* Gabriel sang with GENESIS for seven years before going solo in 1975. As a solo artist, he released four albums, all called *Peter Gabriel*, between 1977 and 1982. His biggest hit "Sledgehammer" was released in 1986. A champion of world music, Gabriel was always regarded as a serious artist rather than a POP star.

GAILLARD, Slim (1916-91) *Jazz singer, pianist, and guitarist* Gaillard first achieved success in the 1930s as half of "Slim and Slam" with bassist Slam Stewart. Their radio show, presented in "vout"—a kind of jive talk—was a huge success. His career also encompassed acting, comedy, and cabaret.

GARBAGE *Rock band* Formed in 1993, Garbage found fame through MTV. Their 1996 single "Stupid Girl," was an international hit. The band feature Butch Vig, producer of NIRVANA's classic *Nevermind* album, and singer Shirley Manson from the group Goodbye Mr. McKenzie. Their second album *Version 2* was released to critical acclaim in 1998.

GARDINER, Sir John Elliot (1943-) *Conductor* Born in England, Gardiner studied at Cambridge where he formed the Monteverdi Choir in 1964. He originally established his reputation in the Baroque repertoire and with period instrument ensembles in music by Handel, Gluck, and Mozart. He went on to perform and record all of Beethoven's symphonies, Berlioz's *Symphonie fantastique,* and other major works of the 19th century on replicas—or actual instruments—of the period. He is known for his meticulous attention to the details of the composers' intentions, such as the controversial metronome markings of Beethoven.

GAY, Noel (1898-1954) *Composer and lyricist* In 1937, Gay wrote the most successful British stage musical of the 1930s, *Me and My Girl.* Composer of the music for a number of other shows as well, Gay is mostly remembered for novelty songs, such as "Run Rabbit Run" and "The Sun Has Got Its Hat On."

GAYNOR, Gloria (1947-) *Soul singer* Despite having several DISCO hits, such as "Never Can Say Goodbye" (1974), and "Reach Out and I'll Be There" (1975), Gaynor's 1979 single "I Will Survive" is the song for which she will always be remembered. Its theme of independence in adversity helped it to be adopted as a feminist anthem.

GERRY AND THE PACEMAKERS *Pop group* Part of the Merseybeat boom coming out of Liverpool, England, in the 1960s, Gerry and the Pacemakers vied with the BEATLES for a while as Britain's top group. They had hits with "You'll Never Walk Alone" (1963), "I Like It" (1964), and "Ferry Across the Mersey" (1965).

GIESEKING, Walter (1895-1956) *Pianist* French-born, but of German extraction, Gieseking was admired both in the mainstream repertoire of Mozart and DEBUSSY, and for his playing of SCHOENBERG and Busoni. Gieseking enjoyed worldwide fame in the postwar years for his recordings and his recitals.

GILBERTO, Astrud (1940-) *Jazz singer* Brought along to a session with Stan GETZ by her husband, singer and guitarist, Joao Gilberto, Astrud was persuaded against her will to sing on "The Girl From Ipanema." The resulting single became a worldwide hit. Born in Brazil, Astrud struggled to repeat her surprise success, and remains forever associated with that one song.

GIMBLE, Johnny (1926-) *Country musician* Gimble played fiddle and banjo with the Shelton Brothers and with Bob WILLS during the 1950s. In the 1960s he moved to Nashville and became one of the top COUNTRY session musicians, recording with artists such as Merle HAGGARD.

GINASTERA, Alberto (1916-83) *Composer* Argentine-born Ginastera composed BALLET and modern dance music, and scores expressing Argentine culture and character. His career was highlighted by two OPERAS: *Don Rodrigo* (1964) and *Bomarzo* (1967), which set contemporary problems, like sex and violence, in the tradition of grand opera.

GIUFFRE, Jimmy (1921-) *Jazz musician* Clarinetist, saxophonist, and composer, Giuffre began his career in an army band but was soon working with Buddy Rich (1948) and Woody Herman (1949). During the 1950s and 1960s he became an important figure in avant-garde JAZZ.

GIULINI, Carlo Maria (1914-) *Conductor* Giulini made his debut in Rome in 1944, and was appointed principal conductor at La Scala in Milan in 1953. After concentrating on OPERA for the early part of his career, he turned to the concert repertoire in 1967. He was later associated with the Philharmonia Orchestra in London, the Chicago Symphony Orchestra, and the Los Angeles Philharmonic Orchestra. His most noted skill was with the music of Verdi.

GODOWSKY, Leopold (1870-1938) *Pianist and composer* Born in Poland, Godowsky began touring as a pianist at the age of nine, making his U.S. debut in 1884. He was particularly associated with Chopin, on whose Etudes he wrote a series of studies.

GOEHR, Alexander (1932-) *Composer* English composer of German birth, Goehr studied in Manchester alongside Birtwistle and Maxwell Davies in the 1950s. He wrote ORCHESTRAL MUSIC, as well as vocal works and some CHAMBER MUSIC. He was appointed Head of Composition at Cambridge, England, in 1976 and became an influential teacher.

GO-GO's, The *Rock band* Formed in 1978 in California the all-female Go-Go's hit No.1 with their first album *Beauty and the Beat* (1981), and had hits with singles "Our Lips Are Sealed" (1981) and "We Got the Beat" (1982). Following the group's break-up in 1984, singer Belinda Carlisle pursued a successful solo career.

GOLDIE (1965-) *Jungle DJ and producer* Early 1993 saw Goldie working under the name Metalheads, releasing an EP called *Terminator*. Other releases saw him as unofficial spokesman for the new JUNGLE scene. With his 1995 album *Timeless*, another critical success, Goldie's influence seemed to have enabled jungle to take its place in mainstream dance music.

GOODMAN, Steve (1948-84) *Country singer-songwriter* Though never sustaining commercial success, Goodman had important associations with Kris KRISTOFFERSON, Bob DYLAN, and Emmylou HARRIS. He wrote the classic COUNTRY song "City of New Orleans" (1970), but is best heard on the album *Steve Goodman* (1972).

GOOSSENS, Sir Eugene (1893-1962) *Conductor and composer* British-born Goossens, a member of the famous musical family, is best remembered as the conductor at the U.K. premiere of STRAVINSKY's *The Rite of Spring* in 1921. But his main contribution was his talent for bringing difficult work to the public.

GOOSSENS, Leon (1897-1988) *Oboist* Brother of Eugene, Leon was regarded as the finest oboist of his day. His ability gave the oboe new standing as a solo instrument. BRITTEN, ELGAR, and VAUGHAN WILLIAMS all wrote pieces for him. He also wrote a seminal book on the instrument with Edwin Roxburgh in 1976 entitled *The Oboe*.

GÓRECKI, Henryk Mikolaj (1933-) *Composer* Górecki studied in his native Poland, and in Paris with MESSIAEN. His music—mostly for orchestra and chamber ensemble, and some of the most original in the 20th century—had its roots in ancient Polish sacred music. He achieved great commercial success, particularly with his Symphony No. 3 (1991).

GRAINER, Ron (1922-81) *Musical director and composer* Born in Australia, Grainer wrote music for theater, TV, and film. He is best known for his British television soundtracks, such as *Dr. Who* and *Tales of the Unexpected*.

GRAND FUNK RAILROAD *Rock group* Formed in 1968, Grand Funk had phenomenal success in the early 1970s. Famous for being one of the loudest bands ever heard in concert, they also had some chart success with their brand of HEAVY METAL. Their biggest hits came with "We're an American Band" (1973), "The Loco-Motion," and "Some Kind of Wonderful" (both 1974).

GRANDMASTER FLASH AND THE FURIOUS FIVE *Rap group* From the Bronx, New York, Joseph Saddler (Grandmaster Flash) was a top rank DJ. Teaming up with rappers the Furious Five, he recorded a series of hit singles, such as "The Message" (1982) and "White Lines (Don't Do It)" (1983), the former is regarded as the first RAP record to crossover into the ROCK market.

GRAPPELLI, Stéphane (1908-98) *Jazz violinist* Born in Paris, Grappelli worked with guitarist Django REINHARDT in Quintette du Hot Club de France during the 1930s, and was hailed as one of the first non-American JAZZ giants. But his career really took off in the 1970s when he began performing with classical violinist Yehudi MENUHIN to great acclaim around the world.

GRATEFUL DEAD, The *Rock group* Though strongly linked to the flower power era of the 1960s, the Grateful Dead outlasted all their contemporaries in popularity and reputation, and went into the 1990s as the biggest grossing band in the U.S. Led by guitarist Jerry Garcia until his death in 1995, the Dead produced a host of classic albums and legendary live performances. Best heard on the albums *Live/Dead* (1970), and *Grateful Dead* (1972). The band continued to record and tour in the 1990s as the Other Ones.

GRAVEDIGGAZ *Rap group* An offshoot of the Wu Tang Clan, Gravediggaz developed their own gothic/horror style best heard on their single "Diary of a Madman." They toured in the U.S., and in 1994 released the album *Niggamortis.*

GREEN, Al (1946-) *Soul singer* Possessor of one of the sweetest voices in SOUL music, Green's career took off when he began working with producer Willie Mitchell in Memphis in 1969. "Tired of Being Alone" (1970), "Let's Stay Together," and "I'm Still in Love with You" (both 1972) established his reputation. He is best heard on the album *Call Me* (1973). Green turned to religion in the mid-1970s and his material reflected this new faith.

GRIFFIN, Johnny (1928-) *Tenor saxophonist* Griffin played with Thelonious MONK, Bud POWELL, and with Art BLAKEY's Jazz Messengers in New York during the late 1950s. Renowned for the tone of his playing, he was regarded as one of the fastest sax players ever heard.

GRIFFITH, Nanci (1953-) *Country singer-songwriter* From a musical family, Texas-born Griffith made her first album, *There's a Light Beyond These Woods,* in 1978. Several albums followed, with particular success greeting *Storms* in 1989 and *Other Voices Other Rooms* in 1993. Griffiths' material veered between COUNTRY and FOLK, and she continued to build her reputation and popularity by recording and touring during the 1990s.

GRISMAN, David (1945-) *Country musician and composer* Primarily a bluegrass player, Grisman played mandolin with many artists, such as Emmylou HARRIS, Dolly PARTON, and Jerry Garcia. During the 1970s and 1980s he championed traditional American music, setting up the Acoustic Disc label in 1990.

GROSSMAN, Stefan (1945-) *Folk and blues guitarist* Active on the Greenwich Village FOLK MUSIC scene in New York in the 1960s, Grossman was a virtuoso guitar player. Best heard on the album *Ragtime Cowboy Jew* (1970), Grossman started Kicking Mule Records to take advantage of the folk and BLUES revival at the end of the 1970s.

GROVES, Sir Charles (1915-92) *Conductor* British-born Groves worked with all the major English orchestras. He was a popular conductor, best known for his interpretation of 20th-century choral music.

GUNS N' ROSES *Rock group* This Los Angeles-based HEAVY METAL band had huge commercial success with both albums and singles in the late 1980s. Their first album *Appetite for Destruction*, released in 1987, sold over 17 million copies worldwide. Led by vocalist Axl Rose and guitarist Slash, Guns n' Roses remained in the headlines during the 1990s for their behavior as well as for their music.

GUTHRIE, Arlo (1947-) *Folk rock musician* Son of Woody GUTHRIE, Arlo released his first album in 1967, at the height of the FOLK MUSIC boom. The song "Alice's Restaurant" became a cult hit and established Guthrie's reputation. He remains a popular performer on the folk scene.

HACKETT, Bobby (1915-76) *Jazz cornetist* Hackett worked with Glenn MILLER, Benny GOODMAN, and Tony BENNETT, among others. A highly versatile cornetist, he showed the influence of Louis ARMSTRONG and was a natural successor to Bix BEIDERBECKE. He also played JAZZ guitar.

HADEN, Charlie (1947-) *Jazz double bass player* Closely associated with Ornette COLEMAN and Keith JARRETT, Haden's 1982 album *The Ballad of the Fallen* showcases much of his most important work. Haden was probably the first bassist to apply the freedoms of the avant-garde to his instrument.

HAGGART, Bob (1914-) *Jazz musician* An important figure in the history of NEW ORLEANS JAZZ, Haggart played double bass in the Bob Crosby band and later in the Lawson-Haggart Jazz Band—widely considered to be the best of its kind. He wrote an instructional book on how to play double bass, and in the 1960s jointly led the hugely successful World's Greatest Jazz Band.

HAIG, Al (1924-82) *Jazz pianist* Haig joined Dizzy GILLESPIE's band in 1945. He also had important associations with Stan GETZ, Fats Navarro, and Charlie PARKER. He was a fine accompanist and one of the first pianists to develop an idiomatic BEBOP style.

HALL, Adelaide (1904-) *Jazz singer* Hall's career began in the 1920s, singing in shows and reviews. She recorded with Duke ELLINGTON, Art TATUM, and Fats WALLER in the 1930s, and her best known recording is "Creole Love Call."

HALL & OATES *Rock group* This white SOUL duo—made up of Darryl Hall, vocals, and John Oates, vocals and guitar—made four albums before having a U.S. No.1 with "Rich Girl" in 1977. Playing what was known as "blue-eyed soul," they had a string of huge hits between 1981 and 1985. including "Kiss on My List" and "I Can't Go for That (No Can Do)" (both 1981), and "Maneater" (1982). They are the second most successful rock duo behind the EVERLY BROTHERS. They continued to play into the 1990s.

HALL, Edmond (1901–67) *Jazz clarinetist* Hall first recorded with Eddie Condon and became a member of Louis ARMSTRONG'S All Stars in 1955 (replacing Barney Bigard). He played in a distinctive style reminiscent of Benny GOODMAN.

HALL, Tom T. (1936–) *Country singer-songwriter* Hall began his career as a radio DJ but went on to have COUNTRY No.1 hits both as singer ("A Week in the County Jail") and songwriter ("Harper Valley PTA," a hit for Jeannie C. Riley). He has written four books and hosted the TV show *Pop Goes the Country*.

HALLIDAY, Johnny (1943–) *Pop singer* France's one real ROCK'N'ROLL star, Halliday never had a hit in the U.S. or the U.K., but has sold over 15 million records in Europe. Singing mostly cover versions of songs by American artists, he projected a rebellious image that lasted him well into the 1990s.

HAMBRAEUS, Bengt (1928–) *Composer* Swedish-born Hambraeus studied at DARMSTADT, later becoming professor at McGill University, Montreal. He wrote avant-garde music for organ and many of his works are influenced by medieval and Japanese music.

HAMPTON, Lionel (1909–) *Jazz musician* Hampton played JAZZ vibraphone and drums. From 1936 to 1940 he played with Benny GOODMAN and recorded over 90 tracks in a quartet with Goodman, pianist Teddy Wilson, and drummer Gene Kruper—the greatest talents of the time—producing some of the best records of the SWING era. In 1940 he formed his own big band which became the longest-running jazz orchestra in 1986.

HAPPY MONDAYS, The *Rock group* Indie-dance pioneers, the Happy Mondays' combined ROCK and DANCE

MUSIC to produce the distinctive "Madchester" sound (named after their home town Manchester) that dominated British music in the early 1990s. Their third album *Pills'n'Thrills and Bellyaches* was a U.K. No.1. In 1993, in the face of a poorly received fourth album, the bankruptcy of their record company and the escalating drug problems of members of the band, they split.

HARNONCOURT, Nikolaus (1929–) *Conductor and cellist* Born in Graz in Austria, Harnoncourt studied in Vienna. In 1953 he founded the Vienna Concentus Musicus to perform early music in style and with appropriate instruments. An expert in period performance, he also recorded a wide repertoire including all the Bach Cantatas, Monteverdi, and much Baroque music.

HARPER, Heather (1930–) *Opera singer* British-born soprano Harper made her debuts in the U.K. at the Royal Opera House, Covent Garden, and at Glyndebourne in the 1960s. She also sang at Bayreuth and has been particularly associated with the music of Benjamin BRITTEN.

HARRIS, Wynonie (1915–69) *Blues singer* Harris sang with the Luck Millinder Big Band. In 1945 he began a solo career that produced a number of R&B hits—including "Good Rockin' Tonight." Harris was the only serious rival of Big Joe Turner in R&B, and his BLUES-shouter style and lascivious stage moves influenced many ROCK'N'ROLL artists.

HARRISON, George (1943–) *Rock musician* In the early 1970s Harrison was one of the most successful ex-BEATLES, producing two No.1 hits: "My Sweet Lord" (1970) and "Give Me Love" (1973); two successful albums: *All Things Must Pass* (1970) and *Living in the Material World* (1973); and organizing the benefit gig *Concert for Bangladesh* (1971). However, his creative momentum failed in the mid-1970s, only returning in the late 1980s with the Traveling Wilburys—a supergroup consisting of Bob DYLAN, Roy Orbison, Tom Petty, Harrison, and Jeff Lynne; and with another No.1 single "Got My Mind Set on You" (1987).

HARTFORD, John (1937–) *Country musician* Hartford played a range of instruments, but is best remembered as the composer of the song "Gentle on My Mind," which was recorded by many singers including Glen Campbell, Frank SINATRA, and Elvis PRESLEY.

HARTY, Sir Hamilton (1879–1941) *Composer and conductor* Born in Ireland, Harty conducted the London Symphony Orchestra and the Hallé Orchestra giving many British premieres, notably of STRAUSS and MAHLER. His compositions include the *Irish symphony*, a violin concerto, and CHAMBER and VOCAL works.

HARVEY, Jonathan (1939–) *Composer* Harvey studied with Hans Keller and Milton Babbitt. His music shows the influence of BRITTEN and STOCKHAUSEN, and later works made extensive use of electronics, for example, *Madonna of Winter and Spring* (1986).

HARVEY, P.J. (1970–) *Rock singer* British-born Polly Jean Harvey attracted considerable attention with her intensely personal debut album *Dry* (1992). Two further albums have followed—*Rid of Me* (1993) and *To Bring You My Love* (1995)—both released to critical acclaim.

HASKIL, Clara (1895-1960) *Pianist* Romanian-born Haskil studied in Vienna and Paris. She played recitals and recorded with CASALS and Grumiaux. A brilliant concert pianist, despite her small size and apparent ill-health, she was particularly admired for her performances of Mozart, Schubert, and Beethoven.

HAVENS, Richie (1941–) *Rock singer-songwriter* New York-born Havens has his musical roots in GOSPEL and DOO-WOP. He was a regular in the folk clubs of Greenwich Village. He gained his reputation with a mixture of his own songs and excellent cover versions—a pattern established on his third album *Mixed Bag* (1967). Havens' finest three hours came with his performance at the Woodstock festival in 1969. His final song "Freedom" brilliantly captured on film in D.A. Pennabaker's documentary of the famous rock festival.

HAWKINS, Screamin' Jay (1929-) *Rock singer* In 1956 Hawkins had phenomenal success with the single "I Put a Spell on You." Hawkins's notoriety and the disturbing sound of the track ensured it sold a million copies—although it never made it onto the *Billboard* charts. Hawkins' live shows involved snakes and skulls, combining tongue-in-cheek horror with ROCK'N'ROLL. However, his career progressed in fits and starts and his influence on artists like Alice Cooper and Ozzy Osbourne far outstripped his record sales.

HAYES, Isaac (1942-) *Blues and soul singer-songwriter* Hayes began his career writing songs for artists such as Otis REDDING and Sam & Dave. Between 1967–73, Hayes recorded 7 albums containing largely instrumentals that often lasted over ten minutes—including his classic reworking of "The Look of Love." In 1971 he wrote the score for *Shaft*, and the single of the theme tune became a No.1 hit in the U.S. Although Hayes went out of fashion in the late 1970s his work was rediscovered in the late 1980s.

HEATH, Percy (1923-) *Jazz double bass player* A superb bass player, Heath worked with Miles DAVIS, Dizzy GILLESPIE, and Charlie PARKER and was a founding member of the MODERN JAZZ QUARTET.

HEFTI, Neal (1922-) *Jazz composer* Hefti began his career as a trumpeter but was soon arranging for Woody Herman. He wrote for Charlie PARKER and Count BASIE, and by the late 1950s was working full-time writing film scores and music for TV.

HENDRICKS, Barbara (1948-) *Opera singer* American soprano Hendricks made her debut in San Francisco in 1974. She gained an international reputation for Mozart roles such as Susanna and Pamina, and for Verdi's Nannetta and Gilda.

HENEKER, David (1906-) *Composer and lyricist* Heneker had his first hit with *There Goes My Dream* in 1940. He also had success with several MUSICALS both in London and on Broadway, in particular *Half a Sixpence* and *Charlie Girl*.

HEPTONES *Reggae group* The Heptones were the definitive rocksteady and REGGAE trio, leading the way for Jamaican harmony groups. Led by bassist and vocalist Leroy Sibbles, they made their most successful album, *Party Time*, with Lee Perry producing, in 1976.

HERMAN, Woody (1913-87) *Jazz musician* Herman worked as bandleader, clarinetist, alto saxophonist, and singer. His band Herman's Herd was internationally known and featured artists such as Stan GETZ. Herman's Herd evolved over 50 years, constantly updating its sound—for example, acknowledging the influence of HARD BOP—without forgetting its early roots.

HERMAN'S HERMITS *Pop band* Formed in Manchester, England, in 1963, Herman's Hermits had a U.K. No.1 in 1964 with "I'm into Something Good." Other hits included "Mrs. Brown, You've Got a Lovely Daughter" and "I'm Henry VIII, I Am," both of which reached No.1 in the U.S.

HESS, Dame Myra (1890-1965) *Pianist* English pianist, Dame Myra Hess, was admired for her playing of Mozart, Beethoven, and Schumann. She wrote a famous arrangement of Bach's *Jesu, Joy of Man's Desiring*. She arranged wartime recitals in London's National Gallery, during a time when all concert halls were closed, as part of the war effort.

HEYWOOD, Eddie (1915-) *Jazz musician and composer* Heywood began as a pianist, forming his own sextet which recorded classic tracks with Billie HOLIDAY, Ella FITZGERALD, and Bing CROSBY. After a bout of illness Heywood began to concentrate on orchestration and composing. He wrote several big hits, including "Canadian Sunset," "Land of Dreams," and "Soft Summer Breeze."

HILLER, Lejaren (1924-) *Composer* American composer Hiller studied with Sessions and Babbitt. He was one of the first to use computers in composition, such as on *Illiac Suite* (1957). He also lectured extensively and wrote articles on computer music.

HINES, Earl (1903-83) *Jazz pianist and bandleader* Hines was one of the greatest classic JAZZ pianists, perhaps only bettered by Art TATUM. In the 1920s he was a close associate of Louis ARMSTRONG. In 1928 he formed his own band which lasted 20 years. In the 1960s his career reached new heights and he spent the rest of his life touring worldwide.

HODES, Art (1904-) *Jazz pianist* Born in the Ukraine, Hodes played as a soloist in Chicago in the late 1920s. In 1938 he moved to New York where he formed his own band in 1941. Hodes was also a DJ, edited *The Jazz Record*, hosted a TV series— one of his programs won an Emmy— and was a pioneering lecturer in JAZZ at schools and colleges.

HOFFNUNG, Gerard (1925-59) *Tuba player and humorist* A refugee from Nazi Germany, Hoffnung is remembered for his comedy illustrations of singers and instrumentalists. He also created the short-lived but successful Hoffnung Music Festival in London in 1956 for which composers wrote humorous works.

HOGWOOD, Christopher (1941-) *Harpsichordist and conductor* Hogwood studied with harpsichordist Gustav Leonhardt and worked with David Munrow, before founding the Academy of Ancient Music. He is widely known as a conductor and harpsichordist and has written books on Handel and the *Trio Sonata* (1979).

HOLLAND/DOZIER/HOLLAND *Composing and production team* Legendary MOTOWN songwriting and production team Brian Holland, Lamont Dozier, and Eddie Holland made their production debut with the Marvelettes' "Locking Up My Heart" in 1963. They went on to achieve huge success both for Motown and for themselves with the Isley Brothers: "This Old Heart of Mine"; the Four Tops: "(It's the) Same Old Song"; and in particular Diana ROSS and the Supremes, for whom they wrote a succession of chart toppers, including "Where Did Our Love Go," "You Can't Hurry Love," and "You Keep Me Hangin' On." They left Motown in 1967 to form their own Invictus and Hot Wax labels.

HOLLIES, The *Pop group* Rivaling even the BEATLES and the ROLLING STONES for popularity at one time, the Hollies had a succession of chart hits between 1966 and 1974, including "Bus Stop" (1966), "Carrie-Anne" (1967), and "He Ain't Heavy, He's My Brother" (1970). Singer and founder member Graham Nash left in 1968 to join Crosby, Stills and Nash.

HOLLIGER, Heinz (1939-) *Oboist and composer* Swiss-born Holliger achieved an international reputation for his large repertoire including contemporary music. His compositions showed the influence of BOULEZ, with whom he studied.

HOLMBOE, Vagn (1909-) *Composer* Holmboe studied in his native Denmark and Berlin. He has written symphonies, string quartets, OPERAS, and CHAMBER MUSIC in a style influenced by NIELSEN and STRAVINSKY.

HONEGGER, Arthur (1892-1955) *Composer* A member of LES SIX, Swiss-born Honegger wrote symphonies, CHAMBER MUSIC, and incidental music, as well as two large-scale oratorios, *Le roi David* and *Jeanne d'Arc au Bûcher*.

HORNE, Marilyn (1934-) *Opera singer* American mezzo-soprano Horne made her debut in Los Angeles in 1954. She had great success in the roles of Carmen in 1972 and Handel's Rinaldo in 1975. She was particularly admired for performing the work of Rossini and Bellini, often appearing with Dame Joan SUTHERLAND.

HORTON, Johnny (1925-60) *Country singer* Horton first achieved fame with COUNTRY hits such as "All Grown Up" and "Honky Tonk Hardwood Floor." From 1959 he recorded story songs such as "When It's Springtime in Alaska" and the title song of the John Wayne film *North to Alaska*.

HORTON, Walter "Shakey" (1918-81) *Jazz and blues musician* Known also as "Big Walter" and "Mumbles," Horton played harmonica on recordings with Buddy Doyle, Muddy WATERS, and Jimmie RODGERS, handling his instrument with remarkable skill.

HOTTER, Hans (1909-) *Opera singer* German-born Hans Hotter took part in the premieres of several OPERAS by Richard STRAUSS, but is principally remembered for his interpretation of the great bass-baritone roles of Wagner, in particular Wotan.

HOVHANESS, Alan (1911-) *Composer* Of Armenian and Scottish descent, Hovhaness wrote religiously inspired music drawing on Armenian and Far Eastern influences. His output includes ORCHESTRAL, CHAMBER MUSIC, and VOCAL AND CHORAL MUSIC.

HOWARTH, Elgar (1935-) *Conductor, trumpeter, and composer* Howarth played in the Royal Philharmonic Orchestra and the Philip Jones Brass Ensemble. He conducted a number of important premieres at London's Covent Garden, such as *Gawain* by Harrison Birtwistle. His own compositions were mainly for brass instruments. He was part of the "Manchester School" with Peter Maxwell Davies, Birtwistle, and Alexander Goehr.

HOWELL, Peg Leg (1888-1966) *Blues singer* Howell's BLUES vocal style was a mixture of street vendors' cries, fragments of narrative ballads and gamblers' slang. He worked with guitarist Henry Williams and fiddler Eddie Anthony.

HOWLIN' WOLF (1910-76) *Blues singer* Born Chester Burnett, Howlin' Wolf developed his BLUES style into what was known as the Chicago Sound of the 1950s. A Chess Records artist, Wolf played guitar and harmonica and sang on classics such as "Smokestack Lightning," "Killing Floor," and "Little Red Rooster."

HUMES, Helen (1913-81) *Jazz and blues singer* Humes replaced Billie HOLIDAY in Count BASIE's orchestra in 1938. She later had hits with "Be-ba-ba-le-ba" and "Million Dollar Secret," and toured with Red Norvo.

HUNTER, Alberta (1895-1984) *Blues singer* Hunter sang with Louis ARMSTRONG, Fats WALLER, and Sydney Bechet in New York. She also wrote "Downhearted Blues" in 1923—a hit for Bessie SMITH. In 1934 she appeared in the film *Radio Parade*.

HUNTER, Rita (1933-) *Opera singer* Hunter studied with Eva Turner and had her greatest success as Brünnhilde in the English National Opera's production of *The Ring* in London in 1970. During her international career she was renowned for her interpretation of Wagner, and Bellini's Norma.

HURT, Mississippi John (1894-1966) *Blues singer and guitarist* Hurt made a number of traditional ragtime recordings in the late 1920s, such as "Frankie" and "Stack O'Lee Blues." After 1928 he took a 35 year break from music and worked on a farm. Prompted by a BLUES fan, Hurt returned to music in 1963, rerecording old songs as well as new material, and influencing a whole new generation of blues singers.

HÜSKER DÜ *Rock group* Formed in Minneapolis in 1979, Hüsker Dü were an influential PUNK ROCK trio—precursors to the 1990s GRUNGE scene. Their early output was ferociously hardcore but their best albums, *Candy Apple Grey* (1986) and *Warehouse: Songs and Stories* (1987) revealed a more melodic, but still powerful approach. The band split in 1987 when Bob Mould went on to form Sugar, and Grant Hart formed Nova Mob.

IBERT, Jacques (1890-1962) *Composer* Ibert studied in Paris and wrote in a light impressionistic style recalling DEBUSSY and POULENC. His most notable works are his string quartet of 1942 and *Divertimento* of 1930.

IBRAHIM, Abdullah (1934-) *Jazz pianist and composer* Also known as Dollar Brand, Ibrahim formed his first band, the Jazz Epistles, in 1961, but the next year he left his native South Africa. After hearing him play, Duke ELLINGTON arranged for him to appear at the Newport Jazz Festival in 1965. During the late 1960s Ibrahim became involved in the FREE JAZZ scene. However, his best music came after he had rejected free jazz and rediscovered his African roots. In 1982 Ibrahim produced *Kalahari Liberation Opera*, a multimedia collage of dance, drama, and music. During the 1990s Ibrahim was spending more time in his native South Africa.

ICE T (1958-) *Rapper* West Coast rapper Ice T, made his first record "The Coldest Rapper" in 1983, but it was with "Ya Don't Know" that his reputation began to be established. One of the original gangsta rappers, Ice T is a controversial figure—sparking public outrage with his song "Cop Killer." Apart from his RAP albums, he has also made forays into HEAVY METAL with the band Bodycount.

IDOL, Billy (1955-) *Rock singer* Inspired by the example of the SEX PISTOLS, Billy Idol formed his own PUNK group Generation X. Moving to America, he began a solo career in 1981. His single "Mony Mony" went to No.1 in both the U.S. and U.K. charts, and his album *Rebel Yell* (1984) reached No.6 in the U.S. His 1990 album *Charmed Life* was perhaps his best—certainly the most expensive, costing $1.5 million—but it failed to equal his previous successes.

IFIELD, Frank (1937-) *Pop singer* One of the most successful pop artists of the 1960s, Ifield had three consecutive U.K. No.1 records in 1963. In the 1970s he appeared regularly in stage shows, before concentrating on COUNTRY music and touring the U.S. and Australia.

IGLESIAS, Julio (1943-) *Pop singer* Spanish singer Iglesias had international success with "Manuela" and "Hey" in the 1970s and with "Begin the Beguine" which topped the U.K. charts in 1981. The album *Julio* sold over a million copies, and his next album featured duets with Willie NELSON and Diana ROSS.

IMBRIE, Andrew (1921-) *Composer* Imbrie studied with Roger Sessions whose influence can be heard in his symphonies, concertos, and quartets. His OPERA *Angle of Repose* (1976) shows a fusion of American FOLK MUSIC with atonality.

INXS *Rock group* Formed in Australia in 1977, INXS developed a style bringing together characteristics of African-American DANCE MUSIC and white SOUL. Their fourth album *The Swing* gained them international recognition and success followed with their next two albums, *Listen Like Thieves*

(1985) and *Kick* (1987). In 1988 the band swept the board at the MTV awards. INXS continued to be successful until the untimely death of lead singer Michael Hutchence in 1997.

IRELAND, John (1879-1962) *Composer* Ireland studied at the Royal College of Music in London with Sir Charles Stanford and was influenced by DEBUSSY, RAVEL, and STRAVINSKY. His best known works are the symphonic rhapsody *Mai-Dun* (1920) and the piano concerto of 1930.

ISAACS, Gregory (1951-) *Reggae singer* Dubbed the "Cool Ruler," by 1980 Isaacs was the biggest star in REGGAE, touring widely in the U.S. and U.K. at the time. A prolific songwriter, Isaacs has produced hundreds of singles and albums during his career, featuring his unique cool vocal delivery. He is best heard on the albums *Soon Forward* (1979), *Night Nurse* (1982), and *Out Deh!* (1983).

ISLEY BROTHERS, The *Rock and R&B band* An incredibly eclectic group, the Isley Brothers, from Cincinnati, mixed R&B, SOUL, GOSPEL, and ROCK'N'ROLL. In 1959 they wrote and recorded their first hit "Shout," and in 1962 they had their first Top 20 hit with "Twist and Shout"—later a huge hit for the BEATLES. In the 1960s the Isley Brothers signed to MOTOWN but this association was largely unsuccessful. They had two further Top 10 hits with "That Lady" (1973) and "Fight The Power" (1975), and continued to perform and record into the 1990s.

IVES, Burl (1909-95) *Folk singer and actor* Illinois-born Ives appeared in Broadway shows and had his own radio program *Wayfaring Stranger*. His first chart success came in 1948, singing with the ANDREWS SISTERS on "Blue Tail Fly." He continued to be successful in the U.S. charts throughout the 1950s and early 1960s.

JACKSON 5 *Soul group* Made up of five brothers, with Michael JACKSON, the youngest, singing lead vocals, the Jackson 5 won numerous talent contests before signing to MOTOWN in 1968. In 1970 their first four singles— "I Want You Back," "ABC," "The Love You Save," and "I'll Be There"—all

topped the U.S. charts. They were the subject of an American cartoon series and hosted their own TV show. However, as Michael Jackson's solo career took off, the rest of the Jacksons were increasingly eclipsed.

JACKSON, Benjamin "Bull Moose" (1919-89) *Jazz musician* Jackson played alto and tenor saxophone with Freddie Webster's Harlem Hotshots. He later played tenor saxophone for Lucky Millinder and had hits with "I Love You, Yes I Do" and "All My Love Belongs to You."

JACKSON, Chuck (1937-) *Soul singer* Jackson sang on the Dell Vikings' Top 10 hit "Whispering Bells." His uptown SOUL style can be heard on "Something You Got" with Maxine Brown (1965), and Freddie Scott's "Are You Lonely for Me Baby?" (1967).

JACKSON, Janet (1966-) *Pop singer* Janet Jackson, sister of Michael JACKSON, had an early career as a TV actress. She made her breakthrough with her third album *Control*— produced by dance music producers Jimmy Jam and Terry Lewis. Her next album, *Janet Jackson's Rhythm Nation 1814* (1989) produced seven Top 5 singles, including four No.1s, and earned her a Grammy. Her next album *Janet* went straight to No.1 in the U.S. in 1993. In 1995 Jackson renegotiated her contract with Virgin securing $80 million and the most lucrative contract in recording history.

JACKSON, Milt "Bags" (1923-) *Jazz vibraphonist* "Bags" Jackson played the vibraphone in BEBOP style and was one of the finest performers ever heard on this instrument. He played with Dizzy GILLESPIE, Thelonious MONK, and Woody Herman, and was a member of the MODERN JAZZ QUARTET. His harmonic-based improvisations and instantly recognizable tone made him one of the most popular modern JAZZ musicians.

JACQUET, Illinois (1922-) *Tenor saxophonist* Jacquet played with Floyd Ray and Lionel Hampton before working with Count BASIE and with Norman GRANZ's Jazz at the Philharmonic. He began a new style in saxophone playing—the "Texas tenor style"—managing to combine the toughness of the best BLUES players with the harmonic mobility of men like Buddy Tate.

JAGGER, Mick (1943-) *Rock singer* With his exaggerated posturing and energetic stage performances, Jagger, lead singer of the ROLLING STONES, virtually invented the modern rock star persona. He was also responsible for many of the group's lyrics, including "I Can't Get No Satisfaction." In 1985 Jagger finally launched his solo career with the album *She's the Boss*, which reached No.13 in the U.S. Since then he has released two solo albums with moderate success.

JAM, The *Rock band* Emerging from the PUNK movement and strongly influenced by R&B, THE WHO and the BEATLES, the Jam's first U.K. chart success came with the single "All Around the World" closely followed by "Down in the Tube Station at Midnight" in 1978. In the early 1980s they had several U.K. No.1 records and attracted a fanatical following for their electric live performances, but they failed to make a major impression in the U.S.

JAMES, Elmore (1918-63) *Blues singer and guitarist* James is best remembered for the song "Dust My Broom" on which he sings and plays slide guitar, but he was also a great influence on other BLUES players, including B.B. KING. During the 1950s James and his backing group, the Broomdusters, had a number of R&B hits. He also wrote songs that were recorded by Jimi HENDRIX, Duane Allman of the Allman Brothers, and Fleetwood Mac.

JAMES, Etta (1938-) *R&B singer* James was discovered by Johnny Otis with whom she toured in the 1950s. She had hits in the 1960s with "All I Could Do Was Cry" and "Something's Got a Hold on Me." She continued to perform in the 1990s.

JAMES, Rick (1948-) *Soul singer* Inspired by George Clinton, James developed an overtly sexualized style of music he called "funk'n'roll," and had a number of successes in the late 1970s and early 1980s, including

"Give It to Me Baby," which topped the R&B charts for five weeks, and "Super Freak (Pt. 1)." James also produced other artists, including the Stone City Band, Teena Marie, and Eddie Murphy.

JAMES, Skip (1902-69) *Blues singer and guitarist* James was one of the finest COUNTRY-BLUES performers of all time. His best known songs are "Skip James Today," "Devil Got My Woman," and "I'm So Glad," which was later recorded by CREAM. In 1942 he became a baptist minister.

JAMIROQUAI *Funk group* Jamiroquai, the creation of vocalist Jason Kay, is one of the leading acid jazz bands in the U.K. In 1993 they had their first hit with "Too Young to Die," which reached the U.K. Top 10. They have had two hit albums, *Emergency on Planet Earth* (1993) and *Return of the Space Cowboy* (1994), showcasing their brand of hip-hop rhythms coupled with an essentially acid jazz/FUNK approach. In 1998 they recorded "Deeper Underground," the theme song to the movie *Godzilla*.

JAN AND DEAN *Pop duo* Jan Berry and Dean Torrence had only intermittent success until they became involved in the California SURF MUSIC scene in 1963. That year they had their first No.1 hit with "Surf City," co-written with BEACH BOYS leader Brian Wilson. The Beach Boys contributed to other Jan and Dean hits and Dean Torrence—although uncredited—sang lead vocals on the Beach Boys' "Barbara Ann." Jan Berry was seriously injured in a car crash in 1966 and the duo's success faded.

JANE'S ADDICTION *Rock band* Jane's Addiction was formed by Perry Farrell in 1986 to pursue his personal vision of ROCK as art. Their three albums were well received by the critics, but only the last, *Ritual De Lo Habitual* (1990), was a commercial success—reaching the U.S. Top 20. The band remained controversial to the end: their first manager had been a prostitute who greeted the audience topless, while the artwork for their last album was banned from several chain stores. Jane's Addiction split in 1992, following the successful Lollapalooza tour.

JARREAU, Al (1940-) *Soul singer* With a highly individual style showing a variety of influences, Jarreau has made several successful albums, including *Glow* (1976) and *Breaking Away* (1981). Elements of JAZZ, AFRICAN, and Asian music can all be heard in his scat singing and he has won Grammys for his performances in JAZZ, R&B, and POP MUSIC.

JEFFERSON AIRPLANE *Rock group* Jefferson Airplane formed in San Francisco in 1965. The following year they were joined by vocalist and songwriter Grace Slick. "White Rabbit" and "Somebody to Love," from their debut album *Surrealistic Pillow* (1967), both became Top 10 hits. After several albums and successful festival appearances—including Woodstock—the band changed personnel and direction. Renamed Jefferson Starship, they had a number of hits in the same vein as Fleetwood Mac during the 1970s. In 1985 Jefferson Starship became Starship, scoring still more hits with songs such as "We Built This City on Rock and Roll" (1985).

JETHRO TULL *Rock band* Formed in the U.K. in 1967, Jethro Tull gained a reputation for their compelling live shows largely due to the performances of frontman, singer/flautist Ian Anderson. Beginning as a BLUES band, Jethro Tull became one of the more important PROGRESSIVE ROCK bands. The hugley successful *Aqualung* (1971) was the best of their albums.

JOAN JETT AND THE BLACKHEARTS *Rock band* Philadelphia-born Joan Larkin formed Joan Jett and the Blackhearts after the split of all-girl glitter-PUNK band the Runaways. Specializing in powerful, uncomplicated ROCK, they had a U.S. No.1 with "I Love Rock'n'Roll" in 1982. Jett continued to record and made two film appearances. She remains something of a figurehead to female rockers.

JOACHIM, Joseph (1831-1907) *Violinist and composer* Joachim led Liszt's orchestra and gave important performances of Schumann and Brahms. He founded a string quartet, composed violin music, and was a highly influential teacher.

JOCHUM, Eugen (1902-87) *Conductor* Jochum conducted in Munich and in Berlin with the Radio Orchestra and the Philharmonic. He was particularly admired for his interpretation of Bruckner's symphonies.

JOEL, Billy (1949-) *Rock musician* Joel was a classically trained pianist. However, it is in the world of ROCK MUSIC that Joel has made his mark—becoming a major star in the 1980s. He first came to prominence with *The Stranger* (1978), which hit No.2 on the charts—becoming Columbia Records' second biggest-selling album ever. A string of hit singles followed, including the No.1 hit "My Life" (1978) and the pop classic "Uptown Girl" (1983).

JOHNSON, Bunk (1889-1949) *Jazz trumpeter* Johnson played in a number of New Orleans' bands. In 1931 bandleader Evan Thomas was stabbed to death as he played alongside Johnson. Following this event Johnson virtually retired, until he was rediscovered by Frederick Ramsey and William Russell in 1939. He made a comeback in the 1940s leading his own bands, playing with Sidney Bechet, and becoming a crucial figure in the JAZZ revival.

JOHNSON, J.J. (1924-) *Jazz trombonist and composer* Johnson played with Count BASIE in New York and with Charlie PARKER and Dizzy GILLESPIE, adapting the BEBOP style to the trombone. He later worked with Miles DAVIS, before forming his own quartet and sextet. In 1970 he moved to Los Angeles to score film and TV background music, and after that made only occasional appearances as a performer.

JOHNSON, James P. (1894-1955) *Jazz pianist and composer* Johnson recorded a number of his own compositions in the 1920s including "Carolina Shout" and "Keep Off the Grass," as well as recording with other artists, such as Bessie SMITH. In 1923 he composed the score for the Broadway show *Running Wild,* and in the 1930s he wrote a symphony as well as various pieces for the stage. Johnson has been called the "father of stride piano" because he was Fats WALLER's teacher.

JOHNSON, Pete (1904-67) *Jazz pianist* U.S. born, Johnson worked as a soloist in clubs throughout the 1930s and played in the 1938 Carnegie Hall concert "From Spirituals to Swing." He was a member of the Boogie Woogie Trio and later toured with Art TATUM and Erroll GARNER.

JOLAS, Betsy (1926-) *Composer* Born in France, Jolas studied with MESSIAEN and MILHAUD, and wrote music mainly for small groups, in a style similar to BOULEZ. Her major compositions include *Quatuor II* (1964), *Musique d'hiver* (1971) for organ and orchestra, and *D'un opéra de poupée en sept musiques* (1982) for modern electric and traditional wind instruments.

JOLIVET, André (1905-74) *Composer* Deeply influenced by his teacher VARÈSE, French-born Jolivet was an exotic orchestrator. He also wrote incidental music, ballets, choral works, and songs. His music is best illustrated by the piece *Mana* (1935), written for piano, and *Danse incantatoire* (1936), written for orchestra.

JONES, George (1931-) *Country singer-songwriter* Influenced by Roy ACUFF and Hank WILLIAMS, Jones developed a distinctive style in the 1950s. He sang at the Louisiana Hayride and in a highly successful partnership with his one-time wife Tammy WYNETTE, becoming one of the most successful COUNTRY singers of his generation.

JONES, Grace (1952-) *Soul singer* A former model, Jones first achieved commercial success with her 1980 album *Warm Leatherette,* which combined elements of ROCK, REGGAE, and FUNK. A more melodic approach became evident on the 1982 release *Living My Life.* Jones is as famous for her carefully constructed, androgynous image and unpredictable persona as for her music.

JONES, Dame Gwyneth (1936-) *Opera singer* One of the finest dramatic sopranos of her generation, Dame Gwyneth sang Sieglinde at London's Covent Garden in 1965, going on to sing all the Wagner heroines internationally—notably Brünnhilde in the 1976 Bayreuth Festival. She also performed as a compelling Turandot.

JONES, Hank (1918-) *Jazz pianist* Elder brother of Thad and Elvin JONES, Hank Jones was also founder of the Detroit "school" of pianists. He worked with Billy Eckstine and in Norman GRANZ's Jazz at the Philharmonic concerts, before becoming Ella FITZGERALD's accompanist from 1948–53. He was pianist and conductor for the Broadway show *Ain't Misbehavin',* and became a member of the Great Jazz Trio.

JONES, Jo (1911-85) *Jazz drummer* Alabama-born Jones had a long association with Count BASIE, providing the backbone for his superlative All-American Rhythm Section. Later, Jones worked with Duke ELLINGTON, Billie HOLIDAY, and Benny GOODMAN. He was highly influential in all aspects of JAZZ percussion playing, laying the foundations for modern jazz drumming.

JONES, Philly Joe (1923-85) *Jazz drummer* Born in Philadelphia, Jones played with Dizzy GILLESPIE and Charlie PARKER, and later in New York with Miles DAVIS' quintet. Forever associated with the classic Davis quintet, Jones not only masterminded its rhythm section but also created its distinctive sound. Later he led the group Dameronia—dedicated to performing the works of Tadd Dameron.

JONES, Thad (1923-86) *Jazz musician* Brother of Hank and Elvin Jones, Thad played cornet and flugelhorn in addition to composing. He played with Charles MINGUS and Count BASIE before forming an 18-piece band with drummer Mel Lewis in 1965. He formed the Thad Jones Eclipse in 1979 in Denmark, but returned to the U.S. in 1985 to lead the Count Basie Orchestra. His accomplished playing has largely been overshadowed by his reputation as an ARRANGER and composer.

JOPLIN, Janis (1943-70) *Blues and rock singer* In 1966 Janis joined Big Brother and the Holding Company. Her highly individual BLUES style vocals powered their one successful album, *Cheap Thrills* (1968), which stayed at the top of the U.S. charts for eight weeks. She later formed the Kozmic Blues Band and the Full Tilt Boogie Band, with whom she recorded the posthumously released No.1 hit single "Me and Bobbie McGee" and the album *Pearl* (both 1971). Joplin had died of a heroin overdose in 1970.

JORDAN, Louis (1908-75) *Jazz musician* Saxophonist, singer, and bandleader, Jordan formed his own group the Tympany Five in New York in 1938, having worked with artists such as Fats WALLER and Kaiser Marshall. He appeared in several films, composed many songs—including "Five Guys Named Moe" and "Is You Is, or Is You Ain't (Ma Baby)?"— and recorded duets with Bing CROSBY, Ella FITZGERALD, and Louis ARMSTRONG. His music is generally considered to have been an important influence on ROCK'N'ROLL.

JORDAN, Stanley (1959-) *Jazz guitarist* Jordan played at numerous JAZZ festivals and recorded solo albums, the second of which, *The Magic Touch* (1985), was a huge commercial success. He brought an entirely new approach to electric guitar playing, even devising his own tuning system. However, his choice of what to play has been relatively limited and later releases were regarded as disappointing.

JOY DIVISION *Rock group* In their two years of existence, U.K. band Joy Division emerged as one of the most brilliant of their era. Their first album, *Unknown Pleasures* (1979), released on Manchester's Factory record label, quickly attracted a large cult following but they are best heard on the follow-up, *Closer* (1980). In May 1980 vocalist Ian Curtis killed himself. One month later, they scored their biggest hit with the single, "Love Will Tear Us Apart." The remaining members of Joy Division formed New Order— achieving a great deal of success in the 1980s and 1990s.

JUDDS, The *Country duo* During the 1980s, mother and daughter duo Naomi and Wynonna Judd made million-selling albums such as *Rockin' with the Rhythm of the Rain,* and recorded with Emmylou HARRIS and Mark Knopfler. In 1990 Wynonna began a solo career with a magnificent first album, *Wynonna.*

KAEMPFERT, Burt (1923-80) *Composer and orchestra leader* Born and educated in Germany, Kaempfert formed his own orchestra in the 1950s. He had success as a writer as well as an arranger, his biggest hits being "Wooden Heart," which was sung by Elvis PRESLEY in the film *G.I. Blues* (1961), and "Strangers in the Night," which became a million-selling hit for Frank SINATRA (1966).

KAMINSKY, Max (1908-) *Jazz trumpeter* Kaminsky played with Tommy DORSEY and Artie Shaw before arriving in New York, where he played the Carnegie Hall with Eddie Condon. A master of the straight lead—an elusive Dixieland art—his style recalled Louis ARMSTRONG and King Oliver.

KANG, Dong-Suk (1954-) *Violinist* Korean-born Dong-Suk Kang studied in New York. He toured internationally, playing with many of the world's finest orchestras and recording several concertos, including those by SIBELIUS, NIELSEN, and ELGAR.

KARR, Gary (1941-) *Double bass player* Los Angeles-born Karr made his New York debut in 1962. He founded the International Institute for the String Bass in 1967. A great champion of his instrument, Karr has commissioned pieces and given many premieres, such as the double-bass concerto by HENZE. His most famous recording is of Paganini's "Moses" Fantasy.

KATCHEN, Julius (1926-69) *Pianist* American-born Katchen was 11 years old when he made his debut with the Philadelphia Orchestra. He was particularly noted for his interpretations of Mozart, Beethoven, and Brahms. A lover of French music, he lived in Paris for most of his life.

KAYE, Danny (1913-87) *Singer, dancer, comedian, and actor* Kaye appeared in *Straw Hat Revue* on Broadway in 1939 and later in other Broadway shows by Cole PORTER and Ira Gershwin. His film appearances included *The Secret Life of Walter Mitty* (1947) and the MUSICAL *Hans Christian Andersen* (1953).

K.C. AND THE SUNSHINE BAND *R&B dance band* Formed in Florida they had U.K. and U.S. hits such as "Get Down Tonight" and three consecutive No.1s all in a dance-FUNK style. Specializing in party-type R&B, K.C. and the Sunshine Band continued to perform in the 1990s, although their chart success ended in the mid-1980s.

KEITA, Salif (1949-) *Vocalist-composer* Born in Mali, of royal parents, Keita played with the Rail Band and later Les Ambassadeurs, with whom he made three albums. As a soloist he has made several albums, notably *Soro* (1982) and *Ko Yan* (1986). His music is a synthesis of ROCK, electronics, Western music, and traditional African elements.

KELLY, Gene (1912-96) *Actor, singer, dancer, and choreographer* Best known for his performances in films such as *On the Town* and *Singin' in the Rain.* Kelly introduced BALLET sequences into FILM MUSICALS—most notably using GERSHWIN's music to create extended dance sequences for the film *An American in Paris.* In 1960 he directed a JAZZ ballet in Paris.

KEMPE, Rudolf (1910-76) *Conductor* German-born Kempe conducted at the OPERA houses in Leipzig, Dresden, and Munich. He was particularly admired for his interpretations of Richard STRAUSS and Wagner.

KEMPFF, Wilhelm (1895-1991) *Pianist* Kempff studied in his native Germany before touring widely. He made his London debut in 1951 and his New York debut in 1964. He was most closely associated with the piano works of Beethoven, Schumann, and Brahms.

KENDRICKS, Eddie (1939-92) *Vocalist* An original member of the Temptations, Kendricks was lead vocalist on many of their hits, including "The Way You Do the Things You Do" (1964) and "Just My Imagination" (1971). In 1973 he left the band to pursue a solo career. His single "Keep on Truckin'" (1973) was a huge hit and he had smaller successes with "Boogie Down" (1974) and "Shoeshine Boy" (1975). After this, his career slowly lost momentum.

KENNEDY, Nigel (1956-) *Violinist* British-born Kennedy has played most of the concerto repertoire with many of the world's great orchestras. He has cultivated an unconventional image, which has, on occasion, overshadowed the quality of his work. He has made many recordings of the standard works, and is renowned for his ELGAR Concerto and Vivaldi's *Four Seasons*.

KENTNER, Louis (1905-87) *Pianist* Hungarian-born Kentner studied in Budapest but settled in England in 1935. He was much admired for his playing of Chopin and Liszt and gave premieres of works by BARTÓK.

KEPPARD, Freddie (1889-1933) *Jazz cornetist* Keppard formed the Olympia Orchestra in 1906 and later the Original Creole Orchestra, with whom he toured extensively before settling in Chicago. He was the first musician to travel widely in the U.S. with a NEW ORLEANS JAZZ ensemble. Before mutes were invented, Keppard was achieving glissandos and muted tones with a glass or a beer bottle. Eventually surpassed by younger players like Louis ARMSTRONG, and drinking heavily, Keppard ended his career as a sideman.

KERSHAW, Doug and Rusty *Country duo* Brothers Doug and Rusty began recording together in 1955. Their biggest hit came in 1960 with "Louisiana Man." In 1964 the duo disbanded, with Doug going on to a highly successful career as a solo fiddler.

KERTESZ, Istvan (1929-73) *Conductor* Hungarian Kertesz worked in his native country until the 1956 revolution. After leaving Hungary he held appointments in Augsburg and Cologne, and with the London Symphony Orchestra. He was highly regarded, particularly for his performances of 20th-century works.

KHAN, Chaka (1953-) *Soul singer* Khan first found fame with the American FUNK group Rufus. In 1978 she began a solo career, achieving success in 1984 with "I Feel for You"—written by PRINCE and featuring Stevie WONDER. She has since collaborated with David BOWIE and Robert Palmer.

KIEPURA, Jan (1902-66) *Opera singer* Polish tenor Kiepura sang in Vienna, Paris, Buenos Aires, and at La Scala in Milan, before making his U.S. debut in Chicago in 1931. As well as being a popular OPERA singer, he made a number of films and appeared on Broadway.

KING, Ben E. (1938-) *Soul singer* King sang with the Drifters before beginning his solo career in 1960. He had a number of hits in the 1960s such as "Spanish Harlem"—written by Jerry Leiber and Phil SPECTOR—"Stand by Me," and "It's All Over." In 1977 he recorded the album *Benny and Us* with the Average White Band.

KING CRIMSON *Rock band* Formed by Robert Fripp in 1968, King Crimson was at the forefront of PROGRESSIVE ROCK. Their first album *In the Court of the Crimson King* (1969) was a critical and commercial success. Other albums followed, but the group disbanded in 1974. They reformed in 1981, making three albums before disbanding again. In 1994 Fripp reformed King Crimson and released the acclaimed album *Thrak* (1995).

KING TUBBY (1941-89) *Reggae producer* King Tubby pioneered recording techniques such as delay echo, slide fading, and phasing. He trained a generation of REGGAE engineers and was highly influential, particularly in the presentation of dance music and the evolution of dub.

KIRBY, John (1908-52) *Jazz double bass player and bandleader* Kirby played with Fletcher HENDERSON and Chick Webb. In 1937 he formed his own group in New York. During the period from 1938–42, they made many recordings and broadcasts, establishing a large following. However, they went out of fashion and Kirby moved to California.

KIRK, Andy (1898-1992) *Jazz saxophonist and bandleader* Kirk joined George Morrison's Orchestra in 1918 and Terrence Holder's Dark Clouds of Joy Orchestra in 1925, taking over as leader in 1929. They enjoyed success, especially with the song "Until the Real Thing Comes Along" before disbanding in 1948.

KIRK, Roland (1936-77) *Jazz tenor saxophonist* A true original, Kirk played three instruments at once— the stritch, the manzello, both archaic saxophones, and tenor sax—as well as a variety of whistles and flutes. Kirk performed with his own group, the Vibration Society, but his music was unclassifiable, containing elements of JAZZ styles ranging from NEW ORLEANS JAZZ through SWING and BEBOP to avant-garde.

KIRKPATRICK, Ralph (1911-84) *Harpsichordist* American-born Kirkpatrick played a repertoire ranging from Bach to Elliot CARTER on the harpsichord and clavichord. He was also an authority on Domenico Scarlatti, whose harpsichord sonatas he catalogued.

KISS *Rock band* Formed in 1972, Kiss developed a reputation based on their live shows, which were billed as "The Greatest Rock'n'Roll Show on Earth"—complete with glam rock outfits, full makeup, and Alice Cooper-style theatrics. They had their first hit single in 1975, and for the next two years were the biggest HEAVY METAL band in the world. Kiss remained popular in the 1980s and 1990s, *Asylum* (1985) and *Crazy Nights* (1987) being their most successful albums.

KLEE, Bernhard (1936-) *Conductor* German-born Klee worked in Cologne and Salzburg before gaining major appointments in Hanover and Düsseldorf. He made his American debut in 1974, and then conducted in New York, San Francisco, and Chicago. Klee appeared at international festivals and made many recordings.

KLEIBER, Carlos (1930-) *Conductor* Son of Erich, Argentinian conductor Carlos was born in Germany. His first success came with BERG's *Wozzeck* in the late 1960s. He worked mostly in Europe, conducting OPERA, notably works by STRAUSS, Wagner, Verdi, Bizet, and Weber. Not wishing to hold a resident appointment, Kleiber has worked at all the major concert halls in Europe, particularly in Munich, Vienna, Bayreuth, and Covent Garden in London.

KLEIBER, Erich (1890-1956)
Conductor Austrian-born Kleiber was music director of the Berlin Staatsoper, where he conducted the first performance of BERG's *Wozzeck* in 1924. During World War II he worked in Latin America. Kleiber was most admired for his performances of OPERAS by STRAUSS and Mozart. He was the father of the conductor Carlos Kleiber.

KNIGHT, Gladys *Soul singer* Born in the U.S. Gladys Knight is most famous for her work with the Pips. Formed in 1952, they had their first success with "Every Beat of My Heart" (1961). From 1966 they recorded for MOTOWN, making a series of highly successful records. They recorded the classic "Midnight Train from Georgia," a No.1 hit in 1973. The group also had its own TV series, and Gladys appeared in the 1976 film *Pipedream* . She also sang the theme song for the James Bond movie *Licence To Kill*. The Pips disbanded in 1989.

KNUSSEN, Oliver (1952-) *Conductor* English-born Knussen began his career as a composer and wrote several works including three symphonies and the two OPERAS, *Where the Wild Things Are* (1983) and *Higglety Pigglety Pop!* (1985). But he is best known as a conductor, particularly in the field of contemporary music.

KOOL AND THE GANG *Soul group* Formed in 1964, originally as a jazz quartet, Kool and the Gang incorporated SOUL and FUNK into their music, leading to huge success in the U.S. charts with singles such as "Jungle Boogie" (1973) and "Hollywood Swinging" (1974). In the late 1970s and early 1980s, Kool and the Gang moved into DISCO and had a number of hits, including "Ladies Night" (1979), "Get Down on It" (1982), and "Fresh" (1985).

KOOPMAN, Ton (1944-) *Conductor, organist, and harpsichordist* Netherlands-born Koopman founded a number of period instrument ensembles, notably the Amsterdam Baroque Orchestra. He made many recordings as a soloist and conductor, in particular of Bach and Buxtehude.

KORNGOLD, Erich (1897-1957)
Composer An infant prodigy, Korngold wrote ballet scores and OPERAS before moving to Hollywood to write FILM MUSIC. He also wrote ORCHESTRAL MUSIC, including a symphony, a violin concerto, and numerous songs in a highly Romantic idiom.

KRAFTWERK *Electronic rock group* Kraftwerk drew on influences such as Tangerine Dream and the avant-garde to produce a style characterized by synthesizers and tape machines. Despite their radical approach, they had a number of hit albums in the U.K. and U.S.—*Autobahn* (1974), *Trans-Europe Express* (1977), and *The Man Machine* (1978)—and a No.1 single in the U.K. with "The Model" (1981). They remain a huge influence on the electronic music of the 1990s.

KRAUSE, Tom (1934-) *Opera singer* Born in Finland, Krause made his debut in Berlin and went on to sing in all the world's major OPERA houses. His rich bass has been heard in a wide operatic repertory, especially Mozart, Verdi, and Wagner, as well as in recital and oratorio.

KREMER, Gidon (1947-) *Violinist* Latvian-born Kremer studied with David Oistrakh. He had an international career in the standard repertoire and in contemporary music, playing important premieres of works by SCHNITTKE and Reimann.

KRENEK, Ernst (1900-91) *Composer* Born in Austria, Krenek incorporated JAZZ into his early OPERAS and used 12-note SERIALISM in *Karl V* (1938). He moved to the U.S. in 1938 and wrote three more operas. Although showing the influence of many styles and perhaps lacking a distinctive voice, his work was always highly proficient.

KRIPS, Joseph (1902-74) *Conductor* Born in Austria, Krips worked at the Vienna State Opera from 1935 and helped to rebuild Viennese musical life after World War II. He held appointments with major orchestras such as the London Symphony Orchestra and San Francisco Symphony Orchestra, and was most admired for performances of Mozart, Schubert, and Viennese OPERETTA.

KRONOS QUARTET, *String quartet* Formed in Seattle in 1978 by David Harrington, the Kronos Quartet specializes in contemporary music, having given over 150 first performances including works by John CAGE, Thelonious MONK, and Steve REICH. They are at home in both classical and JAZZ venues and are renowned for their unusual and contemporary performance style.

KUBELIK, Rafael (1914-96) *Conductor* Kubelik made his debut with the Czech Philharmonic Orchestra in 1934. Important posts followed with the Chicago Symphony Orchestra, London's Covent Garden, and the Bavarian Symphony Orchestra. In addition to conducting he wrote two OPERAS, a CHORAL symphony, and an orchestral symphony.

KUNZ, Erich (1909-) *Opera singer* The Viennese bass-baritone Kunz is particularly admired for his interpretation of the roles of Papagano, Beckmesser, and Figaro, which he sang internationally throughout the 1940s and 1950s. As well as performing OPERA, he also appeared regularly in popular Viennese OPERETTA.

LABELLE, Patti (1944-) *Blues and soul singer* Patti LaBelle began her career with the band LaBelle, who had a major DISCO hit with "Lady Marmalade." Patti began a solo career in 1976 with mixed success. However, she achieved phenomenal sales for the singles "New Attitude" (1985)—from the soundtrack to *Beverly Hills Cop*—and "On My Own" (1986)—a duet with Michael McDonald.

LABEQUE, Marielle (1952-) and Katia (1950-) *Pianists* French pianists Marielle and Katia Labeque are principally known for their duet repertory. The sisters have appeared with many of the great conductors and orchestras and made many recordings.

LaFARO, Scott (1936-61) *Jazz double bass player* LaFaro began touring with Buddy Morrow's band in 1955, and later worked with Chet BAKER in Los Angeles and Bill EVANS in New York. His recordings with the Bill Evans trio were highly influential in the development of JAZZ bass.

LAFONT, Jean-Philippe (1951-) *Opera singer* French bass-baritone Lafont's career embraced a repertoire ranging from Baroque to the late 19th century. He was particularly admired for his performances in the OPERAS of Mozart and Rossini, and in the roles of Rigoletto and Falstaff.

LAINE, Cleo (1927-) *Jazz singer* U.K.-born Laine joined the John Dankworth Seven in 1952. She later married Dankworth who became her ARRANGER, composer, and music director. She appeared in a number of stage shows, including Kurt WEILL's *The Seven Deadly Sins, Showboat,* and *Colette.* She had a huge vocal range which she employed in all types of music. She is best heard on the 1991 album *Jazz.*

LANCE, Major (1941-94) *Soul singer* Lance had a U.S. Top 10 hit with "The Monkey Time" in 1963 and followed that with several more hits in collaboration with Curtis Mayfield during the mid-1960s. In the late 1970s he briefly enjoyed renewed popularity during a craze for "beach music" which retained an interest in vintage SOUL music.

LANDOWSKA, Wanda (1879-1959) *Harpsichordist* Born in Poland, Landowska was a leading figure in 20th-century harpsichord playing. She moved to Paris in 1900 as a pianist, but made her debut in the U.S. in 1923 as a harpichordist. She settled in the U.S. in 1940. She gave many important premieres, such as the concertos by de FALLA and POULENC.

LANE, Burton (1912-) *Songwriter* Lane began his career writing songs for revues, and went on to write over 40 film scores and several Broadway theater scores. Most famously, he collaborated with Alan Jay Lerner on *On a Clear Day You Can See Forever* (1965) and *Carmelina.*

LANG, Eddie (1902-33) *Jazz guitarist* Lang famously partnered the JAZZ violinist Joe Venuti, with whom he recorded "Stringing the Blues" and "Tiger Rag." He was also Bing CROSBY's staff accompanist when Crosby began his solo career. Lang is widely credited with inventing the solo vocabulary for jazz guitarists.

LANG, k. d. (1962-) *Country singer* k.d. lang made a number of albums including *A Truly Western Experience* (1983) and *Shadowland* (1988) before crossing over into the mainstream with her highly acclaimed album *Ingenue* (1992). A worldwide hit the album spawned the successful singles "Miss Chatelaine" and "Constant Craving." Since her early career, lang has progressed from pure COUNTRY to a lusher, poppier style.

LANGLAIS, Jean (1907-91) *Organist and composer* Born in France, Langlais studied with Dupré, DUKAS, and Tournemire. He toured widely as a soloist and wrote music for the organ and church use, much of it based on Gregorian chants.

LANGRIDGE, Philip (1939-) *Opera singer* English tenor Langridge sung a wide range of roles in all the major OPERA houses. His repertoire included baroque and classical works and he was closely associated with certain 20th-century operas—notably BRITTEN's *Peter Grimes,* SCHOENBERG's *Moses und Aron,* and STRAVINSKY's *The Rake's Progress.*

LAROCCA, Nick (1889-1961) *Jazz cornetist and bandleader* LaRocca cofounded the Original Dixieland Jazz Band in 1916. His style of cornet playing was highly influential on later stars such as Bix BEIDERBECKE. Among his many compositions were "At the Jazz Band Ball" and "Clarinet Marmalade Blues."

LARROCHA, Alicia de (1923-) *Pianist* Born in Spain, Larrocha made her debuts in the U.K. and U.S. before forming a duo with cellist Gaspar Cassado. She gained a strong reputation for her playing of Mozart and Beethoven, and recorded works by Albeniz and GRANADOS.

LAST, James (1929-) *Bandleader and arranger* German-born Last gained huge international success arranging hit singles for his big band. His arrangements of well-known works, both popular and classical, to which he generally added a dance beat, proved widely popular in the 1970s and were the basis for over 20 albums, including *Make the Party Last.*

LAURI-VOLPI, Giacomo (1892-1975) *Opera singer* Italian tenor Lauri-Volpi sang at La Scala in Milan and the Metropolitan Opera in New York, gaining a reputation in particular for his singing of Verdi and PUCCINI.

LAWRENCE, Gertrude (1898-1952) *Actress, singer, and dancer* Lawrence was a charismatic stage actress who starred in a number of musical comedies and MUSICALS, both in her native Britain and in the U.S. George GERSHWIN wrote "Someone to Watch Over Me" for her, and she appeared in *Private Lives* with Noel COWARD, WEILL's *Lady in the Dark,* and RODGERS and HAMMERSTEIN's *The King and I.*

LAWRENCE, Marjorie (1909-79) *Opera singer* Australian-born Marjorie Lawrence studied in Paris before establishing herself as a leading dramatic soprano in roles such as Brünnhilde, Brangane, Salome, and Alceste, which she sang in Europe and the U.S.

LEAR, Evelyn (1928-) *Opera singer* Evelyn Lear made her recital debut in her native New York in 1955. During her career she sang a wide operatic repertoire, but was particularly associated with the soprano roles of Mozart, STRAUSS, and BERG's Lulu.

LEE, Laura (1945-) *Soul singer* Lee had hits with "Dirty Man" and "Uptight Good Man" in 1967. After further successes in the 1970s, she reverted to her GOSPEL roots in 1983 with the album *Jesus Is the Light of My Life.*

LEE, Noel (1924-) *Composer and pianist* Although born in China, Noel Lee studied in the U.S. and toured extensively as a concert pianist. Much of her prodigious output as a composer is for piano and chamber ensembles. Lee has also produced a crucial edition of DEBUSSY's works for two pianos.

LEEUW, Ton de (1926-) *Composer* Born in the Netherlands, Leeuw studied with Badings and MESSIAEN. His early works show the influence of BARTÓK and HINDEMITH, but later compositions reveal a more avant-garde style with Eastern, and in particular Indian, influences.

LEHÁR, Franz (1870-1948) *Composer* Hungarian-born Lehár was the son of a military bandmaster. He is principally remembered for his hugely successful OPERETTAS of which *The Merry Widow* (1905) is the best known.

LEHMANN, Lilli (1848-1929) *Opera singer* German soprano Lilli Lehmann sang a huge repertoire ranging from Mozart and Bellini to Wagner. She took part in the first Bayreuth Festival in 1886, and also sang in Berlin, Salzburg, and New York.

LEHMANN, Lotte (1888-1976) *Opera singer* German-born Lehmann was principally associated with lyric soprano roles such as STRAUSS's Marschallin and Wagner's Eva. She sang widely in Germany and Austria and made her U.S. debut in 1930.

LEINSDORF, Erich (1912-93) *Conductor* Born in Austria, Leinsdorf learned his trade from TOSCANINI and WALTER. He conducted the German operatic repertoire at the Met in New York, and later held important posts with orchestras in London and Berlin. He wrote a seminal book on conducting in 1981 entitled *The Composer's Advocate*.

LEMONHEADS, The *Rock group* Formed in the U.S. in 1987, the Lemonheads made a number of albums before their first commercial success with a cover version of Suzanne Vega's "Luka." In the early 1990s—after personnel changes—they produced two albums of snappy COUNTRY-tinged ROCK music, *It's a Shame About Ray* and *Come on Feel the Lemonheads*—both commercial successes in the U.K.

LENNON, John (1940-80) *Rock musician* Lennon began his solo career before the BEATLES' final split. By 1970 he had made two albums with Yoko Ono and played live with the Plastic Ono Band (which included Eric Clapton). In 1971 the Plastic Ono Band reassembled to make the album *Imagine*—produced by Phil SPECTOR. Over the next four years Lennon produced a number of successful records. Much of his music carried a strong political message, for example "War Is Over If You Want It"

and "Woman Is the Nigger of The World." In 1980 Lennon recorded for the first time in five years, making the album *Double Fantasy* which included the single "(Just Like) Starting Over"—a posthumous No.1—before being shot and killed.

LENOIR, J. B. (1929-79) *Blues singer and guitarist* Mississippi-born Lenoir had his first success with the "Mojo Boogie" in 1953. "Eisenhower Blues" (1954) carried a serious message and in later songs, such as "Down in Mississippi," he closely identified himself with the civil rights struggle.

LENYA, Lotte (1898-1981) *Singer and actress* Lenya was particularly identified with the music of Kurt WEILL, whom she married in 1926. She gained an international reputation for her performance in the role of Jenny in the *Threepenny Opera* and gave many performances of the work he wrote for her—*The Seven Deadly Sins*.

LEONHARDT, Gustav (1928-) *Harpsichordist and conductor* Dutch-born Leonhardt was a leading harpsichordist and conductor of Early Music. He was closely associated with the music of Bach, Frescobaldi, and Froberger.

LEPPARD, Raymond (1927-) *Conductor* British-born Leppard conducted his own editions of OPERAS by Monteverdi and Cavalli in the early 1960s. He was also a harpsichordist and pianist noted for his readings of Handel, Rameau, and Couperin.

LEWIS, Barbara (1943-) *Soul singer* Lewis established her reputation with the single "Hello Stranger" (1963). She had further successes with "Someday We're Gonna Love Again" and "Make Me Your Baby," before retiring from music in 1968.

LEWIS, George (1952-) *Jazz trombonist and composer* A leading figure in avant-garde JAZZ, Lewis's compositions showed the influence of contemporary art music and electronics. In later works, for example *Audio Tick*, he used computers and digital synthesizers. Lewis was not, however, restricted to the avant-garde and his style embraced everything from early roots to BEBOP and FREE JAZZ.

LEWIS, Huey, and the News *Rock group* In their prime Huey Lewis and the News played down-to-earth consumer friendly ROCK with huge success. They reached the U.S. Top 10 with "Do You Believe in Love" from their debut album—*Picture This*. During the mid-1980s, the band scored three U.S. No.1s, including "The Power of Love," taken from the movie *Back to the Future*. By the late 1980s and early 1990s the band's popularity was beginning to fade.

LEWIS, John (1920-) *Jazz pianist and composer* In 1946 Lewis joined Dizzy GILLESPIE's big band, replacing Thelonious MONK. However, he is most closely associated with the MODERN JAZZ QUARTET—for whom he wrote many compositions—and his directorship of the Monterey Jazz Festival from 1958–82. His piano playing was original but recalled the stride style of Fats WALLER.

LEWIS, Meade "Lux" (1905-64) *Jazz pianist* Lewis was one of the most famous of the BOOGIE performers. His "Honky Tonk Train Blues" was not a hit but got him noticed. An important figure in the 1930s, Lewis played with Albert Ammons, Pete Johnson, and later Sidney Bechet, remaining a celebrity until his death.

LIBERACE (1919-87) *Pianist* Liberace made his debut with the Chicago Symphony orchestra in 1940. In the 1950s he cultivated a unique musical persona characterized by ostentatious costumes and staging, which made him hugely popular and commercially successful. His own compositions include "Rhapsody by Candlelight" and "Boogie-Woogie Variations."

LIGGINS, Joe (1916-87) *Blues pianist and composer* Liggins formed his own group, the Honeydrippers, in 1945. They had several hits including "I've Got a Right to Cry" (1948) and "Pink Champagne" (1950), and made numerous albums.

LILL, John (1944-) *Pianist* British-born Lill won the 1970 Tchaikovsky Competition. He achieved international success and was particularly admired for his playing of the Beethoven sonatas and concertos.

LITTLE FEAT *Rock band* Formed in Los Angeles in 1969, Little Feat featured legendary singer, songwriter, and guitarist Lowell George. They played ROCK MUSIC with a boogie beat and George's seductive vocals on top. Renowned for their live shows, they are best heard on the albums *Dixie Chicken* (1973) and *The Last Record Album* (1975).

LITTON, Andrew (1959-) *Conductor* New York-born Litton held positions with the Bournemouth Symphony Orchestra and the Dallas Symphony Orchestra. He conducted the house premiere of *Porgy and Bess* at Covent Garden, in London, in 1992, and has made numerous recordings.

LL COOL J (1969-) *Rap singer* Starting in 1984 with his debut single "I Need a Beat," LL Cool J has had one of the longest and most successful careers in RAP. His debut album *Radio* is considered a classic of the genre and he had his first Top 10 hit with "I Need Love" in 1987. He is best heard on his 1990 album *Mama Said Knock You Out.* In the 1990s he also pursued an acting career, appearing in films such as *The Hard Way* and *Toys.*

LOCKHART, James (1930-) *Conductor* Born in Scotland, James Lockhart was associated principally with OPERA, holding important positions in Germany and the U.K. He was music director of the Welsh National Opera and director of opera at London's Royal College of Music.

LOCKWOOD, Annea (1939-) *Composer* Born in New Zealand, Lockwood studied in Europe. She was involved in experimental music using both traditional and unusual instruments to produce the required notes.

LOFGREN, Nils (1951-) *Rock singer-songwriter and guitarist* One of the best ROCK guitarists of his era, Lofgren appeared on *After the Goldrush* (1970) with Neil Young and toured with him before launching a solo career. In 1976 Lofgren released his most successful album to date, *Cry Tough.* Further albums were less successful and in 1984 Lofgren replaced Steve Van Zandt in Bruce SPRINGSTEEN's band. Lofgren returned to solo work in the 1990s.

LOFTON, Cripple Clarence (1887-1957) *Blues pianist and singer* A pioneer of the BOOGIE-WOOGIE piano style, Lofton entertained in his own saloon in Chicago. He made recordings in the 1930s and 1940s including "Brown Skin Girls" and "House Rent Struggle."

LONG, Marguerite (1874-1966) *Pianist* Born in France, Long taught in Paris before starting her own piano school there. She was an authority on FAURÉ, RAVEL, and DEBUSSY and gave the premiere of Ravel's G Major Concerto.

LORIOD, Jeanne (1928-) *Ondes Martenot player* Loriod took part in many first performances and recordings of music by MESSIAEN and Jolivet. She also wrote the definitive work on this early electronic instrument.

LORIOD, Yvonne (1924-) *Pianist* Loriod gave premieres of piano music by MESSIAEN after they first worked together in 1943. Sister of Jeanne, Yvonne became Messiaen's second wife and played important premieres of other composers' works, in particular Pierre BOULEZ and Barraqué.

LOTT, Felicity (1947-) *Opera singer* Lott had an international career as a lyric soprano. She was particularly admired in Mozart and STRAUSS, to whose music her elegant stage presence was perfectly suited.

LOUVIN BROTHERS *Country music duo* This mandolin and guitar duo were popular radio artists in the 1940s, later making over 100 singles and 20 albums. "When I Stop Dreaming," released in the mid-1950s, was their most successful song. They broke up in 1963, but the EVERLY BROTHERS, among others, always acknowledged their debt to the Louvins.

LOVE *Rock band* Formed in Los Angeles in 1965, Love had almost instant success with the singles "My Little Red Book" and "7 and 7 Is." Led by seminal guitarist Albert Lee, they made a number of albums which were critically acclaimed but had little chart success. Their finest moment was the album *Forever Changes* (1967).

LOVE, Courtney (1965-) *Rock singer and guitarist* Courtney Love played briefly in a number of bands before forming Hole in 1991. Based in Seattle, Hole were an important part of the GRUNGE scene in the early 1990s. Their second album, *Live Through This,* was widely acclaimed. In 1992 Love married Kurt Cobain of NIRVANA. His death in 1994 cast a shadow over the achievements of Love herself. In the late 1990s Love pursued a successful acting career.

LOVETT, Lyle (1957-) *Country singer-songwriter* One of the most eclectic and unclassifiable acts in COUNTRY music, Lovett remains a cult figure. Lovett's songs have been covered with some success by Nanci Griffith but his own albums, while critically well received, have failed to gain commercial success. His 1996 album *The Road to Ensenada* is his most accessible to date.

LOVIN' SPOONFUL, The *Rock group* Formed in New York in 1965, the Lovin' Spoonful had hits with "Do You Believe in Magic?" and "Summer in the City." Led by singer John Sebastian, their style brought together ROCK and urban FOLK MUSIC. However, by 1967 things were beginning to fall apart for the band and their success began to fade. They disbanded in 1969 to pursue solo projects.

LUDWIG, Christa (1928-) *Opera singer* Berlin-born mezzo-soprano Ludwig sang in Salzburg and Vienna before making her Met debut in 1959. She was closely associated with the music of Mozart, STRAUSS, and Wagner, in particular the role of Octavian.

LUNCEFORD, Jimmie (1902-47) *Jazz bandleader* Lunceford formed a student JAZZ band in 1927 that became Jimmie Lunceford's Orchestra. They achieved considerable success in the 1930s and are best heard in songs such as "For Dancers Only" and "Organ Grinder's Swing."

LUPU, Radu (1945-) *Pianist* Born in Romania, Lupu studied in Moscow and won the Leeds Piano Competition in 1969. He became a highly sought-after exponent of the Romantic repertoire, in particular the music of Brahms.

LUTYENS, Elisabeth (1906-83) *Composer* Daughter of the British architect Sir Edwin Lutyens, her early compositions used serial techniques recalling WEBERN. Her large output includes songs, OPERAS, string quartets, and FILM MUSIC.

LYMON, Frankie, and the Teenagers *Soul group* Their debut single "Why Do Fools Fall in Love?" was a huge success both sides of the Atlantic— reaching No.7 in the U.S. charts in 1956, when Lymon was only 13 years old. They had further successes and a sensational U.K. tour, but Lymon's career as a soloist after leaving the group proved less successful and he died of a drug overdose in 1968.

LYMPANY, Moura (1916-) *Pianist* Born in Britain, Lympany made her debut at age 12. In an international career, her performances of Russian music, 20th-century English music, and RACHMANINOV were most notable.

LYNYRD SKYNYRD *Rock group* Lynyrd Skynyrd were leading lights in the Southern ROCK revival of the early 1970s. Their first album *Pronounced Leh-nerd Skin-nerd* (1973) contained their classic "Freebird." They really came to prominence as a supporting act on tour with THE WHO in 1974 and had their biggest hit that same year with "Sweet Home Alabama." They continued to be successful with gold discs and sell-out tours until in 1977, when three members of the band were killed in a plane crash.

MA, Yo-Yo (1955-) *Cellist* Born in France, Yo-Yo Ma studied in New York and made his debut there at the age of 15. He had a major international career working with the world's great orchestras and conductors and playing CHAMBER MUSIC with Yehudi MENUHIN and Emanuel Ax.

MACKERRAS, Sir Charles (1925-) *Conductor* Australian born Mackerras was musical director of English and Welsh National Operas. He was particularly associated with 18th-century performance style and with the OPERAS of JANÁČEK—of which he gave many British premieres— PUCCINI, as well as Gluck and Handel.

MACONCHY, Elizabeth (1907-) *Composer* Maconchy studied composition in London and Prague. She is best known for her CHAMBER MUSIC, although she wrote OPERAS, songs, and choral works. Many of her pieces have a characteristic central European sound and her technical methods were similar to BARTÓK'S.

MADERNA, Bruno (1920-73) *Composer* Italian-born Maderna wrote 12-note serial music in the 1940s and early 1950s before turning to a less rigid avant-garde style. He wrote an OPERA and a great deal of instrumental music, as well as electronically based pieces. In 1972 Maderna won an Italia Prize for the radio electronic piece *Ages*. He played an unequalled part in the postwar development of Italian music as a composer, conductor, and teacher.

MALCOLM, George (1917-97) *Harpsichordist* Malcolm conducted orchestras and choirs, notably the Westminster Cathedral Choir, London, which he raised to a very high standard. In 1959 BRITTEN composed *Missa brevis* for Malcolm and his choir. He was also an accomplished harpsichordist, winning renown for his interpretations of the English virginalists and 18th-century masters.

MAMAS AND THE PAPAS, The *Pop group* Formed in New York in 1965, the Mamas and the Papas became closely associated with the San Francisco "flower people." Their debut single, "California Dreaming" hit No.4 in the charts and a string of hits followed, including "Monday, Monday" and "Dedicated to the One I Love." In 1968 the group disbanded. Cass Elliot (Mama Cass) had a successful solo career until her death in 1974.

MANFRED MANN *Rock band* One of the U.K.'s leading bands in the mid-1960s, they had their first No.1 in 1964 with "Do Wah Diddy Diddy." Another Top 10 hit followed in 1968 with "Mighty Quinn" (a song written by Bob DYLAN). After a series of farewell gigs in 1969, the band finally split. They reformed in the 1970s as Manfred Mann's Earthband, scoring a No.1 hit in 1976 with Bruce SPRINGSTEEN's "Blinded by the Light."

MANGELSDORFF, Albert (1928-) *Jazz trombonist* As JAZZ was banned by Hitler toward the end of the 1930s, the young Mangelsdorff had to attend secret meetings to indulge his early passion for the music. When he began playing he immediately took up the BEBOP style. In 1962 Mangelsdorff released the album *Animal Dance* recorded with American composer John Lewis. Two years later he toured India and became interested in Indian music, recording *New Jazz Ramwong* with Ravi SHANKAR. In the early 1970s he began to develop a multiphonic approach to trombone playing. Mangelsdorff was voted Europe's Jazz Musician of the Year more often than anyone else.

MANNE, Shelly (1920-84) *Jazz drummer* Manne played with Dizzy GILLESPIE and Stan KENTON before he moved to Los Angeles where he played with André PREVIN, ran a JAZZ club—Shelly's Manne-Hole—and founded his own group the L.A.4. Manne was a truly versatile drummer, whose unusual effects helped pave the way for the freer approach to jazz drumming that emerged in the 1960s. He was also a composer of music for movies and TV.

MANTOVANI (1905-80) *Conductor, composer, pianist, and arranger* Italian-born Annunzio Mantovani had hits in the 1930s with "Red Sails in the Sunset" and "Serenade in the Night," and was briefly musical director for Noel COWARD, and for several shows in London's West End. During the next four decades he achieved colossal sales throughout the world with his orchestra—famous for their "cascading strings." He was one of the first popular artists to record albums rather than singles and was instrumental in extending the market for stereo recordings.

MANTRONIX *Rap band* The name Mantronix was made up from the words "man" and "electronics," summing up Mantronix's approach to RAP music. Formed in 1985 their first single "Fresh Is the Word" was hugely successful and their debut album broke new ground in terms of technical wizardry.

MARILYN MANSON *Rock band* Formed in Florida in 1990 Marilyn Manson set out to "explore the limits of censorship." In 1994 they released their debut album *Portrait of an American Family*. Since then, their brand of theatrical, industrial ROCK has proved enduringly controversial and successful in the U.S.

MARKEVICH, Igor (1912–83) *Composer and conductor* Born in Russia, Markevich worked originally as a composer collaborating with Diaghilev and the Ballets Russes. After World War II he worked as a conductor with appointments in Monte Carlo and Boston. He was particularly noted for his performances of 20th-century works.

MARRINER, Sir Neville (1924–) *Conductor and violinist* Born in the U.K. Marriner began his career playing in the Philharmonia Orchestra in London. He helped Thurston Dart form the Jacobean Ensemble specializing in 17th- and 18th-century music, and in 1959 founded the Academy of St. Martin-in-the-Fields, in London, with whom he made a huge number of recordings. He was also director of the Los Angeles Chamber Orchestra.

MARSALIS, Branford (1960–) *Tenor and soprano saxophonist* Brother of trumpeter Wynton MARSALIS, in whose quintet he played, Branford also worked with Art BLAKEY, Dizzy GILLESPIE, Miles DAVIS, and STING—with whom he recorded *The Dream of the Blue Turtles*. As a classical player he worked with the English Chamber Orchestra. Marsalis also led his own trios and quartets, playing forceful neo-bop.

MARTIN, Dean (1917–95) *Singer and actor* Martin first came to prominence working in a series of successful movies with comedian Jerry Lewis. After leaving Lewis, Martin became associated with the Ratpack, appearing alongside Frank SINATRA and Sammy Davis, Jr. In 1964, the first *Dean Martin Show* was broadcast on TV. It was a massive success and was syndicated worldwide. Martin's light, playful delivery of familiar standards and easy humor endeared him to the public in the 1950s and 1960s.

MARTIN, Sir George (1926–) *Record producer* Principally remembered for his work with the BEATLES, Martin worked with a host of artists throughout the 1960s, 1970s, and 1980s. In 1965 he set up his own studios in London and later opened a studio on a Caribbean island where he worked with artists such as Paul McCartney, DIRE STRAITS, and the ROLLING STONES.

MARTIN, Jimmy (1927–) *Country singer and guitarist* Martin worked with Bill Monroe—being rated as the best lead singer and guitarist Monroe had ever worked with—and later the Osborne Brothers, before forming the Sunny Mountain Boys. He was one of the greatest bluegrass performers with chart successes such as "Rock Hearts" and "Widow Maker."

MARTIN, Mary (1913–) *Actress, singer, and dancer* Mary Martin made her breakthrough in 1938 singing "My Heart Belongs to Daddy" in Cole PORTER's *Leave It to Me*. She performed in many Broadway MUSICALS, including *South Pacific, Annie Get Your Gun,* and *The Sound of Music*. She also appeared regularly in movies and on TV.

MARTYN, John (1948–) *Guitarist and vocalist* Over the course of his 25-year career, U.K.-born Martyn has created a unique style of music that combines FOLK, BLUES, JAZZ, and ROCK. A consummate guitarist and singer, he has collaborated with many of the great names of rock music. Martyn made his first album, *London Conversation,* in 1968. Several albums followed on which he collaborated with his wife Beverly. But his best albums are *Solid Air* (1973), *One World* (1977) and *Grace and Danger* (1980).

MARVIN, Hank (1941–) *Guitarist* Marvin joined the Shadows—English ROCK'N'ROLL pin-up Cliff Richard's backing band—in 1958. The Shadows had a string of hits with Richard and some instrumental hits, most notably "Apache," which was a U.K. No.1 in 1960. He was a major influence on a generation of British ROCK guitarists, including Jeff Beck and Ritchie Blackmore. Marvin continued to play, with and without the Shadows, into the 1990s.

MASEKELA, Hugh (1939–) *Jazz musician* South African-born Masekela sang and also played trumpet and flugelhorn. He formed a group in South Africa, the Jazz Epistles, before the worsening political situation effectively ended musical performances. Moving to the U.S. he found himself losing contact with his African roots and began to collaborate with fellow Africans Makhaya Ntshoko, and Dudu Pukwana. The result was the dynamic album *Home Is Where the Music Is.* In the 1980s he collaborated with Paul Simon and produced recordings by his wife Miriam Makeba. In the 1990s he returned to South Africa playing regularly around the Johannesburg area.

MASSIVE ATTACK *Rap band* Unlike most RAP artists, Massive Attack produce ambient, introspective music that has been labeled trip-hop. Their first album, *Blue Lines* (1991), was well received and spawned three hit singles including "Unfinished Sympathy." In 1994 they followed this up with *Protection,* a heady cross-breed of REGGAE, FUNK, and hip-hop. In 1998 they produced another well-received album, *Mezzanine.*

MASTERSON, Valerie (1937–) *Opera singer* British soprano Masterson made her Salzburg debut in 1964. Engagements followed in principal OPERA houses in Paris, San Francisco, and London. Her wide repertoire encompasses Handel and Verdi—she was particularly admired in the Handel roles of Semele and Cleopatra.

MASUR, Kurt (1928–) *Conductor* Masur worked in Dresden and Berlin before becoming conductor of the Leipzig Gewandhaus Orchestra in 1970. He has made numerous recordings and has been much praised for his performances of Bruckner, Tchaikovsky, and the Romantic symphonic repertoire.

MATHIS, Johnny (1935–) *Pop singer* With a voice reminiscent of Nat King COLE, Mathis had a hugely successful career singing love ballads. He made many hit albums as a soloist and *Johnny Mathis' Greatest Hits* (1958) remained on the *Billboard* charts for almost a decade. In the 1970s and

1980s Mathis had a number of hits duetting with artists such as Gladys Knight, Nana Mouskouri, and Dionne Warwick. He is one of the best-selling artists of all time.

MAYALL, John (1933-) *Blues singer and harmonica player* One of the pioneers of British R&B, Mayall was an important influence on a number of young players who would become future ROCK superstars, including Eric Clapton, John McVie, Mick Taylor, and Peter Green. His finest work is heard on *Bluesbreakers with Eric Clapton* (1966) and his best-selling album *The Turning Point* (1969) features outstanding harmonica playing on the track "Thoughts About Roxanne." During the 1970s and 1980s Mayall was less popular, but his 1993 album *Wake Up Call* marked a return to form.

MAYFIELD, Curtis (1942-) *Soul singer-songwriter* Working with the band the Impressions, Mayfield had a number of highly successful singles in the 1960s, including the No.4 hit "It's All Right." The Impressions songs ranged from love songs to social issues and protest songs. His solo career began in 1970, and in 1972 he released the platinum-selling "blaxploitation" soundtrack album, *Superfly*. In 1990 Mayfield was paralyzed after a lighting rig fell on him.

MAYFIELD, Percy (1920-84) *R&B singer-songwriter* Mayfield had a huge hit with "Please Send Me Someone to Love" in 1950. Other successes included "Lost Love" and "Big Question." In the early 1960s Mayfield worked as a songwriter for Ray CHARLES, producing the international hit "Hit the Road Jack."

MC5 *Rock band* Formed in Detroit in 1964, MC5 have garnered a huge amount of retrospective critical acclaim without similar commercial success. In the late 1960s they provided a soundtrack for the anti-establishment politics of the White Panther Party. Despite splitting up in 1974 they reached the peak of their popularity during the PUNK era of the late 1970s. They are best heard on their first two albums: the live album *Kick Out the Jams* (1969), and *Back in the USA* (1970).

MCAULIFFE, Leon (1917-80) *Steel guitarist* One of the greatest exponents of the steel guitar, McAuliffe began his career with Bob WILLS' Texas Playboys. He formed the Western Swing Band in 1946, later changing the name to the Cimarron Boys. They had notable successes with "Steel Guitar Rag" and "Panhandle Rag" and with their own version of "Faded Love."

MCBRIDE, "Big"Tom (c.1948-) *Country singer and guitarist* McBride formed the Mainliners in Eire in 1965, and in 1966 had his first hit with "Gentle Mother"—one of the biggest-selling records of all time in Ireland. Until 1978 McBride and the Mainliners had a string of successes, becoming household names in their native land. In the late 1970s McBride left the Mainliners and had a successful solo career. The band reformed in 1989 and they continue to be a popular attraction in the 1990s.

MCCARTNEY, Paul (1942-) *Singer-songwriter* After leaving the BEATLES McCartney made a solo album, *McCartney*. Led by the excellent "Maybe I'm Amazed," the album shot straight to the top of the charts. In 1971 McCartney formed Wings, with whom he made a number of albums and the hugely successful single "Mull of Kintyre." After the death of John Lennon in 1980, McCartney was silent until 1982, when he released a duet with Stevie WONDER, "Ebony and Ivory." He later collaborated with Michael JACKSON and a number of other ROCK celebrities. Throughout the 1980s and 1990s McCartney has recorded with mixed success. He continued to experiment in many areas, including classical music—his Liverpool Oratorio featured Dame Kiri Te Kanawa and was orchestrated by Richard Rodney-Bennett. He remained, into the 1990s, the most successful songwriter of his generation.

MCCLINTON, Delbert (1940-) *Country singer-songwriter* McClinton first found success as a backing singer for artists such as Sonny Boy WILLIAMSON and Howlin' Wolf. He went solo in the 1970s with albums including *Victim of Life's Circumstances* (1975) and *Love*

Rustler (1977). His only hit single was "Givin' It Up For Your Love" (1980), a Top 10. Emmylou HARRIS had a country No.1 with McClinton's "Two More Bottles of Wine" in 1978.

MCCRACKLIN, Jimmy (1921-) *Blues singer* McCracklin started recording R&B records in 1945, not seeing any chart success until almost a decade later with the single "The Walk." His later intermittent chart successes included "Just Got to Know" (1961) and "Think" (1965). He continued to appeal to more specialized audiences.

MCDOWELL, Mississippi Fred (1904-72) *Blues singer* A lifelong BLUES player, McDowell started recording his traditional bottleneck style at age 60. Scorning rock music, one of his best albums was called *I Don't Play No Rock'n'Roll* (1969). Much praised by rock bands of the time, like the ROLLING STONES, who recorded his "You Gotta Move" on their 1971 album *Sticky Fingers*, McDowell was really the last of the great country bluesmen.

MCEVOY, Johnny (c.1945-) *Country singer-songwriter* From the mid-1960s McEvoy became one of the most important Irish COUNTRY music artists. Recording from 1965, he topped the Irish charts with "Mursheen Durkin" (1966). Other hits included "The Ballad of John Williams," "Michael," and "Rich Man's Garden." He also had his own television shows in Ireland and Britain.

MCFERRIN, Bobby (1950-) *Jazz singer* Born in the U.S. McFerrin trained as a pianist at the Juilliard School in New York. He came to prominence in the late 1970s performing wordless songs, full of noises, pops, and clicks—a kind of human beat box. He hit the big time in 1988 when his song "Don't Worry Be Happy" reached No.1 in the charts.

MCGARRIGLE, KATE AND ANNA *Folk duo* Sisters Kate (1944-) and Anna (1946-) McGarrigle came to prominence in the mid-1970s with a distinctive folk sound. Best heard on their eponymous first album (1975), they remain popular and well respected in folk music circles.

McGregor, Chris (1936-90) *Jazz pianist* South African-born McGregor made his reputation as a leader of the legendary Blue Notes in South Africa in the early 1960s. As a multiracial group they had problems in their native country. When invited to play in France in 1964, they left South Africa for good. Touring regularly in Europe, they made a huge impact with their mixture of FREE JAZZ and South African Township dance music. McGregor also formed a big band, the Brotherhood of Breath, which played successfully during the 1970s and 1980s.

McIntyre, Donald (1934-) *Opera singer* McIntyre was an English bass-baritone of New Zealand birth. He made his debut in 1959, and sang regularly between 1960–67 at Sadler's Wells Opera in London. He became an outstanding singer, notably of Wagner.

McKenzie, Red (1899-1948) *Jazz singer* Although not a great artist himself, McKenzie managed to put together a number of groups and gigs using some great musicians. His Mound City Blue Blowers produced a number of recordings, including two tracks with Coleman Hawkins: "Hello Lola" and "If I Could Be with You One Hour Tonight," which both became classics. He also helped Eddie Condon along the road to stardom.

McLaren, Malcolm (1946-) *Pop manager and singer* McLaren found success during the late 1970s PUNK era managing bands such as the New York Dolls, the Sex Pistols, and later Adam and the Ants. Best known as a businessman, McLaren began singing himself in the 1980s, having hits with "Buffalo Girls" and "Double Dutch." Later successful albums included the dance culture sound of *Would Ya Like More Scratchin'* and *Fans* (both 1984), a fusion of POP and OPERA containing the U.K. Top 20 hit "Madam Butterfly."

McLean, Don (1945-) *Pop singer and songwriter* A New York club singer in the 1960s, McLean had a massive hit with the songs "American Pie" and "Vincent" (both 1971). Both songs are classics of the 1970s. Despite several more albums during the 1980s and 1990s, McLean's career faded.

McPartland, Jimmy (1907-91) *Jazz cornetist* At age 17, McPartland replaced Bix Beiderbecke in the Wolverines. He continued to play in many different bands, often of New Orleans Jazz-orientation, well into his 80s. McPartland was able to drive bands with great force.

McPartland, Marian (1920-) *Jazz pianist* McPartland was British, but moved to America with her husband Jimmy McPartland in the 1940s. She established herself as a leading JAZZ pianist. Her long running radio show, *Piano Jazz* for NBC in New York, established her as one of America's best-known jazz artists. Musicians she worked with included Joe Venuti, Teddy Wilson, and her husband Jimmy.

McPhatter, Clyde (1932-72) *R&B-soul singer* McPhatter was a singer in a number of groups from the late 1940s, including the Drifters. Recording solo from 1956, singles included "Treasure of Love" and "Without Love," some becoming R&B standards. He became a hugely influential figure, with songs covered by artists such as Elvis Presley. Arguably his finest song was "Lover Please" (1962), a Top 10 hit.

McShann, Jay "Hootie" (1909-) *Jazz pianist and bandleader* McShann formed his own band, featuring Charlie Parker, in Kansas City in 1938, and this became the city's top band during the early 1940s. Noted for his singing as well as his playing, McShann played a unique blend of JAZZ, BLUES, and BOOGIE-WOOGIE.

McTell, "Blind" Willie (1901-59) *Blues guitarist and singer* One of the greatest BLUES artists ever, McTell began recording in 1927. Early sessions produced classics such as "Statesboro Blues" and "Georgia Rag." He recorded and performed regularly during the 1940s and 1950s, and remained an influence on blues artists long after his death.

Meatloaf (1947-) *Rock singer* Meatloaf had some minor chart success in the late 1960s, as well as a minor acting career. In 1976 he teamed up with Jim Steinman, and

together they composed a rock opera called *Bat Out of Hell*. The resulting album was released in 1978. Initially ignored, it eventually sold over 30 million copies worldwide, and became the third biggest-selling album of all time. Although still making records into the 1990s, Meatloaf has been unable to reproduce this early success.

Meek, Joe (1929-67) *Record producer* Meek was one of the U.K.'s leading record producers in the early 1960s. He created a unique echoey sound on records for artists such as John Leyton, Mike Berry, and Heinz. But his greatest success was with the Tornadoes' instrumental "Telstar" (1962), which was a huge hit on both sides of the Atlantic.

Mellencamp, John "Cougar" (1951-) *Rock singer* A straightforward rocker, Mellencamp's second album *John Cougar*, released in 1979, reached the U.S. charts. Constant touring during the next few years brought its reward in 1982, when the album *American Fool* went to No.1, and his two singles "Hurt So Good" and "Jack and Diane" both sold a million copies. Mellencamp carried on making albums and touring in the 1990s.

Melvin, Harold, & the Bluenotes *Soul group* Formed in 1954, the Blue Notes were originally a DOO-WOP group. They scored a minor hit with "My Hero" in 1960. A change in line-up, adding Teddy Pendergrass as lead vocalist, and the songwriting talents of Gamble and Huff, led to a string of hits such as "If You Don't Know Me by Now" (1972) and "The Love I Lost" (1973). Internal wrangles in the mid-1970s ended with Pendergrass leaving, and the group failed to recapture their former chart success.

Mengelberg, Willem (1871-1951) *Conductor* Born in Holland, Mengelberg forged an international reputation as conductor of the Amsterdam Concertgebouw from 1895. He held the post for the rest of his working life, making the orchestra among the best in the world. He was noted for his performances of Mahler and Strauss, as well as for much of the Romantic repertoire.

MERMAN, Ethel (1909–84) *Musicals singer* From her first great success singing in GERSHWIN's *Girl Crazy* (1930), Merman became one of the greatest ladies of the Broadway stage. In 1934 she starred in Cole PORTER's *Anything Goes*, the first of five Porter shows in which she appeared. Her longest-running musical was BERLIN's *Annie Get Your Gun* (1946) in which she sang "There's No Business Like Show Business," which became her theme song. At the peak of her career she appeared in SONDHEIM's *Gypsy* (1959).

MERRILL, Robert (1917–) *Opera singer* American baritone Merrill made his debut in New York in 1945. Although based at the Metropolitan Opera in New York, he sang all over the world, mostly in the major French and Italian baritone roles. He was a popular singer with a powerful and vigorous voice. He also sang in musicals, including many performances of *Fiddler on the Roof,* on TV, and on radio.

MERRIMAN, Nan (1920–) *Opera singer* American mezzo-soprano Merriman made her operatic debut in 1942, later making a number of broadcasts and recordings for TOSCANINI. Among her many notable performances was the British premiere of STRAVINSKY's *The Rake's Progress* (1953). She retired at the height of her powers in 1965.

MERRITT, Chris (1952–) *Opera singer* American tenor Merritt made his debut at New York City Opera in 1981. From then he sang at all the major OPERA houses, including the Vienna Staatsoper, La Scala in Milan, and Covent Garden in London. He is renowned for his interpretations of Rossini, as well as for his performance at the premiere of HENZE's *Venus and Adonis*.

MERRIWEATHER, Major "Maceo" (1905–53) *Blues pianist* Born and raised in Atlanta, Merriweather played BLUES piano all over the South. In 1941 he moved to Chicago where he played with Big Bill BROONZY and Sonny Boy WILLIAMSON. He was renowned for the speed of his playing and the smoky quality of his voice.

METALLICA *Rock group* Formed in San Francisco in 1981, Metallica have always been regarded as the most open-minded of HEAVY METAL bands. Albums such as *Master of Puppets* (1988), *Metallica* (1991), and *Load* (1996) show them playing thunderous riffs with a clean commercial edge.

METHENY, Pat (1954–) *Jazz guitarist* Metheny started his musical career in his teens. In 1977 he began a solo career. During the next few years his playing and composing led him to work with all the leading contemporary JAZZ players, such as Paul Bley, Sonny ROLLINS, Mike Brecker, and Ornette COLEMAN, as well as turning him into a jazz superstar. Best heard on the albums *As Falls Wichita, So Falls Wichita Falls* (1981) and *Question and Answer* (1989).

MEYER, Kerstin (1928–) *Opera singer* Swedish born mezzo-soprano Meyer made her debut in Stockholm in 1952. She sang at many of the world's leading OPERA houses, and was a favorite at Glyndebourne in England. She appeared in recital and concert, often performing as a duo with Elisabeth Söderström.

MEZZROW, Mezz (1899–1972) *Jazz clarinetist* Mezzrow's career included some marvelous recordings. As a JAZZ player with BLUES roots, he is best heard on *The Quintessential Milton Mezz Mezzrow* (1928–53) with Sidney Bechet, and *In Paris 1955*.

MIGENES, Julia (1949–) *Opera singer* American-born soprano, Migenes appeared on Broadway and at the New York City Opera in 1965. She appeared at the Vienna Volksoper (1973–78), singing Mozart as well as STRAUSS and PUCCINI. She sang at the Met from 1979 and at Covent Garden in London from 1987.

MILLER, Marcus (1959–) *Jazz musician and composer* Miller first worked in JAZZ bands from the late 1970s developing a reputation for his bass playing and his arrangements. In 1980 he joined Miles DAVIS, later writing music for his album *Tutu* (1986). He also recorded with a number of other jazz and pop musicians, such as Aretha FRANKLIN and Luther Vandross.

MILLER, Mitch (1911–) *Musician, record producer, and arranger* One of the most successful recording artists of the 1950s, Miller also had an influential career as a record producer. He worked with Frankie LAINE, Marty Robbins, Rosemary Clooney, and Johnny Mathis among others, guiding them to success by choosing which songs they should cover and then producing the recordings. His own recording career was also successful. He recorded a series of "singalong" albums in the late 1950s and early 1960s that sold in the millions and even spawned a successful television series.

MILLER, Roger (1936–92) *Country-pop singer-songwriter* The 1960s were the best years in Miller's career. He had success with his first releases "Dang Me" and "Chug-a-Lug" (both 1964), while "King of the Road" (1965) and "England Swings" both became international successes. His star faded during the 1970s, but Miller is also remembered for his rich and fruity voice on the soundtrack to Walt Disney's movie *Robin Hood* (1973).

MILLER, Steve (1943–) *Rock guitarist and singer* Miller started bands as early as 1955. But it was not until 1967 that he found fame after a performance at the Monterey Pop Festival with a band that included Boz Scaggs. Several albums appeared between then and *The Joker* (1973), establishing Miller and his band as a top ROCK act. But Miller's best was saved until 1976, when *Fly Like an Eagle* became a million-copy-seller. *Book of Dreams* in 1977 kept up the momentum and *Abracadabra* (1982) reached No.1 on the U.S. charts.

MILNES, Sherrill (1935–) *Opera singer* American baritone Milnes made his debut in 1960, singing at the Metropolitan Opera in New York with Caballé in 1965. He was one of the most prolific recording artists of his time, with a repertoire including Escamillo, Don Giovanni, and all the leading Verdi baritone roles. He has appeared in concert all over the world to great acclaim, and is regarded as one of the greatest baritones of the 20th century.

MILSAP, Ronnie (1943-) *Country singer* Almost blind at birth, Milsap's sight was completely gone by the time he started his career. His first recordings straddled COUNTRY, SOUL, and BLUES. But in 1971 his first album for Warners featured several country hits. His career, including over 30 country No.1 hits, declined during the 1990s.

MILTON, Roy (1907-83) *Blues singer, drummer, and bandleader* After playing in groups in the 1920s, Milton formed the Solid Senders in 1935. Scaled down, but keeping a big band sound, they recorded "R.M. Blues" which was a hit in 1945. Other hits included "Milton's Boogie," and "Best Wishes." Milton's foresight in reducing the personnel in his band, but keeping the power by introducing driving drums is often seen as having helped prepare the market for ROCK'N'ROLL.

MINISTRY *Rock group* Formed in Chicago in the early 1980s, Ministry didn't find their true direction until *The Land of Rape and Honey* (1988) which displayed their unique brand of guitar-based industrial metal. Fronted by Al Jourgensen, commercial success came in 1991 with the single "Jesus Built My Hotrod," and *Psalm 69* (1992). Ministry's music is solid but eclectic HEAVY METAL.

MINNELLI, Liza (1946-) *Popular singer, dancer, and actress* Daughter of Judy GARLAND and film director Vincente Minnelli, Liza first found success singing in stage musicals in the early 1960s. She released her first album *Liza! Liza!* in 1964, continuing on Broadway and in New York cabaret, notably with material from KANDER & EBB. She began her film career in 1968, and hit the big time in 1972 with a starring role in the film version of *Cabaret*, winning an Oscar for Best Actress. She had many more film and stage successes, and was ultimately seen as a star in her own right rather than as Judy Garland's daughter.

MITROPOULOS, Dimitri (1896-1960) *Conductor* An American of Greek birth, Mitropoulos began conducting in 1924. He worked with the Berlin Philharmonic Orchestra in 1930, and made his American debut in 1936. His greatest achievement was as conductor of the Minneapolis Symphony Orchestra, between 1937–49, giving famous performances of contemporary works by BERG and SCHOENBERG. As well as his interpretations of STRAUSS, he was renowned for his conducting of MAHLER.

MOHOLO, Louis (1940-) *Jazz drummer* Moholo developed a strong, clean style. A member of the legendary Blue Notes, he left South Africa with the band in 1964. As part of Chris McGregor's Brotherhood of Breath, he later made many recordings between the 1970s and the 1990s.

MOISEIWITSCH, Benno (1890-1963) *Pianist* Moiseiwitsch was British of Russian birth who studied in Odessa and Vienna before making his London debut in 1908. He was a powerful and poetic player, particularly in Beethoven and RACHMANINOV. He was a popular performer, appealing to audiences all over the world.

MOLL, Kurt (1938-) *Opera singer* German-born Moll made his debut in 1961. From 1970 he was a member of the Hamburg Staatsoper. He was invited to appear at major opera houses all over the world, particularly for his roles in Wagner.

MONKEES, The *Pop group* The Monkees were formed in 1966 for an American TV show about a struggling pop group. The show's success led to the release of several hit singles, such as "Last Train to Clarksville," "I'm a Believer" (both 1966), "Daydream Believer" (1967), and an eponymous million-selling first album on which the band sang but did not play. The second album *More of the Monkees* (1967) sold over 5 million copies. Again the band only sang. The TV show ended in 1968 and the band split up a year later.

MONNOT, Marguerite (1909-61) *Composer* Monnot first found success in the 1930s, writing songs such as "Mon Légion-naire" (1935), and later many for Edith PIAF, including "The Poor People of Paris," "Milord," and "The Left Bank." But she found her greatest success writing for the musical theater, with shows such as *La A'tilé Lil* (1951) and *Irma La Douce* (1956).

MONTGOMERY, Eurreal "Little Brother" (1906-85) *Blues pianist and singer* Playing barrelhouse BOOGIE-WOOGIE piano, Montgomery became a giant of the BLUES. During the 1920s he played with many great musicians, such as Danny Barker, Big Joe Williams, Blind Blake, and later Kid Ory. His recording career began in 1930, and included classic blues tunes such as "Vicksburg Blues No.2" and "No Special Rider." He spent the remainder of his career performing in the blues clubs of Chicago

MONTGOMERY, Wes (1923-68) *Jazz guitarist* With his highly personal style, Montgomery became one of the most respected JAZZ guitarists of the 1960s. During the late 1940s he played with artists such as Lionel Hampton, Hank Jones, and John COLTRANE. Recording from the late 1950s, his most popular albums included *Movin' Wes, Bumpin'* (both 1965), and *A Day in the Life* (1967). He had an unusual technique, using his thumb to play melodic lines in parallel octaves.

MOODY BLUES, The *Pop group* Formed in 1964 as an R&B group, the Moody Blues had an early hit with the single "Go Now" (1965). In 1967 they released *Days of Future Passed*, a concept album with full orchestral accompaniment. The subsequent single, "Nights in White Satin," became a worldwide hit. The group lost its audience in the 1970s and disbanded.

MOORE, Gerald (1899-1987) *Pianist* Moore became one of the most respected accompanists of the 20th century. In his early career he accompanied singers such as Maria CALLAS. His success was not simply due to his technique or his extensive repertoire, but also to the empathy he found with many of the great singers. He was most noted for his work with SCHWARZKOPF and FISCHER-DIESKAU, particularly in Schubert and STRAUSS.

MOORE, Grace (1901-47) *Opera singer* Born in the U.S., Moore was a versatile soprano who sang on stage, in movies, and on radio. She had a glamorous personality to go with her big and sensuous voice, used most memorably in Opéra-Comique.

MORGAN, George (1924-75) *Country singer* Morgan had his first hit with "Candy Kisses" (1949), a U.S. COUNTRY No.1 hit. One of the first "crooner" country stars, he followed up with hits such as "Please Don't Let Me Love You," "Room Full of Roses," and "Almost." He performed regularly at the Grand Ole Opry, but failed to repeat the fame he had earned during the early 1950s.

MORISSETTE, Alanis (1974-) *Rock singer* After one album, *Jagged Little Pill* (1995), Canadian-born Morissette established herself as an international star. A blend of memorable tunes and personal lyrics ensured that the album enjoyed enormous success.

MORRIS, James (1947-) *Opera singer* The American bass-baritone made his debut in 1967. He was much in demand for roles in operas by Mozart, Offenbach, and Verdi. It was, however, as a singer of Wagner that he made his greatest mark, singing the role of Wotan on two complete *Ring* cycle recordings.

MORTON, Benny (1907-85) *Jazz trombonist* One of the unsung heroes of the SWING era, Morton was hired by Fletcher HENDERSON in 1926, and later played with Chick Webb, Don Redman, and Count BASIE. One of the most sophisticated trombonists of his era, it is said that his self-effacing nature got in the way of his fame.

MOSS, Buddy (1914-84) *Blues singer and guitarist* Moss made his name with a distinctive BLUES style, becoming one of the most popular Atlanta-based singers of the 1930s, recording over 60 tracks between 1933–35. Though he performed with Josh White and later with Sonny TERRY & Brownie McGEE, his career was severely hampered by a prison term, between 1935–40, after he was convicted of murdering his wife.

MOTEN, Bennie (1894-1935) *Jazz pianist and bandleader* By 1920 Moten had become an established bandleader. As an arranger he blended New Orleans concepts with the freeflowing style popular in the Midwest. His big band recorded from 1923 and attracted players such as Count BASIE, Hot Lips Page, Jimmy Rushing, and later Walter Page. By the mid-1930s the band was regarded as one of the finest of its kind. After Moten's untimely death, the band evolved into Count Basie's Big Band.

MOTIAN, Paul (1931-) *Jazz drummer* From the late 1950s Motian played with a huge array of great jazz players such as Bill EVANS, Charlie Hadden, and Keith JARRETT. During the 1970s he fronted his own groups releasing an impressive set of albums including *Tribute* (1974) and *Notes* (1987). In the 1980s he began a long-term association with Bill Frisell and the tenor sax player Joe Lovano.

MOTÖRHEAD *Rock group* Formed in 1975 by bassist and singer Lemmy—formerly with acid rockers Hawkwind—Motörhead were one of the greatest HEAVY METAL rock bands of all time. Their relentless guitars, tight drumming, and pumping bass, fronted by Lemmy's razor-blade voice, produced some of the most memorable live shows ever. Best heard on *Ace of Spades* (1980), *No Sleep 'Til Hammersmith* (1981), and *Orgasmatron* (1986).

MOTT THE HOOPLE *Rock group* Formed in the U.K. in 1969, Mott the Hoople bridged the gap between PROGRESSIVE ROCK and the glam rock scene of the pop charts. Their first hit came in 1972, with a David BOWIE song "All the Young Dudes." "Honaloochie Boogie," and "All the Way from Memphis" (both 1973) followed, establishing the band as a major act. But internal pressures were too strong to resist and Mott disbanded in 1974. Singer Ian Hunter went on to have a moderately successful career in the U.S. with the Ian Hunter Band.

MÜNCHINGER, Karl (1915-) *Conductor* German-born Münchinger was conductor of the Hanover Symphony Orchestra (1941–43). He founded the Stuttgart Chamber Orchestra in 1945, which became one of the foremost chamber orchestras in the world. They toured widely and made many highly acclaimed recordings, particularly of Bach and especially the Brandenburg Concertos.

MUNROW, David (1942-76) *Early wind instrument player and director* Munrow studied at Cambridge and developed a deep interest in early music and authentic performance. In 1967 he formed the Early Music Consort of London, which gave concerts of medieval and Renaissance music on period instruments. The group was responsible for bringing a large, and largely ignored, repertoire of music to a wider audience.

MURPHEY, Michael Martin (1945-) *Country singer-songwriter* Firmly in the middle-of-the-road COUNTRY category, Murphey had a number of hits from the early 1970s, such as "Wildfire" (1975), and *Peaks, Valleys, Honky-Tonks, and Alleys* (1979). But it is as a songwriter that he is best known, writing songs for Cher, John Denver, and the Monkees.

MUTI, Riccardo (1941-) *Conductor* Born and educated in Italy, Muti made his debut in 1968. Conducting in Florence from 1969, he was chief conductor of the New Philharmonia in London (1973–82), and additionally the principal conductor of the Philadelphia Orchestra (1975–82). In 1986 he became musical director of La Scala in Milan. His performances, mostly of 20th-century music, are noted for their vitality and warmth of expression.

MUTTER, Anne-Sophie (1963-) *Violinist* Mutter became an international star after coming to the attention of Herbert VON KARAJAN while playing in Lucerne in 1976. From 1977 she played the standard concerto repertoire all over the world to great acclaim. She is also renowned for her interpretations of STRAVINSKY and premieres of LUTOSLAWSKI.

N'DOUR, Youssou (1959-) *Singer and composer* Born in Dakar, Senegal, N'Dour became one of Senegal's greatest musical exports. He began to record in 1981 with *Tabaski*. His Western releases, *Immigrés* (1985) and *The Lion* (1986), developed worldwide interest and success. Further albums followed and the duet "7 Seconds" (1994) with Neneh Cherry was a hit in the U.S. and Europe. N'Dour continued to record and tour in Europe and the U.S. during the late 1990s.

NANCARROW, Conlon (1912–96)
Composer Nancarrow was a Mexican of U.S. origin who, from the late 1940s, composed exclusively for the player piano—a piano that automatically plays music recorded in perforations on a paper roll. Works displayed rhythmic complexity, textural variety, and a virtuosity far beyond a human performer's abilities. His 37 Studies for Player Piano (1950–68) represent a unique achievement. His music only received serious attention after the 1970s, and is now regarded as an important part of 20th-century music. He also composed Toccata for Violin and Piano, Blues for Piano, and Prelude for Piano (all 1935).

NAT, Yves (1890–1956) *Pianist and composer* Born in France, Nat began his career at an early age. He was sent to the Paris Conservatoire on the recommendation of Saint-Saëns and Fauré. Nat was noted for his playing of Beethoven and Schumann. In the latter part of his life he stopped performing and took to teaching and composing. His best known works were *L'enfer* (1942) and a modal Piano Concerto (1953).

NAVARRO, Fats (1923–50) *Jazz trumpeter* Navarro was playing JAZZ professionally by his mid-teens. In 1943 he joined the Andy Kirk band, two years later joining the BEBOP-oriented band of Billy Eckstine. Later, settling in New York, he played with leading beboppers such as Kenny Clarke, Tadd Dameron, Charlie PARKER, and Dizzy GILLESPIE. Despite an early death from drug abuse, he left a legacy of many recordings, becoming one of the great early bebop soloists.

NELSON, Rick (1940–85) *Pop-country singer* Born into a showbusiness family Nelson had immediate success with his solo debut single "I'm Walkin'" (1957). Further pop hits followed including "Poor Little Fool," and "Travelin' Man," until he changed to COUNTRY in the late 1960s. His biggest hit as a country singer was with "Garden Party" (1971), in which he explained his change from POP MUSIC to country. Nelson was killed in a plane crash on his way to a concert date in Dallas.

NEVILLE BROTHERS *Blues-soul group* From New Orleans, the four Neville brothers—Art, Charles, Aaron, and Cyril—played in bands from the early 1950s. Aaron had some success with solo singles, and Art formed the seminal soul band the Meters. But it was in 1978, when the brothers recorded the album *Yellow Moon,* that they achieved real success. Playing a mixture of R&B, ROCK'N'ROLL, SOUL, FUNK, and JAZZ, the Neville Brothers collectively represent the musical mix present in the Crescent City. Aaron also had a hit in 1989 with "Don't Know Much," a song he sang with Linda Ronstadt.

NEWBURY, Mickey (1940–) *Country songwriter-singer* Newbury's career was primarily as a songwriter. He did make some recordings of his own, but his voice was so mournful that it was thought to put people off. His songs were recorded by artists such as Tammy WYNETTE, Roy Orbison, Willie NELSON, Kenny ROGERS, Jerry Lee LEWIS, Joan BAEZ, and John Denver among others. But his greatest success came in 1972 when Elvis PRESLEY sang his composition "The American Trilogy"—a medley of three Civil War songs.

NEWLEY, Anthony (1931–) *Musical songwriter, actor, and singer* Born in London, Newley starred in a number of films in the 1940s and 1950s. As a singer he had some chart hits in 1961, with songs such as "Why" and "Do You Mind." In 1961 he found success collaborating with Leslie Bricusse, writing the stage musical *Stop the World, I Want to Get Off.* Later successes with Bricusse included the FILM MUSICAL of *Willy Wonka and the Chocolate Factory* (1970).

NEW YORK DOLLS, The *Punk group* The short-lived New York Dolls (formed in 1972) were hugely influential on the development of PUNK and HEAVY METAL bands. Their self-titled debut album (1973) was a landmark in rock history, and met with critical acclaim, though little commercial success. The band's glam rock image, legendary drug taking, and general attitude to life seemed to epitomize the punk movement. Soon after their less successful second album, *Too Much Too Soon* (1974), the group disbanded.

NICHOLS, Red (1905–65) *Jazz cornetist* Heavily influenced as a youth by Bix BEIDERBECKE, Nichols became a highly accomplished player. In New York in the 1920s he formed a number of bands, recording hundreds of tracks that became the largest and richest legacy of 1920s white JAZZ. Musicians he used included Jimmy Dorsey, Joe Venuti, Benny GOODMAN, and Jack Teagarden. His career continued into the 1940s and 1950s as a bandleader, appearing regularly on TV and radio.

NICKS, Stevie (1948–) *Rock singer and songwriter* Nicks had much success when she joined Fleetwood Mac in 1975, writing many of the group's best-known songs, such as "Rhiannon" and "Dreams." She went solo in 1980, achieving platinum sales for the album *Bella Donna* (1981), which remained on the U.S. album charts for over two years. She had a number of hit singles, such as "Stop Draggin' My Heart Around"—a duet with Tom Petty—"Leather and Lace"—a duet with Don Henley—(both 1981) and "Stand Back" (1983). She continued to record into the 1990s, and was the producer on Sheryl Crow's 1998 album *The Globe Sessions.*

NIGHTHAWK, Robert (1909–67) *Blues guitarist and harmonica player* One of the great BLUES slide guitarists, Nighthawk accompanied artists such as Big Joe Williams and Sonny Boy WILLIAMSON during the 1930s. At the end of the 1940s he got a record deal and produced classics such as "Anna Lee Blues" and "Sweet Black Angel." Though he never achieved great financial success, his guitar style remained influential.

NILSSON, Birgit (1918–) *Opera singer* Swedish soprano Nilsson first sang at the Royal Opera, Stockholm, in 1946. Her international career took off after performing at the Bayreuth Festival. She sang at Covent Garden, in London, and the Metropolitan in New York during the 1950s. With her bright and powerful voice she became a distinguished interpreter of PUCCINI and STRAUSS, and it was in the role of Strauss's Electra and as a singer of Wagner that she is best remembered.

NINE INCH NAILS *Rock band* Trent Reznor was the creative force behind Nine Inch Nails, which was formed in 1988. From its first album *Pretty Hate Machine* (1989) and the major U.S. hit single "Head Like a Hole," it found a huge following with its wall of guitar and synthesizer-based sound. Further successes included the single "Wish," a Grammy winner, and the third album, *The Downward Spiral* (1994).

NIXON, Marni (1930-) *Opera and popular singer* Born in the U.S., Nixon had an incredibly varied career, appearing with her light and flexible soprano voice in film and MUSICAL comedy as well as in OPERA and concert. She dubbed the singing voices for the actresses in the film versions of *The King and I, West Side Story,* and *My Fair Lady.* She was also successful singing WEBERN, STRAVINSKY, and IVES, as well as operas by Mozart among others.

NOLAN, Bob (1908-80) *Country-and songwriter* Though born in Canada, Nolan was one of the greatest Western songwriters of all time. After hoboing during the 1920s, he joined the Rocky Mountaineers as a singer and yodeler. He later joined Sons of the Pioneers, who had a number of big hits during the 1940s, such as "Cool Water" and "Tumbling Tumbleweeds."

NOONE, Jimmie (1895-1944) *Jazz clarinetist* From 1918 Noone worked in Chicago with King Oliver. He formed his own band in 1926 with Earl Hines. A consummate player, Noone soon became the idol of many up-and-coming musicians. His classic recordings included "Sweet Lorraine" and "Four or Five Times," both recorded in the late 1920s.

NORRINGTON, Sir Roger (1974-) *Conductor* Born in England, Norrington studied at Cambridge. He conducted, while still a professional tenor, during the early 1960s, becoming musical director of Kent Opera from 1969–84. He is most renowned for his work with the London Classical Players, which he formed in 1978. With them he made many highly regarded authentic instrument recordings, including Beethoven symphonies and Mozart operas.

NORVO, Red (1908-) *Jazz xylophonist and vibraphonist* Starting his career as a xylophone player, Norvo changed to vibes during the 1940s when he played with Benny GOODMAN, Woody Herman, and Billie HOLIDAY. Norvo was one of the few JAZZ musicians to manage the crossover from SWING to BEBOP.

NOTORIOUS BIG (1972-97) *Rap artist* Born in Brooklyn as Christopher Wallace, aka Biggie Smalls, Notorious BIG represented East-Coast based gangsta rap. After a spell in prison, he burst onto the hip-hop scene with his 1994 album *Ready to Die,* renowned for its raps that told the true story of life on the street, like the song "One More Chance." He was shot dead in a Los Angeles drive-by shooting in 1997, allegedly as part of the gangsta rap wars.

NOVELLO, Ivor (1893-1951) *Composer* U.K.-born Novello first found success writing the immensely popular song "Keep the Home Fires Burning" (1914). He became a matinée film idol in the 1920s and 1930s, turning to writing his own MUSICALS (in which he also starred). These included the hugely popular *Glamorous Night* (1935) and *The Dancing Years* (1949). In 1947 he was a founding member of the Songwriters' Guild.

NUGENT, Ted (1949-) *Rock guitarist* Nugent first recorded with his band, the Amboy Dukes, for Frank ZAPPA's Discreet Records. But in 1976 he started a solo career. He made his mark as a live performer, playing loud guitar-based ROCK while portraying a wildman image. Best heard on the album *Double Live Gonzo* (1978). As rock music progressed into the 1980s Nugent was unwilling or unable to change with it and he dropped out of sight.

NUNES, Emmanuel (1941-) *Composer* Born in Portugal, Nunes moved to Paris in 1964, where he became immersed in the French and German avant-garde movements, which hugely influenced his ebullient and individual compositions. He wrote CHAMBER MUSIC as well as ORCHESTRAL MUSIC and choral works.

N.W.A. *Rap group* Formed in Compton near Los Angeles in 1986, allegedly on the proceeds of a narcotics deal, N.W.A (Niggers With Attitude)—comprising Eazy-E, Dr. Dre, and Ice Cube, among others—established the genre of gangsta rap with their first album *Straight Outta Compton* (1988). Originally an underground album, it went on to sell over 2 million copies. Although short-lived, their influence remained when they split up in acrimony in 1989.

O'CONNOR, Sinead (1966-) *Rock singer* With little experience in music, O'Connor recorded her first album, *The Lion and the Cobra,* in 1988. Some catchy tunes and some opinionated interviews raised her profile. Her next single, written by PRINCE, "Nothing Compares 2 U" became a international hit and stimulated sales of her second album *I Do Not Want What I Haven't Got* (1990). She courted controversy during the 1990s and found it difficult to sustain her audience, but she continued to perform—notably on the Lilith Fair roadshow—and record during the 1990s.

O'DAY, Anita (1919-) *Jazz singer* O'Day first found fame singing with Gene Krupa from 1941 and then with Stan KENTON's band. She went solo in 1946 making many fine albums into the 1990s. Highlights include *Anita Sings the Most* with the Oscar Peterson Quartet (1957) and *Rules of the Road* (1993). Her remarkable, rhythmic voice, coupled with a forceful personality, made her one of the leading ladies in JAZZ.

O'DAY, Molly (1923-87) *Country singer* O'Day was regarded by some as the greatest COUNTRY singer of all time. She sang from the 1940s, most notably with the Cumberland Mountain Folks (1946–51), with whom she made many recordings. Her individual, emotional style was heard on songs such as "The Drunken Driver" and "Don't Sell Daddy Any More Whiskey." She championed the work of Hank WILLIAMS, recording and performing many of his songs during her career. She continued working and recording into the 1970s.

O'DONNELL, Daniel (1961-) *Country singer* As a "COUNTRY 'n' Irish" singer, O'Donnell first became popular in his native Ireland. He recorded his first album in England in 1985, where he built up a huge following. His many album successes included *Don't Forget to Remember* (1987) and *The Last Waltz* (1990). O'Donnell is without doubt the biggest-selling Irish singer in the world.

O'FARRILL, Chico (1921-) *Jazz arranger* After playing trumpet in CUBAN bands in the 1940s, O'Farrill forged a career in the U.S. in the 1950s as an ARRANGER for artists such as Benny GOODMAN, Stan KENTON, and Dizzy GILLESPIE. He later toured and recorded with his own band, as well as arranging for Count BASIE.

O'NEAL, Alexander (1954-) *Soul singer* Starting as a backing singer for PRINCE, O'Neal began a solo career in the early 1980s. His eponymous first album contained a number of R&B hits, including "If You Were Here Tonight"—a U.K. Top 20 hit. He broke through to the mainstream American audiences with his second album and singles including "Fake." He continued to record in the 1990s, retaining popularity in the U.K.

ODYSSEY *Soul group* Formed in the 1960s, this vocal group found success during the DISCO boom with the classic "Native New Yorker" (1977). They proved more lastingly successful in the U.K., where they had several more hits including "Use It Up and Wear It Out" (1980) and "Going Back to My Roots" (1981). But they failed to sustain interest and broke up in 1985.

OGDON, John (1937-89) *Pianist* Born in England, Ogdon forged a considerable reputation as an interpreter of 20th-century music, giving first performances of works by Maxwell Davies, TIPPETT, and many others. He had formidable technique, which astounded his audiences, playing a vast range of music—including Viennese classics and the Romantics. He was part of the "Manchester School," with Birtwistle, Maxwell Davies, Alexander Goehr, and Elgar Howarth.

OHIO PLAYERS, The *Soul group* Formed in 1959, the Ohio Players first forged a reputation as a backing group. They recorded in their own right from 1962, not achieving any real success until the early 1970s. Their experimental FUNK suddenly scored a massive R&B hit in 1973 with "Funky Worm." Other hits topping the charts were "Fire" (1974) and "Love Rollercoaster" (1975), followed by their last substantial hit "Who'd She Coo?" (1975).

OISTRAKH, David (1908-74) *Violinist* Born in Russia, Oistrakh made his debut in Leningrad in 1928. His technical mastery and powerful tone were often heard in Soviet music—both SHOSTAKOVICH concertos were dedicated to him. As one of the greatest violinists of his day, he was also a fine interpreter of the great Romantic concertos.

OISTRAKH, Igor (1931-) *Violinist* Born in Russia, Oistrakh studied with his father, David, at the Moscow Conservatory where from 1958 he also taught. A player with a phenomenal technique, his rather detached interpretations were best heard in works such as the BARTÓK concertos, Violin Concerto No.2 in particular.

OLDFIELD, Mike (1953-) *Pop artist* Oldfield will forever be remembered for *Tubular Bells* (1973), a 49-minute piece, combining FOLK, ROCK, and classical melodies and ideas. It sold over 12 million copies, topping the U.K. and U.S. charts, and remaining on both for over 5 years. He continued to produce albums into the 1990s. Other successes included the hit singles "In Dulci Jubilo" (1975) and "Moonlight Shadow" (1983), as well as the music for the movies *The Exorcist* (1973) and *The Killing Fields* (1984). *Tubular Bells III* was premiered in London in 1998.

OLIVER, Joe "King" (1885-1938) *Jazz cornetist and bandleader* Oliver was one of the greatest artists in the classic NEW ORLEANS JAZZ style. He formed his own band in Chicago in 1920 with musicians including Johnny and Baby Dodds and Louis ARMSTRONG. The band became a sensation, making classic recordings in 1923–24. The good times soon stopped, however, when others began to adopt his style, including Armstrong himself. By 1936 Oliver had quit music.

OLIVER, Sy (1910-88) *Jazz trumpeter and arranger* Oliver first found major success as trumpeter and main ARRANGER for the Jimmie Lunceford band—shaping its sound from 1933. He later worked with Benny GOODMAN and Tommy DORSEY. His hits included "Swing High" and "Sunny Side of the Street." The style he developed was undoubtedly responsible for the creation of mainstream BIG BAND JAZZ.

ONO, Yoko (1933-) *Pop singer* Ono found musical fame working with her husband John Lennon, but has also had success in her own right. Her first album *Yoko Ono/Plastic Ono Band* came out in 1970, followed by three more later in the decade. Her music is avant-garde and often difficult, but she has recorded some excellent songs, including "Listen, the Snow Is Falling" and "Woman Power." In the 1980s and 1990s she failed to achieve comparable success.

ORBISON, Roy (1936-88) *Country-pop singer-songwriter* Orbison was one of the leading singers of the 1960s, a master of the epic ballad with a high, powerful voice. "Only the Lonely" was his first hit, and by 1965 he had made the U.S. Top 40 some 20 times, including the No.1s "It's Over" and "Oh Pretty Woman." The 1970s were rather barren, but he bounced back in 1980, winning a Grammy with Emmylou HARRIS for the duet "That Lovin' You Feelin' Again." His posthumously released album *Mystery Girl* was the most successful of his career.

ORBITAL *Techno-dance duo* Formed in 1987, Orbital are a U.K. techno band who do much to bring improvisation to live ELECTRONIC MUSIC, and are one of the most visually exciting live bands in any genre—one of the few British bands to appear at Woodstock 2. They released their first single, "Chime" in 1989, following it with a series of successful albums. They also work as PRODUCERS and remixers for other artists, including MADONNA.

ORMANDY, Eugene (1899-1985) *Conductor* Ormandy first performed as a solo violinist before moving to the U.S. in 1921. He began his long association with the Philadelphia Orchestra in 1936. Under his direction their immaculate technique and full, rich tone became legendary, especially in LATE ROMANTIC and early 20th-century music.

ORTIZ, Cristina (1950-) *Pianist* Born in Brazil, Ortiz studied in Rio de Janeiro and then in Paris. She made her New York debut in 1971, moving to London in 1972. She played with most of the world's leading orchestras. Her extensive repertoire and recordings include RACHMANINOV and Clara Schumann.

ORY, Edward "Kid" (1886-1973) *Jazz trombonist* Ory was one of the most popular musicians and bandleaders in NEW ORLEANS JAZZ at the beginning of the 20th century. He moved to California in 1922, and led the first all-black New Orleans jazz band to make recordings. From 1925 he played with artists such as Joe "King" Oliver, Jelly Roll MORTON, and Louis ARMSTRONG. By the mid-1940s he had become a JAZZ celebrity and he continued to play into the 1960s.

OSBORNE BROTHERS, The *Country duo* The Osborne Brothers recorded the first of many records in 1951. In 1958 they had their first COUNTRY hit with "Once More," and achieved more successes from 1963—including "Rocky Top." They were never afraid to modernize their bluegrass style, surviving the competition of ROCK and POP MUSIC to continue recording and touring into the 1980s.

OSBOURNE, Ozzy (1948-) *Rock singer-songwriter* Osbourne originally found fame as vocalist and songwriter for Black Sabbath, going solo in 1979 with the album *Blizzard of Oz*. His lyrics dealt with the grimmest of subjects from insanity to teenage suicide, often courting controversy. With his drug- and liquor-fueled off-stage antics—now behind him—and bat-eating stage act (after which he was treated for rabies), Osbourne went on to become one of the biggest names in HEAVY METAL.

OSMONDS, The *Pop group* This famous family vocal group first appeared in the 1960s on the *Andy Williams Show*. As a group they had 11 hit singles, such as "One Bad Apple," "Double Lovin'," and "Crazy Horses," as well as 12 hit albums between 1971 and 1978. Lead singer Donny Osmond and his sister Marie both had successful solo careers, recorded duets together, and had their own television show.

OTIS, Johnny (1921-) *Jazz-blues drummer* Otis became one of the big names in the R&B scene of the late 1940s when he was drummer for a number of people including Stan KENTON and Illinois Jacquet. In 1945 he formed his own big band, playing a BLUES-based JAZZ repertoire. He also wrote a number of songs such as "Every Beat of My Heart," a huge hit in the 1960s for Gladys Knight, and discovered the talents of Etta James and Willie Mae Thornton.

OTTER, Ann-Sofie von (1955-) *Opera singer* Swedish mezzo-soprano Otter made her debut in 1982. She performed all over the world as well as on many highly regarded recordings. Her light, pure voice is best heard in the OPERAS of Handel and Mozart, and in the cantatas and masses of Bach.

OUSSET, Cecile (1936-) *Pianist* Ousset was born and studied in France, graduating from the Paris Conservatory at the age of 14. Since her debut she has played all over the world, most notably performing the Romantics, including much Brahms and RACHMANINOV. She was also praised for her performances of the French repertoire, especially DEBUSSY.

OWENS, Buck (1929-) *Country Singer* One of the leading COUNTRY music stars of the 1960s and 1970s, Owens went solo in 1955, having his first hit with "Second Fiddle" in 1959. This prepared the way for over 75 country hits, over 40 reaching the Top 10. Among many No.1s were "Act Naturally" (1963), "Before You Go" (1965), and "Open Up Your Heart" (1966). He became one of the leading exponents of the West Coast sound, recording over 100 albums, and he continued working into the 1990s.

OZAWA, Seiji (1935-) *Conductor* Born in Japan, Ozawa had his earliest conducting experience in Tokyo, later studying in America at Tanglewood. Renowned for his interpretations of large-scale, LATE ROMANTIC works, he was musical director of the Toronto Symphony Orchestra and the San Francisco Symphony Orchestra before beginning a long tenure as musical director of the Boston Symphony Orchestra in 1973.

PABLO, Augustus (c.1954-) *Reggae musician and songwriter* Pablo became successful by putting the melodica on the musical map. "Java," one of his earliest singles, proved to be his biggest and one of the most influential. The album *King Tubby Meets Rockers Uptown* (1977) was regarded by many as one of the finest dub REGGAE albums of all time and was adopted by the PUNK movement in the U.K. Other classic albums included *This Is Augustus Pablo* (1974) and *East of the River Nile* (1978).

PADEREWSKI, Ignacy Jan (1860-1941) *Pianist* Paderewski had a formidable reputation as a concert pianist, beginning his career with a world tour in 1888. His repertoire centered on the Romantics, notably Chopin and Liszt, as well as Beethoven. He was also a composer of note, writing much piano music and an OPERA.

PAGE, Hot Lips (1908-54) *Jazz trumpeter* Born Oran Thaddeus, Page originally found success playing with Walter Page and then Benny Moten. Later he joined Count BASIE and briefly Artie Shaw, as well as leading his own bands. He was an excellent, emotional player, rather overshadowed by Louis ARMSTRONG. He made many recordings, including the hit "Baby, It's Cold Outside."

PAGE, Walter (1900-57) *Jazz bassist and bandleader* After playing in a number of bands, Page formed the legendary Blue Devils, whose members included Hot Lips Page, Jimmy Rushing, Lester YOUNG, and Count BASIE. After it folded he often played with Basie. He was generally considered to be the originator of the "walking bass" style—filling-in the basic harmonic structure.

PAGLIUGHI, Lina (1911–80) *Opera singer* The American soprano Pagliughi made her debut in Milan in 1927 and at Covent Garden in London in 1938. Her light voice was at its best in the OPERAS of Mozart and Donizetti. She retired in 1957.

PALM, Siegfried (1927–) *Cellist* Palm was principal cellist of a number of German orchestras between 1945 and 1967, before embarking on a solo career. He made a name for himself as an interpreter of avant-garde music, giving premieres of works by PENDERECKI, XENAKIS, Zimmerman, and many others.

PALMER, Felicity (1944–) *Opera singer* Born in the U.K., the soprano Palmer originally forged a career as a concert soloist, making her debut singing Purcell in 1970. She developed a wide repertoire singing Rameau to BOULEZ. Her OPERA debut, singing Mozart, was in 1973.

PARKER, Herman "Little Junior" (1927–71) *Blues singer* Parker first found success as leader of Howlin' Wolf's backing group. He then worked with, among others, Bobby "Blue" Bland and B. B. KING. He formed his own band, Blue Flame, in 1951, making a number of acclaimed recordings—at one point for Sam Phillips' Sun Records—such as "Driving Wheel" (1961) and "Man or Mouse" (1966). He was one of R&B's most influential figures.

PARKER, Maceo (1943–) *Funk musician* Saxophonist Parker joined the James BROWN Review in 1964 and was featured on a number of their recordings before leaving to join George Clinton's Parliament-Funkadelic in the early 1970s. Parker also pursued a solo career, forming Maceo and the Kings Men in 1970 and making a number of solo albums with some success, including *For All the King's Men* (1989), *Roots Revisited,* (1990) and *Funkoverload* (1998).

PARSONS, Geoffrey (1929–) *Pianist* Parsons became one of the most renowned accompanists in the latter half of the 20th century, appearing with SCHWARZKOPF, Janet Baker, and many others.

PARSONS, Gram (1946–73) *Country singer* Parsons was undoubtedly a huge influence on a generation of performers from the EAGLES to Elvis Costello. He was a member of a number of bands in the early 1960s, recording the album *Safe at Home* (1968) with the International Submarine Band—widely regarded as a landmark in COUNTRY-ROCK. He then had success as a member of the Byrds and The Flying Burrito Brothers—scoring a hit with his own composition "Hot Burrito #1." After being fired by the band he joined Emmylou HARRIS, who produced his debut solo album *GP* in 1972.

PARTCH, Harry (1901–74) *Composer* Partch was largely self-taught as a composer. He worked from the 1930s with his own adapted instruments, playing music in "just" intonation. His works, for voice and unique instruments, included *Oedipus* (1951) and *And on the Seventh Day Petals Fell in Petaluma* (1966).

PARTRIDGE, Ian (1938–) *Opera singer* The English tenor Partridge had his OPERA debut in 1958. He was particularly noted as a recitalist in the lieder of Schubert and Schumann, as well as of English song.

PASS, Joe (1929–94) *Jazz guitarist* Pass played in a number of bands from his teenage years, including Charlie Barnet's. He reemerged after drug addiction in the 1960s, eventually working with JAZZ's greatest names of the time, such as Oscar Peterson and Count BASIE. As a highly regarded accompanist he worked with several singers, including Ella FITZGERALD, but his phenomenal technique was best seen as a soloist on records such as "Guitar Player" (1976).

PASTORIUS, Jaco (1951–87) *Jazz bass guitarist* Pastorius first developed a cult following playing bass guitar for MOTOWN groups like the Temptations and the Supremes. In 1975 he began recording on his own, but it was as a member of Weather Report from 1976 that he made his mark. He formed his own band, Word of Mouth, in 1980, and continued to record with some of the top names in JAZZ until his death.

PATITUCCI, John (1959–) *Jazz bassist* Playing both electric and acoustic bass, Patitucci was best known for his work with Chick COREA and his Elektric Band and the Akoustic Band trio, with whom he recorded five albums. From the 1980s he worked as a bandleader. Perhaps his best recording is *Sketchbook.*

PATTI, Adelina (1843–1919) *Opera singer* While showing promise from an early age, Italian soprano Patti made her OPERA debut in 1859. She first sang at Covent Garden three years later and became the reigning prima donna there for the next 25 years. She excelled in her interpretations of Donizetti and Verdi.

PAUK, György (1936–) *Violinist* Pauk was a British citizen of Hungarian birth. He made his debut with an orchestra in 1950, appearing in London in 1961. After his London debut he forged an international career, at his best in BARTÓK, as well as Mozart, Beethoven, and Brahms.

PAVEMENT *Rock group* Formed in 1989, their debut release, the EP "Slay Tracks (1933–1969)" (1989) charmed the critics, leading them to the top of the U.S. alternative scene. Their live performances earned a staunch following and further successful albums followed including *Slanted and Enchanted* (1992) and *Wowee Zowee!* (1995).

PEARL JAM *Rock group* A product of the Seattle GRUNGE scene, Pearl Jam made their debut with the powerful and melodic album *Ten* (1991), which included the hit single "Alive." They became superstars almost overnight, the album remaining in the Top 20 for a year and a half, selling over 4 million copies in the U.S. alone. Two later albums *Vs.* (1993) and *Vitalogy* (1994), both met with much success. In the mid-1990s Pearl Jam worked extensively with Neil Young, contributing to his album *Mirror Ball.*

PEARS, Sir Peter (1910–86) *Opera singer* Born in the U.K., Pears studied at the Royal College of Music, singing at Sadler's Wells in London from 1943. His lyrical tenor voice created BRITTEN's Peter Grimes there in 1945. Thereafter Britten wrote all his tenor roles for Pears, including *Albert Herring* (1947). Pears also performed other music, ranging from the 16th to the 20th century. As an accomplished recitalist he was often accompanied by BRITTEN.

PEEL, John (1939-) *Alternative rock disc jockey* Peel is regarded as one of the best and most influential of British DJs. In the early 1960s he began working on American radio, before returning to England in 1967 to join the pirate radio station Radio London. There and later on BBC Radio 1 he led the way in introducing new and progressive acts, including the VELVET UNDERGROUND, PINK FLOYD, Jethro Tull, Rod Stewart, the Fall, and many others.

PEETERS, Flor (1903-86) *Composer and organist* Born in Belgium, Peeters pursued an international career as an organist while teaching at Belgian conservatories. His compositions, mainly of sacred choral and organ music, were influenced by Gregorian chants, Flemish Renaissance polyphony, and FOLK MUSIC.

PENDERGRASS, Teddy (1950-) *Soul singer* Pendergrass became famous as lead singer of the reformed Harold Melvin and the Blue Notes—leading lights in the PHILADELPHIA SOUND of the early 1970s. He went solo in 1976, with hit albums including *Teddy* (1979), which reached No.5 in the U.S. charts. He had a near-fatal car accident in 1982 but returned in 1984 with the hit "Hold Me."

PEPPER, Art (1925-82) *Jazz saxophonist* Pepper played alto saxophone with Stan KENTON, among others, until he started recording under his own name in 1952. After repeated imprisonments for drug offenses, Pepper was finally rehabilitated in the late 1960s. He reemerged in the mid-1970s as a major JAZZ figure, producing a string of recordings showcasing his rich melodic style, including *Living Legend* (1975).

PERAHIA, Murray (1947-) *Pianist* Perahia made his debut at Carnegie Hall in 1968, winning the Leeds International Piano Competition in

1972. He performed all over the world, most notably in Chopin and Schumann, and made highly acclaimed recordings of the complete Mozart concertos, conducting from the keyboard.

PERE UBU *Rock band* Formed in 1975, Pere Ubu took their name from a proto-surrealist play by French writer Alfred Jarry. Heavily influenced by bands like the Stooges, they released their debut album, *Modern Dance,* in 1978. Their music was avant-garde industrial ROCK, overlaid with witty lyrics. Pere Ubu split in 1982 after little commercial success but surprisingly reconvened in 1987, releasing their best album so far, *Raygun Suitcase*, in 1995.

PERKINS, Carl (1932-98) *Country guitarist, singer, and songwriter* Perkins became one of the most renowned rockabilly artists of the 1950s, influencing a generation of rock'n'rollers, including the BEATLES. Signed by Sam Phillips at Sun Records, his major success was "Blue Suede Shoes" (1956), the first COUNTRY record to appear on both the R&B and POP charts, as well as being a country hit. Although further recordings failed to do as well, he was one of ROCK's pioneers and remains a big influence on today's guitar players.

PERLEMUTER, Vlado (1904-) *Pianist* Perlemuter, a Frenchman of Polish birth, became established in the 1920s as a notable interpreter of RAVEL and Chopin. He was a professor at the Paris Conservatory, retiring from the concert platform in 1993.

PERLMAN, Itzhak (1945-) *Violinist* Born in Israel—suffering from poliomyelitis—Perlman studied at the Juilliard School from 1958. He had his American debut at Carnegie Hall in New York in 1963, and played with the London Symphony Orchestra in 1968. Interested in violin music of all kinds, he performed the major concertos all over the world, including BARTÓK, BERG, and STRAVINSKY, as well as giving recitals, notably with BARENBOIM and Zukerman. He is regarded as one of the finest violinists of the 20th century.

PETER, PAUL AND MARY *Folk group* Formed in 1961, this vocal and guitar FOLK trio comprising Peter Yarrow, Paul Stookey, and Mary Travers, had a number of hits including Bob DYLAN's "Blowin' in the Wind" and "Puff the Magic Dragon" (both 1963). Their biggest success was "Leaving on a Jet Plane" (1969). With their folky sound they were one of the era's most distinctive acts. They disbanded in 1970.

PETERSON, Oscar (1925-) *Jazz pianist* Already well known in his native Canada, Peterson made his American debut at Carnegie Hall with Jazz at the Philharmonic in 1949. From then he played with all the greatest jazzmen of the day, making hundreds of recordings. His biggest seller was "Affinity" (1963). From the 1970s he stopped maintaining a regular group but continued to record prolifically, becoming one of the most highly regarded and best-known JAZZ pianists ever.

PETTIFORD, Oscar (1922-60) *Jazz bassist and cellist* During his short life Pettiford performed with some of the best jazzmen of his day, including Roy ELDRIDGE, Coleman HAWKINS, Dizzy GILLESPIE, Thelonious MONK, and Art BLAKEY. Playing with an incredible technique and a superb tone, he appeared with many groups, big and small, often leading, and was a major influence on later BEBOP bass players. He is best heard on the albums *Deep Passion* (1956-57) and *Vienna Blues: The Complete Session* (1959).

PETTY, Tom, & the Heartbreakers *Rock group* Petty first recorded with the Heartbreakers, featuring Benmont Tench and Mike Campell, in 1976, producing their eponymous first album. The third album, *Damn the Torpedoes* (1979), went platinum in the U.S. Further hits and albums followed. Petty toured with Bob DYLAN in the late 1980s, as well as producing a well received solo album that included "Full Moon Fever" (1989). His *Greatest Hits* release in 1993 encouraged a new wave of interest, the album becoming a multi-million-copy best-seller. Petty is regarded as one of the most durable ROCK artists of the 1980s and 1990s.

PHILLIPS, Esther (1935-84) *R&B singer* Phillips was discovered by drummer Johnny Otis in the 1950s. From the late 1960s, Phillips became an international star with hits such as "When a Man Loves a Woman" (1966) and "What a Diff'rence a Day Makes" (1975). She recorded her last album in 1981.

PHILLIPS, Flip (1915-) *Jazz saxophonist* Phillips rose to fame in the JAZZ world first by playing with Benny GOODMAN in 1942 and then with Woody Herman for two years. He then raised his international standing by touring with Jazz at the Philharmonic from 1946 to 1956. He had a welcome comeback in 1975, playing in New York and touring Europe. He was undoubtedly one of the great ballad players, recording from 1949 through to 1993.

PHILLIPS, Sam (1923-) *Record producer* Phillips opened his own recording studio on Union Street, Memphis, Tennessee, in 1950, producing, among others Howlin' Wolf, Ike Turner, and B.B. KING. His early work led to the founding of Sun Records in 1952, where Phillips had his biggest success—launching the career of Elvis PRESLEY and producing his first five singles.

PIATIGORSKY, Gregor (1903-76) *Cellist* Piatigorsky studied in Moscow, leaving Russia in 1921 and settled in America. He was principal cello of the Berlin Philharmonic Orchestra (1924–28) after which he pursued a solo career. He made his New York debut in 1929, and was soon hailed as the leading cellist of his generation. His virtuosic flair and exquisite taste in style was best heard in Romantic music.

PICKETT, Wilson (1941-) *Soul singer* Pickett initially found success as part of the Falcons, writing and singing the lead on the hit single "I Found a Love" (1962). Going solo soon after he had a number of hits in the 1960s and early 1970s including "In the Midnight Hour" (1965), "Mustang Sally" (1966), and "Funky Broadway" (1967). Despite a move to Philadelphia to work with producers Gamble and Huff, Pickett's success faded away in the 1970s.

PINNOCK, Trevor (1946-) *Conductor and harpsichordist* Pinnock made an international name for himself as founder and musical director of the English Consort, an AUTHENTIC PERFORMANCE orchestra. With them and as a soloist he made over 70 recordings, including the orchestral music of Bach and Handel, Scarlatti sonatas, and the complete Mozart symphonies.

PITNEY, Gene (1941-) *Pop singer-songwriter* Pitney first found success writing for others, his own solo career taking off with "I Wanna Love My Life Away" (1961). His impassioned ballads produced a number of hits in the mid-1960s, including "Twenty-Four Hours from Tulsa" (1963), "I'm Gonna Be Strong" (1964), and "Princess in Rags" (1965). He had a further unexpected hit in 1988, topping the U.K. charts with a new version of "Something's Gotten Hold of My Heart," recorded with Marc Almond.

POINTER SISTERS, The *Soul group* This group of four sisters first sang as a backing group, producing their first eponymous album in 1973. Their varied repertoire ranged from SOUL to the COUNTRY-sounding "Fairytale" (1974) which won a Grammy. "Fire" (1979) was a million-selling single and was followed by two further gold discs. They had their last hit "Dare Me" in 1985 after which they failed to capture the sparkle of earlier achievements.

POLICE, The *Rock group* This British REGGAE-influenced POP trio was one of the most successful bands of the late-1970s and early 1980s. Featuring STING on bass guitar, Andy Summers on guitar, and Stuart Copeland on drums, the Police produced five albums, all highly acclaimed. The first two, *Outlandos D'Amour* and *Regatta De Blanc* dominated the U.K. charts for most of 1979. The third album *Zenyatta Mondatta* (1980), including the track "Don't Stand so Close to Me" (their third No.1), was their big worldwide breakthrough. The last and most successful album *Synchronicity* (1983) contained perhaps their greatest song "Every Breath You Take."

PONS, Lily (1898-1976) *Opera singer* Pons, an American soprano, joined the Met in 1931, where she was a sensational success, remaining for 25 years. She also sang widely in other countries. Her voice was best heard in Donizetti, Bellini, and Verdi.

POOLE, Charlie (1892-1931) *Blues banjo player and singer* Poole became famous as leader of the popular and influential string band, the North Carolina Ramblers. One of their classic hits, "Don't Let Your Deal Go Down" (1925), sold over 100,000 copies, and in five years they sold over a million records. Poole played with many other musicians, making his last record in 1930.

POPP, Lucia (1939-) *Opera singer* An Austrian soprano of Czechoslovakian birth, Popp sang at Salzburg and the Vienna Staatsoper from 1963, Covent Garden in 1966, and the Met in 1967. Her light, well-focused voice was best heard in Mozart, Verdi, and Richard STRAUSS.

PORTAL, Michel (1935-) *Jazz-classical clarinetist* Born in France, Portal played with many JAZZ musicians in the 1960s, including Don Cherry, Anthony Braxton, and Derek Bailey. He formed the group Portal Unit in 1972. His many recordings include "Alors!" (1972) and "Men's Land" (1987). His diverse talents were demonstrated playing the Mozart Clarinet Concerto or STOCKHAUSEN.

POUSSEUR, Henri (1929-) *Composer* Born in Belgium, Pousseur was a leading figure in the European avant-garde from the 1950s. His compositions owed much to BOULEZ and STOCKHAUSEN, but also had a crucial harmonic element. His many works included the OPERA *Votre Faust* (1969).

PRESTON, Simon (1938-) *Organist and conductor* English-born Preston studied at the Royal Academy of Music and at Cambridge University, becoming sub-organist at Westminster Abbey (1962–67) and later organist and master of the choristers (1981–87). He was organist and lecturer in music at Christ Church, Oxford (1970–81), where he made notable recordings of Haydn's choral works.

PRETENDERS, The *Rock group* A veteran of the British PUNK scene, American Chrissie Hynde formed the Pretenders in 1978. The band had a string of successes over the course of six albums, from 1986–95. Hynde developed a winning formula for writing tight melodic ROCK songs, including the hits "Brass in Pocket," "I Go to Sleep," and "2,000 Miles."

PRÊTRE, Georges (1924–) *Conductor* Prêtre studied at the Paris Conservatory, conducting in provincial French OPERA houses from 1946. He moved to Paris in the 1960s, working and recording often with singer Maria CALLAS. He was noted for his performances of POULENC.

PRIMAL SCREAM *Rock group* Formed in the mid-1980s, Primal Scream started life as an INDIE BAND releasing their first album *Sonic Flower Groove* in 1987. At the end of the 1980s the band changed direction, adopting acid house influences and creating a hugely popular dance-rock hybrid. The single "Loaded" (1991), became a U.K. Top 10 hit, and the accompanying album *Screamadelica* reaped critical acclaim and big sales. In 1994 they moved nearer their ROCK roots with the album *Give Out But Don't Give Up*. In 1998 they released the well-received *Vanishing Point* and an accompanying dub version of the album, showing the band's continual progression.

PRITCHARD, Sir John (1921–) *Conductor* Pritchard worked at Glyndebourne from 1947, becoming musical director in 1969. As a conductor he achieved worldwide renown, as well as performing a wide repertoire. He gave premieres of works by TIPPETT and BRITTEN.

PROCOL HARUM *Rock group* Procol Harum shot to fame with their classic debut single "A Whiter Shade of Pale" (1967). The Top 10 hit "Homberg" and their eponymous first album followed. They had some success with later albums, but didn't return to top form until *In Concert with the Edmonton Symphony Orchestra and the De Camera Singers* (1972), a U.S. Top 5 hit. Later hits included "Pandora's Box" from *Procol's Ninth* (1975). They broke up in 1977.

PRODIGY, The *Techno band* This U.K. group represent the vanguard of the British rave scene. The big-time came with the U.K. No.3 single "Charly," signaling a crossover of rave music from clubs to the charts. Two well-received albums followed, *The Prodigy Experience* (1992) and *Music for the Jilted Generation* (1994) before they released their most successful work to date, *Fat of the Land* (1997)—containing the singles "Firestarter" and "Breathe."

PROFESSOR LONGHAIR (1918–80) *R&B pianist and singer* Louisiana-born Henry Byrd, better known as Professor Longhair, played a characteristic BOOGIE-WOOGIE piano style. A resident of New Orleans, he was highly influential on players such as Fats DOMINO and Dr. John.

PRYOR, Snooky (1921–) *Blues singer* Pryor made his first record "Telephone Blues" in 1949, and followed it up with more singles in the 1950s and early 1960s, including "Boogie Twist." After leaving the music business, he returned in the early 1970s, making a number of later recordings including "Too Cool to Move" (1992).

PUBLIC ENEMY *Rap group* Possibly the most influential and controversial RAP act to date, Public Enemy was formed in the early 1980s. Their first album *Yo! Bum Rush the Show* (1987) broke new ground, but it was their second album, *It Takes a Nation of Millions to Hold Us Back* (1988), that completed their crossover. With their uncompromising political stance, Public Enemy was open to accusations of inciting violence and anti-Semitism—it was later discovered that the FBI held files on the band. As the 1990s progressed, the band lost its momentum and broke up as members followed other careers.

PUBLIC IMAGE LIMITED *Rock group* Formed in 1978 by ex-SEX PISTOLS member John Lydon, PIL's debut was the epic single "Public Image." Albums followed from 1978 through to 1992. Their music, at first struggling to overcome expectations based on Lydon's past, was epic and difficult, but showed that there was music after punk that retained its raw energy.

PUFF DADDY (1970–) *Rap producer and singer* Born in Harlem, as Sean Combs, Puff Daddy was a mover and shaker on the RAP scene of the early 1990s. He produced huge hits for artists such as Jodeci and Mary J. Blige, whose first album, *What's the 411?*, is regarded as the ultimate hip-hop/R&B fusion album. Puff Daddy survived the gangsta rap wars and went on to become one of the biggest entrepreneurs of the music industry of the 1990s. He also had hits of his own, notably the 1997 single "I'll Be Missing You," a tribute to his murdered friend, the rapper Notorious BIG.

PULP *Rock group* Formed in 1981, Pulp had to wait over a decade for success to come. In 1993 the British backlash against GRUNGE began and BRITPOP was born. Pulp, perhaps the most quirkily English band of all, became steadily more popular. By 1994 lead singer Jarvis Cocker was a sought after media personality and in 1995 they released the hugely successful album *Different Class*, which included the hit single "Common People." Success brought its own problems and Pulp took two years to produce their next album, *This Is Hardcore*.

PUYANA, Rafael (1931–) *Harpsichordist* Born in Columbia, Puyana studied in Boston, first as a pianist and then on harpsichord with Landowska. His virtuoso performances have ranged from Scarlatti to works written specifically for him. His repertoire includes music from the 16th and 17th century as well as contemporary works. He has made many recordings both as a soloist and as part of an ensemble.

QUEEN LATIFAH (1970–) *Rap artist* Born Dana Owens in New Jersey, Queen Latifah's first single "Wrath of My Madness" (1988) was followed by feverish reviews of her first album *All Hail the Queen* (1989). She went from SOUL and RAGGA to hip hop for her third album, *Black Reign* (1993) recorded for Motown. In the 1990s Latifah embarked on a successful career as an actress in television and movies like Spike Lee's *Jungle Fever*.

RABBITT, Eddie (1944-) *Pop-country singer-songwriter* Rabbitt's first success come as a songwriter for others, such as Elvis PRESLEY—for whom he wrote "Kentucky Run" (1970). He had his own first U.S. COUNTRY success with "You Get to Me" (1974). From 1976 he had a string of country chart No.1s, including "Drinkin' My Baby," through to 1988's "I Wanna Dance with You."

RADIOHEAD *Rock group* Formed in Oxford, England, in 1988, Radiohead have gone on to become critically acclaimed stadium superstars. Their first success was the single "Creep" (1992), which became the most requested track on U.S. radio. Building on this success, the band toured the U.S., building a solid following. Their second album, *The Bends*, was a critical and commercial hit on both sides of the Atlantic, but their third album, *OK Computer* (1997) managed to top even that, being widely acclaimed as the best album of that year.

RADULESCU, Michael (1943-) *Composer* A highly influential Romanian composer, Radulescu was the first member of what became known as the "spectral" school during the 1970s and 1980s. These composers used the harmonic—or "spectrum"— series as the basis for their works. Radulescu is also known as a teacher of compositional techniques.

RAITT, Bonnie (1949-) *Blues-country singer and guitarist* Raitt has a powerful, emotive voice and is one of the few women to be recognized as a ROCK guitar virtuoso. However, she didn't have her first U.S. hit until 1977, with a cover of Del Shannon's "Runaway," from her album *Sweet Forgiveness*. After something of a decline she made her comeback with *Nick of Time* (1989), which won three Grammys and produced a U.S. hit single with the title track. Raitt entered the 1990s at the peak of her powers with *Luck of the Draw* (1991) and *Longing in Their Hearts* (1994).

RAMONES, The *Punk band* Formed in 1974, the Ramones were key figures in the emerging music scene centered on the CBGB club in New York. In 1976 they made their debut in London and this, along with their debut album, *Ramones,* kick-started the nascent British PUNK movement. The classic anthem "Sheena Is a Punk Rocker" from *Rocket to Russia* (1977) was their first U.K. Top 30 hit. Two further classic albums followed—*Road to Ruin* and *It's Alive*—but during the 1980s the Ramones became sidelined.

RAMPAL, Jean-Pierre (1922-) *Flautist* Rampal studied in Paris and later taught at the Paris Conservatory. He began an international solo concert career in 1947, as well as being solo flautist at the Paris Opera (1956–62). He is most admired for his performances of 18th-century music, particularly Bach and Mozart.

RATTLE, Sir Simon (1955-) *Conductor* Studying at the Royal Academy of Music, in London, Rattle won a competition with the Bournemouth Symphony Orchestra in 1974. From 1979 he forged a worldwide reputation as principal conductor of the City of Birmingham Symphony Orchestra. He has worked with orchestras and OPERA houses all over the world, most notably in 20th-century repertoire, and has made TV programs popularizing ORCHESTRAL MUSIC.

RAUTAVAARA, Einojuhani (1928-) *Composer* Finnish-born Rautavaara's output has shown a variety of influences, notably Mussorgsky, HINDEMITH, and advanced SERIALISM. He wrote in many genres, including *The True and False Unicorn* (1971) for chorus, orchestra, and tape.

RAWLS, Lou (1935-) *Soul singer* Rawls first managed a crossover hit in 1963 with the album *Black and Blue.* He had two Top 20 singles "Love Is a Hurtin' Thing" (1966) and "Dead End Street" (1967). He found further success in the 1970s with the international hit, "You'll Never Find Another Love Like Mine" (1976).

REA, Chris (1951-) *Pop singer-songwriter and guitarist* U.K.-born Rea was in a number of bands before going solo in the early 1970s. His debut album *Whatever Happened to Benny Santini* (1978) included "Fool (If You Think It's Over)" which reached the U.S. Top 20. Rea had his earliest large-scale success in Germany, breaking through in the U.K. with the album *Shamrock Diaries* (1985). "The Road to Hell" (1989) became his first U.K. No.1.

RED HOT CHILI PEPPERS, The *Rock group* The Red Hot Chili Peppers successfully mixed FUNK and PUNK, producing a succession of well-received albums and forging an impressive live reputation—based partly on their propensity for taking their clothes off onstage. Their second album *Freaky Styley,* was produced by George Clinton and they expanded on this funk-punk theme for the next album, *Uplift Mofo Party Plan* (1988). Their biggest hit came with the single "Under the Bridge" from the 1991 album *Blood Sugar Sex Magik.* In 1995 they produced their best album, *One Hot Minute,* and they continued to perform and record.

REDDY, Helen (1942-) *Pop singer* Australian-born Reddy was a big-voiced interpreter of ROCK ballads in the 1970s who had 14 U.S. Top 40 hits. Her first hit "I Don't Know How to Love Him" (1971), was followed by the No.1 "I Am Woman" (1972). Many other chart-toppers followed, her last Top 20 hit "You're My World" coming in 1977. She also had a successful TV career in the 1970s and appeared in concert and cabaret to the late 1980s.

REDMAN, Don (1900-64) *Jazz musician* Conservatory-trained Redman was an accomplished multi-instrumentalist, joining the Fletcher HENDERSON Band in 1923 as a saxophonist. Over the next four years he became the band's main ARRANGER, transforming their sound. He later formed his own bands, and in 1941 opened an arranging office on Broadway, writing for leaders including Jimmy Dorsey, Paul WHITEMAN, Count BASIE, and Duke ELLINGTON. Redman developed the BIG BAND JAZZ sound and had a huge effect on the development of SWING.

REED, Lou (1942-) *Rock musician* Reed came to fame as founder and songwriter of the VELVET UNDERGROUND (1966–70). Reed went solo in 1971 trying to balance his dark lyrics with prettier music. His first solo album, *Lou Reed,* had a big, lush sound and the follow-up, *Transformer* was a modest success, including the surprise hit single "Walk on the Wild Side" (1973). Throughout the 1970s Reed's music was increasingly misanthropic and difficult, experimenting at times with atonality and avant-garde trends. *New York* (1989) was seen as a return to his best work. A year later Reed reunited with his Velvet Underground partner John Cale to produce the Warhol elegy *Songs for Drella.*

REEVES, Martha, & the Vandellas *Soul group* Formed in 1960 and originally providing backing vocals for Marvin GAYE, Martha and the Vandellas were one of MOTOWN's early successes with 23 Hot 100 entries between 1963–71. Their hits included "Heat Wave," "Dancing in the Street," and "Nowhere to Run." Reeves went solo in 1973 with moderate success, reforming the Vandellas in the late 1980s.

REIMANN, Aribert (1936-) *Composer and pianist* After studying in Berlin, Reimann established himself as a fine pianist, notably as accompanist to FISCHER-DIESKAU. His compositions include OPERAS in an expressionist style such as *Ein Traumspiel* (1965), Melusine (1970), and *Lear* (1978)

REO SPEEDWAGON *Rock group* Formed in 1970, REO Speedwagon—the name taken from an early American fire engine—produced a number of albums through to the 1990s. They had a slow climb to national fame from their eponymous first album, released in 1971, to *Hi Infidelity* (1980), which was their first major breakthrough. That album topped the charts and including the U.S. No.1 single "Keep on Lovin' You." At their best REO Speedwagon were the epitome of Adult Oriented Rock (AOR)—faceless but professional.

REPLACEMENTS, The *Rock group* Formed in 1979, the Replacements remained together until 1990, producing eight albums. They had a winning formula of ROCK'N'ROLL mixed with raw PUNK ROCK. Perhaps their best work was the album *Pleased to Meet Me* (1987), containing "The Ledge" and "Skyway."

RICH, Buddy (1917-87) *Jazz drummer and bandleader* Rich performed on stage from the age of four, playing in a number of bands from the 1930s, including those of Artie Shaw and Tommy DORSEY. Forming his own bands from the late 1940s, he began to record as a vocalist from the 1950s, revealing a stylish singing voice. His recordings included *Big Band Shout* (1956) and *The Voice of Buddy Rich* (1959). Undoubtedly one of the best drummers of the big band era, Rich resurrected the idea of BIG BAND JAZZ in the mid-1960s and continued to play until his death.

RICH, Charlie (1932-95) *Country singer* Rich became one of the most successful COUNTRY singers of the 1970s, his career taking off with "Behind Closed Doors" (1973), a U.S. COUNTRY No.1, and Grammy winner. "The Most Beautiful Girl" became a No.1 in both pop and country. He had many more hits through the 1970s until 1980. The 1980s proved to be a barren period for Rich, but he made a triumphant return with the album *Pictures and Paintings* (1992).

RICHARD, Keith (1943-) *Rock guitarist* Now a ROCK legend, Richard became famous as a founding member and lead guitarist of the ROLLING STONES, writing many of their hits in partnership with Mick Jagger, including "(I Can't Get No) Satisfaction," "Honky Tonk Women," and "Jumpin' Jack Flash." Outside of his work with the Stones, he organized a star-studded 60th birthday concert for Chuck BERRY—turned into the film *Hail! Hail! Rock'n'Roll.* His first solo album, *Talk Is Cheap* (1988), received good reviews. *Main Offender* followed in 1992.

RICHIE, Lionel (1949-) *Soul singer-songwriter* Richie formed a number of R&B groups in the mid-1960s, before becoming lead singer and saxophonist with the Commodores in 1968. Richie wrote and sang many of their biggest hits, including "Three Times a Lady" (1978). He branched out writing for others including Kenny ROGERS and Diana ROSS, and in 1982 he went solo, having a U.K. No.1 with "Truly" from his first

album. *Can't Slow Down* (1983) brought him international superstardom, selling over 15 million copies worldwide and winning two Grammy awards. He continued to score hits in the 1990s, and won an Oscar for the song "Say You, Say Me" from the movie *White Nights.*

RICHMAN, Jonathan, and the Modern Lovers *Rock group* Richman rose to prominence during the early 1970s as leader of the Modern Lovers. The group had success in the U.K. with "Roadrunner" and "Egyptian Reggae" (both 1977) and with their eponymously titled first album. Richman went solo in 1978 with songs including "Ice Cream Man," "My Love Is a Flower," and "I'm a Little Dinosaur." Richman reformed the Modern Lovers in the 1980s, and his eccentric acoustic sound continued to enjoy considerable cult popularity in the U.S. and Europe.

RICHTER, Hans (1843-1916) *Conductor* An Austro-Hungarian, Richter worked closely with Wagner, conducting the first performance of *The Ring* at Bayreuth. A great champion of Wagner, as well as Beethoven, Brahms, and Bruckner, he spent a lot of time in England from 1877, directing the Birmingham Festival and conducting the London Symphony Orchestra and the Hallé. He was also a great admirer of ELGAR, giving the premiere of *The Dream of Gerontius.* Elgar dedicated his first symphony to Richter.

RICHTER, Karl (1926-81) *Conductor and organist* Born in Germany, Richter studied in Leipzig, becoming organist at the famous Thomaskirche in 1947. He became well known as the conductor of the Munich Bach Choir and Orchestra, particularly with the music of Bach and Handel.

RICHTER, Sviatoslav (1915-97) *Pianist* The Russian pianist made his debut in 1934, subsequently giving many early performances of PROKOFIEV's music. He appeared in the West from 1960, winning admiration for his outstandingly poetic performances. He was at his best playing 19th-century Romantic music, notably Schubert and Schumann.

RIDDLE, Nelson (1921-85) *Composer, arranger and conductor* Riddle first played trombone in a number of big bands from the late 1930s. From around 1950 he arranged and conducted for artists such as Judy GARLAND, Dean Martin, Johnny Mathis, and Shirley Bassey. He was best known, however, for his work as arranger for Frank SINATRA starting in 1953. He had his own hits, including the instrumental "Lisbon Antigua" (1955) and the Grammy award-winning album *Cross-Country Suite* (1958). He also had considerable success with film scores, including *Paint Your Wagon, The Great Gatsby* and *The Pajama Game*.

RIGHTEOUS BROTHERS, The *Pop vocal duo* Formed in 1962, The Righteous Brothers—Bill Medley and Bobby Hatfield—had minor success before hitting the big time with "You've Lost That Lovin' Feeling" (1964)—a No.1 in the U.S. and U.K., and one of the biggest pop singles of all time. Further hits included "Just Once in My Life" and "Ebb Tide," but they split in 1968. They regrouped and separated on several more occasions, but with little success.

RIPERTON, Minnie (1947-79) *Pop singer* Originally a member of the Gems and then Rotary Connection—an adventurous African-American psychedelic group—Riperton embarked on a solo career, finding international success in 1975 with "Loving You." She died of cancer only four years later.

ROBBINS, Marty (1926-82) *Country singer* Robbins first recorded in 1951 and had several COUNTRY hits during the next few years. However, it was at the end of the 1950s that his career really took shape. Always interested in the Wild West, Robbins began to write soundtracks for Westerns, like *The Hanging Tree* (1959), which included "El Paso"—and that became his theme song. He had huge success over the next few years, both as a singer and an actor. He continued to perform and write for himself and others, including Frankie LAINE, and wrote movie soundtracks, such as for Clint Eastwood's *Honky Tonk Man* (1982).

ROBINSON, Smokey (1940-) *Soul singer, songwriter, and producer* Robinson enjoyed considerable success as founder and lead singer of the Miracles, who had 46 Hot 100 hits between 1959 and 1975—including "Shop Around" (1961), "I Second that Emotion" (1967), and "The Tears of a Clown" (1970). Most of these hits were written by Robinson. He was also a successful songwriter and PRODUCER for other MOTOWN acts, notably for Mary Wells and the Temptations. In 1972 he went solo, scoring seven Top 40 hits, including "Cruisin'" (1979) and "Being with You" (1981). Robinson remains one of the few POP/SOUL artists to have scored hits throughout a four-decade career.

ROBINSON, Tom (1950-) *Rock musician* Robinson found success after forming the Tom Robinson Band (TRB) in 1975—their first album *Power in the Darkness* included the Top 40 single "2468 Motorway" and the unambiguous anthem "(Sing If You're) Glad to Be Gay." After TRB fell apart, Robinson formed the short-lived Section 27 in 1980. His solo career proved more fruitful with hits including "War Baby" and "Listen to the Radio: Atmospherics" (both 1982). He continued to record and play, regrouping the original band in the 1990s.

ROBLES, Marisa (1937-) *Harpist* Robles made her debut in her home town of Madrid in 1954. She settled in Britain in 1959, after which she developed a very successful concert career, becoming popular following a number of appearances on TV. She is heavily involved with CHAMBER MUSIC as well as performing as a soloist.

RODZINSKI, Artur (1892-1958) *Conductor* Rodzinski was an American of Polish birth who first conducted in Poland in 1920. Based in the U.S. from 1925, he became conductor of the Los Angeles Philharmonic Orchestra (1929–33), the Cleveland Orchestra (1933–43), the New York Philharmonic (1943–47), and the Chicago Symphony (1947). He raised American orchestral standards to new heights, giving energetic performances of a wide repertoire, including concert performances of OPERA.

ROGERS, Roy (1911-98) *Country singer and film star* Rogers—also known as "the singing cowboy"—received his first starring role singing in the film *Under Western Skies* (1938), beginning a career as one of the most popular movie stars of the 1930s and 1940s. His songs included "Blue Shadows on the Trail," "Money Can't Buy Love," and "Happy Anniversary," many becoming COUNTRY hits.

ROGERS, Shorty (1924-94) *Jazz trumpeter, composer and arranger* Rogers first found success playing in the Woody Herman band (1945–50) and then with Stan KENTON (1950–51), for whom he also arranged a number of scores. It was as a leading figure in the West Coast style of JAZZ that he is best remembered. His work as a composer and ARRANGER for big bands and smaller groups was the most important of its day, exploring ostinato, bitonality, and even the 12-note technique.

ROGG, Lionel (1936-) *Organist* Born in Switzerland, Rogg forged a considerable reputation as a Bach specialist, recording his complete organ works in the mid-1960s. He also won the Grand Prix du Disque for his recording of *The Art of Fugue* (1970). As well as performing works by other composers, notably Buxtehude, Couperin, and Liszt, he was a teacher and composer.

ROLAND, Walter (1900-70) *Blues pianist* Although rather an under-rated and relatively unknown musician, Roland appeared on over 40 recordings between 1933–35 with other artists, including the outstanding singers Lucille Bogan and Sonny Scott. His own voice was very expressive and versatile. His recording of the song "Jook It, Jook It" (1933) appears on many anthologies.

ROLFE JOHNSON, Anthony (1940-) *Opera singer* The English tenor Rolfe Johnson first appeared at Glyndebourne in 1973 and later at the English National Opera. With his elegant and lyrical voice he has since sung all over the world, particularly in the works of Mozart, Handel, Monteverdi, and BRITTEN.

ROLLINI, Adrian (1904-56) *Jazz musician* Rollini became one of the few masters of the bass saxophone—an instrument even Coleman HAWKINS struggled with—as well as the vibraphone. From the 1920s he played with many musicians including Bix BEIDERBECKE and Red Nichols and traveled to the U.K. Along with his great flair and swing, he was an important influence on many white JAZZ men in the U.S. and U.K.

ROMBERG, Sigmund (1887-1951) *Composer* The Hungarian Romberg found success when he took up residence in New York, composing for the musical stage. His first great hit was the OPERETTA *The Student Prince* (1924). He followed this with *The Desert Song* (1926) and *The New Moon* (1928), the latter containing the hit songs "Lover, Come Back to Me" and "One Kiss." He continued writing for the stage and films with variable amounts of success.

ROOLEY, Anthony (1944-) *Lutenist* Born in England, Rooley made a name for himself at the forefront of the revival of Renaissance music. He studied and taught at the Royal Academy of Music, London. In 1969 he formed the Consort of Musicke, with James Tyler, which performed and recorded Renaissance music all over the world.

ROSE ROYCE *Soul group* Created by former MOTOWN producer Norman Whitfield, Rose Royce first found success with the soundtrack to the film *Car Wash* (1976), which included the platinum-selling title song. Following this they had hits with "Wishing on a Star" and "Love Don't Live Here Anymore." Rose Royce's *Greatest Hits* album (1980) reached No.1 in the U.K. charts.

ROSEN, Charles (1927-) *Pianist and writer* Rosen studied at the Juilliard School, making his debut as a pianist in 1951. His style was rather severe and intellectual, best suited to Bach, Weber, and Beethoven, as well as the 20th-century composers SCHOENBERG, Elliott CARTER, and BOULEZ. As an academic, his chief literary contribution was *The Classical Style* (1971), establishing a context for classical music.

ROSSI, Francis (1949-) *Rock musician* Rossi was a founder member (guitar/vocals) of the Spectres, which became legendary ROCK band Status Quo in 1967. With Status Quo, Rossi has had almost 50 U.K. hits, selling over 100 million records. In 1991 they celebrated their silver anniversary by playing four charity concerts in four cities in the space of 12 hours.

ROSSI, Mario (1902-) *Conductor* The Italian Rossi made his debut in 1926. He spent many years in the OPERA houses of Florence and La Scala in Milan before becoming the resident conductor of the Turin Radio Symphony Orchestra (1946–69), which became one of the best orchestras in Italy and much admired abroad. His repertoire was mainly symphonic, concentrating on the 20th century.

ROXY MUSIC *Rock group* This popular and influential U.K. band came together in 1971 featuring both Brian Eno and singer Bryan Ferry. Their rise was meteoric from their eponymous debut album in 1972. Two follow-up singles, "Virginia Plain" and "Pyjamarama," both hit the U.K. Top 10. The album *For Your Pleasure* (1973) contained the classics "Do the Strand" and "In Every Dream Home a Heartache." They had their only U.K. No.1 single with "Jealous Guy" (1981), also the year of their last album *Avalon*. Brian Ferry went on to have a successful solo career during the 1980s.

RUN DMC *Rap group* Formed in 1982, Run DMC immediately scored a U.S. underground hit with the singles "It's Like That" and "Sucker MCs," often regarded as the birth of modern hip-hop. Their debut album went gold in 1984, the first RAP album to do so. *Raisin' Hell* (1986) was the first rap album to become an R&B No.1, the first to enter the U.S. Top 10, and the first to go platinum. They have continued recording into the 1990s.

RUNDGREN, Todd (1948-) *Rock musician* As well as a singer, Rundgren is also a songwriter, PRODUCER, and instrumentalist. He first found success by forming the group Nazz in 1967, which produced three albums. He then moved into production before going solo with *Runt* (1970). His third album *Something/Anything* (1972), on which he played all the instruments and acted as producer, contained some of his most popular work including the hit single "I Saw the Light." He also formed the PROGRESSIVE ROCK ensemble Utopia, which released a successful album in 1974. Rundgren's production work has included the classic Meatloaf album *Bat Out of Hell*, while he also scored the music for the film *Dumb and Dumber*.

RUSH *Rock group* This Canadian HEAVY METAL trio were formed in Toronto in 1969. Their first single, "Not Fade Away" (1973), was followed by the album *Rush* (1974). Combining high-pitched vocals and powerful guitar sound with their interest in science-fiction and fantasy, they didn't really become popular until the latter half of the 1970s, with albums like *2112* (1976), *A Farewell to Kings* (1977), and *Hemispheres* (1978). By 1979 they were immensely successful worldwide with the hit single "Spirit of Radio" (1980). Finding a new lease of life in the 1990s, Rush is undoubtedly Canada's leading ROCK group.

RUSH, Otis (1934-) *Blues singer and guitarist* From the mid-1950s, Rush was at the forefront of the Chicago BLUES scene with hits like "I Can't Quit You Baby" (1956). Other successes followed, with "So Many Roads" and "Homework" perhaps becoming his best-known songs. He continued to record into the 1990s, with the album *Ain't Enough Comin' In* (1994) receiving critical praise.

RUSHING, Jimmy (1902-72) *Jazz singer* Rushing was one of the great JAZZ singers. His voice was high and powerful with a dramatic vibrato, and by 1927 he was a full-time singer working with, among others, Jelly Roll MORTON. He became a big star with the Count BASIE band (1935–48), immortalizing classics such as "Boogie-woogie," "Evenin'," and "Exactly Like You," as well as recording with artists such as Bing CROSBY. After 1948 he worked regularly with Benny GOODMAN and Buck Clayton.

RUSSELL, Luis (1902-63) *Jazz pianist, bandleader, and arranger* From 1919 Russell played in many bands, often leading his own. Eventually, in 1935, Russell's band were hired to back Louis ARMSTRONG. The band was dismissed in 1940, but Russell stayed with Armstrong as musical director for three more years. In the early 1940s he formed a new band and toured widely. Although he never achieved the public awareness of many of his contemporaries, he made a serious impact on integrating NEW ORLEANS JAZZ with BIG BAND JAZZ music.

RUSSELL DAVIES, Dennis (1944-) *Conductor* Russell Davies had his conducting debut in 1968 with the Juilliard Ensemble. He forged a reputation as a conductor of contemporary music, most notably with the St. Paul Chamber Orchestra (1972–80), giving first performances of works by composers like CAGE, CARTER, Berio, and GLASS.

RZEWSKI, Frederic (1938-) *Composer and pianist* American-born Rzewski was associated with STOCKHAUSEN between 1962 and 1964, and became a member of Musica Elettronica Viva in 1966. With the latter he explored collective improvisation with FOLK and popular melodies. Works such as *Coming Together* (1972) were characterized by impressive drive and intensity.

SAARIAHO, Kaija (1952-) *Composer* After studying in Helsinki, Finnish-born Saariaho composed much instrumental and ORCHESTRAL MUSIC, having it performed at many major music festivals, including Salzburg. Her works—mostly using electronic instruments and computers—included *Verbledungen* (1984) and *Graal-théatre* (1994).

SACHER, Paul (1906-) *Conductor and patron* Sacher founded the Basle Chamber Orchestra, Switzerland, in 1926. With it and the Collegium Musicum of Zurich (formed in 1941) he performed early classical and contemporary music, commissioning and premiering numerous works by BARTÓK, HINDEMITH, Honegger, STRAUSS, STRAVINSKY, and LUTOSLAWSKI.

SAINT-SAËNS, Camille (1835-1921) *Composer* Saint-Saëns is regarded as one of the greatest French classical composers. His conservative musical style—neat proportions, clarity, polished expressiveness, elegant lines—were seen in most of his works, including much CHAMBER MUSIC, three symphonies, concertos, and OPERAS (especially *Samson et Dalila* and *Le carnaval des animaux*). He wrote one of the earliest film scores *L'assassinat du Duc de Guise* (1908) and *Caprice Andalous* (1904) for violin and orchestra. He was also a renowned organist and pianist.

SALONEN, Esa-Pekka (1958-) *Conductor and composer* Salonen was born in Finland and made his debut as a conductor in 1980. Posts he has held include musical director of the Los Angeles Philharmonic Orchestra, and principal guest conductor of the Philharmonia Orchestra, in London. His repertoire is wide, but he is particularly known for his performances of 20th-century works by composers such as STRAVINSKY, MESSIAEN, and LUTOSLAWSKI.

SALT'N'PEPA *Rap duo* Initially performing as backup singers for other RAP artists, this female duo then brought out singles of their own, including "I'll Take Your Man" and "It's My Beat." When "Push It" was reissued in 1988 they hit the charts in both the U.S. and U.K. Further hits followed as well as a nomination for the first rap Grammy in 1989. Salt'n'Pepa are the most commercially successful female rap group of all time, and were the first to achieve a gold disc.

SAM & DAVE *Soul vocal duo* Arguably SOUL's definitive duo, Sam & Dave met in 1961. In 1965 they signed with Atlantic and began to record at the Stax/Volt studios. Over the next four years Sam & Dave, along with Otis REDDING, would define the Southern soul sound. In 1966 the single "Hold on! I'm a Comin'" topped the R&B charts and crossed over to become a POP hit. A year later "Soul Man" made No.2 in the U.S. charts. Although they had further hits including "Soul Sister, Brown Sugar" (1969), Sam & Dave split in 1970, reuniting occasionally over the next 11 years.

SANDERLING, Kurt (1912-) *Conductor* German-born Sanderling began his musical career as a singing coach at the Berlin Städtische Oper in 1931. Moving to Russia he was the conductor of the Moscow Radio Symphony Orchestra (1936–41), and the Leningrad Philharmonic Orchestra (1941–60). He returned to Germany as conductor of the East Berlin Symphony Orchestra and the Dresden Staatskapelle, touring extensively. His expressive interpretations are widely admired, especially of MAHLER, SIBELIUS, and Russian symphonic music.

SANDERLING, Thomas (1942-) *Conductor* Born in Russia, son of the conductor Kurt, Thomas Sanderling made his debut conducting the Berlin Symphony Orchestra in 1962. He moved to the West in 1983, thereafter conducting worldwide. His wide repertoire ranges from Handel to contemporary music, and included giving the German premiere of SHOSTAKOVICH's symphonies No.13 and No.14.

SARGENT, Sir Malcolm (1895-1967) *Conductor* Sargent became one of the most popular English conductors of the mid-20th century. He conducted many concerts for children and was an outstanding CHORAL conductor. He was chief conductor of the Proms (1948–67) and of the BBC Symphony Orchestra (1950–57), with whom he displayed a wide repertoire.

SCAGGS, Boz (1944-) *Rock singer* Scaggs was a member of a number of bands from his high school days, including the Steve Miller Band. However, it wasn't until his seventh album, *Silk Degrees* (1976), that Scaggs found commercial success. The album included "Lowdown," a U.S. No.3, and "We're All Alone," which has since become a standard. In 1981, Scaggs had his last chart hit when "Miss Sun" reached No.14 in the U.S.

SCELSI, Giacinto (1905-88) *Composer* Italian composer Scelsi's early works covered many styles, although all adopt free tonality and are consistent with his ideal of music as a link to the transcendental. After the 1950s he often used microtones, thin textures, and extremely slow movement as found in his *Quattro Pezzi* (1959).

SCHAFER, R. Murray (1933-) *Composer* Born in Canada, Schafer studied in Toronto. His musical output was large and diverse. Although influenced by the major trends of the 1960s—SERIALISM, indeterminacy, and electronics—his use of all techniques was free and individual. Schafer often used texts of dead languages in a very innovative fashion. His many large-scale works include *Patria* (1972) and *Son of Heldenleben* (1968).

SCHIFF, Andras (1953-) *Pianist* Schiff was born and studied in Hungary. He has won many honors, including the Tchaikovsky and the Leeds International Piano competitions (both 1975), becoming one of the most admired pianists of the latter part of the 20th century. He is particularly renowned for his interpretations of Bach (for which he won a Grammy) and Mozart, as well as for the early Romantics.

SCHIFRIN, Lalo (1932-) *Jazz pianist and composer* Schifrin first played JAZZ in his native Argentina. He studied in Paris with MESSIAEN during the early 1950s, before moving to New York in 1958. He played with Dizzy GILLESPIE between 1960–62, writing the suites *Gillespiana* and *New Continent* for him. He also played with Quincy JONES. From the mid-1960s he became more and more involved with composition, having huge success writing over 150 scores for TV and the movies, including *Mission: Impossible* (1967), *Bullitt* (1968), and *Dirty Harry* (1971).

SCHLIPPENBACH, Alexander von (1938-) *Jazz pianist and composer* Schlippenbach played FREE JAZZ in the 1960s, working with many musicians including Manfred Schoof. In 1966 he formed the Globe Unity Orchestra, establishing itself as the leading free jazz big band of the 1970s and 1980s. He also played in smaller groups, and set up the Berlin Jazz Composer's Orchestra in 1988. Schlippenbach's influences range from SCHOENBERG to Charlie PARKER and Thelonious MONK, and he is one of the major figures of the European free jazz scene. He is best heard on the 1989 album *Smoke* with Sunny Murray.

SCHÖNBERG, Claude-Michel (1944-) *Composer* As a composer of MUSICALS, in collaboration with Alain Boublil, Schönberg found fame with *La Révolution* (1973), the first staged French rock OPERA. Their second musical, *Les Misérables* (1978), became a huge success, playing in London and on Broadway, winning two Tony awards and a Grammy. Their third project, *Miss Saigon,* was just as successful, and has been performed all over the world.

SCHOOF, Manfred (1936-) *Jazz trumpeter* Born in Germany, Schoof played in big bands before forming his pioneering FREE JAZZ quintet in 1965, which included Alexander von Schlippenbach. This formed the nucleus of the Manfred Schoof Orchestra, bringing together EUROPEAN JAZZ artists such as Derek Bailey and Peter Brötzmann. Schoof's 1977 album *Scales* received the German Record Critics' Prize. Schoof has also worked in other musical fields, collaborating on the 1966 OPERA *Die Soldaten* and creating a trumpet concerto in 1969.

SCHREIER, Peter (1935-) *Opera singer and conductor* Born in Germany, Schreier had his operatic debut in 1961 at Dresden. As a lyric tenor he sang many roles, including Mozart's Belmonte and Ottavia, as well as roles by Rossini, Weber, and STRAUSS. He is also well known as the Evangelist in Bach's *Passions*, and for singing lieder. Schreier had his conducting debut in 1970, and has since performed and recorded many works, notably OPERA and CHORAL MUSIC.

SCHULLER, Gunther (1925-) *Jazz musician* Schuller, an American, trained as a classical musician before turning to JAZZ. In the late 1940s and early 1950s he recorded with Miles DAVIS. He subsequently wrote music that blended jazz with classical, including his 1959 work *Conversations* —a type of music known as the "Third Stream." In 1961 Schuller was acting musical director at the Monterey Jazz Festival and in 1962 of the first international jazz festival in Washington, D.C. He has written for musicians including Ornette COLEMAN and Eric DOLPHY, and spends much time writing about, lecturing, and teaching jazz.

SCHUMAN, William (1910-) *Composer* Performing initially in JAZZ bands, Schuman began composing classical music in the late 1930s. His compositions, generally tonal with broad melodic lines, include symphonies, CHAMBER MUSIC, and large-scale choral works. In 1955 he wrote *Credendum* for the U.S. government.

SCHUMANN, Elisabeth (1888-1952) *Opera singer* Schumann made her debut in Hamburg in 1909. In 1919 she joined Richard STRAUSS at the Vienna Staats Opera, gaining wide admiration in Strauss and Mozart roles. She had a beautiful and controlled high soprano that was equally well suited to many of Schubert's songs.

SCHWEITZER, Albert (1875-1965) *Organist and scholar* Music played a big part in the life of this Nobel prize-winning physician. Schweitzer studied the organ under Widor, becoming renowned for his epoch-making study of Bach, looking at the interpretation of his music and AUTHENTIC PERFORMANCE techniques. He also published a historic edition of Bach's complete organ works.

SCOFIELD, John (1951-) *Jazz guitarist* By the 1990s Scofield was one of the most original and talented guitarists in the world, playing with a number of musicians from the 1960s, including Gerry MULLIGAN, Chet BAKER, and Charles MINGUS. Scofield joined Miles DAVIS in 1982, and by 1984 was collaborating with him on compositions. Scofield made his first album in 1977, and secured his reputation in the early 1980s with albums such as *Electric Outlet* (1984), which showcased his uniquely rich and creamy sound. A number of albums have followed, all highly regarded.

SCOTT-HERON, Gil (1949-) *Jazz-funk singer-songwriter* Scott-Heron began his career as a poet. His early work included the album *Small Talk at 125th and Lenox,* which included "The Revolution Will Not Be Televised." In 1976 he had hits with "The Bottle," and "Johannesburg" (1976)—a FUNK workout with a powerful anti-apartheid message. He returned in 1994 with *Spirits,* his first album for ten years.

SCULTHORPE, Peter (1929-) *Composer* The Australian Sculthorpe was originally influenced by composers such as SCHOENBERG and VARÈSE, but he was keen to develop originality with new sonorities, his music showing expressive brilliance of color and vigorous *ostinati*. His works include the OPERA *Rites of Passage* (1974), orchestral and vocal pieces, and a series of string quartets.

SEDAKA, Neil (1939-) *Pop singer-songwriter* Sedaka had his first major success with "Stupid, Cupid" (1958), a hit for Connie Francis. From 1959–63, both as a writer and a soloist, he scored 13 Top 40 hits including "Oh! Carol"—written for singer-songwriter Carole KING— "Happy Birthday Sweet Sixteen," and "Breaking Up Is Hard to Do," a No.1 in 1962. His solo success waned, but he continued to write hits for others, including Peggy LEE and Johnny Mathis. He had a second chart career in the 1970s, with hits including "Laughter in the Rain" (1974), "Bad Blood," and a reworked version of "Breaking Up Is Hard to Do" (both 1975). He continues to be a popular entertainer in the 1990s.

SEEGER, Mike (1933-) *Country musician* Born in New York City into a musical family, Seeger formed the New Lost City Ramblers in 1958. A traditional COUNTRY band they performed a set of traditional American music at the first Newport Folk Festival and went on for another 20 years. An accomplished multi-instrumentalist he also formed the Strange Creek Singers in the late 1960s. As a member of these and other line-ups, as a soloist and a duo with his sister Peggy, he recorded over 50 albums, including *The Depression* and *Old Time Country Music*.

SEEGER, Pete (1919-) *Folksinger and banjo player* Seeger formed the Almanac Singers in 1940 which included Woody GUTHRIE. It was, however, with the WEAVERS (which he formed in 1948) that he had huge success and million-selling hit records, such as "We Shall Overcome" and "Where Have All the Flowers Gone." From 1958 he maintained a high-profile solo career, as well as playing with artists such as Arlo Guthrie, Sonny TERRY, and Big Bill BROONZY. He will be remembered, perhaps more than anything else, as a campaigner for civil rights, peace, and equality through FOLK MUSIC.

SEGER, Bob (1945-) *Rock singer* Michigan-born guitarist and singer Seger spent the 1960s in bands around his Ann Arbor home. Although he had a minor hit in 1969 with "Ramblin' Gamblin' Man," it was not until the release of *Night Moves* (1976) that his career took off. A series of hit singles—"Night Moves," "Mainstreet," and "Still the Same"— highly successful tours, and a powerful follow-up album, *Stranger in Town,* made Seger and his Silver Bullet Band one of the biggest draws in the U.S. at the time.

SEMIEN, "Rockin" Sidney (1938-) *Blues guitarist and harmonica player* Semien played frequently in southern Louisiana from the age of 15. He recorded from 1959 on various labels as well as working the clubs. His songs included "Boogie in the Mud," "If I Could I Would," and "They Call Me Rockin'."

SERKIN, Peter (1947-) *Pianist* Peter Serkin, the son of the pianist Rudolf Serkin, has led a varied musical life. It wasn't until the 1970s that he performed regularly, playing a wide musical repertoire ranging from Bach and Mozart through to SCHOENBERG, WEBERN, and much MESSIAEN. During the 1980s and 1990s, as well as playing solo, he has played with the Guarneri Quartet and the Boston Symphony Chamber Players. Serkin has a reputation as a brilliant instrumentalist.

SERKIN, Rudolf (1903-91) *Pianist* Serkin was born and studied in Austria, making his debut in 1915. He settled in the U.S. in 1939, becoming head of the piano department at the Curtis Institute of Music in Philadelphia. Serkin was undoubtedly one of the greatest pianists of the mid-20th century, known for his profound and precise interpretations, especially of Bach, the Viennese classics, Mozart, and Brahms.

SESSIONS, Roger (1896-1985) *Composer* Sessions became one of the most important American composers, firmly establishing an American style in the 1930s and 1940s. A musical and intellectual prodigy, Sessions felt compelled to leave the U.S. in 1925 to develop his talents. He returned in 1933. His compositions were influenced by STRAVINSKY and SCHOENBERG, but demonstrated his own personal style and progression. His many works included symphonies, concertos, string CHAMBER MUSIC, and two OPERAS. He was also a respected author and teacher.

SHANGRI-LAS, The *Pop group* Formed by two pairs of sisters—Mary and Betty Weiss, and Mary Ann and Marge Ganser—this vocal quartet had six hits between 1964 and 1966. They launched their career with the hit single "Remember," which reached No.5, and followed this with the No.1 hit "Leader of the Pack."

SHAVERS, Charlie (1917-71) *Jazz trumpeter and composer* Shavers took up the trumpet in his teens, playing with a number of bands in the 1930s, becoming famous playing with the John Kirby quintet (1937–44). His compositions included "Pastel Blue" and "Undecided," the latter immortalized by Ella FITZGERALD. As well as performing in his own small groups and solo, he also played with Tommy DORSEY and Jazz at the Philharmonic. Shavers was a popular and original stylist.

SHAW, Artie (1910-) *Jazz clarinetist and bandleader* Along with Benny GOODMAN, Shaw was the leading clarinetist of the SWING era. Shaw formed his own big band in 1937, recording "Begin the Beguine" (1938), which stayed at No.1 for six weeks and became an international hit. As famous for his personal life— including a marriage to film star Lana Turner—as his music, Shaw quit bandleading in 1939 only to return two years later with a new line-up and the hit "Frenesi." He formed and reformed bands until the 1950s, when he retired from music and forged a career as a writer. He made a welcome comeback in the late 1980s.

SHAW, Sandie (1947-) *Pop singer*
Shaw was launched as a teenage POP star in 1964, becoming one of the U.K.'s leading female singers of the mid-1960s. She had two No.1s in 1965, including "Always Something There to Remind Me" and won the Eurovision Song Contest—scoring another No. 1—with "Puppet on a String" (1967). By the end of the 1960s her success had waned. Her career was revived briefly in the 1980s with the Smiths' penned hit single "Hand in Glove" (1984) and the album *Hello Angel* (1988).

SHEARING, George (1919-) *Jazz pianist* Blind from birth, Shearing played in his native Britain before settling in America in 1946. He played JAZZ from an early age, becoming famous with his locked-hands technique of playing block chords accompanied by a rhythm section. In the late 1940s he formed his own quintet and produced a succession of very popular recordings including "September in the Rain," "Lullaby of Birdland," "Conception," and "She." From the late 1960s, Shearing spent more time playing with a trio, as a solo performer, and increasingly in duets with artists such as Peggy LEE and Mel TORMÉ. His work with Stéphane Grappelli is also renowned.

SHEPP, Archie (1937-) *Jazz musician and composer* Shepp played tenor and soprano saxophone, and clarinet in a number of bands during the early 1960s. He developed a fruitful musical relationship with John COLTRANE in 1965, which helped to establish his name and reputation. Shepp's performance at the Newport Jazz Festival in 1965 was coupled with a Coltrane performance for the album *New Thing at Newport*. In the same year, he began to establish himself as a dramatist and his play, *The Communist,* was performed in New York. Although he became associated with the FREE JAZZ movement in the late 1960s, he is in fact an eclectic traditionalist, never forgetting the roots of his music. By the 1980s his all-round JAZZ playing was impossible to pigeon hole. He continued touring and recording into the 1990s.

SHINES, Johnny (1915-) *Blues singer and guitarist* Shines first sang part-time in the 1930s alongside artists such as Robert JOHNSON, with whom he appeared on RADIO in 1937. His career didn't really take off until the mid-1960s, when his slide guitar playing and strong, clear vocals found a large following. Excellent albums including *Last Night's Dream* (1968) and *Sitting on Top of the World* (1972) followed.

SHIRLEY-QUIRK, John (1931-) *Opera singer* The English bass-baritone Shirley-Quirk sang at Glyndebourne in the U.K. in the early 1960s, becoming famous by creating roles in many works by BRITTEN. As well as singing other operatic roles and concert works, he was much admired as a fine interpreter of lieder and English song.

SHIRRELLES, The *Pop group* The Shirrelles became one of the most successful female vocal groups of the early 1960s. Formed in 1958, they had their first hit with "Tonight's the Night" (1958). They secured immortality with "Will You Love Me Tomorrow" (1960), which became one of POP's most treasured recordings. Other hugely successful and memorable singles followed, such as "Dedicated to the One I Love," "Mama Said" (both 1961), and "Baby It's You" (1962). The group had a significant effect on the direction of pop music at the time, influencing among others the BEATLES.

SILLS, Beverly (1929-) *Opera singer* The American soprano Sills made her debut singing on commercial radio at the age of three. Her OPERA debut, however, had to wait until 1947. She joined the New York City Opera in 1955, becoming the company's diva and performing many *bel canto* roles, particularly of Donizetti and Rossini. She sang all over the world, perhaps finding her best suited role in Massenet's *Manon*. She retired from the stage in 1980.

SIMON & GARFUNKEL *Pop duo* Paul Simon and Art Garfunkel were one of the most successful POP-FOLK acts of the 1960s. They made their first album, *Wednesday Morning 3 a.m.,* in 1964,

from which came "Sound of Silence," a U.S. No.1. Two albums followed, *Sounds of Silence* (1965) and *Parsley, Sage, Rosemary & Thyme* (1966), the latter arguably their best work. They contributed to the soundtrack of the film *The Graduate* (1968), which gave them one of their biggest hits, "Mrs. Robinson." *Bridge Over Troubled Water* (1970), with it's classic title track, became one of the best-selling albums of all time. After this they split up. In 1981 the pair reunited for a concert in Central Park in New York and a successful world tour, but Simon broke up the duo again soon after.

SIMON, Carly (1945-) *Pop singer-songwriter* Simon was one of the most popular SINGER-SONGWRITERS of the 1970s, perhaps her most famous song being "You're So Vain" (1972), from her third album. She also had huge success with the James Bond theme song "Nobody Does It Better" (1977). In the 1980s she became increasingly involved with films, writing and performing the score for *Heartburn* (1986), and the Oscar-winning song "Let the River Run" from the film *Working Girl* (1989).

SIMON, Paul (1941-) *Pop singer-songwriter* As a solo artist, Simon recorded with some success throughout the 1970s. In the mid-1980s he found a new direction. Beginning with tapes he had made of South African music, he built the album *Graceland*, a diverse and inventive album that enjoyed huge commercial success. In 1990, Simon repeated the experiment using Brazilian drumming music to produce perhaps his best album so far, *The Rhythm of the Saints*. In 1998 Simon's musical *The Capeman* was staged on Broadway in New York City.

SIMPLE MINDS *Rock group* Formed in 1978, Simple Minds scored their first British hit single in 1982 with "Promised You a Miracle." In 1985 they wrote the soundtrack for the bratpack movie, *The Breakfast Club*, and the resulting single, "Don't You Forget About Me," provided them with their only U.S. No.1. For a period in the mid-1980s, Simple Minds seemed to be vying with U2 for stadium-rock supremacy, but in the 1990s, Simple Minds have fallen out of favor.

SIMPSON, Robert (1921–97) *Composer* Born in England, Simpson joined the BBC music staff in 1951, staying until 1980. His major achievement was his cycle of nine symphonies and eight string quartets, which have been performed widely, especially in Britain. Each of his works, although individual in character, is firmly based in tonality, showing the influence of the great symphonists Beethoven, Bruckner, and SIBELIUS.

SINGLETON, Zutty (1898–1975) *Jazz drummer* Singleton was one of the most influential of all classical JAZZ drummers, the first to play extended solos and to introduce brushes into the jazz drummer's vocabulary. He was a well-liked and respected personality on the jazz scene, working with many leading musicians, from Louis ARMSTRONG to T-Bone WALKER and Charlie PARKER, and leading his own bands. Singleton also appeared in three jazz films in the late 1940s: *Stormy Weather,*with Fats WALLER and Lena HORNE; *New Orleans,* with Louis ARMSTRONG and Billie HOLIDAY; and *Turned-Up Toes.* Singleton is best heard on the 1952 album *Rarities.*

SINOPOLI, Guiseppe (1946–) *Conductor and composer* After studying medicine in Venice and Padua, Sinopoli followed Maderna's and STOCKHAUSEN's courses at Darmstadt and studied conducting in Vienna. In 1975 he formed the Bruno Maderna Ensemble for contemporary music and launched his career as a conductor. As a composer, his work shows the influence of Donatoni and the DARMSTADT SCHOOL of the 1950s.

SISTER SLEDGE *Soul vocal group* This group of four sisters began their recording career in 1971 as backing singers. Their greatest success came with DISCO and the production work of Nile Rodgers and Bernie Edwards—the duo behind the group Chic. In 1979 they had three Top 20 hits, "He's The Greatest Dancer," "We Are Family," and "Lost in Music." They had a minor hit in 1982 with the song "My Guy," but broke up soon afterwards.

SKAGGS, Ricky (1954–) *Country singer and musician* Scaggs performed from the age of five. In 1977 he joined Emmylou HARRIS' Hot Band, and learned his trade there. After going solo Skaggs dominated the U.S. COUNTRY charts in the 1980s with his traditional country style. In 1981 he released *Waitin' for the Sun to Shine,* generally seen as a turning point in country music. In 1982 he was the Country Music Association Male Vocalist of the Year and became the 61st and youngest member of the Grand Ole Opry. His revival of Bill MONROE's "Uncle Pen" became the first bluegrass song to top the country charts since 1963. In the 1990s, he became one of the biggest country performers of his time.

SLADE *Rock group* Formed in the U.K. in 1968, Slade are one of the most fondly-remembered pop groups of the early 1970s, producing many glam rock anthems. Beginning with the album *Play It Loud* (1970) Slade were unstoppable, with 13 British Top 10 hits between 1971 and 1975, including the badly spelled "Coz I Love You," "Mama Weer All Crazee Now," and "Merry Christmas Everybody."

SLADE, Julian (1930–) *Composer* Essentially self-taught, Slade began writing stage MUSICALS around 1950. His most popular work was *Salad Days* (1954), a small-scale musical comedy that ran for six years in London's West End—the longest running British musical of its time. Slade continued to compose throughout the 1970s, and successful revivals of his work were produced in the 1990s.

SLATKIN, Leonard (1944–) *Conductor and composer* Born in the U.S., Slatkin studied at the Juilliard School, New York, and made his conducting debut in 1966. He guested with major orchestras all over the world, as well as holding posts with the St. Louis Symphony Orchestra and the National Symphony Orchestra. Slatkin conducted a wide repertoire including American music, and was a renowned interpreter of ELGAR. His compositions included string quartets, and *The Raven,* after Edgar Allen Poe (1971), for voice and orchestra.

SLEDGE, Percy (1941–) *Soul singer* Along with contemporaries Otis REDDING, Joe Tex, and Wilson Pickett, Sledge defined the mid-1960s sound of Southern SOUL. His debut single "When a Man Loves a Woman" (1966) was an instant hit, No.1 in both the U.S. POP and soul charts, and a U.K. Top 5. He had ten more hits between 1966 and 1969, including "It Tears Me Up" (1967) and "Take Time to Know Her" (1968). He recorded into the 1990s with further minor hits, and continued to tour.

SLIM, Harpo (1924–70) *Blues singer and harmonica player* Along with Lightnin' Slim, Harpo Slim—born James Moore—was a defining influence of the Excello Records' BLUES sound in the 1950s and 1960s, and one of the major exponents of Louisiana swamp blues. He began his solo recording career in 1957, enjoying a string of R&B hit singles including "Raining in My Heart" (1961) and "Little Queen Bee" (1964). "Baby Scratch My Back" (1966) was his most successful single, a U.S. Top 20 pop hit (and R&B No.1).

SLIM, Sunnyland (1907–95) *Blues pianist and singer* Slim has one of the biggest recording catalogs in BLUES, stretching from the 1920s to the early 1990s using a variety of pseudonyms. He became established in the 1950s as a leading figure in the development of Chicago blues, performing with artists such as Muddy WATERS and J.B. Lenoir. His powerful piano work set the standard for underpinning the hard, electric sound associated with Chicago blues.

SLY AND ROBBIE *Reggae duo* Sly Dunbar (drums) and Robbie Shakespeare (bass) began working together in 1975, and quickly became Jamaica's leading rhythm section. They were the basis for the house band at Channel One in Kingston. In 1980 they formed their own label, Taxi, and produced hit records for many artists. For many years Sly and Robbie provided the rhythm section for seminal reggae band Black Uhuru. They made a number of albums under their own names and worked with rock stars as diverse as Bob DYLAN, Ian Dury, and Joe Cocker.

SLY AND THE FAMILY STONE *Rock group*
Formed by Sly Stone in 1967, Sly and the Family Stone were the first group to fuse POP, SOUL, and ROCK to make first-class DANCE MUSIC. The diverse racial makeup of the Family Stone and the crucial role of women instrumentalists were groundbreaking at the time. They became firmly established with the album *Stand!* (1969), which included the No.1 single "Everyday People." Superficially, the songs were breezy FUNK workouts but the lyrics often conveyed a dark humor. "Hot Fun in the Summertime" reached No.2 in the U.S. despite being an ironic commentary on racial unrest. Sadly, by the mid-1970s Sly was wrestling with serious cocaine addiction and the band split up in the early 1980s.

SMALL FACES, The *Rock group*
Formed in London in 1965, the Small Faces became one of the best pop bands of the late 1960s. Their debut single "Whatcha Gonna Do" (1965) went into the U.K. Top 20 and "All or Nothing" reached No.1 the same year. In 1967 the Small Faces released "Itchycoo Park," which became their first American hit. Their last album, *Ogden's Nut Flake* (1968), was a huge commercial and critical success, but that same year the band split. Guitarist Steve Marriott went on to form Humble Pie, and the rest of the band became Rod Stewart's backing band, the Faces.

SMASHING PUMPKINS *Rock group*
Although Smashing Pumpkins had a slow start, they persevered, achieving acceptance and press veneration. Their debut single, "I Am the One" (1990), and first album, *Girls* (1991), announced the group to both INDIE and HEAVY METAL audiences. The follow-up album, *Siamese Dream* (1993), with its pop hooks and rock atmospherics, launched the band onto center stage, reaching the Top 10 in the U.S. *Billboard* charts. In 1995 *Mellon Collie and the Infinite Sadness*—two hour-long CDs—demonstrated an unheard of breadth of style.

SMILEY, Arthur Lee "Red" (1925–72) *Guitarist* Smiley formed a bluegrass duo with banjo player Don Reno in the 1950s, recording and working together at various major venues.

Their recordings included *Instrumentals* (1958) and *Good Ole Country Ballads* (1959), and they achieved a Top 20 COUNTRY chart hit with "Don't Let Your Sweet Love Die" (1961). Smiley was forced to give up touring in 1964 due to the effects of an old war wound, but continued to record with the Bluegrass Cut-Ups.

SMITH, "Big" Maybelle (1924–72) *Blues singer* Smith was one of the great female BLUES "shouters." She began singing professionally in 1936, with the all-female band, the Sweethearts of Rhythm. From the mid-1940s she began a solo career. Smith worked with many great artists such as Jimmy Witherspoon and Quincy JONES, and can be seen in the film *Jazz on a Summer's Day*, performing at the Newport Jazz Festival (1958).

SMITH, Carl (1927–) *Country singer*
Born in Maynardsville, Tennessee, Smith turned professional in the 1950s. He had some minor hits between 1967 and 1970, scoring his first Top 10 with "I've Found Someone of My Own," following it up with a No.1—"Let Old Mother Nature Have Her Way." With his rich, mature voice, Smith scored 41 chart records during the 1950s. During his lengthy career he had 93 hits, a total rarely surpassed.

SMITH, Clara (c.1894–1935) *Blues singer* Smith sang professionally from her mid-teens, becoming a big name in New York by 1923. Called the "Queen of the Moaners," she sang in a low, deeply sensual manner. Her early recordings are melancholic songs of lost love and betrayal. By the mid-1920s she had improved her delivery, and her best recordings include many songs with risqué sexual references. She recorded with some of the best instrumentalists of her time—including Louis ARMSTRONG and Lonnie JOHNSON—and twice sang duets with Bessie SMITH.

SMITH, Clarence "Pinetop" (1904–29) *Jazz pianist* "Pinetop" is considered to be the founder of the BOOGIE-WOOGIE style of piano playing. His fame largely rests on his recording of "Pinetop's Boogie Woogie" (1928), the first documented use of the term. In 1929 at age 25 he was shot and killed.

SMITH, Jimmy (1925–) *Jazz organist*
Smith became the most successful JAZZ organist, popularizing the use of the Hammond organ and bringing BEBOP style lines to organ playing for the first time. His classic albums include *The Sermon*—with Art BLAKEY—and *Houseparty*, both from the 1950s, and his recordings regularly crossed over into the pop charts. Jimmy Smith's influence was not restricted to JAZZ—his style was instrumental in the development of BLUES and FUNK keyboard playing.

SMITH, Mamie (1883–1940) *Blues singer* In 1920 Smith recorded "Crazy Blues," becoming the first black singer to record the BLUES as a soloist. The song was an instant hit, beginning a postwar craze for "Negro blues." Seven more hits between 1921 and 1923 firmly established her reputation, and throughout the 1920s she was a highly successful entertainer. However, as the popularity of the blues declined during the 1930s and 1940s, Smith sank into obscurity.

SMITH, Patti (1946–) *Rock singer*
Smith started her career as a poet, using ROCK MUSIC as a backing to the spoken word. However, by 1975 the Patti Smith Band was signed to Arista and had produced its brilliant first alternative rock album, *Horses*. Despite the lack of a promotional single it reached the *Billboard* Top 50. Her third album, *Easter,* was the most commercial to date, with the Bruce SPRINGSTEEN song "Because the Night" reaching No.13 in the U.S. During the 1980s Smith went back to her poetry and raising her family. However, in 1995 she appeared on stage with Bob DYLAN, and in 1996 she released a new album, *Gone Again*.

SMITH, Trixie (1895–1943) *Blues singer* Trixie Smith made many successful recordings in the 1920s as well as having a career as an actress. Her voice was not as strong as her contemporary namesakes, Mamie, Bessie, and Clara, but her records include outstanding, polished examples of the BLUES—most famously, "Railroad Blues" and "The World Is Jazz Crazy and So Am I"—accompanied by artists such as Fletcher HENDERSON and Louis ARMSTRONG.

SMITH, Willie "The Lion" (1897-1973)
Jazz pianist and composer From the 1920s, Smith was one of Harlem's best-known stride pianists and a major influence on younger, better-known musicians such as Duke ELLINGTON. In the 1930s Smith became famous through recordings like the reflective "Morning Air" and "Echoes of Spring." From the 1940s until his death he toured extensively and starred at JAZZ festivals.

SMITHS, The *Rock group* The Smiths are regarded by many as the most important British band of the 1980s. Their strikingly original music influenced a generation of bands. Critical excitement followed their early singles and propelled "What Difference Does It Make?" into the U.K. Top 10 and the self-titled first album to No.2. Four Top 30 hits followed and the albums, *Meat Is Murder* (1985) and *The Queen Is Dead* (1986), were hailed as two of the finest achievements of the decade. In 1987 guitarist Johnny Marr left, and the Smiths folded a few months later. Singer Morrissey pursued a moderately successful solo career after the breakup.

SMYTH, Ethel (1858-1944) *Composer* Born in the U.K., Smyth's early work was derivative but promising and in 1893 she signaled the scale of her ambitions with a powerful Mass in D. Smyth's central interest was OPERA. Her major work, and greatest success, was the opera *The Wreckers*, first produced in Leipzig in 1906. Throughout her career, Smyth's style remained eclectic, never acquiring a settled personal voice. She did, however, find fame in England, becoming important at the time of a renaissance of English music.

SNOOP DOGGY DOGG (1971-) *Rap artist* In the early 1990s Snoop Doggy Dogg was one of the most successful gangsta RAP artists. Snoop's first recordings were made for fellow Death Row rap star, Dr. Dre. After the success of Dre's album, *The Chronic*, Snoop's own debut *Doggy Style* (1993), became the most eagerly anticipated album in rap history. Combining uncompromising lyrics with FUNK and SOUL backing tracks, it

proved a popular new direction for rap music and *Doggy Style* became the first debut album to enter the *Billboard* chart at No.1.

SNOW, Hank (1914-) *Country singer, guitarist, and songwriter* One of the most successful COUNTRY stars of all time, Snow first found success in Canada, imitating the yodeling style of Jimmie RODGERS. After moving south to the U.S. Snow struggled to maintain his popularity, until the self-penned "I'm Moving On" (1950) hit the charts. It spent 44 weeks in the U.S. country charts, 21 at No.1, and even reached the Top 30 in the pop charts. At this time Snow was firmly established as an international star. He went on to amass 85 country chart hits between 1950 and 1980, including "The Golden Rocket," "I Don't Hurt Anymore," and "Hello Lover."

SÖDERSTRÖM, Elisabeth (1927-) *Opera singer* The Swedish soprano Söderström made her operatic debut in 1947. She was a member of the Swedish Royal Opera throughout her career, but also pursued an international career in a wide variety of roles. Her expressive voice was best suited to the works of Mozart, Richard STRAUSS, and JANÁCEK.

SOLAL, Martial (1927-) *Jazz pianist* Born of French parents in Algiers, Solal moved to Paris in 1950. In Paris he was able to play with many expatriate American JAZZ musicians. In 1968 he began a long association with the saxophonist Lee KONITZ, as well as frequently playing solo. He also wrote a number of film scores including Jean-Luc Godard's *Breathless* (1959). Solal's reputation is international, but his style remains individual and distinctively Gallic.

SOLOMON (1902-88) *Pianist* Born in the U.K., Solomon began his career as a child prodigy, but retired for a period, returning to the stage in 1926 as an accomplished adult. The greatest pianist of his day, his performances, particularly of Mozart and the Romantics, were renowned for their exceptional virtuosity and evocative poetry. In 1965 he suffered a stroke and retired permanently from public performance.

SONIC YOUTH *Rock group* Formed in the U.S. in 1981, Sonic Youth became the best-known underground band in America. Their discordant guitars, impassioned vocals, and compulsive drum patterns first gained widespread exposure in America and the U.K. with their fourth album, *Bad Moon Rising* (1985). Recording throughout the 1980s and 1990s, they established a reputation as godfathers to the alternative ROCK scene, giving support slots to less well-established bands on tour—including the early NIRVANA.

SOUNDGARDEN *Rock group* A U.S. quartet who fused influences including LED ZEPPELIN and early PUNK bands, their sound is characterized by heavy, bass-laden metallic riffs and ranting articulate vocals. With NIRVANA and Green River, Soundgarden defined the GRUNGE sound that dominated early 1990s ROCK. Their second album, *Louder Than Love*, (1990) was considered the best rock album of that year, but it was the fourth album, *Superunknown* (1994), that was the most commercially successful—selling over 3 million copies. Soundgarden continued to record successfully and in 1996 they headlined the Lollapalooza tour.

SPANIER, Muggsy (1906-67) *Jazz cornet player* Throughout the 1920s Spanier worked in Chicago clubs absorbing lessons from the greats—Louis ARMSTRONG, King Oliver, and Tommy Ladnier. In 1938 Spanier formed his own band, the Ragtimers, and recorded 16 Chicago-style DIXIELAND sides—including "Relaxing at the Touro"—which are known to JAZZ fans as "The Great Sixteen." Spanier was one of the great Dixieland bandleaders. Perhaps not technically startling, he played with great economy, timing, and note placement.

SPEARS, Billie Jo (1937-) *Country singer* Spears' first taste of stardom came at the early age of 15, when her first record, "Too Old for Toys, Too Young for Boys," earned her $4,200. However, she didn't record regularly until 1964, scoring her first hit in 1968 with "He's Got More Love in His Little Finger." In 1974 she had a transatlantic smash hit with the song "Blanket on the Ground."

SPECIALS, The *Rock group* The Specials, formed in the U.K. in 1977, started life as a PUNK-REGGAE fusion group. However, by 1979 they were in the forefront of the 2-Tone movement (named after the Special's own record label) to repopularize ska music. After a string of hits they reached their commercial peak with the single "Ghost Town," a British No.1 in 1981. The band split up soon after this.

SPRINGFIELD, Dusty (1939-) *Pop singer* Springfield was one of the great white SOUL singers. Born in the U.K., she originally found fame as part of the folk trio, the Springfields, in the early 1960s. Going solo in 1963, Springfield came up with an instant classic "I Only Want to Be with You," following it with many more hits such as "You Don't Have to Say You Love Me," and "Son-of-a Preacher Man." Her finest work is *Dusty in Memphis* (1969), recorded in the U.S. and featuring compositions by the writers such as BACHARACH-David, Goffin-KING, and Randy Newman. She continued to record sporadically in the 1980s and 1990s, including a hit single with the Pet Shop Boys, "What Have I Done to Deserve This?"

STANLEY BROTHERS, The *Country duo* Leaders of the renowned bluegrass group, the Clinch Mountain Boys, Carter and Ralph Stanley created some of the most beautiful harmonies in COUNTRY music. They made their first recordings in 1947, but the mid-1950s were their golden era, producing classics such as "The White Dove." Carter Stanley died in 1966. After his brother's death, Ralph Stanley reformed the Clinch Mountain Boys and in 1970 started the annual Bluegrass Festival (named in memory of his brother).

STAPP, Olivia (1940-) *Opera singer* The American mezzo-soprano Stapp made her debut at Spoleto in Italy in 1960. She has since sung all over the world including La Scala in Milan, and the Metropolitan Opera in New York City. She has taken roles in OPERAS by composers as diverse as PUCCINI and Verdi through to STRAVINSKY and SHOSTAKOVICH.

STARKER, Janos (1924-) *Cellist* Starker made his debut in his native Hungary when he was just 11 years old. After settling in the U.S. he became principal cello of the Metropolitan Opera Orchestra and then the Chicago Symphony. He is known for his successful solo career, his playing best displayed on the Bach cello suites. He has also been the dedicatee and first performer of concertos by Bernard Heiden and Miklos Rosza. One of his greatest achievements is in being the dedicatee of KODÁLY's sonata for solo cello, now a standard work. Starker is the "cellists' cellist" and is universally regarded as the world's greatest.

STARR, Ringo (1940-) *Rock drummer* Starr became world-famous as a member of the BEATLES—joining in 1962 after the sacking of the original drummer. Many of the Beatles' albums include a vocal track by Starr including the huge hit "Yellow Submarine" (1966). After the Beatles split up Starr pursued a solo career—one of his albums, *Ringo,* achieving platinum status. He continued recording intermittently into the late 1990s, often with a band made up from his superstar friends.

STATLER BROTHERS, The *Country group* The Statler Brothers vocal quartet was formed in 1960. In 1963 they became part of the Johnny CASH roadshow and played with Cash for the next nine years. Their first hit, "Flowers on the Wall" (1966), sold 2 million copies and was followed by a string of hits stretching into the 1990s—including "Bed of Roses" and "I'll Go to my Grave Loving You." The Statler Brothers' annual show—the Old-Fashioned Fourth of July Celebration—in Staunton, Virginia, still attracts over 70,000 people a year.

STATUS QUO *Rock group* London-based ROCK group, Status Quo have been in business for over 30 years and have become an institution in Britain. Since their first hit single "Pictures of Matchstick Men," which reached No.7 in the U.K. charts, they have had hit after hit, based on a 12-bar-blues rock sound. Status Quo have sold over 100 million albums, and they have had over 50 U.K. hit singles.

STEELY DAN *Rock group* Originally formed in 1972 to showcase the songwriting talents of Walter Becker and Donald Fagen, Steely Dan made records featuring JAZZ and latin-tinged melodies backing up bitter, cynical, or impenetrable lyrics. The band had a number of hits in the 1970s, starting with first album, *Can't Buy a Thrill* in 1973. *Pretzel Logic*, in 1974, yielded their biggest hit single, "Ricky Don't Lose that Number." By 1976 Steely Dan had ceased to be a performing band and future recordings were made by Becker, Fagen, and hired session musicians. This approach produced their best album yet, *Aja* (1977). In 1981 the band finally split, only to reform for a comeback tour in 1993.

STEINBERG, William (1899-1978) *Conductor* Steinberg was an American conductor of German birth who began his career in Cologne, Germany, as KLEMPERER's assistant. After the rise of Hitler in the early 1930s, the Jewish Steinberg was severely restricted and in 1936 he emigrated, founding the Palestine Orchestra (later the Israel PO). From 1938 he worked in the U.S., notably as musical director of the Pittsburgh Symphony Orchestra (1952–76). He was at his best conducting LATE ROMANTIC music and his performances of the work of Richard STRAUSS remain unsurpassed.

STEPPENWOLF *Rock group* Formed in 1967, Steppenwolf had an exemplary eponymous debut album in 1968 that included the classic single "Born to Be Wild," which reached No.2 on the U.S. charts. "Born to Be Wild," along with "Pusher"—both featured on the soundtrack to the film *Easy Rider*—proved to be the twin peaks of Steppenwolf's career. They recorded nothing as important after that early high, and broke up in 1972.

STERN, Mike (1954-) *Jazz guitarist* Stern began his career with Blood, Sweat and Tears in 1976, but moved into JAZZ ROCK in 1978 when he joined Billy Cobham's band. In 1981 he was asked to join Miles DAVIS' comeback band. Subsequently he worked with Jaco Pastorius, saxophonists Michael Brecker and Bob Berg, Bunny Brunel, and many others. Perhaps, his best recording is *Odds and Ends* (1991).

STEVENS, Cat (1947-) *Pop singer-songwriter* British-born Stevens wrote a catalog of timeless songs during the 1970s. As well as recording himself, he also wrote for others. Two of his finest songs were "Matthew and Son" and "Sitting." At his peak he had eight consecutive gold albums, including *Tea for the Tillerman* (1970) and *Teaser & the Firecat* (1971), ten hit singles in the U.K. and 14 hit singles in the U.S. Stevens gave up POP MUSIC in 1979, after converting to Islam.

STEWART, Rod (1945-) *Rock singer* Born in the U.K. Stewart was a member of many groups from the early 1960s, becoming well known in R&B and BLUES circles. He gained national exposure with the Jeff Beck Group and then joined the Faces, as well as embarking on a solo career. His second solo album *Gasoline Alley* (1970) made the breakthrough and he followed it up with the albums, *Every Picture Tells a Story*—including the single "Maggie May," a No.1 hit in Britain and the U.S.—and *Never a Dull Moment.* Stewart continued to score hits, becoming a major star. However, he has been unable to recapture the creative high of the early 1970s.

STITT, Sonny (1924-82) *Jazz saxophonist* Part of the BEBOP movement almost from the beginning, Stitt was influenced by Charlie PARKER. In 1945 he settled in New York, working with Dizzy GILLESPIE, and by the late 1940s he had formed the first of many bands he was to lead and colead. For the next 30 years Stitt remained in demand, working with Miles DAVIS among others, producing consistently good work despite his battles with alcohol and narcotics.

STOLZ, Robert (1880-1975) *Composer and conductor* Born in Austria, Stolz was known as a prolific composer of OPERETTAS and FILM MUSICALS. He first found popularity with the operetta *Der Tanz Ins Glück* (1920)—produced in the U.S. as *Sky High.* In 1924 he began writing scores for German film musicals, and after 1940 he wrote for Hollywood. In 1952 he returned to Austria to conduct concerts of Viennese music and write music for more popular audiences.

STONE ROSES, The *Rock group* Formed in Manchester, England, in 1984, the Stone Roses released their debut album *The Stone Roses,* in 1989. It was hailed as a classic and stayed in the British charts for 48 weeks. Its attempt to combine alternative ROCK and DANCE MUSIC proved hugely influential on the next generation of Manchester bands. However, their follow-up album did not appear until 1994. The band could not recover their early momentum and split in 1996.

STOOGES, The *Rock group* Formed in the late 1960s, the Stooges were fronted by Iggy Pop. A reputation as a wild live act helped them to some success. Their third album *Raw Power* (1973), contains two of their best-known songs "Gimme Danger" and "Search and Destroy." In 1974 the band split up in a drug-induced mess, with Iggy being saved by the personal interest of David BOWIE.

STRAIT, George (1952-) *Country singer* After a difficult start, Strait's career took off in 1981 with his first single "Unwound." His style, a throwback to 1950s honky-tonk and reminiscent of Merle HAGGARD and Lefty Frizzell, did him good. Strait produced a string of 18 U.S. COUNTRY chart No.1 hits—including "Nobody in His Right Mind Would've Left Her" and "Am I Blue"—making him the most successful country singer of the 1980s.

STRANGLERS, The *Punk group* The Stranglers are one of the longest-surviving groups from the British PUNK explosion of the late 1970s. Formed in 1974, their debut single "Grip" didn't appear until 1977. Their biggest hit came with the evocative single "Golden Brown" from the album *La Folie* (1981). In 1991 guitarist/vocalist Hugh Cornwall left the band. The Stranglers continued without the excitement or success of earlier years.

STRATAS, Teresa (1938-) *Opera singer* Born in Canada, the lyric soprano Stratas made her debut in 1959. In 1960 she played the title role in Peggy Glanville-Hick's *Nausicaa,* and in 1962 Queen Isabella in FALLA's *Atlántida.* She has taken on various roles, her deep involvement distinguishing all her appearances.

STRAY CATS, The *Rockabilly group* The Stray Cats, formed in New York in 1979, found success in the U.K.—and later the U.S.—with the rockabilly resurgence of the early 1980s. Their debut single "Runaway Boy" reached No.9 in the U.K. charts, but they hit the big time in 1982 with "Rock This Town" and in 1983 with "Stray Cat Strut." They split in 1983 after a short but intense period of chart success, returning less successfully in 1989.

STRAYHORN, Billy (1915-67) *Jazz composer and pianist* Strayhorn began and ended his professional career as the main contributor of original material and arrangements for the Duke ELLINGTON band, writing a total of some 200 pieces, including the Ellington theme "Take the A-Train." Although there are clear differences between Ellington's and Strayhorn's individual work, they were both adept at imitating each other and serious study is now being undertaken on Strayhorn's individual contribution.

STUDER, Cheryl (1955-) *Opera singer* Studer made her debut in her native Germany in 1980. Her flexibility and much-loved voice made her a favorite for Mozart through to Verdi, Richard STRAUSS, and Wagner.

STYLISTICS, The *Soul group* Formed in 1968, the Stylistics had a number of POP/R&B hits between 1971–74. Signed to Philadelphia International Records, the Stylistics were one of the bands that defined the PHILADELPHIA SOUND in the early 1970s. They reached their peak with "You Are Everything" (1971), "Betcha By Golly Wow" (1972), and "You Make Me Feel Brand New" (1974).

SUBOTNIK, Morton (1933-) *Composer* Subotnik, an American, studied with MILHAUD and Kirchner. He then taught in various places, including, from 1969, the California Institute of the Arts. His compositions, realized on Buchla synthesizers, have concentrated on electronic music. His work, often using serial and game theory techniques, included *Silver Apples of the Moon* (1966), the first electronic work written for a recording company.

SUGARHILL GANG, The *Rap group*
The Sugarhill Gang saw international success in 1979 with "Rapper's Delight," the first hip-hop single to break through into the mainstream. Although they only had two further hits, their place in rap's history was already assured. The Sugarhill Gang fell apart in the early 1980s.

SUICIDE *Rock group* Suicide was an electronic NEW WAVE duo, originally formed in 1970 by Alan Vega and Martin Rev. Their potent fusion of rockabilly and relentless keyboards was ahead of its time, and their confrontational performances—including a full-scale riot in Brussels—made it difficult for them to get gigs. They didn't record until 1977, when their eponymous debut album became a cult hit on both sides of the Atlantic. A second album, also self-titled, followed in 1980, but they have recorded only sporadically since then.

SUMMER, Donna (1948-) *Pop singer* Summer was one of the best known of all DISCO divas. Working predominantly with producer Giorgio Moroder, she had 25 Hot 100 singles between 1975 and 1984, 13 hit albums, and won four Grammy Awards. Her first hit was the breathily suggestive "Love to Love You Baby," which sold over a million copies in the U.S., instantly making her an international star. Her other hits included "I Feel Love," Hot Stuff," and "Bad Girls."

SUN RA (1914-93) *Jazz musician* Born in Birmingham, Alabama, as Herman Lee, Sun Ra is one of the most extraordinary figures in 20th-century music. He began as a pianist, arranger, and composer in the mid-1930s, and by the mid-1950s had formed his own ten-piece big band, the Arkestra, recording their debut "Sun Song" in 1956. With unusual instruments for the time—including electric guitar, keyboards, and timpani—they became the most advanced and experimental group of the era, often playing FREE JAZZ years before the experimental period of the late 1960s. Sun Ra became one of the great modern visionaries, recording right up until his death.

SUPERTRAMP *Rock group* Supertramp were a U.K. group formed in London in 1969. After many false starts and changes of personnel, their first hit single, "Dreamer" (1975), was taken from *Crime of the Century*, the first of a string of million-copy-selling albums. Electronic piano and saxophones were their trademark, and they scored many further hits, including their biggest-selling album *Breakfast in America* (1979), which went to No.1 in the U.S.

SUPREMES, The *Soul group* The Supremes, formed in the late 1950s, became easily the most successful female group of the 1960s and the launch pad for MOTOWN's assault on the charts. They had more than two years of flop singles before Diana Ross became their lead vocalist and Holland-Dozier-Holland took over the songwriting. From their first hit, "The Lovelight Starts Shining," they became queens of the pop charts. During the 1960s the Supremes notched up 19 Top 10 hits and 12 No.1s—including "Where Did Our Love Go," "Baby Love" (both 1964), "Stop! In the Name of Love" (1965), and "You Can't Hurry Love" (1966). The group disbanded in 1977.

SUSSKIND, Walter (1918-80) *Conductor* Susskind was a British conductor of Czech birth. He made his debut at the German Opera in 1934, conducting *La Traviata*. In 1938 he went to Britain, where he later became music director of the Scottish (National) Orchestra. He had further posts in Australia, Canada, and the U.S. He was highly regarded for his sound musicality and eagerness to explore the repertoire.

SUZUKI, Shin'ichi (1898-1998) *Violinist and teacher* Although he performed, forming the Suzuki Quartet and the Tokyo String Orchestra, Suzuki will be best remembered as the creator of the hugely successful Suzuki method of violin teaching. Developed in the 1930s, it is based on the learning processes of young children, with instruction by ear and by rote at its core. Suzuki's first pupil was renowned violinist Toshiya Eto. The method has now been adapted to teach a variety of musical instruments.

SYLVESTER (1946-88) *Soul singer* Sylvester recorded his first solo album *Sylvester* in 1977. He scored two massive DISCO hits in 1978 with "Dance" (1978) and "You Make Me Feel (Mighty Real)" (1979), both of which showcased his distinctive high-pitched vocals. He quickly faded in popularity though as the disco movement ran its course.

SZELL, George (1897-1970) *Conductor* An American conductor of Hungarian birth, Szell quickly made his name conducting professionally with the Vienna Symphony Orchestra at the age of 16. In 1939 he moved to the U.S. and became a legend as musical director of the Cleveland Orchestra (1946-70). Szell was particularly praised for his work with the Austro-German repertoire, from Haydn to Richard STRAUSS. Although Szell played relatively little contemporary music, he did champion composers such as BARTÓK, JANÁCEK, and WALTON.

SZERING, Henryk (1918-88) *Violinist* Polish born, Szering made his debut in 1933, but World War II interrupted his career. His fluent command of seven languages led to a post on the staff of General Sikorski, the exiled head of the Polish government. He resumed his concert performances in 1954, and his versatility, elegance, and technical command were widely admired. Having settled in Mexico in 1946, Szering was a strong advocate of native Mexican composers, often playing their work. During the latter years of his life he formed a recording partnership with Polish pianist Artur RUBINSTEIN.

SZIGETI, Joseph (1892-1973) *Violinist* Hungarian-born, but with U.S. citizenship, Szigeti began his concert career as a child prodigy, performing all over the world. However, his music did not really flourish until he reached his 30s. He settled in the U.S. in 1940, but returned to Europe in 1960. He had a huge musical personality, well-suited to the grandeur of Beethoven and Brahms. Szigeti was also a champion of contemporary music, notably PROKOFIEV, BARTÓK, Bloch, and Martin, and many composers dedicated work to him.

TALKING HEADS *Rock group* Emerging from the NEW WAVE movement of the late 1970s, along with Television and Patti Smith, Talking Heads became one of the best and most influential groups of the 1970s and 1980s. From their first single, "Love Goes to Building on Fire," to their last album *Naked* (1988), they followed an idiosyncratic path of uncompromising brilliance. Their first classic album, *Remain in Light* (1980), spawned the hit single "Once in a Lifetime." Throughout their career, the various members of Talking Heads pursued successful individual projects, including David Byrne's solo albums and the Tom Tom Club.

TANGERINE DREAM *Rock group* Formed in Germany in 1967, Tangerine Dream started life as a PINK FLOYD-inspired psychedelic rock band. However, they soon lost interest in rock and concentrated on creating ambient, experimental music—pioneering the use of synthesizers. In 1973 they signed with Virgin and used its superior studio facilities to produce the album *Phaedra* (1974). In 1977 they recorded the first of many film soundtracks for William Friedkin's *Sorcerer*.

TATE, Buddy (1915-) *Jazz saxophonist* Tate was one of the outstanding tenor saxophonists of his time. A direct musical successor to Coleman HAWKINS and Herschel Evans, Tate took Evans' place with Count BASIE after his death in 1939. He took his own band into a residency at the Celebrity Club in New York in 1953, staying there for 21 years. To maintain his profile, Tate recorded regularly during this period. He continued recording and touring into the 1990s.

TATE, Jeffrey (1943-) *Conductor* Born in the U.K., Tate studied at Cambridge and qualified as a doctor. He began conducting in OPERA houses in England, Germany, and later in the U.S. His tastes are wide, but he is particularly admired for his interpretation of Mozart. He has held posts with a number of orchestras, including the Royal Opera House, Covent Garden, in London, the English Chamber Orchestra, and the Rotterdam Philharmonic.

TAUBER, Richard (1891-1948) *Opera singer* Tauber began his career in his native Germany, and by 1919 was a well-known tenor in German-speaking Europe. It was in lighter music, the OPERETTAS of Lehár and others, that he really made his name, and he became one of the most popular tenors of the first half of the 20th century. However, the strain of singing long parts eight times a week left its mark on his vocal chords, and his return to OPERA in the late 1930s was marked by some dubious stylistic elements.

TAVARES *Pop group* Formed in 1964, Tavares had a number of commercial successes in the mid-1970s with their undemanding blend of light SOUL and pop. They had a soul chart-topper and U.S. pop Top 10 hit with "It Only Takes a Minute" (1975), while "Heaven Must Be Missing an Angel" (1976) sold a million copies. In 1978 "More Than a Woman," taken from the soundtrack to *Saturday Night Fever*, gave the band its last significant hit.

TAYLOR, Cecil (1929-) *Jazz pianist* Taylor was a towering figure in post-war avant-garde JAZZ. In the 1950s he became more and more distanced from mainstream jazz, shedding all direct reference to tonality and regular time-keeping. The advent of FREE JAZZ should have made Taylor a star. However, the arrival in New York of Ornette COLEMAN eclipsed Taylor entirely and he spent much of the 1960s practicing at home. During the 1970s he found increasing acceptance—his solo album, *Fly! Fly! Fly! Fly! Fly!* (1981) was a stunning achievement and one of his best.

TAYLOR, James (1948-) *Pop singer and songwriter* After an unsuccessful first album, Taylor released *Sweet Baby James* (1970), which eventually spent two years on the American charts. It contained "Fire and Rain," one of the finest songs of the era. Taylor has become the embodiment of the late 1960s and early 1970s SINGER-SONGWRITER. He built a long-lasting career, made an appearance in the cult movie *Two Lane Blacktop,* and has a continuing public commitment to liberal causes. He released an album of all-new material in 1997 entitled *Hourglass.*

TEAGARDEN, Jack (1905-64) *Jazz trombonist and singer* Teagarden became one of the greatest and best-known JAZZ musicians of his time, setting a new standard for his instrument. Before Teagarden, the trombone had provided band harmonies and light comedy moments. After Teagarden, the trombone achieved a status to match that of Louis ARMSTRONG's trumpet playing. Teagarden's playing was smooth, relaxed, and above all effortless, quite unlike any player before him, gaining respect from musicians like Glen MILLER and Tommy DORSEY. He was also a remarkable singer. With his superlative playing and lazy vocal charm he made many songs his own, including "I'm Coming Virginia" and "Aunt Hagar's Blues."

TEAR, Robert (1939-) *Opera singer* Welsh-born Tear made a name for himself as a lyric tenor. He was particularly noted for his performances of BRITTEN, TIPPETT, and Taverner. In many ways his voice and manner resembled Peter Pears, and he took many of the roles created for Pears. Tear worked frequently with guitarist and lutenist Julian Bream, performing songs by the 17th-century English composer John Dowland.

TELEVISION *Rock group* Television were the first of a number of NEW WAVE bands to come out of New York in the early 1970s, paving the way for such luminaries as Talking Heads, the Ramones, and Blondie. Success eluded Television in their native U.S., but in the U.K. their debut album, *Marquee Moon* (1977) was applauded as one of ROCK's most accomplished debut albums and reached the Top 30. Their second album was less successful and the group split in 1978.

TEMPTATIONS, The *Soul group* A talented vocal group, the Temptations benefited, in their early years, from the attention of Smokey Robinson, who wrote most of their mid-1960s hits, starting with "The Way You Do the Things You Do" (1964). As the 1960s progressed, they became more closely associated with Norman Whitfield, who moved them in a funkier direction. The 1968 hit "Cloud

Nine" was a landmark for the Temptations, signaling a new, funky sound and socially aware lyrics. They had a run of nearly 40 U.S. Top 40 hits, notably "Ball of Confusion (That's What the World Is Today)" (1970), "Just My Imagination" (1971), and "Papa Was a Rollin' Stone" (1972). They continued to perform, albeit with different personnel, into the 1990s.

10CC *Pop group* Formed in England in 1971 to fulfill a contractual obligation, 10cc became one of the most popular groups of the 1970s. Their first single, "Donna," went straight to No.2 in the U.K. charts, beginning a string of hits through to the end of the decade, with "I'm Not in Love" (1975) being the standout hit. Although their music was often less than inspiring, their lyrics revealed a lively wit.

TENNSTEDT, Klaus (1926-97) *Conductor* Born in Communist East Germany, Tennstedt did not become internationally known until the 1970s. Working with orchestras across Europe, he developed a reputation as one of the greatest conductors of his time, being especially acclaimed for his interpretation of the symphonic repertoire, particularly Beethoven and MAHLER.

TERRY, Clark (1920-) *Jazz trumpeter* In his early career, Terry played with musicians such as Count BASIE and Duke ELLINGTON. He became famous when he was one of the first African-American musicians to feature regularly on TV in the *Tonight Show* starring Johnny Carson. Terry played the flügelhorn as well as the trumpet, introducing the instrument as a JAZZ alternative to the trumpet. The very vocal sound Terry produced had a direct influence on Miles DAVIS and a whole generation of trumpeters. Terry is best heard on the 1957 album *Serenade to a Bus Seat.*

TERRY, Todd (c.1958-) *Producer* Terry learned his trade playing early house and hip-hop, and became an important innovator and producer in house music. His distinctive use of samples underpinned all his production and remixing work.

THEM *Rock group* Best known as Van MORRISON's first major group, Them were formed in Ireland in 1963. Their second single, "Baby Please Don't Go," backed with "Gloria," reached the U.K. Top 10. "Gloria" has inspired hundreds of cover versions, including those by Jimi HENDRIX, The Doors, and Patti Smith. An excellent album, *Here Comes the Night,* followed, but the band's fortunes soon began to wane and Van Morrison left in 1966.

THIBAUD, Jacques (1880-1953) *Violinist* French-born Thibaud became one of the greatest violinists in the first half of the 20th century. Particularly noted for his performances of Mozart and the French Romantics, he was also part of a famous trio with CASALS and Cortot, making notable recordings of Schubert and Beethoven. In 1943 he cofounded the Marguerite Long–Jacques Thibaud Competition, a biennial international competition for violinists and pianists.

THIN LIZZY *Rock group* Thin Lizzy's first hit was the single "Whiskey in the Jar" (1973), which popularized the group's blend of Irish FOLK and strident guitar work. The real breakthrough year for Thin Lizzy, however, was 1976 with their acclaimed album *Jailbreak*—featuring the anthem "The Boys Are Back in Town"—hitting the charts in both Britain and the U.S. They continued with further successes, *Live and Dangerous* (1978) perhaps being their finest hour, until bass guitarist and vocalist Phil Lynott, the heart of the band, died from a heroin overdose in 1986.

13TH FLOOR ELEVATORS, The *Psychedelic R&B group* Formed in 1965, this influential group from Austin, Texas, set the pace in psychedelic rock. Their debut *The Psychedelic Sounds of 13th Floor Elevators* (1966) contained their most successful single "You're Gonna Miss Me," and was a forceful piece of propaganda for the hallucinogenic counter-culture. The band produced a second classic album, *Easter Everywhere* (1968), before disintegrating a year later.

THOMAS, Irma (1941-) *Soul vocalist* Thomas became known as the Soul Queen of New Orleans, although she never had a major hit record. In 1960 "(You Can Have My Husband But Please) Don't Mess with My Man" reached No.22 on the R&B charts, and four years later "Wish Someone Would Care" climbed to No.17. Thomas continues to record into the 1990s, remaining a popular live attraction, but has never been able to cross over into the mainstream.

THOMAS, Jesse "Babyface" (1911-) *Blues pianist and guitarist* Thomas made his debut recording in 1929. By the time he returned to the studio in 1948, he had developed an individual electric guitar style of great fluency, stemming from formal training, an acquaintance with JAZZ, and serious attempts to transfer his piano technique to guitar. He recorded intermittently into the 1980s, most tracks remaining firmly in the Texan BLUES tradition.

THOMAS, Michael Tilson (1944-) *Conductor* Born in the U.S. Thomas is a brilliant conductor noted for his interpretations of 20th-century music, and has conducted widely in the U.S. and abroad, being the principal conductor of the London Symphony Orchestra and musical director of the San Francisco Symphony Orchestra since 1995. He has a wide breadth of interest and his repertoire ranges from Pérotin to STOCKHAUSEN and REICH. He also has a knack for building original yet harmonious musical programs. He is seen as an eloquent spokesman for classical music.

THOMPSON, Hank (1925-) *Country singer and bandleader* Thompson became the most successful exponent of Western SWING from the late 1940s through to the 1980s. In 1946 he formed the Brazo Valley Boys and produced a string of hits, beginning with the "(I've Got a) Humpty Dumpty Heart" (1948) and including the most successful "The Wild Side of Life," a No.1 in 1952. In 1959, Thompson became the first COUNTRY artist to record in stereo and the first to record an "in concert" album, *Live at the Golden Nugget.* He continued to tour with success into the 1990s.

THOMPSON, Richard (1949-) *Rock guitarist, vocalist, and songwriter* Thompson forged his reputation as a member of Fairport Convention in the 1960s. His sensitive compositions included "Meet on the Ledge," and his innovative guitar style brought a distinctive edge to the band. He made an impressive solo debut album, *Henry the Human Fly* (1972), as well as forming a duo with his wife, Linda, recording highly regarded albums. With a reputation for his guitar playing and a catalog of beautiful songs, he continued as a solo artist into the 1990s.

THORNHILL, Claude (1905-65) *Jazz pianist and bandleader* In the early 1930s, Thornhill played in many bands including those of Paul WHITEMAN and Benny GOODMAN. Later in the 1930s he began arranging pieces for several bands and singers, including the huge hit "Loch Lomond" for singer Maxine Sullivan. He began recording under his own name from 1937, forming his own band around 1940. He soon earned great respect, his complex harmonies being influential on JAZZ arrangers such as Gil Evans.

THORNTON, Willie Mae "Big Mama" (1926-84) *Blues singer* Thornton's most famous hit and first R&B No.1 was "Hound Dog" in 1953. However, her importance extends far beyond one song. A musical descendant of the classic BLUES singers, Ma RAINEY and Bessie SMITH, Thornton was the link between this early tradition and 1960s blues-rock. In the 1960s Thornton moved to San Francisco, successfully resuscitating a fading career and becoming a legendary figure. Her 1975 album *Jail* features live versions of "Hound Dog" and "Ball and Chain."

THUNDERS, Johnny (1952-91) *Rock guitarist* Thunders first gained recognition as a member of the New York Dolls. After the Dolls split he formed the Heartbreakers, recording prolifically and achieving much popularity. In 1976 the Heartbreakers joined the SEX PISTOLS on their "Anarchy Tour." In 1978 Thunders began a solo career with the album *So Alone* (1978), but increasing drug dependence blighted his career during the 1980s.

TILLMAN, Floyd (1914-) *Country singer, guitarist, and songwriter* Tillman became famous as a writer of classic COUNTRY songs, such as "They Took the Stars out of Heaven" (1944), which gave him a No.1 U.S. country chart hit. His songs proved even more successful when recorded by other artists, for example Ernest TUBB's version of "Slippin' Around." Tillman is credited as being the first to use electric guitar on a country recording.

TOMLINSON, John (1946-) *Opera singer* Born in England, Tomlinson was one of the greatest dramatic basses in the world, particularly known for his performances of Wagnerian characters. His repertoire stretched from Handel to late 20th-century works. He sang all over the world, and made many appearances at the Bayreuth Festival.

TORKANOWSKY, Werner (1926-) *Conductor* Born in Germany, Torkanowsky became an American citizen in 1952. He made his conducting debut at the Spoleto Festival in Italy in 1959. From 1963–77 he was the musical director of the New Orleans Philharmonic. He conducted most of the major American orchestras as well as many OPERA companies, and his repertoire ranged from the Baroque to 20th-century avant-garde.

TORTELIER, Jan-Pascal (1947-) *Conductor* Born in France, the son of Paul Tortelier, Jan-Pascal Tortelier has conducted major orchestras throughout the world. He was principal conductor of the Ulster Orchestra (1989–92) and then moved to the BBC Philharmonic in 1992. He gained a reputation for his interpretations of French composers, notably DEBUSSY and RAVEL.

TORTELIER, Paul (1914-90) *Cellist and composer* Born in France, Tortelier made his debut at the Concerts Lamoureux in Paris in 1931. He quickly became an international soloist, known for his interpretations of the Bach suites and the Romantic repertoire, bringing to them both enthusiasm and tender expression. His experiences are documented in his book *How I Play, How I Teach* (1975).

TOUGH, Dave (1907-48) *Jazz drummer* Undoubtedly the best white drummer of his generation, Tough had a career with the finest big bands of the SWING era, including Tommy DORSEY, Red Norvo, Benny GOODMAN, Artie Shaw, and above all Woody Herman's. Tough cared intensely about his music, once walking off stage after only eight bars with B.A. Rolfe's showband, because he was too angry about their commercial music.

TOUSSAINT, Allen (1938-) *Pianist, songwriter, and producer* Toussaint made his recording debut in 1958 with *Wild Sounds of New Orleans,* but he had greater success as a PRODUCER. Many of Toussaint's artists recorded songs he had written under the pseudonym Naomi Neville, such as the Lee Dorsey singles, "Ride Your Pony" and "Working in the Coal Mine." Toussaint's solo career was inconsistent but his production and songwriting skills were in continual demand. The Band, Dr. John, Labelle, and Paul Simon are just a few of those who have called upon his talents.

TOWNSHEND, Pete (1945-) *Songwriter and guitarist* Born in the U.K., Townshend will chiefly be remembered as one of rock's best-known and finest guitarists, and as a founding member of THE WHO. He wrote many of their classic songs such as "I Can See for Miles" (1967) and "Pinball Wizard" (1969). He also composed the rock opera *Tommy* (1969). But the band are also remembered for their 1971 album *Who's Next.* The Who have continued to reform intermittently, while Townshend has pursued a solo career with some success.

TRAFFIC *Rock group* Formed in the U.K. in 1967, Traffic's first single "Paper Sun" immediately hit the charts in the U.K., reaching No.5. It was followed by their first album, *Mr. Fantasy* (1967), which incorporated a variety of styles from psychedelia to knockabout humor. Their next album, the eponymously titled *Traffic* (1968), showed how far the band had progressed, both compositionally and technically, in a short time. Soon after that the band split for the first time. In 1970 they reformed and made six more albums, including an excellent live album, *On the Road* (1973), before splitting again. Steve Winwood went on to have a successful solo career.

TRAVIS, Randy (1959-) *Country singer* Travis had a hit with his debut album *Storms of Life* (1986). It included four Top 10 COUNTRY singles, won a Grammy, and became the first country album to sell a million copies within a year of its release. In 1987–88 he registered six more country No.1s, and entered the 1990s as a superstar.

TRICKY (1964-) *Rap artist* Born in the U.K. and based in Bristol, Tricky began his career as a member of the collective Massive Attack, rapping on their album *Blue Lines*. Never really part of the nucleus of the band, Tricky struck out on his own, issuing a solo single "Aftermath," followed by the critically acclaimed album *Maxinquaye* (1995). Difficult to characterize, Tricky's trip-hop style combines eerie studio effects and blunted rhythms often with disturbing lyrics.

TROGGS, The *Pop group* Formed in the U.K. in the 1960s, the Troggs found success with "Wild Thing," a U.K. No.2 and U.S. No.1. Led by singer Reg Presley, their next single "With a Girl Like You" went straight to No.1 in the U.K. Two more Top 10 hits followed in 1966, but thereafter the going got tough. Musically unaccomplished and lacking any real direction, the Troggs' appeal was in their rough and ready sound and their no-nonsense approach. Internal arguments at their lack of continued success caused them to split up in the late 1960s.

TROUBLEFUNK *Funk group* Troublefunk were at the forefront of Washington's go-go music scene in the 1980s. Their call-and-response vocals anticipated the emergence of RAP, notably on the singles "Drop the Bomb" and "Woman of Principle." They were still active in the 1990s.

TUCKWELL, Barry (1931-) *Horn player* Born in the U.K., Tuckwell played professionally from the age of 15, later becoming principal of the

London Symphony Orchestra (1955–68). After that he mainly played solo and chamber music, having recorded the Mozart concertos and all the standard repertoire. He was one of the leading horn players of his generation and had a number of works composed for him.

TURNER, Dame Eva (1892-1990) *Opera singer* One of the foremost English sopranos of her day, Turner sang in OPERAS ranging from Mozart through to PUCCINI. In 1924 TOSCANINI'S assistant heard her singing and sent her to Milan to sing for Toscanini himself. She made her debut at La Scala in Milan in 1924. In 1926 she sang Turandot for the first time, a role with which she was to be closely associated for the next 20 years.

TURNER, Ike (1931-) *Rock musician* Turner formed the Kings of Rhythm during the late 1940s, producing "Rocket '88'" in 1950, considered to be the first ROCK'N'ROLL recording. His band was later joined by a singer who became his wife, the legendary Tina TURNER. They had a number of hits as a duo including "It's Gonna Work Out Fine" (1961), the Phil SPECTOR produced "River Deep, Mountain High" (1966), "Proud Mary" (1971), and "Nutbush City Limits" (1973).

TURNER, Joe (1907-90) *Jazz pianist and singer* Turner worked in New York in the 1920s with many leading JAZZ musicians, including Louis ARMSTRONG and the singer Adelaide Hall. He also worked extensively in Europe, eventually settling in Paris, where from 1962 he was resident at the Calvados club.

TWITTY, Conway (1933-93) *Country singer* Twitty was a singer of rock ballads in the late 1950s, but turned to COUNTRY in 1965. By the time of his death, Twitty had had 61 Top 10 hits, 31 of those reaching No.1. His most popular song was "You've Never Been This Far Before" (1973), which reached No.22 on the pop charts. Of his ROCK'N'ROLL numbers, "It's Only Make Believe" was the biggest hit and it continued to be the focal point of his stage show throughout his life. During his career, Twitty had more chart toppers than any other artist.

ULMER, James "Blood" (1942-) *Guitarist, vocalist, and composer* Ulmer is an uncategorizable musician although he could be described as an avant-garde bluesman. In the 1970s he played at the famous BEBOP venue Minton's Playhouse in New York, playing and recording with artists such as Art BLAKEY, Joe HENDERSON, and Ornette COLEMAN. He sang like Jimi HENDRIX, but his guitar playing was rhythmic and harmonically inventive, with a cutting tone often creating an irresistible, intense, brooding momentum. He is best heard on the 1997 album *Revealing*.

UNDERTONES, The *Rock group* Formed in Northern Ireland in 1978, the Undertones were a much-loved PUNK-POP quintet, regarded as one of the most refreshing groups of the time. By 1979 the band had entered the U.K. Top 20 with "Jimmy Jimmy," gaining considerable acclaim for their debut album *The Undertones*. The follow-up album, *Hypnotised* (1980), also produced hit singles. However, as the band's output became more sophisticated, its popularity declined and the group split in 1983. Singer Feargal Sharkey went on to have a successful solo career during the mid-1980s, which saw him record several hit singles, such as "A Good Heart."

VALENS, Ritchie (1941-59) *Rock singer* Born Richard Valenzuela, Valens was the first Hispanic-American ROCK'N'ROLL star, best remembered for his classic 1950s hit "La Bamba." There were other hits, including "Donna" (1958) and "Little Girl" (1959), but Valens' promising career was cut short in 1959 when he died in a plane crash—following a concert in Clear Lake in Iowa—with Buddy HOLLY and the Big Bopper.

VAN CLIBURN, (1934-) *Pianist* Born in the U.S. Van Cliburn began his career in 1954, playing with the New York Philharmonic. He achieved wider fame in 1958 when he won the International Tchaikovsky Competition. With his technical command and massive tone he is known for his interpretations of the Romantics, particularly Tchaikovsky and RACHMANINOV. He also set up a piano competition in his own name in the U.S.

VAN DAM, José (1940-) *Opera singer* Born in Belgium, the bass Van Dam made his debut in 1960 in Brussels and then transferred to the Paris Opera (1961–65). His powerful deep voice extended well into the baritone range, making him suitable for many roles, including Mozart's Figaro.

VANDROSS, Luther (1951-) *Soul singer* Vandross began his career as a session vocalist, backing artists such as David BOWIE—arranging all the vocal parts on *Young Americans*—and Barbra STREISAND. He broke free as a solo artist in the 1970s, but had little success until 1980 with "Glow of Love." A year later "Never Too Much" became an R&B No.1. Duets with Cheryl Lynn and Dionne Warwick also became hits. Vandross was widely considered to be one of the finest SOUL singers of the 1980s and 1990s. He has also worked as a producer with artists such as Diana ROSS and Whitney HOUSTON.

VANGELIS (1943-) *Composer* Born in Greece, Vangelis was a child prodigy on the piano. In the early 1960s he joined the pop group Aphrodite's Child with Demis Roussos. He started a solo career in the 1970s and in 1981 he composed the soundtrack to the film *Chariots of Fire,* the theme song of which went straight to the top of the charts. Further success followed, notably on "I Hear You Now" (1980) and "I'll Find My Way Home" (1982), both collaborations with former YES vocalist Jon Anderson. Vangelis continues to write and record in the 1990s, particularly for the movies.

VAN HALEN *Rock group* Formed in 1974, Van Halen became one of America's most successful HEAVY METAL bands, their eponymous first album (1978) selling a million copies within a year. Marked out by the lightning fretwork of guitarist Eddie Van Halen, and the larger-than-life stage persona of vocalist Dave Lee Roth, Van Halen made four multi-platinum albums in the late 1970s and early 1980s, peaking with the album *1984* and the single "Jump." Roth left the band in 1985 to pursue a solo career, but Van Halen continued to ply their trade into the 1990s.

VASARY, Tamas (1933-) *Pianist and conductor* Vasary was born in Hungary but left for Western Europe after the 1956 uprising. As a pianist he recorded most of Chopin's work and a great deal of Liszt, playing with seductive phrasing and a delicate virtuosity. Regarded as a Romantic, he also enjoyed playing Bach, Beethoven, and Mozart. He made his long-awaited debut as a conductor in 1979, becoming musical director of the Northern Sinfonia (1979–82) and then the Bournemouth Sinfonietta, both English chamber orchestras.

VAUGHAN, Stevie Ray (1954-90) *Blues guitarist* After playing in various bands, Vaughan formed Double Trouble in 1979. Their albums, *Couldn't Stand the Weather* (1984) and *In Step* (1989) both won Grammy Awards and critical acclaim. He also played with many of the best musicians of the time, including David BOWIE (providing the powerful guitar sound on the album *Let's Dance*), Bob DYLAN, and Eric Clapton. Vaughan's style was warm yet powerful. His best was perhaps yet to come when he was killed in a helicopter accident.

VEASEY, Josephine (1930-) *Opera singer* A dramatic mezzo-soprano, Veasey made her debut at Covent Garden in London in 1955, after which she sang all over the world. Her voice was rich, vibrant, and well focused, and she has made several roles her own, including Wagner's Fricka.

VEGA, Suzanne (1959-) *Rock singer-songwriter* Vega is a highly literate SINGER-SONGWRITER who found international success in the late 1980s. "Marlene on the Wall" (1985) was her first hit, with "Luka" (1987), a song about child abuse, becoming an unlikely hit in the U.S. and Britain. She continued to record and perform into the 1990s.

VENUTI, Joe (1903-78) *Jazz violinist* A larger-than-life figure and inveterate joker, Venuti was as famous for his off-stage antics—pouring Jello into a sleeping Bix BEIDERBECKE's bath, for example—as he was for his musical talents. From the 1920s Venuti played in various bands, most notably Paul

WHITEMAN's, and finally formed his own in 1935. He also appeared with many artists, including Eddie Lang, with whom he recorded the classic Venuti-Lang "Blue Four."

VERVE, The *Rock group* Formed in Wigan, England, in 1990, the Verve found success in the U.K. with their mix of ROCK, JAZZ, and ambient textures. But it was with their elegiac third album, *Urban Hymns* (1997), that they finally achieved mainstream success. The album spawned three successful singles, including the haunting "Bittersweet Symphony," adapted from a Jagger-Richard composition and "The Drugs Don't Work," written by the group's singer Richard Ashcroft.

VICKERS, Jon (1926-) *Opera singer* The Canadian tenor Vickers sang regularly for Canadian radio in Wagner concerts before joining the Royal Opera House, Covent Garden, London, in 1957. He sang at all the major OPERA houses and festivals worldwide and was considered one of the finest interpreters of the heroic tenor roles, in particular Florestan in Beethoven's *Fidelio*.

VIERNE, Louis (1870-1937) *Composer and organist* Vierne succeeded Charles-Marie Widor as the organist at St. Sulpice, Paris, and as professor at the Paris Conservatory. In 1900 he moved to Notre Dame. He is chiefly remembered for his organ compositions, which include his six symphonies (1899–1930).

VILLAGE PEOPLE, The *Pop group* The Village People, from New York, were assembled by PRODUCER Jacques Morali to perform his DISCO songs. They are best remembered for their single "Y.M.C.A.," which went to No.2 in the U.S. in 1978, earning a platinum disc. However, as the disco boom faded, the band became less visible.

VINCENT, Gene (1935-71) *Rock singer* Vincent sang with the Bluecaps and their first single "Be-Bop-A-Lula" (1956) stormed to No.7 in the U.S. Despite one or two further successes, his career never really took off, though he was more popular in the U.K., scoring eight Top 40 hits between 1956 and 1961.

VINSON, Eddie "Cleanhead" (1917–88) *Jazz saxophonist, singer, and bandleader* Vinson became an R&B stalwart, also highly regarded in JAZZ circles. On joining Cootie Williams in 1942, he became one of the best BIG BAND vocalists of the 1940s. He formed his own band in 1945 scoring several hits, including "Juicy Head Baby" (1961). Vinson was also the composer of "Tune Up" and "Four," both originally attributed to Miles DAVIS and recorded by him in the 1950s.

VIOLENT FEMMES *Rock group* Formed in Milwaukee in 1981, Violent Femmes initially presented themselves as school geeks. Their lyrics, consisting of sarcastic put-downs and self-mockery, were laid over simple basslines and choppy guitars. The eponymous first album (1983) was a hit with college RADIO, but the work that followed never lived up to the success of their debut.

VON STADE, Frederica (1945–) *Opera singer* The American mezzo-soprano had her OPERA debut in New York in 1973. After that she appeared with most of the world's leading opera houses, performing Mozart and Bellini through to STRAUSS and DEBUSSY. She was also a soloist with orchestras and a recitalist, as well as a crossover artist, recording songs from Broadway MUSICALS.

WAGNER, Siegfried (1869–1930) *Conductor and composer* The son of Richard Wagner, Siegfried is chiefly remembered for Bayreuth Festival productions of his father's works (1906–30). He wrote symphonies and OPERAS which were often performed in Germany during his lifetime, but have since faded in popularity.

WAGONER, Porter (1930–) *Country singer-songwriter* Wagoner began his long run of success in 1955 with the No.1 COUNTRY single "A Satisfied Mind." Between 1955 and 1983, scarcely a year passed without Wagoner appearing in the country charts. In 1960 Wagoner was given his own TV show, and by the early 1970s it was syndicated to over 100 stations. From 1967 Dolly PARTON appeared as a regular on the show, launching her own career.

WAITS, Tom (1949–) *Singer-songwriter* Waits used his distinctive whispering, tobacco-stained voice to good effect chronicling the lives of the losers and outsiders of America. The album *The Heart of Saturday Night* (1974) was his first success. In the mid-1980s he recorded his three most ambitious albums, *Swordfish-trombones, Rain Dogs,* and *Frank's Wild Years*. His songs have been successfully covered by artists as diverse as Rod Stewart and Bruce SPRINGSTEEN. Waits also appeared successfully in a number of films during the 1980s and 1990s.

WALKER BROTHERS, The *Pop group* Although American, the Walker Brothers had much greater success in the U.K., with nine Top 30 singles between 1965–67. They excelled at dramatic ballads, including the two No.1 singles, "Make It Easy on Yourself" and "The Sun Ain't Gonna Shine Anymore." Internal pressures split the band in 1967, but they briefly reunited in the late 1970s, producing "No Regrets," a Top 10 single in the U.K. Scott Walker managed to construct a solo career at the same time. He was successful, but his fame was really based on the hits of his former group.

WALLACE, Beulah "Sippie" (1898–1986) *Jazz singer and pianist* Wallace recorded her first single "Up the Country Blues" in 1923. It was an immediate hit. Artists she recorded with included Louis ARMSTRONG, Clarence Williams, Sidney Bechet, and later Albert Ammons. In 1983 she saw her last album, *Sippie,* nominated for a Grammy.

WALLENSTEIN, Alfred (1898–1998) *Conductor and cellist* Born in the U.S., Wallenstein began his career as a cellist playing with the San Francisco Symphony Orchestra. He went on to join the Chicago Symphony Orchestra and the New York Philharmonic under TOSCANINI. He conducted his first orchestral performance in 1931, and went on to become musical director of the Los Angeles Philharmonic in 1943 and a member of the faculty at the Juilliard School of Music, New York, in 1968. He was also an active educator.

WAR *Soul-funk band* Formed in California, War had their first success as the backing band to Eric Burdon, former lead singer with the Animals. After he left the band (mid-tour) they made 15 hit albums, with six singles in the Top 10 between 1970 and 1978. Their potent fusion of FUNK, R&B, and rock produced a progressive SOUL sound best heard on the albums *All Day Music* (1971) and *The World Is a Ghetto* (1972). War's back catalog remains influential in African-American music, especially hip-hop.

WARREN, Harry (1893–1981) *Composer* One of the greatest and most prolific composers of FILM MUSICALS, Warren had his first great successes working with lyricist Al Dubin in the 1930s. Their scores included *42nd Street* and the *Gold Diggers* series—from which "Lullaby of Broadway" earned him his first Oscar. Warren was equally successful working with different lyricists and his later work included "I, Yi, Yi, Yi, Yi, (I Like You Very Much)" for Carmen Miranda and "Chattanooga Choo Choo" for a film featuring Glen MILLER's band.

WARWICK, Dionne (1940–) *Soul-pop singer* From 1962 Warwick had more than 50 hit singles, including the classic "Walk on By" (1964), and 30 hit albums. Her best-known work was recorded during her long association with Burt BACHARACH and Hal David (1962–72) but her first No.1 was "Then Came You" (1974) with the Spinners. After a lull her commercial standing picked up in the 1980s, when she collaborated with the Bee Gees, Elton JOHN, and Stevie WONDER.

WASHINGTON, Geno (1945–) *Soul singer* After leaving the air force, ex-U.S. serviceman Washington remained in Britain to form the Ram Jam Band, which he started in 1965. Their first success was the album *Hand Clappin'–Foot Stompin'–Funky Butt–Live!* (1966), which reached the U.K. Top 10. The group split at the end of the 1960s, but Washington tentatively returned to the stage in the late 1970s with a ROCK trio. In 1980 Dexy's Midnight Runners eulogized Washington in the song "Geno," a U.K. No.1.

WASHINGTON, Grover, Jr. (1943–) *Saxophonist and composer* Washington began his career in JAZZ, but became more popular as he moved into a lighter, pop style. "The Two of Us" reached No.2 in the U.S. pop charts, and his album *Winelight* (1980), which mixed DISCO, SOUL, and BLUES, achieved platinum status, and won two Grammy Awards.

WATSON, Doc (1923–) *Folk guitarist* Undiscovered until 1960, Watson was recognized as one of the greatest flat-pickers of all time. He made many recordings, winning Grammys for *Then and Now* (1973) and *Two Days in November* (1974).

WATSON, Johnny "Guitar" (1935–96) *Rock guitarist* Watson made a name for himself playing FUNK and R&B in the 1970s, but he started in the 1950s playing ROCK'N'ROLL. Watson toured with LITTLE RICHARD in the late 1950s, and his flamboyant stage persona was an important influence on Jimi HENDRIX. His first hit "Those Lonely, Lonely Nights," a bluesy ballad, came in 1955, but major success had to wait until 1976 when his album *Ain't That a Bitch* went gold. By the late 1980s Watson had virtually retired, making cameo appearances on Frank ZAPPA albums but doing little else.

WEBB, Chick (1909–39) *Jazz drummer and bandleader* One of the greatest SWING-JAZZ drummers of all time, Webb became popular when his band began a residency at the Savoy Ballroom, in New York, in 1931. His career was further enhanced when he hired Ella FITZGERALD as vocalist in 1935. His bands had a number of hits, featuring Fitzgerald's vocals, including "A-Tisket, A-Tasket" (1936) and "Undecided" (1938).

WEBB, Jimmy (1946–) *Singer-songwriter* Webb became one of America's most successful songwriters in the late 1960s with hits such as "Up, Up and Away" (a hit for Fifth Dimension) and "By the Time I Get to Phoenix" (sung by Glen Camp-bell). His own singing was first recorded in 1967, and his most commercially successful albums were *Letters* (1972) and *El Mirage* (1977). Among the artists who have recorded Webb's

work are Frank SINATRA, Waylon JENNINGS, Donna Summer, Johnny CASH, Kris KRISTOFFERSON, and Art Garfunkel.

WEINGARTNER, Felix (1863–1942) *Conductor* Born in Austria, Weingartner was thought of as one of the most eminent conductors of his day, particularly noted for his inter-pretation of classical composers. His many prestigious posts included director at the Vienna Court Opera (1908–11)—where he succeeded MAHLER—and conductor of the Vienna Philharmonic until 1927. He also worked in the U.S. and the U.K.

WEIR, Gillian (1941–) *Organist* A New Zealander by birth, Weir became one of the best recital organists in Britain, touring widely in Europe and the U.S. She is noted for her interpre-tations of Bach and 20th-century music, particularly MESSIAEN.

WELLS, Dicky (1907–85) *Jazz trombonist* In the 1930s, when the trombone was only just beginning to be taken seriously, along came Dicky Wells to put the comedy right back into the trombone repertoire—albeit with style and sophistication. Wells played with the Count BASIE band from 1938 until 1950, and established a reputation as one of the finest trombone soloists with a stylishness and exemplary technique.

WELLS, Junior (1934–) *Blues harmonica player and singer* One of the most highly regarded blues-men of his generation, Wells helped to define the Chicago BLUES harp sound of the 1950s. He played with Muddy WATERS during the 1950s, but it was with Buddy GUY that he had his greatest success, producing one of the finest Chicago blues albums, *Hoodoo Man Blues* (1966). Their association lasted until the late 1980s.

WELLS, Kitty (1919–) *Country singer* One of the first queens of COUNTRY music, Wells was thinking of retiring when her career suddenly took off in 1953 with the single "It Wasn't God Who Made Honky Tonk Angels"—making her the first female artist to have a country No.1. In total she had 81 hits, with over 450 singles and 40 albums released by 1973.

WELLS, Mary (1943–92) *Soul singer* Wells was one of the first and most popular MOTOWN stars of the 1960s. Her version of her own song "Bye Bye Baby" became the label's first Top 50 hit in 1960. In 1964 her single "My Guy," went to No.1.

WERTHEN, Rudolf (1946–) *Violinist and conductor* Born and raised in Belgium, Werthen appeared as a soloist with the NDR Symphony Orchestra and was also a professor at the Robert Schumann Institute in Ger-many. From 1977 he was conductor of the Flanders Chamber Orchestra and from 1992 director of the Flanders Opera at Anvers in his native Belgium.

WESLEY, Fred (1943–) *Trombonist* Wesley made his name as the front man of the James BROWN ensemble. His most successful single "Doin' It to Death" topped the R&B charts in 1973. He also performed in other groups and as a solo artist, perform-ing well into the 1990s, notably with alto sax player Maceo Parker and Pee Wee Ellis—both ex-members of Brown's JBs.

WESTON, Randy (1926–) *Jazz musician* A pianist and composer with a unique voice, Weston's music was greatly influenced by his interest in AFRICA and the West Indies. Much of his work was with his own trios and quartets. His best-known tunes include "Summer Eyes," "Hi-Fly," and "Little Niles," and, like many pianists influenced by Thelonious MONK, Weston was at his best playing his own compositions.

WHITE, Barry (1944–) *Pop-soul singer* White performed in a number of groups and made several records in the early 1960s but only became a star in the early 1970s after forming Love Unlimited and the 40-piece Love Unlimited Orchestra. Using his trademark deep, breathy delivery, White had six Top 10 single hits between 1973 and 1977, including "Never, Never Gonna Give Ya Up," "Can't Get Enough of Your Love, Babe," and "You're the First, the Last, My Everything" (both 1974) being the biggest. He continued to record into the 1990s.

WHITE, Josh (c.1915-69) *Blues-folk singer* White was a versatile performer, covering BLUES in local or more nationally popular idioms. A contemporary of Woody GUTHRIE, he also sang social protest songs, and as the Singing Christian he recorded religious material. His repertoire was an odd mixture, covering everything from traditional ballads such as "Lord Randall" to popular songs like "Scarlet Ribbons."

WHITMAN, Slim (1924-) *Country singer* Whitman made his name as a light-voiced balladeer and yodeler. His first hit was "Love Song of the Waterfall," which he quickly followed up with "Indian Love Call" (1955), which spent 11 weeks at the top of the U.K. charts. Other hits followed although, surprisingly, Whitman has never topped the U.S. COUNTRY charts.

WIDOR, Charles-Marie (1844-1937) *Composer* French-born Widor is chiefly remembered for his Romantic compositions for the organ, notably the Toccata from Symphony No.5. He was also a fine organist, being professor of both organ and composition at the Paris Conservatory, and the organist at St. Sulpice, in Paris, for over 60 years.

WILLCOCKS, Sir David (1919-) *Conductor and organist* British-born Willcocks was organist at King's College Chapel, Cambridge, from 1957-74, making many recordings with the choir there. In 1960 Willcocks became conductor of the London Bach Choir, giving the first London performances of works such as Fricker's *The Vision of Judgement* and Crosse's *Changes.*

WILLIAMS, Big Joe (1903-82) *Blues singer and guitarist* Williams's recording career stretched from the 1930s to his death in 1982. Through it all he kept the Delta BLUES tradition alive. Between the wars, Williams lived the life of the archetypal traveling bluesman, playing for change or food, and sleeping in railroad cars. He performed for many years with Sonny Boy WILLIAMSON. After World War II he continued to play across the U.S., and in the 1970s Williams became popular in Europe and Japan.

WILLIAMS, Clarence (1898-1965) *Jazz pianist and composer* Williams had formed his own publishing company by the age of 21 and had great success as a BLUES composer, writing songs for artists such as Bessie SMITH and Sara Martin. His most famous works include "Baby Won't You Please Come Home" and "West End Blues." In the recording studio he also performed with Louis ARMSTRONG, Coleman HAWKINS, and King Oliver, among others.

WILLIAMS, Cootie (1911-85) *Jazz trumpeter and bandleader* Williams was an unsurpassed master of SWING-style JAZZ trumpet playing. By 1929 he had joined the Duke ELLINGTON orchestra, where he stayed for 11 years, becoming famous in his own right. In 1940 he left Ellington for Benny GOODMAN's band and then formed his own outfit in 1941. Williams' band featured a string of young talent, including Charlie PARKER, Bud POWELL, and Eddie "Cleanhead" Vinson. Williams ended his career where it had begun, with Duke Ellington.

WILLIAMS, Don (1939-) *Country singer* Williams is one of the most popular COUNTRY artists with his gently paced love songs—in the mold of Jim REEVES—and his laid-back style. His solo debut "The Shelter of Your Eyes" in 1972 became a U.S. country hit and a stream of hit singles followed, including the country No.1s "You're My Best Friend," "Till the Rivers All Run Dry," and "Some Broken Hearts Never Mend." During latter years he has also made successful appearances in films, including *Smokey and the Bandit 2* (1980).

WILLSON, Meredith (1902-84) *Composer* Willson was a great composer of MUSICALS and film scores, writing music for films as diverse as Charlie Chaplin's *The Great Dictator* (1940) and *Dark at the Top of the Stairs* (1960). He had his first Broadway hit in 1957, with *The Music Man* (including the classic hit songs "Seventy-Six Trombones" and "Trouble"), and followed it up with *The Unsinkable Molly Brown* (1960).

WILSON, Jackie (1934-84) *Pop-soul singer* Wilson was one of the most talented and prodigious POP-SOUL singers, with a career spanning from the early 1950s to the mid-1970s. In 1953 Wilson became lead vocalist with the Dominoes and went solo in 1957. He had 35 R&B hits and 54 Hot 100 pop singles, 'Doggin' Around' reaching No.1 in the R&B charts in 1960, his most successful year. Despite being shot by a crazed fan in 1961, Wilson continued performing until he suffered a heart attack on stage in 1975 after which he retired from performing. He is best remembered for the 1967 classic "(Your Love Keeps Lifting Me) Higher and Higher."

WILSON, Sandy (1924-) *Composer and lyricist* Born in the U.K., Wilson made his first impact in the early 1950s by contributing songs for revues in London's West End. His big break, securing his fame, came in 1953 with his musical comedy *The Boy Friend,* which became one of the longest running shows in London's theater history.

WILSON, Teddy (1912-86) *Jazz pianist and arranger* In 1931 Wilson teamed up with Art TATUM and was quickly spotted as a rising talent. After moving to New York, Wilson began performing with small groups, often featuring the singer Billie HOLIDAY. He became one of the most important pianists of the SWING period and the first African-American musician to play in the Benny GOODMAN band.

WINTER, Johnny (1944-) *Blues guitarist* Hailed as America's answer to British BLUES-ROCK stars, Eric Clapton, Jimmy Page, and Jeff Beck, Winter's debut album, *Johnny Winter* (1969) cemented his reputation as one of the most fluid blues-rock guitarists of the era. Many further hit albums followed into the 1970s and 1980s, the most successful of which was *Johnny Winter And* (1970), which included the song "Rock'n'roll Hoochie Coo." Winter has also worked as a producer. Two albums he produced for Muddy WATERS, *Hard Again* and *I'm Ready,* won Grammys and helped resuscitate Waters' career.

WISHBONE ASH *Rock group* Formed in 1969, Wishbone Ash's unique twin guitar attack, of Andy Powell and Ted Turner, played heavy BLUES riffs over a solid rhythm section. In 1973 they released *Argus,* their biggest-selling album, combining folk and hard rock with medieval imagery—song titles included "The King Will Come" and "Throw Down the Sword." In 1980 the band became tax exiles from Britain. They reformed in 1998 and toured extensively in the U.S. and the U.K.

WITHERS, Bill (1938-) *Soul singer-songwriter* Withers met Booker T. Jones (of Booker T. & The MGs) in 1970 and Jones quickly helped Withers get a contract with Sussex Records. He secured an immediate success with "Ain't No Sunshine," a No.3 hit. Withers' light, folksy-SOUL voice continued to score further hits for Sussex, most notably with the song "Lovely Day" (1977), and he continued to record and tour into the 1980s.

WITHERSPOON, Jimmy (1923-) *Blues singer* Although Witherspoon has crossed over into ROCK, JAZZ, and R&B, his deep mellow voice places him firmly as a fine BLUES singer. His first hit was in 1949 with "T'ain't Nobody's Business," an R&B No.1. In the late 1950s, as the popularity of blues began to fade, Witherspoon moved toward jazz. Despite treatment for throat cancer, he continued to perform into the 1990s.

WOMACK, Bobby (1944-) *Soul singer and guitarist* An accomplished vocalist and guitarist, Womack is regarded as having an influence on the development of SOUL music. He worked as Sam COOKE's guitarist, before starting a solo career. He is also associated with Sly Stone, Wilson Pickett, for whom he wrote many songs, and the ROLLING STONES.

WOMACK & WOMACK *Soul duo* This husband and wife team had notable success as writers and performers of SOUL music. "Love TKO" was a hit for Teddy Pendergrass in 1980. Their own performances have included the hit singles, "Love Wars" (1984) and "Teardrops" (1988), the latter reaching the U.K. Top 3.

WOOD, Sir Henry (1869-1944) *Conductor* Wood's greatest achievement was founding the Queen's Hall Promenade Concerts in London in 1895, which continue today. The series later moved to the Royal Albert Hall where Wood remained in sole charge until 1940. Although the Proms will always be associated with his name, he was also important in the general raising of standards of British orchestral performance. He gave early British performances of works by SCHOENBERG, BARTÓK, and SIBELIUS.

WOODS, Oscar "Buddy" (c.1900-56) *Guitarist* Woods was one of the most impressive prewar slide guitar BLUES stylists and an important member of the early Shreveport, Louisiana, blues scene. Woods worked with, among others, Jimmy Davis and Alan LOMAX. He spent the late 1940s/early 1950s performing in the Shreveport area.

WU TANG CLAN *Rap group* Formed in New York in the early 1990s, the Wu Tang Clan's debut album *Enter The Wu Tang* (1993)—heavily influenced by martial arts culture—quickly went gold, setting the underground hip-hop scene on fire. More of a collective than an actual group, the Clan featured no less than eight MCs—including Method Man, Ol' Dirty Bastard, Raekwon, and Ghost Face Killa—many of whom have gone on to solo success.

XTC *Rock group* Formed in 1976, XTC achieved enormous popularity in the U.K. in the late 1970s and early 1980s. Their jangly guitar sound and pop art lyrics earned them a reputation as one of the most original bands of the era. Albums included *Go2* and *Drums and Wires*, while they also charted with the singles "Making Plans for Nigel" (1979) and "Senses Working Overtime" (1982).

YANCEY, Jimmy (1898-1951) *Pianist, singer, and composer* Yancey was one of the prime movers in establishing the brief popularity of the original blues BOOGIE-WOOGIE. A prime mover in the Chicago blues and JAZZ scene, he made many records and performed widely in the 1930s and 1940s, with hits including "Yancey Stomp" and "State Street Special."

YARDBIRDS, The *Rock group* Formed in the U.K. in 1963, the Yardbirds' style was based on Chicago R&B. Early success came with the release of the album *Five Live Yardbirds* in 1964, featuring Eric Clapton on guitar. Clapton was later replaced by Jeff Beck, who in turn gave way to Jimmy Page. Further hits followed, including "For Your Love" and "Heart Full of Soul" (both 1965), but the group split in 1968. Although short-lived, the Yardbirds retained enormous credibility as pioneers of British R&B, classic experimental pop and heavy rock.

YELLO *Techno dance band* Formed in Switzerland by Dieter Meier, a millionaire entrepreneur, and Boris Blank, a composer of electronic music, Yello had the same beat-driven Euro appeal as bands like Tangerine Dream and Kraftwerk. Early albums, such as *Solid Pleasure* (1980) and *You Gotta Say Yes to Another Excess* (1983), proved popular, but wider commercial success was sought. With tracks such as "Vicious Games," "Oh Yeah," and "Domingo," the album *Stella* (1985) provided that success. "The Race" (1988) was a massive dance hit across Europe, reaching the U.K. Top 10.

YEPES, Narciso (1927-98) *Classical guitarist and composer* Yepes was born and studied in Spain, where he made his concert debut in 1947. He toured widely, performing on a ten-string guitar of his own design—which extended the bass range—becoming a specialist in Spanish and Baroque music. He also composed the music for a number of films.

YOAKAM, Dwight (1956-) *Country singer-songwriter* After a short-lived attempt at breaking into the Nashville COUNTRY scene, Yoakam became successful after signing for Warner Bros. in 1984, registering two Top 5 U.S. country chart hits two years later. His country-rock style made him popular with rock fans but less so with purist country fans.

YOUMANS, Vincent (1898-1946) *Composer* American-born Youmans was a composer and producer of stage MUSICALS during the 1920s and 1930s. His many Broadway successes include *No, No Nanette* (1925).

Young, Faron (1932-) *Country singer* Greatly influenced by Hank Williams, Young become a major recording star in the late 1950s and throughout the 1960s with many U.S. country chart hits. His biggest success came with "Hello Walls" (1961) which was written by Willie Nelson. He also appeared in a number of Western films.

Young, Neil (1945-) *Rock guitarist and songwriter* Canadian-born Young is one of the foremost songwriters and performers of the rock music scene. After a brief stint with the Buffalo Springfield, Young started to make his own albums featuring the band Crazy Horse. An innovative guitarist, Young's mainstream popularity always fluctuated. Huge success with albums such as *After the Goldrush* (1970) and *Harvest* (1972) was mixed with critical and commercial disasters. His highest-profile venture was as a member of the group Crosby, Stills, Nash, and Young. Without doubt, Young's reputation as a maverick of the rock scene is well deserved. He continued to tour, record and innovate into the 1990s.

Ysaÿe, Eugène (1858-1931) *Violinist, conductor, and composer* Born in Belgium, Ysaÿe became an international soloist, most notably for performing and conducting contemporary Belgian and French music. His style of playing was intense but also poetic, and his compositions—mostly for the violin—were of a post-Romantic style. His six sonatas for unaccompanied violin have since become part of the central repertoire for violin virtuosi.

Yun, Isang (1917-) *Composer* Korean-born Yun studied and taught composition in Japan. Moving to Paris he began studying in the West in the 1950s and took German nationality in 1971. His compositions fused Asian imagination and practices with Western instruments and techniques, and he developed an increasingly individual style.

Zabaleta, Nicanor (1907-) *Harpist* Born in Spain Zabaleta performed all over the world. He was noted for trying to increase the number of works available for the harp by

uncovering neglected pieces and encouraging contemporary composers to write new music for the instrument.

Zawinul, Joe (1932-) *Jazz keyboard player, composer, and bandleader* Born in Austria, Zawinul emigrated to the U.S. in 1959, where he formed the group Weather Report with Wayne Shorter in 1970. Their style of modern jazz was popular with rock fans. Through his work with the group, Zawinul became one of the most original, prolific, and influential jazz composers of the 1970s. He worked extensively with Miles Davis between 1969 and 1970.

Zender, Hans (1936-) *Conductor and composer* Zender studied and worked in his native Germany and became particularly associated with contemporary music, most notably with the composer Bernd Zimmerman. His compositions were in the mold of Pierre Boulez.

Zevon, Warren (1947-) *Rock singer-songwriter* Never part of rock's main stream, Zevon has always received critical acclaim for his darkly comic piano-led rock'n'roll. Born in Chicago, Zevon was a classical music child prodigy. Hearing Bob Dylan's songs pushed him toward a career in rock'n'roll and he recorded his first album in 1969. Fame arrived when Linda Ronstadt recorded three of his songs in 1978. Best heard on *Excitable Boy* (1978) and the live album *Stand in the Fire* (1981). Zevon's only chart success came in 1978 with the song "Werewolves of London."

Zimbalist, Efrem (1890-1985) *Violinist and composer* Zimbalist studied at the St. Petersburg Conservatory with the Hungarian violinist Leopold Auer and emigrated to America in 1911. Thought of as one of the great violinists of his day, his performances were noble but never extrovert. He taught at the Curtis Institute in Philadelphia from 1928 and was director there from 1941 to 1968. His compositions included an opera and several orchestral works.

Zimmerman, Bernd Alois (1918-70) *Composer* Zimmerman was born and studied in Germany, where he

developed an individual style of composition in which quotation from all periods played a prominent part. It wasn't until after his death in 1970 that his music became appreciated, with his only opera *Die Soldaten* acknowledged as the most important in German since those of Alban Berg.

Zorn, John (1953-) *Composer and instrumentalist* Zorn was born in New York, becoming an active contributor to the downtown music scene. Known as a composer of dense, loud aural canvases—likened to the work of abstract artist Jackson Pollock—he also received acclaim as a performer (keyboards, saxophone) with various avant-garde and rock musicians. Zorn is best heard on his two 1987 albums *Spy Vs Spy* and *News for Lulu*.

Zukerman, Pinchas (1948-) *Violinist, violist, and conductor* Zukerman was born and studied in Israel and later at the Juilliard School in New York. He performed as a violinist with the world's leading orchestras and was also known for playing chamber music. He made his conducting debut in London in 1974.

Zwilich, Ellen Taaffe (1939-) *Composer, violinist and lecturer* Zwilich studied at Florida State University and was the first woman to receive a doctorate in composition from the Juilliard School in New York. Her major teachers were Elliott Carter and Roger Sessions. She wrote three symphonies, several concertos, and chamber music, especially for strings.

Z.Z. Top *Rock group* Formed in Houston, Texas, in 1969, this blues-rock Southern boogie trio—Billy Gibbons, Dusty Hill and Frank Beard—achieved national fame with several hit singles and gold albums. International success came when they signed with Warner Brothers in 1978. They evolved a new musical style, combining their blues roots with modern computer wizardry, launching them as one of the world's greatest live acts. Worldwide sales of the album *Eliminator* (1983), featuring songs like "Gimmie All Your Lovin'," "Sharp Dressed Man," and "Legs," topped 8 million copies at the end of 1985.

GLOSSARY

Words that appear in **BOLD SMALL CAPITALS** refer to other entries within the glossary; words or names that appear in SMALL CAPITALS refer to articles in the main part of the encyclopedia.

A CAPPELLA — literally: as the church. Choral music with no instrumental accompaniment. In the early church, only voices were used—instruments were regarded as only suitable for secular music. Barbershop quartets, unaccompanied GOSPEL groups, and all unaccompanied close harmony vocal groups perform a cappella singing.

ACCENT — the stressing of a note by the performer, either by playing it more loudly or by lengthening it.

ANTIPHONY — music that employs opposing groups of instruments or voices. These are usually spatially separated, though the contrast can also be achieved through differences in **TIMBRE**, range, and **DYNAMICS**.

ARTICULATION — the way successive notes are connected to each other in performance; also the way particular notes are played: e.g., staccato (which means short and detached), or legato (which means that the notes are joined together smoothly). Legato is indicated by a **SLUR**—a curved line.

ATONAL — music that is not in a **KEY** and has no tonal center (that is, it has no particular key chord, or triad, that the composer uses as a point of departure and return). Early atonal music was both a progression from, and a conscious denial of, the tonal harmonic system. An example is SCHOENBERG's *Five Orchestral Pieces.*

AVANT-GARDE — vanguard. Music that embraces experimentation and originality of composition with, sometimes, **IMPROVISATION,** to discover new forms of musical expression. The term is also used to refer to composers or artists working in this field.

BACKBEAT — a term describing the use of the second and fourth beat of a 4/4 (or 12/8) bar. The backbeat came to prominence in the 1950s with the advent of ROCK'N'ROLL.

BALLAD — a traditional song form used in FOLK MUSIC. It usually consists of four-line stanzas, with or without a refrain, and it often tells a story. Many popular songs are in the ballad form, and in JAZZ ballad has come to mean a slow tune in a relaxed tempo.

BEL CANTO — literally: "beautiful song." A style of singing at its height in 17th- and 18th-century Italian opera, distinguished by a light, rapid, and ornamental melodic line, as opposed to the more dramatic 19th-century style.

BITONALITY — the simultaneous use of two **KEYS** within the same work, in order to effect musical tension by having two tonal centers. Examples of this can be found in STRAVINSKY's *The Rite of Spring.*

BRASS — tubular instruments made of brass or other metals that are activated by the player blowing a column of air through a mouthpiece, and also by varying the lip pressure against the mouthpiece. Early marching bands were composed entirely of brass instruments. In the orchestra the brass section consists of horns, trumpets, trombones, and tubas.

CADENCE — the chord sequence ending a musical phrase. In tonal music there are four types: Perfect, V-I; Imperfect, I-V; Plagal, IV-I; and Interrupted, V-VI.

CANONIC IMITATION — a type of **COUNTERPOINT** where the lines are the same but separated in time. This is done so that, at any one time, the listener hears different parts of the "same" line, giving a sense of imitation of one part by another. This can be done with two or more lines. It is a

typical device in Renaissance and Baroque music, and was continued into the classical period, especially by Haydn, Mozart, and Beethoven.

CHORUS — the refrain of a song that is repeated after each verse. In JAZZ, this is generally the main theme, since jazz players do not usually play the verse of a song.

CHROMATIC — a type of **SCALE** or **HARMONY** based on the division of the octave into 12 semitones, in contrast to **DIATONIC.**

COMPING — a technique in JAZZ that provides a solid harmonic background to the soloist-dominated (linear) sound of a band. It is usually done by the pianist or guitarist, and is essentially the articulation of the important chords at regular or rhythmically necessary points.

CONCERTO — a (usually) large-scale work for a solo instrument and orchestra, where the musical development is formed by a dialogue between the soloist and orchestra.

COUNTERPOINT — the simultaneous combination of separate lines or parts in a composition. Also known as polyphony, "true" counterpoint is that which has harmonic implications (not necessarily tonal) in the progression of **INTERVALS** formed by the meeting of the lines. The minimum number of lines required is two, and there is no upper limit. An example of multi-voice counterpoint is the 16th-century composer Thomas Tallis's motet *Spem in alium* for 40 separate voices.

COVER — a recording of a song written and already recorded by another artist. The word came into use in the early 1950s, when record sales became financially significant. In the 1950s, white artists started "covering" songs by black **RHYTHM AND BLUES** artists. In the 1970s and 1980s covers often revived old songs and made more money for the original composers. A covers band is one that plays only the music of other people, usually in performance.

DEGREES OF THE SCALE — the seven notes that make up the **SCALE** in the tonal harmonic system and the chords based on each of these notes. The names of the degrees, beginning from the root, or keynote, going up are: Tonic (I), Supertonic (II), Mediant (III), Subdominant (IV), Dominant (V), Submediant (VI), and Leading note (VII).

DEVELOPMENT SECTION — the part of a composition that develops the material after the initial presentation of the themes. This is usually done through the use of **MODULATION** into different **KEYS**, **SEQUENCES**, and the lengthening or modification of parts of the themes.

DIATONIC — a type of **SCALE** or **HARMONY** based on the division of an octave into five whole-tones and two semitones, to make the seven-note major scale from which the minor scales can be derived.

DOUBLING — a device for bringing out a line by playing or singing it on more than one instrument or voice, in unison, at the octave, or other interval, above or below.

DRONE — a held note against which other parts are composed to give a combined sense of stasis and activity. It is often used in Eastern Orthodox Church music, Indian music, and many kinds of FOLK MUSIC such as Scottish bagpipe music. It is usually called a pedal point in Western classical music as it was often held by the pedal in Baroque organ music.

DUB — a version of REGGAE music, in which tunes are stripped of all their elements, except the drum and bass rhythm section, which is then bombarded with echo. The original instruments and/or vocals are often held in place, but are mixed in and out by the producer. Dub music was most popular during the late 1970s. Prominent exponents of this music include Lee "Scratch" Perry, Augustus Pablo, and King Tubby.

DYNAMICS — the element of actual volume in music used for expressive purposes: e.g., *piano* means soft and *forte* means strong or loud. Dynamics can occur suddenly or gradually: for example, *crescendo* means gradually get louder.

FEEDBACK — the note(s) produced when a microphone or guitar pickup is pointed at its own speaker. This causes a loop in the signal which begins to pick up itself, thereby increasing its amplitude. At the same time it produces a pitch that is usually a related harmonic (or **OVERTONE**) of the note last played on the instrument or the natural **FREQUENCY** of the microphone diaphragm.This note steadily increases in volume. Feedback is often used for expressive purposes in ROCK music.

FIDDLE — a FOLK term for violin.

FINGERING — the pattern of finger movement used by a performer in order to play a work or passage. Particular fingerings are applied for ease of execution and also for expressive purposes, such as playing a theme or even an entire work on the bottom (G) string on a violin. This ensures a unified tone and exploits the rich, sonorous quality of this string.

FLAT — the symbol is ♭, and, when it is placed immediately before a note, it is called an accidental and lowers it by a semitone. When flats are placed at the beginning of a line or piece, they form a **KEY** signature that flattens the notes to which they refer for the entire piece, or until they are neutralized by a natural ♮ sign.

FORM — the overall shape or structure of a piece. Popular song form is usually ABA, AABA, or ABACADA, with the letters referring to sections containing about four lines of text. In classical music, form is more complex because works are usually longer. Typical symphonic form of the 18th and 19th centuries consisted of four separate movements, each having their own internal structure. Modern classical pieces employ many different types of form, a common one being the single movement, encapsulating the functions of the different forms in earlier music.

FREQUENCY — the scientific, or precise, measurement of pitch described as Hertz or cycles (vibrations) per second. The concert A, which is used as a standard for tuning, is 440 Hz.

FUGUE — a work using **COUNTERPOINT**, having a set theme or subject and counter-subject from which all the material is derived. It usually has at least three parts or voices and makes use of devices such as **INVERSION**.

FULL SCORE — a manuscript or printed score that shows the parts for all the players. Usually orchestral.

FUSION — a type of music that combines two or more distinct musical styles, e.g., JAZZ ROCK. It usually occurs when two cultures meet through immigration or increased communication. Another example is BHANGRA BEAT, which combines Indian music with popular DISCO or club music.

GIG — A booking for a band to play for one night only. However, the term is also used simply as another word for a concert.

GLAM ROCK — a British musical movement from the early 1970s that was closely tied to fashion. Featuring artists such as the Sweet, Gary Glitter, T. Rex, Slade, and David BOWIE, bands and fans of the music wore extravant clothes, glitter, platform shoes, and make up.

GLEE — a vocal form developed in the 18th century in which unaccompanied (usually male) voices sing in close **HARMONY**. This was adopted by many U.S. university glee clubs that survived into the 20th century. Close harmony singing groups were the precursors of DOO-WOP.

GLISSANDO — a sliding effect. Sounding a succession of notes rapidly on instruments such as the piano or guitar. The notes are not played individually but are produced by moving the hand quickly across the keyboard or fingerboard. Glissandos can also be produced on bowed string instruments but these, like brass instruments, are more suited to **PORTAMENTOS**.

GRACE NOTE — ornament. A decoration of the melodic line with (usually unaccented) extra notes. These are either written as small notes in the score or are improvised by the player.

HARMONICS — see **OVERTONE SERIES.**

HARMONY — how notes are combined to produce chords, and how the chords are used to produce chord progressions through a piece of music. Harmony usually consists of concordant and dissonant **INTERVALS** that are combined according to certain rules to provide a sense of necessity in the progress of the music.

HEAD — the main tune on which JAZZ performers base their **IMPROVISATION.**

HOUSE MUSIC — a type of dance music that originated in the Warehouse Club in Chicago in the mid-1980s. Produced electronically, typically with 120 beats-per-minute, house music did not need instruments or performers, and boosted the importance of the DJ. Quite influential in the U.S., its importance in Europe was great, with dance music almost entirely produced electronically in the late 1980s and 1990s.

IMPROVISATION — the art of creating music in real time during performance. Improvised music, with few exceptions, obeys musical laws that are either agreed upon beforehand or are intuitively learned from the performer's cultural background. Examples occur all over the world and include such diverse styles as FLAMENCO, JAZZ, and Indian classical music. From the 17th century to the late 19th century, improvisation was an integral part of the performance skills of a classical musician, who would always be expected to improvise the cadenza in a **CONCERTO** in order to display their virtuosity.

INTERPRETATION — the way in which a performer or conductor transmits a work to the listener. The choices made by the performer include **TEMPOS**, **DYNAMICS**, nuances of **RUBATO**, and also many things that cannot be written in by the composer—hence the importance of a good interpretation in realizing the meaning of a work.

INTERVAL — the distance between the pitch of two notes. There are 12 measured intervals, including the octave: the minor/major second, minor/major third, perfect/augmented fourth (or tritone), perfect fifth, minor/major sixth, minor/major seventh, and the octave. These intervals can be used in various contexts, allowing for a huge diversity in music all based on the same building blocks.

INTONATION — the type of tuning used by singers and performers of instruments with no fixed pitch, such as the violin. The term can also be used to describe a system of pre-performance tuning (temperament) used on fixed pitch instruments, in various musical periods and by composers concerned with the modification of the standard intervals.

INVERSION — the modification of a theme by turning it upside down. This is done simply by inverting the **INTERVALS** of which it is constructed. This was a compositional device used widely in the Baroque period and also in the early 20th century movement known as SERIALISM.

IRRATIONAL RHYTHM — a rhythm, or group of notes, whose value is other than that of the pulse value in the **TIME SIGNATURE**. The one most commonly used is the triplet, where three notes are played in the time of two. There is no theoretical limit to irrational rhythms, and quintuplets (five) and septuplets (seven) are often used in contemporary classical music to create a fluidity of rhythm. Brian Ferneyhough is a composer who has taken the use of irrational rhythm to its physical limit.

JIG — a lively dance usually associated with Ireland but which is common in the north of England and with antecedents in many European countries.

JUMP MUSIC — a type of JAZZ music that began at the end of the 1930s. The term applied literally to the energy of dance music being made by BIG BANDS of the time. However, during the 1940s, many of the bands playing jump music got smaller, often down to saxophones, piano, bass, and drums. Jump music is often regarded as being an early version of **RHYTHM AND BLUES**.

KEY — the pervading pitch color of a work that causes one particular note to be felt as the most important in a hierarchy. The tonic triad (the first, third, and fifth notes of the scale) is felt as the home chord, with related chords having a close relationship with it, and unrelated chords being used less frequently and having a more distant relationship to the key. For example, the key of D major has the A major triad as its Dominant (see **DEGREES OF THE SCALE**), G major as its Subdominant, and B minor as its Submediant or Relative Minor. Other chords are not related and are therefore further down the ladder of the tonal hierarchy of this key.

LIBRETTO — the text written for an OPERA or MUSICAL.

LIEDER — the German word for "songs." Usually applied to German art songs of the 19th century, particularly those of Schubert and Hugo Wolf, who set contemporary poetry to illustrative piano accompaniments.

LINE — a part, or a sequence of notes that make up a theme or accompanying "voice."

LYRIC — usually used to mean the words of a song, but "lyrical" implies an especially graceful melodic style. Can also describe a type of **VOICE**, e.g., lyric tenor.

MASTER TAPE — the final version of a recording after the final mix, which is used to make the compact disc or record for commercial use.

MELISMA — a type of vocal ornament where the singer elaborates a note into a short phrase. Used in Western Baroque music, GOSPEL, and SOUL; and also in Islamic, FLAMENCO, and Indian singing styles.

METALLOPHONE — the group of percussion instruments that consists of tuned metal bars or slabs, such as the vibraphone and the Javanese saron.

METER — the way in which time is organized in music by the "horizontal" spacing of notes to give a sense of a regular pulse or beat.

METRIC MODULATION — a rhythmical device developed and extensively employed by composers such as the American Elliott CARTER. It is the changing of perspective of an **IRRATIONAL RHYTHM,** such as a triplet, so that the pulse of the irrational becomes the actual **METER**. This causes a **TEMPO** change to take place, but the pulse is not heard to speed up or slow down until one perceives a new irrational in relation to the old irrational, which is now the meter. The process can also be reversed.

MIXER — a machine used in recording that controls the dynamic, tone, and position in the stereo field of each channel that has been previously recorded separately.

MODAL — refers to music written in a **MODE**, usually one of the Greek modes or a mode used in FOLK MUSIC. Because the arrangement of intervals is different from those of the major and minor scales, modal music has a distinctive flavor.

MODE — a sequence of notes, usually within the octave, separated by particular **INTERVALS**. The original modes came from Ancient Greece, and they can be played using only the white notes on the keyboard. For instance, the Dorian mode (D to D) starts on D and is played on white notes only. However, once the pattern of intervals is fixed, the mode can be transposed to start on another note. The major and minor **SCALES** are derived from two of the Greek modes. Modes are important in JAZZ, and are used in MODAL JAZZ.

MODERNISM — mostly used to refer to a particular movement in the early 20th century that rejected **TONALITY**. The essential concept of modernism is the idea of going forward to find new means of expression in order to avoid populism and cliché.

MODULATION — the process used to change from one **KEY** to another, usually to further the development of a piece. Traditionally, a piece is modulated to a more or less closely related key, but composers such as Beethoven greatly increased the range of keys used.

MOTIF — a short phrase or theme used as a basis for a work. Also used as a unifying device to keep a work together. Wagner used leitmotifs, also spelled leitmotivs, meaning "leading motifs," to represent the central characters in his music dramas, either to mark their entrance onto the stage or to underline a reference to them in the plot.

MULTIPHONICS — the production of **INTERVALS** or chords on an instrument that usually only plays single lines. It is done by holding a fundamental note and fingering a prominent **HARMONIC** above. Voice multiphonics are extensively used in the indigenous Mongolian music called Khöömiy chanting.

MUSICIANSHIP — the general skills acquired by a professional musician. They can include taught subjects such as understanding of basic harmonic movement, rapid sight-reading, ability to play in ensemble, and other skills that are more intuitive, such as **IMPROVISATION** and a subtle sense of rhythm.

MUSIQUE CONCRÈTE — a type of early electronic music that used recorded natural sounds, which could then be manipulated in various ways so that the composition uses the actual sounds rather than a score.

MUTE — a device used on many instruments, initially designed to reduce the volume. Because of the difference in tone color caused by the use of a mute (especially on brass instruments) many players adopted the muted sound as part of their approach—Miles DAVIS, for example. Many different types of mute have been developed to obtain certain tone color. A popular trumpet mute is the Harmon mute, which has a movable stem to allow different filtering of the required frequencies. Mutes are often used in orchestral music, especially on the strings, where the silvery muted sound can still prevail, even though a considerable volume of sound is being created because of the number of players. In contemporary music, the use of mutes has been extended to include practice mutes (which nearly silence the instrument) and mutes made by stuffing cloth in the end of the instrument (e.g., clarinet) to get an exact balance of volume and tone.

NOCTURNE — a work, usually for solo piano, suggesting night and subjects associated with night. The earliest examples are those of the Irish 19th-century composer John Field, which Chopin studied before he wrote his own nocturnes. Chopin's piano nocturnes are now universally regarded as the finest in the genre. DEBUSSY also wrote an orchestral piece in three parts entitled *Nocturnes*.

NOTATION — the system of writing used to convey the composer's intentions to the performer. Many cultures do not write down music at all. Western notation has a generally standard base, with many variations according to the type of music.

OPEN TUNING — known in classical music as *scordatura*. The alteration of the pitch of one or more strings on a string instrument to give a particular intervallic or harmonic color to the instrument. It is commonly used in FOLK and BLUES **SLIDE GUITAR** playing. An example of its use in the classical repertoire is KODÁLY's Sonata for solo cello.

ORCHESTRATION — the craft of combining instruments to clarify the composer's musical ideas, such as particular themes or harmonic progressions. The term was originally applied only to the use of the orchestra, but it now encompasses all types of ensemble. Classical (18th and 19th century) orchestration uses the strings to carry the main body of the music, with the woodwind used for highlighting important **LINES** and the brass and percussion often saved for "tutti" climaxes or **ACCENTS**. Modern orchestration lays more emphasis on the woodwind, brass, and percussion sections, with the strings often used in an accompanying role, as, for example, in Harrison Birtwistle's *Earth Dances*.

OSTINATO — a repeated rhythmical and harmonic pattern used as an accompanying device in music.

OVERDUBBING — the superimposition of recorded material on tape in order to make multilayered music or combinations of words and music not actually performed together. This is particularly important in POP MUSIC.

OVERTONE SERIES — also known as the Harmonic series. It is a naturally occurring phenomenon whenever a pitch is produced (excepting the SINE WAVE, which is an artificially created note without any harmonics). The overtone series is an unchanging set of pitches, known as harmonics, that are present above the main note (called the fundamental). It is made up of an octave, a perfect fifth, a perfect fourth, a major third, and so on, with the intervals reducing in size. The tone color of an instrument is largely defined by which of the harmonics are prominent. The overtone series was first measured and quantified by the Greek philospher Pythagoras, and provided the basis for the major scale and hence the modal and tonal systems of music.

PENTATONIC SCALE — a type of MODE made up only of the intervals of a major second and a minor third. The black notes of a piano make up the pentatonic scale.

PERCUSSION — instruments played by shaking or striking.The main instruments in the percussion section of an orchestra are timpani (kettle drums), bass drums, side drums, tenor drums, cymbals, gong, tambourine, triangle, xylophone, and tubular bells. Other instruments that may be used include castanets, woodblock, claves, wind machine, and many others.

PHRASING — how a line in music is interpreted and divided. Phrases are analogous to sentences in prose. The correct phrasing of a piece is essential to its being clearly understood.

POLYPHONY — see COUNTERPOINT.

POLYRHYTHM — two or more rhythms played simultaneously, producing a complex overall rhythmic pattern.

POLYTONALITY — an extension of BI-TONALITY where three or more KEYS are used simultaneously, sometimes known as pan-tonality.

PORTAMENTO — in contrast to GLISSANDO, portamento or a "slide" can only be done on string instruments, woodwind, trombone, timpani, and more unusual instruments such as the

musical saw and slide whistle. This is because these instruments can pass from one note to another without any break. Instruments on which portamento is impossible include the piano and other fixed-pitch instruments.

POST-MODERNISM — a reaction to the extreme MODERNISM of the 1950s and 1960s. The movement originated in architecture and literature. In music it is a style or language that consciously uses devices and harmonies of older music (especially 19th-century music) and mixes them with AVANT-GARDE effects. This was sometimes done for ironic effect by composers such as SCHNITTKE, who took actual themes and harmonic progressions from Baroque music. Other composers have tried to integrate techniques of old and new music into one language with varying degrees of success.This approach can be found in the music of PENDERECKI.

PSYCHEDELIA — a musical movement associated with San Francisco and the flower-power movement of the mid-1960s. Expounding hippy theories, such as free love and the use of mind-expanding drugs as recreation, the movement was also represented by artwork, clothes, and posters. Bands most associated with psychedelia are the 13th Floor Elevators, the Jefferson Airplane, and the Grateful Dead.

REEL — an ancient and indigenous Scottish dance. Also used in American FOLK and square dances.

REVERB — reverberation. A reflection of a sound off its surroundings, usually walls, that is heard as a slight lengthening of a note. The length of the sound of the reverb is determined by the type of material the surroundings are made of and the size of the room. Cathedrals can often have a reverb time of close to a minute in length. It is also possible to produce reverb electronically.

RHYTHM AND BLUES — a genre of African-American music that emerged in late 1930s and early 1940s. Originally called "race music," the term applied to up-tempo "popular" pieces, whether JAZZ, GOSPEL, or BLUES, that featured humorous lyrics. White musicians, aware of

the popularity of this kind of party or JUMP MUSIC, started to adopt its qualities in the late 1940s. Bands got smaller while the beat got stronger, guitars began to dominate the sound, and vocalists became more important. In 1949, *Billboard* magazine changed the name of its African-American music chart from Race Records to Rhythm and Blues. In the mid-1950s white kids started to buy African-American hits, particularly dance music. White musicians, notably Elvis PRESLEY, started to record the music for themselves, and ROCK'N'ROLL was born—a kind of white version of rhythm and blues. In the 1960s, white bands started to COVER R&B tunes from the 1940s and 1950s. Although *Billboard* changed the name of its R&B chart to SOUL in 1969, the term R&B has remained as a musical genre on its own. British R&B refers specifically to the beat groups of the 1960s, such as John Mayall, Alexis Corner, and the Animals, who played versions of the Chicago style of rhythm and blues.

RHYTHM SECTION — a term applied to the part of a band or group, such as drums and bass guitar, that supplies the rhythm of a piece of music. In JAZZ, this can be extended to include other instruments, i.e., guitar, piano, banjo, tuba, etc.

RIFF — a term used in JAZZ and ROCK MUSIC for a shortish solo phrase, usually played on the electric guitar, and usually repeated many times in the course of the piece. Also known as a "lick."

RUBATO — literally: "robbed" time, implying that one note or phrase is subtly lengthened at the expense of another, often in performance. Generally, it means flexibility in time rather than metronomic regularity.

SAMBA — a popular form of music and dance found in BRAZIL, which had its roots in AFRICA.

SAMPLING — a process used in ELECTRONIC MUSIC and TECHNO dance music where a short digital recording of a sound (usually from one to 15 seconds) is used as an instrumental color for composition. Sampling is often used to fake the sound of a real instrument, which can then be "played" on a keyboard. More adventurous uses include sampling the sound of striking metal or other materials and this can then be altered to make an electronic percussion instrument.

SCALE — a sequence of notes, ascending or descending, that has a set order of **INTERVALS** separating the notes within the compass of an octave. Essentially the same as a **MODE**, but in Western art music it is used as a basis for the tonal system of composition, where the basic chords (triads) are derived directly from the major and minor scales. One type of major scale and two types of minor scale are recognized in **TONALITY**.

SCAT SINGING — a JAZZ term for using the voice as an instrument for **IMPROVISATION**, using not words, but rather syllables related to the sound of instruments, such as "shulie-a-bop."

SEQUENCE — a musical phrase that is repeated rhythmically but at a different pitch, or with different harmonic implications or context. An essential part of **FUGUE** composition.

SHAPE NOTE — a type of notation used in rural American sacred music where the note heads have particular shapes (usually simple geometrical triangles or squares) representing the syllables of the do, re, mi nomenclature of the **SCALE**.

SHARP — to sharpen a note is to raise it by a semitone or half step. The symbol is # and, when it is placed immediately before a note, it affects that particular note only, and is called an accidental. As with the **FLAT** sign, when sharp symbols are placed at the beginning of a line or work, they form a key signature and affect all subsequent notes to which they refer.

SHORT SCORE — a reduction or original sketch for an orchestral or large ensemble work. It is written for one or two pianos and is used for rehearsal with soloists, for harmonic analysis, or as a basis for student **ORCHESTRATION**. It is also known as a piano reduction or, when it is part of an OPERA score, a vocal score.

SHOUT — a term used in JAZZ denoting an energetic delivery, not necessarily vocal. Thus, a **STRIDE** pianist can play a shout and a BLUES singer can shout rather than sing. Shout also refers to the last full **CHORUS** in a BIG BAND performance.

SINE WAVE — an electronically produced pitch, free of all **HARMONICS**, used as a basis for sound synthesis.

SLIDE GUITAR — a style of BLUES playing also known as bottleneck playing because the original slides were sometimes made from the necks of bottles. The slide is worn on a finger of the left hand and is held on the strings at the required note to produce the pitch. Its special function is that it can slide between notes producing a very expressive **PORTAMENTO**. The foremost exponent of slide guitar playing in the 20th century was Ry COODER.

SLUR — a slur is made when two or more notes are played in the same breath or bow, or without a break between them, on instruments such as the piano. It is indicated by a curved line either connecting two notes or, when more than two are to be slurred, reaching over the set of notes to be included, connecting the two outer notes of the group.

SOLO — a work for one performer. Also refers to the part that dominates a work for soloist and ensemble, such as a concerto. In a JAZZ or ROCK context it is the **IMPROVISED** line played by the soloist. Other terms referring to the number of players include duo, trio, quartet, quintet, sextet, septet, octet, etc. All of these terms can also be used to refer to the actual works played by that number of people. More specific terms are used in classical music, such as piano trio, which is a piece for violin, piano, and cello (or an ensemble of three musicians playing those instruments together).

SPRECHSTIMME — literally: German for speech-voice, also known as Sprechgesang (speech-song). A type of vocal production somewhere between singing and speaking that was used extensively by SCHOENBERG. BERG also used it, but defined the actual pitches,

whereas Schoenberg gives interval size only. It was also used by later composers such as BOULEZ and HENZE.

STRIDE PIANO — a style of piano playing especially used by ragtime musicians and reaching its apogee with Art TATUM. The stride bass typically used widely spaced left-hand chords, alternately at the bottom and middle of the keyboard, creating an urgent, driving bass line.

STRINGS — a term describing instruments that produce sound through the vibration of strings. They include the violin family, piano, harp, and guitar. In the orchestra "strings" refers specifically to the large section of instruments comprising violins, violas, cellos, and double basses.

SYMMETRY — usually refers to phrases or formal sections that are the same in length and that balance each other rhythmically. It can also refer to the two halves of a serial **TONE-ROW,** which are made up of the same intervals, but with one being the **INVERSION** or retrograde of the other. It can also be applied to a type of harmonic construction that has some aspect of mirror image as its basis. Phrase and serial symmetry can be found in the works of WEBERN.

SYNCOPATION — a rhythmic device, essential to JAZZ and ragtime, where there is a secondary pulse occurring between the beats of the main meter. It is also known as cross-rhythm. Syncopation was common in European art music after the Renaissance and was used extensively in the Baroque period by composers such as J. S. Bach and Domenico Scarlatti.

TECHNO — a form of **HOUSE MUSIC.** Originating in Detroit in 1990, it developed into a term to describe hard, mainly instrumental, dance music. It was very popular in Northern Europe.

TEMPO — the "speed" of the music: for example, ♩ = 92 means 92 quarter notes in one minute. In contemporary music, the tempo is usually indicated using the above notation because of the proliferation of musical styles and concepts. In older music, especially the mainstream classical repertoire,

Italian terms such as *presto* (quick) and *andante* (at a walking pace) were used either in conjunction with, or instead of, exact tempo markings.

TIE — a curved line connecting two notes with the same pitch. It is usually used to make one note with the combined time value of the two notes together, and is therefore used across a bar line where the one long note could not be written. The tie is also used to combine two notes of differing value that could not be written as one note, even within a measure, because of the irregularity of their values: for example, a half note and a dotted eighth note.

TIMBRE — tone color, the actual sound of an instrument or instrumental combination. The timbre is determined by the type of attack and by which notes are prominent in the **HARMONIC SERIES**. These are initially determined by the type of sound production; for example, a bowed string, a strike on a stretched membrane, or a vibrating column of air. Other factors include the size of the instrument, the material it is made from, and especially the performer who is playing it.

TIME SIGNATURE — the number of certain metric values in each measure. The one most often used, also known as common time, is 4/4. This indicates that there are four quarter notes in each measure. Time signatures fall into two main categories of simple and compound time. Common 4/4 time is simple, while 6/8 is an example of compound time (it is divisible by more than two). Other types of time are used in the more complex languages of contemporary music, such as 11/8, which may also be written as 5/8 + 6/8. Time signatures such as this are also used in Greek and Bulgarian FOLK MUSIC. Time signatures such as 7/8 + 1/16 are common in the works of Peter Maxwell Davies, giving a flowing, unmetered sense of rhythm.

TONALITY — the main system of harmony in Western music used from the end of the Renaissance up to the mid-20th century. It is still widely used in popular music. Its basis is that of the major and minor **KEYS** and the tensions created by the traveling to and away from a tonic or home key. Tonality to a large extent also determined the form of music by using other keys as reference points in the flow of the music.

TONE CLUSTER — a very densely packed chord made up mainly of halftones. Tone clusters were used by many **AVANT-GARDE** composers, especially in piano music, in order to achieve a percussive effect without having to be committed to a particular pitch, interval, or harmony.

TONE-ROW — or note-row. The sequences of notes used in 12-note (or dodecaphonic) composition, developed especially by **SCHOENBERG**. The tone-row is made up of all 12 semitones of the **CHROMATIC** scale, used in an arbitrary order decided on by the composer, where no note is more important in the composition than any other (as opposed to the tonic and dominant of the ordinary **KEY**).

TRIPTYCH — a work in three parts. The name is taken from the three-part construction of a painting, engraving, or sculpture for a church altar in which the two outer parts form doors that can close onto and obscure the central portion.

TRITONE — the **INTERVAL** of an augmented fourth, or diminished fifth. It is made up of three whole tones, hence the name. Its dissonant nature, the fact that it exactly divides the perfect interval of the octave, and its connection with numerical perfection caused its use to be banned in early church music.

12-BAR BLUES — the harmonic and formal basis for the BLUES and much of early JAZZ. It is a simple cycle of 12 bars, and three chords and conformed to strict rules of composition. It consists of four bars of the tonic chord (for example, A major), followed by two bars of the subdominant (D major), then two bars of the tonic again. This is followed by one bar of the dominant (E major), one bar of the subdominant, then two further bars of the tonic. The sequence is therefore I, I, I, I, IV, IV, I, I, V, IV, I, I. In jazz, this chord sequence is often heavily modified by using substitute chords, but with reference to the same underlying harmonic structure.

VIBRATO — a rapid but small fluctuation of pitch above and below a note produced by a singer or instrumental performer. The vibrato in singing occurs naturally in a trained voice and is consciously reproduced on instruments, particularly string instruments such as violins, in order to mimic the voice and add expression to music.

VOICE TYPES — types of voices fall into the main categories of soprano, mezzo-soprano, and contralto for women and countertenor, alto, tenor, baritone, and bass for men. In opera, the particular voice type is usually chosen for the kind of dramatic role required. For example, the role of hero or lead is usually given to the tenor, with the baritone playing the father or uncle figure, that is, a man of wisdom or age. The leading roles for women are usually sopranos, and the secondary roles are usually sung by contraltos. The other voices are used mainly in concert works and in choirs. In some choirs, particularly church choirs, boys' voices are used instead of women sopranos because of their purity of tone and ability to sing very high notes effortlessly.

VOICING — the way in which the notes of a chord are distributed. A chord can be said to be in an open or closed position, depending on the size of the **INTERVALS** between the notes, and this gives either a sense of clarity or density. Voicing is extremely important when the chord is part of a progression, because the movement from any one note in one chord to a note in the next chord makes a discernible **LINE**, which is called voice leading.

WOODWIND — tubular instruments originally made of wood, but the group now includes metal instruments such as the flute and saxophone. They are played by blowing a column of air through the mouthpiece, either through a reed, or over an edge. Different notes are produced by covering or uncovering fingerholes along the length of the tube. The woodwind section of an orchestra consists of flutes, oboes, clarinets, and bassoons. Other woodwind instruments are the recorder, the saxophone, and the piccolo.

CONTRIBUTORS

Jim Allen
Music Journalist

Ramona Sohn Allen
Music Department
Scripps College
Claremont, California

Terry Atkinson
Music Journalist

Alison Bay
Music Journalist

Thomas Betts
Music Department
Hartnell College
Salinas, California

Alan Blackwood

Greg Bower
Music Journalist

David Brock
Music Department
Scripps College
Claremont, California

Richard Conviser
Music Journalist

Donna Cox
Department of Music
University of Dayton
Dayton, Ohio

Linda Dailey Paulson

Todd Denton
Editorial Director,
Music Boulevard

Dave DiMartino
Executive Editor, 2Way Media

Douglas Dunston

Judi Gerber
Music Journalist

Rebecca Giacosie

Joseph Goldberg
Music Department
University of Chicago
Chicago, Illinois

Ina Gonzalez

Charlotte Greig

Stuart Harling

Stan Hieronymus
Music Journalist

Joanne Hsia

Hao Huang
Music Department
Scripps College
Claremont, California

Rachel Vetter Huang
Music Department
Scripps College
Claremont, California

Renee Jinks
Music Journalist

Gregg Juke
Musician and Producer

Jeff Kaliss
Music Journalist

Matty Karas
Music Journalist

Tracey Kelly
Film Music Composer

Brett Allan King
Music Journalist

Timothy Kloth
Department of Music
University of Dayton
Dayton, Ohio

Allan Kozinn
Music Journalist and
Beatles Specialist

Daria Labinsky
Music Journalist

Kathleen J. Lamkin
Music Department
Scripps College
Claremont, California

Michael Lamkin
Music Department
Scripps College
Claremont, California

Richard Langham Smith
Department of Music
University of Exeter
Exeter, U.K.

Spencer Leigh

Christopher Lengefeld
Music Department
Scripps College
Claremont, California

Sarah Lowe

Esther J. Luo

Graham McColl

Linnie Messina

Elaine Musgrave

Jane Prendergast
Music Journalist

Alan Rich
Author, Music Journalist
and Critic

Todd Ridder
Music Department
University of Dayton
Dayton, Ohio

Paul Rinzler
Music Department
University of California
Santa Cruz, California

Michael R. Ross
Music Journalist

Herb Scher
Musician and
Music Journalist

Alyn Shipton
Author and
Jazz Broadcaster

Chris Slawecki
Music Journalist

Jim Tosone
Music Journalist

Richard Trombley
School of Music
University of Oregon
Eugene, Oregon

James Tuverson
Music Journalist

Steve Valdez
School of Music
University of Oregon
Eugene, Oregon

Eleanor Van Zandt

Llyswen Vaughan
Musician

Michael Weber
Classical Music
Consultant

Jim Whipple

Joan Wildman
Music Department
University of Wisconsin
Madison, Wisconsin

BIBLIOGRAPHY

Abrahams, Roger. *The Smithsonian-Folkways Book of American Folk Songs* (New York: HarperPerennial Library, 1995).

Acuff, Roy, and William Neely. *Roy Acuff's Nashville: The Life and Good Times of Country Music* (New York: Putnam, 1983).

Alker, Frank, and John McDonough, eds. *Down Beat: 60 Years of Jazz* (Milwaukee, WI: H. Leonard Publishing, 1995).

Allen, B., ed. *The Blackwell Guide to Recorded Country Music* (Cambridge, MA: Blackwell, 1994).

Alpert, Hollis. *Broadway!* (New York: Arcade, 1991).

Alten, Stanley R. *Audio in Media: The Recording Studio* (Belmont, CA: Wadsworth, 1996).

Alvera, Pierluigi, trans. Raymond Rosenthal. *Respighi* (New York: Treves Publishing Company, 1986).

Amburn, E. *Buddy Holly: A Biography* (New York: St. Martin's Griffin, 1995).

Ancelet, Barry J. *Cajun Music: Its Origins and Development* (Lafayette, LA: Center for Louisiana Studies, University of Southwestern Louisiana, 1989).

Andersen, C. P. *Madonna, Unauthorized* (New York: Simon & Schuster, 1991).

Andrews, Maxene, and Bill Gilbert. *Over Here, Over There: The Andrews Sisters and the USO Stars in World War II* (Thorndike, MA: Thorndike Press, 1994).

Antokioletz, Elliott. *The Music of Béla Bartók* (Berkeley, CA: University of California Press, 1984).

——. *Twentieth-Century Music* (Englewood Cliffs, NJ: Prentice Hall, 1992).

Appignanesi, L. *The Cabaret* (New York: Universal Books, 1976).

Appleby, D. *The Music of Brazil* (Austin, TX: University of Texas Press, 1989).

Ardoin, John. *The Furtwängler Record* (Portland, OR: Amadeus Press, 1994).

——. *The Stages of Menotti* (New York: Doubleday, 1985).

Arganian, Lillian. *Stan Kenton: The Man and His Music* (East Lansing, MI: Artistry Press, 1989).

Armbruster, G. *The Art of Electronic Music* (New York: William Morrow, 1984).

Arnold, Gina. *Route 666: On the Road to Nirvana* (New York: St. Martin's Press, 1993).

Artis, Bob. *Bluegrass: The Story of an American Musical Tradition* (New York: Hawthorn Books, 1975).

Ashkenazy, Vladimir, and Jasper Parrot. *Ashkenazy: Beyond Frontiers* (New York: Atheneum, 1985).

Atkins, C. *Off the Record* (Pacific, MO: Mel Bay, 1976).

Ayala, Cristóbal Diaz. *The Roots of Salsa: The History of Cuban Music* (New York: Excelsior Music Publishing, 1995).

Aznavour, Charles. *Aznavour by Aznavour: An Autobiography* (Chicago IL: Cowles Book Co., 1979).

Bach, Bob, and Ginger Mercer. *Our Huckleberry Friend: The Life, Times and Lyrics of Johnny Mercer* (Seacaucus, NJ: Lyle Stuart, 1982).

Baez, Joan. *And a Voice to Sing with* (New York: Summit Books, 1987).

——. *Joan C. Baez: And Then I Wrote* (New York: Big Three Music Corp., 1979).

Bailey, K. *The Twelve-Note Music of Anton Webern* (New York: Cambridge University Press, 1991).

Bailey, Rebecca. *The Kinks: Reflections on 30 Years of Music* (Morehead, KY: Trillium Publications, 1994).

Bailey, Walter B., ed. *The Arnold Schoenberg Companion* (Westport, CT: Greenwood Press, 1998).

Baker, Chet. *As Though I Had Wings* (New York: St. Martin's Griffin, 1997).

Baker, James M. *The Music of Alexander Scriabin* (New Haven, CT: Yale University Press, 1986).

Baldock, Robert. *Pablo Casals* (Boston MA: Northeastern University Press, 1993).

Balliett, Whitney. *New York Notes: A Journal of Jazz in the Seventies* (New York: Da Capo Press, 1977).

Barenboim, Daniel. *A Life in Music* (New York: C. Scribner's Sons, 1992).

Barnes, K. *The Crosby Years* (New York: St. Martin's Press, 1980).

Barnouw, E. and S. Krishnaswamy. *The Indian Film* (New York: Oxford University Press, 1980).

Barrett, Mary Ellen. *Irving Berlin: A Daughter's Memoir* (New York: Simon & Schuster, 1994).

Basie, Count, with Albert Murray. *Good Morning Blues* (New York: Random House, 1985).

Becker, Judith. *Traditional Music in Modern Java* (Honolulu, HI: University of Hawaii Press, 1980).

Beckerman, Michael. *Janáček as Theorist* (Stuyvesant, New York: Pendragon Press, 1994).

Beecham Society. *Sir Thomas Beecham Discography* (Westport, CT: Greenwood Press, 1978).

Beecham, Sir Thomas. *A Mingled Chime* (Westport, CT: Greenwood Press, 1976).

Bego, Mark. *Aretha Franklin: The Queen of Soul* (New York: St. Martin's Press, 1989).

——. *I Fall to Pieces: The Music and the Life of Patsy Cline* (New York: Adams Publishing, 1995).

Béhague, Gerard H. *Music and Black Ethnicity: The Caribbean and South America* (New Brunswick, NJ: Transaction Publications, 1994).

——. *Music in Latin America* (New York: Garland, 1985).

Behr, Edward. *Thank Heaven for Little Girls: The True Story of Maurice Chevalier's Life and Times* (New York: Villard Books, 1993).

Bennett, Tony. *What My Heart Has Seen* (New York: Rizzoli, 1996).

Berger, Ed., et al. *Benny Carter: A Life in American Music* (Metuchen, NJ: Scarecrow Press, 1982).

Berger, Melvin. *Guide to Chamber Music* (New York: Anchor, 1989).

Bergman, Billy, and Andy Schwarz. *Hot Sauces: Latin and Caribbean Pop* (New York: Quill, 1985).

Bergreen, Laurence. *As Thousands Cheer: The Life of Irving Berlin* (New York: Da Capo Press, 1996).

Berkenstadt, J., and C. R. Cross. *Nevermind: Nirvana* (New York: Schirmer Books, 1998).

Berlin, Edward. *A King of Ragtime: Scott Joplin and His Era* (New York: Oxford University Press, 1995).

Bernard, Jonathan W. *The Music of Edgard Varèse* (New Haven, CT: Yale University Press, 1987).

Bernard, Matthew. *Mario Lanza* (New York: MacFadden-Bartell Corp., 1971).

Bernstein, Leonard. *Young People's Concerts* (New York: Doubleday Anchor, 1992).

Berry, Chuck. *Chuck Berry: The Autobiography* (New York: Simon & Schuster, 1988).

Bierley, Paul E. *John Philip Sousa, American Phenomenon* (Columbus, OH: Integrity Press, 1986).

Bing, Sir Rudolf. *5000 Nights at the Opera* (Garden City, NY: Doubleday, 1972).

Birnbaum, L. "Machito: Original Macho Man" (*Down Beat,* vol. xlvii, no. 12, 1980, p.25).

Blair, John. *The Illustrated Discography of Surf Music, 1961-1965* (Ann Arbor, MI: Popular Culture Ink, 1995).

Blancq, Charles. *Sonny Rollins, The Journey of a Jazzman* (Boston, MA: Twayne, 1983).

Blau, Eric. *Jacques Brel Is Alive and Well and Living in Paris* (New York: E. P. Dutton, 1971).

Blesh, R. *USA: Eight Lives in Jazz* (New York: Da Capo Press, 1971).

Bluestein, Gene. *Poplore: Folk and Pop in American Culture* (Amherst, MA: University of Massachusetts Press, 1994).

Blum, David. *Casals and the Art of Interpretation* (New York: Holmes & Meier, 1977).

Blumenthal, Bob. *Cool, Man: A Swing Through the World of Jazz* (Los Angeles, CA: General Publishing Group, 1997).

Boardman, Gerald. *American Operetta* (New York: Oxford University Press, 1981).

Bockris, Victor, and Gerald Malanga. *Up-Tight: The Story of the Velvet Underground* (New York: Omnibus Press, 1995).

Boggs, Vernon W. *Salsiology: Afro-Cuban Music and the Evolution of Salsa in New York City* (New York: Greenwood Press, 1992).

Böhm, Karl. *A Life Remembered* (New York: Marion Boyars, 1992).

Bois, Mario. *Iannis Xenakis: The Man and His Music* (Westport, CT: Greenwood Press, 1980).

Bonds, Ray. *The Illustrated Encyclopedia of Black Music* (New York: Harmony Books, 1982).

Booker, C. and A. Winkler. *Bob Marley: An Intimate Portrait by his Mother* (New York: Viking, 1996).

Bookspan, Martin, and Ross Yockey. *André Previn: A Biography* (Garden City, NY: Doubleday, 1981).

——. *Zubin: The Zubin Mehta Story* (New York: Harper & Row, 1978).

Boot, Adrian, and Chris Salewicz. *Punk: The Illustrated History of a Music Revolution* (New York: Penguin, 1996).

Bordman, Gerald. *American Musical Theater* (New York: Oxford University Press, 1978).

——. *Jerome Kern: His Life and Music* (New York: Oxford University Press, 1980).

Borovsky, Victor. *Chaliapin: A Critical Biography* (New York: Alfred A. Knopf, 1988).

Bowen, Jimmy, and Jim Jerome. *Rough Mix: An Unapologetic Look at the Music Business and How It Got that Way* (New York: Simon & Schuster, 1997).

Bowers, Faubion. *Scriabin, A Biography* (New York: Dover, 1996).

Bowler, Dave, and Brian Dray. *Genesis: A Biography* (New York: Macmillan, 1992).

——. *R.E.M.: From "Chronic Town" to "Monster"* (Secaucus, NJ: Carol Publishing Group, 1995).

Bowman, Jeffrey. *Diva* (New York: HarperCollins, 1995).

Bowman, Rob. *Soulsville, U.S.A.: The Story of Stax Records* (New York: Schirmer Books, 1997).

Boyer, Horace Clarence. *How Sweet the Sound: The Golden Age of Gospel* (Washington, DC: Elliott & Clark, 1995).

Brendel, Alfred. *Music Sounded Out* (New York: Noonday, 1992).

Breslin, Herbert H. *The Tenors* (New York: Macmillan, 1974).

Bret, David. *The Piaf Legend* (New York: Robson Books, 1989).

Britt, Stan. *Long Tall Dexter, Dexter Gordon: A Musical Biography* (New York: Da Capo Press, 1989).

Bronson, Fred. *The Billboard Book of Number One Hits* (New York: Billboard Publications, 1985).

Broonzy, William, with Yannick Bruynoghe. *Big Bill Blues: William Broonzy's Story* (New York: Da Capo Press, 1992).

Broven, John. *South to Louisiana: The Music of the Cajun Bayous* (Gretna, LA: Pelican Publishing, 1983).

Brown, J. *James Brown: The Godfather of Soul* (New York: Macmillan, 1986).

Brown, Jonathan. *Puccini* (New York: Simon & Schuster, 1995).

Brown, Malcolm Hamrick. *Russian and Soviet Music* (Ann Arbor, MI: University of Michigan Research Press, 1984).

Brown, Peter Harry, and Pat H. Broeske. *Down at the End of Lonely Street* (New York: Dutton, 1997).

Brown, Royal S. *Overtones and Undertones* (Berkeley, CA: University of California Press, 1994).

Brown, Wesley. *Boogie Woogie and Booker T* (New York: Theater Communications, 1987).

Bruce, Graham. *Bernard Herrmann: Film Music and Narrative* (Ann Arbor, MI: University of Michigan Research Press, 1985).

Bruhn, Siglind. *Images and Ideas on Modern French Piano Music: The Extra-musical Subtext in Piano Works by Debussy, Ravel and Messiaen* (Stuyvesant, NY: Pendragon Press, 1997).

Büchmann-Møller, Frank. *You Just Fight for Your Life: The Story of Lester Young* (New York: Greenwood Press, 1990).

——. *You Just Got To Be Original, Man* (New York: Greenwood Press, 1990).

Budwig, A., and G. Chase. *Manuel de Falla: A Bibliography and Research Guide* (New York: Garland, 1986).

Bufwack, M. A. and R. K. Oermann. *Finding Her Voice: The Illustrated History of Women in Country Music* (New York: Henry Holt, 1995).

Burckholder, J. Peter. *Charles Ives and His World* (Princeton, NJ: Princeton University Press, 1996).

Burton, Gary. *A Musician's Guide to the Road* (New York: Watson-Guptill, 1981).

Burton, Humphrey. *Leonard Bernstein* (New York: Doubleday, 1994).

Butler, Dougal. *Full Moon* (New York: Quill Books, 1982).

Calt, Stephen, and Gayle Wardlow. *King of the Delta Blues: The Life and Music of Charlie Patton* (Newton, NJ: Rock Chapel Press, 1988).

Campbell, Don G. *Master Teacher, Nadia Boulanger* (Washington, DC: Pastoral Press, 1984).

Campbell, Lisa D. *Michael Jackson: The King of Pop* (Boston, MA: Branden Books, 1993).

Cantwell, Robert S. *When We Were Good: The Folk Revival* (Boston, MA: Harvard University Press, 1996).

Card, Caroline, ed. *A Tribute to Alan P. Merriam* (Bloomington, IN: Indiana University Press, 1981).

Carley, Lionel. *Delius: A Life in Letters 1901-34* (Brookfield, VT: Gower Publishing, 1988).

Carmichael, Hoagy. *The Stardust Road* (New York: Greenwood Press, 1969).

——, with Stephen Longstreet. *Sometimes I Wonder: The Story of Hoagy Carmichael* (New York: Da Capo Press, 1976).

Carner, Mosco. *Alban Berg: The Man and the Work* (New York: Holmes & Meier, 1977).

Carr, Ian. *Keith Jarrett: The Man and His Music* (New York: Da Capo Press, 1982).

——. *Miles Davis: A Biography* (New York: William Morrow, 1982).

Carr, J. and A. Munde. *Prairie Nights to Neon Lights: The Story of Country Music in West Texas* (Lubbock, TX: Texas Technical University Press, 1995).

Carter, Alan. *U2: The Road to Pop* (Boston: Faber and Faber, 1997).

Carter, Janette. *Living with Memories* (Hiltons, VA: Carter Family Memorial Music Center, 1983).

Caruso, Dorothy. *Enrico Caruso: His Life and Death* (Westport, CT: Greenwood Press, 1987).

Caruso, E., Jr., and A. Farkas. *Enrico Caruso: My Father and Family* (Portland, OR: Amadeus Press, 1997).

Casell, Chuck. *A&M Records: The First Ten Years—a Fairy Tale* (Hollywood, CA: A&M Records, 1972).

Cass-Beggs, Barbara. *Your Baby Needs Music* (North Vancouver, B.C.: Douglas & McIntyre, 1978).

Cavicchi, David. *Tramps Like Us: Music and Meaning among Springsteen Fans* (New York: Oxford University Press, 1998).

Chambers, Jack. *Milestones I & II: The Music and Times of Miles Davis* (Toronto, Canada: University of Toronto Press, 1985).

Chanan, Michael. *Repeated Takes: A Short History of Recording and its Effects on Music* (New York: Verso, 1995).

Charlton, Andrew. *Jazz and Commercial Arranging* (Englewood Cliffs, NJ: Prentice Hall, 1982).

Charlton, Katherine. *Rock Music Styles: A History* (Madison, WI: Brown & Benchmark, 1994).

Charnin, Martin. *Annie: A Theatre Memoir* (New York: Dutton, 1977).

Chasins, Abram. *Leopold Stokowski: A Profile* (New York: Da Capo Press, 1979).

Chesterman, Robert. *Conductors in Conversation* (New York: Limelight Editions, 1992).

Chilton, John. *The Song of the Hawk: The Life and Recordings of Coleman Hawkins* (Ann Arbor, MI: University of Michigan Press, 1990).

Chylinska, Teresa, trans. John Glowacki. *Karol Szymanowski: His Life and Works* (Los Angeles, CA: University of Southern California, 1993).

Cimino, Al. *Great Record Labels* (New York: Apple, 1992).

Clarke, Donald. *The Rise and Fall of Popular Music* (New York: St. Martin's Press, 1995).

——. *Wishing on the Moon: The Life and Times of Billie Holiday* (New York: Viking, 1994).

Clarke, Steve. *Genesis: Turn It on Again* (New York: Omnibus, 1984).

Clifford, Mike, ed. *The Harmony Encyclopedia of Rock* (New York: Harmony Books, 1992).

Cohn, L., ed. *Nothing but the Blues: The Music and the Musicians* (New York: Abbeville Press, 1993).

Cole, Bill. *John Coltrane* (New York: Da Capo Press, 1993).

——. *Miles Davis: A Musical Biography* (New York: William Morrow, 1974).

Collaer, Paul. *Darius Milhaud* (San Francisco, CA: San Francisco Press, 1988).

Collier, James Lincoln. *Duke Ellington* (New York: Oxford University Press, 1987).

——. *The Making of Jazz: A Comprehensive History* (New York: Dell, 1979).

Collier, Simon. *Tango: The Dance, the Song, the Story* (New York: Thames and Hudson, 1995).

Collins, John. *West African Pop Roots* (Philadelphia, PA: Temple University Press, 1992).

——, and Sylvia Moore. *African Pop Roots* (New York: W. Foulsham, 1985).

Connelly, Will. *The Musician's Guide to Independent Record Production* (Chicago, IL.: Contemporary Books, 1981).

Connor, D. Russell. *Benny Goodman: Wrappin' It Up* (Lanham, MD: Scarecrow Press, 1996).

Conrad, Peter. *A Song of Love and Death* (Saint Paul, MN: Graywolf Press, 1996).

Cook, Pansy. *The Saga of Jim Reeves: Country and Western Singer and Musician* (Los Angeles, CA: Crescent Publications, 1977).

Cooke, M., and P. Reed. *Benjamin Britten: Billy Budd* (New York: Cambridge University Press, 1993).

Cooper, B. Lee, and Wayne S. Haney. *Rock Music in American Popular Culture II: More Rock'n'Roll Resources* (New York: Harrington Park Press, 1997).

Cope, David. *New Directions in Music* (Dubuque, IA: Brown & Benchmark, 1993).

Copland, Aaron. *Composer from Brooklyn* (New York: W. W. Norton, 1984).

——. *Our New Music* (New York: W. W. Norton, 1968).

Coroniti, Joseph. *Poetry as Text in Twentieth-Century Vocal Music: from Stravinsky to Reich* (Lewiston, NY: E. Mellen Press, 1992).

Coryell, Julie, and Laura Friedman. *Jazz Rock Fusion: The People, the Music* (New York: Dell Publishing, 1978).

Covach, John, and Graham M. Boone, eds. *Understanding Rock: Essays in Musical Analysis* (New York: Oxford University Press, 1997).

Craig, Warren. *Sweet and Lowdown: America's Popular Song Writers* (Metuchen, NJ: Scarecrow Press, 1978).

Crain, S. R., et al. *You Send Me* (New York: William Morrow, 1995).

Crawford, John C. and Dorothy L. *Expressionism in 20th-Century Music* (Bloomington, IN: Indiana University Press, 1993).

Crimp, Susan, and Patricia Burstein. *The Many Lives of Elton John* (New York: Carol Publishing Group, 1992).

Crosby, B., with P. Martin. *Call Me Lucky* (New York: Da Capo Press, 1993).

Crosland, Margaret. *Piaf* (New York: Fromm International, 1987).

Cross, Charles R. *Backstreets: Springsteen: The Man and His Music* (New York: Crown, 1992).

Cuellar, Carol. *Money for Nothing* (Burbank, CA: Warner Brothers, 1988).

Cuniff, Albert. *Waylon Jennings* (New York: Kensington Publishing Corporation, 1985).

Cunningham, Merce. *Changes: Notes on Choreography* (New York: Something Else Press, 1968).

Damrosch, Walter. *My Musical Life* (Temecula, CA: Reprint Services, 1991).

Dance, Helen Oakley, *Stormy Monday: The T-Bone Walker Story* (Baton Rouge, LA: Louisiana State University Press, 1987).

Danchin, Sebastian. *Blues Boy* (Jackson, MS: University Press of Mississippi, 1998).

Daniel, Oliver. *Stokowski: A Counterpoint of View* (New York: Dodd, Mead, 1982).

Dannen, Frederic. *Hit Men: Power Brokers and Fast Money Inside the Music Business* (New York: Vintage, 1991).

Darby, W., and J. Dubois. *American Film Music: Major Composers, Techniques and Trends 1915-90* (New York: Schirmer Books, 1997).

Davis, Francis. *The History of the Blues* (New York: Hyperion, 1995).

Davis, Miles, with Quincy Troupe. *Miles: The Autobiography* (New York: Simon & Schuster, 1989).

Davis, Stephen. *Bob Marley: Conquering Lion of Reggae* (New York: Doubleday, 1985).

——. *The Hammer of the Gods* (New York: Boulevard Books, 1997).

Day, Doris, and A. E. Hotcher. *Doris Day: Her Own Story* (New York: Morrow, 1976).

De Barres, Pamela. *Rock Bottom: Dark Moments in Music Babylon* (New York: St. Martin's Press, 1996).

Deane, Basil. *Albert Roussel* (New York: Greenwood Press, 1980).

DeCurtis, Anthony, et al. *Illustrated History of Rock & Roll* (New York: Random House, 1992).

Delaunay, Charles, trans. Michael James. *Django Reinhardt* (New York: Da Capo Press, 1982).

DeLong, Thomas. *Pops: Paul Whiteman, King of Jazz* (Piscataway, NJ: New Wind Publishing, 1983).

Demarquez, Suzanne, trans. Salvator Attanasio. *Manuel de Falla* (New York: Da Capo Press, 1983).

DeVeaux, Scott. *The Birth of Bebop: A Social and Musical History* (Berkeley, CA: University of California Press, 1995).

DeWitt, Harry A. *Chuck Berry: Rock'n'Roll Music* (Ann Arbor, MI: Pierian Press, 1985).

Dibango, Manu, and Danielle Rouard. *Three Kilos of Coffee: An Autobiography* (Chicago IL: University of Chicago Press, 1994).

Dickson, Harry Ellis. *Arthur Fiedler and the Boston Pops* (Boston, MA: Houghton Mifflin, 1981).

——. *Gentlemen, More Dolce Please!* (Boston MA: Beacon Press, 1974).

Dishef, Robert K. *The New Breed* (Minneapolis, MN: Lerner Publications, 1978).

Dixon, W., with D. Snowden. *I Am the Blues: The Willie Dixon Story* (New York: Da Capo Press, 1989).

Dodge, Consuelo. *The Everly Brothers: Ladies Love Outlaws* (Starke, FL: CIN-DAV, 1991).

Donice, Darlene. *Mahalia Jackson* (Los Angeles, CA: Melrose Square, 1992).

Donington, Robert. *The Interpretation of Early Music* (New York: St. Martin's Press, 1974).

Doran, James M. *Erroll Garner: The Most Happy Piano* (Metuchen, NJ: Scarecrow Press and the Institute of Jazz Studies, Rutgers University, 1985).

Dorsey, Thomas A. *Great Gospel Songs of Thomas A. Dorsey* (Milwaukee, WI: H. Leonard, 1988).

Drake, James A. *Richard Tucker: A Biography* (New York: Dutton, 1984).

Dubal, David. *Evenings with Horowitz* (New York: Birch Lane Press, 1991).

Duckworth, William. *Talking Music: Conversations with John Cage, Philip Glass, Laurie Anderson, and five Generations of American Experimental Composers* (New York: Schirmer Books, 1995).

Dunaway, David. *How Can I Keep From Singing: Pete Seeger* (New York: Da Capo Press, 1990).

Easton, Carol. *Straight Ahead: The Story of Stan Kenton* (New York: Da Capo Press, 1981).

Eatherly, Pat Travis. *In Search of my Father* (Nashville, TN: Broadman Press, 1987).

Eberly, Philip K. *Music in the Air: America's Changing Tastes in Popular Music, 1920-1980* (New York: Hastings House, 1982).

Edwards, A. *Flawed Words and Stubborn Sounds: A Conversation with Elliott Carter* (New York: W. W. Norton, 1971).

Edwards, Ann. *Streisand: A Biography* (New York: Little, Brown, 1997).

Eliot, Marc. *To the Limit: The Untold Story of the Eagles* (Boston: Little, Brown and Co., 1997).

Ellington, Duke. *Music Is My Mistress* (Garden City, NY: Doubleday, 1973).

Emmons, Shirlee. *Tristanissimo: The Authorized Biography of Heroic Tenor Lauritz Melchior* (New York: Schirmer Books, 1990).

Eremo, Judie, ed. *Country Musicians: from the Editors of Guitar Player, Keyboard and Frets Magazines* (Cupertino, CA: Grove Press, 1987).

Erenberg, Lewis A. *Swingin' the Dream* (Chicago, IL: University of Chicago Press, 1998).

Escott, Colin, et al. *Hank Williams: The Biography* (Boston, MA: Little, Brown & Co., 1995).

Escott, Peter. *Good Rockin Tonight* (New York: St. Martin's Press, 1991).

Evans, P. *The Music of Benjamin Britten* (New York: Oxford University Press, 1996).

Ewen, David. *All the Years of American Popular Music* (Englewood Cliffs, NJ: Prentice Hall, 1977).

——. *American Songwriters* (New York: H. W. Wilson, 1987).

——. *Great Men of American Popular Song* (Englewood Cliffs, NJ: Prentice Hall, 1972).

——. *Musicians Since 1900* (New York: H. W. Wilson & Co., 1978).

——. *The World of 20th Century Music* (New York: Prentice Hall, 1968).

Ewens, Graeme. *Africa O-Ye!* (New York: Da Capo Press, 1992).

Farrell, Gerry. *Indian Music and the West* (New York: Oxford University Press, 1997).

Faulkner, Robert R. *Music on Demand: Composers and Careers in the Hollywood Film Industry* (New Brunswick, NJ: Transaction Books, 1983).

Feather, Leonard. *Inside Jazz* (New York: Da Capo Press, 1992).

——. *The Jazz Years: Earwitness to an Era* (New York: Da Capo Press, 1987).

——. *The Passion for Jazz* (New York: Da Capo Press, 1990).

Feiler, Bruce. *Dreaming out Loud: Garth Brooks, Wynonna Judd, Wade Hayes, and the Changing Face of Nashville* (New York: Avon Books, 1998).

Ferguson, J, ed. *The Guitar Player Book* (New York: Grove Press, 1983).

Fernando, S. H., Jr. *The New Beats* (New York: Doubleday, 1994).

Ferris, Jeri. *What I Had Was Singing: The Story of Marian Anderson* (New York: First Avenue Editions, 1994).

Fiedler, Johanna. *Arthur Fiedler: Papa, the Pops, and Me* (New York: Doubleday, 1994).

Figueroa, Rafael. *Salsa and Related Genres: A Bibliographical Guide* (Westport, CT: Greenwood Press, 1992).

Fink, Michael. *Inside the Music Industry: Creativity, Process, and Business* (New York: Schirmer Books, 1996).

Finletter, Damrosch G. *From the Top of the Stairs* (Temecula, CA: Reprint Services, 1993).

Firedwald, W. *Jazz Singing* (New York: Da Capo Press, 1996).

Firestone, Ross. *Swing, Swing, Swing* (New York: W. W. Norton, 1993).

Fischer-Dieskau, Dietrich, trans. Ruth Hein. *Reverberations: The Memoirs of Dietrich Fischer-Dieskau* (also known as *Echoes of a Lifetime*) (New York: Fromm International, 1989).

Fisher, James. *Al Jolson* (Westport, CT: Greenwood Press, 1994).

Flanagan, Bill. *U2 At the End of the World* (New York: Delacorte Press, 1995).

Fleischer, Leonore. *Joni Mitchell* (New York: Flash Books, 1976).

Fliege, Richard. *Amps!: The Other Half of Rock'n'Roll* (Milwaukee, WI: H. Leonard Publishing, 1993).

Flippo, Chet. *On the Road with the Rolling Stones* (New York: Doubleday, 1985).

Follet, Robert. *Albert Roussel: A Bio-bibliography* (New York: Greenwood Press, 1988).

Fonseca, Isabel. *Bury Me Standing: The Gypsies and Their Journey* (New York: Alfred A. Knopf, 1995).

Ford, Robert. *Children's Rhymes, Children's Games, Children's Songs, Children's Stories* (Detroit, MI: Singing Tree Press, 1968).

Fordin, Hugh. *Getting to Know Him* (New York: Da Capo Press, 1995).

Frame, P. *The Complete Rock Family Trees* (New York: Omnibus, 1993).

Frank, Gerold. *Judy* (New York: Harper & Row, 1975).

Fraser, Angus. *The Gypsies* (Cambridge, MA: Blackwell, 1992).

Freedland, Michael. *All the Way: A Biography of Frank Sinatra* (New York: St. Martin's Press, 1998).

——. *Jerome Kern* (New York: Stein and Day, 1981).

——. *Maurice Chevalier* (New York: Morrow, 1981).

——. *Sophie: The Sophie Tucker Story* (London: Woburn Press, 1978).

Frew, Timothy. *Scott Joplin and the Age of Ragtime* (New York: Friedman/Fairfax Publishers, 1996).

Friedwald, Will. *Jazz Singing* (New York: Da Capo Press, 1996).

Froud, Nina, and James Hanley, eds. *Chaliapin: An Autobiography as Told to Maxim Gorky* (New York: Stein and Day, 1967).

Furia, Philip. *The Poets of Tin Pan Alley: A History of America's Greatest Lyricists* (New York: Oxford University Press, 1990).

Furlong, William B. *A Season with Solti: A Year in the Life of the Chicago Symphony* (New York: Macmillan, 1974).

Gaar, G. *She's a Rebel* (Seattle, WA: Seal Press, 1992).

Gabel, E. F. *Stan Kenton: The Early Years, 1941-47* (Lake Geneva, WI: Balboa Books, 1993).

Gaines, Steven. *Heroes and Villains* (New York: Da Capo Press, 1995).

Galkin, Elliott W. *The History of Orchestral Conducting* (New York: Pendragon Press, 1989).

Galway, James. *An Autobiography* (New York: St. Martin's Press, 1979).

Gänzl, Kurt. *The British Musical Theatre* (New York: Oxford University Press, 1983).

——. *The Encyclopedia of the Musical Theater* (New York: Schirmer, 1994).

Garland, Peter. *Americas: Essays on American Music and Culture* (Santa Fe, NM: Soundings Press, 1982).

Garon, Paul, and Beth Garon. *Woman with Guitar: Memphis Minnie's Blues* (New York: Da Capo Press, 1992).

Garretson, Robert L. *Choral Music: History, Style, and Performance Practice* (Englewood Cliffs, NJ: Prentice Hall, 1993).

Garrod, Charles. *The Andrews Sisters* (Zephyrhills, FL: Joyce Record Club, 1992).

——, and Peter Johnston. *Harry James and His Orchestra* (Zephyrhills, FL: Joyce Record Club. 1996).

——, et al. *Tommy Dorsey and His Orchestra* (Zephyrhills, FL: Joyce Music, 1988).

Garvin, R. M., and E. G. Addeo. *The Midnight Special: The Legend of Leadbelly* (New York: B. Geis Associates, 1971).

Gavin, James. *Chet Baker* (New York: Random House, 1998).

Gelb, Alan. *The Doris Day Scrapbook* (New York: Grosset & Dunlap, 1977).

George, Nelson. *Where Did Our Love Go? The Rise & Fall of the Motown Sound* (New York: St. Martin's Press, 1987).

Gerard, Charlie. *Salsa: The Rhythm of Latin Music* (Crown Point, IN: White Cliffs Media Company, 1986).

Giddins, Gary. *Riding on a Blue Note: Jazz and American Pop* (New York: Oxford University Press, 1981).

Gigli, Beniamino. *Memoirs of Beniamino Gigli* (New York: Arno Press, 1977).

Gillespie, John and Anna. *Notable 20th-Century Pianists, Vol. 2* (Westport, CT: Greenwood Press, 1995).

Gillett, Charlie. *The Sound of the City: The Rise of Rock and Roll* (New York: Pantheon Books, 1983).

Gilliam, Bryan. *Richard Strauss and his World* (Princeton, NJ: Princeton University Press, 1992).

Gillman, P. and L. *Alias David Bowie* (New York: Henry Holt, 1987).

Gioia, Ted. *The History of Jazz* (New York: Oxford University Press, 1997).

Girard, Sharon. *Funeral Music and Customs in Venezuela* (Tempe, AZ: Center for Latin American Studies, Arizona State University, 1980).

Gitler, Ira. *Jazz Masters of the Forties* (New York: Da Capo Press, 1983).

Gobbi, Tito. *Tito Gobbi on His World of Italian Opera* (New York: Franklin Watts, 1984).

——. *Tito Gobbi: My Life* (New York: Doubleday, 1980).

Godbolt, Jim. *A History of Jazz in Britain, 1950–70* (New York: Quartet, 1989).

Goggin, Jim, and Pete Clute, *The Great Jazz Revival* (San Rafael, CA: Ewald Publications, 1994).

Goldberg, Joe. *Jazz Masters of the 1950s* (New York: Da Capo Press, 1983).

Goldman, Albert. *Disco* (New York: Hawthorn Books, 1978).

Goldrosen, J., and J. Beecher. *Remembering Buddy* (New York: Da Capo Press, 1996).

Gonzalez, Doreen. *Gloria Estefan* (Springfield, NJ: Enslow Publishers, 1996).

Goodman, Fred. *The Mansion on the Hill* (New York: Times Books, 1997).

Gorbman, Claudia. *Unheard Melodies* (Bloomington, IN: Indiana University Press, 1987).

Gordy, Berry. *To Be Loved: The Music, the Magic, the Memories of Motown* (New York: Warner Books, 1995).

Goss, Glenda Dawn, ed. *The Sibelius Companion* (Westport, CT: Greenwood Press, 1996).

Gourse, Leslie. *Billie Holiday: The Tragedy and Triumph of Lady Day* (New York: Franklin Watts, 1995).

——. *Blowing on the Changes: The Art of the Jazz Horn Players* (New York: Franklin Watts, 1997).

——. *Dizzy Gillespie and the Birth of Bebop* (New York: Atheneum, 1994).

——. *Mahalia Jackson: Queen of Gospel Song* (New York: Franklin Watts, 1996).

——. *Sassy: The Life of Sarah Vaughan* (New York: C. Scribner's Sons, 1993).

——. *Straight, No Chaser: The Life and Genius of Thelonious Monk* (New York: Schirmer Books, 1977).

——. *The Ella Fitzgerald Companion: Seven Decades of Commentary* (New York: Schirmer, 1998).

——. *Unforgettable: The Life and Mystique of Nat King Cole* (New York: St. Martin's Press, 1992).

Govenar, Alan. *Meeting the Blues* (Dallas, TX: Taylor Publishing, 1988).

Gracie, Andrew. *Kurt Cobain* (Broomall, PA: Chelsea House Publishers, 1997).

Gradenwitz, Peter. *The Music of Israel* (Portland, OR: Amadeus Press, 1996).

Grafton, David. *Red, Hot, and Rich! An Oral History of Cole Porter* (New York: Stein and Day, 1987).

Gray, Marcus. *It Crawled from the South: An R.E.M. Companion* (New York: Da Capo Press, 1997).

Green, Benny. *The Reluctant Art: Five Studies in the Growth of Jazz* (New York: Da Capo Press, 1991).

Green, Richard L. ed. *A Salute to Historic Blacks in the Arts* (Chicago, IL: Empak, 1996).

Green, Stanley. *Broadway Musicals: Show By Show* (Milwaukee, WI: H. Leonard Publishing, 1985).

——. *The World of Musical Comedy* (New York: A. S. Barnes & Co., 1980).

Greer, Jim. *R.E.M.: Behind the Mask* (Boston MA: Little, Brown & Co., 1994).

Gregory, Hugh. *One Thousand Great Guitarists* (San Francisco, CA: GPI Books, 1994).

Gribin, Anthony J., and Matthew M. Schiff. *Doo-wop: The Forgotten Third of Rock'n'Roll* (Iola, WI: Krause Publications, 1992).

Gridley, Mark C. *Concise Guide to Jazz* (Upper Saddle River, NJ: Prentice Hall, 1998).

——. *Jazz Styles: History and Analysis* (Englewood Cliffs, NJ: Prentice Hall, 1985).

Griffiths, Paul. *Modern Music: A Concise History* (New York: Thames and Hudson, 1994).

——. *Stravinsky* (New York: Schirmer Books, 1993).

Gruden, Heidi von. *The Music of Lou Harrison* (Metuchen, NJ: Scarecrow Press, 1995).

Gruen, John. *Menotti: A Biography* (New York: Macmillan, 1978).

Guilbault, Jocelyne, et al. *Zouk: World Music in the West Indies* (Chicago, IL: University of Chicago Press, 1993).

Guralnick, Peter. *Last Train to Memphis: The Rise of Elvis Presley* (Boston, MA: Little, Brown & Co., 1994).

——. *Searching for Robert Johnson* (New York: E. P. Dutton, 1992).

Guthrie, Woody. *Pastures of Plenty: A Self-Portrait* (New York: HarperCollins, 1990).

——. *Seeds of Man* (Lincoln, NE: University of Nebraska Press, 1995).

Haa, Erikka. *Boogie Nights: The Disco Age* (New York: Friedman/Fairfax, 1994).

——. *Soul* (New York: Friedman/Fairfax Publishers, 1995).

Haggard, Merle, and Peggy Russell. *Sing Me Back Home* (New York: Times Books, 1981).

Haggin, B. H. *Conversations with Arturo Toscanini: Contemporary Recollections of the Maestro* (New York: Da Capo Press, 1989).

Halbreich, Harry, trans. Roger Nichols. *Arthur Honegger* (Portland, OR: Amadeus Press, 1998).

Haley, John W. and John von Hoelle. *Sound and Glory: The Incredible Story of Bill Haley* (Wilmington, DE: Dyne-American, 1990).

Hall, Fred. *It's About Time: The Dave Brubeck Story* (Fayetteville, AR: University of Arkansas Press, 1996).

Hamlisch, M., et al. *A Chorus Line: The Book of the Musical* (New York: Applause Musical Library, 1991).

Hamm, Charles. *Yesterdays: Popular Song in America* (New York: W. W. Norton, 1979).

Hardinge, Melissa. *Elvis Presley* (Philadelphia, PA: Chelsea House, 1997).

Harpole, Patricia W. *Los Mariachis! An Introduction to Mexican Mariachi Music* (Danbury, CT: World Music Press, 1989).

Harris, Craig. *The New Folk Music* (Crown Point, IN: White Cliffs Media Co., 1991).

Harris, Daphne. *Black Pearls: Blues Queens of the 1920s* (New Brunswick, NJ: Rutgers University Press, 1988).

Harris, Michael W. *The Rise of Gospel Blues: The Music of Thomas Andrew Dorsey in the Urban Church* (New York: Oxford University Press, 1992).

Hart, Philip. *Conductors: A New Generation* (New York: C. Scribner's Sons, 1983).

Haskins, James. *Queen of the Blues: A Biography of Dinah Washington* (New York: W. Morrow, 1987).

——, and Kathleen Benson, *Lena: A Biography of Lena Horne* (New York: Madison Books, 1991).

Hasse, John Edward. *Beyond Category: The Life and Genius of Duke Ellington* (New York: Simon & Schuster, 1993).

Hawes, Esme. *The Life and Times of Frank Sinatra* (Philadelphia, PA: Chelsea House, 1997).

Headlam, Dave. *The Music of Alban Berg* (New Haven, CT: Yale University Press, 1996).

Hebdige, Dick. *Cut 'n' Mix: Culture, Identity, and Caribbean Music* (New York: Methuen, 1987).

Heilbut, Antony. *The Gospel Sounds: Good News and Bad Times* (New York: Limelight, 1997).

Hemming, Roy. *The Melody Lingers On: The Great Songwriters and Their Movie Musicals* (New York: Newmarket Press, 1986).

Hennessee, Don A. *Samuel Barber: A Bio-bibliography* (Westport, CT: Greenwood Press, 1985).

Henze, Hans Werner. *Music and Politics* (Ithaca, NY: Cornell University Press, 1982).

Herman, Jerry, and Marilyn Stasio. *Showtune: A Memoir* (New York: Donald I. Fine, 1978).

Hess, Carol A. *Enrique Granados: A Bio-bibliography* (New York: Greenwood Press, 1991).

Hewitt, Paolo. *Getting High: The Adventures of Oasis* (New York: Hyperion, 1997).

Heylin, Clinton. *From the Velvets to the Voidoids* (New York: Penguin, 1993).

Heyman, Barbara. *Samuel Barber* (New York: Oxford University Press, 1992).

Heyworth, Peter. *Otto Klemperer: His Life and Times* (New York: Cambridge University Press, 1996).

Hill, Dave. *Prince: A Pop Life* (New York: Harmony Books, 1989).

Hill, Edward Burlingame. *Modern French Music* (Westport, CT: Greenwood Press, 1970).

Hill, Peter, ed. *The Messiaen Companion* (Portland, OR: Amadeus Press, 1995).

Hillmore, Peter. *Live Aid: World-Wide Concert Book* (Parsipanny, NJ: Unicorn Publishing House, 1985).

Hirschhorn, Clive. *The Hollywood Musical* (New York: Portland House, 1991).

Hirshey, Gerri. *Nowhere to Run: The Story of Soul Music* (New York: Da Capo Press, 1994).

Hoare, Philip. *Noel Coward: A Biography* (Chicago, IL: University of Chicago Press, 1998).

Hodkinson, Mark. *Queen: The Early Years* (New York: Omnibus, 1995).

Hoffman, Matthew. *Tony Bennett* (New York: MetroBooks, 1997).

Hogan, Peter. *The Complete Guide to the Music of Queen* (New York: Omnibus, 1994).

Holmes, T. B. *Electronic and Experimental Music* (New York: C. Scribner's Sons, 1985).

Holorny, Linda. *Blur: An Illustrated Biography* (New York: Omnibus, 1996).

Holroyde, Peggy. *The Music of India* (New York: Praeger, 1972).

Holst, Imogen. *Gustav Holst: A Biography* (New York: Oxford University Press, 1988).

Hopkins, J. *Bowie* (New York: Macmillan, 1985).

Horowitz, Joseph. *Conversations with Arrau* (New York: Limelight, 1984).

Hotchner, A. E. *Blown Away: The Rolling Stones and the Death of the Sixties* (New York: Simon & Schuster, 1990).

Howard, Brett. *Lena Horne: Singer and Actress* (New York: Holloway House, 1991).

Howard, Quentin. *Sukay Workbook* (San Francisco, CA: Sukay, 1988).

Howell, Tim. *Jean Sibelius: Progressive Techniques in the Symphonies and Tone Poems* (New York: Garland Publications, 1989).

Hyland, William G. *Richard Rodgers* (New Haven, CT: Yale University Press, 1998).

Ivashkin, Alexander. *Alfred Schnittke* (New York: Phaidon Press Inc., 1996).

Jablonski, Edward. *Harold Arlen: Rhythm, Raincoat, and Blues* (Boston, MA: Northeastern University Press, 1996).

Jackson, John A. *Big Beat Heat: Alan Freed and the Early Years of Rock'n'roll* (New York: Schirmer Books, 1991).

Jackson, Stanley. *Letters of Giacomo Puccini* (New York: AMS Press, 1971).

Jacobson, Bernard. *Conductors on Conducting* (Frenchtown, NJ: Columbia Publishing Co., 1979).

James, Burnett. *Bix Beiderbecke* (New York: A. S. Barnes & Co., 1988).

——. *Coleman Hawkins* (New York: Hippocrene Books, 1984).

Jameux, Dominique. *Pierre Boulez* (Cambridge, MA: Harvard University Press, 1990).

Janácek, Leos, et al. *Janácek: Leaves from His Life* (New York: Taplinger Publishing, 1982).

Jarman, Douglas. *Kurt Weill, An Illustrated Biography* (Bloomington, IN: Indiana University Press, 1982).

Jasper, Tony. *Eurythmics* (Port Chester, NY: Cherry Lane, 1985).

Jefferson, Alan. *Elisabeth Schwarzkopf* (Boston, MA: Northeastern University Press, 1995).

Jelavich, P. *Berlin Cabaret* (Cambridge, MA: Harvard University Press, 1993).

Jennings, Waylon, with Lenny Kaye. *Waylon: An Autobiography* (New York: Warner Books, 1996).

Jones, Hettie. *Big Star Fallin' Mama: Five Women in Black Music* (New York: Viking, 1995).

Jones, Liz. *Purple Reign: The Artist Formerly Known as Prince* (Secaucus, NJ: Carol Publishing Group, 1998).

Jones, M. *Patsy* (New York: HarperCollins, 1996).

Jones, Peter. *Tom Jones* (Chicago, IL: Regnery, 1970).

Jost, Ekkehard. *Free Jazz* (New York: Da Capo Press, 1994).

Kalet, Beth. *Kris Kristofferson* (New York: Quick Fox, 1979).

Kamhi de Rodrigo, Victoria, trans. Ellen Wilkerson. *Hand in Hand with Joaquin Rodrigo: My Life at the Maestro's Side* (Pittsburgh, PA: Latin American Literary Review Press, 1992).

Kamin, Philip, and Peter Goddard. *The Who: The Farewell Tour* (New York: Beaufort Books, 1983).

Karpp, Phyllis. *Ike's Boys: The Story of the Everly Brothers* (Ann Arbor, MI: Pierian Press, 1988).

Kasha, Al, and Joel Hirschhorn. *Notes on Broadway* (New York: Simon & Schuster, 1987).

Kaufman, Frederick, and John P. Guckin. *The African Roots of Jazz* (Sherman Oaks, CA: Alfred Publishing, 1979).

Kaufmann, Walter. *The Ragas of South India* (Bloomington, IN: Indiana University Press, 1976).

Kavanaugh, Lee Hill. *Quincy Jones: Musician, Composer, Producer* (Springfield, NJ: Enslow, 1997).

Keck, George R. *Francis Poulenc: a Bio-bibliography* (New York: Greenwood Press, 1990).

Keetman, Gunild, and Carl Orff. *Music for Children* (New York: Schott, 1963).

Kehler, George. *The Piano in Concert, Vol. 2* (Metuchen, NJ: Scarecrow Press, 1982).

Keith, Michael C. *Voices in the Purple Haze: Underground Radio and the Sixties* (Westport, CT: Praeger, 1997).

Kemp, Ian. *Tippett, The Composer and His Music* (New York: Da Capo Press, 1984).

Kennedy, Michael. *Portrait of Elgar* (New York: Oxford University Press, 1995).

——. *Richard Strauss* (New York: Schirmer Books, 1996).

——. *Turn of the Century Masters* (New York: Norton, 1984).

Kesting, Jürgen, trans. John Hunt. *Maria Callas* (Boston, MA: Northeastern University Press, 1993).

——, trans. Susan H. Ray. *Luciano Pavarotti: The Myth of the Tenor* (Boston, MA: Northeastern University Press, 1991).

Kiersh, Edward. *Where Are You Now, Bo Diddley?* (Garden City, New York: Doubleday, 1986).

King, B. B., and David Ritz. *Blues All Around Me: The Autobiography of B. B. King* (New York: Avon, 1996).

Kirk, H. L. *Pablo Casals: A Biography* (New York: Henry Holt, 1974).

Kirkeby, W. T., ed. *Ain't Misbehavin': the Story of Fats Waller* (New York: Da Capo Press, 1975).

Kislan, Richard. *The Musical: A Look at the American Musical Theater* (New York: Applause Theater Books, 1995).

Klein, Joe. *Woody Guthrie: A Life* (New York: Alfred A. Knopf, 1980).

Klinkowitz, Jerome. *Listen, Gerry Mulligan: An Aural Narrative in Jazz* (New York: Schirmer Books, 1991).

Koerner, Julie. *Swing Kings* (New York: Friedman/Fairfax Publishers, 1994).

Koseluk, Gregory. *Eddie Cantor: A Life in Show Business* (Jefferson, NC: McFarland, 1995).

Kostelanetz, Richard, ed. *The Frank Zappa Companion: Four Decades of Commentary* (New York: Schirmer Books, 1997).

——. *John Cage (ex)plain(ed)* (New York: Schirmer Books, 1996).

Kressley, David, and Charles Garrod. *Guy Lombardo and His Royal Canadians* (Zephyrhills, FL: Joyce Record Club Publications, 1995).

Kreuger, Miles. *Show Boat: The Story of a Classic American Musical* (New York: Applause, 1995).

Krishef, Robert K. *Loretta Lynn* (Minneapolis, MN: Lerner Publications Co., 1978).

——, and Stacy Harris. *The Carter Family: Country Music's First Family* (Minneapolis, MN: Lerner Publications Co., 1978).

Krugman, Michael. *Oasis: Supersonic Supernova* (New York: St. Martin's Griffin, 1997).

Kurtz, Michael, trans. Richard Toop. *Stockhausen: A Biography* (Boston, MA: Faber and Faber, 1992).

La Grange, Henry-Louis de. *Gustav Mahler* (New York: Oxford University Press, 1995).

Lacoren, Nelson. *Mercedes Sosa Poems: The New Woman* (New York: Latin Culture Productions, 1990).

Laine, Frankie. *That Lucky Old Son: The Autobiography of Frankie Laine* (Ventura, CA: Pathfinder, 1993).

Lambert, Philip. *The Music of Charles Ives* (New Haven, CT: Yale University Press, 1997).

Large, Brian. *Martinu* (New York: Holmes & Meier, 1976).

Laubich, Arnold, and Ray Spencer. *Art Tatum, a Guide to His Recorded Music* (Metuchen, NJ: Scarecrow, 1982).

Layton, Robert. *Sibelius* (New York: Schirmer Books, 1993).

Lebrecht, Norman. *The Maestro Myth* (Secaucus, NJ: Carol Publishing Group, 1991).

Ledbetter, Gordon T. *The Great Irish Tenor* (New York: Charles Scribner's Sons, 1977).

Lee, Peggy. *Miss Peggy Lee: An Autobiography* (New York: D. Fine, 1989).

Lees, Gene. *Inventing Champagne: The Worlds of Lerner and Loewe* (New York: St. Martin's Press, 1990).

——. *The Singer and The Song* (New York: Oxford University Press, 1987).

Legrand, Michel, with George Mendoza. *Michel's Mixed-up Musical Bird* (Indianapolis IN: Bobbs-Merrill, 1978).

Lennon, Nigey. *Being Frank: My Time with Frank Zappa* (Los Angeles, CA: California Classic Books, 1995).

Lester, James. *Too Marvellous for Words: The Life and Genius of Art Tatum* (New York: Oxford University Press, 1994).

Lewis, G. H. *All That Glitters: Country Music in America* (Bowling Green, OH: Bowling Green State University Popular Press, 1993).

Lewis, M., with M. Silver. *Great Balls of Fire!* (New York: St. Martin's Press, 1989).

Lieb, Sandra. *Mother of the Blues: A Study of Ma Rainey* (Amherst, VA: University of Massachusetts Press, 1983).

Linakis, Steven. *Diva: The Life and Death of Maria Callas* (Englewood Cliffs, NJ: Prentice Hall, 1980).

Lindenberger, H. *Opera in History: from Monteverdi to Cage* (Stanford, CA: Stanford University Press, 1998).

Lindrall, Marianne. *ABBA: The Ultimate Pop Group* (Edmonton, Canada: Hurtig, 1977).

Litweiler, John. *Ornette Coleman* (New York: Da Capo Press, 1994).

——. *The Freedom Principle: Jazz After 1958* (New York: Da Capo Press, 1984).

Lochner, Louis P. *Fritz Kreisler* (St. Clair Shores, MI: Scholarly Press, 1977).

Loesser, Susan. *A Most Remarkable Fella: Frank Loesser and the Guys and Dolls in His Life: A Portrait by his Daughter* (New York: Donald I. Fine Inc., 1993).

Logan, Nick, and Bob Woffinden. *The Illustrated Encyclopedia of Rock* (New York: Harmony Books, 1977).

Lomax, Alan. *Folk Song Style and Culture* (Cambridge, MA: Harvard University Press, 1996).

——. *Mister Jelly Roll* (New York: Pantheon Books, 1993).

——. *The Land Where the Blues Began* (New York: Pantheon Books, 1993).

Lomax, John, III. *Nashville: Music City USA* (New York: Abrams, 1985).

Lombardo, Guy, with Jack Altshul. *Auld Acquaintance: An Autobiography* (New York: Doubleday, 1975).

Loney, Glenn. *Twentieth-Century Theater, Vol. 2* (New York: Facts on File Publications, 1983).

Lulow, Kalia. *Barry Manilow* (New York: Ballantine Books, 1985).

Lynch, K. *David Bowie: A Rock'n'roll Odyssey* (New York: Proteus, 1984).

Lynn, Loretta, with George Vecsey. *Loretta Lynn: Coal Miner's Daughter* (New York: Da Capo Press, 1996).

Lyons, Len. *The Great Jazz Pianists: Speaking of Their Lives and Music* (New York: Da Capo Press, 1983).

Lyttelton, Humphrey. *Basin Street to Harlem: Jazz Masters and Masterpieces 1917-30* (New York: Taplinger, 1979).

Macan, Edward. *Rocking The Classics: English Progressive Rock and the Counterculture* (New York: Oxford University Press, 1997).

MacDonagh, Don. *The Complete Guide to Modern Dance* (New York: Doubleday, 1976).

MacDonald, Bruno. *Pink Floyd: Through the Eyes of the Band, Its Fans, Friends, and Foes* (New York: Da Capo Press, 1997).

MacDonald, Ian. *Revolution in the Head: The Beatles Records and the Sixties* (New York: Henry Holt, 1994).

MacFarlane, Colin. *Tom Jones: The Boy from Nowhere* (New York: St. Martin's Press, 1988).

Maconie, Robin. *The Works of Karlheinz Stockhausen* (New York: Oxford University Press, 1990).

Maggin, Donald L. *Stan Getz: A Life in Jazz* (New York: W. Morrow & Co., 1996).

Major, Norma. *Joan Sutherland: The Authorized Biography* (Boston, MA: Little, Brown and Co. 1994).

Makower, Joel. *Woodstock: The Oral History* (New York: Doubleday, 1989).

Malm, William P. *Music Cultures of the Pacific, the Near East, and Asia* (Englewood Cliff, NJ: Prentice Hall, 1995).

Mancini, Henry, with Gene Lees. *Did They Mention the Music?* (Chicago, IL: Contemporary Books, 1989).

Manilow, Barry. *Sweet Life: Adventures on the Way to Paradise* (New York: McGraw-Hill, 1987).

Manion, Martha L. *Writings About Henry Cowell* (New York: Institute for Studies in American Music, 1982).

Mann, William. *James Galway's Music in Time* (New York: Abrams, 1983).

Manuel, Peter, ed. *Essays on Cuban Music: North American and Cuban Perspectives* (Lanham, MD: University Press of America, 1991).

——, et al. *Caribbean Currents: Caribbean Music from Rumba to Reggae* (Philadelphia, PA: Temple University Press, 1995).

March, Robert C. *Dialogues and Discoveries* (New York: C. Scribner's Sons, 1998).

Marcus, Greil. *Invisible Republic: Bob Dylan's Basement Tapes* (New York: Henry Holt, 1997).

Marmorstein, Gary. *A Hollywood Rhapsody: Movie Music and its Makers 1900-75* (New York: Schirmer Books, 1997).

Marsalis, Wynton. *Sweet Swing Blues on the Road* (New York: W.W. Norton, 1994).

Marsh, Dave. *Born to Run* (New York: Thunder's Mouth Press, 1996).

——. *George Clinton and P-Funk: An Oral History* (New York: Avon, 1998).

Marsh, G., and G. Callingham, eds. *California Cool: The Album Cover Art* (San Francisco, CA: Chronicle Books, 1962).

Martin, Bill. *Listening to the Future: The Time of Progressive Rock, 1968–1978* (Chicago, IL: Open Court, 1999).

——. *Music of Yes: Structure and Vision in Progressive Rock* (Chicago IL: Open Court, 1996).

Martyn, Barrie. *Rachmaninov: Composer, Pianist, Conductor* (Brookfield, VT: Grover Publishing Co., 1990).

Mason, Michael, ed. *The Country Music Book* (New York: C. Scribner's Sons, 1985).

Mathews, M. V., and J. R. Pierce. *Current Directions in Computer Music Research* (Cambridge, MA: MIT Press, 1989).

Mawer, Deborah. *Darius Milhaud: Modality and Structure in Music of the 1920s* (Brookfield, VT: Ashgate, 1997).

May, Elizabeth. *Musics of Many Cultures* (Berkeley, CA: University of California Press, 1983).

McAleer, D. *The Fab British Rock'n'Roll Invasion of 1964* (New York: St. Martin's Press, 1994).

McArthur, Edwin. *Flagstad: A Personal Memoir* (New York: Alfred A. Knopf, 1965).

McBrien, William. *Cole Porter: A Biography* (New York: Alfred A. Knopf, 1998).

McCabe, John. *George M. Cohan: The Man Who Owned Broadway* (New York: Da Capo Press, 1980).

McCalla, James. *Twentieth-Century Chamber Music* (New York: Schirmer, 1996).

McCarthy, Albert. *Big Band Jazz* (New York: Berkeley Publishing, 1977).

McClelland, Doug. *Blackface to Blacklist* (Metuchen, NJ: Scarecrow Press, 1987).

McEwen, Joe. *Sam Cooke* (New York: Sire Books, 1977).

McGilligan, Patrick. *Yankee Doodle Dandy* (Madison, WI: University of Wisconsin Press, 1981).

McGowan, Chris, and R. Pessanha. *The Brazilian Sound: Samba, Bossa Nova, and the Popular Music of Brazil* (Philadelphia, PA: Temple University Press, 1997).

McKissack, Pat. *Paul Robeson: A Voice to Remember* (Hillside, NJ: Enslow Publishers, 1992).

McKnight, Gerald. *Andrew Lloyd Webber* (New York: St. Martin's Press, 1984).

McMahon, Jacqueline Higuera. *Salsa* (Lake Hughes, CA: Olive Press, 1986).

McNeil, Legs, and Gillian McCain. *Please Kill Me: The Uncensored Oral History of Punk* (New York: Penguin, 1997).

McSquare, Eddie. *Good Times Bad Times* (New York: Bobcat Books, 1991).

Melba, Nellie. *Melodies and Memories* (Freeport, NY: Books for Libraries Press, 1970).

Mellers, Wilfrid. *Francis Poulenc* (New York: Oxford University Press, 1993).

——. *Percy Grainger* (New York: Oxford University Press, 1992).

Menuhin, Yehudi. *Unfinished Journey: Twenty Years Later* (New York: Fromm International, 1977).

Merriam, Alan P. *African Music in Perspective* (New York: Garland, 1995).

Mertens, Wim. *American Minimal Music: La Monte Young, Terry Riley, Steve Reich, Philip Glass* (New York: Broude, 1983).

Miller, Jim. *The Rolling Stone Illustrated History of Rock & Roll* (New York: Random House/Rolling Stones Press, 1980).

Miller, Mina, ed. *The Nielsen Companion* (Portland, OR: Amadeus Press, 1995).

Mingus, Charles. *Beneath the Underdog* (New York: Penguin Books, 1980).

Minturn, Neil. *The Music of Sergei Prokofiev* (New Haven, CT: Yale University Press, 1997).

Mitchell, Timothy. *Flamenco Deep Song* (New Haven, CT: Yale University Press, 1994).

Moldenhauer, H. and R. *Anton von Webern* (New York: Alfred A. Knopf, 1978).

Monk, R. *Edward Elgar: Music and Literature* (Brookfield, VT: Ashgate Publishing, 1993).

Monteux, Doris. *It's All in the Music* (New York: Farrar, Straus & Giroux, 1965).

Moran, William R. *Nellie Melba: A Contemporary Review* (Westport, CT: Greenwood Press, 1985).

Morehouse, Ward. *George M. Cohan* (Westport, CT: Greenwood Press, 1972).

Morella, Joseph, and George Mazzei. *Genius and Lust: The Creativity and Sexuality of Cole Porter and Noel Coward* (New York: Carroll & Graf, 1995).

Morgan, Robert P. *Twentieth Century Music* (New York: W. W. Norton, 1991).

Moriarty, Frank. *Johnny Cash* (New York: Metro Books, 1977).

Morse, Tim. *Yesstories: Yes in Their Own Words* (New York: St. Martin's Press, 1996).

Morton, Brian, ed., and Pamela Collins. *Contemporary Composers* (Chicago, IL: St. James Press, 1992).

Murphy, Agnes G. *Melba: A Biography* (New York: Da Capo Press, 1977).

Murray, Charles Shaar. *Crosstown Traffic* (New York: St. Martin's Press, 1989).

Nectoux, Jean-Michel, trans. Roger Nichols. *Gabriel Fauré: A Musical Life* (New York: Cambridge University Press, 1991).

Negus, Keith. *Producing Pop: Culture and Conflict in the Popular Music Industry* (New York: Routledge, Chapman, and Hall, 1992).

Nelson, P. *"Folk Rock" from The Rolling Stone Illustrated History of Rock'n'roll* (New York: Random House, 1992).

Nelson, Willie, and Bud Shrake. *Willie: An Autobiography* (New York: Simon & Schuster, 1988).

Neumeyer, David. *The Music of Paul Hindemith* (New Haven, CT: Yale University Press, 1986).

Newsom, Jon, ed. *Perspectives on John Philip Sousa* (Washington, DC: Library of Congress, Music Division, 1983).

Nichols, Roger. *Ravel Remembered* (New York: W. W. Norton, 1988).

Nicholson, Lois P. *Michael Jackson* (New York: Chelsea House, 1994).

Nicholson, Stuart. *Ella Fitzgerald* (New York: C. Scribner's Sons, 1993).

——. *Jazz Rock: A History* (New York: Schirmer Books, 1998).

——. *Jazz: The 1980s Resurgence* (New York: Da Capo Press, 1995).

Nikart, Ray. *Sting and The Police* (New York: Ballantine Books, 1985).

Nisbet, Alec. *The Sound Studio* (Boston, MA: Focal Press, 1995).

Nisenson, Eric. *Ascension: John Coltrane and His Quest* (New York: St. Martin's Press, 1993).

Norman, Philip. *Elton John* (New York: Simon & Schuster, 1993).

Norris, Geoffrey. *Rachmaninov* (New York: Schirmer Books, 1994).

Noss, Luther. *Paul Hindemith in the United States* (Urbana, IL: University of Illinois Press, 1989).

Obrecht, Jas. *Blues Guitar* (Milwaukee, WI: H. Leonard Publishing, 1990).

O'Connell, Charles. *The Other Side of the Record* (Westport, CT: Greenwood Press, 1970).

O'Donnell, Red. *Country Gentleman* (New York: Amereon, 1976).

Ohtake, Noriko. *Creative Sources for the Music of Toru Takemitsu* (Brookfield, VT: Ashgate, 1993).

Old, Wendy C. *Louis Armstrong: King of Jazz* (Springfield, NJ: Enslow, 1998).

Oldfield, Michael. *Dire Straits* (New York: Quill, 1984).

Oliver, Paul. *The Story of the Blues* (New York: Chilton Book Co., 1969).

Olsen, Dale A. *Music of the Warao of Venezuela: Song People of the Rain Forest* (Gainesville, FL: University Press of Florida, 1996).

Orenstein, Arbie. *Ravel: Man and Musician* (New York: Dover Publications, 1991).

Orledge, Robert. *Satie the Composer* (New York: Cambridge University Press, 1990).

Owens, Thomas. *Bebop: The Music and Its Players* (New York: Oxford University Press, 1995).

Palmer, Christopher. *Delius: Portrait of a Cosmopolitan* (New York: Holmes & Meier, 1976).

——. *Impressionism in Music* (New York: C. Scribner's Sons, 1974).

Palmer, Robert. *Baby, That Was Rock and Roll: The Legendary Leiber and Stoller* (New York: Harcourt Brace Jovanovich, 1978).

——. *Deep Blues* (New York: Penguin Books, 1981).

Parks, Richard S. *The Music of Claude Debussy* (New Haven, CT: Yale University Press, 1989).

Parton, Dolly. *Dolly: My Life and Other Unfinished Business* (Thorndike, ME: Thorndike Press, 1995).

Passman, Donald S. *All You Need to Know About the Music Business* (New York: Simon & Schuster, 1991).

Pavarotti, Luciano, and William Wright. *My World* (New York: Crown Publishers, 1995).

Payzant, Geoffrey. *Glenn Gould: Music and Mind* (Toronto, Canada: Key Porter, 1992).

Peare, Catherine. *Aaron Copland: His Life* (New York: Holt, Rinehart, and Winston, 1969).

Perle, George. *The Operas of Alban Berg* (Berkeley, CA: University of California Press, 1980–84).

Peterson, David, and Dick Denney. *The Vox Story: A Complete History of the Legend* (Westport, CT: Bold Strummer, 1993).

Pettinger, Peter. *Bill Evans: How My Heart Sings* (New Haven, CT: Yale University Press, 1998).

Peyser, Joan. *Boulez: Composer, Conductor, Enigma* (New York: Macmillan, 1976).

Pischl, A. J., and S. J. Cohen, eds. *Composer/Choreographer* (New York: Dance Perspectives, 1963).

Platt, John. *Disraeli Gears: Cream* (New York: Schirmer Books, 1998).

Polic, Edward F. *The Glenn Miller Army Air Force Band* (Metuchen, NJ: Scarecrow Press, 1989).

Polk, Keith. *German Instrumental Music of the Late Middle Ages: Players, Patrons, and Performance Practice* (New York: Cambridge University Press, 1992).

Porter, Lewis, ed. *A Lester Young Reader* (Washington, DC: Smithsonian Institution Press, 1991).

——. *Jazz: A Century of Change* (New York: Schirmer Books, 1997).

——. *John Coltrane: His Life and Music* (Ann Arbor, MI: University of Michigan Press, 1997).

Porterfield, Nolan. *Jimmie Rodgers: The Life and Times of America's Blue Yodeler* (Champaign, IL: University of Illinois Press, 1992).

Potash, C., ed. *Reggae, Rasta, Revolution: Jamaican Music from Ska to Dub* (New York: Schirmer Books, 1997).

Prendergast, Roy. *Film Music: A Neglected Art* (New York: W. W. Norton, 1977).

Previn, André. *No Minor Chords: My Days in Hollywood* (New York: Doubleday, 1991).

Pride, Charley, with Jim Henderson. *Pride: the Charley Pride Story* (New York: W. Morrow, 1994).

Pride, Dominic. *Jungle: The Beat Goes On* (Billboard, April 15, 1995).

Priestley, Brian. *Mingus: A Critical Biography* (New York: Da Capo Press, 1984).

Pritchett, James. *The Music of John Cage* (New York: Cambridge University Press, 1993).

Pruter, Robert. *Doo-wop: The Chicago Scene* (Urbana, IL: University of Illinois Press, 1996).

Pugh, Ronnie. *Ernest Tubb: The Texas Troubadour* (Durham, NC: Duke University Press, 1996).

Quellette, Fernand, trans. Derek Coltman. *Edgard Varèse* (New York: Da Capo Press, 1981).

Rasponi, Lanfranco. *The Last Prima Donnas* (New York: Alfred A. Knopf, 1982).

Reed, Lou. *Between Thought and Expression* (New York: Hyperion Books, 1991).

Reilly, Jack. *The Harmony of Bill Evans* (Milwaukee, WI: H. Leonard Publishing, 1982).

Respighi, Elsa, et al. *Fifty Years of a Life in Music, 1905–55* (Lewiston, NY: E. Mellen Press, 1993).

Rettenmund, M. *Encyclopedia Madonnica* (New York: St. Martin's Press, 1995).

Ribowsky, Mark. *He's a Rebel* (New York: Dutton, 1989).

Rich, Alan. *Classical Music: Orchestra* (New York: Simon & Schuster, 1980).

Richart, Robert W. *György Ligeti: A Bio-bibliography* (New York: Greenwood Press, 1990).

Richman, Saul. *Guy: The Life and Times of Guy Lombardo* (New York: RichGuy Publishing, 1978).

Ritz, David. *Divided Soul: The Life of Marvin Gaye* (New York: Da Capo Press, 1986).

——. *Ray Charles: Voice of Soul* (New York: Chelsea House, 1994).

Robbins, Ira. *The Trouser Press Record Guide* (New York: Collier, 1991).

Roberts, Paul. *Images: The Piano Music of Claude Debussy* (Portland, OR: Amadeus Press, 1996).

Robinson, Paul. *Opera and Ideas: From Mozart to Strauss* (Ithaca, NY: Cornell University Press, 1986).

——. *Solti* (Toronto, Canada: Lester and Orpen, 1979).

Robinson, Ray. *Krzysztof Penderecki: A Guide to His Works* (Princeton, NJ: Prestige Publications, 1983).

Rodgers, Carrie C. W. *My Husband, Jimmie Rodgers* (Nashville, TN: Country Music Foundation, 1975).

Rodgers, Richard. *Musical Stages: An Autobiography* (New York: Da Capo Press, 1995).

Rogan, Johnny. *Wham! Death of a Supergroup* (New York: Omnibus Press, 1987).

Rolfe, Lionel Menuhin. *The Menuhins: A Family Odyssey* (San Francisco, CA: Panjandrum/Aris Books, 1978).

Roman, Zoltan. *Gustav Mahler's American Years, 1907-11* (Stuyvesant, NY: Pendragon Press, 1989).

Rooney, James. *Bossmen: Bill Monroe and Muddy Waters* (New York: Da Capo Press, 1991).

Rose, C. *Living in America: The Soul Saga of James Brown* (New York: Serpent's Tail, 1991).

Rosen, Charles. *Arnold Schoenberg* (Chicago, IL: University of Chicago Press, 1996).

Rosensteil, Léonie. *Nadia Boulanger: A Life in Music* (New York: W. W. Norton, 1982).

Rosenthal, David H. *Hard Bop: Jazz and Black Music 1955-65* (New York: Oxford University Press, 1992).

Ross, Courtney. *Back on the Block: A Portrait of Quincy Jones* (New York: Warner Books, 1990).

Ross, Diana. *Secrets of a Sparrow: Memoirs* (New York: Villard Books, 1993).

Rostropovich, M., with C. Samuel. *Mstislav Rostropovich and Galina Vishnevskaya: Russia, Music and Liberty* (Portland, OR: Amadeus Press, 1988).

Rowe, M. *Chicago Blues: The City and the Music* (New York: Da Capo Press, 1979).

Rubinstein, A. *My Many Years* (New York: Alfred A. Knopf, 1980).

Ruppli, Michel. *The Clef/Verve Labels: A Discography* (New York: Greenwood Press, 1986).

Russell, Tony. *The Blues: From Robert Johnson to Robert Cray* (New York: Schirmer Books, 1998).

Ruttencutter, Helen Drees. *Previn* (New York: St. Martin's/Marek, 1986).

Ruuth, Marianne. *Nat King Cole* (Los Angeles, CA: Melrose Square Publishing, 1992).

Sachs, Harvey. *Rubinstein: A Life* (New York: Grove Press, 1995).

——. *Toscanini* (Rocklin, CA: Prima Pub., 1995).

——. *Virtuoso: The Life and Art of . . . Fritz Kreisler* (New York: Thames and Hudson, 1982).

——. *Virtuoso: The Life and Art of . . . Glenn Gould* (New York: Thames and Hudson, 1982).

Sadie, J. A., and R. Samuel, eds. *Grove Dictionary of Women Composers* (New York: Norton, 1994).

Saerchinger, César. *Artur Schnabel: A Biography* (Westport, CT: Greenwood Press, 1973).

Salvador-Daniel, Francesco. *The Music and Musical Instruments of the Arab* (Portland, ME: Longwood Press, 1976).

Salzman, Eric. *20th-Century Music: An Introduction* (Englewood Cliffs, NJ: Prentice Hall, 1988).

Samson, Jim. *The Music of Szymanowski* (New York: Taplinger, 1981).

Samuel, Claude. *Prokofiev* (New York: Marion Boyars, 1998).

Sansevere, J. R., and E. Farber. *Grunge—Inside Seattle's Music* (Racine, WI: Western Publishing Co., 1993).

Santoro, Gene. *Dancing in Your Head: Jazz, Blues, Rock, and Beyond* (New York: Oxford University Press, 1994).

Sargeant, Winthrop. *Divas* (New York: Coward, McCann & Geoghegan, 1973).

Saunders, Susan. *Dolly Parton, Country Goin' to Town* (New York: Puffin Books, 1986).

Savage, Jeff. *Whitney Houston* (Parsippany, NJ: Dillon Press, 1998).

Savage, Jon. *England's Dreaming* (New York: St. Martin's Press, 1992).

——. *The Kinks: The Official Biography* (Boston, MA: Faber and Faber, 1984).

Scaduto, A. *Bob Dylan* (New York: Putnam, 1972).

Schaffner, N. *The British Invasion* (New York: McGraw-Hill, 1983).

Schiesel, Jane. *The Otis Redding Story* (Garden City, NY: Doubleday, 1973).

Schiff, David. *Gershwin: Rhapsody in Blue* (New York: Cambridge University Press, 1997).

——. *The Music of Elliott Carter* (New York: Eulenberg, 1983).

Schneider, Wayne. *The Gershwin Style* (New York: Oxford University Press, 1998).

Schoenberg, Harold C. *Horowitz: His Life and Music* (New York: Simon & Schuster, 1992).

——. *The Great Pianists* (New York: Simon & Schuster, 1987).

Schoffman, Nachum. *From Chords to Simultaneities: Chordal Indeterminacy and the Failure of Serialism* (New York: Greenwood Press, 1990).

Schonzeler, Hans-Hubert. *Furtwängler* (Portland, OR: Amadeus Press, 1990).

Schuller, Gunther. *Early Jazz* (New York: Oxford University Press, 1986).

——. *The Swing Era: The Development of Jazz, 1930–1945* (New York: Oxford University Press, 1989).

Schumacher, Michael. *Crossroads: The Life and Music of Eric Clapton* (New York: Hyperion, 1995).

Schutz, Susan Polis, ed. *You've Got a Friend: Poetic Selections from the Songs of Carole King* (Boulder, CO: Blue Mountain Press, 1978).

——. *What the World Needs Now Is Love* (Boulder, CO: Blue Mountain Press, 1979).

Schwartz, Boris. *Great Masters of the Violin* (New York: Simon & Schuster, 1983).

Schwinger, Wolfram, trans. William Mann. *Krzysztof Penderecki: His Life and Work* (New York: Schott, 1989).

Sclappi, Elizabeth. *Roy Acuff: The Smoky Mountain Boy* (Gretna, LA: Pelican Publishing Co., 1993).

Scoey, Lola. *Willie Nelson, Country Outlaw* (New York: Zebra Books, 1982).

Scruggs, Earl. *Earl Scruggs and the Five String Banjo* (Philadelphia, PA: Theodore Presser, 1980).

Sebesky, Don. *The Contemporary Arranger* (Van Nuys, CA: Alfred Publishing Co., 1994).

Secrest, Meryle. *Leonard Bernstein: A Life* (New York: Vintage Books, 1995).

———. *Stephen Sondheim: A Life* (New York: Alfred A Knopf, 1998).

Seeger, Pete, and Bob Reisner. *Everybody Says Freedom: A History of the Civil Rights Movement in Songs and Pictures* (New York: W. W. Norton, 1989).

Segal, Harold. *Turn-of-the-Century Cabaret* (New York: Schirmer Books, 1996).

Segovia, Andrés. *Andrés Segovia: An Autobiography of the Years 1893–1920* (New York: Macmillan, 1976).

Sellers, Robert. *Sting: A Biography* (New York: Omnibus Press, 1989).

Selvin, Joel. *Monterey Pop: San Francisco* (San Francisco: Chronicle Books, 1992).

Sennett, Ted. *Hollywood Musicals* (New York: Harry N. Abrams, 1981).

Shankar, Ravi. *Drops of Light: Discourses in Santa Barbara* (Santa Barbara, CA: Art of Living Foundation, 1990).

———. *Learning Indian Music: A Systematic Approach* (Ft. Lauderdale, FL: Onomatopoeia, 1979).

Shapiro, H., and C. Glebbeek. *Electric Gypsy* (New York: St. Martin's Press, 1990).

Shapiro, Marc. *The Long Run: The Story of the Eagles* (New York: Omnibus, 1995).

Shapiro, Nat, and Nat Hentoff, eds. *The Jazz Makers* (New York: Da Capo Press, 1979).

Shapiro, Robert. *Germaine Tailleferre: A Bio-bibliography* (Westport, CT: Greenwood Press, 1994).

Shaw, Arnold. *Black Popular Music in America* (New York: Schirmer Books, 1986).

Sheafer, Silvia Anne. *Aretha Franklin: Motown Superstar* (Springfield, NJ: Enslow Publishers, 1996).

Shelton, Robert. *No Direction Home: The Life and Music of Bob Dylan* (New York: Da Capo Press, 1997).

Shepard, Sam. *Rolling Thunder Logbook* (New York: Viking, 1977).

Sheridan, Chris. *Count Basie: A Bio-discography* (Westport, CT: Greenwood Press, 1986).

Sherlaw Johnson, Robert. *Messiaen* (New York: Oxford University Press, 1994).

Sherman, B. D. *Inside Early Music* (New York: Oxford University Press, 1997).

Shiloah, Amnon. *The Dimension of Music in Islamic and Jewish Culture* (Brookfield, VT: Variorum, 1993).

Shipman, David. *Judy Garland: The Secret Life of an American Legend* (New York: Hyperion, 1992).

Shipton, Alyn. *Fats Waller: His Life and Times* (New York: Universe Books, 1988).

Shirley, David. *Every Day I Sing the Blues: The Story of B. B. King* (New York: Franklin Watts, 1995).

Shore, Bernard. *The Orchestra Speaks* (Freeport, NY: Books for Libraries Press, 1972).

Short, Michael. *Gustav Holst: The Man and His Music* (New York: Oxford University Press, 1990).

Silvester, Peter J. *A Left Hand Like God: A History of Boogie Woogie Piano* (New York: Da Capo Press, 1989).

Simms, Bryan R. *Music of the Twentieth Century: Style and Structure* (New York: Schirmer, 1986).

Simon, George. *Glenn Miller and His Orchestra* (New York: Da Capo Press, 1988).

———. *The Big Bands* (New York: Schirmer Books, 1981).

Simone, Nina, and Stephen Cleary. *I Put a Spell on You* (New York: Pantheon, 1991).

Simpson, Robert. *Carl Nielsen: Symphonist, 1865-1931* (Westport, CT: Hyperion Press, 1979).

Sklar, Rick. *Rocking America: An Insider's Story: How the All-Hit Radio Stations Took Over* (New York: St. Martin's Press, 1984).

Smith, Betty. *Journey to Valhalla: The Lauritz Melchior Story* (New York: Paragon House, 1992).

Smith, Carolyn J. *William Walton: A Bio-bibliography* (New York: Greenwood Press, 1988).

Smith, Steven C. *A Heart at Fire's Center* (Berkeley, CA: University of California Press, 1991).

Smith-Brindle, Reginald. *The New Music: The Avant-garde Since 1945* (New York: Oxford University Press, 1987).

Somosko, V., and B. Teppeman. *Eric Dolphy: A Musical Biography and Discography* (New York: Da Capo Press, 1996).

Sousa, John Philip. *Marching Along: Recollections of Men, Women, and Music* (Westerville, OH: Integrity Press, 1994).

Spada, James. *Streisand: Her Life* (New York: Crown Publishers, 1995).

Spycket, Jerome. *Nadia Boulanger* (Stuyvesant, NY: Pendragon Press, 1992).

Stefoff, Rebecca. *Placido Domingo* (New York: Chelsea House, 1992).

Stehman, Dan. *Roy Harris: An American Musical Pioneer* (Boston, MA: Twayne Publisher, 1984).

Steine, J. B. *The Grand Tradition* (Portland, OR: Amadeus Press, 1993).

Stevens, Gary, and Alan George. *The Longest Line: Broadway's Most Singular Sensation* (New York: Applause Theater Books, 1995).

Stewart, Gary. *Breakout: Profiles in African Rhythms* (Chicago, IL: University of Chicago Press, 1992).

Stewart, Rex. *Jazz Masters of the Thirties* (New York: Da Capo Press, 1988).

Stockdale, Robert L. *Tommy Dorsey: On the Side* (Metuchen, NJ: Scarecrow Press, 1995).

Stokes, Niall. *Into the Heart: The Stories Behind Every U2 Song* (New York: Thunder's Mouth Press, 1998).

Storbe, Ilse. *Louis Armstrong: The Definitive Biography* (New York: Peter Lang, 1996).

——, and Klaus-G. Fischer. *Dave Brubeck: Improvisations and Compositions: The Idea of Cultural Exchange* (New York: P. Lang, 1994).

Stowe, David W. *Swing Changes: Big Band Jazz in New Deal America* (Cambridge, MA: Harvard University Press, 1994).

Strait, R., and T. Robinson. *Lanza: His Tragic Life* (Englewood Cliff, NJ: Prentice Hall, 1980).

Stravinsky, Igor. *An Autobiography 1903-34* (New York: Marion Boyars, 1990).

Strickland, Edward. *Minimalism: Origins* (Bloomington, IN: Indiana University Press, 1993).

Stucky, Steven. *Lutoslawski and His Music* (New York: Cambridge University Press, 1981).

Stuessy, Joe. *Rock and Roll: Its History and Stylistic Development* (Englewood Cliffs, NJ: Prentice Hall, 1994).

Suarez, Virgil. *Latin Jazz* (New York: Simon & Schuster, 1990).

Suskin, Steven. *Show Tunes: 1905-91: The Songs, Shows, and Careers of Broadway's Major Composers* (New York: Limelight Editions, 1992).

Sutherland, Joan. *A Prima Donna's Progress: The Autobiography of Joan Sutherland* (Washington, DC: Regnery Pub., 1997).

Swafford, Jan. *Charles Ives: A Life with Music* (New York: W. W. Norton, 1996).

Swain, Joseph P. *The Broadway Musical: A Critical and Musical Survey* (New York: Oxford University Press, 1990).

Swenson, John. *Bill Haley: The Daddy of Rock'n'Roll* (New York: Stein and Day, 1983).

——. *The Who: Britain's Greatest Rock Group* (New York: Tempo, 1979).

Symonette, L. and K.H. Kowalke, eds. *Speak Low: Letters of Kurt Weill and Lottie Lenya* (Berkeley, CA: University of California Press, 1996).

Tacka, Phil., and Michaeál Houlahan. *Zoltán Kodály: A Guide to Research* (New York: Garland, 1998).

Tait, Robin. *The Musical Language of Gabriel Fauré* (New York: Garland, 1989).

Takemitsu, Toru, et al. *Confronting Silence* (Berkeley, CA: Fallen Leaf Press, 1995).

Taraborrelli, J. Randy. *Call Her Miss Ross: The Unauthorized Biography of Diana Ross* (New York: Ballantine Books, 1989).

Tarasti, Eero. *Heitor Villa-Lobos: The Life and Works, 1887–1959* (Jefferson, NC: McFarland, 1995).

Taylor, Arthur, ed. *Notes and Tones: Musician-to-Musician Interviews* (New York: Da Capo Press, 1993).

Taylor, Paula. *Carole King* (Mankato, MN: Creative Education, 1976).

Taylor, Theodore. *Jule: The Story of Composer Jule Styne* (New York: Random House, 1979).

Thomas, J. C. *Chasin' the Trane* (New York: Garden City Publishing, 1971).

Thompson, C. *Bing: The Authorized Biography* (New York: McKay, 1976).

Thompson, D. *Never Fade Away: The Kurt Cobain Story* (New York: St. Martin's Press, 1994).

Thompson, Wendy. *Claude Debussy* (New York: Viking, 1993).

Thomson, Virgil. *American Music Since 1910* (New York: Holt, Rinehart, and Winston, 1971).

——. *Music With Words: A Composer's View* (New Haven, CT: Yale University Press, 1989).

Tippett, Michael, and Meirion Bowen, ed. *Tippett on Music* (New York: Oxford University Press, 1995).

Titon, Jeff Todd, et al. *Worlds of Music: An Introduction to the Music of the World's Peoples* (New York: Schirmer Books, 1996).

Tobler, John. *ABBA Gold: The Complete Story* (New York: St. Martin's Press, 1993).

——, and Stuart Grundy. *The Guitar Greats* (New York: St. Martin's Press, 1984).

Tommasini, Anthony. *Virgil Thomson: Composer on the Aisle* (New York: W. W. Norton, 1997).

Tormé, Mel. *It Wasn't All Velvet: An Autobiography* (New York: Viking, 1988).

Tosches, Nick. *Country: The Twisted Roots of Rock'n'Roll* (New York: Da Capo Press, 1996).

——. *Hellfire: The Jerry Lee Lewis Story* (New York: Dell Publishing, 1982).

Touma, Habib Hassan. *The Music of the Arabs* (Portland, OR: Amadeus Press, 1996).

Towe, Ronald. *Here's to You: The Complete Bio-discography of Miss Peggy Lee* (San Francisco, CA: R. Towe Music, 1986).

Traubner, Richard. *Operetta, A Theatrical History* (New York: Doubleday, 1983).

Tucker, Mark, ed. *A Duke Ellington Reader* (New York: Oxford University Press, 1993).

Tucker, Sophie. *Some of These Days* (Garden City, NY: Doubleday, Doran, 1945).

Turk, Ruth. *Soul Man* (Minneapolis, MN: Lerner, 1996).

Turner, Steven. *Van Morrison: Too Late to Stop Now* (New York: Viking, 1993).

Turner, Tina, and Kurt Loder. *I, Tina* (New York: Avon, 1986).

Vallee, Eleanor, and Jill Amadio. *My Vagabond Lover: An Intimate Biography of Rudy Vallee* (Dallas, TX: Taylor Publishing, 1996).

Vallee, Rudy. *Let The Chips Fall* (Harrisburg, PA: Stackpole Books, 1975).

Vaughan Williams, Ursula. *RVW* (New York: Oxford University Press, 1984).

——, and Imogen Holst, eds. *Ralph Vaughan Williams and Gustav Holst, Correspondence* (Westport, CT: Greenwood Press, 1980).

Vaughan, Robert. *Herbert von Karajan: A Biographical Portrait* (New York: W. W. Norton, 1985).

Vincent, Rickey. *Funk: The Music, the People, and the Rhythm of the One* (New York: St. Martin's Griffin, 1996).

Vincent, Ted. *Keep Cool* (Boulder, CO: Pluto Press, 1995).

Volkov, Solomon, ed., Antonia W. Bouis, trans. *Testimony: The Memoirs of Dmitry Shostakovich* (New York: Limelight Editions, 1984).

Wade, Graham. *Segovia: A Celebration of the Man and His Music* (New York: Allison & Busby, 1983).

Walker, Robert Matthew. *Rachmaninov* (New York: Omnibus Press, 1984).

Waller, Johnny. *"Sweet Dreams": The Definitive Biography of Eurythmics* (Wauwatosa, WI: Robus, 1985).

Walser, Robert. *Running with the Devil: Gender and Madness in Heavy Metal Music* (Hanover, NH: Wesleyan University Press, 1993).

Walsh, Michael. *Andrew Lloyd Webber: His Life and Works* (New York: Harry N. Abrams, 1989).

Walter White, Eric. *Stravinsky: A Critical Survey 1882–1946* (Mineola, NY: Dover, 1997).

Walter, Bruno. *Theme and Variations: An Autobiography* (Westport, CT: Greenwood Press, 1981).

Walton, Susana. *William Walton: Behind the Façade* (New York: Oxford University Press, 1989).

Ward, Ed., et al. *Rock of Ages* (New York: Rolling Stone Press/Summit Books, 1986).

Warner, Brigitte. *Orff Schulwerk: Applications for the Classroom* (Englewood Cliffs, NJ: Prentice Hall, 1991).

Washabaugh, William. *Flamenco* (Washington, DC: Berg, 1996).

Waters, Edward N. *Victor Herbert: A Life in Music* (New York: Da Capo Press, 1978).

Watkinson, Mike, and Pete Anderson. *Crazy Diamond: Sid Barrett and the Dawn of Pink Floyd* (New York: Omnibus Press, 1993).

Weaver, William, and Simonetta Puccini. *The Puccini Companion* (New York: W. W. Norton, 1994).

Webern, Anton. *The Path to the New Music* (Bryn Mawr, PA: Presser, 1963).

Weinstein, Deena. *Heavy Metal* (New York: Lexington Books, 1991).

Weisbard, Eric. *The Spin Alternative Record Guide* (New York: Vintage, 1995).

Werner, Otto. *The Latin Influence on Jazz* (Dubuque, IA: Kendall/Hunt Publishing Co., 1992).

———. *The Origin and Development of Jazz: Readings and Interviews* (Dubuque, IA: Kendall/Hunt, 1989).

Weschler-Vered, Artur. *Jascha Heifetz* (New York: Schirmer Books, 1986).

West, Sarah Ann. *Deep Down Hard Blues: A Tribute to Lightnin' Hopkins* (Lawrenceville, VA: Brunswick, 1995).

White, Charles. *The Life and Times of Little Richard: The Quasar of Rock* (New York: Da Capo Press, 1994).

White, Gary. *Instrumental Arranging* (Dubuque, IA: Brown & Benchmark, 1992).

White, George R. *Bo Diddley: Living Legend* (New York: Harvill Press, 1997).

Whiting, Steven Moore. *Satie the Bohemian: From Cabaret to Concert Hall* (New York: Oxford University Press, 1998).

Whittall, Arnold. *Romantic Music: A Concise History from Schubert to Sibelius* (New York: Thames and Hudson, 1987).

Whitton, Kenneth S. *Dietrich Fischer-Dieskau: Mastersinger* (New York: Holmes & Meier, 1981).

Wilcock, Donald E. with Buddy Guy. *Damn Right, I've Got the Blues* (San Francisco, CA: Woodford Press, 1993).

Wild, D., and M. Cuscuna. *Ornette Coleman 1958-79: A Discography* (Ann Arbor, MI: Wildmusic, 1980).

Wilde, Laurent de. *Monk* (New York: Marlowe, 1997).

Wilder, Alec. *American Popular Song: The Great Innovators, 1900–1950* (New York: Oxford University Press, 1990).

Williams, Richard. *Out of His Head, the Sound of Phil Spector* (New York: Outerbridge & Lazard, 1972).

Wills, Rosetta. *The King of Western Swing: Bob Wills Remembered* (New York: Billboard Books, 1998).

Wilson, Elizabeth. *Shostakovich: A Life Remembered* (Princeton, NJ: Princeton University Press, 1994).

Wilson, John Stuart. *Jazz: The Transition Years, 1940–60* (New York: Da Capo Press, 1983).

Wilson, Paul. *The Music of Béla Bartók* (New Haven, CT: Yale University Press, 1992).

Wise, Nick. *The Beach Boys in Their Own Words* (New York: Omnibus, 1994).

Woideck, Carl. *Charlie Parker: His Music and Life* (Ann Arbor, MI: University of Michigan Press, 1996).

———. *The Charlie Parker Companion* (New York: Schirmer Books, 1998).

Wolfe, Charles. *The Devil's Box: Masters of Southern Fiddling* (Nashville, TN: Vanderbilt University Press, 1997).

———, and K. Lornell. *The Life and Legend of Leadbelly* (New York: HarperCollins, 1992).

Wolff, Konrad. *Schnabel's Interpretation of Piano Music* (New York: W. W. Norton, 1979).

Wolliver, Robbie. *Hoot!* (New York: St. Martin's Press, 1994).

Wood, Jack. *Surf City: The California Sound* (New York: Friedman/Fairfax Publishers, 1995).

Woog, Adam. *The Beatles* (San Diego, CA: Lucent Books, 1998).

Worth, Paul, and Jim Cartwright. *John McCormack: A Comprehensive Discography* (New York: Greenwood Press, 1986).

Wright, David K. *Paul Robeson: Actor, Singer, Political Activist* (Springfield, NJ: Enslow Publishers, 1998).

Wright, Simon. *Villa-Lobos* (New York: Oxford University Press, 1992).

Wynette, Tammy, with Joan Drew. *Stand by Your Man* (New York: Simon & Schuster, 1979).

Xenakis, Iannis. *Formalized Music* (Bloomington, IN: Indiana University Press, 1971).

Yeomans, David. *Bartók for Piano* (Bloomington, IN: Indiana University Press, 1988).

Young, Alan. *Woke Me Up This Morning: Black Gospel Singers and the Gospel Life* (Jackson, MS: University Press of Mississippi, 1997).

Young, Percy M. *Zoltán Kodály: A Hungarian Musician* (Westport, CT: Greenwood Press, 1976).

Yuzefovich, Victor, et al. *Aram Khachaturyan* (New York: Sphinx Press, 1985).

Zadan, Craig. *Sondheim and Company* (New York: Da Capo Press, 1994).

Zak, Albin, III. *The Velvet Underground Companion* (New York: Schirmer Books, 1997).

Zanderbergen, G. *Nashville Music: . . . Charley Pride* (Mankato, MN: Crestwood House, 1976).

Zingg, Jim, and Joe Gattuso. *America's Great Festivals: A Legacy of Entertainment* (Lake Havasu City, AZ: Events U.S.A., 1992).

INDEX